THE SEARCH FOR THE ANCIENT NOVEL

The Search for
the Ancient Novel

EDITED BY

James Tatum

THE

JOHNS HOPKINS UNIVERSITY PRESS

BALTIMORE AND LONDON

This book has been brought to publication
with the generous assistance of
the David M. Robinson Publication Fund.

The Johns Hopkins University Press
2715 North Charles Street
Baltimore, Maryland 21218–4319
The Johns Hopkins Press Ltd., London

Frontispiece: Hans Baldung Grien, *Aristotle Ridden by Phillis,* 1503. Pen and
ink drawing. Cabinet des Dessins, Musée du Louvre; Cliché des Musées
Nationaux, Paris. Photo courtesy of Département des Arts Graphiques,
Musée du Louvre.

Library of Congress Cataloging-in-Publication Data

The Search for the ancient novel / edited by James Tatum.
p.   cm.
Includes bibliographical references.
ISBN 0-8018-4619-6. — ISBN 0-8018-4621-8 (pbk.)
1. Classical fiction—History and criticism.   2. Rhetoric, Ancient—
Congresses.   3. Literary form—Congresses.   I. Tatum, James.
PA3040.S4   1994
883'.0109—dc20   93-13210

A catalog record for this book is available
from the British Library.

For
Jane Lincoln Taylor
and
Gail M. Vernazza

CONTENTS

Contents

Contents

PART VIII
How Antiquity Read Its Novels

PREFACE

A gracious note in the November 1990 issue of the *Giornale italiano di filologia classica* introduced a sequence of four papers from the July 1989 Dartmouth-NEH international conference, *The Ancient Novel: Classical Paradigms and Modern Perspectives,* by observing that only a volume of abstracts had appeared by that date.* Since the conference's diligent organizer had not been able to guarantee publication of all ninety papers, the note continued, conference papers would appear in various journals, in various countries. And so they have: aside from the *Giornale,* in the *American Journal of Philology,* Lisbon's *Euphrosyne,* the *Zeitschrift für Papyrologie und Epigraphik,* the *Groningen Colloquia on the Novel,* and Oxford's *Classical Quarterly.*

As the *solerte organizzatore* in question, I should also point out that many participants were giving previews of work scheduled for publication elsewhere, in articles (Panagiotis Agapitos, Marie-Françoise Baslez, Helen Elsom) as well as books (Shadi Bartsch, Niall Slater, Giuseppe Zanetto), while others were discussing projects in their earlier stages (Bracht Branham, Stephen J. Harrison).

This volume presents twenty-four essays out of the original ninety papers, a ratio of more than one to four. It aims to show how different critical perspectives can be brought together on a single occasion; its contributors are all captured, as it were, in midflight. Some translate or revise work they have presented elsewhere (Merkle, Zeitlin); others offer work they would go on to publish, or shortly will publish (Montague, Romm, Konstan). The moment is crystallized for readers in classics, comparative literature, and modern language departments, especially English. All the contributors endeavored to write something interesting for those reading or teaching ancient novels, in any field, for any reason.

Books written for a wide audience have their narrow aspects, and this one is no exception. Aside from whatever issues the conference itself failed to address, there were a number of important contributions that seemed likely to be of interest mainly to other specialists. Most who attended generously recognized that fact of market analysis and did not mistake it for a criticism.

---

*It is in fact more pretentious than that; see J. Tatum and G. M. Vernazza, eds., *The Ancient Novel: Classical Paradigms and Modern Perspectives* (Hanover, N.H., 1990).

The essays in the present volume represent the range of that conference, at many of its most interesting moments. As noted in the conference proceedings of 1990, we attempted to cover every aspect of the novelists of ancient Greece and Rome: the recovery of their texts; their reception, ancient and modern; their place in literary history and theory. John J. Winkler could not attend, yet his work was as important a contribution to the occasion as any. His essay included here is the sort of thing he would have been likely to say, if he had been present; in fact he really did say it, some years before, in the Fall 1982 issue of *Laetaberis*. I am grateful to the editors of that journal and the California Classical Association for permission to reprint "The Invention of Romance," with a few changes made at its author's suggestion.

The only thing more daunting than the initial prospect of ninety contributions has been the speed with which other conference participants have published their work, beginning with the 1990 issue of the precocious *Giornale*. This book appears four years after the event because we preferred to follow the old, characteristically American ways, slowly, carefully taking whatever time was needed to see that each essay reached its best possible form. I am grateful to all the contributors for their considerable patience, either in responding to often substantial demands for revision, or in simply waiting for the volume to appear. Although many editors of such a collection thoughtfully include an extended contribution of their own, I decided not to delay publication even further by attempting that. A relevant essay will appear, one of these days, elsewhere. As editor, I gained some much-needed detachment from a consuming project; for the reader, as Ovid says, at least the punishment will be lighter.

Eric Halpern expressed strong interest in something like this book well before the conference itself. His support has been crucial at every stage of its preparation, as has been that of Johns Hopkins's managing editor, Barbara B. Lamb, and her colleagues at the Press. Two anonymous main readers and a small army of specialists targeted to individual essays provided helpful criticism and suggestions. The costs of preparing the manuscript have been met by funds from the original conference grant of the National Endowment for the Humanities, Washington, D.C., the Faculty Committee on Research at Dartmouth, and the office of the Dean of the Faculty at Dartmouth.

Many other friends and colleagues gave valued advice in the dozen or so different academic fields represented in this collection. Among those who were so incautious as not to forbid me to mention their names as a condition for serving in this regard were Susan Ackerman, Carla Freccero, Brenda Silver, Kevin Reinhart, Christopher P. Jones, Ann Ellis Hanson, Lia Schwartz Lerner, Robert H. F. Carver, Margaret Alexiou, Robert A.

Oden, Jr., Robert Fogelin, Peter W. Cosgrove, David Quint, B. P. Reardon, Daniel L. Selden, Susan A. Stephens, Ole Smith, and Walter Stephens. Virginia L. Close of the Baker Library at Dartmouth helped me track down the representation of Phyllis and Aristotle that I most wanted to use, before I knew I wanted to use it.

Finally, the most important collaborators of all: Gail M. Vernazza, who prepared the drafts of an alarmingly expanding and contracting manuscript in Hanover with the same efficiency she brought to the conference and its published proceedings. And Jane Lincoln Taylor, in New York City: she edited the entire copy through its many stages, remarkably and perceptively, as is her custom. Their names appear on another page and mark the end of our imaginary voyage together—at long last!—in search of the ancient novel.

THE SEARCH FOR THE ANCIENT NOVEL

The Search for the Ancient Novel

James Tatum

A STORY, OR FABLE, OR PARABLE, OR HISTORY, OR WHATEVER YOU WANT TO CALL IT

According to the poet Henri d'Andeli and the cardinal Jacques de Vitry (d. 1240), Alexander the Great found his tutor Aristotle's warnings about the dangers of eros so tedious that he decided to teach his famous tutor a lesson. He arranged for his beautiful mistress, Phyllis, to seduce Aristotle; with the effortlessness characteristic of this kind of tale, she did. But as the price for her favors she demanded that Aristotle allow himself to be saddled and ridden about the palace garden like an ordinary beast of burden. The spectacle of love's power over reason provided much amusement for Alexander and his court and was the subject of a number of entertaining sculptures in Rouen, Lyons, Caen, San Gimignano, the Bargello, and other monuments in the cities of medieval Europe.[1] There would be many other versions of this story of the philosopher in love, some more morally improving than others. It does not appear in ancient Alexander fiction like the *Alexander Romance* of Pseudo-Callisthenes, but was added to the ever-growing body of Alexander legends well before de Vitry's and Henri d'Andeli's canon-bashing times. In the thirteenth century the pagan Aristotle was widely perceived as a leading representative of an oppressive classical tradition and a popular target for ridicule.[2]

A fable about the inefficacy of teaching ends with still more teaching. As many an outwitted scholar might, Aristotle tries to have a last, authoritarian word: all the more reason for Alexander to heed his warnings. If an older man who was the embodiment of reason itself could fall victim to love, to what dangers might a young prince like Alexander not fall prey? Moralizing and misogyny mingle with storytelling, with everyone involved scoring a point: Phyllis in her power over men, Aristotle in his resilience as a teacher, Alexander in his wit, and most of all, the poets and artisans who delighted in ridiculing the folly of a teacher of legendary austerity. The story explodes classical antiquity's claims on moral education; at another level, the impulse to discipline and define is frustrated by an equally basic impulse: in this instance, it seems, lust.

Those already familiar with the fiction of ancient Greece and Rome may recognize a continuum of scholarly response to such tales: Aristotle pontificating, Aristotle humiliated, Aristotle calmly attempting to reassert his control, all told in a story that purports to be ancient when it is in fact deeply inauthentic. Dürer's pupil Hans Baldung Grien captured the most notorious moment with great delicacy.[3] The subject and the drawing will serve admirably as an emblem for a book on the search we are about to undertake.

OXYMORON

"The ancient novel" is not an overly hasty typification. Classical philology traditionally dates its inquiry into the subject from 1876 and the publication of Erwin Rohde's book on the Greek novel and its predecessors (*Vorläufer*).[4] As Rohde well knew, this kind of speculation about the origins of fiction could be found much earlier than 1876. When Cervantes (d. 1616) used the verb *novelar* to describe his writing of fiction, he may or may not have thought that his ancient masters Heliodorus and Apuleius were engaged in the same activity as he was.[5] By the time of Pierre-Daniel Huet's *Traité de l'origine des romans* (1670), however, moderns saw clear forerunners of contemporary fiction in classical antiquity.[6] Adding the Roman novel, as represented by Petronius and Apuleius, made the claim seem even more plausible;[7] together with five complete Greek novels by Heliodorus, Chariton, Xenophon of Ephesus, Achilles Tatius, and Longus, the works of these ancients themselves could be perceived as the *Vorläufer* of later novels.

Antiquity offered specific models for imitation and adaptation by later writers: scandalous tales from Apuleius's *Golden Ass* reworked and sprinkled over the *Decameron*, to equally scandalous effect; Lucian's *True History* begetting *Gulliver's Travels*; Heliodorus's *Ethiopian Story*, Cervantes' *Trials of Persiles and Sigismunda*, Richardson's *Clarissa*, and Burney's *Wanderer*. It also achieved levels of sophistication equaling anything an aficionado of later fiction could name. "Borges and Nabokov," as John Winkler asserted in his 1985 narratological study of *The Golden Ass*, "have nothing on Apuleius."[8]

New ancient novels are still being published, thanks to the discoveries of Greek papyrology. Modern estimates of both the chronology and the characteristics of antiquity's fiction change regularly, and often fundamentally, because of new fragments of ancient fiction.[9] The Greek Lollianus's *Phoenician Story* has tales of banditry that duplicate, imitate, or follow a common source for similar episodes in the Latin of Apuleius's *Golden Ass*.[10] The uniqueness once perceived in Petronius's *Satyricon* now seems far from unique with the discovery of fragments of *Iolaus,* a Petronianesque narrative of low life narrated in high style.[11] Gerald Sandy's version will give a good sense of how much is and is not there:

> Noble Iolaus, greetings! And you, *cinaedus* [sc., passive male prostitute], silence! I have become a *gallus* [sc., eunuch] initiated into the mysteries [and shall] exhort [you in] words [known] to initiates . . . Iolaus, for [your sake]. Nicon . . . so that [you] would have [me] as a *gallus* . . . who knows everything. I know to whom you . . . I know everything, the familiarity . . . the oath . . . [unburied body] . . . of someone . . . the bastard . . . everything [has happened] . . . wailing . . . your house, mother, your bedroom, I know of [your] father's lamentations, [Eurycleia], that [she] is aware . . . Nicon, [trickery], *cinaedus,* and the [birthday] . . . I know of the invitation and the *cinaedus* [joking] . . . how he joked, how he fled . . . solution, assertion, cutting off . . . that you intend to screw by deceit . . . Therefore conceal nothing from me . . . and I want your . . . , Iolaus . . . and you will know. For the interval . . .[12]

Virtually unintelligible on its own, the tattered *Iolaus* has more than enough to bring a gleam to the eye of an experienced reader of Petronius—though more than enough in what sense, and with what consequence, remain matters of debate. The practical effect of such discoveries is that it becomes less and less easy to say confidently what is typical of such fiction.[13]

The ancient novel is thus a self-consciously young subject, with a first, field-defining conference in 1976 to commemorate the centennial of Rohde's *Griechischer Roman,*[14] a sequel conference (from which the present volume of essays comes) in 1989,[15] and in that same year, the first complete set of English translations.[16]

At once youthful and venerable, ancient novels do not lack evangelists. In one communication after another, the hope is expressed that those not yet acquainted with them will eventually come to know this oxymoronic subject, the newest chapter in ancient literature.[17] Literary theory is now as much at home with ancient fiction as with any other part of classics.[18] As Aristotle teaches us in the *Nicomachean Ethics*—it seems Aristotle is hard to ignore, after all—such openness and generosity are more typical of the young than of the old.[19]

The more the news about ancient novels spreads, however, the more mixed the reception. Outside classical studies, "the novel" has long been widely assumed to be one literary form that was a characteristic invention of early modern Europe.[20] To claim it for the languages of Sophocles or

Vergil—worse, to define it as a distinct, new field anticipating modern developments by a millennium and more—seems an unexamined effort to coopt modernity. In effect, one could be charged with writing not so much a new chapter in ancient literary history as a new chapter in the Battle of the Books. For more than one reader, "the ancient novel" is an unwelcome piece of anachronistic literary taxonomy. As J. Paul Hunter observes at the beginning of *Before Novels: The Cultural Contexts of Eighteenth-Century English Fiction:*

> Other attempts to broaden or diffuse the definition of the novel—to include a variety of early Continental traditions, classical prose of several kinds, and narratives of China, India, and Japan—muddle the cultural and formal issues in similar ways, however useful they are in extending knowledge of narrative generally. The question of beginnings is a real one, with significant implications for generic definition and ideas of temporality and continuity, but it is easily blurred into pedantry, triviality, and the stalking of game that has been chosen for the chase. Making all prose fiction, from all ages and places, into the novel is not a serious way of dealing with either formal or historical issues.[21]

Hunter is an able guardian, kind to friends and harsh to strangers, writing in instinctive reaction against the prospect of Arthur Heiserman or anyone else attempting to modify a concept long ago defined by Ian Watt as "the rise of the novel."[22] Watt and his followers have the solid claim not only of multiple texts that purport to be or not be "novels," "romances," or "histories"; they have theoretical and lexicographical documentation from the novelists and romancers as well.[23] Hunter's prophylactic warning seems justified.

As Socrates points out about the original guardians, however, the disposition of a culture's *phylakes* depends on the *paideia* or training they receive.[24] They instinctively sniff out what is familiar, and just as instinctively chase away what is not. Hunter's rejection of attempts to broaden the conception of the novel beyond what is tolerable for English literature is appropriate for his project, yet his guardianship of "the novel" is itself a construction of a *paideia* peculiar to American English departments. To onlookers of the terrain recently mapped by Gerald Graff, professing literature often seems to permit such a narrowing of focus to a single language and literature that the new discipline is pursued, for all practical purposes, in nationalistic terms, with no more than passing reference to traditions lying beyond whichever pale one thinks needs to be defended.[25]

Claiming "the novel" for antiquity is problematic, as several essays in this book will make clear;[26] but, as several others will make equally clear, rejecting that claim may be no less so. To some English novelists—

4

Richardson, Fielding, Burney—a connection with ancient or Continental fiction played as important a role in the shaping of their fiction as anything else did.[27] Yet the names Heliodorus and Cervantes do not appear in *Before Novels,* nor does Boccaccio's, who, because of the prestige of the *Decameron* and its *novelle,* is often credited with being an inventor, not only of "the novel," but of the word *novel* itself.[28]

WHO GUARDS THE NOVEL?

Current theory about literary genre is much concerned with just such issues of naming and typification.[29] As Hayden White observes, the beginning of all understanding is classification.[30] If the very act of naming ancient prose fiction "novels" is a crucial issue for Hunter, it may be because classification, White's "beginning of all understanding," is also the beginning of all control. Genesis 2:19–20 suggests that the acts of naming and establishing domination precede romance (the human experience, not the literary form): "So God formed out of the ground all the wild animals and all the birds of heaven. He brought them to the man to see what he would call them, and whatever the man called each living creature, that was its name. Thus the man gave names to all cattle, to the birds of heaven, and to every wild animal; but for the man himself no partner had yet been found." Through the power of naming, all the animals are made subordinate to the man. They become his inferiors, not his equals.[31] When woman is made from man and brought to him, the man (Adam) names her, in Genesis 2:23: "Now this, at last—bone from my bones, flesh from my flesh—this shall be called woman [Hebrew, *ishshah*], for from man [*ish*] was this taken." Both classifying and naming will henceforth be necessary preludes to the control of whatever activity human beings undertake. Naming is an enterprise as much for contest as for clarification. There is always the possibility of refutation, change, demolition. It is in this sense that contests for classification are contests for control.

More than one writer of fiction, modern as well as ancient, seems to have understood these higher uses of literary terminology and taken considerable pains to thwart them, often with great success. Furthermore, to the intense frustration of modern scholars' efforts to control the form, their ancient and Byzantine colleagues thought it unnecessary to develop a different classification for "the novel."[32] Rather uneasily, they tended to see fiction as a variation of established norms, such as history, myth, or comedy, and then to refer to those elements that distinguished it from the real (generic) thing.[33] Eroticism, falsehoods, things patently fictive (Latin, *ficta*) and made-up (Greek, *plasmata*), all enable a reader to tell the difference between a Chariton and a Thucydides, and, within the work of a single writer, to separate rather easily Apuleius's delightful *Golden Ass* from his respectable but less engaging treatise *On the God of Socrates*.

The stage would seem to be set for the kind of practical accommodation Alistair Fowler explores in *Kinds of Literature*. It has been the favored solution of those who could not find an ancient term for what they wanted to describe: "The word is late, but the thing is ancient. For Seneca's Epistles to Lucilius, if one mark them well, are but essays—that is, dispersed mediations, though conveyed in the form of epistles."[34] Bacon's advice is to give the thing priority over the word and get on with whatever needs to be said (or done).

But *novel* has an ancient history: from Latin *novella* to French *nouvelle*, thence English *novelle* simplified to *novél*, and finally the modern pronunciation *nóvel*.[35] As Curtius once demonstrated with an etymology of the economic origins of the word *classic* in Aulus Gellius's reference to the top Roman tax bracket, this kind of genealogy need not be a mere antiquarian exercise.[36] What is not often noted about *novel* is that the word itself carried the characteristics of the literary form it would describe, before it actually described it. One might say it was the word that was ancient, and the thing that was new.

The diminutive *novellus* (from *novus*), meaning "young" or "new," first described horticulture and animal husbandry (vines, goats, chickens), then anything new in a general sense. By the sixth century A.D. it referred to the series of supplementary laws instituted by Justinian and his successors, which from the twelfth century became a supplement to the *Corpus juris civilis*. Mostly issued in Greek, some in Latin and Greek, and some only in Latin, depending on the needs of various parts of the empire, these statutes became known in western Europe as the *novellae constitutiones* or simply the *novellae*, the "new laws" or "novels" of Justinian.[37] For those concerned with literary history, it would seem natural enough to pass by this first, nonliterary appearance of *novella* as form and go straight to Boccaccio, by whose time it could mean a story true or fictional, new or simply unusual, written or recited.[38]

But there is good reason to pause at the novels of Justinian. In one important respect they anticipate what is thought to be most characteristic of the novel as a literary form. The code of Roman civil law assembled in the *Digest* had an "almost inpenetrable vastness," often "concealing rather than precisely setting forth the principles of the law."[39] Justinian and his advisers wrote their *novellae constitutiones* (new laws or amendments) when they no longer had the obligation to reproduce and preserve the Roman legal heritage in all its volume and complexity. The *novellae* were chiefly concerned with an extensive remodeling of the law of family and inheritance, displaying a kind of legal dialogic imagination markedly different from that of the *Digest*.[40] In this sense, Justinian's novels mark an interesting turn in the prehistory of the word *novel*.[41]

Boccaccio knew well that the word *novella* carried these legal connotations; pseudolegalistic classifying and defining abounds in the *Decameron*, as it does throughout one of its important ancient models, *The Golden Ass*. "There begins the book called *Decameron*, also named *Prince Galeotto*, in which there are told one hundred stories [*novelle*] in ten days, by seven women and three young men" (proem, 1.4.1). This careful, mathematically precise description of the 7 + 3 × 10 *novelle* is immediately undercut by another round of definitions. "My intention is to relate one hundred stories [*novelle*], or fables [*favole*], or parables [*parabole*], or histories [*istorie*], or whatever you want to call them [*che dire le vogliamo*]" (proem, 1.4.5). Like attempts to write a history of the form, then, tracing the history of the word *novel* yields a series of moments in which the concept can be seized and used to mean, as in eighteenth- and nineteenth-century English and American fiction, exactly what its users want it to mean.[42] Yet the legal historian has as much claim on the word *novel* as does the literary critic.

A brief genealogy, but perhaps enough to suggest that the rise of the novel (Justinian's *novellae constitutiones*) took place a thousand years before the rise of the novel (J. Paul Hunter's and Ian Watt's English version), and that neither of these novels was the same as the novel that, according to Rohde and the classicists, rose in the ancient world.

THE SEARCH FOR THE ANCIENT NOVEL: TWENTY-FOUR ESSAYS

Given the power of Boccaccio and other artists to outwit even the most determined guardians, it seems prudent to take a more heuristic approach to the ancient novel (to continue to be bold about the term) or ancient prose fictional narratives, whether conceived of as realistic novels or ideal romances (to use all the weasel words currently in play in English). A heuristic approach is what many of the contributors to this book, though certainly not all of them, have taken. It is at any rate the approach the present order and arrangement seek to underscore.

A centripetal impulse to find the familiar and the contemporary in antiquity encouraged unitary perceptions of many ancient literary forms, not only novels. An opposite, centrifugal movement is now more characteristic of literary theory and critical inquiry, as we realize that much that had been lost to time and then found again was perhaps not so familiar as had at first been supposed.[43] I rehearse these Newtonian formulations to remind us that the ancient novel is as subject to reconception and redefinition as any other area of literature.[44] The essays also cover many texts and periods in the history of the ancient novel, from its ancient audiences to the present, but they do not add up to a chronological survey of ancient fiction.[45] There are a number of good introductions that survey it more completely than any collection with many contributors would ever be able to.[46] In this sense it is an advanced collection, presupposing the ready availability of introductions, if needed. Here you will find the kind of critical and theoretical debates that characterize many areas in present-day scholarship.[47]

Ancient fiction is the most elusive of literary subjects, the search for it, exceptionally unstraightforward. In the following pages we shall encounter the anonymous authors of *Apollonius, King of Tyre* and *The Apocryphal Acts of Peter*, Racine, Lucian, Achilles Tatius, Frances Burney, Heliodorus, Apuleius, Cervantes, Rabelais, Eusthathius Macrembolites, Nikos Kazantzakis, Tasso, Antonius Diogenes, Samuel Richardson, Petronius, Chrétien de Troyes, "Dictys of Crete" (overseas correspondent of the Trojan War), the Harlequin romance writer "Margery Hilton," and Abû 'l-Ḥasan al-Masʿûdî, chronicler of Al-Iskandar, the founder of Alexandria. A developmental scheme or division along purely departmental or chronological lines (Greek vs. Roman, ancient vs. modern) would obscure the very things we most want to show about ancient fiction: not only its richness and variety, but its abiding presence in literature, whether in Islam, Byzantium, or western Europe, from antiquity to the present.

Where we do aim to be comprehensive is in our desire to represent the many ways it is possible to engage with ancient fiction. Cervantes or Burney will show how much Apuleius or Heliodorus gains when either ceases to be the exclusive property of a single field. Some of the most important work of a century and more of research will be assessed here, as well as arguments radically dissenting from that tradition. Each section brings together affinities of argument as well as divergent approaches, with parts 1 and 8 framing the collection: we begin with ancient fiction's identity today and end with its identity in antiquity.[48] Within this frame appear the other parts (2 through 7), each devoted to earlier writers' engagements with that fiction, from antiquity to the present.

Theorizing Ancient Fiction (part 1). *Theôria* (viewing or contemplation) is an abstract way of describing the experience of being a spectator in whichever *theatron* one thinks one is in, or wants to be in. In this sense, as is often observed, theory is inevitably present, even when denied.[49] The first two essays articulate a theoretical approach, each proceeding a different way. John J. Winkler's early "Invention of Romance" is a graceful overture, exploring ancient romances not simply as love stories, but as love-leading-to-marriage stories, from the moment of initial desire to its consummation. It is deliberately seductive—no footnotes—exploring a characteristic feature of ancient fiction, as well as a characteristic modern desire to search for its origins.[50] By the time Daniel L. Selden came to write his essay, Winkler's narratological reading of Apuleius had set new directions for his work and for the field generally.[51] Selden's paper is self-consciously written in that context, with the field itself the object of inquiry. "Genre of Genre" is a polemical exploration of the critical and interpretive issues the volume raises, ending with the constructive proposal that we read ancient fiction according to the rhetorical figure of syllepsis, which, Selden argues, is so characteristic of ancient prose fiction as to constitute a kind of master trope. Syllepsis satisfies one sense, one code, one logic at the same time as another; essentially it is a travesty and an undoing of the very possibility of genre.[52]

Remembering and Revising (part 2). Each contributor deals with the reception of Winkler's and Selden's ancient forms, examining how later writers knew, read, copied, parodied, imitated, or were otherwise inspired by the fiction of classical antiquity. Each of these essays describes western European constructions of a literary past where the dialogue between antiquity and the present becomes the center of a present literary reality. Walter Stephens's argument in "Tasso's Heliodorus and the World of Romance" is that Torquato Tasso thoroughly grasped the narrative technique of Heliodorus's *Ethiopian Story* and reinscribed his themes of exile, return, and marriage under a Christian dialectic and the metaphors of eternal salvation and damnation. Nor is Tasso merely Christianizing the Greek text's version of providence; he is also answering the desacralization of providence in Ariosto's *Orlando furioso,* condensing its vast plot, so that the ancient Heliodorus becomes a compact "original" and "exemplar" who corrects the diffuse and complex plots of Ariosto.

Toda comparación es odiosa (*Don Quixote,* 2.23). And yet that is how most criticism of fiction has proceeded, nowhere more overtly than in work on the novel from which this never-to-be-taken-literally tag is drawn. In "Homage to Apuleius," Diana de Armas Wilson shows how Cervantes' *Persiles* pays more than oblique homage to Apuleius's *Golden Ass,* in what is customarily billed as a Heliodoran romance.[53] Her argument suggests that modern readers might begin to construct their own *comparación odiosa* of Heliodorus and Apuleius, still as separated in our imaginations as Greek is from Roman. Cervantes' joining of the two is more than opportunistic.[54]

In "Novels beyond Thule," James Romm shows how the *voyages imaginaires* of antiquity played an important role in the development of the novel in both antiquity and the Renaissance. These are narratives situated in an intermediate zone between truth and invention, where the reader is left unsure whether or when the author crosses the boundary between what is truth and what is falsehood. The discovery of Seneca's *ultima Thule* in 1492 made real an event that formerly belonged to pure fantasy.

In "Heliodorus Rewritten," Margaret Anne Doody focuses on questions of gender: can a woman as well as a man (re)write the Heliodoran novel? What changes must be made if she does? Even more than Richardson in *Clarissa,* Frances Burney widens the form of the Heliodoran novel by including what is usually ignored. *The Wanderer* works on the edges of prior narrative, dealing with its gaps and spaces. A significant difference emerges in a woman's telling of a story in which a woman is the focal point: she resists the temptation to end the novel as a complete story; as in life itself, true ending in harmony is as far off as ever.

For exploring *Romance in Its Ancient Landscape* (part 3), I have juxtaposed two essays employing different modes of scholarship and approaches to the problems of ancient fiction that are also complementary. The first poses a question about the "fable, not a rational account" (*mythos ou logos*) of Longus's pastoral *Daphnis and Chloe;* the second gives possible answers to the dialectic of eros perceived in the novel. In "Μῦθος οὐ λόγος: Longus's Lesbian Pastorals," B. P. Reardon uses the occasion of the five-hundredth anniversary of the publication of *Daphnis and Chloe* to interrogate the text through its reception and especially through its profile in critical debates about its form since Rohde. He argues that the story is a parable framed by realistic details; the interplay of its two levels is the essential element in its presentation of love. In "Gardens of Desire in Longus's *Daphnis and Chloe,*" Froma I. Zeitlin examines the proem and its relation to the two other significant examples of the narrator's pictorial and rhetorical skills: Philetas's garden of eros and the grand garden park of the urban gentleman Dionysophanes that serves as the theater for the denouement. She traces the way the novel unfolds consistently from its opening ecphrastic moment, in a steady development altogether typical of the literary strategies of the Second Sophistic.[55]

In *Romance at a Critical Distance* (part 4), we move from what is commonly regarded as the most characteristic element of ancient fiction—idealized, romantic love—to two works that hold that typical pattern at a distance.[56] This juxtaposition calls into question the typicality of ancient fiction, showing how a widely used pattern of romance in antiquity could be treated not just with the irony of Achilles Tatius's *Leucippe and Clitophon,* or the parodic Roman fictions of Petronius and Apuleius, but in two works that are indisputably melodramatic and not at all comic.[57] David Konstan's "*Apollonius, King of Tyre* and the Greek Novel" appropriates the form of Greek romance, invoking the separation and reunion of a primary couple, but the couple in question are a father and daughter. Conjugal love is de-eroticized, and, to the extent eros exists, it does so primarily as an anxiety over incest. In a critically similar move, Stefan

Merkle in "Telling the True Story of the Trojan War: The Eyewitness Account of Dictys of Crete" describes a narrative that revises canonical images of heroism in the *Iliad* from beginning to end. The tendency of Greeks under the Roman Empire was to ignore Rome and concentrate on the glories of the past.[58] Sharing that tendency, Dictys is strongly anti-Trojan, but equally critical of the Greeks, in tracing their moral decline as victors. He casts his fiction in the form of a military record or memoir, a tactic misconstrued by less curious readers as a sign of limited talent. Merkle's Dictys emerges as a far more interesting, far less simpleminded writer than before. Somewhat like Euripides in the *Iphigenia at Aulis* or *The Trojan Women,* he shifts radically from the familiar themes of Hellenic patriotism and the heroic paradigm of the *Iliad* to a revelation of the disastrous effects of war on human character.

The search for an ancient novelist's representations of reality has for the most part been directed toward human, political institutions.[59] But our encounter with ancient novelists and their relationship to *The Real World* (part 5) begins with a rather broader perspective than that. W. Geoffrey Arnott's "Longus, Natural History, and Realism" plays Longus's novel against present knowledge of the natural history of the island of Lesbos, as well as what can be inferred about antiquity's knowledge of the same subject. His analysis reflects the connections Adena Rosmarin has drawn between literary and scientific description.[60] The impulse to identify literary form (*Daphnis and Chloe,* a "realistic pastoral romance") is related to the process by which natural species are identified in their environment (*Hirundo rustica, Columba palumbus*). Under Arnott's guidance, philology recapitulates ornithology.

Although they do not yet have much of a reputation for it, *Daphnis and Chloe* and other novels often reflect the changing urban landscapes of later antiquity. In "The City in the Greek Novel," Suzanne Saïd considers the images of the Greek city at the time of the Roman Empire and the ways in which these images may be reflected in ancient fiction. Far from being entirely inside a never-never land that modern theories of romance tend to describe,[61] the ancient novels are nuanced in their locations, often having quite particular resonances with the world of the contemporary ancient city.

The next two arguments bring us to more familiar modes of contextualizing fiction. Since Erich Auerbach's classic essay, the story of the banquet of Trimalchio has been the ancient text most renowned for its representation of reality.[62] John Bodel's "Trimalchio's Underworld" brings together the literary and the sociological in a single reading. While Trimalchio's obsession with the underworld has an obvious relation to the high culture of the *Aeneid*'s underworld, it is also a natural result of his ambivalent status as a freedman; as a former slave he bears the indelible marks of his servitude. Trimalchio is a free man in appearance only: he lacks the essential quality of having been born free. Hence the melancholy that pervades the determined merriment of Trimalchio's table; hence also his preoccupation with death, the final emancipation. Once property, now propertied, he and his freedmen friends live against the clock, struggling to make up for a past that can be neither redeemed nor effaced.

From constraints of slavery, we move to constraints of gender, a relatively recent perception gained through feminist theory. Brigitte Egger begins "Women and Marriage in the Greek Novels" by observing that legal regulations regarding women tended to be more conservative than other aspects of reality, but that in late Hellenistic society they were not so conservative or constraining a discourse as that of the Greek romance. Though the novels are by modern definition innovative as a literary form, they are in fact conservative and nostalgic about the social institution that is so often the center of their action. The narratives concentrate on the attractiveness and emotions of their women protagonists, and in this sense are gynocentric, but the world of romance is dominated in every other respect by its men.

Fictions Sacred and Profane (part 6). Novelists who belonged to religious communities confronted an interesting problem when they attempted to harmonize an imaginary world of fiction with religious experience. They might adapt its systems of belief and ritual to their narratives to give them structure—in a move analogous to what we have just seen in our explorations of the real world. They might simply create a fictional world with techniques similar to those in other fiction. But the writing of fiction itself could come to be the central problem, not in the sense that it had been in classical antiquity, when the temptation to draw invidious comparisons with the high genres of history, epic, or philosophy was always close at hand, but rather in the sense that the values and many of the actions of ancient fiction could too easily be perceived as alien, pagan in the Christian sense, or outside European contexts, as products of the infidel in the world of Islam. Four essays define the collisions of as well as the collusions between fiction and religious belief.

The first two consider primary religious texts. In "Novel and Aretalogy," Reinhold Merkelbach returns to one of the most provocative and widely known arguments about ancient fiction and its relation to the mystery cults in antiquity, in this instance focusing on three specimen texts of statements about the mighty deeds by which a divinity demonstrates its powers.[63] In "The Social World of the *Acts of Peter*," Judith Perkins argues that the *Acts* preserve signs and strategies of an emerging representational and political contest. Like the Greek novels, which have been described as reflecting certain societal and individual needs, the *Acts* are narratives designed to build and maintain new structures, written for a community that conjoins religion with a social and political agenda.[64]

The second pair shows how ancient fiction could be restructured to fit the needs of later, quite different religious communities. Suzanne Mac-Alister's "Ancient and Contemporary in Byzantine Novels" is concerned with the twelfth-century Byzantine revival of ancient fiction, which Mac-rembolites, Prodromus, and Eugenianus all treated from the enlightened perspective of Christianity. Each of these writers created texts for which, had charges of heresy been brought forward, a defense was readymade. For the Muslim and Arabic audience of Islam, Greco-Roman fiction required equally fundamental revisions. Under the influence of Islamic pietism, cities and their pretensions were invitations to cosmic refutation, ruins-to-be rather than monuments to the eternal glory of their founders. Faustina C. W. Doufikar-Aerts's "Legacy of the *Alexander Romance* in Arab Writings: Al-Iskandar, Founder of Alexandria" describes an adaptation of the Alexander legend by Abû 'l-Hasan al-Mas'ûdî (born ca. A.D. 896), who had scarcely less radical changes to perform. This Alexander is at all times the pious servant of God, filled with wise sayings, exemplary behavior, contemplative visions. Under the guidance of al-Mas'ûdî, Alexander, already transformed from historical reality in the romantic fictions of Pseudo-Callisthenes, becomes a sober, religious Muslim, and Alexandria, once the center of eternal prosperity, a backward settlement with unfavorable prospects.

Pursuing the Idea of Ancient Fiction (part 7). However debatable the notion of ancient novels may be, one effect of its creation and of the proliferation of studies in the field has been to attract the notice of those working in other, potentially related areas of narrative. Three essays argue for connections with ancient fiction: where none were thought possible (in medieval French romance); where they were possible, but none was wanted, because of the modest reputation of the form (in nineteenth- and twentieth-century Greece); and where any possible connection between ancient fiction and contemporary culture is vigorously denied (in feminist inquiry into the connections between ancient and contemporary mass market romance). David Rollo's "From Apuleius's Psyche to Chrétien's Erec and Enide" is an examination of the way Chrétien de Troyes explores issues of gender, and for that purpose Apuleius's story of Cupid and Psyche provides an illuminating paradigm. For Rollo, there are too many parallels to be accidental, even though Apuleius is not supposed to have been accessible to Chrétien. Strategic changes in the Apuleian, Platonic model turn Chrétien's romance into an allegory through which the drama of the soul (Psyche) and carnality (Cupid) is reenacted in both postlapsarian man and woman, a transformation Rollo concludes is more easily explained by literary filiation than by folklore.

In "The Reemergence of Greek Prose Fiction in the Nineteenth and Twentieth Centuries," Peter Bien explores the ironies of associating ancient and modern fiction: modern Greece itself did not recover the very thing ancient Greece was credited with inventing. Even when prose fiction becomes a viable genre, by the time of Kazantzakis, it never overshadows poetry. Prose fiction gains status in Kazantzakis's *Saint's Life of Zorbas* only when ways are discovered to make it poetic, a record of the virtues of a hero of orality as opposed to a despised, unvital, and un-Greek pen pusher who, until he meets Zorbas, is misled by the West. Holly W. Montague's "From *Interlude in Arcady* to *Daphnis and Chloe*" is a similar exercise in retrospection: in this instance, from the feminist perspective on contemporary Harlequin romances (a reading as much against that kind of text as with it) to ancient romances. She is concerned with the manner in which novels both ancient and modern encourage erotic fantasy on the part of their readers. Considered as erotic fantasies, ancient and modern romances not only lend themselves to similar readings; some feminist approaches to the erotic novel apply better to ancient works than to contemporary ones.

How Antiquity Read Its Novels (part 8). The final section completes the frame we began with: from modern theoretical approaches to the ancient novel, to material and historical evidence for its ancient readership. Thanks in no small part to the associations that follow from terming ancient fiction "novels," a good many common assumptions, recent and not so recent, have been applied to the past. It has been tempting to speculate that the same conditions of readership and production obtained in antiquity as in early modern Europe and later. Each of these essays contests that move. While the audience of any given novel cannot really be demonstrated, it is possible to reconstruct readerships in general ways, and from a variety of perspectives.

Susan A. Stephens asks "Who Read Ancient Novels?" and tries to answer the question by surveying the fragments of ancient books from the one region of the Greco-Roman world where they have survived, Roman Egypt. She argues that statistics cannot tell us precisely who read novels, but that they do suggest that one group of ancient readers owned fewer of them than copies of Homer, Demosthenes, or Thucydides. She concludes that there is now less reason than ever for classicists to attempt to borrow the arguments of Ian Watt and Michael McKeon to explain the development of fiction in the ancient world. This is confirmation via material evidence that writers like Heliodorus and Achilles Tatius did indeed write from within the highest of a high culture, and for a significantly more limited readership than we once imagined.

In "The Roman Audience of *The Golden Ass*," Ken Dowden shifts the inquiry about readership both to the western and Latin-speaking parts of the empire and to the issue of a single author and his work. Dowden's argument is with the double-decentering that has characterized our view of Apuleius and his novel, removing him not only to the margins of Latin literary history, but away from Rome itself, to the provincial cities of Carthage and Sabratha. Doubting the efficacy of continuing to speak of a genre called "the Roman novel," he reconstructs the ancient readership of literary and philosophical works in the second century and places *The Golden Ass* squarely in the middle of a Roman audience, in Rome.

In "The Readership of Greek Novels in the Ancient World," Ewen Bowie brings our search to a close with an examination of previous arguments about the readership of fiction in antiquity. Though it is not his aim, Bowie's argument incidentally does much to relate the whole question of ancient fiction to explorations of novels in other traditions. He points out that the production of the Greek genre covers a relatively short span of time, from A.D. 60 to 320, with a concentration in the period A.D. 150–250. This gives ancient fiction a *floruit* comparable to what historians in other traditions of fiction have typically described, not only in England, but in China.[65] In restricting his search to a carefully defined field, of which the five major extant novels are the leading examples, Bowie also creates the kind of coherent view that Watt and McKeon achieve, but constructed from entirely different sources, and with quite different results. The educated (*pepaideumenoi*) were familiar with what we term novels, and their authors expected their readers to be of the same sort as those of other serious literature. The notion that they were women, juveniles, or the poor in spirit (in other words, anything but canonical, serious readers) has little to recommend it.

Envoy: *Laetaberis*

In these ways our perception of ancient fiction can rise to something like a level Heliodorus, Cervantes, or Burney would recognize, even if we learn to call this P. G. Wodehousian what-is-it of antiquity by other names. One of the best of the ancients offers as good a reason as any for turning to the essays that follow: *Lector, intende: laetaberis*—"Reader, attend: you shall be delighted."[66] In the hope that Apuleius's prediction is once again proved correct . . .

Notes

1. W. Stammler, *Wort und Bild: Studien zu den Wechselbeziehungen zwischen Schrifttum und Bildkunst im Mittelalter* (Berlin, 1962), 12–44; cf. *Lexikon des Mittelalters* (Munich, 1980), 947–48; *Reallexikon zur deutschen Kunstgeschichte* (Stuttgart, 1937), 1:1027–40; R. Van Marle, *Iconographie de l'art profane* (The Hague, 1932), figs. 519–20.

2. O. Springer, "A Philosopher in Distress," in *Germanic Studies in Honor of Edward*

Henry Sehrt (Coral Gables, Fla., 1968), 203–18; cf. G. Cary, *The Medieval Alexander* (Cambridge, 1956), 231–32.

3. J. H. Marrow and A. Shestack, *Hans Baldung Grien* (Washington, D.C., 1981), 170–71; cf. H. Fischer, ed., *Schwankerzählungen des deutschen Mittelalters* (Munich, 1962), 5–15.

4. E. Rohde, *Der griechische Roman und seine Vorläufer,* 3d ed., ed. W. Schmid (Leipzig, 1914).

5. W. L. Reed, *An Exemplary History of the Novel: The Quixotic versus the Picaresque* (Chicago, 1981), 39–42.

6. This is merely an anticipation of the far more developed account of "origins" provided by Daniel L. Selden in "Genre of Genre."

7. Cf. P. G. Walsh, *The Roman Novel* (Cambridge, 1969), 224–43.

8. J. J. Winkler, *Auctor and Actor: A Narratological Reading of Apuleius' "Golden Ass"* (Berkeley and Los Angeles, 1985), vii.

9. N. Holzberg, *Der antike Roman* (Munich, 1986), 60.

10. A reading not without controversy; cf. A. Henrichs, *Die Phoinikika des Lollianos* (Bonn, 1972), and J. J. Winkler, "Lollianos and the Desperadoes," *Journal of Hellenic Studies* 100 (1980): 155–81.

11. P. J. Parsons, "A Greek *Satyricon?*" *Bulletin of the Institute of Classical Studies* 18 (1971): 53–68; cf. B. P. Reardon, ed., *Collected Ancient Greek Novels* (Berkeley and Los Angeles, 1989), 816.

12. Reardon, *Collected Ancient Greek Novels,* 817–18.

13. This is a major theme of the new collection edited by S. A. Stephens and J. J. Winkler, *Ancient Greek Novels: The Fragments* (Princeton, 1993).

14. B. P. Reardon, ed., *Erotica Antiqua: Acta of the International Conference on the Ancient Novel* (Bangor, Wales, 1977).

15. J. Tatum and G. M. Vernazza, eds., *The Ancient Novel: Classical Paradigms and Modern Perspectives* (Hanover, N.H., 1990).

16. Reardon, *Collected Ancient Greek Novels.*

17. Tatum and Vernazza, *Ancient Novel,* 23–24.

18. J. P. Sullivan, "The Relevance of Modern Critical Approaches to the Roman Novel," in Tatum and Vernazza, *Ancient Novel,* 90–101.

19. Aristotle, *Nicomachean Ethics* 8.3, esp. 1156b1: *kai erôtikoi hoi neoi* (the young are prone to desire).

20. See G. P. Firmat, "The Novel as Genre," *Genre* 12 (1979): 269–92.

21. J. P. Hunter, *Before Novels: The Cultural Contexts of Eighteenth-Century English Fiction* (New York, 1990), 7. This comment is made in reference to the kind of argument advanced by A. Heiserman in *The Novel before the Novel* (Chicago, 1977).

22. I. Watt, *The Rise of the Novel* (Berkeley and Los Angeles, 1957).

23. For the historic continuity of the romance and the novel in English literature, see M. McKeon, *The Origins of the English Novel, 1600–1740* (Baltimore, 1987); cf. L. J. Davis, *Factual Fictions: The Origins of the English Novel* (New York, 1983). For a Hispanist's critique of Anglocentric theories of the novel, cf. Reed, *An Exemplary History,* 12, 19–42.

24. Plato, *Republic* 2.374e ff.

25. Cf. the discussion of "the classical college" in G. Graff, *Professing Literature: An Institutional History* (Chicago, 1987), 19–35.

26. See in particular those by Daniel L. Selden, Susan A. Stephens, and Ken Dowden; on the problematic aspects of using a unitary ideal romance as the canonical form, see the essays of David Konstan and Stefan Merkle.

27. As argued by Margaret Anne Doody, James Romm, and Diana de Armas Wilson;

see also the essays of Suzanne MacAlister and Faustina C. W. Doufikar-Aerts, as well as those of David Rollo, Peter Bien, and Holly W. Montague.

28. R. J. Clements and J. Gibaldi, *Anatomy of the Novella: The European Tale Collection from Boccaccio and Chaucer to Cervantes* (New York, 1977), 1–8; cf. S. Battaglia, *Grande dizzionario della lingua italiana* (Turin, 1961), 11:601, s.v. "novella."

29. It is also aware of the limits of this kind of inquiry; in general, see A. Fowler, *Kinds of Literature* (Cambridge, Mass., 1982), esp. 37: "Genre is much less a pigeonhole than a pigeon."

30. H. White, *Topics of Discourse: Essays in Cultural Criticism* (Baltimore, 1978), 22; cf. White, *Validity in Interpretation* (New Haven, 1967), 68–163.

31. P. Trible, *God and the Rhetoric of Sexuality* (Philadelphia, 1978), 88ff.; cf. G. Anderson, "Celibacy or Consummation in the Garden? Reflections on Early Jewish and Christian Interpretations of the Garden of Eden," *Harvard Theological Review* 82 (1989): 121–48.

32. For ancient theorizing and terminology, see H. Kuch, *Der antike Roman: Untersuchungen zur literarischen Kommunikation und Gattungsgeschichte* (Berlin, 1989), 11–51, esp. 13–18; for the preference for the word *novel*, see T. Hägg, *The Novel in Antiquity* (Berkeley and Los Angeles, 1983), 1–5 ("The Ancient Novel: A Contradiction in Terms?"), and Fowler, *Kinds of Literature,* 120: "We probably do best to retain the broader concept 'novel.' It is too deeply in the grain of criticism to be removed without endangering continuity"—an accommodation Daniel L. Selden argues we should not be so quick to make.

33. One theme in G. W. Bowersock's Sather Classical Lectures, *Fiction as History: Nero to Julian* (Berkeley and Los Angeles, forthcoming).

34. Bacon is quoted in Fowler, *Kinds of Literature,* 131.

35. *Oxford English Dictionary,* s.v. "novel"; cf. Clements and Gibaldi, *Anatomy of the Novella,* 4–8.

36. E. R. Curtius, *European Literature and the Latin Middle Ages* (New York, 1953), 249–50; cf. Aulus Gellius, *Noctes Atticae* 19.8.15. For the Bakhtinian spin on Curtius's observation, cf. P. Stallybrass and A. White, *The Poetics and Politics of Subversion* (London, 1986).

37. A. Berger, *Encyclopedic Dictionary of Roman Law* (Philadelphia, 1953), vol. 43, p.2.

38. Clements and Gibaldi, *Anatomy of the Novella,* 4; cf. now *Oxford Latin Dictionary,* s.v. "novellus." For an interesting assessment of the novella that ranges beyond the literary focus of Clements and Gibaldi, see W. Trimpi, *Muses of One Mind* (Princeton, 1983), 328–44.

39. H. J. Wolff, *Roman Law: An Historical Introduction* (Norman, Okla., 1951), 169–70.

40. Wolfgang Kunkel, *An Introduction to Roman Legal and Constitutional History* (Oxford, 1973), 175–76.

41. *The Dialogic Imagination: Four Essays by M. M. Bakhtin,* ed. M. Holquist, trans. C. Emerson and M. Holquist (Austin, Tex., 1981), 41–83; esp. 42–43.

42. *Oxford English Dictionary,* s.v. "novel," 2b–c; cf. Davis, *Factual Fictions,* 102–22, and A. Rosmarin, *The Power of Genre* (Minneapolis, 1985), 25ff.

43. This will be the argument of a number of contributions to a collection of essays, *Lies and Fiction in the Ancient World,* ed. C. Gill and T. P. Wiseman (Austin, Tex., forthcoming).

44. As Tzvetan Todorov observes, the difference between a scientific genre and a literary genre is that every new utterance in art is potentially ungrammatical, thereby altering an established species; see Todorov, *The Fantastic: A Structural Approach to a Literary Genre* (Cleveland, 1973).

45. Cf. the design of the collection of conference papers in *The Greek Novel, A.D. 1–1985,* ed. R. Beaton (London, 1988): they actually appear more in the order of A.D. 1985 to A.D. 1.

46. See E. L. Bowie, "The Greek Novel," in *The Cambridge History of Classical Literature,* ed. P. E. Easterling and B. M. W. Knox (Cambridge, 1985), 1:683–99. Cf. also Hägg, *Novel in Antiquity;* G. Anderson, *Ancient Fiction: The Novel in the Greco-Roman World* (Totowa, N.J., 1984); and B. P. Reardon, *The Form of Greek Romance* (Princeton, 1991).

47. E.g., K. Galinsky, "Introduction: The Current State of the Interpretation of Roman Poetry and the Contemporary Critical Scene," in *The Interpretation of Roman Poetry: Empiricism or Hermeneutics?* ed. K. Galinsky (Frankfurt am Main, 1992), 1–40.

48. As the work of Daniel L. Selden and Susan A. Stephens shows, the opening is not exclusively theoretical, nor is the closing simply historical, but an adaptation of Tzvetan Todorov's familiar opposition of theoretical and historical approaches to genre; see Todorov, "The Origin of Genres," *New Literary History* 8 (1976): 159–67.

49. E.g., T. Eagleton, *Literary Theory* (Minneapolis, 1983) 12–16.

50. As noted in the Preface, this essay was first published in *Laetaberis,* in 1982.

51. J. Winkler, *Auctor and Actor;* cf. Tatum and Vernazza, *Ancient Novel,* ii, 24, and 96.

52. Cf. Lennard Davis's comment on ideology and the novel in *Factual Fictions:* "It can be said that novels are framed works (even if they are apparently unframed) whose attitude toward fact and fiction is constitutionally ambivalent" (212).

53. Hägg, *Novel in Antiquity,* 201–5; cf. A. K. Forcione, *Cervantes' Christian Romance* (Princeton, 1972).

54. Winkler provides narratological readings of both authors; in addition to his book on Apuleius, *Auctor and Actor,* see "The Mendacity of Kalasiris and the Narrative Strategy of Heliodoros' *Aithiopika,*" *Yale Classical Studies* 27 (1982): 93–158.

55. See E. L. Bowie, "The Greeks and Their Past in the Second Sophistic," *Past and Present* 46 (1970): 3–41.

56. See in general Reardon, *Form of Greek Romance;* for the concept of "the ideal Greek romance," cf. B. E. Perry, *The Ancient Romances* (Berkeley and Los Angeles, 1967).

57. For three of the most recent studies, see S. Bartsch, *Decoding the Ancient Novel: The Reader and the Role of Description in Heliodorus and Achilles Tatius* (Princeton, 1989); N. Slater, *Reading Petronius* (Baltimore, 1989); C. C. Schlam, *The Metamorphoses of Apuleius: On Making an Ass of Oneself* (Chapel Hill, N.C., 1992).

58. Cf. Bowie, "Greeks and Their Past."

59. One of the earliest and most influential historical explorations of the connection between social realities and ancient fiction is P. Veyne, "Vie de Trimalcion," *Annales ESC* 16 (1961): 213–47.

60. Rosmarin, *Power of Genre,* 8, 167; for the similarity of logic, cf. Aristotle, *Topics* 121b1–122a and *On Plants* 816a.

61. See N. Frye, *The Secular Scripture: A Study of the Structure of Romance* (Cambridge, Mass., 1976).

62. E. Auerbach, *Mimesis: The Representation of Reality in Western Literature* (Princeton, 1953), 24–49.

63. R. Merkelbach, *Roman und Mysterium in der Antike* (Munich, 1962); cf. also Merkelbach, *Die Hirten des Dionysos: Die Dionysos-mysterien der römischen Kaiserzeit und der bukolische roman des Longus* (Stuttgart, 1988). For two recent assessments of Merkelbach's 1962 study (and the related work of Karl Kerenyi), see Winkler, *Auctor and Actor,* 230–33, and Reardon, *Form of Greek Romance,* 171–75.

64. This comparatively recent reading of religious texts as novels appears to me to be

an extension of Friedrich Schleiermacher's program of bringing *hermeneutica profana* to bear on sacred texts; cf. White, *Validity in Interpretation,* 112, and R. Pervo, *Profit with Delight: The Literary Genre of the Acts of the Apostles* (Philadelphia, 1987).

65. See A. H. Plaks, "Chinese Narrative Theory," in *Chinese Narrative: Critical and Theoretical Essays* (Princeton, 1977), 309–53.

66. Apuleius, *The Golden Ass* 1.1.

PART I

Theorizing
Ancient Fiction

CHAPTER ONE

The Invention of Romance

John J. Winkler

In the year 1658, Jean Racine was the sole remaining pupil at the Abbey of Port-Royal des Champs, the famous Jansenist school that had recently been closed by the Jesuits. His favorite pastime was to walk through the woods reciting Sophocles and Euripides, much of which he knew by heart, for he was quite proficient in Greek. One day he came across a text of Heliodorus's *Aethiopica*. The sacristan, his Greek teacher, discovered him reading it and threw the book into a fire. A week later Racine obtained another copy, but it suffered the same fate. When he obtained a third copy, he set himself to learn it by heart, and when he had done so he himself presented the book to the sacristan, to be burned.

This striking conjunction of attitudes toward the same work—one person's contempt, another's devotion—is a perfect emblem of the genre we now call the ancient novel, or romance. In their own time the Greek and Latin novels were widely read, but the professional custodians of literature—the ancient sacristans, so to speak—dismissed them with hardly a word. And not only in their own day were the novels both treasured and trashed: the thirteenth-century Laurentianus manuscript, which contains three of the Greek novels, has buried them in the center pages of the folio; they are preceded and followed by theological treatises of remarkably little interest even by monastic standards. It does look as if this manuscript was some scribe's or abbot's private storehouse of recreational reading.

The collision of wills between the sacristan and the pupil, between the

At the author's request, all translations of the *Aethiopica* come from the version of J. R. Morgan, in *Collected Ancient Greek Novels,* ed. B. P. Reardon (Berkeley and Los Angeles, 1989), 349ff. Readers interested in exploring the art that is concealed by this essay's art should consult J. J. Winkler, "The Mendacity of Kalasiris and the Narrative Strategy of Heliodoros' *Aithiopika,*" *Yale Classical Studies* 27 (1982): 93–158, published in the same year as this essay; *Constraints of Desire: The Anthropology of Sex and Gender in Ancient Greece* (London, 1990); and D. M. Halperin, J. J. Winkler, and F. I. Zeitlin, eds., *Before Sexuality: The Construction of Erotic Experience in the Ancient Greek World* (Princeton, 1990). Many of the themes of those later works found their first articulation here.

old grammarian and the adolescent dreamer, raises an issue. The school-teacher insists on waking the boy up from his daydream of love and adventure. The unreality of this particular dream is not to be indulged. Now perhaps if it consisted in fighting with monsters in exotic lands, we could understand the sacristan to mean that such things should not be confused with reality. But the essential unreality of the novel, the unreality that constitutes the genre, is the plot of two persons (almost always a young man and a young woman) who fall in love; this event in their lives immediately puts them in mind of marriage! This plot is a romance, and the novels with such plots were called romances. These are not just "love stories": eros (love, lust, passion, desire) is an old theme in Greek litera-ture, but romances are a rather late development. These are a quite spe-cialized form of erotic story: these are love-leading-to-marriage stories, in which the necessary goal of passion itself is lawful matrimony. I was raised to think that life was like that. Nowadays it seems to me more accurate to say that it is one particularly fine fantasy, which life sometimes resembles, and that it can be a useful fantasy, provided we know that we're dreaming.

The question I want to pose here has two sides: How did the romance as a literary form come into being at all? and How was it that a literary form whose substance was largely in contrast to the demands and consider-ations by which marriages were actually arranged came to be a privileged social norm? This is a study in the relations of popular culture (folk tales, novels, stories) and social identity. There have been, we know, remarkable changes over the ages in the assumed categories that give sense to our personal identities and shape our projects of life. Michel Foucault studied these categories in his *History of Sexuality,* or rather *Sexualité,* the French word having a connotation of social institution and ideology that the English word lacks. I must leave to him and to others the working out of the answer or answers to the second question. My contribution, as a historian of classical culture, will be to make the *problem* come to life, so that we can see, at least in a brief and suggestive sketch, the concreteness and complexity of a culture in which romance was excluded rather than cultivated. This is a study in the *early* history of romance, and I hope only to cast some light on the first problem.

First we need an example—a paradigmatic case. There is none better than Heliodorus's *Aethiopica.* Pardon me if I here display a special enthusi-asm for an author and an entire genre that, when read, are often misread, and because misread despised, and because despised unread. I do not pro-pose to discuss in detail a novel that (I would guess) is probably not fresh in the minds even of most classicists. But I will spend a short time on a few features of the *Aethiopica* which will liven our sense of its greatness, and make us understand the testimonials not only of Racine but also of Shake-speare, Cervantes, Rabelais, Sidney, and many others to this masterpiece.

This phase of my essay is like a movie preview: it is meant simply to capture attention, rouse curiosity, and plant the idea that the work itself might be worth considering.

Page 1: As day dawned and the sun lit up the mountain peaks, some men dressed as bandits had just reached the ridge of a hill overlooking the westernmost mouth of the Nile. They looked out over the ocean, scanning the horizon for ships that might be plundered, but seeing nothing in the distance they turned their eyes to the shore below them, and there they saw a merchant vessel, heavily laden with cargo (as they could tell from the depth of water it drew) but with no one on deck. On the shore itself they saw a litter of corpses newly slain, some just breathing their last, all lying in the midst of overturned tables and a rich banquet of food, so that wine and blood were now mingling on the sand. No plunder had been taken, and most had died from impromptu weapons—table knives, blunt objects, firebrands, such things as lay to hand during the banquet, though a good number had been shot with arrows. At a loss to explain what had taken place, the Egyptian bandits counted themselves the victors and clambered down the hill to possess themselves of the booty. As they approached the ship they came upon a still stranger sight: a white maiden of divine beauty seated on a rock, her head crowned with laurel, an unstrung bow in her left hand, her cheek resting on the palm of her right hand, as she gazed intently on the ground where a young man lay, cruelly wounded, his white skin stained with blood; he seemed to be just waking up from a deathlike sleep, and as he did their eyes met and were held fixed on each other. "My darling," he whispered, "are you really alive, or were you another victim of the fighting and now cannot bear to be separated from me, even after death? Does even your ghost, your soul, still care what befalls me?" "It depends on you," replied the girl, "whether I live or die. Do you see this?" She indicated a sword that lay on her knees. "Till now it has been idle, stayed so long as you draw breath" (1.2). And as she spoke she leaped from the rock.

The men watching were struck with terror as if lightning had flashed, for as she arose and moved she seemed even more like a goddess: the arrows rattling in her quiver as she leaped, the sun glinting from her garments inwrought with gold, her hair spreading over her shoulders like that of a bacchant. All this and their own ignorance filled them with terror, as they dove for cover behind bushes and rocks, thinking her some goddess—Artemis, maybe, or the local Isis—or else a priestess who in a god-inspired frenzy had wrought the massacre they saw before them. So they variously thought, and did not grasp the truth. The maiden quickly came to the youth and, folding him in her arms, with tears and kisses, began to nurse him. Seeing this, the Egyptians began to think, Can this be a goddess who is so attentive to a man near death? And recovering themselves they began to draw near. The noise of their armor and their shadows falling across her view caused the young woman to raise her head and look directly at them. She saw that their skin was black and their appearance wild and unkempt. "If you are the ghosts of those who here lie dead," she said, "you are wrong to trouble us. Most of you died at one another's hands. Those that we slew we slew in self-defense and in retribution for your outrage against chastity. But if you are living men, you lead the life of brigands, it seems. Your appearance is timely. Set us free from the woes that beset us! Kill us and so bring our story to a close!" (1.3).

So spoke the fair tragedian; but they, not comprehending a word of the language she spoke, left the young couple safe in their weakness and fell to plundering the ship and ransacking its cargo: gold, silver, precious gems, and costly clothes. As they were piling up their booty on the shore, another troop of brigands appeared, led by two men on horseback. Since they numbered thirty to the first group's ten, there was a quick rout. The second group was equally amazed by the tableau, and struck by the beauty and spirit of the young woman and her patient. Communicating by gestures, the bandit chief promised safety to them both and the pair were mounted on the horses. The entire group, laden with booty from the ship, left the scene, making its way back to the pirates' secret city in the marshes.

There are even more spectacular scenes in the novel: the marsh city of the pirates set ablaze at night, the woman falsely accused of murder and led to her execution on a burning pyre, a witch's necromantic rites on a moonlit battlefield, the siege of Assuan in which the river Nile is diverted so as to flow around the city like a moat, the pageantry of the games at Delphi and the love intrigues of the Egyptian wizard who deciphers at last the mysterious signs embroidered on the clothes in which the heroine was exposed as a baby, or the exciting scene where the captain of the bandits, realizing that he will never obtain the young woman as his bride, runs into the labyrinthine cave where she has been placed for safety during a battle and thrusts his sword into her chest up to the hilt. (The Duke in *Twelfth Night* alludes to this scene as one well known to his audience.) Thrill as you watch the vain attempts of the holy Ethiopian monks to halt the rites of human sacrifice, whose latest victims are to be Theagenes and Chariclea (the heroes of this novel): will the king of Ethiopia unwittingly condemn his own daughter to such a death? Well . . . not likely, but the suspense is kept high, and the recognition scene, when it comes, contains not only every subcategory of anagnorisis enumerated by Aristotle but also surprises that may elude even the craftiest reader.

I will quote two more excerpts from the *Aethiopica*, to illustrate the extremes of tone—low humor and high sentiment—that it contains. When the crafty old priest Calasiris had helped the lovers escape from Delphi and they had stopped at the island of Zacynthus, he looked around for lodging. "I had not gone far when I saw an old fisherman sitting at the door of his house repairing the mesh of a torn net. I accosted him and said: 'Good morning, my friend. Could you please tell me where one might find lodgings?' 'Just here, by the headland,' he replied. 'It got snagged on a sunken rock yesterday, and now it is full of holes!' 'That is not what my question was about,' I said, 'but it would be very helpful of you if you could find room for us yourself, or tell me someone else who might.' 'It was not me,' he replied. 'I was not out with them. No! I hope Tyrrhenos never gets so old and silly as to do such a stupid thing. It is those young whippersnappers who are to blame: they do not know their way around the reefs and put down their nets in the wrong place'" (5.18).

And so it goes. I quote this throwaway silliness partly because there is a notion about that the Greek romances are monotonously ideal, whereas in fact they are as various in tone as any good literature ever is. My final excerpt displays one of those exalted moments of exquisite feeling on which the ordinary reputation of the Greek novels was based. It is the moment when the lovers first glimpse each other, and (as one expects in this genre) feel something like love at first sight. The event is a feature of the form; what is worth noting is the ceremonious style and the psychological subtlety with which the type-scene is carried out. The hero is Theagenes, leader of a mission of the Aenianes to Delphi to perform sacrifices in honor of Neoptolemus during the Pythian games; the priest of Apollo is Charicles, and his foster daughter Chariclea is a ministrant holding the torch:

> On an enormous altar they heaped countless twigs, and on top they laid all the choicest parts of the sacrifices, as custom demanded. Then they asked the priest of Pythian Apollo to commence the libation and light the altar fire. Charikles replied that it was his office to pour the libation, "But the leader of the sacred mission should be the one to light the fire, with the torch that he has received from the hands of the acolyte. This is the usage laid down by ancestral custom."
>
> With these words he began the libation, and Theagenes made to take the fire; and in that instant it was revealed to us, Knemon, that the soul is something divine and partakes in the nature of heaven. For at the moment when they set eyes on one another, the young pair fell in love [*horôn kai erôn*], as if the soul recognized its kin at the very first encounter and sped to meet that which was worthily its own. For a brief second full of emotion they stood motionless; then slowly, so slowly, she handed him the torch and he took it from her, and all the while they gazed hard into one another's eyes, as if calling to mind a previous acquaintance or meeting. Then they smiled a fleeting, furtive smile, discernible only as a slight softening of their expressions.

And then they blushed, as if they were embarrassed at what had occurred, and a moment later—I suppose as their passion touched their hearts—the color drained from their faces. In short, in the space of an instant, an infinity of expression passed across both their faces, as every imaginable alteration in complexion and countenance bore witness to the waves that pounded their souls.

No one but me seemed to see any of this; they were all taken up with their own concerns and thinking their own thoughts. (3.5)

These are two chaste and innocent souls, quite young and untouched as yet by any worldly passion. In fact, they will *never* feel any eros, any erotic passion, but this one for each other, and it will survive incredible trials and temptations until they are at last properly married in Ethiopia. The final page indeed presents the consummation of their marriage (*gamos*), of their sexual passion (eros), and of the book itself. In fact the entire form of the Greek romance can be considered an elaboration of the period between initial desire and final consummation. That falling in love is an event occurring only once in a life, and that it leads to marriage, are notions that strike me as highly unrealistic, though they seem to be a privileged ideal and (roughly speaking) a convention by which many people still live. More to the point, they are notions quite at variance with the literary and social conventions of Greek culture in earlier days. The word from earlier erotic literature that became taboo in the conventions of the later Greek love story is *dêute*, "once again"; as Sappho and Alcman and others say, "once again I have fallen in love, once again Eros has made me his victim." Love in the Greek novels is rather like birth or death—it only happens once. It is also characteristic of earlier Greek love literature that falling in love and being in love are explored as activities almost wholly unrelated to the question of marriage (*gamos*). The appropriate concerns of marriage were such things as property, dowry, family, legitimate heirs, stability, and harmony, but not private passion, not that special kind of helpless victimization or fevered feeling celebrated under the name *eros*.

I refer to my problem or subject as the invention of romance. By romance I mean love-in-marriage, or that plot in which a young person falls suddenly and completely in love with another young person (usually of the opposite sex), finds that love perfectly reciprocated, and in spite of various obstacles and trials eventually consummates the passion in marriage. Romance in this sense is today both a plot of literature and a plot of life, both a literary form and a social norm. The problem of romance is simply to understand how, when, and why these two spheres of activity—call them *gamos* and eros—came to be defined together, so that, in my image, the two spheres converged and were, ideally at least, coextensive. As Sinatra sang, "Love and marriage, love and marriage, go together like a horse and carriage; Dad was told by Mother, you can't have one without the other." There is a pleasantly antiquated feeling about that image of a horse and carriage—expressing perhaps that romance in the sense in which I have defined it is always and everywhere at best a never-quite-realized ideal. The first stage in understanding the problem is to appreciate the independence of those two spheres in the societies of the Mediterranean basin whose records are in Greek and Latin.

By referring to this problem as the *invention* of romance, I am simply calling attention to the fact that for a long time there was no such thing: not that people who fell in love never got married, or that married persons never loved each other, but rather that the coincidence of eros and *gamos* was not a privileged norm, not an important and sought-after ideal, and further that the typical literary treatment of love and the atypical practical advice about marriage noted that eros is a dangerous and upsetting experience, in principle an unstable passion, and that one is better off keeping eros to a minimum, certainly not letting it interfere with the important business of marriage.

By using the word *invention* I mean to refer to the gradual processes of cultural reformulation and social adaptation, not to the act of some single genius who discovered or invented the idea. That is, however, exactly the thesis of one book that takes this problem seriously. Most studies of love in the Western world, such as Denis de Rougemont's, ignore the ancient period, whereas treatments by classicists, such as Lesky's *Vom Eros der Hellenen* (Göttingen, 1976), do not see the problem. But a book published in London in 1896 (reprinted in Groningen in 1970), *Antimachus of Colophon and the Position of Women in Greek Poetry,* by E. F. M. Benecke, does pose the question. The curious thesis of this interesting book is that romance, which he defines in a male-centered way as being in love with one's wife, was first presented to the public in a poem by Antimachus of Colophon, *Lyde,* which was a lengthy collection of unhappy love stories from mythology brought together in elegiac form to honor the memory of the poet's dead wife. Benecke's thesis is that the attitude of conjugal devotion struck men as a felicitous one and they rushed to imitate Antimachus not only by writing romantic literature but by falling in love with their wives. We know that there have been odd cultural fashions which have unexpectedly caught on for a time, such as the rash of romantic suicides after the publication of Goethe's *Werther,* but the theory that the joint definition of erotic passion and marriage was discovered and successfully promulgated by a single literary gent really won't bear scrutiny.

Further, Antimachus is a poet of the late fifth century B.C., and virtually all the documentation I am aware of tends to show that a dissociation of passion and marriage was the rule for both life and literature. I have in mind two series of texts: on the one hand, love stories and love poetry; on the other, discussions of love and marriage by commentators from Xenophon to John Chrysostom.

To take the latter series first, we should perhaps leave to one side the advice of Hesiod and Theognis on marriage. They fit with my thesis, to be sure. In *Works and Days* (695–705), Hesiod recommends a careful choice of wife, one young enough to be trained in her domestic duties; Theognis condemns marriages made for money, saying marriages ought to be made solely with regard to good family and aristocratic bloodlines, not wealth (183–92). Theognis provides a particularly clear example of the differentiation of eros and *gamos*. *Gamoi* are family interrelationships guaranteeing security of property, while *erotika* are relationships among men of older and younger generations that serve more political functions—friendship alliances, particularly alliances representing the city's future and the uncertain mixture of hopes, desires, and disappointments that future will bring—all this symbolized by the image of the beautiful, fickle boy. All this, I say, should probably be left to one side, because of its ambiguous status as perhaps a literary pose. But we are on more solid ground when we come to Xenophon's *Economicus* 7–10. To be sure, this is a fiction also— the fictional sketch of an ideal patriarch running an Athenian household; the young bride who listens to a catechism of her duties from the patriarch is a lifeless type, representing Xenophon's ideal of wifely obedience. But the *Economicus* is the sort of social fiction written not to entertain but to instruct; its purpose is the inculcation of an ideal of behavior. Its lack of reality, if any, lies in the excessive passivity of the young wife, who shows no signs of resistance to her husband's dominance, rather than in the absence of erotic passion.

In the long series of discussions of marriage over the next thousand years, are there any changes in this fundamental pattern of social recommendation? The answer is yes, but not many. To illustrate the sameness, consider the incidental (and therefore revealing) remark of Diodorus Siculus (19.23) when explaining the Hindu custom of suttee: this is essentially related, he says, to the Hindu convention that husband and wife choose each other rather than accept the choice of their parents. One oddity is explained by another, young romance and wife burning are equally unreal in the Greek world. And in the late fourth century A.D., John Chrysostom gives an interesting picture of marriage ideals in three sermons in *Patrologia graeca* (51.207–42). One of his basic concerns is to insist that divorce is not allowable except on grounds of adultery; therefore, when a man is visiting the marriage broker and entering into complex negotiations over the exact terms of property settlement and future contingencies (what if her father dies after she has two children but while her brother is still alive?), he should not forget to consider the character and personality of his intended bride. For if she is a shrew or a laggard or an alcoholic, he is stuck with her, just as he would be stuck if he went blind in one eye or one hand withered away. One doesn't amputate a limb simply because it is useless; no more may one divorce a wife who is a lost cause (228). In the three sermons there is some mention of harmony and considerateness, but none of passion.

Against this cantus firmus there are some grace notes. I would call it a tiny step in the direction of romance when the author of the third book of the Pseudo-Aristotelian *Economics* advises that a husband's erotic adventures outside marriage are a kind of injustice to the wife (3.2, adumbrated in 1.4.1). The argument is pragmatic: since a wife will feel that her honor has been insulted, that she has lost face, she may be unfaithful by way of revenge. But even the practical consideration of the wife's feelings and interests, treating her as a personal agent rather than a chattel, and the recommendation that the *husband* must modify his ways to account for this are important shifts toward a more bipartisan view of marriage.

The author who is closest to viewing marriage in a possibly romantic light, however, is Plutarch, and even he is far from writing the essential romantic plot whereby young persons fall in love and then get married. But he does speak of marital cooperation not only in terms of duties and responsibilities but also as a locus of occasional passion. In his *Eroticus* he contrasts the instability of eros, of love affairs (usually between men), with the calmer friendship of marriage.

> In the case of lawfully wedded wives, physical union is the beginning of friendship, a sharing, as it were, in important sacred rituals. The pleasure is minimal, of course, by comparison with love affairs, but the respect and kindness and affection . . . [are great]. Homer was right to call such intercourse *philotes* ["friendship," "intimacy"], and Solon is proved to be an experienced legislator concerning marriage when he prescribed that a man should sleep with his wife no less than three times per month, not for the sake of pleasure, of course, but as cities renew their treaties of mutual peace from time to time, so he wanted a marriage to be renewed by such an act of tenderness and thereby freed from the complaints and grudges which accumulate all the time. (769a)

Eventually husband and wife may even develop a special kind of erotic intimacy, to explain which Plutarch resorts to metaphors from Stoic to Epicurean physics. The Stoics postulated that two substances may thoroughly interpenetrate—the so-called *di' holon krasis,* or perfect blending. The Epicurean atoms, on the other hand, collide with each other and rebound; they may get stuck together but they do not blend. Plutarch says, "It is just as with the mixing of two liquids, love seems at first to cause some bubbling and excitement but as time goes on it becomes a stable solution, the impurities settle out, and it displays the steady coherence [of a single element]. This is what should truly be called a 'perfect blending,' that of a passionate couple; whereas the union of those who merely live together without passion is like the grappling and embracing of Epicurean atoms which bump together and then rebound and never create the kind of unity which Eros makes when he takes hold of a marital union." I believe this is the closest any ancient commentator on the social ideals of marriage comes to romance. Romance, for Plutarch, is something that may happen within an arranged marriage, and represents the closest accommodation between eros and *gamos* that was possible in real life.

Turning to the second series of texts, the literature of Eros, I would like to focus not on the well-known complaints of the destructive power of that god in lyric and tragedy. We have often heard the heartrending complaints of characters in drama who want to be released from life because they cannot be released from eros, try as they might. I will look rather at the art of popular narrative, at folk tales associated with particular locations and reported from generation to generation as instructive. Fortunately, these narratives have been collected by Erwin Rohde in his *Griechischer Roman* (1876) from historians, geographers, and mythographers—generally, from the byways of classical literature, frequented mainly by shepherds, by peasants, by women on their way to the well, and by a few ancient scholars like Pausanias who wanted to track down old oral traditions. In surveying this body of popular narrative concerning eros we are struck by the proportion of unhappy to happy tales, which is about fifty to one. I will tell you the one, but first let me tell you some of the fifty.

My first tale comes from Pausanias's *Guidebook to Greece:*

> After the Charadrus River you come to some ruins, not particularly impressive, of the city Argyra, to the spring Argyra on the right of the high road, and to the river Selemnus going down to the sea. The local people tell a tale about Selemnus—that he was a handsome lad who used to feed his flocks here. Argyra, they say, was a sea nymph, who fell in love [that's *eros*] with Selemnus and used to come up out of the sea to visit him and to sleep with him. After no long while Selemnus no longer seemed handsome, and the nymph would not visit him. So Selemnus, deserted by Argyra, died of love, and Aphrodite turned him into a river. This is the tale told by the people of Patrae. Since Selemnus continued to love [*era*] Argyra even when he was turned into water, just as Alpheus in the legend continued to love Arethusa, Aphrodite bestowed on him a further gift, by blotting out the memory of Argyra. I heard too another story about the water, how it is a useful remedy for both men and women when in love [*es erotos iama*]; if they wash in the river they forget their passion. If there is any truth

in the story the water of the Selemnus is of more value to humankind than great wealth. (7.23.1–3)

This same attitude informs the folk songs Athenaeus records from earlier scholars in the fourteenth book of his *Deipnosophists* (619c–620a). He lists four that deal with love. The first is a pastoral song in which Eriphanis laments her rejection by a hunter named Menalcas; the wild animals of the forest lament along with her. Stesichorus is credited with a song sung by women in olden days about the desire of a maiden named Calyce for a young man named Euathlus; he rejects her and she commits suicide. Third, there is a song contest among maidens known as the Harpalyce, after a maiden who fell in love, was rejected, and died. Finally, among the Mariandynians in Bithynia there is a festival at which an ancient song is sung about an especially handsome young man named Bormus who went to fetch water for the reapers and never returned. Evidently this is in the same family of stories as that of Hylas.

In most of the narratives the mere mention of eros is already a signal to the audience of peril, danger, and an unhappy ending. So common was the narrative of unhappy love leading to death that Lucian could parody it in a dialogue set in the underworld. He represents one of the Fates counting off a checklist of the dead who are arriving on the latest boatload into Hades —this batch includes seven who killed themselves because of unhappy love, including the philosopher Theagenes, who loved a courtesan from Megara.

The programmatic tale of instability in royal succession told by Herodotus at the beginning of his *Histories* concerns the ousting of Candaules by Gyges. This story was told in various ways; we have a folkloric version in Plato that involves an underground chamber of mysterious origin and a ring of invisibility. Herodotus's account begins: "Now Candaules fell in love with his own wife." This formulation may surprise us; what should be emphasized is that within the social conventions and narrative patterns Herodotus is using, it automatically strikes an ominous note.

Two other eros stories from Herodotus have happy endings, but neither is romantic. Both have that mark of oral tradition, the site or monument the locals talk about to travelers.

Amasis, king of Egypt, concluded a pact of friendship and alliance with Cyrene, and to show his goodwill, or perhaps merely because he wanted a Greek wife, decided to marry a woman from that city. The woman he chose was Ladice, daughter . . . of one of the leading citizens. For a time the marriage was not consummated, for whenever the king went to bed with her, he was unable to have intercourse, while with his other wives he did. This happened frequently, until at last Amasis told her that she must have bewitched him, and there was no escape for her therefore from a most miserable death. Ladice denied the charge, but in vain; the king's anger was not softened, so she made a silent vow to Aphrodite that if that very night—the last that could save her from death—the marriage could be consummated, she would present a statue to the temple of the goddess of Cyrene. Her prayer was at once answered; Amasis lay with her successfully, and continued to do so on every occasion afterward, and came to cherish her deeply [stergein]. Ladice fulfilled her vow to Aphrodite; she had the statue made and sent it to Cyrene, where it still remained up to my own time, looking outward from the city. (Herodotus 2.181)

No doubt a special statue of Aphrodite in her temple could have many tales told about it, especially if it was commissioned by a native daughter who had made good. The practical tensions of ordinary social life that make this story work are quite astonishing (though also, as usual, familiar): Ladice is held responsible for her husband's impotence, and she accepts that responsibility. Here eros is not portrayed as a force destructive to marriage but as one of the duties of marriage: her business is his pleasure. If the fundamental requirements of a marriage (which may be children, domestic work, sex) are satisfied, then a certain affection is allowed to grow. Although this story contains a strand of the romantic plot—his eros, which presumably leads to the marriage—this is not what we would call a romance.

To illustrate another variation on the same material, consider the following story whose plot you may know from the romanticized versions in the brothers Grimm and Walt Disney: it occurs in Strabo's account of Egypt. In addition to the two largest pyramids near Memphis there is a third, smaller one, made of black stone brought all the way from Ethiopia. It is called the Tomb of the Courtesan, having been built by the lovers of Doricha, who lived in the time of Sappho. The fabulous story is told that, when Doricha was bathing, an eagle snatched one of her sandals from her maid and carried it to Memphis; while the king was administering justice in the open air, the eagle when it arrived above his head dropped the sandal into his lap, and the king, stirred by the occurrence, sent men in all directions into the country in quest of the woman who wore the sandal. When she was found in the city of Naucratis, she was brought up to Memphis and became the wife of the king, and when she died she was honored with the abovementioned pyramid (17.1.33). There is here a certain coincidence of love and marriage, but remember too that the king had many "wives," that Doricha was a courtesan, and that the pyramid was built by her lovers. Herodotus's version of the tale told about the same pyramid (2.126) is that Cheops made his daughter a prostitute, and that in addition to the fee each customer was required to pay to the royal treasury she demanded that each man give her a block of stone; from these stones the pyramid was erected.

Now for a bit of melodrama: in Calydon, according to Pausanias again

(7.21.1–5), a priest of Dionysus named Coresus fell madly in love with a maiden named Callirhoe, but she would have nothing to do with him. Praying for help to his god, Coresus obtained the favor from Dionysus that all the people of Calydon went stark, raving mad, and the oracle at Dodona explained that the madness would only be removed if Callirhoe or a substitute were sacrificed to Dionysus. Callirhoe could find no one to take her place, so she was eventually led to the altar, where the ministrant of course was Coresus himself. At the last minute, his hurt at being rejected gave way to his love and he slew himself in her place. She realized then how much he really loved her and was ashamed that she had rejected him, so she cut her throat beside a spring, which to this day is called Callirhoe.

And so it was that the people of Greece personalized their environment with images of their own hopes and fears, reading into place names and seasonal rituals the stories of what was possible and impossible in daily life. Before psychiatry and marriage counseling, folk tales were among the regular institutions that helped people adjust their fantasies and desires to the stricter demands of a pretechnological society.

The rare story of falling in love that has a happy ending is represented by an episode from early Asian history recorded by Chares of Mytilene in the tenth book of his Alexander history. An Armenian prince and a Russian princess see each other in a dream and fall in love telepathically. The prince journeys north across the river Don and arrives just at the moment when her father has summoned his nobles to a banquet at which his daughter Odatis must choose her husband by handing one of them a wine cup. She hears this command and looks around the room in dismay, for she does not see the man of her dreams. As she stands at the sideboard near the kitchen door slowly pouring the wine into the cup, the prince, whose name is Zariadres, appears at her side dressed in a Russian cloak and hood; they recognize each other and with help from the servants make their escape back to his kingdom. Chares concludes: "Now this love story is a very popular tale among the barbarians of Asia; they have pictures of this tale in their temples and palaces and even in private homes; and most kings name their daughters Odatis" (Athenaeus 13.575). Orientalists (reported in Rohde, Der griechische Roman, 49–55) trace the pattern of this story to the Iranian saga of Firdusi, in which a princess chooses her husband from those assembled by her father at a banquet; she sees in the group and chooses the hero who had previously appeared in her dreams.

On the basis of the small selection of evidence I have presented here it begins to look as if the narrative pattern of romance (as I have defined it) is a resident alien in Greek culture, a literary form born in and (presumably) appropriate to the social forms of a Near Eastern culture, and which has been Hellenized in the wake of Alexander's conquests.

A remarkable supporting argument for this line of thought appeared in an article by Gerald Gresseth on the *Odyssey* and the *Nalopakhyana,* an Indian epic (*Transactions of the American Philological Association* 109 [1979]: 63–85). He argues quite well, as far as I can judge, that the story pattern of the *Odyssey* is the same as that of the *Nalopakhyana.* The key event in both, toward which all the action leads, is the Indian ceremony known as *svayamvara,* literally "self-choice," a ceremony in which a woman chooses her own husband. The husband in both cases is in disguise. The paradox of the plot is essentially that the ceremony of "self-choice" whereby the wife would have chosen a new husband and forsaken her first husband is exactly what brings about the reunion. This reading of the *Odyssey* as an adaptation of an Indian romance would be an interesting parallel to the hypothesis of a later Hellenization of Near Eastern romances after Alexander, but what makes it especially exciting is that it isolates as crucial the ceremony of *svayamvara,* which is also the central scene of the story of Zariadres and Odatis. It has long seemed that the *Odyssey* is a kind of protoromance of which the Greek novels are a distant development—certainly it has many of the same elements, though in different combinations (the youthful experiences of Nausicaa and Telemachus, the affectionate reunion of husband and wife). But now it appears that perhaps both the *Odyssey* and the later Greek novels are Hellenizations of Eastern tales—Iranian, Persian, and Sanskrit.

This is, to be sure, a general speculation, and I am aware that I have not introduced into this sketch the numerous variables of class, period, country, and so forth that are necessary. What I have tried to argue here is that love-in-marriage was a fully formed artistic entity in the Greco-Roman world of the first few centuries of our era, even though it had virtually no representational value for the lives of its readers, and further—most strangely and importantly—that it was somehow prophetic of a social order to come. For the era did arrive (and I presume is still going on) when young romance became an expectation of life.

A more precise analysis of this state of affairs may be reached by considering an analogous case. The earliest portrayal of a women's political movement occurs in several plays of Aristophanes—*Lysistrata,* the *Congresswomen,* and a lost play entitled *Skenas Katalambanousai* (The women taking over the stage). This last was apparently a development of the theme in other plays that the proper married ladies of Athens objected to the slanderous female stereotypes employed by male tragedians. And their protest is a radical action: they occupy the theater itself. Yet this artistic image of women speaking out, demanding a reordering of political life to include them as they are, was not a realistic portrayal of what was actually happening in Athens. I should call it a fantasy of the significantly impossible. Social rules constantly and insistently forbade women—actually men in drag—to lift their veils, to break their silence, to act with autonomy.

Therefore these acts came to exist in certain male myths (of the Amazons, for example) and on the festivals when the rules of ordinary decorum were systematically violated.

Such an analysis goes some way toward explaining the development of romantic stories from the first century B.C. on: why they caught people's fancies and at the same time seemed beneath serious consideration. They are—like the protofeminist politics in Aristophanes—a fantasy of the significantly impossible. They express the same thing, but in a different light; they *are* the prohibitions of folk tales about the danger of eros, but cast in a fantasy mode. Just as we expect Aristophanic comedy to reverse the roles and violate the boundaries of daily life, and by that expression to reinforce our sense of them, so the emergence of romantic plots in a nonromantic culture is not entirely strange.

What most interests me in this is the curious phenomenon that an artistic pattern may endure for a long time in a gray area of irrelevance to actual life and then much later take on new existence as a concrete social norm. If I can to a certain extent make sense of the emergence of the literature of romance, that only leaves the other part of the problem crying for explanation—the much later infiltration of that idle daydream from a lazy summer afternoon. Shall we call this situation precisely a desert mirage? That is, the encounter with an insubstantial image, deeply satisfying to the thirsty wanderer but, alas, unreal because the oasis itself exists in reality far away?

Let me conclude with a joking text which points the issue even more acutely. The first occurrence of true-love-lasting-forever that I know in classical culture is the Aristophanic myth in Plato's *Symposium*. The discussion of eros in that dialogue has an evident lack of relation to *gamos*. Aristophanes' account of the origin of sexual desire is a fabulous fable: the primal people were roly-polies, four arms, four legs, a head with two faces—creatures who were split down the middle for their impiety and sewn up so the skin was knotted at (what we now call) the navel and whose heads were twisted backward. The ineradicable longing for completion with another being is thus explained, by a joke, as the memory of a formerly complete self. This also explains the varieties of desire, of men for men, of women for women, and of some men and women for each other. The implications are wholly romantic—there is only one "other half" who will answer the deepest cry for wholeness, and if such lovers were asked what they wanted more than anything else, they would reply, "To be joined together as a single body, in a permanent melting union of one with the other," which presumably would last forever, like the happy marriages which conclude the Greek novels. But this crazy suggestion, this outrageous joke, a parody of romantic feelings and an implicit rejection of them, is the very myth that was to become the romantic plot.

How extraordinary it is, and what fun, to watch one person's joke on an absurd possibility become a popular form of escape literature, and then to see (precisely when and how I do not yet know) that daydream become a sort of waking hallucination, a pleasant enough dream, like those from which we are aroused but which are so satisfying that we turn off the alarm and go back to sleep.

CHAPTER TWO

Genre of Genre

Daniel L. Selden

> The night before, two doubtful words had halted him at the beginning
> of the *Poetics*. These words were *tragedy* and *comedy*. He had encountered
> them years before in the third book of the *Rhetoric;* no one in the whole
> world of Islam could conjecture what they meant.
>
> —J. L. Borges, "Averroës' Search"

For some time now, it has been assumed that we could shed light on the
prose fiction of late antiquity by determining its genre. I would like to
pursue this problem a bit further by posing the question the other way
around: What can the prose fiction of antiquity contribute to an understanding of our own sense of generic order?

In the first place, genre is not simply one critical question among others
that one brings to classical prose fiction; it is an issue of intrinsic structural
importance. Greek and Roman writers worked within a highly elaborated
field of generic classifications (εἴδη) which admitted several overlapping
systems of distinction. Difference was recognized at every level of the
discourse: pragmatic (epic, lyric, drama), syntactic (ode, elegy, epigram),
and semantic (*kômos, propemptikon, sôtêria*).[1] Poetic production aimed less
at internally complete or highly individuated texts than at creativity in the
selection, combination, and revision of generic topoi.[2] Pindar already
speaks of his obedience to the law (τεθμός) of the encomium and hymn,[3]
and his younger contemporary, Choerilus of Samos, stresses that Greek
writers do not have free rein for innovation, since literature is divided up
(δέδασται) into fixed modes of composition.[4] The vocabulary here betrays
specific social connotations: τεθμός, in particular, belongs to the semantic
sphere of θέμις, the unwritten code of divine origin that prescribes the
rights and duties of the individual under the jurisdiction of the gentilitial
chief.[5] All ancient genres originated in important and recurrent real-life
situations,[6] and their institutionalization as patterns of regular response
supplied part of the fundamental architecture (θέμεθλα) for the social order.[7] It comes as no surprise, then, that a formal theory of literary genres
first emerged as part of political philosophy. Plato attempts in the *Republic*
to identify the single genre that will most successfully inculcate civic virtue
as the "pure imitator of propriety,"[8] though Socrates' hard line yields in

the *Laws* to greater toleration for a spectrum of different literary forms. In spite of this concession, Plato is adamant about one thing: literary kinds must remain distinct and, in fact, the mixture of genres serves the Athenian Stranger as the principal paradigm for political degeneration. Originally, he argues,

> our music was divided [διῃρημένη] into several kinds and patterns, and it was not permissible to misuse one type of melody for another. In the course of time, however, the poets became increasingly possessed by a frantic lust for pleasure; they mixed laments with hymns and paeans with dithyrambs, actually imitated the strains of the flute on the harp, and thereby created a universal confusion among forms [πάντα εἰς πάντα συνάγοντες]. Compositions of this kind naturally inspired in the multitude a contempt for poetic order, and a pretense to general knowledge and disrespect for law [παρανομία] has ultimately followed in its train. What might be the outcome of this sort of license?—a refusal to submit to magistrates, emancipation from the authority of parents and elders, efforts to escape obedience to the law and, when that goal is all but reached, disregard for oaths and complete contempt of all religion. Thus, the legendary spectacle of the Titans is replayed, and man returns to his old condition, a wretched life of unrelenting misery.[9]

Whether or not Plato is seriously suggesting that generic mixture is the leading source of Athens's decadence, there is a close connection in his thought between generic prescription and political hierarchy, in this case the institutional authority of fathers, magistrates, and gods. Even in the wake of Aristotle's remarkable effort to displace discussion to the realm of natural forms,[10] the idea of genre in antiquity never sheds its social overtones. Cicero, for instance, recognizes that each genre (*genus dicendi*) has its own peculiar nature, but correlates their differences with discrepancies in the rank (*honos*), authority (*auctoritas*), and duty (*officium*) of the respective subjects that each treats. Political propriety grounds the decorum of literary kinds, so it would be wholly inappropriate, he argues, to address the *maiestas* of the Roman people in a menial style.[11] Horace similarly enjoins the poet to observe the boundaries between genres: *versibus exponi tragicis res comica non vult*.[12] The assertion suggests a property essential to each kind, though the text goes on to liken the way tragedy eschews satiric language to a Roman matron who chastely avoids mingling with the lascivious crowd.[13] Long after the different genres ceased to be occasional and to fulfill specific social functions,[14] they continued to bear the marks of status, class, ethnicity, and gender,[15] and for writers to uphold the propriety of these distinctions was felt implicitly to validate a social order.

In this case, theory stands in dialectical relation to authorial practice.

The hybridization of which Plato complains in the *Laws* was already fact, and however strongly critics reinforced the notion of generic purity, the hallmark of Hellenistic letters became the crossing of literary kinds.[16] Often, as in Herodas's *Mimiamboi* or the *Epistulae Heroidum* of Ovid, two genres are conflated, though in later imperial writers, like Lucian and Apuleius, disparate generic forms are brought together piecemeal and collocated side by side. An episode from the *Satyricon* is particularly illuminating in this respect.

> *Encolpius enters a picture gallery hung with mythological scenes of rape. There he encounters the indigent old poet Eumolpus, who tells him a racy story and then speculates on the reason for the decadence of painting. The poet extemporizes some verses on the fall of Troy, and the two men beat a hasty exit from the gallery when they are pelted with stones by strollers in the colonnade.*[17]

This short sequence presents the reader with a dazzling display of generic composition: ecphrasis, satire, a Milesian tale, diatribe, and epyllion all follow in rapid succession, juxtaposing vulgar with elite, poetry with prose, anecdote with declamation. The separate pieces are connected by the common theme of decadence, physical as well as moral, which each develops from its own generically specific point of view. The result is a series of prismatic contrasts in perspective, which are most extensively worked out in the two interpolated compositions given to Eumolpus. The *Troiae Halosis* is a miniature epic,[18] which, in an arcane diction removed from contemporary speech,[19] returns us to a heroic world and to a moment, in particular, that the *Aeneid* canonizes as the mythic origin of the Roman state.[20] In a series of lapidary vignettes, the narrator retells how Troy was taken, as witnessed from the Trojan side: the construction of the wooden horse, the testimonial of Sinon, Laocoon's incredulity and death, imprudent reveling, the slaughter of the Trojans in their sleep. The poem focuses principally on acts of duplicity (*fraus*), which it ultimately valorizes from the vantage point of military conquest, national enterprise, and world-historical significance.[21]

By contrast, the colloquial Milesian tale is an anonymous account that unfolds in contemporary Asia Minor within the privacy of the bedchamber.[22] Here too, however, is a story of seductions: while billeted at Pergamum on military duty, a government official beguiles his hosts, but bribes their teenage son with promises of gifts, the most lavish of which is a horse, until he successfully corrupts him; when the youth's sexual appetite turns out to be voracious, it is the officer who threatens to reveal the whole ruse to the parents if the boy will not let him get a few hours' sleep. All the imagery of the *Troiae Halosis* quite strikingly recurs here, and in roughly the same order, though in the tale violence and destruction are consistently transmuted into amatory coupling and sexual awakening. To take just one example: the ghastly serpents who strangle the sons of Laocoon before their father's eyes (*repente tergoribus ligant angues corusci*) become, in the Milesian tale, a phallic figure for the officer as he worms his way into the boy's backside: "dum dicit 'patrem excitabo' irrepsi tamen et male repugnanti gaudium extorsi." *Irrepere* is the *vox propria* for how snakes move,[23] and, among other things, the narrative diptych here plays off two radically different types of penetration.

We find, then, that a single matrix of figures gives rise to two divergent textual elaborations, realized along opposing generic lines. The one composition conforms to a genre privileged by the literary establishment at Nero's court,[24] while the other is a popular, scurrilous, and unofficial mode of storytelling.[25] Modern readers have generally preferred the Milesian tale on various aesthetic grounds, but insofar as it is Eumolpus, a single character, who gives voice to both of them, the point is surely to experience the differences, and similarities, between the two. The text itself poses the syncrisis in a more provocative way on grounds that are political. The story of the boy at Pergamum, which unfolds while the paterfamilias is off guard or sound asleep,[26] thematizes a reversal in values and authority exactly parallel to the way in which the tale itself challenges official taste. The generic tension is part of a more far-reaching critique of social values and, to the same extent that the boy's seduction is both a liberation and a scandal, the achievement of the tale, literary as well as ethical, remains ambivalent.[27] As such, the episode requires of its readers a precise familiarity with the principles of Greek and Roman generic composition, whose social implications, in particular, it both exploits and exposes by distinction. To this end, the sequence runs the gamut of Hellenistic literary forms, though characteristically its social engagement cannot be halted here. Both the *Troiae Halosis* and *Boy of Pergamum,* set on the Eurasian border, represent an encounter between East and West,[28] and, as it turns out, the composition of the picture gallery segment as a whole finds its closest parallels in Oriental fiction. The run-in with a threadbare literary charlatan, the mixture of poetry and prose, and the conjunction of moral diatribe with stories of seduction are established generic features of the classical Arabic *maqâmât.*[29] Published examples first appear in the fourth century A.H., but parallels with folklore and with the Sanskrit *Panchatantra* suggest much older currency throughout the Middle East.[30] It would seem, then, that Petronius has taken a popular type of Semitic-Oriental narrative, itself based on principles of hybridization, and infused it with a farrago of Greek and Roman genres. Like the banquet of Trimalchio, with its motley crew of guests, the *Satyricon* itself is a site of meeting and engagement for the most socially and ethnically diverse literary forms.

What happens when this type of text is ascribed to a unitary genre? As is well known, classical antiquity had no generic rubric for complex prose fiction,[31] and the texts themselves tend to refer to their own eclectic nature. Apuleius promises *sermone Milesio varias fabulas conseram;*[32] Heliodorus's narrative is specifically τὸ σύνταγμα τῶν περὶ Θεαγένην καὶ Χαρίκλειαν Αἰθιοπικῶν,[33] and Longus characterizes his writing as a dialectical response (ἀντιγράψαι).[34] Not surprisingly, later critics have had some difficulty in categorizing this work. Byzantine readers connected the texts variously with history, rhetoric, and drama,[35] and from the fifteenth century, when they began to resurface in the West, attempts at generic categorization were equally diverse.[36] In the principal poetic handbooks of the High Renaissance (Scaliger, Tasso, Sidney, Pinciano), the *Aethiopica* serves as a model for heroic epic;[37] at the same time, however, *The Golden Ass* figures among comic texts,[38] while Petronius is assimilated to satire.[39] In fact, there is no evidence that before the modern era the range of texts that we have come to call the "ancient novel" were ever thought of together as constituting a coherent group. The realignment occurred gradually over the course of the seventeenth century and found its definitive articulation in Pierre-Daniel Huet's *Traité de l'origine des romans,* which appeared in 1670.[40] With considerable lucidity as to the character of his own myth-making,[41] Huet achieves generic synthesis by postulating the novel (*roman*) as a natural impulse of the human spirit "common to all men, at all times and in all places."[42] Most of his ideas about the formal components of the genre had been in circulation for at least a century, but no one before Huet had tried to systematize them as integrants of a coherent code.[43] Like all genres in the Grand Siècle, Huet's novel possessed unity, verisimilitude, and propriety, and aimed through pleasure at instruction.[44] The form is distinguished from other kinds of narrative, however, by a series of binary oppositions that define the type of signifier, signified, and referent proper to its code: the novel is in prose, not verse; it deals with love, not politics or war; and its narrative is fictional, not fact.[45] Above all, the novel "must conform to a specific set of rules; otherwise," Huet asserts, "[the genre] would be a confused mass, lacking order and all beauty."[46]

This "rule of the rule" is what grounds the entire system, and it allows the treatise to make two further points regarding antiquity. First, Huet devises the concept of the Greco-Roman novel and synchronically defines its field.[47] His colleague, Nicholas Boileau, had stated categorically, "There are not only genres of poetry in which the Latins have not surpassed us, but with which they were wholly unfamiliar; for example, those poems in prose that we call novels."[48] Much of the burden of Huet's treatise is to revise this received idea by redistributing the lines of filiation among the ancient texts. Photius had perceived a formal similarity between the "Greek romances,"[49] and Huet extends the network of these connections and normalizes them on the basis of their conformity to his novelistic code. Accordingly, Heliodorus, Iamblichus, and Achilles Tatius set the standards for the genre;[50] Longus, Petronius, Lucian, and Apuleius are appreciably germane, but structurally "less regular," and at the outer limits there are aberrant or incompletely realized instances of the form, like the *Erotika pathêmata* or *Barlaam and Joasaph*.[51] In this way, the essay configures the field of the novel in antiquity around a core of ideal narratives, against which all other examples of the type in the Greco-Roman world are to be judged. Second, Huet constructs a diachronic history for the form. Jean Chapelain's *Lectures des vieux romans* (1647) went back no further than the Middle Ages, but Huet sets out to trace an unbroken genealogy of prose fiction. Not surprisingly, his itinerary reconfirms *translatio studii* and the Westering of culture: from the Orient, we move through Greece and Rome to medieval France and thence to modern Europe. Heliodorus, Achilles Tatius, Longus, Petronius, and Apuleius constitute the apogee of this world-historical development, so that the treatise is ultimately organized around the origins, analysis, and heritage of these focal texts. In Huet's thinking, uniformity of structure, integrity of genre, and continuity of history are three related pressures, which dovetail in the essay to define and validate the novel as a classical generic form.

Huet's treatise is not a philological monograph of the type familiar from the nineteenth century. It appeared first as a letter, prefaced to Mme de La Fayette's *Zayde,* and has a precise place in the literary polemics of seventeenth-century France. Although Huet is obviously prescient in championing modern prose fiction, in most respects the basic impulse of the essay is conservative. Among other things, it attempts to supply for the novel a codification equivalent to d'Aubignac's *Pratique du théâtre,* Boileau's *Art poétique,* and Le Bossu's *Traité du poème epique,* the triad of genres of which the century officially approved.[52] By 1670 the *nouvelles françaises* were intensely controversial and offered a radically progressive challenge to the cultural establishment.[53] Huet's response was to ennoble the genre with an impeccable pedigree of Greco-Roman precedents and to diffuse its potentially disruptive force by subsuming it within the canons of orthodox neoclassical aesthetics.[54] By the time of Huet's death, this vision of the novel was already out of date,[55] and for the history of modern fiction his essay is today little more than an intellectual curiosity. This is not the case, however, for its synthesis and exposition of the Greek and Roman texts, which has proved definitive for scholarship on ancient fiction in the modern era. From Hugh Blair through Rohde and Perry,[56] articles and surveys have not only continued to ascribe to the generic coordinates laid out by Huet's treatise; they continue to follow its critical agenda and often reproduce its very structure.

Of the many examples one might adduce to illustrate this point, I take the first International Conference on the Ancient Novel, held in Bangor, Wales, in 1976, which has the advantage of being a type of collective text, representative of the general *état de la question*.[57] At its opening session, the conference reaffirmed that ancient fiction is a "synchronic order of coexisting works," whose *système romanesque* subsequent papers attempted to work out in some detail.[58] Individual panels were devoted to Heliodorus, Xenophon,[59] Longus, Petronius, and Apuleius, and throughout the range of the proceedings these authors remained the center of attention. Participants were recurrently reminded that in their structure the *Satyricon* and *Golden Ass* conform less regularly to the standards of the genre, and a session on "near-novels" defined its outer "fringe." At the same time, the conference accorded complementary emphasis to the evolution of the novel and to establishing a "chronology for the form." Panels on "origins" and "the novel-tradition" argued for the "fundamental continuity" of the genre's history, which various speakers traced from the Assyrian *Life of Ahikar* through Níkos Kazantzákis.[60] One of the purposes of this gathering was to acknowledge the centennial of Erwin Rohde's *Griechische Roman* and, among other things, the proceedings commemorated the advances scholars have made on individual texts, their antecedents and tradition, in this century. Coincidentally, however, the decade also marked the tercentenary of Huet's treatise, and one might equally have wondered at how little progress has been made in our concept of ancient fiction as a genre in the past three hundred years.[61]

It is not my intention to adjudicate whether there is or is not a literary kind that can be called "the ancient novel." Tzvetan Todorov is probably right that genres exist if readers think they exist,[62] though if we take this observation seriously, it leads us from questions of taxonomy and form back to the sociology of fiction. As Todorov puts it, "each era has its own system of genres, which is in relation with the dominant ideology."[63] The question is not simply whether there is a coherent corpus of prose fiction from antiquity, but why and under what historical conditions it becomes both possible and desirable to conceive of it as such. From Michael McKeon we have learned how deceptively "simple abstractions" like *romance* or *novel* enclose complex historical processes, marking sites of dialectical tension within the emergent ideology of modern bourgeois culture.[64] How ancient fiction has been implicated in this enterprise can be indicated briefly by looking at the way character is handled in contemporary criticism. In general, studies of this aspect of the Greco-Roman novel tend to be not descriptive, but judgmental. They show a marked preference for the "effortlessly natural representation of [an] unforgettable individual,"[65] where a premium is placed on the fullness of the portrait and the impression of psychological depth. Thus, critics invariably praise figures who are "distinctive," "many-sided," "integrated," "consistent," and "convincing," while they deplore those that remain "predictable," "simplistic," "underdeveloped," or "absurd."[66] Ultimately, each character must have a purpose and, wherever possible, contradictions in behavior are resolved *a fortiori* by integration into a more complex scheme.[67]

What is most significant about this line of criticism is the predictability of the approach. It is well known to modernists that this norm for characterization crystallized in the eighteenth century;[68] it dominated thinking about the novel for the next few generations,[69] and remains popularly entrenched today among writers of prose fiction.[70] The semiological configuration of the system has been well studied, most memorably by Barthes,[71] and for some time now the entire set of discursive practices has been rigorously resisted by the Left. An ideological critique of its conventions was already sketched by Marx in the notebooks of 1857, in which he observes that the "aesthetic illusion" (*Schein*) of autonomous individuation appeared in Western letters precisely at the point when social relations were in fact the most developed.[72] Brecht made this insight a cornerstone of his anti-Aristotelian aesthetics and, more than any other critic, he worked to demystify the ways in which subjective characterization (*Einzelpersönlichkeit*) entails specific ideological assumptions about the relation of the individual to society.[73] In particular, Brecht noted how the continual focus on personally distinctive traits systematically opposes the individual to the collective. Since the demand for character development simultaneously precludes any but the most individual solutions, the strategy as a whole effectively obscures both the need and the possibility for large-scale social change. One of the things that makes this deflection so enormously seductive, he suggested, is the way the typical "well-rounded" character substitutes for the ceaseless "inner shuffling" of human personality a fiction of consistency and closure.[74] What bothered Brecht was how this semblance of completeness falsifies the reality of modern sociopersonal relations, though more recent theorists of the novel have seen it as a discursive practice deeply embedded in its age. Lennard Davis, for example, relates the reification of the subject required to produce a character to the market economy that gave rise to modern fiction and on which it manifestly thrives:

> The novel works . . . by turning personality into controlled character. In effect, personality is rendered a form of property—quite literally if you consider the author's ownership of his or her creation through copyright laws—and a commodity in the sense that readers buy novels in some sense to have access to these controlled personalities. By placing so much emphasis on the process of desire, and the feeling that this activity of novel reading is so dependent on Eros to solve personal problems and reshape character, the novel in effect

becomes a social form that changes the complexity of personality into a rather simplified commodity of desire. Like a desirable commodity that seems to offer the promise of an improved life, or like an objectified fashion model who beckons the user of the targeted product into the frame of an advertisement, character holds out the possibility of personal fulfillment in a world that is increasingly making such fulfillment inconceivable.[75]

It would seem, then, that behind the deceptively simple device of subjective characterization lies a complex literary mechanism that concomitantly exploits, advances, and mystifies the prevailing socioeconomic order. By rediscovering this strategy, however rudimentary, in ancient fiction, the academy accomplishes at least two things: it reinforces the great novelistic myth that character as such is universal, and it ensconces modern prose uncritically as the acme of literary, and by implication social, evolution.[76] To write, for example, that "Heliodorus can hardly hold his own against . . . the modern masterpieces of prose fiction" entails an aesthetic judgment, but leaves an ideological remainder.[77]

"Genres," Fredric Jameson observes, "are essentially literary *institutions,* or social contracts between a writer and a specific public, whose function is to specify the proper use of a particular cultural artifact."[78] Whatever one's politics or aesthetic predilections, it is clear that the subscription of ancient fiction to the genre of the novel has not served these texts particularly well. While before the seventeenth century they were extremely highly prized, in the wake of Huet's treatise their reputation only plummeted. Scaliger, for instance, advised the public: "Every epic poet should read the *Aethiopica* with care and regard it as the very best of models [*quasi pro optimo exemplari sibi proponendum*]."[79] Three centuries later, Rohde reviewed the same book as part of *The Greek Novel and Its Antecedents* and found only *leere und schaale Gebilde* there; he wrote: "Dem Leser . . . wird es bei dieser Art der [Dichtung] graulich 'er reitet geschwind', um aus dieser Barbarei zu entkommen."[80] Whereas Rohde's repugnance for the ancient novel could not be clearer, his allusion to the final lines of Goethe's "Erlkönig" casts Greek fiction as a kind of Doppelgänger, the ghostly other or repressed of modern literary sensibility, which threatens to return to claim its due. Recent years have witnessed a remarkable rebirth of interest in the ancient novel, though whether this new work will resist the centripetal force of current generic orderings remains unclear.[81]

I would like to conclude with a brief consideration of this possibility by way of a well-known tale from Apuleius.

A young adulterer pays a visit to the wife of a day laborer who is temporarily off work. Suddenly the husband returns: what are they to do? The woman hides her lover in an old crock stashed in the corner of the bedroom, but when the husband enters, he goes immediately to fetch the tub, which he has arranged to sell for six denarii. His wife berates him for his lack of business sense: she, a mere woman, has not only found someone who will buy the crock at seven, but the man is already down inside the jar inspecting its insides. The husband is delighted to see a prospect for financial gain and, when the lover emerges to complain that the tub is caked with grime, he jumps into the crock to clean it. Now the wife leans across the vessel and, as her lover has his way with her outside, she directs her husband where to scrape the dirt within. With both jobs finished, the young man pays his money and the husband is enlisted to cart the old jar to his rival's home.[82]

What is scandalous about this story is not that a woman cuckolds her husband, but that her behavior satisfies two orders of logic simultaneously that were diametrically opposed in the Roman mind.[83] On the one hand, she is the epitome of the artful adulteress (*lasciva, temeraria, fallaciosa*), who hoodwinks her husband practically before his eyes.[84] On the other, she is completely provident of her domestic economy: as materfamilias, she manages the household and ingeniously ensures that there is money for supper in the till.[85] When the two men show up seriatim on her doorstep,[86] she plays one set of expectations off against the other and has the best of both of them: she enjoys the youth as she serves the marriage.[87] Her actions are consistently legible within both plots until, spread over the tub between her husband and her lover, it is no longer possible to tell to which scenario her posturing belongs: "She kept pointing out with her finger spots to be rubbed, saying, 'There . . . here . . . there . . . there . . .'"[88] These ejaculations are diegetically pure copula, and climax comes precisely at the point of suture between the two irreconcilably divergent codes. Each of the men here winds up in some way losing out,[89] but for the *mulier perastutula* the concurrence is a windfall, which yields her augmented profit and unconditioned pleasure.

The interest of this anecdote for the text of Apuleius, and indeed for the corpus of ancient fiction as a whole, hinges on its rhetorical construction. The piece is organized around a trope that classical rhetoricians called syllepsis.[90] In its most basic form, the handbooks define this as a linguistic mismatch (ἁμάρτημα μετὰ λόγου πεποιημένον)[91] in which one word is taken simultaneously in two different senses.[92] Pope, for example, in *The Rape of the Lock*, wonders whether Belinda will "stain her honor or her new brocade."[93] The sentence is entirely grammatical, but in the first clause the blot is metaphoric, while in the second it would be quite real. Ancient rhetoricians recognized that this same figure can also govern actions (τὸ ἄλλως πραχθὲν ἐφ' ἕτερον ἕλκουσα) as well as more complex narrations (διήγησις),[94] and this is precisely what we find in Apuleius's tale. Here a single fact, the lover's presence in the tub, receives one interpretation in the first part of the story (amatory), but another in the second (commercial). The narrative elaborates this syllepsis comically, and ultimately thematizes it in the body of the matron who yields herself up simultaneously to the different uses of her two men.[95] Puttenham called this figure "double supply," commenting that it "conceiv[es], and, as it were, comprehend[s] under one, a supplie of two natures, and may be likened to a man that serves many masters at once, being of strange Countries or kinreds."[96] What interests Apuleius is precisely the institutional character of these "two natures," the figural potential to comply equally with differing political or social ends. In the tale, the emphasis falls on mutually resistant models of housewifery, though as a general device for double coding, syllepsis is a figure manifestly operant throughout *The Golden Ass*. From Apuleius's diction, which Eduard Norden once compared to "an honorable Roman matron gone a-whoring,[97] to the narrative's notorious thematic "alternative . . . between Milesian ribaldry and Platonic mysticism,"[98] the *Asinus aureus* consistently supplies the reader with a double logic. The result is what John J. Winkler calls a series of "asymmetric syzygies": the "surreal conjoining . . . of hermeneutic alternatives . . . , which gives to each [passage] a stereoscopic quality of unresolved differences in perspective on the same item."[99] This "double-directedness," Winkler argues, constitutes the fundamental architecture of the text, so that, among other things, the woman in the tale of the tub functions as a figure for Apuleian fiction. Perpetually deployed between divergent codes, Apuleius's narrative is neither hybrid nor ambiguous, but a delirious seam edging incompatible systems of order, which by no means always see each other face-to-face.

One of the reasons it is worthwhile to review *The Golden Ass* tropologically along these lines is that it brings the text into relation with other fictions of late antiquity. Georges Molinié has already noted that syllepsis constitutes one of the principal resources of the "Greek romance," engendering such topoi as the *Scheintod* and transvestism,[100] but if we extend his sample, we find that the scheme informs all the basic mimetic categories of these texts—gender (*True Stories:* the wives and mothers of the Moonmen are actually younger males),[101] identity (*Letters of Themistocles:* a double correspondence develops two coherent, yet incompatible, personae for the statesman, each of which implicitly critiques the other),[102] class (*Satyricon:* a Semitic immigrant is simultaneously a freedman and an effigy of the emperor at Rome),[103] race (*Aethiopica:* the white heroine finds out midway through the book that she is the child of black parents).[104] Many of these texts unfold along the borders between two cultures and can be read divergently within each one. Thus, the *Confession and Prayer of Aseneth,* which issues from the confluence of Greek and Jewish communities in Egypt, is both a πάθος ἐρωτικόν of the type familiar from Xenophon of Ephesus or Chariton and a drama of mystical conversion (μετάνοια) closely linked to the apocrypha and pseudepigrapha of the Hebrew Bible.[105] These two dimensions of the text do not stand in either metaphoric or ironic relation,[106] but emerge simultaneously without one reinforcing or, alternatively, interfering with the other: details of the narrative that may seem odd or irrelevant to one interpretive community are fully motivated for the other.[107] Key passages, in fact, like the ecphrastic opening of Achilles Tatius, are culturally bivalent:

> A Greek-speaking traveler enters the sanctuary of Astarte in Sidon to sacrifice in thanks for a safe passage. Among the temple offerings, he sees a painting of a woman riding on a bull at sea. With one hand, the woman steers her mount, clasping to its horn, and with the other holds her veil, which billows up behind her in the breeze. The water deepens from red to blue, and a small boy leads the way, as a troop of girls looks on beside a grove, spring, and meadow on the shore. While the traveler is admiring this panel, he notices a Phoenician standing to his side: this, it turns out, is Clitophon. The two men start up a conversation, and at the traveler's request, the protagonist recounts his past adventures, which occupy the remainder of the book.[108]

The image in the temple here is subject to a double determination. The foreigner identifies the picture as the rape of Europa,[109] and the iconography for this is well established in Greek sculpture and painting from the archaic era on.[110] Clitophon, however, calls the figure represented in the scene Selene, an attribution so oblique to Hellenists that they have inclined, in general, to emend the text.[111] It is Lucian, in his essay *On the Syrian Goddess,* who clarifies the issue: while some people say the great temple in Sidon belongs to Europa, it is actually dedicated to Astarte, whose Greek equivalent, the polymath suggests, would be Selene.[112] In fact, the crescent moon is among the most widespread of Astarte's emblems,[113] and Clitophon, who is from Tyre,[114] evidently takes the temple-offering to be her votive image.[115] Nor is this, given his background, necessarily a misprision, for the mythological conjunction of goddess,[116] bull, and sea belongs to the oldest strata of Syro-Palestinian religion. In Ugaritic poetry, for instance, Anat couples with an ox along the shore,[117] and later tesserae and stelae regularly depict Astarte standing or seated on a bull.[118] The motif takes its significance from the animal's symbolic association with her consort, Baal,[119] whence it forms part of a complex system of imagery that expresses the supremacy of Astarte in Phoenician cult.[120]

As Erich Neumann puts it, "The bull on which the goddess stands is the symbol of the masculine, the fertilizing male partner god, whose representation as an animal makes him inferior to the goddess: . . . riding on the bull, she tames the masculine and bestial."[121] Since the sea is traditionally a refuge of Astarte,[122] within the iconography proper to West Semitic culture, Achilles Tatius's picture unequivocally displays the goddess mastering her consort on her own ground.[123] As such, however, the image yields a significance almost symmetrically inverse to that which the traveler initially elicits from it: whereas Europa is overcome by Zeus and helplessly forced out to sea,[124] the marine goddess Astarte assumes dominion over Baal.[125] The text strategically accommodates both possibilities,[126] so that depending on the reader's frame of reference, Hellenic or Phoenician,[127] the image can be decoded in two opposing ways.[128] This doubleness reveals that any assumption about gender, mutability, or power here is culturally contingent. If, as has often been observed, the painting "foreshadows the key elements in [Achilles Tatius's] plot,"[129] its ambivalence projects an antithetical reception for Clitophon's adventures according to Syriac norms.[130]

From Roman Jakobson we know that different literary periods or movements tend to be characterized by the predominance of one rhetorical figure over others.[131] For the fiction of late antiquity, this master trope turns out to be syllepsis, which is what effectively distinguishes these narratives—formally, thematically, intertextually—from other fictions that we know.[132] At the same time, however, the figure refuses to define a genre in any classical understanding of the term. Structurally, syllepsis always exceeds the law and, by satisfying one sense, one code, one logic at the same time as another, it constitutes a travesty and an undoing of the very possibility of genre. While these texts successfully maintain the separation between kinds enjoined by Plato, they serve no single order, but through syllepsis operate as shifters across the basic categories of cultural construction (class, ethnicity, gender, race). The tale of *Barlaam and Joasaph* is, in this respect, exemplary, for the saint's conversion, from one socio-spiritual community to another,[133] is realized in the historical destiny of the text's millenary passage from India across the Middle East.[134] Such books admit no hierarchy among themselves and have no communal history, but like the wife in Apuleius's tale, they capitalize paranomically on societal distinctions to their own advantage. *Vocis immutatio desultoriae scientiae stilo respondet:* it is their ability to negotiate their way between our canonical configurations of the world—vulgar and elite, Greek and Roman, pagan and Christian, East and West, classical and modern—that generates the power, and the pleasure, of these late-antique texts.[135]

NOTES

1. For the triad semantic-syntactic-pragmatic, see C. Morris, *Writings on the General Theory of Signs* (The Hague, 1971), 28–64. Distinctions were also based on the materiality of the signifiers (e.g., dialect) and, occasionally, on the graphics of the text (e.g., *technopaignia*).

2. See, in general, F. Cairns, *Generic Composition in Greek and Roman Poetry* (Edinburgh, 1972). For preliterate generic composition, see G. Nagy, *The Best of the Achaeans* (Baltimore, 1979).

3. See Pindar, *Olympian* 7.88, 13.29; *Nemean* 4.33; *Isthmian* 6.20; *Paean* 6.57.

4. Choerilus of Samos, frag. 1 (Kinkel): ἀκήρατος ἦν ἔτι λειμών. / νῦν δ' ὅτε πάντα δέδασται, ἔχουσι δὲ πείρατα τέχναι (2–3). For this reading of the passage, see L. Rossi, "I generi letterari e le loro leggi scritte e non scritte nelle letterature classiche," *Bulletin of the Institute of Classical Studies* 18 (1971): 76.

5. See E. Benveniste, *Le vocabulaire des institutions indo-européenes*, 2 vols. (Paris, 1969), 2:99–105.

6. See esp. B. Gentili, *Poesia e pubblico nella Grecia antica* (Rome, 1985).

7. The Sanskrit cognate *dhâman* denotes both "law" and "creation"; cf. Avestan *dâmi-*, "creator." By extension the withering away of a genre could be perceived as a deterioration of the social order. Thus, Aristophanes' point of departure in the *Frogs* is the decline of tragic competition (λωβηταὶ τέχνης, / ἃ φροῦδρα θᾶττον, ἢν μόνον χορὸν λάβῃ, / ἅπαξ προσουρήσαντα τῇ τραγῳδίᾳ [93–95], and the motivation for Aeschylus's utopian return to Athens is explicitly political renewal (ἵν' ἡ πόλις σωθεῖσα τοὺς χοροὺς ἄγῃ [1419]).

8. Plato, *Republic* 397d4.

9. Plato, *Laws* 700a–701c (abridged).

10. Aristotle, *Poetics* 1448b4–5; ἐοίκασι δὲ γεννῆσαι μὲν ὅλως τὴν ποιητικὴν αἰτίαι δύο τινὲς καὶ αὗται φυσικαί. Cf. the remarks on the development of tragedy at 1449a13ff.

11. Cicero, *Orator* 70–75.

12. Horace, *Ars poetica* 89. For connections among the generic theories of Plato, Aristotle, Cicero, and Horace, see R. Hack, "The Doctrine of Literary Forms," *Harvard Studies in Classical Philology* 27 (1916): 1–65.

13. Horace, *Ars poetica* 231–33.

14. Shifts in the systematization of literary kinds do not affect the point; see A. Harvey, "The Classification of Greek Lyric Poetry," *Classical Quarterly*, n.s. 5 (1955): 157–75. For the continuity of generic categories from archaic Greek poetry through late antiquity, see Cairns, *Generic Composition*, chap. 2.

15. Some obvious examples—*stephanôtikos* (victor: Menander Rhetor, *On Epideictic Speeches* 423), *skolion* (aristocratic: Aristophanes, *Wasps* 1216ff.), *fabula Atellana* (Oscan: Livy, *Ab urbe condita* 7.2.13), *threnos* (gynecian: Plutarch, *Solon* 21.4).

16. The basic study is still W. Kroll, "Die Kreuzung der Gattungen," in *Studien zum Verständnis der römischen Literatur* (Stuttgart, 1924), 202–24.

17. Petronius, *Satyricon* 83–90.

18. For the generic type, see Moschus's *Europa* or Catullus's *Peleus and Thetis*.

19. The language is directly reminiscent of Seneca and Vergil; see J. Sullivan, *The Satyricon of Petronius* (Bloomington, Ind., 1968), 186–89.

20. The poem is in effect an epitome of *Aeneid* 2; for the connections to Vergil, see F. I. Zeitlin, "Petronius Romanus," *Latomus* 30 (1971): 56–82.

21. These are the traditional Roman literary values par excellence, as canonized, for example, in Cicero's speech *pro Archia*.

22. For the genre of the so-called Milesian tale, see B. Perry, *The Ancient Romances* (Berkeley and Los Angeles, 1967), 92–95 and 361 n. 7; S. Trenkner, *The Greek Novella in the Classical Period* (Cambridge, 1958); and Q. Cataudella, *La novella greca* (Naples, 1957).

23. See Festus, *De verborum significatu* 351M.

24. See J. Sullivan, *Literature and Politics in the Age of Nero* (Ithaca, N.Y., 1985), chap. 2.

25. The contrast here conforms closely to M. Bakhtin's distinction between *epos* and *roman;* see *The Dialogic Imagination: Four Essays by M. M. Bakhtin,* ed. M. Holquist, trans. C. Emerson and M. Holquist (Austin, Tex., 1981), 3–40.

26. The point is emphasized at the beginning of both halves of the story. *Satyricon* 85.1: "Excogitavi rationem qua non essem patri familiae suspectus"; 87.1: "Ut intellexi stertere patrem, rogare coepi ephebum ut reverteretur in gratiam mecum."

27. The same ambivalent logic of inversion is expressed throughout the *Troiae Halosis,* most succinctly in the following lines: "Ibat iuventus capta, dum Troiam capit" (27), "Contraque Troiam invocat Troiae sacra" (65).

28. The interpretation of the Trojan War and similar instances of rape as a cross-cultural conflict between East and West is set by Herodotus at the opening of his *Histories.*

29. For the parallels, see Perry, *Ancient Romances,* 206–10, and G. Anderson, *Ancient Fiction: The Novel in the Greco-Roman World* (London, 1984), 183–84. For moral diatribe, see, e.g., al-Hariri, *Maqâmât* 1; for pederastic seduction, al-Hamadhani, *Maqâmât* 35.

30. See A. Beeston, "The Genesis of the *maqâmât* Genre," *Journal of Arabic Literature* 2 (1971): 1–12; J. N. Mattock, "The Early History of the *maqâma,*" *Journal of Arabic Literature* 15 (1984): 1–18; and F. Malti-Douglas, "*Maqâmât* and *Adab,*" *Journal of the American Oriental Society* 105 (1985): 247–58. On the relation to Indic narrative in this and other connections, see F. Lacôte, "Sur l'origine indienne du roman grec," *Mélanges d'Indianisme offerts par ses élèves à M. Sylvain Lévi* (Paris, 1911), 249–304.

31. For an overview of the problem, see C. Müller, "Der griechische Roman: Die Einheit der Gattung," in *Griechische Literatur,* ed. E. Vogt (Wiesbaden, 1981), 387f.

32. Apuleius, *Asinus aureus* 1.1.

33. Heliodorus, *Aethiopica* 10.41.

34. Longus, *Poemenica* 1.1.

35. For the connection with history, see the discussion by C. Roueché, "Byzantine Writers and Readers," in *The Greek Novel: A.D. 1–1985,* ed. R. Beaton (London, 1988), 123–33; for rhetoric: Josephus Pinarus Rhakendytes, Σύνοψις ῥητορικῆς 2, in *Rhetores Graeci,* ed. C. Walz, 9 vols. (Stuttgart, 1832–36), 3:526; for drama: Photius, *Bibliotheca* cod. 73 and passim; cf. H. Hunger, *Die hochsprachliche profane Literatur der Byzantiner,* 2 vols. (Munich, 1978), 2:123.

36. For the medieval period, references to Greek writers are naturally absent in the West; for the sparse, intermittent, and largely secondhand acquaintance with Roman writers, see A. Collignon, *Pétrone en France* (Paris, 1905), 1–20, and E. Haight, *Apuleius and His Influence* (New York, 1927), chap. 4.

37. J. Scaliger, *Poetices libri septem* [1561], ed. A. Buck (Stuttgart, 1964), 144; T. Tasso, *Discorsi del poema heroico* [1594], ed. L. Poma (Bari, 1964), 108; P. Sidney, *A Defence of Poetry* [1595], ed. J. Van Dorsten (Oxford, 1966), 24, 27; L. Pinciano, *Philosophia antigua poetica* [1596], ed. A. Carballo Picazo, 3 vols. (Madrid, 1953), 3:165–67.

38. See, for example, D. Erasmus's prefatory letter to the *Encomium moriae,* or Sidney, *Defence of Poetry,* 67.

39. Collignon stresses in particular that Sorel, Scarron, and Furetière, among other novelists of the early seventeenth century, failed to exploit the *Satyricon* as a model for their writing, largely because they perceived his work as belonging to a different genre; *Pétrone en France,* 43ff.

40. *Zayde Histoire Espagnole, par Monsieur de Segrais. Avec un traitté de l'Origine des Romans, par Monsieur Huet* (Paris, 1670); references are to the critical edition of A. Kok (Amsterdam, 1942), which reproduces the text and pagination of 1711, the last edition to be revised by Huet before his death.

41. See, for example, the remarks on Oriental accounts of the origins of storytelling:

"Je diray seulement en passant, qu'il faut se souvenir que les Histoires de ces peuples d'Orient, selon le témoinage de Strabon, sont pleines de mensonges, qu'ils sont peu exacts & peu fideles, & qu'il est assez vray-semblable qu'ils ont esté fabuleux en parlant de l'Auteur & de l'origine des Fables, comme en tout le reste" (Huet, *Traité*, 30). Strabo here is not only an unlikely source; since *vraisemblance* is, according to Huet, the novelistic category par excellence (10), there is at least reason to suspect that his account is at this point essentially a fiction about a fiction about fictions. Cf. also the discussion of Plato's Porus and Penie (194ff.), which effectively folds the historical projection of the essay back into an allegorical scheme, or the closing lines of the treatise, which pointedly collapse the previous distinctions, posing the question whether a chronicle of Louis XIV's "regne merveilleux . . . seroit une Histoire ou un Roman" (227–28).

42. The reasoning is notably circular: "Après estre convenu des ouvrages qui meritent proprement le nom de Romans, je dis qu'il faut chercher leur premiere origine dans la nature de l'esprit de l'homme, inventif, amateur des nouveautez & des fictions, désireux d'apprendre, & de communiquer ce qu'il a inventé, & ce qu'il a appris; & que cette inclination est commune à tous les hommes de tous les temps, & de tous les lieux" (ibid., 12). The passage first appears in 1711.

43. Huet's position in seventeenth-century theory of the novel is most conveniently summarized by Kok in the introduction to his critical edition of the *Traité*, 51–69.

44. For the terms, see R. Bray, *La formation de la doctrine classique en France* (Paris, 1926).

45. These are the main distinctions; see Huet, *Traité*, 2–12.

46. Ibid., 4.

47. The only reference I have found to an ancient text as a "novel" before Huet is in Georges de Scudery's preface to *Ibrahim* (1641), which calls the *Aethiopica* a *roman*. The whole of this piece reads like an unsystematic rough draft of Huet's *Traité*.

48. N. Boileau, "A M. Perrault," in *Oeuvres complètes,* ed. F. Escal (Paris, 1966), 572; the statement dates from about 1698.

49. Photius, *Bibliotheca* cod. 166; for Huet's dependence on this passage, see *Traité*, 61ff.

50. To be more precise, Heliodorus is the only unimpeachable exemplar, the "meilleur modele de Roman, qu'[on] pust choisir" (*Traité*, 108); Iamblichus and Achilles Tatius, along with Antonius Diogenes, are slightly less perfect examples of the genre.

51. Huet, *Traité*, 60–153.

52. M. Magendie, *Le roman français au XVIIe siècle* (Paris, 1932), 118.

53. For the subversive force of the novel within seventeenth-century cultural politics in France, see E. Harth, *Ideology and Culture in Seventeenth-Century France* (Ithaca, N.Y., 1983), 129–221, and M. McKeon, *The Origins of the English Novel, 1600–1740* (Baltimore, 1987), 25–64.

54. Huet is quite explicit about the Aristotelian impress of his enterprise, and in his thinking, metaphor, mimesis, and narration cooperate conspicuously as parts of a coherent system that propels the novel teleologically from pleasure to instruction (*Traité*, 5, 185–87, 192–93, 198–200, 214–16); for the basic components of the system and its metaphysical implications, see J. Derrida, *Margins of Philosophy,* trans. A. Bass (Chicago, 1982), 207–71. In fact, the generic reorganization of ancient fiction in the seventeenth century coincides with a remarkable shift in the way these pieces are perceived. For example, in the first part of *Don Quixote* (1605), Cervantes has the canon say: "Las fábulas que llaman milesias . . . son cuentos disparatados, que atienden solamente a deleitar, y no a enseñar . . . No he visto ningún . . . que haga un cuerpo de fábula entero con todos sus miembros, de manera que el media corresponda al principio, y el

fin al principio y al medio, sino que los componen con tantos miembros, que más parece que llevan intención a formar una quimera o un monstruo que a hacer una figura proporcionada" (*Don Quijote de la Mancha*, ed. V. Gaos, 3 vols. [Madrid, 1987], 1:905–7). A century later, Johann Christoph Gottsched looked at the same material, but what he saw there was completely the reverse: "Die milesische Fabel [machet] wohl mittelmäßiger, ja ganz unbekannter und erdichteter Personen ihr Hauptwerk . . . Eine einzige Haupthandlung, die auf eine Liebe hinausläuft, ist derjenige Zweck, wohin alles abzielet. Dieses ahmet nun der Natur nach, die in allen ihren Meisterstücken viele Glieder unter einem Haupte und Herzen vereiniget. Ja, wenn gleich eine doppelte Handlung in einem solchen Gedichte zu seyn scheint, so bezieht sich doch die eine auf die andere, und macht sie desto vollkommener" (*Versuch einer Critischen Dichtkunst* [1751], ed. J. Birke and B. Birke, in *Ausgewählte Werke* [Berlin, 1973], 6.2: 463; Huet already anticipates the point [*Traité*, 96–97]). The organic metaphors come right out of Aristotle (*Poetics* 1450b27ff.), but whereas in the early modern period it was still possible to appreciate at least certain types of Greco-Roman fiction as aberrant and heteromorphic, over the course of the seventeenth and eighteenth centuries the ancient texts came increasingly under a normative and integrating eye.

55. According to the traditional literary histories, the watershed was the publication of Mme de La Fayette's next novel, *La princesse de Clèves* (1678), and with the appearance of Defoe's *Robinson Crusoe* (1719) the entire picture changed. Huet died in 1718.

56. Blair's discussion of "Fictitious History" in the *Lectures on Rhetoric and Belles Lettres*, 2 vols. (London, 1783), 2:303–10, is typical of the eighteenth-century reception of Huet's ideas. The full syllabus is laid out for the first time by J. Dunlop, *The History of Fiction: . . . From the Earliest Greek Romances to the Novels of the Present Age* (London, 1814). For all their differences, E. Rohde, *Der griechische Roman und seine Vorläufer* (Leipzig, 1876), and B. Perry, *Ancient Romances,* the two principal landmarks in modern thinking on the ancient novel, both leave Huet's construction of the field essentially unquestioned.

57. My source is the published proceedings of the conference: B. P. Reardon, ed., *Erotica Antiqua: Acta of the International Conference on the Ancient Novel* (Bangor, Wales, 1977).

58. The proceedings state more precisely: "Il y a pourtant une grammaire du roman antique, à son tour subordonnée à la grammaire du roman en général" (ibid., 120).

59. The texts of Xenephon of Ephesus and Chariton, first published in the mideighteenth century, were readily assimilated to the canon established by Huet.

60. The basic agenda, which the conference went on to confirm, was succinctly summarized by G. Schmeling in the first session: "Without trying . . . to pass off generic study for more than it is, I believe that we can approach the *Satyricon* by making use of the concepts behind the novel to help us better see the novel (and thus the *Satyricon* 'as a synchronic order of coexisting works.' These concepts stress the similarities between the *Satyricon, Metamorphoses,* ancient Greek romances, and *Tom Jones.* The approach to the novel through a diachronic sequence complements this and points out those elements which develop and change (or remain static), and also makes us aware of how much we learn about the nature of one specific novel from reading earlier and later examples of the genre" (Reardon, *Erotica Antiqua,* 6–7).

61. In fact, other than articles on texts or fragments unknown to the seventeenth century, I find only one paper delivered at the conference that did not deal with a problem already formulated by Huet: class structure in Xenophon of Ephesus.

62. More precisely: "We [shall agree] to call 'genres' only those classes of texts that have been perceived as such in the course of history . . . The *historical* existence of genres is indicated by the discourse on genres; that does not mean, however, that genres

are only metadiscursive, and no longer discursive notions" (T. Todorov, "The Origin of Genres," *New Literary History* 8 [1976]: 162).

63. Ibid., 163.

64. McKeon, *Origins of the English Novel*, 1–22.

65. Anderson, *Ancient Fiction*, 72.

66. These adjectives, pro and con, are all taken from recent surveys or monographs on the ancient novel.

67. See, for example, R. Beck, "Eumolpus *poeta,* Eumolpus *fabulator:* A Study of Characterization in the *Satyricon,*" *Phoenix* 33 (1979): 239–53, or G. Sandy, "Characterization and Philosophical Decor in Heliodorus' *Aethiopica,*" *Transactions of the American Philological Association* 112 (1982): 141–67.

68. I. Watt, *The Rise of the Novel* (Berkeley and Los Angeles, 1957). For cultural antecedents, see F. Barker, *The Tremulous Private Body: Essays in Subjection* (London, 1984).

69. H. James, in a well-known passage, both epitomizes and puts in question the line of thought: "There is an old-fashioned distinction between the novel of character and the novel of incident which must have cost many a smile to the intending fabulist who was keen about his work . . . What is character but the determination of incident? What is incident but the illustration of character? What is . . . a novel that is *not* of character? What else do we seek and find in it?" (*Partial Portraits* [London, 1888], 392–93).

70. An American popular manual on fiction from the 1930s reads s.v. "characterization": "The depicting, in writing, of clear images of a person, his actions and manners of thought and life. A man's nature, environment, habits, emotions, desires, instincts: all these go to make people what they are, and the skillful writer makes his important people clear to us through a portrayal of these elements" (W. Thrall and A. Hibbard, *A Handbook to Literature* [Garden City, N.Y., 1936]).

71. R. Barthes, *S/Z* (Paris, 1970), 74–75 and passim.

72. K. Marx, "Einleitung [zur Kritik der politischen Ökonomie]," in *Werke* (Berlin, 1964), 13:615–16. The passage opens with the programmatic assertion "gesellschaftlich bestimmte Produktion der Individuen ist natürlich der Ausgangspunkt," in which the ambiguity of the genitive (possessive or objective) epitomizes Marx's point.

73. See, in particular, B. Brecht, *Gesammelte Werke,* 20 vols. (Frankfurt am Main, 1967), 15:229–336; however, comments on character are scattered throughout his writings on the theater.

74. In an early interview, Brecht is quoted as saying: "Auch wenn sich eine meiner Personen in Widersprüchen bewegt, so nur darum, weil der Mensch in zwei ungleichen Augenblicken niemals der gleiche sein kann. Das wechselnde Aussen veranlaßt ihn beständig zu einer inneren Umgruppierung. Das kontinuierliche Ich ist eine Mythe. Der Mensch ist ein immerwährend zerfallendes und neu sich bildendes Atom. Es gilt zu gestalten was ist" (*Die literarische Welt,* Berlin, 30 July 1926, 2).

75. L. Davis, *Resisting Novels* (New York, 1987), 128.

76. The clearest example is P. Turner, "Novels, Ancient and Modern," *Novel* 2 (1968): 15–24.

77. T. Hägg, *The Novel in Antiquity* (Berkeley and Los Angeles, 1983), 73. Overall, this is an excellent survey of the field and I quote it in this context for that reason.

78. F. Jameson, *The Political Unconscious* (Ithaca, N.Y., 1981), 106.

79. Scaliger, *Poetice,* 144d1.

80. Rohde, *Der griechische Roman,* 1 and 530. The latter remarks are made in connection with Prodromus's *Rhodanthe and Dosicles.*

81. While genre study no longer predominates in scholarship on ancient fiction today, work in the field continues to consider categorization a prerequisite for exegesis.

To cite one example among many, critics as different in temperament as B. P. Reardon and F. I. Zeitlin both initiate their discussions of Longus by reestablishing the position of *Daphnis and Chloe* within "th[e] corpus [of] five love-and-adventure romances that have come to be regarded as constituting the canon in this form"; cf. B. P. Reardon, ed., *Collected Ancient Greek Novels* (Berkeley and Los Angeles, 1989), 1–16, and Zeitlin, "The Poetics of Eros," in *Before Sexuality: The Construction of Erotic Experience in the Ancient Greek World*, ed. D. M. Halperin, J. J. Winkler, and F. I. Zeitlin (Princeton, 1990), 417–64. The point is not that scholars working in this area are unaware that the rubrics "novel" and "romance" are problematic, but that course offerings, conferences, and publications persist in massively reinforcing these categories as "a matter of convenience," while remaining for the most part oblivious of the critical consequences this entails.

82. Apuleius, *Asinus aureus* 9.5–7.

83. Compare, for example, the two Claudiae of *Corpus Inscriptionum Latinarum* (Berlin, 1863–), 1.1007, and Cicero, *Pro Caelio* 49.

84. Summarized at 9.7.6: "Maritum suum astu meretricio tractabat ludicre."

85. The woman is addressed as materfamilias at 9.7.1; cf. her reproaches to her husband, which are only partially ironic: "Sicine vacuus et otiosus insinuatis manibus ambulabis mihi nec obito consueto labore vitae nostrae perspicies et aliquid cibatui parabis?" (9.5.5); "Magnum istum virum ac strenuum negotiatorem nacta sum, qui rem, quam ego mulier et intra hospitium contenta iam dudum septem denariis vendidi, minoris distraxit" (9.6.4). The story opens by stressing the couple's economic straits: "Is gracili pauperie laborans fabriles operas praebendo parvis illis mercedibus vitam tenebat" (9.5.1).

86. Contrary to the preconceptions that tend to creep into translations, the Latin gives no indication that the woman has ever seen the young man before, or that she has previously been unfaithful to her husband: "Dum matutino ille ad opus susceptum proficiscitur, statim latenter inrepit eius hospitium temerarius adulter. Ac dum Veneris conluctationibus securius operantur, maritus ignarus rerum ac nihil etiam tum tale suspicans inprovisus hospitium repetit" (9.5.2). The text describes the woman as *postrema lascivia* and *ad huius modi flagitia perastutula;* this certainly insinuates that she was a seasoned adulterer, but it may mean no more than that she liked a good joke and was extremely clever. Throughout the tale the emphasis is on the woman's resourcefulness and ingenuity.

87. At 9.5.5, the woman herself alludes to the common Roman epitaphic formula *domum servavit, lanam fecit.*

88. This is Jack Lindsay's suggestive mistranslation (*The Golden Ass* [Bloomington, Ind., 1960], 189), which captures the important point: "Hoc et illud et aliud et rursus aliud purgandum demonstrat digito suo" (9.7.6). In Latin, the pun centers on *purgandum*—to the Roman mind the genitalia are intrinsically unclean or foul; see A. Richlin, *The Garden of Priapus* (New Haven, 1983), 26–30 and passim. Soranus, who was active in Rome a generation before Apuleius, reports the popular opinion that, like the old tub in the tale, women collect residue by sitting idly around the house and hence require regular purgation (κάθαρσις): ὁρῶσα τοίνυν τοὺς ἄρρενας γυμνασίοις τὸ περιττὸν ἀποκενοῦντας, τὰς δὲ θηλείας διὰ τὸ οἰκουργὸν καὶ καθέδριον διάγειν βίον πλῆθος ὑποσυλλεγούσας, προνοοῦσα τοῦ μηδὲ ταύτας κινδύνῳ περιπεσεῖν, διὰ τῆς καθάρσεως ἐπενόησεν [ἡ φύσις] τὸ περιττὸν ἀποχετεύειν (*Gynaeceia* 1.8). Sexual intercourse was thought directly to facilitate this process: οὕτως καὶ ἡ περὶ τὰ γυναικεῖα μόρια συγκίνησις ἐν τοῖς ἀφροδισίοις συναναχαλᾷ τὸν ὄγκον ὅλον· διὰ τοῦτο δὲ καὶ τὴν ὑστέραν ἀνίησιν, ὥστε καὶ τὴν κάθαρσιν ἀπαραπόδιστον φυλαχθῆναι (ibid., 1.9). Celsus employs the term *purgare* in particular to designate vaginal cleansing of this type: "Quae

menstruis non purgatur, si sanguinem ex naribus fudit, omni periculo vacat" (*De medicina* 2.8.16).

89. Their stories are in fact symmetrically inverse: the lover indulges his desire, but winds up paying for a dilapidated tub; the husband is saddled with a debauched wife, but manages to fill his stomach. The parallel between the jar and the woman is explicit in the text: "At vero adulter belissimus ille pusio inclinatam *dolio* pronam uxorem fabri superincuruatus secure *dedolabat*" (9.7.5).

90. I am indebeted here to T. Todorov's analysis of an analogous tale in Boccaccio; see *Poétique de la prose* (Paris, 1971), 35–36.

91. L. Spengel, *Rhetores Graeci*, 3 vols. (Leipzig, 1856), 3:171.

92. Ibid. 3:100: σύλληψις δὲ ὅταν τὸ τῷ ἑτέρῳ συμβεβηκὸς κἀπὶ θατέρου λαμβάνηται. Cf. H. Lausberg, *Elemente der literarischen Rhetorik* (Munich, 1963), 105–6.

93. A. Pope, *The Rape of the Lock*, 2.107.

94. See Spengel, *Rhetores Graeci* 3:158, 211, and 224.

95. The fact that the figure here affects both *histoire* and *discours*—for the distinction, see E. Benveniste, *Problèmes de linguistique générale* (Paris, 1966), 238ff.—complicates the point.

96. G. Puttenham, *The Arte of English Poesie* [ca. 1570], ed. G. D. Willcock and A. Walker (Cambridge, 1936), 165.

97. E. Norden, *Die antike Kunstprosa*, 2 vols. (Leipzig, 1923), 2:601. The basic study is L. Callebat, *Sermo Cotidianus dans les Métamorphoses d'Apulée* (Caen, 1968).

98. P. Walsh, *The Roman Novel* (London, 1970), 143. Both issues are surveyed by J. Tatum, *Apuleius and "The Golden Ass"* (Ithaca, N.Y., 1979).

99. J. J. Winkler, *Auctor and Actor: A Narratological Reading of Apuleius's "Golden Ass"* (Berkeley and Los Angeles, 1985), 123–24.

100. G. Molinié, *Du roman grec au roman baroque* (Toulouse, 1982), 278–94.

101. Lucian, *True Stories* 1.22, reaffirms gender roles as it effaces sexual difference: γάμοις γὰρ τοῖς ἄρρεσι χρῶνται καὶ οὐδὲ ὄνομα γυναικὸς ὅλως ἴσασι. μέχρι μὲν οὖν πέντε καὶ εἴκοσι ἐτῶν γαμεῖται ἕκαστος, ἀπὸ δὲ τουτῶν γαμεῖ αὐτός. In part, the theme is motivated by the grammatical anomaly of the proper name οἱ Σεληνῖται, in which the "masculine" article is coupled with a characteristically "feminine" ending; cf. ὀχεύουσι καὶ πλησιάζουσι τοῖς γαμέταις τοῖς ἑαυτῶν (ibid.), where the morphological alternation τοῖς, -ταις, -τοῖς explicitly foregrounded. Declensional discrepancies of this type were a constant cause of concern to ancient critics from at least the time of Aristophanes of Byzantium; see R. Pfeiffer, *History of Classical Scholarship from the Beginnings to the End of the Hellenistic Age* (Oxford, 1968), 202–3.

102. See the excellent analysis by J. Penwill, "The Letters of Themistokles: An Epistolary Novel?" *Antichthon* 12 (1978): 83–103.

103. The correspondences between Nero and Trimalchio are collected by H. Crum, "Petronius and the Emperors," *Classical World* (1951–52): 161ff., most sensibly evaluated by Walsh, *Roman Novel,* 137–39.

104. Persinna's apostrophe to Chariclea is decoded by Calasiris at *Aethiopica* 4.8: σε λευκὴν ἀπέτεκον, ἀπρόσφυλον Αἰθιόπων χροιὰν ἀπαυγάζουσαν . . . , οὕτω σε γενομένην ἐξεθέμην. The disclosure requires, on the one hand, a wholesale reevaluation of the foregoing narrative constructions (εἰσήει γάρ με πολλὴ ἔννοια, τίνων μὲν γενομένη τίνων ἐνομίσθη πόσῳ δὲ τῷ μεταξὺ τῆς ἐνεγκούσης ἀπήχθη, κεκλήρωτο δὲ θυγατρὸς ὄνομα νόθον, ἀποβαλοῦσα τὸ γνήσιον Αἰθιόπων καὶ βασίλειον γένος [4.9]), and on the other, an immediate change in the course of action (τῷ γένει προσέδραμε καὶ "τί οὖν χρὴ ποιεῖν;" ἠρώτα [4.12]).

105. Compare the divergent readings of S. West, "Joseph and Asenath: A Neglected

Greek Romance," *Classical Quarterly* 24 (1974): 70–81, and M. Philonenko, *Joseph et Aséneth* (Leiden, 1968).

106. In this respect syllepsis differs fundamentally from the type of *Doppelsinnigkeit* described by R. Merkelbach in *Roman und Mysterium in der Antike* (Munich, 1962): i.e., the Greek romance plot does not function as an allegory for Judaic verity. Even granting the possibility that a Hellenic audience might have read the story as a *Mysteriendrama*, this understanding would not coincide with the text's Hebraic proselytism. While the narrative by no means precludes allegory, structurally the syllepsis overrides it.

107. For the principle, see S. Fish, *Is There a Text in This Class? The Authority of Interpretive Communities* (Cambridge, Mass., 1980); cf. Philonenko, *Joseph et Aséneth*, 72.

108. Achilles Tatius, *Leucippe and Clitophon* 1.1–2.

109. Ibid., 1.2.1: Εὐρώπης ἡ γραφή.

110. For the iconography, see O. Jahn, "Die Entführung der Europa auf antiken Kunstwerken," *Denkschriften der kaiserlichen Akademie der Wissenschaften,* Philosophisch-historische Classe (Vienna) 19 (1870): 1–54.

111. Achilles Tatius, *Leucippe and Clitophon* 1.4.3: τοιαύτην εἶδον ἐγώ ποτε ἐπὶ ταύρῳ γεγραμμένην Σελήνην. To be more precise, two out of the three manuscript traditions read "Selene" (αF: Σελήνην, β: Εὐρώπην); for the authority of αF here, see Achilles Tatius, *Leucippe and Clitophon,* ed. E. Vilborg (Stockholm, 1955), lxxxv, and E. Vilborg, *Leucippe and Clitophon: A Commentary* (Stockholm, 1962), ad loc. Vilborg (*Commentary,* 22) explains Clitophon's attribution as follows: "Selene is sometimes depicted as riding on a bull (see Roscher, s.v. Selene); so A.T. could use her to give associations to Europe." Roscher, however, knows of only three instances of a Selene ταυροπόλος, and of these, only in the passage of *Leucippe and Clitophon* under discussion is that attribution certain. In effect, the argument is circular; see W. Roscher, *Über Selene und Verwandtes* (Leipzig, 1890), 31–32, 169–71, and *Ausführliches Lexikon der griechischen und römischen Mythologie* (Hildesheim, 1965), 2.1:3136ff. Both these publications review the possible connections between Europa and Selene in Greek mythology.

112. Lucian, *On the Syrian Goddess* 44: ἔνι δὲ καὶ ἄλλο ἱρὸν ἐν Φοινίκῃ μέγα, τὸ Σιδώνιοι ἔχουσιν, ὡς μὲν αὐτοὶ λέγουσιν, ᾿Αστάρτης ἐστίν· ᾿Αστάρτην δ᾿ ἐγὼ δοκέω Σεληναίην ἔμμεναι· ὡς δέ μοί τις τῶν ἱρέων ἀπηγέετο, Εὐρώπης ἐστὶ τῆς Κάδμου ἀδελφεῆς. ταύτην δ᾿ ἐοῦσαν ᾿Αγήνορος τοῦ βασιλῆος θυγατέρα, ἐπειδή τε ἀφανὴς ἐγεγόνεεν, οἱ Φοίνικες τῷ νηῷ ἐτιμήσαντο καὶ λόγον ἱρὸν ἐπ᾿ αὐτῇ ἔλεξαν, ὅτι ἐοῦσαν καλὴν Ζεὺς ἐπόθεε καὶ τὸ εἶδος εἰς ταῦρον ἀμειψάμενος ἥρπασε, καί μιν ἐς Κρήτην φέρων ἀπίκετο. τάδε μὲν καὶ τῶν ἄλλων Φοινίκων ἤκουον, καὶ τὸ νόμισμα, τῷ Σιδώνιοι χρέωνται, τὴν Εὐρώπην ἐφεζομένην ἔχει τῷ ταύρῳ τῷ Διί· τὸν δὲ νηὸν οὐκ ὁμολογέουσιν Εὐρώπης ἔμμεναι. The point of the passage, which is roughly contemporary with the composition of Achilles Tatius, is specifically to *differentiate* Europa from Astarte/Selene. For the general reliability of Lucian's account, see H. Attridge and R. Oden, *The Syrian Goddess* (Missoula, Mont., 1976), 1–5. In fact, after Herodotus, the Europa saga was transferred from its original locale in northern Greece to the Syrian coast, but there is no evidence that she was actually thought to be Astarte or that she played any role within Phoenician cult (see Escher, "Europe," in *Real-Encyclopaedie der classischen Altertumswissenschaft,* ed. A. Pauly and G. Wissowa [Stuttgart, 1894–1963], 6.1:1289–91). Lucian lists a number of Greek divinites who were identified with the Syrian goddess, but Europa is not among them (*On the Syrian Goddess* 32).

113. For an overview of the iconography, see Roscher, *Lexicon* 1.1:652–53. Throughout the Middle East, Astarte was consistently invoked as *dea caelestis* (Syria: H. Donner and W. Röllig, eds., *Kanaanäische und aramäische Inschriften,* 2d ed., 3 vols.

[Wiesbaden, 1966–69], no. 14.16; Palestine: Jeremiah 7:18 and 44:17–18; Egypt: stele from the reign of Merenptah, F. Petrie et al., *Memphis,* 6 vols. [London, 1909–15], 1:8 and 19, plate 15, 37). Herodian reports in connection with the emperor Elagabalus: Λίβυες μὲν οὖν αὐτὴν Οὐρανίαν καλοῦσι, Φοίνικες δὲ Ἀστάρτην [codd. Ἀστροάρχην] ὀνομάζουσι, σελήνην εἶναι θέλοντες. ἁρμόζειν τοίνυν λέγων ὁ Ἀντωνῖνος γάμον ἡλίου καὶ σελήνης τό τε ἄγαλμα μετεπέμψατο καὶ πάντα τὸν ἐκεῖθεν χρυσόν (5.6.4). Coins from Sidon frequently show the cart of Astarte bearing a crescent or lunar disk (e.g., G. Hill, *Catalogue of the Greek Coins of Phoenicia* [London, 1910], Sidon, nos. 244ff.); of particular interest to the present context, the city's coinage from the first century A.D. displays a bust of Astarte beside a crescent moon, while the exergue on the reverse reads ΣΙΔΩΝΟΣ ΘΕΑΣ (ibid., nos. 170–82). Both Astarte and Selene come from commonplace roots that, in their respective languages, mean "bright" or "shining," which may not have been lost on such bilingual writers and readers as Lucian and Achilles Tatius; see W. Albright, *Yahweh and the Gods of Canaan* (Garden City, N.Y., 1968), 134, and Plato, *Cratylus* 409b12.

114. Clitophon's origin is stressed specifically at the outset of his narration: ὁ δὲ ἄρχεται τοῦ λέγειν ὧδε· Ἐμοὶ Φοινίκη γένος, Τύρος πατρίς, ὄνομα Κλειτοφῶν (1.3.1). For Astarte's position in the pantheon at Tyre, see R. du Mesnil du Buisson, *Nouvelles études sur les dieux et les mythes de Canaan* (Leiden, 1973), 32–69.

115. The identification of Phoenician deities in Greek texts by their Greek names is standard for the imperial period, both in treatises on local religion (e.g., Philo of Byblus, *Phoenician History*) and in inscriptions; see M. Avi-Yonah, "Syrian Gods at Ptolemais-Accho," *Israel Exploration Journal* 9 (1959): 1–12.

116. Historically, the Canaanite pantheon identified three major goddesses ('Anat, 'Ashtart, and 'Asherah), who were subsequently fused into Atargatis. In all periods, however, their attributes and worship overlapped so fully that there is little to be gained by distinguishing between them here; to simplify the presentation, I have retained Achilles Tatius's term *Astarte.* For identities and intersections, see M. Pope and W. Röllig, "Syrien," in *Wörterbuch der Mythologie,* vol. 1, ed. H. W. Haussig (Stuttgart, 1965), s.vv., supplemented by R. Oden, Jr., *Studies in Lucian's "De Syria Dea"* (Missoula, Mont., 1977), 58–107, and F. Hvidberg-Hansen, *La Déesse TNT,* 2 vols. (Copenhagen, 1979), 1:69–112. The basic diachronic study is W. Albright, "The Evolution of the West-Semitic Divinity 'An-'Anat-'Attâ," *American Journal of Semitic Languages and Literatures* 41 (1925): 73–101.

117. Ras Shamra table IV AB ii, in A. Herder, *Corpus des tablettes en cunéiformes alphabétiques,* 2 vols. (Paris, 1963), no. 10; J. Pritchard, *Ancient Near Eastern Texts,* 3d ed. (Princeton, 1969), 142. There is an Egyptian version of the same scene in a magical papyrus from the Nineteenth Dynasty: W. Helck, *Die Beziehungen Ägyptens zu Vorderasien im 3. und 2. Jahrtausend v. Chr.,* 2d ed. (Wiesbaden, 1971), 461. Coins from Byblus of the fourth century B.C. show the lion of Astarte atop the body of a bull, with a maritime scene on the obverse: Hill, *Coins of Phoenicia,* Byblus, nos. 2–11.

118. The goddess rides a lion, horse, or bull; the fundamental survey is J. Leclant, "Astarté à cheval d'après les représentations égyptiennes," *Syria* 37 (1960): 1–67. The basic type is illustrated in J. Pritchard, *The Ancient Near East in Pictures,* 2d ed. (Princeton, 1969), 163–65. For representations of Astarte mounted on a bull, see Leclant, "Astarté à cheval," fig. 29; du Mesnil du Buisson, *Nouvelles études,* 116, 118; E. Neumann, *Die grosse Mutter* (Zurich, 1956), plate 54; S. Moscati, ed., *The Phoenicians* (Milan, 1988), 403; H. Ingholt et al., *Recueil des tessères de Palmyre* (Paris, 1955), no. 170; S. Moscati, *The World of the Phoenicians,* trans. A. Hamilton (New York, 1968), 57. A common variant of the type of particular interest to the present context shows a crescent or lunar disk surmounting the humped back of a bull; for example, Ingholt, *Tessères de*

Palmyre, nos. 155, 383, 471, 599; Moscati, *Phoenicians,* 326; M. Rostovtzeff, *American Journal of Archaeology* 37 (1933), plate 9. Coins from Aradus have a bust of Astarte on the obverse with a bull on the reverse: Hill, *Coins of Phoenicia,* Aradus, nos. 324ff.

119. The lion is the regular fetish for Astarte, the bull for Baal Hadad; see Lucian, *On the Syrian Goddess* 31. The basic iconography for Baal is illustrated by Pritchard, *Ancient Near East in Pictures,* 167. The fullest survey of the field, inevitably from a Hellenizing point of view, is A. Cook, *Zeus,* 3 vols. (Cambridge, 1914), 1:549–644. More focused are Pope and Röllig, *Wörterbuch,* 255, and, especially, P. Bauer et al., eds., *The Excavations at Dura-Europos: Preliminary Report of Third Season of Work* (New Haven, 1932), 107–39.

120. The primacy of Astarte over Baal is a central and recurrent theme in Syro-Palestinian religion. Already in Ugaritic narrative, El asks, "Am I a slave, an attendant of Asherah? Am I a slave?" (II AB iv 59–60). A widely disseminated figural motif shows Astarte, in either human or lion form, leaping on a bull as it cowers from below; see R. du Mesnil du Buisson, *Etudes sur les dieux phéniciens hérités par l'empire romain* (Leiden, 1970), 20–28. On a tessera from Palmyra, the lion attacks under a crescent moon, while on the reverse Astarte sits enthroned facing a giant fish; Ingholt, *Tessères de Palmyre,* no. 432. The same relationship is expressed spatially in the famous relief of Atargatis and Hadad from Dura-Europus; as P. Bauer puts it, "Atargatis is given twice as much space as her consort occupies, her footstool is twice as broad, and her lions are more than twice the size of his bulls. All this clearly shows her predominance in northern Syria. She is paramount mistress, her husband only a partner by necessity" (*Excavations,* 128–29). The ritual castration and haircutting associated with Astarte also belong within this field of ideas; see E. Neumann, *Ursprungsgeschichte des Bewusstseins* (Zurich, 1949), 73–75, 91–92, 176–77. Similarly, Philo of Byblus reports: ἡ δὲ Ἀστάρτη ἐπέθηκεν τῇ ἰδίᾳ κεφαλῇ βασιλείας παράσημον κεφαλὴν ταύρου (H. Attridge and R. Oden, Jr., eds., *Phoenician History* [Washington, D.C., 1981], frag. 2D, 20–21). Astarte crowned by Nike is a popular theme in coinage along the coast; see Hill, *Coins of Phoenicia,* index 2, s.v. "Nike."

121. Neumann, *Die grosse Mutter,* 141 n. 66 and 265.

122. In Ugaritic texts, Asherah has clear marine connections: her cult titles are "Lady Asherah of the sea" and "She who treads on the sea (or, sea dragon)"; see Pope and Röllig, *Wörterbuch,* 247, and Hvidberg-Hansen, *La Déesse TNT* 1:74–75. R. Coote remarks, "Whether Asherah treads *on* the sea in cosmogonic battle with the sea dragon, as does her younger counterpart Anat, or whether she treads *by* the sea as the consort of El who lives at the source of the double deep or as the goddess of any one of the several Canaanite towns, or whether she treads *through* the sea as the goddess represented as the serpent in the sea, the *yammu* of her epithet [*rabbatu 'athiratu yammi*] cannot be totally divorced from the *yammu* who is the sea dragon" (*The Serpent and Sacred Marriage in Northwest Semitic Tradition* [Ph.D. diss., Harvard University, 1972], 111). The coinages of Sidon, Tyre, and Berytus all depict Astarte as a marine deity; see Hill, *Coins of Phoenicia,* index 2, s.v. "Galley."

123. The description specifically stresses this control: ἡ παρθένος μέσοις ἐπεκάθητο τοῖς νώτοις τοῦ βοός . . . τῇ λαιᾷ τοῦ κέρως ἐχομένη, ὥσπερ . . . ἡνίοχος χαλινοῦ· καὶ γὰρ ὁ βοῦς ἐπέστραπτο ταύτῃ μᾶλλον πρὸς τὸ τῆς χειρὸς ἕλκον ἡνιοχούμενος (1.1.10). For παρθένος as a standard epithet for the goddess, see Oden, *Studies in Lucian's "De Syria Dea,"* 104.

124. In Greco-Roman literary treatments, the abduction of Europa is uniformly treated as an act of violence in which Europa is an unwilling and passive victim. Cf., for example, Moschus, *Europa* 78; Lucian, *Dialogues of the Sea Gods* 15.2; Ovid, *Metamorphoses* 2.873–75; Horace, *Odes* 3.27.57–58. For the history of the Europa saga in

Daniel L. Selden

Greco-Roman literature, see W. Bühler, *Die Europa des Moskhos* (Wiesbaden, 1960), 17–29.

125. A Canaanite myth preserved in a Hittite version depicts Ashertu as the sexual aggressor who ensnares Baal; see E. von Schuler, "Kleinasien," in Pope and Röllig, *Wörterbuch*, 159.

126. This double reading encompasses not only the central figure in the painting, the woman on the bull, but its subsidiary details as well. On the one hand, the picture can be set within the mimetic traditions of Greco-Roman art; see E. Harlan, "The Description of Paintings as a Literary Device and Its Application to Achilles Tatius (Ph.D. diss., Columbia University, 1965), 96–106. On the other, it can be read according to Syro-Palestinian figural conventions in which details of a symbolic nature are "set within the available space with little or no meaningful visual connection" (A. Perkins, *The Art of Dura-Europas* [London, 1973], 117; cf. H. Seyrig, "Représentations de la main divine," *Syria* 20 [1939]: 189–94). Thus, the principal components described by the traveler as naturalistic features of the landscape have other connotations within Phoenician cult. Four examples: (1) θάλασσα ὑπέρυθρος—the festival of Adonis, Astarte's lover, commences when his eponymous river turns blood-red, flows into the sea, and colors a large part of it (see Lucian, *On the Syrian Goddess* 8; W. Baudissin, *Adonis und Esmun* [Leipzig, 1911]); (2) δένδρων φάλαγξ—tree worship seems to have been integrally associated with the cult of Astarte; thus, in the Septuagint, the name ʿAsherah is regularly translated as ἄλσος, and trees regularly appear on coins and engravings in conjunction with Astarte (see B. Soyez, "Le Bétyle dans le culte de l'Astarté phénicienne," *Mélanges de l'Université Saint-Joseph* 47 [1972]: 152; J. Pritchard, *Palestinian Figurines in Relation to Certain Goddesses Known through Literature* [Philadelphia, 1943], 62; Hill, *Coins of Phoenicia*, Tyre, nos. 275–87); (3) χορὸς παρθένων—throngs of women were notoriously associated with Astarte, not as virgins but as "temple prostitutes" (see W. Kornfeld, "Prostitution Sacrée," in *Supplément au Dictionnaire de la Bible*, fasc. 47 [1972], cols. 1358–59); (4) μικρὸν παιδίον—the goddess is frequently shown accompanied by a child (occasionally winged), who is either some sort of "acolyte" or the junior member of a divine family triad (see Baudissin, *Adonis und Esmun*, 10–55; J. Teixidor, *The Pagan God* [Princeton, 1977], 34–39; B. Trell, "The World of the Phoenicians, East and West," in *Proceedings of the Ninth International Congress of Numismatics*, ed. T. Hackens and R. Weiller, 2 vols. [Louvain-La-Neuve, 1982], 1:421–43); Ingholt, *Tessères de Palmyre*, no. 415; C. Bonnet et al., *Religio Phoenicia* [Namur, Belgium, 1986], 275; J. Rouvier, "Numismatique des villes de la Phénicie: Sidon," *Journal international d'archéologie numismatique* 5 [1902]: no. 1539).

127. The number of bilingual readers in the early empire in command of both cultural traditions should not be underestimated. For the cultural climate in Syria, see E. Boucher, *Syria as a Roman Province* (Oxford, 1916), 1–18; F. Millar, "The Problem of Hellenistic Syria," in *Hellenism in the East*, ed. A. Kuhrt and S. Sherwin-White (London, 1987), 110–33; and G. Bowersock, *Hellenism in Late Antiquity* (Ann Arbor, Mich., 1990), 29–40. The strong evidence for biliteracy is surveyed by R. Schmitt in *Die Sprachen im römischen Reich der Kaiserzeit*, ed. G. Neumann and J. Untermann (Cologne, 1980), 198–205, and W. Harris, *Ancient Literacy* (Cambridge, Mass., 1989), 187–90. Beyond this, F. Cumont stresses the extent to which Syro-Phoenician observance penetrated even the highest echelons of imperial society: "La diffusion des cultes sémitiques en Italie, qui commença insensiblement sous la République, s'intensifia surtout à partir du Ier siècle de notre ère. Leur expansion et leur multiplication furent rapides, et ils atteignirent l'apogée de leur puissance au IIIe siècle. Leur influence devint presque prépondérante quand l'avènement des Sévères leur valut l'appui d'une cour à demi syrienne. Les fonctionnaires de tout ordre, les sénateurs et les officiers rivalisèrent de

piété envers les dieux protecteurs de leurs souverains et protégés par ceux-ci. Des princesses intelligentes et ambitieuses—Julia Domna, Julia Maesa, Julia Mamaea—dont l'ascendant intellectuel fut si considérable, se firent les propagatrices de leur religion nationale . . . Ainsi les souverains, à deux reprises [Héliogabale et Aurélien], voulurent remplacer par un dieu sémitique le Jupiter capitolin, faire d'un culte sémitique le culte principal et officiel des Romains. Ils proclamaient la déchéance de la vieille idolâtrie latine au profit d'un autre paganisme emprunté à la Syrie" (*Les religions orientales dans le paganisme romain,* 4th ed., rev. [Paris, 1929], 105–7). Where precisely Achilles Tatius's work falls within this historical development is still uncertain, though it is clear that from at least the first century A.D. on, there would have been a sufficiently large audience not only in the Levant, but throughout the Roman Empire, competent to read a Greek/Syrian bicultural text; for the diffusion of Syrians in the West, see H. Solin in Neumann and Untermann, *Die Sprachen der römischen Reich,* 301–30. On the other hand, the extent to which the two pagan traditions were still felt to be fundamentally quite different, despite widespread syncretism, can be gauged from the virulent reaction provoked by Elagabalus when he attempted to establish normal Syrian religious practices at Rome; see Cassius Dio 80.11.1–2.

128. The textual problem at 1.4.3 is ultimately a red herring, for the Syro-Phoenician iconography is established by the narrative independent of any reference to Selene. The initial description of the painting is already set up to evoke ambivalent responses in readers competent in one system of representation or the other. Sidonian coins of the first century A.D. play the same game: they depict a female figure riding a bull, but do not identify her; see Hill, *Coins of Phoenicia,* Sidon, nos. 163ff. To my knowledge, only one coin, minted during the reign of Valerian (A.D. 253–60) at Tyre, actually bears the exergue ΕΥΡΩΠΗ; its pictorial composition, however, is completely different: a woman stands erect right of center as the torso of a bull approaches her out of the water from the lower left (ibid., Tyre, no. 468).

129. R. Garson, "Works of Art in Achilles Tatius' *Leucippe and Clitophon,*" *Acta Classica* 21 (1978): 83.

130. Narratological science of Syro-Palestinian literature is, at the moment, so rudimentary that it is difficult to carry such a reading forward. At least one point, however, can be made: while the rape of Europa looks forward to the abductions of Calligone and Leucippe, the icon of Astarte prefigures all the controlling thematic motifs of the plot. The Syrian goddess is not only mistress of the seas, but intimately associated with fortune (Tyche), love (Aphrodite), war, virginity, androgyny, death, and resurrection.

131. See R. Jakobson, "Randbemerkungen zur Prosa des Dichters Pasternak," *Slavische Rundschau* 7 (1935): 357–74, refined in Jakobson and M. Halle, *Fundamentals of Language* (The Hague, 1956), and complicated by P. de Man, "The Rhetoric of Temporality," in *Blindness and Insight,* 2d ed., rev. (Minneapolis, 1983), 187–228, and H. White, *Metahistory* (Baltimore, 1973), 1–42; cf. also R. Wellek and A. Warren, *Theory of Literature,* 3d ed. (New York, 1962), 193–99. For the term "master trope," see K. Burke, *A Grammar of Motives* (Berkeley and Los Angeles, 1969), 503–17.

132. This is not to say that syllepsis does not occur elsewhere in ancient literature, even quite commonly, but that in ancient fiction it becomes the central narrative device. What is also peculiar to these texts is the way syllepsis is used to stage differences in cultural perspectives or world-views.

133. The Greek recension describes the convert as δυσὶ παλαίοντος λογισμοῖς (261). As such, the historical principle at stake here is clearly not the reductive secularization of Oriental myth described by K. Kerényi ("religiöses Gut gleichsam zu säkularisieren, kultisches Material in profanen Beziehungen zu verwenden"), nor its redemptive aestheticization ("eine nichtliterarische Erzälungsform—diejenige von Göttersagen,

Mythennovellen oder -märchen, Aretalogien und volkstümlichen Romangeschicht-en—zur hochliterarischen zu erheben") under the aegis of a Hellenizing humanism ("die vollständige Vermenschlichung nichthumanen Stoffes"); see *Die griechisch-orientalische Romanliteratur in religionsgeschichtlicher Beleuchtung,* 3d ed. (Darmstadt, 1973), 229ff.

134. The most complete account of how the Buddha became a Christian saint is D. Lang, *The Wisdom of Balahvar* (New York, 1957). The Sanskrit sources are summarized more fully by E. Budge, ed., *Baralâm and Yewâsef,* 2 vols. (Cambridge, 1923), 2:xi–cxxi.

135. Tag: Apuleius, *Asinus aureus* 1.1.6.

PART II

Remembering
and Revising

CHAPTER THREE

Tasso's Heliodorus and the World of Romance

Walter Stephens

Torquato Tasso (1544–95) is perhaps the foremost example of a successful epic poet who was also highly influential as a theorist of heroic narrative. His earliest systematic commentators, Scipione Gentili and Giulio Guastavini, already observed that the biography of the warrior Clorinda in *Gerusalemme liberata* is based in part on that of Chariclea in Heliodorus's *Aethiopica*.[1] As we might expect from a writer who was both poet and theorist, the story of Clorinda constitutes a reading of the themes and theoretical implications of Heliodorus's text. The convergence of theory and theme in the story of Clorinda does indeed illuminate both texts, but not in ways that simply vindicate Tasso's theory as an adequate or definitive description of his compositional practice. Rather, the convergence points beyond Tasso's explicit theory to epitomize his praxis of intertextuality and exemplify a theory of romance that may not have been fully articulated at any conscious level, and that is strongly reminiscent of Mikhail Bakhtin's theory of romance.

In all likelihood, Tasso read the *Aethiopica* not in Warschewicski's Latin translation of 1552, or in the Greek original available since 1534, but rather in the Italian translation done by Leonardo Ghini, published in 1556, 1559, 1560, and thereafter. Despite his abilities in Latin and Greek, Tasso was wont to read Italian translations of narrative when they were available,[2] and this one, published by the well-known Venetian printer Gabriel Giolito de' Ferrari, would have been far more widely available than either the original or the Latin translation. In addition, given his birthdate, Tasso could have read Ghini's translation for pleasure in adolescence, even before he began to theorize about the epic. Ghini's very title would have attracted the future theorist of epic and romance: *Heliodorus's History of Things Ethiopian, in Which, among Divers Pathetic Adventures of Two Lovers, Are Contained Single Combats, Descriptions of Foreign Countries, and Many Other Things Both Useful and Delightful to Read*. Ghini's title claims that he translated directly from Greek into Tuscan, and, if he was the son of the botanist and physician Luca Ghini, who founded the botanical gardens of Pisa and Florence for the grand duke of Tuscany, Ghini would have been well equipped for a direct translation.[3]

In his letters and theoretical works, Tasso mentions or alludes to Heliodorus only a few times, and the opinions he expresses have often been discussed, most notably by Alban Forcione.[4] Following the neo-Aristotelian definition of his time, which was independent of the question of verse, Tasso classified the *Aethiopica* as a heroic "poem," and in his early *Dell' arte poetica* (probably finished by 1566), he used the example of Theagenes and Chariclea to defend the appropriateness of love as an epic subject.[5] Elsewhere he maintained in a similar vein that "noble" erotic themes were suited to the heroic poem.[6] In a letter of 1575, Tasso went even further; like Jacques Amyot, he praised Heliodorus's use of *in medias res* narration to create suspense, and compared the *Aethiopica* to his own technique in the subplot of the Muslim princess Erminia.[7] As Forcione points out, however, Giulio Cesare Scaligero was the first to recommend Heliodorus's technique as a model for the epic poet.[8] Scipione Gentili remembered Scaliger when commenting on Tasso's Clorinda. Suggesting that Heliodorus should be read diligently by lovers of poetry, he notes that "a worthy man of our time . . . has proposed that fabulous history as a perfect model or paradigm [*esempio, o argomento*] of epic poetry."[9] However, Gentili appears to have read Scaliger through the filter of Tasso's own pronouncements: Forcione observes that although Scaliger took Heliodorus as "a model for the disposition of an epic," he did not "admit the possibility of an epic in prose," as did Tasso and some other theorists of the time.[10]

Still, Scaliger had implicitly compared Heliodorus to Vergil by reference to the stories of Chariclea and Camilla. He proposed Camilla as a model for the successful integration of "relevant episode and main plot" to achieve both suspense and variety, but added, "You [also] observe this most splendid manner of constructing a work in Heliodorus's *Ethiopian History,* a book which I think should be read with great attention by the epic poet and which should be proposed to him as the best model possible."[11] Tasso may have been struck by this mention of Camilla in the same context as Heliodorus, for he also compares Heliodorus to Vergil on the basis of the *in medias res* technique, proclaiming Vergil the master.[12] More importantly, in *Gerusalemme liberata,* and again in *Gerusalemme conquistata,* the warrior Clorinda's biography draws extensively on both Chariclea and Camilla. Despite his Aristotelian training, which inclined him to conceptualize the *Aethiopica* as an epic, and despite his definition of the romance as a species of heroic composition inferior to the epic,[13] Tasso clearly appreciated what Bakhtin defines as the quintessentially romance aspects of

Heliodorus's text, and adapted them to mitigate Clorinda's resemblance to the tragic Camilla.

Most scholars' attention since Guastavini and Gentili has been focused on the obvious adaptation of Heliodorus in Tasso's account of Clorinda's birth.[14] Both heroines are portrayed as the anomalously white offspring of the king and queen of Ethiopia. Each mother, fearful that her daughter's whiteness will be interpreted as a sign of adultery, abandons her child soon after birth. Each text attributes the accident of the daughter's complexion to the influence of the painted representation of a white maiden seen by the mother. Both heroines leave Ethiopia in infancy, wander extensively in the Near East, and spend significant portions of their lives in Egypt. Chariclea learns of her origins from the Egyptian priest Calasiris, who soon becomes her foster father, while Clorinda hears her life story from the Egyptian eunuch Arsete, who has raised her from infancy. Arsete, in fact, appears almost as an epitome of those numerous foster fathers of Chariclea: Sisimithres, Charicles, Calasiris, and the Persian eunuch Bagoas, who actually delivers her to her biological father Hydaspes.

Yet the decisive Clorinda may seem an unlikely avatar of the stereotypically feminine Chariclea. At her first appearance, Clorinda rescues a pair of young Christians who are about to be burned at the stake by the Muslim king of Jerusalem. But intertextuality invests the scene with irony, for, although scholars have traditionally seen the source of this episode in a novella of Boccaccio (*Decameron, 5.6*), any reader of Heliodorus can also see behind Tasso's Christian couple the serenity of Chariclea and the vacillations of Theagenes in their trials by fire.[15] Further, like Theagenes and Chariclea, Sofronia and Olindo are married immediately after their release.[16] The happy end of Chariclea's story hangs over the beginning of Clorinda's, whose empathy with Sofronia is a narrative marker of the intertextual kinship both heroines have with Chariclea.

The end of Clorinda's subplot is likewise permeated with dramatic and ideological ironies that make its relation to Heliodorus less evident. Seeking to return to Jerusalem after a nighttime sortie in which she and a male companion have burned the Christians' principal siege-engine, Clorinda is trapped outside the walls by Tancredi, the Christian warrior who loves her unrequitedly. Initially recognizing her as a "pagan" but not as his beloved, Tancredi mortally wounds her in a duel, and then, at her request, baptizes her the instant before she dies.

From a strictly thematic vantage point, any similarities between the two plots appear negligible or even questionable. Chariclea's story is overtly a narrative of quest for identity and return, and ends with her recognition by her parents, her reintegration into their society, and her marriage to the faithful Theagenes. Conversely, Clorinda never returns to Ethiopia or to her parents; indeed, on the same night she learns her identity, Clorinda is separated from the foster father who has been her only family since birth, is fatally wounded by her would-be husband, is converted, is baptized, and dies (GL, 12.1–69).

Resemblances are equally problematic from a more theoretical standpoint. Mikhail Bakhtin identifies the "chronotope" of a Greek romance like the *Aethiopica* as the "alien world in adventure-time."[17] According to Bakhtin, passage through this world "takes place in an extratemporal hiatus between two moments of biographical time" and "leaves no trace" on the individual, but merely affirms "the identity between what had been at the beginning, and what is at the end." "There is no potential for evolution, for growth, for change . . . nothing . . . is destroyed, remade, changed, or created anew."[18] Bakhtin's observation would seem to negate the few parallels that scholars have noticed between Heliodorus's and Tasso's heroines, for Clorinda undergoes the most radical changes imaginable in a few hours' time. Her story apparently conforms more to what Bakhtin calls "Christian crisis hagiographies," which show "how an individual becomes other than what he was" by presenting two separate "images" of him.[19] Unlike the adventure-time typified by the *Aethiopica,* this sort "leaves a deep and irradicable mark on the man himself as well as on his entire life," and within it, "the primary initiative . . . belongs to the hero himself and to his own personality."[20] In fact, within the Christian theological tradition, conversion and baptism are both presented as the death of an old self and the birth of a new one.[21]

In contrast to the unfailingly energetic Clorinda, Heliodorus's heroine is often passive, even quietistic. Her happy ending is only marginally a result of her initiative. Gerald N. Sandy describes it thus: "The *Aethiopica* is a complex blend of divinely orchestrated and naturally motivated events presented from multiple points of view without linear chronological progression. The apparent disorder may, as Heiserman suggests, be intended to duplicate the mysterious unfolding of Destiny. Chariclea refers to 'events whose beginnings the divine power from the outset laid down in a complex way' (9.24.4); and the sage Sisimithres, as the wondrous events begin to unravel themselves at Meroë, waits 'for the revelations to be disclosed with certainty by divine will.' "[22] What Sandy refers to as destiny would have appeared to Tasso and his contemporaries as a view of divine providence, the more so since they believed that Heliodorus had been an apostate Christian.[23]

Bakhtin was not unaware of this religious correlative to narrative structure, and observed that an essential feature of "Greek adventure-time" is the tendency of "chance" to assume the guise of "nonhuman forces—fate, gods, villains—and it is precisely these forces, and not the heroes, who take all the initiative."[24] Bakhtin's account of the afterlife of "Greek adventure-time" could also describe the romance significance Tasso found in Heliodorus's view of providence: "Whenever Greek adventure-time appears in the subsequent development of the European novel, initiative is handed over to chance, which controls meetings and failures to meet—either as an impersonal, anonymous force in the novel, or as fate, as divine foresight, as romantic 'villains' or romantic 'secret benefactors.'"[25] A general congruence thus emerges from the welter of contrasts in plot: both Tasso's and Heliodorus's are narratives in which divine providence plays the central role, almost as if it were one of the dramatis personae.

To say that Tasso Christianized Heliodorus is to describe how he looked beyond the differences between a "chronotope" that leaves indelible traces and one that does not, to see their similarities, which reside in the form of temporality. Bakhtin observes that both kinds of narrative unfold outside what he calls "biographical" time, depicting only "exceptional and unusual events, events determined by chance, . . . [by] fortuitous encounters (temporal junctures) and fortuitous nonencounters (temporal disjunctions)."[26] What Tasso actually said in his theoretical works about the relation between epic and romance must be measured against the critique of Heliodorus's notion of providence implicit in Clorinda's story.

As with Chariclea, the biography of Tasso's heroine is determined—in all senses—by the theme of return, which manifests itself as a cancellation of the effects of time. In both texts the successful return is dependent on dramatic recognition, which in turn depends on a play of physical resemblance to represented images at widely separated moments in time. The heroine's movement from discovery to recovery of identity, the revelation of her own biography, which creates the rationale for Clorinda's last-minute conversion, is actually Tasso's largest debt to Heliodorus. Clorinda's return to Christianity is her trope of Chariclea's return to Ethiopia.

In both texts, providence enables recognition and reintegration by an activity that resembles writing. In fact, the intertextual dynamics between the narratives of Chariclea and Clorinda appear most succinctly in their inscribed correlatives to what Bakhtin calls the "signs" or "marks" left on the individual by "adventure-time." The *Aethiopica* is characterized by numerous signs, signals, and representations: it displays an extensive thematic network of black and white, and foregrounds the act of writing, both as a metaphor for providence and as the self-conscious literary praxis of rewriting. By transforming and reinscribing these signs, Tasso redefines the meaning of an "alien world" of romance in terms both religious and literary.

Within the *Aethiopica,* both resemblance and return depend on writing as the vehicle for identification. Though Chariclea bears no psychological "mark" of development in Bakhtin's sense, her white skin is already something of a text, the presumed sign of her mother's sexual infidelity. It is a "blank" that seems to lack the mark of her black father. Thus the infant girl is sent out into the world laden with signs and writing. She is wrapped in swaddling clothes, and this involucrum of cloth is a kind of second "skin" that counteracts her whiteness: it is explicitly a text, on which the true biography of Chariclea is written "in the blood and tears" of her own mother. Furthermore, it includes a hypothetical script for Chariclea's future providential salvation.[27] Calasiris, who translates the document for the reader, remarks transparently that "on reading this, . . . I perceived the hand of the gods and marvelled at the subtlety of their governance."[28] In addition, Chariclea bears the "hand" or signature of her father, in the form of his signet ring, which Tasso's translator Ghini describes inaccurately, but appropriately, as a wedding ring.[29]

Chariclea's recognizability as the child of her father depends in large part, but not entirely, on her possession of these portable graphic tokens. The truly climactic moment occurs when Sisimithres, Chariclea's first foster father, remembers the birthmark on her arm. This birthmark, as Ghini translates, was "like a little circle of ebony placed around ivory," and it is her mother's recognition of this *corporeal* sign that proves her legitimacy.[30] The sign on Chariclea's body is doubled by the signet ring, which externalizes Hydaspes' mark or seal of sexual possession, as "impressed" on the physiognomy of his wife's child. The ring's jewel, a *pantarbe* or "all fear," externalizes Persinna's acceptance of her husband's sexual authority; when transferred to Chariclea, it appears to externalize the fear and awe her beauty inspires. This transformation of paternal charisma is responsible for protecting her from death by fire, and ultimately, from sacrifice by her own father.[31]

Chariclea is thus definitively recognized and restored to her origins thanks to the letter O, which is imprinted on her body, and repeated in the circles of her father's ring, of the swaddling cloth around her waist, and of her mother's necklaces.[32] As a circle and an omicron, it prefigures the course of Chariclea's "odyssey," her circular wanderings from Ethiopia to Greece and Egypt and back to Ethiopia. At another level, in terms anachronistic for Heliodorus but not for Tasso, the mark on Chariclea's skin is the cipher zero. It externalizes the cancellation of the entire interval between Persinna's first recognition that her infant bears the white "mark of Andromeda" and her recognition of a grown daughter's tokens of "blackness," and it negates the period of wanderings and travails that constitutes most of Chariclea's life. After a plethora of reunions with her biological parents, her surviving foster fathers, and her native religion, Chariclea assumes her mother's identity, supplanting her as priestess of the moon, deity of cycles. This closure of the circle is a moment of conjugal union as well as reunion, for Chariclea is finally allowed to marry Theagenes, who supplants her father as priest of the sun. Here it can be said with Bakhtin that the rites of passage through an "alien world in adventure-time" have left no mark on Chariclea, or at most only a null sign.

In the *Aethiopica,* there are three providential "scripts" Chariclea acts out with varying degrees of consciousness. In the most superficial, Apollo or Helios is the inscribed "author" to whom Chariclea attributes her deliverance from peril. But Chariclea's mother sends her into the world bearing a second script, which she cannot read: the swaddling garment inscribed with hieroglyphs, which prescribes an ideal process of Chariclea's adoption, preservation, and reunion. The third and master script is both genetic and intertextual; it is "written" at the moment of Chariclea's conception, by Persinna's glance at a painting of Andromeda, represented in the moment of her rescue by Perseus. Tasso saw that, to the extent that Chariclea resembles Andromeda through predicament as well as physiognomy, her adventures are epitomized in her mother's painting of Perseus.

Tasso masterfully transfuses this overt and redundant graphology into the allusive substrate of a romance about the fundamental ritual of Christianity. He rewrites Heliodorus microscopically by changing one detail concerning the birth of Clorinda: she owes her anomalous color not to a single glance during the moment of conception, but to her mother's daily prayers before an image of Saint George liberating the white maiden from the dragon.[33] As the specific agent of providence in Clorinda's salvation, Saint George is the Christian Perseus. He performs as if he were one of those guardian angels in whom Counter-Reformation Catholics were expected to believe literally. The world of romance is most succinctly described in the allusivity of this substitution.

This slight deviation from Heliodorus creates the conditions for macroscopically Christianizing the theme of return by transforming the definitions of the "alien world" and of "adventure-time." By Christianizing Perseus, Tasso is not only modifying Heliodorus's religious version of providence, but also alluding to the deeper structure of repetition and return that underlies both romance plots and the writing of romance. The broader congruence with Heliodorus contextualizes the many obvious differences in detail between Clorinda's biography and Chariclea's, some of which derive from a self-conscious *contaminatio* with other sources. By mixing his sources, Tasso translates Heliodorus's plethora of inscribed signs and scripts into a plurality of inscribed *texts,* so as to find metaphorical or allusive equivalents for writings that are present more or less literally in Heliodorus's narrative.

Like Chariclea's, Clorinda's biography describes the almost indefinite postponement of ceremonial reunion and union (*GL,* 12.39.1–8; 12.64.1–69.8). But Tasso reinscribes the Heliodoran themes of exile, return, and marriage under a Christian dialectic of eternal salvation and damnation. The last wish of Clorinda's mother is not that Arsete guarantee her return home, but that he have her baptized (*GL*, 12.36.5–8). This change is reflected in the Christianization of the image: while Chariclea's fate was foretold by Andromeda's marriage to Perseus, the story of Saint George and the maiden is one of baptism and conversion, like Clorinda's own career.[34] Yet through her vocabulary Clorinda's mother invokes the Pauline notion of baptism as a marriage of the soul to Christ, for her hypothetical script for her daughter's salvation describes her as a faithful handmaiden (*fida ancella*) of God.[35] In a similar vein, the Tridentine hagiographer who undertook to purge the legend of Saint George from its fantastic imitation of the Perseus and Andromeda plot had concluded that George's own deepest significance—rather than that of the maiden—was as a perfect spouse of Christ.[36]

Like Chariclea, Clorinda's life is a "zero sum," but not on the literal plane of plot, since she does not actually return to Ethiopia. Similarly, the zero imprinted on Chariclea's flesh, which secures her reunion with family, nation, and religion, has no literal correlative in *Gerusalemme liberata*. Rather, it corresponds to what Catholic dogmatists of Tasso's day called the "character" of baptism, a literal but invisible impress made on the soul by performance of the sacrament. Without this mark the soul cannot enter heaven.[37] Though Tasso never mentions "character," his substitution of baptism as the goal of his Chariclea-figure strongly implicates it. David Quint's analysis demonstrates that Tasso was aware of Catholic uneasiness toward Ethiopian (Coptic) baptismal practices in his day. Although Catholics had hoped to find doctrinal as well as geopolitical support in Ethiopia, Coptic practices, relating both to the postponement of infant baptism and to the repeated baptism of adults, showed disturbingly close resemblances to Protestant heresies, especially those of the Anabaptists.[38] Unbaptized infants who died were damned, according to the Catholic way of thinking, and the Catholic prohibition of repeated baptisms derived precisely from a conviction that the *character* must not be "overwritten." This prohibition was so important that the Catholic formula for baptizing anyone other than a newborn began by stating: "If you are already baptized, I do *not* baptize you again."[39]

While it is not written on her body, the sign of the zero is proleptically present in Clorinda's infancy, when Arsete flees with her across a river into Egypt. Although this river scene is adapted from Vergil's story of Camilla's infancy (*GL*, 12.34–36; *Aeneid* 11.547ff.), its most significant feature is the substitution of a whirlpool, which Tasso calls a *cerchio,* for the raging flood in Vergil's story. The circular movement of the water is a visual symbol of the "character" of baptism, but also of the enduring struggle between Catholicism and heresy for possession of Clorinda's soul: as long as the Muslim Arsete clutches her and attempts to swim, the whirlpool drags them ever downward, but as soon as he releases her, it reverses direction and pushes the infant safely to shore (*GL*, 12.35). Later, Saint George boasts to Arsete in a dream that it was he who gave intelligence (*mente*) to the waters (12.37.1–2). The circle of Clorinda's odyssey is a journey between the banks of two streams: the first one, the one with the whirlpool, is crossed in infancy with Arsete, as they move from the Christian territory of Ethiopia into Egypt, the land of Muslim "paganism" (or heresy); the second stream is the *picciol rio* (*GL*, 12.67.2) where she will be baptized in the instant before death. The banks are the external markers of a juxtaposition of bodily and spiritual births and deaths, for in Christian dogmatics from Saint Paul onward, baptism is described as a moment of spiritual death and rebirth that annuls the previous life of the individual. In addition, as both John Freccero and David Quint have observed, all baptismal water is identified with the water of the Jordan in Catholic tradition, so in a sense, Clorinda's two rivers are one.[40]

Like the zero, Chariclea's ring has no literal equivalent in Clorinda's story, which is instead subtended by the twin valences of *fede,* a word that in Tasso's day signified both religious faith and sexual fidelity.[41] Like Heliodorus's ring, however, *fede* is intimately tied to paternal authority: while Chariclea's mother Persinna feared that society as a whole would accuse her of infidelity, the mother of Tasso's heroine feared only the wrath of her husband, a man so jealous that he hid her from the very glances of the sun by locking her in a tower (*GL*, 12.22). Conversely, while the ring of Chariclea externalizes her circular movement from biological father through foster fathers and back again, *fede* represents for Clorinda a sort of Augustinian movement away from earthly fathers to the lap of God (*in grembo a Dio*, 12.92.3). Moreover, this sublimation of fatherhood has a sexual dimension, as Clorinda escapes from the aggressive sexual jealousy of her natural father (12.22) to the sexless Arsete, a eunuch "involved in womanish employment among the flocks of handmaidens [*ancelle*, 12.21.5–6],"[42] who is doubled by the fearsome yet maternal Saint George (12.36–37), to a "heavenly father" whose *grembo* is always a sign of maternity in *Gerusalemme liberata,* since it is a womb as well as a lap. It is surely not coincidental that Tridentine doctrine defines baptism as the very sacrament of *fede,* and that through it, initiates into Christianity receive new fathers.[43]

In this context, the body of the girl-child as misinterpreted signifier of broken faith, which Heliodorus represented so prolifically by ring and swathes and birthmark, is condensed by Tasso so as to render oxymoronic the symbolism of black and white. In Ghini's translation, Persinna says that Chariclea's color seemed to inscribe or "denote" maternal adultery: "'l color tuo mi *notava* d'adulterio."[44] Tasso's Arsete makes a paradox of the white sign or note, saying that Clorinda's father would have deduced from the infant's "candid" whiteness that the faithfulness (*fede*) of his wife was not white.[45] As Clorinda's life began from a problem of *fede,* so it ends: her final discussion with Arsete concerns whether she should change religious *fede.* As foretold by the symbol of the whirlpool, he "releases" her from adherence to Islam. But paradoxically, she, the "born" Christian, refuses the "heretic's" plea for conversion to Christianity, thus dramatizing the humanly poignant dimension of religious faith as culture, or learned *faithfulness* to a societal convention:

> Rasserenando il volto, al fin gli dice:
> —Quella fé seguirò che vera or parmi,
> che tu co 'l latte già de la nutrice
> sugger mi fèsti, e che vuoi dubbia or farmi;
> né per temenza lascierò, né lice
> a magnanimo cor, l'impresa e l'armi,
> non se la morte nel più fer sembiante
> che sgomenti i mortali avessi inante.—

Clearing her countenance, at last she says to him: "I shall follow that faith that seems to me true at this moment, that once you caused me to drink in with my nurse's milk, and that now you wish to make me doubtful of. Nor shall I abandon out of fear (nor is that permitted the magnanimous heart) my enterprise and my weapons: not if I had before me Death in the fearfullest shape in which he terrifies mortal men."[46]

Providence overrides the social dimension of faith, however, for Clorinda's instantaneous conversion is caused by an infusion of *fede* as one of the three theological virtues.[47] So her circular journey away from and back toward Christian *fede,* initiated by her jealous father's obsession with infidelity, substitutes for Chariclea's physical return to Ethiopia.[48] (The circle is in fact somewhat "broken" by providence, for although born a Copt, Clorinda is baptized a Catholic. Still, she has no remaining time for action or exercise of will, and this makes such distinctions irrelevant; from the Tridentine doctrinal point of view, she enters heaven immediately, as a baptized infant would.)

In Tasso as in Heliodorus, the ultimate deliverance of the heroine is foreshadowed and theatrically prescribed by the visually represented fable of deliverance, and is dependent on the motif of resemblance to a painted image. The theme of black and white relating to the body of the heroine is already so strongly foregrounded in both texts as to seem allegorical of writing. But each also implicates the issue of literary representation, since the heroine's odyssey takes place in a period demarcated by resemblance to the visual representation of a literary legend. In infancy, the representation is believed somehow to cause the daughter's estrangement from her moth-

er, while the adult daughter's proven resemblance coincides with her reintegration into the community. In Heliodorus, Chariclea's and Persinna's
perfect chastity is the basis for a psychological resemblance masked by
physical dissimilarity;[49] likewise, in some paradoxical sense, Tasso's
white Clorinda symbolizes the "immaculate" chastity of her "brown but
beautiful" mother.[50]

In Heliodorus, the penultimate in an increasingly climactic series of
recognitions occurs when Chariclea, who bears no superficial resemblance
to her black parents, is proved to be the living facsimile of the painted
image of Andromeda at which her mother was gazing during the moment
of impregnation. Chariclea's resemblance to her mother is thus mediated
by the represented white maiden: true to the assertions written on the
swathes, she resembles her mother's *mental* "conception" rather than her
physique. By this point in the text, the reader, like Tasso, has long since
noticed that Chariclea's endless predicaments mirror those of Andromeda,
the archetypal "damsel in distress." Then, there is a suspicion that this
visual resemblance is as much natural (genetic) as magical (sympathetic),
since Andromeda is also Chariclea's ancestor.[51] In fact, Tasso's commentator Gentili was uncertain whether heredity or sympathetic influence was
responsible for the parallel "historical" cases he mentioned.[52]

Chariclea's reintegration is effected by her father's acceptance of this
occult resemblance to her mother. Hydaspes' paternal authorization and
legitimation are similarly mediated, for it is not he but the high priest
Sisimithres, Chariclea's first foster father, who orders that "the exemplar"
of Andromeda be brought and placed alongside Chariclea to confirm the
resemblance.[53] Indeed, the presence of all Chariclea's foster fathers save
the dead Calasiris provides a continuum of paternal recognitions and au-
thorizations that leaves no moment in her life unaccounted for, and explicitly enumerates all the bases for resemblance and legitimacy.

Tasso further sublimates and attenuates the dynamics of resemblance,
since religious reintegration alone is the goal of his narrative, whereas in
Heliodorus, Chariclea's reintegration into her native religious community
was subordinated to reunion with her parents. And whereas Chariclea's
biography is demarcated by two moments of resemblance to the "exemplar" of Andromeda, Clorinda's is bounded by resemblance to two separate painted images of two different virgins. In Tasso's story, furthermore,
the relations of causality have been reversed: it is Clorinda's return to her
mother's religious faith that evinces an enduring resemblance, mediated
by images, between mother and daughter. At the moment of death,
Clorinda's white face is described as beautifully pallid, as if violets had
been mixed with lilies.[54] This description recalls the white and vermilion
face of the virgin rescued by Saint George in her mother's devotional
picture, and combined with George's supervision of Clorinda's baptism,

it implies that he is her rescuer from the "old serpent" Satan.[55] But Clorinda's resemblance to her mother's "conception" is doubled by her allusive (and elusive) physiognomic resemblance to her mother, based on a paradoxical play of black and white. When she abandoned her infant to an unknown fate, Clorinda's mother fainted, and Arsete describes her face as "painted with pallid death."[56] The black woman's pallor assimilates her both to the white damsel represented in her painting and to her pallid daughter, both as "candid" infant and as dead woman in the distant future.

True to Tasso's associative play between black and white and *fede,* the pallor of the dead adult Clorinda is preceded by a mediated return to the blackness of her mother's skin. In preparation for her fatal heroic sortie, Clorinda exchanges her heraldic white armor, which is recognized by friend and foe, for a black and rusty suit, so as to avoid detection in the dark.[57] This "illegible" black involucrum paradoxically functions like the textualized swaddling clothes of Chariclea. As a reminder of Clorinda's origins, the sight of it moves Arsete to disclose the story of her life, since he interprets the shift from white to black as an ill omen (*infausto annunzio*) (GL, 12.18.4). The black armor also causes the dramatic irony whereby Clorinda's Christian *soupirant* Tancredi initially "recognizes" her militarily as an enemy, but not personally as his beloved (GL, 12.51.5–8). Tancredi's personal recognition of Clorinda both enables and coincides with her return to Christianity, for Tasso postpones it until after Clorinda, realizing she is fatally wounded, requests baptism. Thus Tasso further exaggerates the postponement tactics of Heliodorus, whereby the almost infinite delay of recognition and return completely annuls the identity of the heroine as established by the narrative; conversely, the end of the narrative denies us any glimpse of her performance in her new identity—which is actually the original or "real" identity that was initially foreclosed by the accident of her color. As the narrator says, Tancredi will kill Clorinda with iron only to give her life with water (GL, 12.67.5–68.4), but that new life is outside the narration, and is not vouchsafed by it.

Like causality, the chronology of resemblance has been reversed in Tasso's plotting of the biography. The primal image that appears to determine Clorinda's physiognomy is only described on the last day of her life, which is only narrated at the end of her biography. A second image, which appears to foreshadow her conversion a few weeks before the end of her life, appears chiastically, at the beginning of her biography. At her entry into the poem, Clorinda rescues the Christian Sofronia and her timid *soupirant* Olindo from death on a pyre. They stand accused of having stolen an icon of the Virgin Mary from a mosque, where it had been profaned by a Muslim sorcerer, who sequestered it to create a kind of palladium for the magical preservation of Jerusalem (GL, 2.1–53). There is a double irony, for Clorinda, a formidable enemy of Christianity, requests the liberty of the Christian couple as a boon in exchange for her service in the Muslim cause. But there is a deeper proleptic irony: the narrator's vocabulary creates allusive links of virginity and veiling between Sofronia and the image of Mary, and of pallor and "candor" between Sofronia and Clorinda.[58] There is thus a kind of double *mise en abîme:* Clorinda rescues a virgin who is accused of rescuing *the* Virgin (who may be operating through Sofronia to rescue the Christian community of Jerusalem). As the "Saint George" who rescues the "white virgin" Sofronia, Clorinda foreshadows her own eventual deliverance, which, we will learn ten cantos later, was already foreshadowed by her mother's picture of George and the dragon.[59] Thus the two images reflect and gloss each other at a distance of exactly half the poem.

In the *Aethiopica,* the thematic system of black and white, repetition, and representation is related to the fundamental praxis of rewriting the *Odyssey,* whereby Heliodorus presents Chariclea as a kind of feminine Odysseus.[60] This is most explicit in Calasiris's dream of Odysseus on the eve of a fateful sea voyage,[61] but the scar that enables Odysseus's recognition in Ithaca already has an implied equivalent in Chariclea's birthmark.[62] In addition, there is a further thematic dimension of writing and rewriting, for Chariclea's *segno nero* will cause her to be recognized as royal and priestly, which enables her to enact in reverse Heliodorus's own eccentric biography of the *Odyssey*'s author. In an apparent digression in book 3, Calasiris notes that Homer was actually an Egyptian: "Ostensibly he was the son of a high priest, but in actual fact, his father was Hermes, whose high priest his ostensible father was: for once when his wife was sleeping in the temple in the performance of some traditional rite, the god coupled with her and sired Homer, who bore on his person a token of this union of human and divine, for . . . one of his thighs [*ho meros*] was covered with a shaggy growth of hair."[63]

When Homer came of age and was elected to the priesthood, his putative father banished him, because, as Ghini translates, the *sign* on his body declared his bastardy: "Al *segno* ch'egli havea nel corpo, fu conosciuto bastardo."[64] Thus Homer pretended to be a Greek and went into exile, "and by concealing his true place of origin he was claiming the whole world as his own."[65] Likewise, Perseus had been born of a divine father and a human mother, and was exiled at birth.[66] Although the script of "fortune" written by her mother on Chariclea's swaddling clothes may seem to determine her biography, the preexisting scripts of Perseus, Homer, and Odysseus are tacitly invoked by the *Aethiopica* as truer subtexts of providence.[67]

It would have been hard for a Christian of Tasso's day to read Heliodorus's anecdote of a union of human and divine that seems "illegitimate" and not be reminded of Christ, as well as Homer and Perseus.[68] In addition, the finale of the *Aethiopica,* in which Chariclea's deliverance ends the Ethiopian practice of human sacrifice, might have had the same effect, since she is nearly sacrificed by her own father. More importantly, the relation of this story about Homer to Chariclea's biography resembles the Christian theory of narrative repetition known as typology or *figura,* in which one person's life is foreshadowed by that of another. As in Heliodorus, Clorinda's sign—or rather, her unwitting quest for the invisible *character* left on the soul at baptism—indicates a number of parallels between her life and the lives of males, whose biographies become a script she unwittingly reenacts. The two lives Tasso's heroine most obviously reenacts in her infancy are the two most important in Christian *figura,* those of Christ and Moses.

In Tasso's text, the three lives are intimately related through the motifs of water, escape from death in infancy, and foster parents. Like Christ, Clorinda flees into Egypt in infancy to avoid being recognized and killed by a jealous king; like Moses, she is adopted in infancy by an Egyptian, and saved from a slaughter of the innocents by being hidden in a basket "among flowers and fronds."[69] These resemblances reflect and extend the most conventional exemplification of *figura:* the symbolism of baptism, as established through the lives of Moses and Christ. Since Saint Paul, Christian interpretation of the Hebrew Bible had always construed the Israelites' crossing of the Red Sea and the Jordan River as a prefiguration of the salvation of the individual soul through the sacramental effect of baptismal waters.[70]

Tasso's thematic use of Egypt in *Gerusalemme liberata* gives that country new meaning as the "alien world" of romance, to use Bakhtin's term. Egypt was the land of exile for Chariclea throughout much of the *Aethiopica,* but in a Christian context, it had always been construed as the symbol of *spiritual* exile and captivity, as in the traditional exegesis of Psalm 114, "In exitu Israël de Aegypto." The "alien world" of the Christian romance of salvation is always *this* world, the Egypt through which the individual must pass in exile on a journey that begins and ends in heaven. Throughout his poem, Tasso makes Egypt synonymous with *errore,* in the double sense of the wandering associated with romance and the sinfulness of straying.[71] As intimated by the scene with Arsete in the whirlpool, Clorinda's reception of the *character* of baptism frees her definitively from the grasp of Egypt. It assimilates her to the Christian males of the poem, those "erring companions" of Goffredo whom providence "brought back beneath the sacred *signs.*"[72]

Figura is a theory of providence, because "foreshadowing" is always read as the expression of a divine intentionality behind individual and collective salvation. Tasso extrapolates the dynamics of *figura* to provide a preexisting "script" for Clorinda to enact. He not only reads Moses' life as an unwitting prefiguration of Christ's, but also depicts Clorinda's life as an unwitting repetition or *imitatio* of both. Thus for Clorinda baptism becomes analogous to the multiplex reunions of Chariclea at the end of her "odyssey." Closing the circle of an existence lived between the crossing of two thresholds—two rivers and two births—baptism ends her wandering through an Egypt that, as always with *figura,* was both literal and figurative. Even more so than Chariclea, Clorinda lives life as a zero sum: once she has been baptized, the sign that the sacrament leaves on her soul effectively erases the rest of her existence, all those moments between the time her mother prayed for her baptism and the moment that prayer was answered. This providential cancellation of every moment between birth and death annuls her story: *sub specie aeternitatis,* it is as if she had died a baptized infant.

There is one further dimension to Tasso's adaptation of the Heliodoran world of romance, and that is its unavoidably polemical relation to Ariosto's *Orlando furioso.* This is not the place to rehearse Tasso's anguished relation to his illustrious predecessor, but the resentment he felt has left its traces in the adaptation of Heliodorus.[73] First, Tasso names Clorinda's father "Senapo." This name is so distinctive that it can only be a deliberate recall of Ariosto's portrayal of an Ethiopian king named Il Senapo. It is also undeniably provocative in itself. Since it suggests the Latin and Italian words for mustard, it seems undignified, if not comic; indeed, these are qualities of the Ariostan Senapo, and they clash with the tragic tonalities of Clorinda's story. There is a further point of contact, for in *Orlando furioso* the subplot of Astolfo in the land of Senapo is bisected by another subplot: the climactic adventures of the warrior Marfisa, a Camilla-figure and an obvious precursor of Clorinda. While Astolfo is in Ethiopia, Marfisa is reunited with her foster father, the magician Atlante, and with her twin brother, Ruggiero. The poem has led the twins into the fratricidal situation Atlante had always feared, after having entertained the possibility of their incest, which Ruggiero's jealous betrothed Bradamante—herself a virgin warrior with a male twin—has feared. As brother and sister duel, unaware (like Tancredi and Clorinda) of each other's identity, Atlante's voice issues from within the tomb where he is buried, revealing their history and foreclosing the two dangers.[74] Later, the narrator describes Astolfo's return to Senapo's Ethiopia (*OF,* 38.26), just after recounting how Marfisa was baptized by Turpino, with Carlomagno as her godfather (*OF,* 38.23).

The similarities of Marfisa's story to the "romance" of Clorinda, which are reinforced by interweaving Astolfo's adventures in Ethiopia, are further magnified by the omnipresent figure of Perseus. Atlante reveals that the Ariostan twins' biography resembles that of Perseus: like Danae, the twins' pregnant mother was abandoned in a tiny boat on the high seas, and died giving birth. Atlante rescued them and raised them as his own until Marfisa was stolen by Arab bandits. Not only does Perseus appear as the "exemplar" of Ruggiero and Marfisa's infancy, but his rescue of Andromeda is the archetype of adventure in *Orlando furioso,* especially when both Orlando and Ruggiero mimic it in their ironically juxtaposed rescues of Olimpia and Angelica (10.92–11.60). As *Orlando furioso* shows, the Perseus and Andromeda plot determines the deeper structure of repetition and return that underlies not only providential romance plots but also the praxis of writing romance, as surely as it determined the fate of Chariclea.

The Marfisa subplot, like the biographies of Chariclea and Clorinda, is overtly governed by the theme of providence. Atlante had his tomb built on the site where he had foreseen that Ruggiero and Marfisa were destined to duel (*OF,* 36.58–67). Clearly, the "undead" Atlante is proposed as an agent of providence not only through his actions and vocabulary (*Fortuna, caso, destino, predire, prevedere*), but also in his act of speaking from the grave, which bears a remarkable similarity to the earlier incident where the "undead" sorcerer Merlino had predicted Bradamante's providential marriage to Ruggiero and foundation of the Estense genealogy (*OF,* 3.9–64). Furthermore, the adventures of Astolfo and Marfisa are saturated with the question of *fede.* Aside from the dynamics of jealousy and personal faith among Bradamante, Marfisa, and Ruggiero, Ariosto's Senapo is a Prester John figure whose name alludes to the mustard seed of Christ's parable about religious faith, and his literal blindness symbolizes his lack of faith.[75] More importantly, the Astolfo and Marfisa subplots are the junction point of a thematic exploration of divine providence: Astolfo delivers Senapo while on his way to repossess the wits of Orlando from the cosmic lost-and-found office on the moon. Supposedly, both Orlando's insanity and his cure at the hands of Astolfo are ordained by providence, and this assertion is made through a "figural" comparison with the punishment of Nebuchadnezzar (*OF,* 34.61–67), which was responsible for the release of Israel from the Babylonian captivity (itself a repetition of the captivity in Egypt).

By Christianizing Heliodorus's Perseus, Tasso is not merely Christianizing the Greek text's version of providence. He is also answering what he undoubtedly chose to read as the desacralization of providence in *Orlando furioso.*[76] In that work, the concept of providence often seems to be reduced to the status of a well-crafted exercise in plotting: ironic, self-reflexive, often facetious, always dizzyingly complex. In Clorinda's birth story, Tasso allusively condenses and reduces the vast intertwined Marfisa- and Astolfo-plots of *Orlando furioso* by means of an extremely limited *imitatio* of Heliodorus. Just as importantly, Tasso finds in Heliodorus a compact "original" or "exemplar" of the diffuse and multiplex Ariostan plot configuration. Thereby he makes his claim to outdo Ariosto, for on his Ferrarese predecessor's text he performs in miniature that reduction of romance wandering to the "sacred signs" of epic that underlies both his story of Clorinda's redemption and his aspirations for the literary form and religious ideology of the heroic poem.

NOTES

1. S. Gentili, *Annotationi di Scipio Gentili sopra la "Gerusalemme liberata" di Torquato Tasso* (Leiden, 1586); G. Guastavini, *Discorsi e annotationi sopra la "Gerusalemme" del Tasso* (Pavia, 1592). For these commentators, I have cited the somewhat reduced versions appended to the edition of the poem published by B. Castello at Genoa in 1617, *La "Gerusalemme" di Torquato Tasso, figurata da Bernardo Castello* (Genoa, 1617), 44–45 bis, 19 ter. The poem was completed in 1576, but was not published until 1581. Quotations from *Gerusalemme liberata* (hereafter cited as *GL*) are from the edition of L. Caretti (1957; reprint, Milan, 1979).

2. Tasso is also known to have used the Crusade chronicle of William of Tyre, his principal historical source, in the Italian translation by G. Orologi (William of Tyre, *Historia della guerra sacra di Gierusalemme, della terra di promissione, e quasi tutta la Soria ricuperata da' Christiani: Raccolta in XXIII. libri* [Venice, 1562]).

3. On Luca Ghini (ca. 1490–4 May 1556), see G. Gentile, ed., *Enciclopedia italiana di scienze, lettere, ed arti,* 36 vols. (Rome, 1929–39), 16:916–17.

4. A. K. Forcione, *Cervantes, Aristotle, and the "Persiles"* (Princeton, 1970), 11–87, esp. 66–68, and Forcione, *Cervantes' Christian Romance: A Study of "Persiles y Sigismunda"* (Princeton, 1972).

5. Forcione, *Cervantes, Aristotle, and the "Persiles,"* 67.

6. T. Tasso, *Le lettere di Torquato Tasso disposte per ordine di tempo,* ed. C. Guasti, 5 vols. (Florence, 1852–55), 1:160–61, 180.

7. Ibid. 1:78.

8. Forcione, *Cervantes, Aristotle, and the "Persiles,"* 68.

9. Gentili, *Annotationi,* 44–45 bis.

10. Forcione, *Cervantes, Aristotle, and the "Persiles,"* 64–68.

11. Ibid., 66; Forcione's translation.

12. Tasso, *Lettere* 1:78.

13. See Tasso's *Discorsi dell' arte poetica* and *Discorsi del poema eroico,* in *Scritti sull' arte poetica,* ed. E. Mazzali (1959; reprint, Turin, 1977), esp. 22ff., 231ff.

14. Aside from Guastavini, *Discorsi,* and Gentili, *Annotationi,* see M. Oeftering, *Heliodor und seine Bedeutung für die Litteratur* (Berlin, 1901), 114–15; the parallel is obligatory in editions and criticism of *GL*. The main exception is D. Della Terza, whose two studies have little to do with my analysis: *Forma e memoria: Saggi e ricerche sulla tradizione letteraria da Dante a Vico* (Rome, 1979), 4–9, and "History and the Epic Discourse: Remarks on the Narrative Structure of Tasso's *Gerusalemme liberata,*" *Quaderni d' Italianistica* 1 (1980): 30–45.

15. Heliodorus, *An Ethiopian Story,* trans. J. R. Morgan, in *Collected Ancient Greek Novels,* ed. B. P. Reardon (Berkeley and Los Angeles, 1989), 349–588 (hereafter cited as Morgan, *Ethiopian Story*). See 526–30, 563ff.

16. Tasso's couple goes *dal rogo a le nozze* (from the pyre to the wedding) (*GL,* 2.53.5).

17. M. Bakhtin, *The Dialogic Imagination: Four Essays,* ed. M. Holquist, trans. C. Emerson and M. Holquist (Austin, Tex., 1981), 86–110.

18. Ibid., 89–90, 110.

19. Ibid., 115.

20. Ibid., 116.

21. Colossians 2:12; Romans 6:1–11; *Catechismo, cioè istruttione, secondo il decreto del Concilio di Trento, a' parochi, publicato per comandamento del Santiss. S. N. Papa Pio V,* trans. A. Figliucci (Venice, 1568), 168–70.

22. G. N. Sandy, *Heliodorus* (Boston, 1982), 41; see also the excerpt from E. Rohde, *Der griechische Roman und seine Vorläufer,* in *Il romanzo greco: Guida storica e critica,* ed. P. Janni (Bari, 1987), 5–26.

23. Sandy, *Heliodorus,* 3–4.

24. Bakhtin, *Dialogic Imagination,* 95.

25. Ibid.

26. Ibid., 116.

27. Morgan, *Ethiopian Story,* 432–34.

28. Ibid., 434.

29. L. Ghini, trans., *Historia di Heliodoro delle cose etiopiche: Nella quale fra diversi, compassionevoli avenimenti di due Amanti, si contengono abbattimenti, discrittioni di paesi, e molte altre cose utili, e dilettevoli a leggere* (1556; reprint, Venice, 1560), 141: *l'anello con cui tuo padre mi sposò.* (Note recurrences of *segno, disegnare,* etc.) J. R. Morgan translates, "it was a gift that your father gave me during our courtship," in Morgan, *Ethiopian Story,* 433.

30. Ghini, *Historia,* 370–71: "Come un cerchietto di ebeno posto intorno ad avorio, che le tingeva il braccio"; Morgan, *Ethiopian Story,* 569: "a mark, like a ring of ebony staining the ivory of her arm!"

31. Morgan, *Ethiopian Story,* 433, 526, 529.

32. Ibid., 567–68, 404.

33. *GL,* 12.23; on Saint George and Perseus, see F. Caraffa et al., *Bibliotheca sanctorum,* 13 vols. (Vatican City, 1961–70), 6:515–16.

34. Jacobus a Voragine [Giacomo da Varazze], *Legenda aurea vulgo historia longobardica dicta,* 3d ed., ed. T. Graesse (1890; reprint, Osnabrück, Germany, 1965), 260–62. But note that the story of Saint George and the maiden is, like that of Heliodorus, a celebration of the end of human sacrifice.

35. *GL,* 12.28.5; cf. 12.65.7–8, 11.9.3, and 20.136.7. In *GL,* the term *ancella (ancilla)* always carries resonances of "feminine" submission, corresponding to Saint Paul's use of the term *subdita* to describe perfect wives in Ephesians 5:22, Colossians 3:18, and Titus 2:3–5. See W. Stephens, "Saint Paul among the Amazons: Gender and Authority in *Gerusalemme liberata,*" in *Discourses of Authority in Medieval and Renaissance Literature,* ed. K. Brownlee and W. Stephens (Hanover, N.H., 1989), 169–200, esp. 174–75, 193–99.

36. "Apte in martyrem Georgium cadunt, ut cum Christo sponso coniunctum, ea quae in cantico de Christi sponsa Ecclesia scripta sunt, cuius formosi corporis membrum quoddam preciosissimum martyr ipse est: 'Veni a Libano, sponsa,' quoniam non per gratiam tantum, sed & propriorum operum suavi odore, sui amatorem ac sponsum Deum effecit, morte ipsa eundem oblectans, factus perfecta victima, eique in odorem suavitatis accepta . . . digna quoque est martyris anima, quae ab eodem Domino & hoc audiat, 'En ut pulchra, propinqua mea, es, tota pulchra, & macula non est in te'" (L. Lippomano, *De vitis sanctorum ab Aloysio Lipomano, episcopo Veronae, viro doctissimo, olim conscriptis: Nunc primum a F. Laurentio Surio Carthusiano emendatis, & Auctis,* 6 vols. [Venice, 1581], 2:255ᵛ).

37. Baptism, confirmation, and ordination share "il carattere, il quale a l'anima imprimono." According to the Tridentine catechism, Paul's phrase "signavit nos" in 2 Corinthians 1:22, "Chiaramente descrisse il carattere, di cui è proprio segnare, & notare

qualche cosa. Perilché il carattere non è altro che un certo segno impresso a l'anima & a quella in perpetuo unito, il quale non si può per tempo alcuno scancellare" (*Catechismo,* 166).

38. Quint's analysis will appear in a book on epic and empire. He demonstrates that Tasso was indeed aware of Ethiopian practices as related by European explorers.

39. "Si baptizatus es, te iterum non baptizo; si vero nondum baptizatus es, ego te baptizo in nomine Patris & Filij, & Spiritus Sancti" (*Catechismo,* 198). On 197–98 it is stated that the Church baptizes only once because of the *character,* because Christ died only once (repeating the theme of baptism as death).

40. *Catechismo,* 168–204, esp. 171–72, 177; J. Freccero, "The River of Death: Inferno II, 108," in *Dante: The Poetics of Conversion,* ed. R. Jacoff (Cambridge, Mass., 1986), 61–62; D. Quint, *Origin and Originality in Renaissance Literature: Versions of the Source* (New Haven, 1983), 119–30.

41. E.g., "Fede, cioè quella fideltà ch'è tra il marito e la moglie, i quali havendo dato scambievolmente l'uno a l'altro la potestà del proprio corpo, conservano inviolabilmente la fede maritale" (S. Antoniano, *Tre libri dell' educatione christiana de i figliuoli* [Verona, 1584], fol. 9ᵛ; Silvio Antoniano was one of Tasso's chosen censors of the GL). The modern (nineteenth-century) Italian word for wedding ring, *fede,* preserves the resonances of both religious faith and sexual fidelity.

42. T. Tasso, *Jerusalem Delivered,* trans. R. Nash (Detroit, 1987), 259 (hereafter cited as Nash, *Jerusalem*).

43. According to Augustine, baptism is also called "sacramento di fede, perché quelli che lo ricevono fanno professione di tutta la fede de la Christiana religione" (*Catechismo,* 169; cf. G. Alberigo, ed., *Conciliorum oecumenorum decreta* [Bologna, 1972], 673). On *padrini* or *sponsores,* see *Catechismo,* 181–83. The "spiritual kinship" incurred by godparents was real enough to occasion marriage taboos, which the Council of Trent carefully redefined (*Catechismo,* 181–83; Alberigo, *Conciliorum oecumenorum decreta,* 757).

44. Ghini, *Historia,* 140.

45. "Avria dal candor che in te si vede, / argomentato in lei non bianca *fede*" (*GL,* 12.24.7–8).

46. *GL,* 12.41; Nash, *Jerusalem,* 263.

47. *GL,* 12.64–65, esp. 65.4–7: "Disse le parole estreme; / parole ch'a lei novo un spirto ditta, / spirto di fé, di carità, di speme: / virtù ch'or Dio le infonde" (Her last words: words that a new spirit is teaching her, a spirit of faith, of charity, of hope: [virtues] that God now [infuses in] her). This is a slight modification of Nash's translation; cf. Nash *Jerusalem,* 268.

48. Tasso describes the jealousy (*gelosia*) of Clorinda's father as *folle zelo GL,* 12.22), recognizing the semantic and etymological affinities of jealousy and religious zeal. Likewise, the *Catechismo* (383) describes God as a jealous (*zeloso*) lover of the souls wed to him, while stipulating that God's *zelo,* unlike the human kind, has no passion or perturbation.

49. Morgan, *Ethiopian Story,* 433, 564.

50. *GL,* 12.26.7–27.2; 21.8. Clorinda's mother is herself a symbol of the Church as spouse of Christ, the "black but beautiful" spouse of Lebanon of the Song of Songs, according to traditional exegesis (see the quotation from Lippomano, above, n. 36).

51. Morgan, *Ethiopian Story,* 432, 561.

52. Gentili, *Annotationi,* 44–45 bis.

53. Morgan, *Ethiopian Story,* 569.

54. "D'un bel pallore ha il bianco volto asperso, / come a' gigli sarian miste viole" (*GL,* 12.69.1–2).

55. "Vergine, bianca il bel volto e le gote / vermiglia" (*GL,* 12.23.3–4).

56. *E di pallida morte si dipinse* (*GL*, 12.28.8).

57. *GL*, 12.18.4, *ruginose e nere*; cf. *GL*, 6.108.3, *spoglie candide e leggiadre*.

58. *GL*, 2.5–8, 14–26, 47. Ironically, as David Quint reminds me, Clorinda uses the occasion to accuse her Islamic coreligionists of having been corrupted by the "Christian—that is, Catholic—vice of idolatry" (*GL*, 2.50). There is a complex allusiveness between religious strife in the poem (Catholic, Coptic, Muslim) and in Tasso's milieu (Catholic, Anabaptist, Protestant "iconoclast").

59. The correspondences are extremely precise: King Aladino, who wishes to put Sofronia to death, has previously been described as a serpent (*angue*) when he begins the persecutions of Christians that Sofronia opposes (*GL*, 1.85.5–8).

60. Sandy, *Heliodorus*, 47–48, 64. See also 83–89 on quotations from Homer.

61. Morgan, *Ethiopian Story*, 462.

62. Sandy, *Heliodorus*, 85. Morgan, *Ethiopian Story*, 569n, traces the "simile of colored ivory" to *Iliad* 4.141 (Menelaus's bleeding leg). I hardly need mention E. Auerbach's classic chapter "Odysseus' Scar," in *Mimesis: The Representation of Reality in Western Literature* (Princeton, 1968), 3–23. Morgan points out (449n) that Theagenes' showing Chariclea "a scar on his knee that he had got hunting boar" as an identifying countersign recalls this passage (*Odyssey* 19.392–475); Chariclea's reciprocation by showing her father's ring enriches the network of associations around Odysseus.

63. Morgan, *Ethiopian Story*, 420.

64. Ghini, *Historia*, 118.

65. Morgan, *Ethiopian Story*, 421.

66. For the Perseus story, see R. Graves, *The Greek Myths*, 2 vols. (1955; reprint, Harmondsworth, 1977), 1:237–45, esp. 238 and 242. Both Chariclea's and Clorinda's biographies extensively reenact the plot of Perseus's infancy.

67. "Fortune's uncertain mercies"; "The secrets of fortune cannot be read by men" (Morgan, *Ethiopian Story*, 433, 434).

68. "Now the birth of Christ was thus: When Mary, his mother, was espoused to Joseph, before they came together, she was found with child of the Holy Ghost. Whereupon Joseph, her husband, being a just man, and not willing publicly to expose her, was minded to put her away privately. But while he thought on these things, behold the angel of the Lord appeared to him in his sleep, saying: Joseph, son of David, fear not to take unto thee Mary thy wife: for that which is conceived in her, is of the Holy Ghost" (Matthew 1:18–20, Douai version).

69. *GL*, 12.29–35; Matthew 2, esp. 1–16; Exodus 1:7–2:10. The most telling reference is made through an echo of Petrarch. Arsete's declaration that he took Clorinda into Egypt from a "little village" (*picciol borgo, GL*, 12.32.3) recalls a sonnet of Petrarch's (4.12), where the phrase anchors a comparison between Laura and Christ.

70. See Freccero, "River of Death," 55–69, and Quint, *Origin and Originality*, 69–75, 92–132.

71. Cantos 3, 13, 16, 17, and 20 contrast Jerusalem as a figure of heaven with Egypt as a figure of hell.

72. "Sotto a i santi / segni ridusse i suoi compagni erranti" (*GL*, 1.1.7–8).

73. Tasso's attitude to Ariosto was explored by S. Zatti in "Exorcising Romance: Tasso versus Ariosto," in *The Ancient Novel: Classical Paradigms and Modern Perspectives*, ed. J. Tatum and G. M. Vernazza (Hanover, N.H., 1990), 46–47. Zatti convincingly reads Tasso's correspondence with Orazio Ariosto, grandnephew of the *Furioso* poet, as a classic text of Bloomian anxiety of influence. The paper would serve as an ideal preface to his earlier *L'uniforme cristiano e il multiforme pagano: Saggio sulla "Gerusalemme liberata"* (Milan, 1983), wherein he explores "pagan" romance multiformity as the repressed desire that continually returns to subvert Tasso's ideal of Christian and epic uniformity.

(See also M. W. Ferguson, *Trials of Desire: Renaissance Defenses of Poetry* [New Haven, 1983], 54–136.) However, by excluding any interpenetration between the terms *Christianity* and *romance,* and by making the latter term practically synonymous with Ariosto's poetics, Zatti excludes or minimizes the textual relationships I examine here.

74. For what follows, see L. Ariosto, *Orlando furioso,* ed. L. Caretti (1966; reprint, Turin, 1971), cantos 36–39 (hereafter cited as *OF*), and A. R. Ascoli, *Ariosto's Bitter Harmony: Crisis and Evasion in the Italian Renaissance* (Princeton, 1987), 369–76.

75. On Senapo and the question of faith, see Ascoli, *Ariosto's Bitter Harmony,* 264ff., esp. 268n.

76. This "answer" is sometimes point for point: while Ariosto's twins were suckled by a lion whom Atlante had charmed with magic (*OF,* 36.62). Clorinda was suckled by a tiger mysteriously moved by Saint George (*GL,* 12.29–32).

CHAPTER FOUR

Homage to Apuleius:
Cervantes' Avenging Psyche

Diana de Armas Wilson

Mira . . . que no mires a ese hermoso Cupido.
—*Persiles* 3.17

The monitory line "Remember . . . not to look at that handsome Cupid" is spoken by the primary narrator of Cervantes' last romance, *Persiles and Sigismunda,* a book whose avowed intention is to compete not with Apuleius but with Heliodorus.[1] In one of the dozen interpolated tales of the *Persiles* (3.16–17), Cervantes' nameless narrator frenetically warns a Scottish countess not to look at the sleeping "Cupid" she is about to kill. The warning recalls the similar prohibition for Psyche in the Castilian version of *The Golden Ass* available to Cervantes, Diego López de Cortegana's translation of *El asno de oro* (ca. 1513). Cortegana's Castilian Cupid warns his Psyche not to try to discover *el gesto y figura de su marido* (the face or figure of her husband), lest such a "sacrilegious curiosity" (*sacrílega curiosidad*) cause her to lose him.[2] Later in the text, Cupid will repeat the admonition during his tirade against Psyche's sisters: "Ellas te quieren persuadir que tu veas mi cara, la cual, como muchas veces te he dicho, tú no la verás más, si la ves" (They want to persuade you to look at my face, which, as I've often told you, having seen it once, you'll not see it again) (157). But the parallel warning of Cervantes' narrator, as it turns out, is put forward in such a way as to make it unreceivable. It is entirely in the ironic mode: if the heroine looks at Cupid, "the whole machinery" (*toda la máquina*) of her thoughts will be instantly dismantled (389). Since the machinery of her thoughts is fueled by a morbid, quirky, and bloodthirsty desire for revenge, looking at Cupid turns out to be a smart thing to do. In Cervantes, as we shall see, the wages of sight is not Cupid's flight but his capture.

My intention is to examine the presence of the "Cupid and Psyche" tale, as well as other textual formations from Apuleius, in Cervantes' story.[3] Although it may be an impossible task (at least without divine or magical aid) to unravel the tangle of subtexts under this Cervantine episode, I will attempt, without any definitive closing of the question, to account for the sophisticated allusiveness to Apuleius in the *Persiles*. What I see there is a dialectical imitation, a transformation of the model that, structurally and rhetorically, pays a more than oblique homage to Apuleius.[4]

Before the legendary look discussed above, Cervantes' Psyche figure is prepared to kill her "Cupid" with an instrument similar to the one in the *Metamorphoses:* Apuleius's *novacula(m) praeacuta(m)* becomes Cortegana's *navaja bien aguda* (162) and, in turn, Cervantes' *agudo cuchillo* (388).[5] In all three versions, the knife drops out of Psyche's hand: Apuleius's *ferrum timore tanti flagitii* (230) becomes Cortegana's *por el temor se le cayó la navaja de la mano* (164), which may have motivated Cervantes to *hacerle caer el cuchillo de la mano* (make the knife drop from her hand) (389). Between Apuleius and Cervantes, the Latin oil lamp (*stillam feruentis olei super umerum dei dextrum* [162]) is metamorphosed into a Spanish lantern with a wax candle. Like Psyche, Cervantes' heroine drops her source of light: "Se le cayó la lanterna [*sic*] de las manos sobre el pecho de Croriano, que despertó con el ardor de la vela" (The lantern fell from her hands onto Croriano's chest, who awoke with the burning of the candle) (390). Apart from virtually shouting out the name "Cupido," in short, this whole bedside routine loudly signals its debt to Apuleius. But what kind of debt?

The critical writing on the indebtedness of the *Persiles* to the *Asno* is scarce, lightly documented, and at variance.[6] Other writings of Cervantes that gesture to Apuleius have had more press. In *The Colloquy of the Dogs,* Cervantes represents a well-read witch, Cañizares, who knows her Apuleius. Her recipe for disenchanting the talking dogs, she laments, could not be "tan fácil como el que se dice de Apuleyo en *El asno de oro,* que consistía en sólo comer una rosa" (as easy as the one mentioned by Apuleius in *The Golden Ass,* which only consisted in eating a rose). The witch's allusion notwithstanding, critical responses to considering Apuleius a model for the *Coloquio* have been widely divergent.[7] More recently the focus has intriguingly shifted to the implausibility of Cervantes' witch— or, indeed, of any of the witches of his day—being learned enough to read, let alone to cite, Apuleius.[8] Menéndez y Pelayo claimed power, if not literacy, for Cervantes' witches, one of whom he compared favorably to *las antiguas hechiceras de Tesalia* (the ancient witches of Thessaly).[9]

Cervantes' links with Apuleius, however, are best known through the homicide of the walking wineskins (what Robert Graves calls the "wine-skinicidal mania") that both Lucius and Don Quixote commit in their respective novels.[10] What perhaps has not been remarked enough in the context of Don Quixote's wineskin episode concerns the rhetoric of double interpolation: the whole event of the hero's sleepwalking violence is interpolated into an interpolated tale (*The Curious Impertinent*) about a man (Anselmo) who, like both Psyche and Lucius, suffers from a "sacrilegious curiosity."[11] But comparisons between Apuleius and *Don Quixote* occasionally move beyond the wineskin episode: one critic, for instance, who sees *The Golden Ass* as "the bitterest of comedies" writes of "the masochistic enslavement of a hero who suffers more blows than Don Quixote and Sancho Panza together."[12]

Least well known of all the intertextualities in question, however, is the role of *The Golden Ass* in the *Persiles,* a work in which Cervantes strings together for us a dozen tales, "in the Milesian style" only insofar as they involve the marvelous—talking wolves, flying women, and oversexed witches—though not the obscene.[13] Renaissance Aristotelians regarded the Milesian tale, as Alban K. Forcione explains, as "the most decadent type of fiction in its lack of truth and its erotic subject matter." Apuleius's work, in particular, was judged not only as "a low order of fiction, one which fails to observe verisimilitude in its invented matter," but also as "totally reprehensible."[14] Cervantes' imitation of Apuleius, which abides by contemporary Aristotelian norms insofar as it avoids the salacious, is welded together by all that stuff of the marvelous that we find in Apuleius. One eighteenth-century Spanish critic even praised Cervantes for his *jocosidad milesia* (Milesian jocoseness).[15]

Setting aside Don Quixote's categorical (and self-deceiving) judgment that *toda comparación es odiosa* (all comparisons are odious) (2.23), let us now compare how each of these tales—Latin model and Spanish imitation—segments its world. Apuleius's tale of "Cupid and Psyche" has a nameless crone as a narrator: the drunken old lady who cooks for the bandits tells the tale in order to console the captive heroine Charite. The corresponding story in the *Persiles,* however, is the collective product of two men who spy on the heroine in various bedrooms. The narrative is introduced by her squire, a senile misogynist dressed in mourning; then taken up by the narrator of the *Persiles,* who intervenes vigorously in the story, addressing both the heroine and us in the second person; and, finally, closed by the indirect discourse of the same woman-hating squire. The story, in short, is "framed" by a misogynist, a detail that seems to me not fortuitous.

This is a tale of a triangle, although the heroine, a Scottish countess called Ruperta, is the only survivor when the story opens. She is obsessed with securing blood vengeance for the murder of her husband, treacherously slain by another Scottish nobleman who had once been a rival for her hand. En route to Rome to seek political aid for her plotted revenge, Ruperta finds that her enemy's son has checked into the same Italian inn where she is lodging. She gains access to his bedroom, lantern and knife in hand, in order to exact vengeance on him as a stand-in for his father, but his Cupid-like attractions cause her to drop the lantern on his chest. In the ensuing altercation, the heroine renounces all thoughts of vengeance, her intended victim reveals that his father is dead anyway, and the couple embrace. The next morning finds them still in each other's arms.

This banal abstract scarcely does justice to the charm of the story, which depends on its Cervantine ironies. The faintly ridiculous names of the characters—the Countess Ruperta, her defunct husband Lamberto de Escocia, and the killer and his son, Claudino and Croriano Rubicón[16]—all invoke heroic figures from the romances of chivalry, the "bestsellers" of sixteenth-century Spain. There are also various chivalric shards in the countess's response to her husband's death. Directly after his burial, the grieving widow orders his corpse to be decapitated and the head unfleshed by appropriate chemicals ("Se le cortó la cabeza, que en pocos días, con cosas que se le aplicaron, quedó descarnada y en solamente los huesos") (385). But Ruperta's project also has some unchivalric analogues: it has faint affinities, for example, with the enterprise of the "honorable gentlewoman" in John Skelton's poem, who sends the poet a dead man's skull (an "ugly token") to remind him of his mortality ("Upon a Dead Man's Head," ca. 1498). A closer and more bourgeois analogue occurs in Boccaccio's story of Isabetta (*Decameron,* 4.5), who pots the head of her lover, murdered by her three merchant brothers, and grows basil in it. Keats would imitate this narrative in "Isabella, or the Pot of Basil," and Cervantes may have pondered the Boccaccian theme of a too-much-loved head. In the *Persiles* tale, however, the clinical detail of the preservation of a spousal body-part for veneration by a widow invokes for us Cervantes' ultimate parody of a bankrupt chivalric order: the Cave of Montesinos episode in *Don Quixote* (2.23), where Montesinos carefully documents the salting and mummifying of Durandarte's heart (*un corazón de carnemomia*) as a token for his wife, Belerma. In the *Persiles* story, Ruperta carts the grisly relic of her husband's skull all around Europe in a silver chest (a kind of carry-on luggage), together with two bloodstained relics: the shirt he died in and the sword that killed him.[17] Cervantes' episode mordantly ridicules the literary codes of chivalry—the codes inscribed in the books it was his avowed intention to topple. The overarching structures of this episode, however, advertise its derivation from Apuleius.

Cervantes' heroine (a widow, not a maid) uses her husband's skull as a prop for her secret rites of blood vengeance, a tirade of vivid rhetorical threats. As a postscript to an erudite digression on the sources of anger, Cervantes' psychologically minded narrator shares with us the etiology of her compulsion: "Mientras se amenaza, descanza el amenazador" (While in the act of threatening, the threatener feels at rest) (387). Until Ruperta accomplishes what she admits is her *no cristiano deseo* (not very Christian desire), she swears to remain, Hamlet-style, in all "the trappings and the suits of woe" (1.2.86): "que mi vestido será negro, mis aposentos lóbregos, mis manteles tristes y mi compañía la misma soledad" (that my dress shall be black, my dwellings dark, my dinner table sad and my company, solitude itself) (386). This *juramento* or ritual swearing famously recalls the archaic formulas of the chivalric oaths of vengeance, such as the one Cervantes parodied in Don Quixote's comic identification with the Marqués de Mantua's oath "de no comer pan a manteles, ni con su mujer folgar" (not to eat bread at table, nor to sleep with his wife) (1.10).[18]

Ruperta's dark and secret rites have so excited the sympathy of her servant that he invites lodgers at the inn to her room as voyeurs, tapping, perhaps, into what Heiserman calls "our aroused desire to spy on shameful witches."[19] These spectators (and we) are allowed to overhear one of Ruperta's soliloquies, in which she commands herself to forget that she is the weaker sex in preparation for the task of blood vengeance: "Olvídate de que eres mujer" (Forget that you are a woman) (388), she tells herself, in a mandate that recalls Lady Macbeth's gender-coded invocation to the infernal powers, her request that they "unsex" her for the work of murder (Macbeth, 1.5.42). More to our point, however, Ruperta's situation seems dimly similar to that of Apuleius's Psyche when, on the verge of killing Cupid, she undergoes a sex change: sexum audacia mutatur (2.30).[20]

But in Cervantes' text, so does Cupid, since he is described as having the properties of Medusa, a glimpse of whose face would turn men to stone.[21] Ruperta's specular discovery petrifies her: "Halló en él la propiedad del escudo de Medusa, que la convirtió en mármol" (She found in him the property of Medusa's shield, which converted her into marble) (389). Some remarkable gender confusion arises here: Cupid in the role of a petrifying Medusa with Psyche as his marbleized victim would seem to be a sly deviation from their presumed sexes. Medusa is a woman, whether in Hesiod or in Freud (who famously equated Medusa's severed head with castration).[22] She is even a woman earlier in Cervantes—or at least an extremely feminine personification called "Sensuality"—whose glance turns the hero of the Persiles and all his male companions to stone: they are pictured como si . . . de dura piedra formados (as if . . . formed of hard rock) (243). Cervantes' Cupid figure, then, invested with the properties of the Medusa, is here feminized. By the same token, Cervantes gives us a hyper-masculinized heroine, one who compares herself to Judith ("Judic") taking vengeance on Holofernes (388). Such a Golden Age Judith may even invite the Freudian label of castrating woman—a kind of phallic Psyche. Freud, we may recall, saw the biblical Judith as "the woman who castrates the man who has deflowered her."[23] Readers who resist that kind of psycho-analytic labeling, however, may still wonder at the aggressiveness of Ruperta's access to her new lover: "¡ . . . cuán mejor eres tú para ser mi esposo que para ser objeto de mi venganza!" (. . . how much better might you be for my husband than for the object of my vengeance!) (389). This woman's access to her man, as the narrator later explains, serves the "holy holocaust" of her pleasure: "No le escogió para víctima del cruel sacrificio, sino para holocausto santo de su gusto" (She did not choose him as the victim of a cruel sacrifice, but rather for the holy holocaust of her pleasure) (389).

After Ruperta drops her lantern on his chest, Croriano awakens and runs about the dark bedroom until he bumps into her, instantly recognizing her as the woman his father made into a widow. Just as quickly, he offers her restitution for the offense (la ofensa) his father committed in killing her husband (390). But first he wants to touch her honestamente (chastely), to make sure she is not any kind of fantasma come to harm him. Ruperta launches into a long defense of her position, at the close of which speech she resolutely gives up her mania for vengeance: "Yo no quiero más venganzas ni más memorias de agravios" (I wish for no more vengeances nor memories of affronts) (391). In return, her intended victim gives up his single status and begs to become her husband: "Recíbeme por tu esposo, si ya, como he dicho, no eres fantasma que me engañas" (Take me as your husband, if, as I have said, you are not a phantom deceiving me)" (391). The literary image of woman as a deceiving phantom seems distinctly Apuleian, given the many witches in Thessaly who operate in that mode. But the notion of any phantasmic nuptials is brought up only to be studiously rejected by Cervantes' heroine. In answer to her lover's worries about her being a phantom, she asks for an embrace that will document the materiality of her body: "Dame esos brazos . . . y verás, señor, cómo este mi cuerpo no es fantástico" (Take me in your arms, and you will see, sir, that there is nothing fantastic about my body) (391). The lovers then fall back into bed in yet another of those "canonically irregular" relationships so frequent in Cervantes (391n).

Eros has overcome anger (la ira) in this story, an anger specifically gendered by Cervantes' intrusive narrator: "Que la cólera de la mujer no tiene límite" (There is no limit to the anger of women), he confides to the reader (386). He follows this generalization, later in the text, with three rhetorical questions: "¿Qué no hace una mujer enojada? ¿Qué montes de dificultades no atropella en sus disignios [sic]? ¿Qué inormes [sic] crueldades no le parecen blandas y pacíficas?" (What won't an angry woman do? What jungle of difficulties won't she trample underfoot with her scheming? What enormous cruelties won't seem to her gentle and peaceful?) (389). It is no surprise, then, that this disenchanted narrator gives, via indirect discourse, the last word in the tale to Ruperta's squire, a kind of Golden Age stand-in for Juvenal.[24] This aged servant mutters all the old misogynist topoi as he removes the grisly relics—skull, sword, and shirt—from the inn and from Ruperta's life: "Murmuró de la facilidad de Ruperta, y en general, de todas las mujeres, y el menor vituperio que dellas dijo fue llamarlas antojadizas" (He carried on about the easy virtue of Ruperta and, in general, of all women, and the least vituperation he expressed was to call them all willful) (392). In The Golden Ass, Lucius has a similar moment of "vituperation" about the "easiness" of women. Upon seeing Charite perk up when she hears Haemus the Thracian Bandit (really her bridegroom Tlepolemus) mention, in Cortegana's translation, *el nombre del suzio y hediondo burdel* (the name of the filthy and stinking brothel), Lucius reflects that *todo el linaje de las mujeres merecía ser vituperado* (the whole lineage of women deserved to be vituperated). Misreading Charite's virtuous laughter, Lucius turns misogynist and puts the character of the whole female sex on trial, hanging upon what the narrator, distancing himself from Lucius, calls "the judgment of an ass"—the *juicio de un asno* in the Cortegana translation (203). The judgmental squire who frames Cervantes' tale is also an ass and a bad reader. He likes his mistress only when she is driven by her morbid vengeance, hooked into the exhausted norms of the chivalric code of honor.

Cervantes' interpolated tale, then, is a visible product of his reading into writing, a metamorphosis of the *Metamorphoses*. With its twenty-seven interpolated stories, Apuleius's text may have reoriented Cervantes' notions of interpolation. If, indeed, Cervantes had projected some of these notions onto Cide Hamete—who chose to eliminate, albeit grudgingly, any interpolated episodes from part 2 of *Don Quixote*—the *Persiles* offered Cervantes a fresh narrative field to rupture at will with multiple episodes. One of these, the Cupid and Psyche story, is structurally intriguing because Cervantes has transferred what was a frame in Apuleius into a center.

Taking our cue from Cervantes' Arab historian, who asks to be celebrated for *lo que ha dejado de escribir* (what he has not written) (*Don Quixote,* 2.44), consider what Cervantes chose *not* to write in his imitation of Apuleius—the discarded images. What are the elements that did not jump the cultural divide between the two writers? The most obvious difference, of course, is that in Cervantes all the gods are gone, including the shrewish Venus. Cervantes does not allow his "Cupido" to have Venus for a mother. The goddess is displaced by a ridiculous and grumbling squire, the only person who objects to Ruperta's falling in love. Cervantes, in other words, demythologizes and, in a way, disenchants Apuleius. Psyche's sisters are also missing, those treacherous bitch-wolves or *perfidae lupulae* (228) whom Cortegana had rendered as *aquellas lobas sin fe* (157). Psyche's "bridal tests," which would have been wasted on a tough Renaissance widow, have also been eliminated. Gone, too, is the invitation to allegory: Cervantes deallegorizes the Cupid and Psyche story and, in the process, gives Psyche (Soul) back the body that over a millennium of allegorical readings since Fulgentius—depicting the exalted progress of the soul toward love—had so relentlessly erased.[25]

What *did* Cervantes imitate, then, from *The Golden Ass?* An imitative work need not slavishly follow its model, of course, but the model, as

Thomas Greene puts it, "must count as a major presence if one is to speak of imitation in a valid sense." *The Golden Ass* is, to my mind, a major presence in Cervantes' story, a "*determinate* subtext" playing a constitutive part in it, well beyond the noisy allusion to Cupid.[26] I would argue that Cervantes borrowed the structures of his tale of the Countess Ruperta from *The Golden Ass,* not from the tale of Cupid and Psyche but from the tale that frames it (bks. 4–8): the story of Charite and Tlepolemus (Carites and Lepólemo in the Spanish translation). Charite, the beautiful and high-born maiden who has been kidnapped by bandits on the eve of her wedding, is the primary audience for the hag-cook's tale of Cupid and Psyche (not including Lucius the Ass and the reader, who overhear it). Directly after the hag's narrative, Charite is rescued from the bandits' cave by her husband and settles down to a short and happy married life. At the beginning of book 8 of *The Golden Ass,* however, we hear, by way of a servant, a dismaying postscript to the marriage of Charite and Tlepolemus—and this I believe to be the major subtext of Cervantes' tale. A servant tells the story of how Charite's husband Tlepolemus was treacherously murdered by Thrasyllus, a disappointed man who had been a rival suitor for her hand (bk. 8.2–14). The ghost of the murdered husband returns to tell all, much as the skull of Countess Ruperta's husband—*esa cabeza sin lengua* (that tongueless head), in Cervantes' phrase—seems to be saying to her: "¡Venganza, dulce esposa mía, que me mataron sin culpa!" (Vengeance, my sweet wife, since I have been killed blamelessly!) (388).

As a result of her husband's precipitous murder in *The Golden Ass,* Charite changes into a female revenger. She becomes a "fury," as James Tatum puts it, undergoing one of the "violent psychological transformations" in *The Golden Ass,* her long speech or "coloratura aria" (8.12) revealing a "taste for feverish rhetoric."[27] All the above strengthens her candidacy, I think, as the model for Cervantes' heroine. Unlike Ruperta, however, who undergoes a conversion from vengeance—the kind of subjective transformation we may call a metamorphosis—Charite remains an avenging fury to the end, gouging out her enemy's eyes with a hairpin before she kills herself at her husband's tomb. The basic structures of Charite's tale, however—a happy marriage destroyed by a disappointed and murderous suitor who turns the wife into an avenging widow—are all present in Cervantes, transformed into what we may call a Golden Age "revenger's comedy." Should Cervantes have needed more fuel for his revenge motif, he could always have turned to Apuleius's Venus, who, as she herself admits, is relentlessly associated throughout the Cupid and Psyche tale with *el placer de tanta venganza* (the pleasure of so much vengeance) (170). Both Venus and Charite are linked to Cervantes' Ruperta by a mania for vengeance that is stressed in Ruth El Saffar's cogent summary of Cervantes' tale: "Though heavily overlaid with literary associations, and presented so as to resemble a puppet show more than an actual event, the story carries the concept of vengeance to its extreme."[28]

Beyond the adoption of such eccentric themes and structures, however, Cervantes' fervid and extravagant writing in this particular episode has many of the stylistic mannerisms of Apuleius's work: florid, self-conscious, highly artificial prose, with balanced phrases and unexpected diction, including one or two rhetorical set pieces and an addiction to alliteration. Let me give a few examples from Cervantes' arsenal of rhetorical resources. In the middle of the scene in which some guests at the inn spy on Ruperta, swearing her oaths with her right hand *sobre la cabeza del marido* (over her husband's head), the narrator turns suddenly to address the reader in the second person in a passage that combines, minimally, the rhetorical figures of *aversio, anaphora, demonstratio, interpretatio, incrementum,* and, that favorite scheme of Apuleius, *isocolon:* "¿Veisla llorar, veisla suspirar, veisla no estar en sí, veisla blandir la espada matadora, veisla besar la camisa ensangrentada, y que rompe las palabras con sollozos?" (Do you see her weeping, do you see her sighing, do you see her in ecstasy, do you see her flashing that killer sword, do you see her kissing the bloody shirt, and disrupting her words with sobs?) Adding the figures of *promissio* and *hyperbole,* the narrator then assures us that if we wait to hear how the story ends the next morning, we shall have a topic of conversation for *mil siglos* (a thousand centuries) (387). Various passages in Cervantes' two-chapter episode, with their involved, lurid, and erudite language, buttonhole the reader in a similar way.

At another point, the narrator turns from the reader to address the heroine in an explosive speech that opens with three oxymora: "Bella matadora, dulce enojada, verdugo agradable: ejecuta tu ira, satisface tu enojo, borra y quita del mundo tu agravio" (Beautiful killer, sweet fury, pleasing executioner: act out your ire, satisfy your anger, erase and remove from the world your injury) (389). If Cortegana's Spanish translation of Apuleius had tempered, as Menéndez y Pelayo claimed, "the violent and tormented Latinity" of Apuleius, Cervantes' imitation would seem to have returned to it with a vengeance.[29]

One of the narrator's more piquant eruptions in the *Persiles* shows, I think, a close point of connection with Apuleius. When Ruperta is about to launch into her spellbinding soliloquy, the narrator explains that he cannot imagine how it came to be known that she had spoken *estas o [sic] otras semejantes razones* (these or other such words) to herself (388). A similar interrogation of omniscience occurs in the millhouse episode of *The Golden Ass,* when Lucius anticipates that some "scrupulous reader" (*lector escrupuloso*) might question his knowledge: "Tú, asno malicioso, ¿dónde pudiste saber lo que afirmas y cuentas que hablaban aquellas mujeres en secreto?" (You, wicked ass, how could you have known what you say those ladies spoke in secret?) (262).[30]

In sum, then, although the structures of Cervantes' imitation are borrowed from Apuleius's frame tale of Charite and Tlepolemus—a frame that would itself be transformed into a tale at the beginning of book 8 of the *Asno*—Cervantes alters his model. Apuleius's harrowing revenge narrative of Charite and Tlepolemus is hollowed out, transmuted into a comic romance, a tale of countesses and Cupids that closes with a merry, if hugger-mugger, pre-Tridentine wedding. But Apuleius's darker narrative of eye-gouging vengeance offered a cultural expression especially appealing to a writer who claimed to have been the first to represent *los pensamientos escondidos del alma* (the hidden thoughts of the soul).[31] Cervantes' imitation rewrites the convention, reproduced by both his narrator and his model, that woman's anger (*la cólera de la mujer*) has no limits (386). The representation of female revenge, in its most subjective manifestations, Cervantes saved for the *Persiles*, a text that has been called his "most studied work, the one for which he did most research."[32] Apuleius, we must conclude, was a pivotal figure in that research.

NOTES

1. M. de Cervantes, *Los trabajos de Persiles y Sigismunda,* ed. J. Bautista Avalle-Arce (Madrid, 1969), 389. Further references to this text will be cited parenthetically by page number. The English translation of the epigraph is from M. de Cervantes, *The Trials of Persiles and Sigismunda,* trans. C. R. Weller and C. A. Colahan (Berkeley and Los Angeles, 1989), 282. All further English translations are my own, unless otherwise noted.

In a prepublication advertisement in 1613, Cervantes announced that the forthcoming *Persiles* "dares to compete with Heliodorus" (*libro que se atreve a competir con Heliodoro*). See "Prólogo al lector," *Novelas ejemplares,* in *Obras completas, Cervantes,* 2 vols., ed. A. Valbuena Prat, 18th ed. (Madrid, 1986), 2:10. For more about this competition, see the opening chapter ("Kidnapping Romance") in D. de Armas Wilson, *Allegories of Love: Cervantes's "Persiles and Sigismunda"* (Princeton, 1991), 3–23.

2. Apuleyo, *El asno de oro,* ed. C. García Gual (Madrid, 1988), 153. See García Gual's splendid introduction—entitled "El libro de oro" (The book of gold)—to his recent edition of the 1513 Spanish translation of Apuleius by Diego López de Cortegana (1455–1524). All further references to the *Asno* will be to this edition and be parenthetically documented. I have also consulted the edition of Amberes, 1551, on microfilm at the Doe Library, University of California at Berkeley. Other Castilian editions of the *Asno* appeared in Zamora, 1536 and 1539; Medina del Campo, 1543; Antwerp, 1551; Alcalá de Henares, 1584; Madrid, 1601; and Valladolid, 1601.

3. In the non-narratological context of my essay, the title "Cupid and Psyche" is, I think, less "abusive" (pace John J. Winkler) than it is conventional and handy. See Winkler's stricture about this title in *Auctor and Actor: A Narratological Reading of Apuleius's "Golden Ass"* (Berkeley and Los Angeles, 1985), 89.

4. I am indebted here to T. M. Greene's remarks on "dialectical imitation," one

boundary of which he calls parody. See *The Light in Troy: Imitation and Discovery in Renaissance Poetry* (New Haven, 1982), 46.

5. Apuleius, *The Golden Ass: Being the Metamorphoses of Lucius Apuleius* [1566], trans. W. Adlington, Loeb Classical Library (London, 1965), 228. Further references to the Latin text will parenthetically cite this Loeb edition.

6. The 1914 editors of the *Persiles,* Rodolfo Schevill and Adolfo Bonilla, call Cervantes' scene a *reminiscencia* (reminiscence) of the Amor and Psyche episode (*Persiles y Sigismunda,* [Madrid, 1914], 2:167n); María Rosa Lida de Malkiel argues that Cervantes knew Apuleius *de oídas, que no de vista* (by hearsay, not firsthand) ("Dos huellas del *Esplandián* en el *Quijote* y el *Persiles,*" *Romance Philology* 9 [1955]: 160–62); and Juan Bautista Avalle-Arce finds in Cervantes' episode a cluster of chivalric readings, over which there floats (*sobrenada*) the Cupid and Psyche myth (*Persiles,* 384n).

7. See Pierre-Daniel Huet's 1670 claim that Apuleius or Lucian was the apparent model for the *Coloquio* (*Traité de l' origine des romans* [Paris, 1670]); Marcelino Menéndez y Pelayo's 1902 declaration that Apuleius did not "necessarily" serve as Cervantes' model (*Bibliografía hispano-latina clásica* [Madrid, 1902], 1:146–47); Agustín Amezúa y Mayo's 1912 discounting of the influence of Apuleius in favor of Lucian (*El casamiento engañoso y el colloquio de los perros* [Madrid, 1912], chap. 4); Francisco A. de Icaza's flat denial, in 1917, of any influence (*Supercherías y errores cervantinos puestos en claro* [Madrid, 1917]); and, coming full circle, Antonio Oliver's claim, in 1953, that Cervantes acquired the philosophy of the Cynics from Apuleius ("La filosofía cínica y el *Coloquio de los perros,*" *Anales Cervantinos* 3 [1953]: 291–307). All the above are cited in D. B. Drake's *Cervantes' "Novelas ejemplares": A Selective, Annotated Bibliography,* 2d ed. (New York, 1981).

8. Editor Francisco Rodríguez Marín finds it implausible and, it would seem, irritating, that the witch Cañizares would present herself as knowing Apuleius. The witches of Cervantes' day, he insists, were women who did not read or write, nor did they practice skills other than those learned from teachers as brutish (*maestras tan toscas*) as they were (*Cervantes: Novelas ejemplares,* 2 vol., [Madrid, 1975], 2:294n). Juan Bautista Avalle-Arce also appears concerned about the plausibility of a witty witch; *tantos conocimientos librescos* (so much literary knowledge) does not square with witchcraft (*Novelas ejemplares* [Madrid, 1982], 3:295n). The sanest focus on this witch is provided by Ruth El Saffar, for whom Cañizares "converts the story from an idle animal fable to one of deep moral dimensions" (*Cervantes: "El casamiento engañoso" and "El coloquio de los perros"* [London, 1976], 63).

9. M. Menéndez y Pelayo, *Historia de los heterodoxos españoles,* ed. Artigas, 5:371; cited by R. Porras Barrenechea, *El Inca Garcilaso en Montilla (1561–1614)* (Lima, 1955), 239.

10. In *The Golden Ass,* Lucius mistakes three inflated wineskins for burglars: "Nam cadavera illa iugulatorum hominum erant tres utres inflati variisque secti foraminibus" (3.9). In *Don Quixote,* the innkeeper tells Sancho the truth about the wineskins Don Quixote punctured in his sleepwalking dream (1.35). Mikhail Bakhtin sees (somewhat preposterously) the "transformation of blood into wine" in this episode as a theme "developed even more strikingly in the 'Golden Ass' of Apuleius" (*Rabelais and His World,* trans. H. Iswolsky [Cambridge, Mass., 1968], 209n). Graves's phrase is from his translation of *The Golden Ass* (Harmondsworth, 1950), 86.

11. If curiosity, as James Tatum puts it, "might even be said to be Lucius' tragic flaw" (*Apuleius and "The Golden Ass"* [Ithaca, N.Y., 1979], 34), it must certainly be that of Anselmo. Alexander Scobie is rare in looking to Apuleius for those "traces of a preoccupation with *curiositas*" occurring in Cervantes' *Curious Impertinent.* See Scobie's "*El curioso impertinente* and Apuleius," *Romanische Forschungen* 88 (1976): 75–76. F. A.

De Armas explores Apuleian curiosity in his essay "Interpolation and Invisibility: From Herodotus to *Don Quixote*," *Journal of the Fantastic in the Arts* 4 (1992): 8–28.

12. A. Heiserman, *The Novel before the Novel* (Chicago, 1977), 165.

13. "The exact character of the 'Milesian tales' is disputable, though they were certainly thought to be obscene," writes Heiserman. The tales were "short stories about conjugal betrayal, comic contretemps, and sardonic or cruel trickery resolved in surprising but not supernatural ways. The anthology of such stories compiled in the first century B.C. by Aristides of Miletus (from which the type gets its name) was infamous for its obscenity but has not survived" (ibid., 231n and 151).

Note the interesting parallels between Cervantes' "flying woman," the *mujer voladora* who is wafted on her skirts safely to the ground in the *Persiles*—two chapters earlier than the Cupid and Psyche imitation (3.14)—and the flights of Psyche and her sisters off what Heiserman calls "Execution Rock" (ibid., 158).

14. On this anti-Apuleius stance, see Tasso, *Del poema eroico*, 83–84; El Pinciano, *Philosophía antigua poética*, 2:8, 12–13; 3:153–54, 177; and Carvallo, *Cisne de Apolo*, 1:81–82 (cited by A. K. Forcione, *Cervantes, Aristotle, and the "Persiles"* [Princeton, 1970], 92n).

15. G. Mayáns y Siscar, *Oración en que se exhorta a seguir la verdadera idea de la elocuencia española*. In *Orígenes de la lengua española* [1737]; cited by E. Carilla, ed., in his introduction to *Los trabajos de Persiles y Sigismunda* (Salamanca, 1971), 13.

16. See another reference to *Rubicón* (from Latin *rubeo* = to be red) in *Don Quixote* (2.8). The Rubicon, which is a small river (the modern Pisatello?) on the east coast of Italy, formed the boundary between Italy and Cisalpine Gaul.

17. Lida de Malkiel locates this skull as "probably" in the Arthurian tradition and suggests, as analogues, the *Perlesvaus*, where a maid carts the head of a knight about in a rich ivory vessel (*una rica vasija de marfil*), and the *Mabinogion*, where two maids carry a man's head about on a large dish. Lida de Malkiel cites R. S. Loomis, *Arthurian Tradition and Chrétien de Troyes* (New York, 1949), 395, for data on the *Perlesvaus* (lines 8678–8710), and J. Loth's edition (Paris, 1913), 2:64 and 119, for the *Mabinogion*. See Lida de Malkiel, "Dos huellas," 161.

18. The Marqués de Mantua appears in *Don Quixote* (1.5) and twice again in part 2, where his ballad is praised by the Countess Trifaldi.

19. Heiserman, *Novel before the Novel*, 154.

20. In Adlington's 1566 translation, "by her audacity she changed herself to masculine kind" (231); in Graves's 1950 translation, "Psyche was neither very strong nor very brave but the cruel power of fate made a *virago* out of her" (133, emphasis added).

21. See Ovid, *Metamorphoses* 4.803, where Minerva wears the snake-haired head of Medusa, the Gorgon slain by Perseus, in the aegis of her armor. See also Hesiod, *Theogony* 270–83.

22. See the equation in "Medusa's Head" (1922) between "to decapitate" and "to castrate." Freud claims that "the terror of Medusa is . . . a terror of castration that is linked to the sight of something" (*The Standard Edition of the Complete Psychological Works of Sigmund Freud*, trans. J. Strachey, 24 vols. [London, 1953–74], 18:273). For an excellent psychoanalytic reading of Cervantes' uses of Medusa, see M. A. Garcés, "Zoraida's Veil: 'The Other Scene' of the *Captive's Tale*," *Revista de estudios hispánicos* 23, no. 1 (1989): 65–98.

23. Freud, *Complete Works* 11:207.

24. Writing of the tradition of cataloguing the vices of women, a convention that begins with Semonides in the mid-seventh century B.C., James Tatum cites Juvenal's *Satire* 6 (ca. A.D. 116) as the longest example of this kind of dispraise in Latin (*Apuleius*, 74).

25. Fulgentius's *Mythology* (sixth century) included a summary of the Cupid and Psyche tale together with a long allegorical reading. Not every reader sees the tale as an allegory: Heiserman, for instance, finds it "impossible to discover a cogent allegorical significance in this sardonic little romance" (*Novel before the Novel*, 159).

26. Greene, *Light in Troy*, 50.

27. Tatum, *Apuleius*, 72, 31, and 148.

28. R. El Saffar, *Beyond Fiction: The Recovery of the Feminine in the Novels of Cervantes* (Berkeley and Los Angeles, 1984), 156.

29. Menéndez y Pelayo's judgment of Cortegana's translation is cited by Adolfo Bonilla y San Martín in his "Advertencia" in Menéndez y Pelayo's *Orígenes de la novela* (Madrid, 1915), 4:149.

30. E. C. Riley calls attention to these passages in *Cervantes's Theory of the Novel* (Oxford, 1962), 207n.

31. Cervantes uses this phrase in the context of bringing moral figures to the stage. See his prologue to *Ocho comedias y ocho entremeses,* in Prat, *Obras completas* 1:210.

32. Riley, *Theory of the Novel,* 191.

CHAPTER FIVE

Novels beyond Thule: Antonius Diogenes, Rabelais, Cervantes

James Romm

At the conclusion of his earliest effort in narrative fiction, *Pantagruel,* Rabelais charts a course for his hero's coming adventures. In future books, he promises, the reader will learn "how Pantagruel found the Philosopher's Stone, together with the manner of his finding it and using it; also how he crossed the Caspian Mountains, how he sailed across the Atlantic Sea, how he defeated the Cannibals and conquered the Perlas Islands; . . . and how he visited the regions of the moon, to find out whether that orb would not be whole but for the fact that women have three-quarters of it in their heads; together with a thousand other little jests, all of them true."[1] Unfortunately, most of these promises go unfulfilled; Pantagruel never reaches the "Perlas Islands," that is, the Antilles, or the moon, much as one would have liked to see him explore those places. However, it is telling that Rabelais, at this early stage of his authorial career, envisioned his hero reaching these exotic locales, and later did in fact send him across the Atlantic on a route paralleling that of contemporary explorers. Once a fictional hero has been created and set loose, Rabelais suggests, the natural places for him to go are the New World and the moon. A similar, though reversed, travel impulse stands behind the novel that Cervantes meant to be his crowning achievement, *The Trials of Persiles and Sigismunda.* In this case Cervantes' heroes come *from* a remote Atlantic locale—the island of Thule, roughly equivalent to Iceland in the minds of his contemporaries—and spend about half the novel crisscrossing that northerly region, before voyaging overland to Rome on their quest for a Christian marriage.

The use of such *voyages imaginaires* in early prose fiction has traditionally been explained as a way of imparting credibility to otherwise outlandish inventions. Torquato Tasso, for example, in a passage of the *Discourses on the Epic Poem* that is often cited in discussions of Cervantes' *Persiles,* urges his contemporaries to "take matter . . . from Gothland, Norway, Sweden, Iceland, the East Indies, or countries recently discovered in the vast Ocean beyond the Pillars of Heracles" in order not to be exposed as out-and-out liars.[2] But this explanation seems only partly satisfactory, since it depicts the voyage only as a device designed to solve an author's practical dilemma rather than as a resource offering its own peculiar benefits and rewards. Nor does it account for cases like that envisaged by Rabelais, in which the plot's movement toward locales like the New World assumes a hyperbolic course and ends up on the moon. In such cases, the effect of geographical distance is not to instill belief, as Tasso assumes, but the precise opposite: to make belief impossible.

This tension between differing uses of *voyages imaginaires* in fiction, as a way of making inventions credible or of sacrificing credibility to invention, can be found in ancient literary theory as well, in particular in critical debates over the Phaeacian tales of the *Odyssey*. Eratosthenes of Cyrene, for example, anticipates Tasso in explaining the *Odyssey*'s use of distant locales as *dia to eukatapseuston,* on account of the ease with which lies can there be concealed.[3] On the other hand, Lucian of Samosate cites the same text as a model not of credible fictions but of obvious frauds. In the prologue to the *True Histories*—a work that explicitly abandons verisimilitude for the sake of imaginative freedom—Lucian traces his own authorial pedigree back through a series of literary voyagers: Ctesias, who recorded Indian wonders purely of his own invention; Iambulus, who wrote a fiction *gnôrimon hapasi,* "obvious to everyone"; and finally Homer's Odysseus, whose lies were only convincing enough to fool the simpleminded Phaeacians.[4] Thus when Lucian himself describes a journey that, like the one forecast above in *Pantagruel,* takes him across the Atlantic and then to the moon, he appropriates the *Odyssey* not as a species of *eukatapseuston* narration but as an example of extreme and unrestricted fictional license.

The tension between these two approaches to *voyages imaginaires* is worth exploring further, especially since this species of narrative has played a major role in the development of both the ancient and the Renaissance novel. Erwin Rohde, in *Der griechische Roman und seine Vorläufer,* posited *Reisefabulistik* as one of two literary traditions that had fused to give rise to the Greek novel (the second being stories of star-crossed love familiar from New Comedy); to illustrate this seminal role of the voyage narrative Rohde seized on an obscure, lost novel as a paradigm, the *Wonders beyond Thule* of Antonius Diogenes.[5] His claims for this work turned out hollow, since subsequent papyrus finds revealed a fully developed travel-romance tradition antedating it, and Diogenes' novel, stripped of temporal priority, faded back into the obscurity from which Rohde had briefly rescued it. However, I believe that the *Wonders beyond Thule* again deserves our attention, though for reasons different than those put forth by Rohde.

In its movement toward such places as Thule and the moon, this novel stands in the family line of Rabelais's *Quart Livre* and, *mutatis mutandis,* Cervantes' *Persiles,* and like these two later texts can be seen as a theoretical exercise designed to test the limits of the voyage narrative's credibility. By mediating between the two poles outlined above, at times inviting his audience to believe and at other times warning it not to, Diogenes demonstrates that neither is in and of itself an adequate approach to prose fiction.

The *Wonders beyond Thule,* a work tentatively assigned to the second century A.D., may seem an anomalous text from which to launch any far-ranging or theoretical discussion, since it is almost entirely lost and has become known to us only by way of the epitome of the Byzantine patriarch Photius.[6] Fortunately, however, Photius's notes on the novel are extensive enough to give us a good sense of the original and to reveal some of its prominent connections with the exploration literature of its day. However, we must make allowances where appropriate for the limitations of Photius's redaction and for the ways in which the epitomizer may have privileged certain elements of the novel over others.[7]

The first feature of the *Wonders beyond Thule* with which Photius presents us, and one of several for which we have independent confirmation,[8] is its title, *Apista huper Thoulên* in Greek. This title immediately foregrounds the novel's irreverent stance toward canonical standards of criticism, which found *apista*—literally, "unbelievable things"—artistically improper. The author of the treatise *On the Sublime,* for example, probably a near contemporary of Diogenes, censures the *Odyssey*'s Phaeacian tales as a "journey through fables and *apista*" (9.13). There was, however, one literary setting in which *apista* were not only acceptable but desirable: in collections of natural wonders or *paradoxa;* one such paradoxographical work actually carried the word *apista* as its title,[9] implying a meaning closer to "strange but true" than to "obviously false."[10] Thus Diogenes, by using the same word in his title, seems to be applying to narrative fiction the credibility standards appropriate to descriptive or pseudoscientific literature, in which it is taken for granted that *paradoxa,* things contrary to expectation, will turn out to be true. In so doing he distances himself not only from the author of *On the Sublime* but also from Aristotle, who in the *Poetics* had deemed implausibilities (*apithana*) in fiction a serious flaw (24.19–22, 25.27–28).[11]

The second element of Diogenes' title, "beyond Thule," helps clarify and confirm the implications of the first; Thule was a place that stood poised between truth and fiction in the ancient scientific record. The island had first been reported around 300 B.C. by the Greek explorer Pytheas of Massilia, who approached it (but did not land) in the course of a voyage along Europe's western coast. But Pytheas's account of Thule, and indeed his entire voyage, had subsequently become a topic of heated debate among geographers. Some accepted it but others, arguing that it placed an inhabited land beyond the northernmost limit of the habitable world, disbelieved.[12] By evoking this elusive and unverifiable island in his title, therefore, Diogenes seems to situate his entire narrative in an intermediate zone between truth and invention, leaving us unsure as to where, or whether, he has crossed the boundary between the two. In this he can be distinguished from Lucian, who had likewise used famous tales of exploration as models for the *True Histories,* but had assured his readers that those antecedents could not be believed.[13]

As a final gloss on the programmatic title *Wonders beyond Thule* we should note that Diogenes, in aiming his narrative beyond the known world, steers away from the historiographical concerns of the traditional romance and toward an undefined future era. Unlike the locative names of other Greek novels—*Aethiopica, Ephesiaca, Babyloniaca*—Diogenes avoids the tradition-steeped vistas of Egypt, Asia Minor, and the Levant, and instead evokes the raw and unexplored realm of Thule in the farthest Northwest.[14] This mysterious outpost, as its Latin epithet *ultima* implies, represented a last frontier of Mediterranean culture; to go beyond this frontier, as Vergil and Seneca make clear in their poetry, would be to escape history altogether and usher in a new age of civilization.[15] It is this sort of escape that Diogenes seems to have attempted. This is not to deny that the *Wonders beyond Thule* was actually set in the distant past (around 500 B.C.) or that the novel's external frame—recounting how the story had thereafter been found by Alexander the Great on a set of inscribed wooden tablets—served to anchor it in historical time. However, these devices seem to have been handled with a light, perhaps even parodic, touch. Outside the Alexander frame stood another in which Diogenes acknowledged himself to be the *real* author of the story, perhaps as a way of mocking the conceit by which fictional narratives were tied to famous personages. In general the impression conveyed by Photius's summary is that of a timeless world that only rarely coincides with a recognizable historical landscape.[16]

All that has been deduced above from the title *Wonders beyond Thule* concerning Diogenes' interest in discovery, novelty, and the problem of belief finds expression in his use of a voyage of exploration to structure his plot. The first phrase of Photius's summary (109a13f.) has the novel's hero, one Deinias of Arcadia, sailing away in pursuit of scientific knowledge, *kata zêtêsin historias*—a phrase that recalls Pytheas of Massilia, since he was one of few, in contrast to the normal ancient pattern of mercantile and military exploration, to undertake a true voyage of research.[17] Deinias's expedition takes him through the Black Sea and into the Scythian Ocean, then east to the rising-place of the sun to escape the unbearable cold, then by way of a "circle," presumably a *periplous* around all Asia and Africa, to Thule in the northwest corner of the world. There Deinias and his crew decide to make a *stathmos,* or layover, before continuing their journey; however, after Deinias meets Dercyllis, a noblewoman from Tyre with many tales to tell, his stop is extended—throughout nearly all the rest of the novel. His journey of exploration is not resumed until the novel's final episode.

Deinias's initial *periplous* can be understood, on one level, as Diogenes' way of moving immediately to the "blank page" outside the *oikoumenê* and avoiding the sites associated with classical Greek history.[18] On another level, though, this move had obvious implications in terms of literary credibility, the issue considered above in connection with the Phaeacian tales of the *Odyssey.* The tendency for Odysseus's ship to wander outside the *oikoumenê* had been attacked, by Eratosthenes for instance, as an *exô- keanismos,* a kind of exotic fantasy linked in the Greek mind with the waters of Ocean. The geographer Strabo, for his part, countered Eratosthenes by claiming that Homer had possessed real knowledge of Ocean, and had only imported the exotic in order to please his audience; but the vehemence with which Strabo advances his argument only reveals how damaging the charge of *exôkeanismos* was felt to be, since even Homer, the prince of Greek poets, had to be rescued from it at all costs.[19] The same charge, moreover, might well have been leveled against Pytheas, whose log—entitled *Concerning Ocean (Peri Ôkeanou)*—smacked of the exoticism typical of an *exôkeanismos.*[20] What, then, are we to think of Antonius Diogenes, who in the first episode of the *Wonders beyond Thule* sends his hero through a wider swath of Ocean then either Odysseus or Pytheas had ever seen? Surely this willful *exôkeanismos* was intended by Diogenes as a demonstration of his freedom from generic constraints— just as his choice of title was meant as a response to the critical ethic that had ruled *apista* out-of-bounds.

After this initial round-the-world excursion, then, the island of Thule becomes the setting for the static middle portion of the novel, in which Deinias falls in love with Dercyllis while hearing her convoluted story. Dercyllis and her brother had fled their home in Tyre after Paapis, an evil Egyptian sorcerer who had been adopted by the household, tricked them into casting a spell on their parents. They and their traveling companions, at times split into two groups, sojourn across the breadth of Europe three times, always pursued by the evil Paapis, and always encountering *apista.* In some cases, in fact, the Tyrians' adventures seem to have been built out of the material quarried from paradoxographical tracts. For example, in one episode Dercyllis's friend Astraeus, whose eyes had the miraculous property of growing larger and smaller in connection with the phases of the moon, manages to solve a dispute between two rival monarchs by directing them to rule by turns during alternate lunar phases (109b25–33). The bizarre *auxomeiôseis* of Astraeus's eyes may have been suggested by an *apiston* found in paradoxographical tracts, according to which mouse livers similarly expand and contract with the phases of the moon—a marvel that had become proverbial as an emblem of nature's mysterious powers.[21] Other *apista* encountered by the Tyrians have similar precedents in pseudoscientific writers, including Eudoxus, Poseidonius, and Pseudo-Aristotle.[22] But adventures of a more mythic cast, such as an *Odyssey*-style descent to the underworld, were also included in Dercyllis's itinerary.

Eventually all the travelers arrive on Thule, including the sorcerer Paapis, who puts a spell on Dercyllis and her brother, causing them to live by night and fall into a deathlike trance by day. At this point we emerge from Dercyllis's retelling of her history and return to "live action"— although it is "live" in only a qualified sense, for there are several larger frames beyond this one serving to encapsulate and distance the narrative.[23] In any case the heroine and her brother are soon freed from Paapis's spell by Azoulis, a member of Deinias's crew, after an antidote is discovered among the effects of Paapis (who has by now been killed by an outraged Thulan native). He and Dercyllis's party all return to Tyre, where they succeed in expiating the guilt of their family crime and prepare to live happily ever after. In this way Diogenes concludes what might be called the "inset romance" of the *Wonders beyond Thule,* the story of Dercyllis and her brother and their nemesis Paapis, and along the way generates a love affair (however passive) between Dercyllis and the auditor of her tales, Deinias of Arcadia.

But the larger narrative that began in book 1 with Deinias's departure *kata zêtêsin historias* remains unresolved, as the epitomizer Photius impatiently points out.[24] In the novel's final episode, which (as Photius informs us) occupied the latter part of the twenty-fourth and last book, Deinias separates from Dercyllis to resume his voyage of exploration, steering at last for the promised region "beyond Thule." The point of this final, climactic voyage has confused some commentators,[25] but it becomes intelligible if we recall that Thule had been for Deinias only a *stathmos* in a longer journey, implying that his quest for knowledge had not been fulfilled in his initial sweep around the *oikoumenê*. Moreover, in terms of the literary-critical "waters" Diogenes has been navigating, involving the credibility problems implied in the terms *apista* and *exôkeanismos,* the leap "beyond Thule" forms a natural last step. Having posed the implicit question of how far belief can be stretched in matters of natural science, the author now prepares to carry this question to its logical extreme.

The idea that this final voyage represents a test of the elasticity of *apista,* their ability to unite the otherwise opposing poles of belief and incredulity, is supported by the way the novel's wonders trace a rising curve of implausibility. As Photius tells it,

> Deinias claimed here to have seen what the devotees of astronomy speculate about, for instance that there are some men who live beneath the Great Bear, and that the night can be a month long, or more or less, or even six months, or even a year . . . And he reports having seen other things of that sort, tribes of men and other curiosities, which he says no one had seen, nor heard of, nor even imagined before. And, most incredible of all, he claims that in his voyage north he approached the moon, as if toward some exceedingly pure version of Earth, and there saw the kinds of things you might expect from such a fictionalizer of outlandish fables. (111a4–11)

In other words, Deinias's experiences initially remain within the bounds of accepted scientific theory, and closely approximate the findings of his predecessor, Pytheas; Pytheas too had discovered men "beneath the Great Bear,"[26] as well as six-month nights,[27] and according to one source at least, yearlong nights,[28] in the farthest North. At a second stage, however, Deinias's findings grow more exotic and strange, involving phenomena "never seen, nor heard of, nor even imagined" previously. Finally he approaches the moon, or perhaps even lands on it (Photius's language is ambiguous); and the corresponding amplification of the *apista* he describes is evidenced by Photius, who has thus far raised no objection to any of Diogenes' inventions, at last losing patience and disdaining to continue his summation. As a result we know only that Deinias discovered the moon to be a "pure version of Earth" (*gên katharôtatên*), a phrase that admits of no certain interpretation.[29] But it is at least evident that Deinias's long-delayed journey followed a hyperbolic course in this final episode, bringing him at last to a point where his reader, Photius, refuses to follow him.

After attaining this pitch of unbelievability Diogenes swiftly concludes his story, bringing in a benevolent sibyl to whisk Deinias back to Tyre and there reunite him with Dercyllis and her brother. But the novel does not quite conclude even after this second resolution. Photius reports an addendum to the *Wonders beyond Thule* written in the author's own persona, perhaps attached to the end of book 24,[30] in which Diogenes reveals himself to be the inventor of it all—thus abandoning the elaborate historical deceit of the buried tablets. Diogenes then turns to address the issue of his *apista,* and here his statements, as recorded by Photius, become extremely puzzling: "Concerning himself, he says he is a poet of Old Comedy, and that, even if he invents *apista* and lies, nonetheless for most of his fabulous tales has the support of the ancient sources from which he has energetically collected them; and he prefaces each book with names of the men who dealt with such material before him, so that his *apista* might not seem to lack witnesses" (111a34–40). If we understand this summary correctly, Diogenes seems here to admit his predilection for the kinds of fables appropriate to Old Comedy, perhaps in imitation of plays like Aristophanes' *Birds*.[31] But at the same time he claims scientific authority for these marvels, and even supplies a bibliography of the sources from which they were drawn.[32] We are thus faced with the paradox of an author who cites real sources for made-up information, who casts himself both as a comic poet and as a compiler of scientific fact. Nor does his duplicitous role become any clearer when we learn from Photius that his source list included Antiphanes of Berga—another "explorer" whose accounts of a northern voyage into Ocean were notorious for their bald-faced mendacity.

In this closing epistle, then, Diogenes has the last laugh on his audience by leaving unresolved the tension inherent in the term *apista,* a word that stands poised between "true" and "false." If geographical literature can be said to define a spectrum of credibility, stretching from obvious fictions like that of Antiphanes of Berga to wholly reliable accounts like those of Eudoxus and Poseidonius, then in the *Wonders beyond Thule* Diogenes moves up and down the scale with reckless abandon. Mostly, though, he situates his novel squarely in the middle, where Thule and other elements derived from Pytheas's *Concerning the Ocean* reside. In cultivating this middle ground, and in flaunting his freedom of movement in both directions, Diogenes in effect defies his readers to apply the standards of credibility by which narrative fictions, beginning with Homer's *Odyssey,* had conventionally been judged. Though we may, like Photius, take exception to the material at the "Bergaean" end of the spectrum,[33] we are nevertheless unable to say exactly where the boundary between acceptable and unacceptable *apista* is to be drawn; the shadings of the marvelous advance by increments, like the gradual extension of nighttime during the course of Deinias's northward journey, until we are finally engulfed.

There we must leave our inquiry into the *Wonders beyond Thule,* for the loss of Diogenes' original text prevents us from venturing further. But we have already learned enough about Diogenes' technique to connect him with certain Renaissance fiction writers, among whom the "novel beyond Thule" particularly thrived. Nor should we balk at making such a comparison. Despite obvious discontinuities there is a close harmony between the literary-critical concerns of the two periods, as attested by the Renaissance's intense engagement with the Greek romance and with self-conscious fictions like Lucian's *True Histories*.[34] Whether the *Wonders beyond Thule,* or Photius's epitome of it, had a direct influence on Renaissance writers, as Lucian's *True Histories* certainly did, is unclear, and I do not wish to imply by my remarks here that such was the case. However, I would submit that Diogenes' techniques supply a close analogue for much of what went on in Renaissance fiction, and for a quite specific reason. In the early modern period the voyage of exploration, as exemplified by recent discoveries made in the New World, had once again become a prominent and problematic literary model.

Columbus's voyage to the Americas, after all, had itself been a journey beyond Thule, in two separate senses. First, Columbus, according to his sixteenth-century biographers, had as a youth sailed a hundred leagues past Thule (then identified with Iceland) on a reconnaissance mission, the object of which was to demonstrate that his later transatlantic crossing would not be impeded by climatic extremes.[35] Thus Thule had again become a *stathmos* for nautical journeys into the great unknown. Second, and more important, the subsequent discovery of the Americas was widely interpreted in the Renaissance as a fulfillment of the "prophecy" contained in the verses of Seneca mentioned earlier, which described a day when *ultima Thule* would no longer limit the progress of travel.[36] Thus the Renaissance had reason to define the New World as the "land beyond Thule," the discovery of which had made real an event that had formerly seemed the stuff of purest fantasy.

In the aftermath of such a reversal, prose fiction came increasingly to blend *voyages imaginaires* with real explorers' logs as a way of establishing its own ambiguous brand of veracity. Thus François Rabelais, at the outset of the *Quart livre* (1548), places a thinly veiled version of Jacques Cartier on board the flagship that will bear Panurge and Pantagruel to the Holy Oracle of Bacbuc,[37] and the route his heroes follow, although described in obscure language, nevertheless replicates the real and contemporary quest for a northwest passage to India. The conjunction of actual and fantastic voyages is then carried on in the fleet's first port of call (4.2), when the island of Medamothy ("Nowhere") is pointedly compared with its real-world correlate, Canada.[38] Similarly Johannes Kepler, as I have shown elsewhere, admits to having blended ancient *voyages imaginaires* like that of Lucian's *True Histories* with the 1598 account of a Dutch expedition to Nova Zembla in composing his own voyage text, the *Somnium* (1634).[39] In imitation of both these sources, he sends his hero, Duracotus, to Thule—Iceland—before launching him toward his ultimate destination, the moon.

Of particular interest in relation to the *Wonders beyond Thule,* however, is the Cervantes novel mentioned at the outset of this chapter, *The Trials of Persiles and Sigismunda.* Here, as Alban Forcione and others have demonstrated,[40] Cervantes constructs an elegant example of literary theory in practice, an experiment in stretching the credibility standards of the conventional romance—much as I have tried to illustrate above for Antonius

Diogenes. Moreover, Cervantes, like Diogenes, adopts the island of Thule as the testing ground for this experiment. Although his heroes eventually travel inward from Thule rather than outward, Cervantes manages to bring back the truth-fiction question in its most extreme form in the novel's penultimate episode, just before the climactic resolution of his romance plot.

Though Cervantes may not have known the *Wonders beyond Thule*,[41] he was certainly well versed in Heliodorus's *Aethiopica,* and the project of the *Persiles* was in many ways conceived as a response to that great narrative paradigm.[42] Whereas Heliodorus had situated his adventures in the farthest southeast corner of the *oikoumenê,* Cervantes, in a gesture both of imitation and of transgression, locates his in the farthest northwest corner. The story begins in a place identified only as an *isla barbara,* located vaguely in the Ocean Sea, but the northern setting soon becomes apparent from the wonders therein encountered: frozen wastes, perpetual darkness, and strange creatures like the barnacle bird (1.12) borrowed from popular compendiums of septentrional lore.[43] The hero and heroine, who at this point are known to us as Periandro and Auristela, are conveyed throughout the first two books of the novel from this barbarian island to other, equally vague points in the North Atlantic, some of which can be tentatively identified with the British Isles;[44] there are also many encounters with other travelers, à la Heliodorus, each of whom recounts a new tale of northern adventures or helps fill in the background of the plot. At the beginning of book 3 the novel assumes a new, more linear course when Periandro and Auristela, seeking a Christian marriage in the city of Rome, cross over into the known world, reaching Lisbon after some twenty days of sailing (3.1). In this latter, European half of the novel Cervantes also leaves behind the wonders of nature with which he had filled the first half—seemingly in accord with Tasso's notion that only in the North would a romancer's inventions find safe refuge.

However, even in the North, Cervantes forces the reader to confront various credibility problems associated with his wonders, as if probing the nature of the truth-fiction divide. In one prominent episode, for example, a character named Rutilio tells of killing a werewolf—a mythic creature supposedly prevalent in northern parts—and his companions proceed to debate the veracity of his account. Mauricio, the rationalist of the group, suggests that Rutilio had merely been bewitched into imagining a werewolf, since those creatures do not really exist; as part of his polemic he cites a passage of Pliny's *Natural History* describing a lycanthropic transformation undergone by the ancient Arcadians, another example, he concludes, of imagined experience standing in for reality. With this reference to Pliny—one of few explicit source citations in the *Persiles*—Cervantes moves the credibility problem surrounding Rutilio's narrative to a literary-critical domain. To take stories from Pliny as truth, he implies, is no different than mistaking a hallucination for real experience. But Pliny's text was itself extremely problematic, having been accepted by some Renaissance authors as an accurate scientific treatise, but parodied by others (including Rabelais) as a collection of fables.[45] Like Diogenes, then, Cervantes seems here to be assimilating into his own narrative the truth-fiction ambivalence he had found in ancient collections of apista.

Nor is this sort of ambivalence limited to the first, northwestern half of the Persiles; it is carried straight into Rome, the center of the inhabited world. In the two chapters prior to the novel's conclusion (4.12f.), the hero and heroine, still known to us as Periandro and Auristela, have arrived at their destination, but are prevented from marrying by complications arising from their as-yet-undisclosed past. To set the resolution in motion Cervantes brings on Periandro's boyhood tutor, Seráfido, who reveals that the disguised lovers are in reality Persiles, prince of Thule, and Sigismunda, princess of an adjoining island named Frisland, which (as Seráfido goes on to say) had been discovered in 1380 by Nicholas Temo of Venice. After the true identity of the protagonists has thus been revealed, the stage is set for the unraveling of the tangled romance plot. But nothing in that plot requires Cervantes to insert the reference to "Temo," also known as Zeno, nor to add to the end of Seráfido's speech a description of another island even more remote than Frisland:

> It's named Greenland and on one of the headlands there's a monastery called Saint Thomas where there are monks from four nations . . . This island is buried in snow, and at the top of a low mountain there's a spring, marvelous and worth knowing about. From it spills and pours forth a great abundance of water so hot that when it flows into the sea it not only thaws a large part of it, but heats it as well, so that incredible numbers of fish congregate in those waters. The monastery and the whole island support themselves by fishing . . . This spring also produces some viscous material from which a sticky cement is made and used to build houses similar to those constructed of solid marble. I could tell you other strange facts about this island, which seem to place its veracity in doubt but which are in fact the truth.[46]

In this last, most anomalous wonder—also taken from Zeno, possibly by way of a sixteenth-century commentary on Pliny's Natural History[47]—Cervantes continues to raise the credibility questions implied in his earlier use of apista. By deriving his picture of the North from the Zeno brothers' Due viaggi (1558)—a text that, though initially embraced as true, had by the early seventeenth century come under suspicion[48]—Cervantes situates his entire narrative on shifting and ambiguous ground, leaving the reader less certain than ever as to the boundary between fact and fiction. In the

Zeno log, that is, Cervantes finds the same sort of vehicle Diogenes had found in Pytheas's *Concerning Ocean:* a means of carrying his story beyond Thule, in both the geographic and the narratological senses of that expression. But whereas Diogenes' journey is one of science, bringing his hero into contact with the "pure" world in the moon, Cervantes' is rather a leap of faith, offering a vision of Christian grace—the spring that feeds and houses the monks of Saint Thomas—working its miracles even on Greenland's purest shore.

Notes

1. F. Rabelais, *Pantagruel*, bk. 2, chap. 34. Trans. J. M. Cohen in the Penguin Classics edition (*Gargantua and Pantagruel*, New York, 1955), 277.

2. T. Tasso, *Discourses on the Epic Poem*, trans. M. Cavalchini and I. Samuel (Oxford, 1973), 50. Among the critics who refer this passage to Cervantes' project in the *Persiles* is E. C. Riley, *Cervantes's Theory of the Novel* (Oxford, 1962), 190.

3. Strabo 1.2.19 (C 26). Since Eratosthenes himself claimed to see through the strategy (cf. Strabo 1.2.7 [C 18]), he presumably meant this *eukatopseuston* with reference to an audience of Homer's contemporaries.

4. Lucian, *True Histories* 1.3–4. The train of thought that introduces this literary family tree has been partly obscured by a mistaken emendation of the text, introducing a *hoios* or *hón* before Ctesias's name (proposed by Bekker, endorsed most recently by Macleod in the Oxford Classical Text). The effect of this subordinating conjunction is to make the names that follow examples of authors Lucian intends to *spoof,* rather than those he intends to *imitate.* I follow Joseph Dane (*Parody: Critical Concepts versus Literary Practices, Aristophanes to Sterne* [Norman, Okla., 1988], 76) in rejecting both the lacuna assumed before *Ctésias* in the standard texts and the *hos* that, in some manuscripts, immediately follows.

5. This is discussed at the conclusion of E. Rohde, *Der griechische Roman und seine Vorläufer,* sect. 2, 250–87 in the first edition (Leipzig, 1876) (hereafter cited as *GR*). In thus prioritizing the *Wonders beyond Thule,* Rohde allied himself with the Byzantine patriarch Photius, who had read a complete version of the work in the ninth century and remarked that it seemed not only the "source and root" of Lucian's *True Histories* and the Lucianic *Ass* but also a "paradigm" of all the erotic romances: "Nicht mit Unrecht aber hält er ihn für ein *Vorbild* der späteren Romanschreiber" (275).

6. Cod. 166, 140–49, in vol. 2 of R. Henry's Budé edition of the *Bibliotheca* (Paris, 1960); translation and commentary forthcoming shortly in *The Ancient Greek Novels: The Fragments,* ed. S. A. Stephens and J. J. Winkler (Princeton, 1993) (I am indebted to these authors for showing me a preliminary version of their work). There are other analyses by O. Schissel von Fleschenberg, *Novellenkränze Lukians* (Halle, 1912), 101–9; L. Di Gregorio, "Sugli *Apista Hyper Thoulên* di Antonio Diogene," *Aevum* 42 (1968): 199–211; K. Reyhl, *Antonios Diogenes* (Ph.D. diss., University of Tübingen, 1969); and J. R. Morgan, "Lucian's *True Histories* and the *Wonders beyond Thule* of Antonius Diogenes," *Classical Quarterly* 35 (1985): 475–90. A translation of the Photius epitome is now available in *Collected Ancient Greek Novels,* ed. B. P. Reardon (Berkeley and Los Angeles, 1989).

7. Tomas Hägg, who has made an extensive study of Photius's reliability (*Photios als Vermittlere antiker Literatur,* Studia Graeca Upsaliensia 8 [Uppsala, 1975]), cautions

against the kind of reconstruction I have attempted here (chap. 9), but when the critic is offered as many tantalizing clues as are contained in the *Wonders beyond Thule* epitome it is hard to resist the temptations. Hägg himself contemplates undertaking an analysis of the Diogenes epitome (195 n. 1).

8. See Porphyry's *Life of Pythagoras*, chap. 10 (where it is reported as *ta huper Thoulên apista*), and Epiphanius's *Against the Heretics* 1.33.8 (cited simply *ta apista*, but perhaps in abbreviated form). I am indebted to Stephens and Winkler, *Ancient Greek Novels*, for these citations. In addition, the title *ta huper Thoulên apista* seems to have been applied to the novel by Antonius Diogenes himself, if Photius's words at 111a32f. are a quote (as seems likely).

9. The work is attributed to Isigonus of Nicaea, first century B.C.; see A. Giannini, "Studi sulla paradossografia Greca," part 2, *Acme* 17 (1964): 124f. and n. 150.

10. The duality of meanings is noted in O. Weinreich, "Antiphanes und Munchhausen," *Sitzungsberichte der Akademie der Wissenschaft im Wein* 220 (892):33f. and n. 4. Our own word "incredible" works the same way, since it is often used as an exclamation to greet startling revelations of the truth.

11. Cf. also *Problems* 18.10, where it is asserted that "we disbelieve [*apistoumen*] things far from our experience, and that which we disbelieve gives us no pleasure." The case of the *apiston* as "incredible but true" is, however, admitted in the *Rhetoric* (2.23.22).

12. Cf. Strabo 2.5.8 (C 114); also 2.4.2 (C 104), 1.4.2 (C 63). For the larger debate, see R. Dion, "La renommée de Pythéas dans l'antiquité," *Revue des etudes latines* 43 (1965): 443–66. On Diogenes' relationship to Pytheas, see especially di Gregorio, "Sugli *Apista Hyper Thoulên*," 206f., and Stephens and Winkler, *Ancient Greek Novels*, sect. 1.2 of the introduction.

13. A parallel difference in the tone of the two works—explicitly parodic in Lucian's case, shifting and semiserious in Diogenes'—is remarked by Stephens and Winkler, *Ancient Greek Novels*, sec. 1.3.

14. As noted by M. Cary and E. H. Warmington, *The Ancient Explorers* (London, 1929), 204f., I have here assumed no specific location for Thule; "somewhere beyond the British Isles" will do, although other, more northerly sites have been proposed. For the arguments on this issue, see R. Carpenter, *Beyond the Pillars of Heracles* (N.p., 1965), chap. 5.

15. Vergil, *Aeneid* 6.795–98 and *Georgics* 1.30; Seneca, *Medea* 375–79.

16. For instance, when Diogenes' plot called for several of the main characters to be hauled before a Sicilian ruler, he chose to set his scene not at the court of a Hippocrates or a Gela but at that of the little-known Ainesidemus of Leontini (110a6; see *GR*, 265 n. 2). Even the novel's close connection with Pythagoras, moreover, can be seen as a way of detaching it from history. Pythagoras himself was a transhistorical personage, a multiply reincarnated time-traveler whose past lives were said to extend all the way back to the Trojan War. By contrast, the *Aethiopica* of Heliodorus, another novel set in the early fifth century B.C., continually evokes features of that setting familiar from Herodotus and other historiographers, as revealed by J. R. Morgan's study ("History, Romance, and Realism in the *Aithiopika* of Heliodorus," *Classical Antiquity* 1 [1982]: 220–65).

17. See Rohde's note, *GR*, 259 n. 2.

18. Rohde thinks Diogenes would have brought many of the wonders of the East and South into play here (*GR*, 259f. n. 4), but if so they would likely have been mentioned by Photius, who loves to retail such material. It seems more likely to me that the "much time and various adventures" mentioned in the epitome (190a21f.) reproduces a truncation of the original text; it was Diogenes, not Photius, who whisked his hero around the world in short order.

19. Strabo 1.2.37 (C 44), 1.2.40 (C 46). See H. Berger, *Geschichte der Wissenschaft-*

lichen Erdkunde der Griechen (Leipzig, 1903), 536f., and D. M. Schenkeveld, "Strabo on Homer," *Mnemosyne* 29 (1976): 52–64. Appollonius Rhodius, who in his *Argonautica* strove in various ways to steer his heroes to terra incognita, studiously and self-consciously avoids having them commit an *exôkeanismos,* as if acknowledging to his readers the impropriety of such a move. See L. Pearson, "Apollonius of Rhodes and the Old Geographers," *American Journal of Philology* 59 (1938): 443–59.

20. At 2.3.5 (C 120), Strabo lumps Pytheas together with Euhemerus and Antiphanes of Berga, implying that his hoax had been motivated by literary ambition.

21. Antigonus Carystius 136, in *Paradoxographorum Graecorum reliquiae,* ed. A. Giannini (Milan, 1965). Cf. also Plutarch, *Quaestiones conviviales* 4.5 (670b). Other, similar lunar wonders are cited by Stephens and Winkler, *Ancient Greek Novels,* sec. 3 of the introduction.

22. See the extensive annotation of this section by Rohde, *GR,* 259–67.

23. Deinias's experiences are recounted, within the scheme of the novel, to Cymbas, an Arcadian envoy sent to fetch him home; this long flashback is in turn dictated to an Athenian scribe, Erasinides, and the resulting text (engraved on the aforementioned wooden tablets) is finally transcribed some one hundred fifty years later by one Balagrus, a member of Alexander the Great's cohort, after it is recovered from the graves of the principal heroes. The "Chinese box" technique of inset narratives in the *Wonders beyond Thule,* though fascinating, is not directly relevant to my topic here. See sec. 4 of Stephens and Winkler, *Ancient Greek Novels.*

24. Photius, *Bibliotheca* 110b16–20: "Thus the twenty-third book of the *Wonders beyond Thule* reaches its close; yet the work has thus far revealed nothing about Thule, save for a few bits at the beginning."

25. Partly because Deinias's exploration of the moon had gotten tangled (thanks to Photius's scattershot remarks at 111b35–37) with a similar lunar voyage described in Lucian's *True Histories;* the recent disentangling of the two works (by J. R. Morgan, "Lucian's *True Histories,*" and J. Hall, *Lucian's Satire* [London, 1984], 342–47) has made matters easier. Nevertheless, Stephens and Winkler (*Ancient Greek Novels,* note to 110b33ff.) seem at a loss to explain Deinias's reasons for going on.

26. Strabo reports Pytheas as the source for "men who live beneath the Great Bear" (2.5.8), a notion that was otherwise deemed impossible due to extreme cold (cf. Herodotus 5.9).

27. Pliny, *Natural History* 2.71.187, 4.16.104; Geminus, *Eisagôgê* 6.9.22.

28. Cosmas Indicopleustes 116d; see Berger, *Geschichte,* 343f. and n. 1. Perhaps the most suggestive link between Pytheas and Deinias, however, derives from the former's alleged discovery, according to a text probably contemporary with the *Wonders beyond Thule,* of the moon's role in producing the ebb and flow of oceanic tides (cf. Plutarch, *De placitis philosophorum* 3.17 [987b]). The existence of this theory enables us to see a Pythean tinge not only in Deinias's exploration of the moon but perhaps in other *Wonders* episodes that take the lunar phases as their organizing principle, e.g., the waxing and waning of Astraeus's eyes.

29. I have given the most literal sense of Photius's phrase *gên katharôtatên,* for which several possible meanings have been proposed: "bright," "bare," "geniune." G. N. Sandy, the most recent translator, gives "a completely stripped land" (Reardon, *Collected Ancient Greek Novels,* 781).

30. I will not pursue the question of where this letter was placed in relation to the narrative, a question left open by Photius and variously debated scholars. The most natural way to read an epitome would be to assume that it follows the sequence of its original, unless otherwise noted (as, for example, at 111a41); thus Photius's description of the letter to Faustinus (111a30–40), which occurs at the conclusion of his plot summary, probably reflects its placement at the end of the novel.

31. Hence di Gregorio ("Sugli *Apista Hyper Thoulên*," 200 n. 1), approved by Stephens and Winkler (*Ancient Greek Novels*), in opposition to scholars like Rohde (*GR*, 251 n. 2), who would take the term *palaias kômôidias* less literally.

32. This bibliography must have preceded the entire novel, just as Pliny's occupies book 1 of the *Natural History*. A papyrus fragment of the novel (*POxy.* 3012) shows that the source citations were *not* given before individual books (see Stephens and Winkler, *Ancient Greek Novels,* introduction). On the tradition of parodic source-citation in antiquity, see E. Gabba, "True and False History in Classical Antiquity," *Journal of Roman Studies* 72 (1981): 54.

33. "Bergaean" is a term derived from Antiphanes of Berga, which Strabo (1.3.1 [C 47], 2.4.2 [C 104]) and others apply to fabulous and incredible travel tales.

34. The shared concerns of antiquity and the Renaissance over the boundary between truth and fiction in literary texts is explored by W. Nelson in "The Boundaries of Fiction in the Renaissance: A Treaty between Truth and Falsehood," *English Literary History* 16 (1969): 30–58. For the prominence of Lucian's *True Histories* as a model for sixteenth-century fiction, see J. C. Dunlop, *A History of Prose Fiction,* 2 vols. (London, 1911), 2:511–38, and C. Mayer, *Lucien de Samosate et la Renaissance Française* (Geneva, 1984), esp. chap. 5.

35. This is described in one of Columbus's letters as quoted by his son Fernando, *Historia del Almirante,* chap. 4, and Bartolomé de las Casas, *Historia de las Indias,* 1.3; cited by C. De Lollis in *Scritti di Cristoforo Colombo* (Rome, 1894), 1.2:524f. The story has been accepted as accurate by S. E. Morison in *Admiral of the Ocean Sea: A Life of Christopher Columbus* (1942; reprint, Boston, 1983), 24–26, but is disputed by other historians.

36. See F. H. A. von Humboldt, *Histoire de la géographie du nouveau continent,* 5 vols. (Paris, 1864), 1:101–6, 161–67; E. G. Bourne, "Seneca and the Discovery of America," in *Essays in Historical Criticism* (New York, 1901), 221–24; J. Imbelloni, "Las 'Profecias de America' y el Ingreso de Atlantida en le Americanista," *Boletin de la Academia Nacional de la Historia de Buenos Aires* 12 (1939): 115–21; and J. Ronn, "New World and *Novos Orbes:* Seneca in the Renaissance Debate over Knowledge of the Americas," *The Classical Tradition in the Americas,* vol. 1 (1993), forthcoming.

37. In F. Rabelais, *Quart livre,* chap. 1, the captain of Pantagruel's fleet is identified as Jamet Brayer, a name that, although taken from an associate of Rabelais's family, is conspicuous both because of its phonic resemblance to "Jacques Cartier" and because it was inserted by the author only into the work's second (1552) edition. The identification with Cartier was greatly strengthened by A. Lefranc in *Les navigations de Pantagruel* (Paris 1905), 214–17; A. Tilley raised some doubts in "Rabelais and Geographical Discovery," part 2, *Modern Language Review* 3 (1908): 209–17, but agreed that the letters of Cartier are used throughout the voyage narrative in any case. For a comparison of the two texts in respect of technique, see J.-P. Beaulieu, "La description de la nouveauté dans les récits de voyage de Cartier et de Rabelais," *Renaissance and Reformation* 9 (1985): 104–10.

38. See Lefranc, *Les navigations de Pantagruel,* 44ff. In an appendix (293–95), Lefranc ingeniously suggests that the name Medamothy was coined by Rabelais as a punning equivalent of "Canada," which had itself been formed, according to one folk etymology, from Spanish *aca nada,* or "nothing here."

39. Note 2 to the *Somnium,* in vol. 8 of C. Frisch's *Johannis Kepleri astronomi opera omnia* (Frankfurt, 1870), 40f.; discussed by E. Rosen in *Kepler's "Somnium"* (Madison, Wis., 1967), 35 n. 22. On the whole topic, see J. Romm, "Lucian and Plutarch as Sources for Kepler's *Somnium,*" *Classical and Modern Literature,* 9 (1989): 97–107.

40. In A. K. Forcione, *Cervantes, Aristotle, and the "Persiles"* (Princeton, 1970) and *Cervantes' Christian Romance: A Study of "Persiles y Sigismunda"* (Princeton, 1972). See

also Riley, *Cervantes's Theory of the Novel,* and T. D. Stegmann, *Cervantes' Musterroman "Persiles": Epentheorie und Romanpraxis um 1600* (Hamburg, 1971). I am also indebted in what follows to D. de Armas Wilson, "Cervantes on Cannibals," *Revista de estudios Hispanicos* 22 (1988): 1–25, and E. González, "Del *Persiles* y la Isla Bárbara: Fábulas y reconocimientos," *Modern Language Notes* 94 (1979): 222–57.

41. The suggestion that he did has been entertained, however; cf. T. Hägg, *The Novel in Antiquity* (Berkeley and Los Angeles, 1983), 203, where the particular critic referred to is not cited. The Photius epitome had been published in Latin translation in a 1606 edition of the *Bibliotheca,* well before the composition of the *Persiles* (see the introduction to vol. 1 of R. Henry's Budé edition). Antonius Diogenes goes unmentioned in the extensive review of the *Persiles'* Greek sources conducted by R. Schevill ("Studies in Cervantes I: *Persiles y Sigismunda,*" *Modern Philology* 4 [1906]: 1–24).

42. See Forcione, *Cervantes, Aristotle, and the "Persiles,"* chap. 2, and *Cervantes' Christian Romance,* chap. 1.

43. In this case (and many others), from Olaus Magnus's *Historia de gentibus septentrionalibus* (1555). On the sources of Cervantes' northern material, see K. Larsen, "Cervantes' Vorstellungen vom Norden," *Studien zur vergleichenden Literaturgeschichte* 5 (1905): 273–96, and R. Beltrán y Rózpide, "La pericia geográfica de Cervantes," *Boletín de la Real Sociedad Geográfica* 64 (1923): 270–93.

44. See the appendix on "Cervantes' Far North" in the English edition of the novel, *The Trials of Persiles and Sigismunda,* trans. C. R. Weller and C. A. Colahan (Berkeley and Los Angeles, 1989), 363–66.

45. Compare, for example, Montaigne's assessment (*Essais* 1.27) with that of Rabelais (*Gargantua,* chap. 6). The assessment of Pliny in the *Persiles* is the more ambiguous in that the passage cited by Mauricio (8.34.81) actually rejects, rather than endorsing, the legend of the werewolves of Arcadia.

46. Weller and Colahan, *Trials of Persiles and Sigismunda,* 346, with the final sentence modified. R. H. Major discusses the report of real hot springs on the coast of Greenland in his introduction to the English translation of the Zeno log (*The Voyages of the Venetian Brothers Nicoló and Antonio Zeno,* Hakluyt Society, ser. 1, vol. 50 [London, 1873], lxxxff).

47. Gerónimo de Huerta's marginal note to Pliny 6.34, cited in the R. Schevill and A. Bonilla edition of the *Persiles* (Madrid, 1914), 2:324, contains virtually all the material used by Cervantes from the Zeno narrative, and also provides a precedent for his corrupt spelling of the name.

48. The degree to which the Zeno account was embraced as true in Cervantes' day has been overstated by commentators, including Beltrán y Rózpide ("La pericia geográfica de Cervantes," 274f. and n. 1) and L. Astrana Marin (*Vida ejemplar y heroica de Miguel de Cervantes de Saavedra* [Madrid, 1958], 7:421–25). Samuel Purchas, for instance, in *Purchas His Progress* (13.18, Hakluyt Society, vol. 13 [Glasgow, 1906], 417), admits to serious doubts: "This Historie I have thus inserted at large, which perhaps, not without cause in some things, may seem fabulous; not in the Zeni, which thus writ, but in the relations which they received from others." Hakluyt gives a stronger, though still circumspect, endorsement. According to Justin Winsor, the Zeno narrative was "equally the subject of belief and derision" even in its earliest history, despite its strong influence on cartography (see *Narrative and Critical History of America,* ed. J. Winsor [Cambridge, Mass., 1889], 1:74, 111–15 n. H).

CHAPTER SIX

Heliodorus Rewritten:
Samuel Richardson's *Clarissa*
and Frances Burney's *Wanderer*

Margaret Anne Doody

In 1789 there appeared a new English edition of Heliodorus's *Aethiopica*, translated as *The Adventures of Theagenes and Chariclea: A Romance*. This two-volume novel contains a prefatory "Advertisement" by the translator, recommending the Greek novelist:

> Heliodorus may be considered as the Homer of romance, and if it cannot be said of him, as it may of the great father of epic poetry, that he has never been excelled or equalled by any of his successors, it may with truth be affirmed that he has very seldom been so. In clear, spirited, elegant narration, Cervantes is not his superior—in the just, warm, and delicate delineations of the passions, particularly that of love, he equals Rousseau or Richardson. If his work abounds not with the striking and varied representations of character which we admire so much in the works of the latter, and in those of his great rival in this, as well as in many other of his excellencies, Miss Burney, several passages of his book lead one to imagine, that it might be rather owing to the different and more confined state of society and manners when he wrote, than to any deficiency of talent.[1]

This last is a rather condescending statement, which certainly gives pride of place to two of Heliodorus's recent successors. The new translator estimates how Richardsonian Heliodorus may be, or how Burneyesque. "Miss Burney" was famous at the time for *Evelina* (1778) and *Cecilia* (1782), and, although in 1789 she was still in durance at the court of Queen Charlotte, and not writing prose fiction, two more novels were yet to come. This handsome compliment may well have come to her notice, and it is not impossible that she might have been moved at some point to look into the two little volumes. But we need not invoke a direct influence in order to pose the question whether Frances Burney, in her last novel, *The*

Wanderer (1814), offers an example of a new *Aethiopica,* or at least proves herself Heliodoran.

The Heliodoran novel is of immense importance to European literature in general, and certainly to English literature in particular. It is visible everywhere in Sir Philip Sidney's *Arcadia,* and it was from the *Arcadia* that Samuel Richardson took the name—and more than the name—of the heroine of his first novel, *Pamela* (1741–42).[2] His next heroine, the central character of *Clarissa* (1747–48), seems a Chariclea *rediviva,* and the novel seems an experiment with the Heliodoran novel, an experiment that takes it into tragedy. Even the index supplied for *Clarissa* is after a fashion a Heliodoran allusion, modeled after Renaissance indexes to the *Aethiopica.* Whether or not Frances Burney was stimulated to read Heliodorus for herself, she was the inheritor of a fictional tradition stemming directly from his work.

Yet as soon as we start to consider Burney's novel in this light, we come upon the gender factor. Can a woman write—or rather, rewrite—the Heliodoran novel? Can it become a novel not written by "a good bishop," or one thought to have been such, but a work reflecting another sort of view? What changes must be made in the Heliodoran novel if a woman is going to write it? Frances Burney's novel *The Wanderer,* the most gothic and most "feminist" of her works, a novel that incorporates the views of Mary Wollstonecraft and the history of the French Revolution, seems in its own strange way to offer an answer to these questions.

We should at the outset consider the beginnings of both novels—the *Aethiopica* and *The Wanderer.* Here is the opening of the *Aethiopica* as it appears in the translation of 1789:

> The day began to dawn, the sun had already enlightened the tops of the hills, when a band of men, in appearance pirates, gained the summit of a mountain that extended nearly to the Heracleotic mouth of the Nile: here they made a stand, and contemplated the sea that was expanded before them. When they saw nothing on the water that gave them hopes of a booty, they cast their eyes upon the opposite shore; the situation of things there was as follows: A ship lay at anchor, with no soul on board of her; but in appearance laden with merchandize, as she was sunk deep in the water. The beach was strewn with bodies newly slaughtered; some quite dead, others dying, yet still breathing, gave signs of a combat recently ended. Yet it appeared not to have been a designed engagement; but there were mingled with these dreadful spectacles the fragments of a feast, that seemed to have concluded in this horrible manner. (1:1–2)

(Note how the eighteenth-century translator makes Heliodorus sound like a writer of the eighteenth century, just as Amyot and Underdowne make him sound like a writer of the Renaissance.) We begin Heliodorus's novel by seeing a scene of confusion on a beach—a puzzle to which there is no ready solution. Our first view is implicated, contaminated; we share the view of the band of marauders, looking from a distance at the disordered scene, not with pity but with a desire for plunder. The apparent recent breakup of the "unlucky banquet" (to borrow Underdowne's phrase) contains strange echoes of the *Odyssey,* but this is evidently not the *Odyssey.* None of the viewers of the scene can make sense of it here, or relate the various phenomena.

After they notice the puzzling scene of slaughter, the bandits see the puzzling young woman: "A spectacle presented itself which perplexed them more than any which they had yet seen. A virgin of uncommon and almost heavenly beauty sat upon a rock; she seemed deeply afflicted . . . but . . . preserved an air of dignity . . . at her rising she appeared still greater and more divine. Her shafts sounded as she moved; her golden garments glittered in the sun; and her hair flowed, under her laurel diadem, in dishevelled ringlets down her neck" (1:4–5).

This resplendent heroine is reflected in Richardson's Clarissa; the hero-villain of Richardson's novel, Robert Lovelace, frequently refers to her as "the divine Clarissa" and describes her in terms as refulgent as those in which Heliodorus describes Chariclea. He speaks, for instance, of "the presence of my charmer, flashing upon me all at once in a flood of brightness," and describes her physical appearance in detail: "Thou hast heard me also describe the wavy Ringlets of her shining hair, needing neither art nor powder; of itself an ornament, defying all other ornaments; wantoning in and about a neck that is beautiful beyond description" (3:28).[3]

If Richardson's description sounds also like Milton on Eve—why, Milton had read Heliodorus too (and the translator of 1789 had read both Milton and Richardson). Both Chariclea and Clarissa are seen at a disadvantage—each looks tremendously goddesslike but is also fearfully vulnerable. The first description of Chariclea incorporates the view of vulgarians who could destroy her. She guesses as much, and speaks to them in a speech combining hauteur and pathos, pointing out that she has been engaged in a struggle to repel the violence offered to her chastity, and begging them satirically to deliver herself and the young man she loves (Theagenes) from their sorrows by death, thus putting an end to "our drama" (ἡμῶν δϱᾶμα). It is an eloquent speech, but the brigands are unheeding, "not understanding what she said." Her language is not intelligible to them. Throughout Heliodorus, we come upon the problem of different languages, the need for translation; the story emphasizes (in Calasiris) the value of the polyglot. The goddess-woman who is not to be understood and the injured young man she tends are both seized by yet another band of marauders; the first party, the group with whom we came in, vanish from the scene into the wilds of savage inarticulateness, matching the disarticulate and fragmented heap of bodies and bowls on the beach. Abducted before she has identified herself, participating in the action and yet remaining unknown, the girl insists on remaining a riddle. We as readers are required to sympathize with the maiden and the young man—particularly with the beautiful girl—before we know who they are. We learn eventually how to name them. But Chariclea's parentage and inheritance are not explained to us until later—indeed, there is information she herself does not possess. We are marshaled into the novel having to take much on trust, and striving to unriddle what led to the mysterious first scene. Our first relation is to violence and mystery.

In Heliodorus's novel, we learn after other puzzling accounts, Chariclea is the white daughter of black African parents, King Hydaspes and his queen, Persinna. The mother bore the daughter and secretly gave her away, not acknowledging her existence to the child's father because the child was white, and would seem to accuse the mother, by her presence, of adultery. Denied her inheritance because she was the "wrong" color, Chariclea was adopted and even "wrongly" named after Charicles, her adoptive father. It is her task (though she does not know it at the outset) to vindicate her Ethiopian inheritance. Chariclea must return "home" to a foreign place and be reconciled with parents who do not even know she is alive, and who appear to be of a different race. The end of the novel represents, as it were, a becoming-black. Chariclea's task is to reconcile blackness and whiteness, to fulfill the prophecy:

Then shall the gods reward your pious vows,
And wreaths of triumph bind your sable brows.

(The 1789 translator in a sarcastic footnote registers the puzzle: "Why sable brows? . . . I am not obliged to explain oracles" [1:124].) The heroine must incarnate a blackness that is whiteness, a whiteness that is blackness. Incompatible racial identities are harmonized as the answer to the novel's oracular prophetic riddle. Hero and heroine will indeed arrive at the paradoxical region, the dark land of the Sun, and be given the prize that changes them: "white garlands on dusky brows," as Hadas translates it (λευκὸν ἐπὶ κροτάφων στέμμα μελαινομένων).[4] Heliodorus's novel hinges on that black/white opposition, his S/Z.

Frances Burney's novel is figurally self-conscious (to borrow the allegories permitted in modern criticism). Yet *The Wanderer* is certainly not self-conscious in the manner of Heliodorus, who insistently points to and jests about the "made-ness," the "written-ness," of his story, and suggests the literary habits it may be expected to assume. When, for instance, Theagenes complains of "the deity who persecutes us," who "makes sport, in short, with us and our fortunes, and gives them the appearance of a continually shifting scene, and sadly varied drama" (1:216), he is at one level referring to the author. The author is the hostile deity who persecutes the characters for sport, like the demonic sage enchanter complained of by Don Quixote. (Cervantes is probably the world's most attentive reader of Heliodorus.) There is, I think, a jest hidden behind the agitating dream of Charicles that Calasiris so soothingly interprets. Charicles dreams that he sees Apollo's eagle snatch his (adopted) daughter away from him and "bear her away to some corner of the earth, full of sooty and shadowy forms" (1789, 1:188). Charicles believes this means that Chariclea will die and go to Hades; Calasiris, lying, assures him the dream portends his daughter's marriage. We come to believe that the narrative logic demands that Char-iclea return to Ethiopia—a far land full of dark people, hence "dark and shadowy phantoms" (γῆς . . . ζοφώδεσί τισιν εἰδώλοις καὶ σκιώδεσι πλῆ-θον).[5] But there is another meaning as well. Chariclea is, after all, captured in the Apollonian art of writing, and must take her existence in and through the "shadowy phantoms" of the written word. She is condemned to be one of the εἴδωλα—not only phantasms or specters but also images in the mind. She is one of the *eidôla* of fancy, and leaves her "real" life as Charicles' daughter for the shady existence of a novelistic character, leav-ing Charicles as bereft as Keats's little white town, depopulated by the absence of citizens who became part of a work of art.

Richardson picks up some of the complicated jesting about the written, while avoiding any device that lets us dwell on Clarissa's unreality. Yet in a story in which all the characters are authors (for *Clarissa* is famously epis-tolary), the variations of point of view connect us with the idea of "written-ness." Lovelace takes upon himself the role of sage enchanter, consciously endeavoring to write Clarissa's story for her, and acting the part of the novelist, setting himself up as a "hostile deity" who will subject his lady to new trials. Like Heliodorus, he denies his heroine a tragic ending; Clarissa speaks in a "violent Tragedy speech" that amuses Love-lace (5:89), while Chariclea initially speaks in a tragic vein (ἐπετραγῴδει) not commensurate with the outcome of her story.

Burney avoids the direct question of authorial control and makes no such jokes about the structure of the novel. Yet she is quite willing to abandon "realism" for intermittent symbols, and she breaks her narrative up not only with puzzles but with puns. Her interest lies largely in the idea of woman's fate as something often determined, like what is conceived of as her nature, determined by cultural pressures that make a woman very difficult to see. Her novel works on edges, and deals with gaps and spaces—but in this, too, it adopts Heliodorus.

Heliodorus's novel opens on a seashore (τῷ πελάγει), a favorite setting for opening scenes or important occasions in novels; we often encounter a beach, a seastrand, a riverbank. Some sandy or muddy margin, some dirty place of clayey incarnation, seems sought by the novel (as a genre). In George Eliot's *Mill on the Floss,* for instance, the heroine and her narrator both stand at the beginning of the novel "at the edge of the water"; Maggie's mother complains of the child, "wanderin' up and down by the water, like a wild thing; she'll tumble in some day."[6] On the narrative bank, one is threatened by the humbling dirt of earthiness and by the hazards of launching out upon dangerous depths. Heliodorus insists on the violence of opening; we stand on a savage margin. *Clarissa* opens with great violence, with the fight between James Harlowe and Lovelace. James's passion is cooled "on seeing his blood gush plentifully down his arm" (1:2), but his father and uncles represent the crime it would be in *Clarissa* "to encourage a man, who is to wade into her favour . . . thro' the blood of her Brother" (1:3). The shore that is visibly bloody in Heliodorus becomes metaphorically so in *Clarissa,* but the blood and conflict, the violence and mystery, are literal again in *The Wanderer.* The novel begins with the sense of danger, with mystery, hostility, and multiple languages; here are its opening paragraphs:

During the dire reign of the terrific Robespierre, and in the dead of night, braving the cold, the darkness and the damps of December, some English passengers, in a small vessel, were preparing to glide silently from the coast of France, when a voice of keen distress resounded from the shore, imploring, in the French language, pity and admission.

The pilot quickened his arrangements for sailing; the passengers sought deeper concealment; but no answer was returned.

"O hear me!" cried the same voice, "for the love of Heaven, hear me!"

The pilot gruffly swore, and, repressing a young man who was rising, peremptorily ordered every one to keep still, at the hazard of discovery and destruction . . .

"Oh listen to my prayers!" was called out by the same voice, with increased, and even frightful energy; "Oh leave me not to be massacred!"

"Who's to pay for your safety?" muttered the pilot.

"I will!" cried the person whom he had already rebuffed, "I pledge myself for the cost and the consequence!"

"Be lured by no tricks"; said an elderly man, in English; "put off immediately, pilot."

The pilot was very ready to obey.

The supplications from the land were now sharpened into cries of agony, and the young man, catching the pilot by the arm, said eagerly, "'Tis the voice of a woman! where can be the danger? . . ."

"Take her in at your peril, pilot!" rejoined the elderly man.

Rage had elevated his voice; the petitioner heard it, and called—screamed, rather, for mercy. (1:1–3)[7]

At first we, like the passengers, see nothing, and hear only a voice—a voice speaking French. Only as it reiterates supplications can it be identified as "the voice of a woman." As it is identified its articulation ceases, and it is capable of forming expressive sounds rather than words: "cries of agony" and screams. This woman is implicated in whatever violence is natural to that shore, and she is certainly not in control of it, though there is a certain violence registered in herself. A slaughter seems to have been going on—people must have been "massacred," but we do not see the bodies, as we do in Heliodorus's opening paragraphs. Yet the mystery of the corpse-laden shore is unriddled for us in the first phrase of the novel's first sentence. This is a blood-soaked, corpse-laden shore because the action is set "during the dire reign of the terrific Robespierre." History explains—up to a point. The Terror is a phenomenon of history that all can identify, even if no one can fully explain it.

The screaming female is, after all, to be the heroine. She is taken aboard the vessel of escape, at the particular urging of the young man (Albert Harleigh, the novel's "hero"—of sorts). The woman taken aboard does not offer a clear outline to the view; she is a Chariclea obscured, as it were. She speaks, but some on board cannot understand her French language. She cannot at first be distinctly seen, and what can be made out is uninteresting: "There was just light enough to shew him a female in the most ordinary attire" (1:3). The young English lady among the passengers, Elinor Joddrel, the antiheroine (or secondary heroine) of the novel, begins to speculate on the riddle that this unknown young lady, this "Incognita," represents: "I wonder what sort of a dulcinea you have brought amongst us! though I really believe, you are such a complete knight-errant, that you would just as willingly find her a tawny Hottentot as a fair Circassian" (1:5). Elinor's gibe that Harleigh has a "dulcinea" refers to the beloved of Cervantes' Don Quixote, who is, as Don Quixote more than half admits, the product of his own imagination; this touch reminds us of the "madeness" of heroines, who are, after all, *eidôla* manufactured for the purpose of story.

Elinor's words are also prophetic, for as the day begins to dawn over the English Channel, the passengers begin to discern in the stranger further alarming manifestations of difference. This female may indeed be the "tawny Hottentot" rather than the "fair Circassian." When the unnamed woman takes off her gloves, she "exhibit[s] hands and arms of so dark a colour, that they might rather be styled black than brown." The "elderly man," rough Mr. Riley, asks the dark foreigner, "Pray, Mistress . . . what part of the world might you come from? The settlements in the West Indies? or somewhere off the coast of Africa?" (1:21).

Burney's as yet nameless heroine may be taken as a sort of Chariclea reversed. She seems at the outset to be an African, but is not. Chariclea's problem (from birth) is that she seems not to be an African, but is. Chariclea rises majestically upon the view of the criminal intruders who first see her, so that they wonder if she is a goddess. Burney's heroine looks at first not at all like a goddess, and her vulgar middle-class companions wonder if she is a housemaid. Chariclea has lived through what was apparently a major battle of some sort, and has escaped unscathed. Burney's Incognita has come from the scene of violence represented by France itself. (History, as Heliodorus suspected, provides all the horrifying excitement a story could want.) We see no symptoms of recent battle around the heroine of *The Wanderer,* and yet this girl seems wounded; she wears "a large black patch, that covered half her left cheek, and a broad black ribbon, which bound a bandage of cloth over the right side of her forehead" (1:22). These mystifying signs of pain elicit only comic speculation from the cruder passengers: "Why, Mistress, have you been trying your skill at fisty cuffs for the good of your nation? or only playing with kittens for your private diversion?" (1:23).

It can be said of Heliodorus's protagonist and Burney's that they are both unnamed in the sequence that introduces them, and that both are the objects of ruthless inspection. That last could be said of Clarissa, also—as it is said by Anna Howe in the first letter of the novel: "Every eye, in short, is upon you." Now "pushed into blaze," Clarissa is metaphorically watched "with the expectation of an example" (1:3–4). Both Chariclea and Burney's heroine prove to be exemplary, but the original gazers do not expect them to be so. Burney picks up, as it were, the strange humility and social unfixedness of Chariclea's position, while employing an emphatic contrast to the usual objects offered for reader gratification. We expect heroines to be beautiful and dazzling. Chariclea and Clarissa do dazzle us.

The heroine of *The Wanderer* may, however, be seen as borrowing in advance from Chariclea's other aspects. It is in the nature of Heliodoran heroines to go disguised at some point. Clarissa will eventually be disguised as a housemaid, and thus escape from the brothel. In disguising themselves, Burney's heroine, and Richardson's, may be seen as imitating Chariclea (among other fictional characters). Chariclea, in fact, does later go in exactly the same kind of disguise as Burney's distressed refugee. In the sixth book of the *Aethiopica,* Clarissa disguises herself by rubbing soot and mud on her face. (The translator of 1789 does not like these dirty facts, and merely says that the heroine "stained her cheeks with a composition prepared for that purpose, and threw an old and torn veil negligently over her face" [2:26]). The manuscripts leave it in doubt whether Heliodorus's heroine concealed one eye or both, but the old veil was not very clean. The hero and heroine, both in disguise, take their predicament in good humor: "When the metamorphosis was completed they could not help smiling at each other's appearance" (2:27).

In Burney's novel, the protagonist has no companion in her guising, and she is the occasion for the scornful pleasantries of others. Her strange attire declares her not a whole person, but rather an inarticulate or disarticulated ensemble. Nasty Mrs. Ireton sarcastically inquires "whether you always travel with that collection of bandages and patches? and of black and white outsides? or whether you sometimes change them for wooden legs and broken arms?" (1:84). As the Incognita reveals herself to be "fair" under the "black," the other characters are disconcerted. Metamorphosis means that sense impressions prove incorrect. Eyes are untrustworthy. Mrs. Ireton complains vigorously: "You have been bruised and beaten; and dirty and clean; and ragged and whole; and wounded and healed; and a European and a Creole, in less than a week. I suppose, next, you will dwindle into a dwarf; and then, perhaps, find some surprising contrivance to shoot up into a giantess. There is nothing that can be too much to expect from so great an adept in metamorphoses" (1:85).

This young woman seems capable of multiplicity; she reminds others uncomfortably of change and possibilities, just as her languages remind them of the desirability of being polyglot. Many of the English speak no other language than their own, and detest Frenchness, as they detest un-knowns. Like the metamorphosing Chariclea, this woman is a nameless riddle. She looks at first like a victim only, possessing none of the power that Chariclea the archer wields. We learn later, however, how she came to be in this plight. Much later—for we find that, as in the case of Helio-dorus's novel, we really begin *in medias res,* and long flashbacks are neces-sary, as in the *Aethiopica,* to tell us how the heroine came to be on that beach in such distress. The heroine came to be where she was because of her heroic deed in endeavoring to protect a man: her unofficial guardian, the bishop, the uncle of her best friend. The phrase "the good bishop" in the notes of the translator of 1789 refers to Heliodorus the author (1:245); in Burney's novel it is the unseen object of the heroine's self-sacrifice. This elder priestly character is definitely not a Calasiris, protector and spiritual father of Heliodorus's heroine. Unlike such Calasiris-like characters in eighteenth-century fiction (for example, Dr. Harrison in Fielding's *Amelia* [1751]), he offers no advice, and does not even appear until the end of the novel. Far from being of assistance, this substitute father is a responsibility and a burden to the heroine, who must preserve him at high cost to herself—including the cost of painful and mysterious discretion. The reader knows from the beginning that the mysterious female character is good, and that she is the heroine; yet the reader cannot explain who the heroine is or what may appropriately befall her.

In Heliodorus's novel also, the reader starts in a condition of unknowing, and is required to make judgments with incomplete information. In the *Aethiopica,* too, the reader's view is contaminated. We share the point of view with a band of (not very bright) brigands; in *The Wanderer,* we share it with the ship of fools. A construct of paradoxes, the émigrée is given a name, yet it is not a "real name" but a combination of syllables based on the two letters of the alphabet under which she receives letters: L.S. Misunderstanding, a character calls her "Ellis," and the name becomes both first and last name. In itself this no-name name seems like a riddle or pun. Elle is. She is.

As well as representing a riddle, the strange woman enacts one—a narrative riddle—during the voyage out: "the pilot proclaimed that they were half way over the straits. A general exclamation of joy now broke forth from all, while the new comer, suddenly casting something into the sea, ejaculated in French, 'Sink and be as nothing!' And then clasping her hands, added, 'Heaven be praised, 'tis gone for ever!'" (1:8). The elderly man asks outright, "Pray what have you thrown overboard, Mistress?" but goes "unanswered" (1:8–9). We are left to tease ourselves with the puzzle. What is it that a woman might want to throw into the deep of the sea, into the midst of that dark blank that separates two shores?

Another novel of antiquity begins with a sea scene, and a voyage. Achilles Tatius's *Clitophon and Leucippe* opens with the representation of Europa's story. In this famous ecphrasis, the narrator describes the picture showing Europa's maiden companions rushing to "the margin of the sea," while the bull "was painted in midsea, riding on the waves," the woman riding sidesaddle, traveling "as if on board a cruising ship, using her veil as a sail."[8] The veil that modestly conceals becomes an instrument of power, a means of escape and movement. The figure of Europa, who gives her name to such a diverse continent, is a figure of the Novel itself, of narrative and novel-making. Richardson uses the emblem of veiled Europa on her bull (not unlike the figure painted in words by Achilles Tatius) as a printer's ornament in *Clarissa.*[9] There it serves to foreshadow and comment on Lovelace's rape of Clarissa. The "rape of Europa" is not, however, a rape like Clarissa's, but a reincarnation, an exploration. It represents abandonment of the known margin, with Eros or desire of life leading the way. It is a figure of beginning.

Yet an emblem of rape of any kind, including the "rape of Europa," is dangerous to women. It calls for radical revision and reinterpretation. Richardson reinterprets by focusing his whole long novel on rape as fact and idea, pointing out what it means to men and women to live in a rape-culture such as ours, with its consequent devaluation of human beings. The heroines of the Greek novels are righteous virgins threatened by rape and reacting heroically against that threat; one sees clearly the connection between Richardson and Heliodorus on that score. In fact, Richardson is playing upon the reader's being accustomed to the quick saves and happy endings endemic to the Greek novel, with its scenes of sexual threat. The reader is so accustomed to "this sort of story" that a "happy ending" seems securely predictable—until we find out it is not going to happen.

Frances Burney's novel, the subtitle of which is *Female Difficulties,* likewise includes the sort of rape threats found in the Greek novel. The heroine's real name proves to be "Juliet," a name allying her to the Shakespearean heroine who evaded unwanted marriage and maintained her own choice of love through a sleight of *Scheintod.* Marriage as rape menaces Burney's heroine. The price of the bishop's life was Ellis-Juliet's marriage to Robespierre's brutal commissary. Escaping the loathsome husband, yet keeping the bishop alive by the force of the commissary's hope of her (and of her dowry), the heroine flees through a provincial English world. Seen from her ironic angle, complacent English society reveals its stultification, obtuseness, and powers of oppression. Ellis-Juliet is threatened by many dangers, as was Chariclea. (*Chariclea, or Female Difficulties?*) The threats to Burney's protagonist include an Arsacé in the jealous Elinor Joddrel—who is, however, no spoiled, exotic princess, but a lively young woman, bored with Sussex and fascinated, not without reason, by the new doctrines of the Rights of Man, and the Rights of Woman. Elinor, alas, can interpret these rights only as her own right to Albert Harleigh, as Arsacé thought she had a right to Theagenes. Harleigh, a much less forceful character than either of the women, is not even the second character in his own novel—but then, it is often remarked that Theagenes is barely the second character in his story.[10]

The most disagreeable character in Burney's novel, Mrs. Ireton, another Arsacé figure, has a summerhouse called "the Temple of the Sun." This strange structure mocks the Apollonian order, and reminds us of power; Mrs. Ireton is as powerful in her way as Robespierre is in his, and Robespierre's power can create "the shrine of unmeaning though ferocious cruelty" (5:78), the temple and theater of the scaffold and guillotine. The story that history books tell is the Apollonian history of control, the fictions that belong to the realm of the Temple of the Sun—as indeed they do in Heliodorus, where the temple in Ethiopia is designed for the offering of human sacrifices to Sun and Moon. It takes the gymnosophist at the end to persuade Hydaspes to put an end to human sacrifice.

The Wanderer is also a plea for an end to human sacrifice—not only the sacrifice of history's cruellest dramas of torture and execution, but the hidden, dull, old story of overworked and underpaid labor. Ellis-Juliet becomes one of the working poor, one of the nameless; as music teacher, companion, milliner, seamstress, teacher in a dame school, she plunges into the depths of the inarticulate, the unhistorical history of the working poor.

The realm of hidden history in Heliodoran fiction is always the realm of the displaced or wandering woman, whose lot it is to undergo enslavement, imprisonment, even the descent into the tomb. The life Ellis-Juliet leads opens to her eyes (and to the readers' eyes) the life that is as dull or invisible as the young woman herself, who was at first merely a scream from the shore that others wish not to heed. The most powerful argument for immortality, the heroine concludes, must be the sight of the inequity and suffering in this world, in the here and now, "oppression in the very face of liberty" (4:339).

The form of the novel first suggested by Heliodorus is to be widened, Burney's work suggests, by including what is usually ignored. The heroine's postconclusion wedding is here not of great significance. Richardson in *Clarissa* focused our attention so fully on his shining heroine and her demon lover that we could take her tragedy as a complete story. That story is so good and so powerful that it may make us look less at the world around the heroine than Richardson himself wishes; that at least is one construction that can be put on the pile of material Richardson wishes to add to the end of the book, after Clarissa's death. *The Wanderer* certainly does not allow us to look at the wedding as a full consummation of the story; the bonds that connect a Theagenes and a Chariclea have been loosened. Ellis-Juliet may be in love with Albert Harleigh, and he, in his timid, anxious way, in love with her, but she can get along without him. This is forcefully suggested by the riddle that takes so long to be answered in the narrative. "Sink and be as nothing!"

What was the object Ellis-Juliet threw overboard? The answer is "a wedding ring." Juliet threw off her false wedding ring (from the civil marriage to the vile commissary) once she was fairly launched on the deep—in an in-between place, equidistant from the hostile shores, in the middle of nowhere. At one level, the casting-off of the wedding ring can be viewed as a casting-off of the masculine story—the story of a woman as Heliodorus or Richardson might tell it. Eros is also found in this apparently antierotic gesture, casting off the notion of Woman as the object only of desire, the currency ("Ellis" = £sd?) as well as merchandise of bargain and sale. The heroine will not be passive. Here we have a new Europa coming from Europe and setting forth on some new voyage.

At the same time, the wedding ring thrown into the sea signifies that Ellis-Juliet weds the deeps, like a doge. Here is the figure of Europa the voyager without her taurine god. The possibilities for reconciliation must begin here, with the usual symbol of reconciliation thrown overboard.

There is no structure that will figure reconciliation, that will hold opposites together in concord and harmony. Heliodorus can end with a temple, a strong place, even though Hydaspes' temple needed the correction of wisdom, an enlightenment to bring it up to the level of the temple at Delphi, where the worship of Apollo has been (puzzlingly) tempered by worship of Artemis/Isis. In Richardson's novel, the temples (the churches) are strong structures with strange congregations—as at the service Lovelace attends at Saint Paul's (3:323–26).

The temple becomes Clarissa herself, as Lovelace intimates in a quotation from Dryden: "Mark her majestic fabric!—She's a temple / Sacred by birth, and built by hands divine" (3:329).[11] The last temple to appear in *Clarissa* is the church as place of burial, and we descend with the narrator and the heroine's corpse into the tomb that in this case (as not in the Greek novels) will truly confine forever the body of the heroine. It is as if Richardson were tightening the temple image found at the end of the *Aethiopica*—everything becomes firmly enclosed: "In that little space, said Mr. Mullins, is included all human excellence!" (8:89).

If the temple structure in Richardson becomes unduly tight, in Burney's novel it is deliberately loosened. Stonehenge is a ruin, with strong objects placed at intervals, objects that once might have made an enclosure but can do so no longer. Structure is done away with; there is only the ruined circle amid "unpeopled air, and uncultivated waste" (5:134). Stonehenge, which, as Sir Jaspar Herrington believes, was once a Druid temple, has lost its religious and hierarchical authority and has become a feminine place. The shape of the circle has been anticipated in the earlier figure of the *tombeau* that Ellis-Juliet's friend Gabriella made for her dead child: "a small elevation of earth, encircled by short sticks, intersected with rushes" (3:9). This is a place of the Mother, not a stone monument but a biodegradable little riddle, delicate, perishable, and humbly unauthoritarian. It is a place associated with the women and with the otherness of foreign language. (The conversation between Juliet and Gabriella beside this *tombeau* is conducted wholly in French.)

Circles are feminine, but Burney creates broken circles: tentative, unconstraining, incomplete. There is no assured figure for the reconciliation of opposites. Burney shows us that she desires reconciliation—the harmony of the enemies England and France. But this is a phenomenon not historically visible in 1794, or even in 1814. Burney wishes for an end to what Juliet calls "unmeaning though ferocious cruelty" (5:78), but Juliet cannot succeed like a gymnosophist in banishing human sacrifice. Heliodorus could end his story with reconciliation, πρὸς συμφωνίαν, "a pleasing concert at the last act and unravelment of this complicated story, where so many different interests were to meet, and so many contraries and improbabilities were to be explained and reconciled" (2:269).

Heliodorus proffers a satisfying figure in fulfillment of the riddling oracle:

> Then shall the gods reward your pious vows,
> And wreaths of triumph bind your sable brows.

Narrative completion is figured in the satisfactory complete circles of the crowns. Burney's intermittent circles have gaps for investigation. The important figures are of circles that do not enclose, and cannot be completed. The last word of Burney's novel is, significantly, "hope." It is not that the righteous virgin has not triumphed in Burney's story, as in that of Heliodorus. After her disguises and flights about England, and after all her hard work, Ellis-Juliet is delivered. The man who lays wrongful claim to her is killed by the revolution whose dirty work he did. The heroine's chastity is preserved; she may properly marry the (unsatisfactory) hero. Her birth is at last acknowledged by her father's family, and she will receive her rightful inheritance. All of this is very Heliodoran, surely. Yet Burney makes us feel the degree to which these happy points of fiction are fictitious. These are the *eidôla* required by the necessity of making endings. The true ending, with harmony between peoples and the social institution of justice, is as far off as ever. There is no mysterious syzygy of race and race, nation and nation, class and class. Despite the hopes of the characters, differences triumph still. Yet in raising the possibility of reconciliation, and in pointing to the severity of difference everywhere to be found in our harsh human history, Burney took more than a leaf from Heliodorus's book.

NOTES

1. "Advertisement" to *The Adventures of Theagenes and Chariclea: A Romance, Translated from the Greek of Heliodorus*, 2 vols. (London, 1789), 1:vi–vii. Quotations from this translation will be cited by volume and page in the text. I use this translation not because it is the best (for it certainly is not) but because it has a certain eighteenth-century charm, and there is the slender chance that Frances Burney herself read it. It might seem scholarly to use Underdowne, but later translations were the ones read in the eighteenth century; Richardson, for instance, could have read the translation by a "Person of Quality" and Nahum Tate, or the 1717 edition. For the Greek and for generally helpful material, I have drawn on R. M. Rattenbury and T. V. Lumb, eds., and J. Maillon, trans., *Les Ethiopiques*, 3 vols. (Paris, 1960).

2. For a discussion of Richardson's use of Sidney's *Arcadia* in *Pamela*, see G. Beer, "*Pamela*: Rethinking *Arcadia*," in *Samuel Richardson: Tercentenary Essays*, ed. M. A. Doody and P. Sabor (Cambridge, 1989), 23–29.

3. All references to Richardson's *Clarissa* are to the third edition of 1751 (8 vols.) as reproduced in *The Clarissa Project* under the general editorship of Florian Stuber (New York, 1990), cited by volume and page.

4. Heliodorus, *An Aethiopian Romance,* trans. M. Hadas (1957; reprint, Westport, Conn., 1976), 66. J. R. Morgan translates the last couplet of the oracular riddle as

> Where they will reap the reward of those whose lives are passed in virtue:
> A crown of white on brows of black.

See *An Ethiopian Story* in *Collected Ancient Greek Novels,* ed. B. P. Reardon (Berkeley and Los Angeles, 1989), 409.

5. Morgan, in Reardon, *Collected Ancient Greek Novels,* 437.

6. G. Eliot, *The Mill on the Floss,* ed. A. S. Byatt (Harmondsworth, 1979), 60.

7. F. Burney, *The Wanderer, or Female Difficulties,* 5 vols. (London, 1814), cited in the text by volume and page.

8. Achilles Tatius, *Leucippe and Clitophon,* trans. J. J. Winkler, in Reardon, *Collected Ancient Greek Novels,* 176–77.

9. The ornament appears at the end of the fifth volume. The figure is reproduced in Doody and Sabor, *Samuel Richardson,* 266, and in Stuber, *The Clarissa Project* 5:358.

10. "CHARICLIA is evidently the chief character of the ensuing Poem (for . . . I must call it so, tho' in Prose . . .) 'tis on her the Author bestows his utmost mastery, and in her he has drawn a perfect Character of the Social Virtues. THEAGENES has but the second place, and is every where subservient to the setting her Excellence in a more ingenuous Light" (translator of *The Adventures of Theagenes and Chariclia* [London, 1717]). But one might argue that Calasiris is the character in second place, and that Theagenes comes in a poor third. Even Cnemon, cowardly, kind, and talkative, vies with him. Incidentally, "a perfect Character of the Social Virtues" is a splendid eighteenth-century phrase that might well be used to describe Clarissa.

11. Lovelace is quoting from a description of the heroine in John Dryden's play *Don Sebastian, King of Portugal* (1690), 2.1. The idea of the body as a temple of the spirit goes back to antiquity, and is not improperly pursued in connection with ideas abroad in Christian and other circles during the age of Heliodorus. See P. Brown, *The Body and Society: Men, Women, and Sexual Renunciation in Early Christianity* (New York, 1988). Dryden himself approaches body and spirit from a Roman Catholic viewpoint, but he was a reader of Heliodoran novels, and almost inevitably of the *Aethiopica.*

PART III

Romance in
Its Ancient Landscape

CHAPTER SEVEN

Μῦθος οὐ λόγος: Longus's Lesbian Pastorals

B. P. Reardon

In 1988 the British Library mounted an exhibition on *Daphnis and Chloe,* with several dozen versions of the book on display; it was called *Daphnis and Chloe: The Markets and Metamorphoses of an Unknown Bestseller.*[1] Bestseller it certainly has been: according to Giles Barber's catalogue for the exhibition, in the five hundred years since the first printed reference to the work, by Poliziano in 1489, some five hundred different editions, translations, and adaptations have appeared, in various languages. An impressive average. Perhaps its perennial appeal is due in part to its tantalizing quality, for readings of it have varied widely. This chapter will look at some of them, and at some general questions of structure and interpretation.

First, the interpretation that sees the book as trivial, nothing more than a charming idyll, without pretensions, "a most sweet and pleasant pastoral romance for young ladies," as George Thornley's celebrated seventeenth-century translation puts it.[2] And there is a variant of this interpretation, which sees the story as trivial, certainly, but not at all charming; rather, unhealthy, indeed immoral, in its emphasis on the sexual experimentation its heroes participate in; as near-pornography, in fact, written by a mere littérateur, a "sophist" in a pejorative sense, quite lacking in sincerity. That was what Rohde thought.[3] Nowadays few people would go as far as Rohde did; but as we shall see, the questions he asked have not gone away. More recently we have seen interpretations of a quite different kind: *Daphnis and Chloe* as a serious novel, a religious novel, or a symbolic one. Or again, as above all an exercise in literary composition in which the plot is relatively unimportant, and whose effectiveness depends largely on the reader's receptiveness to the author's literary methods; the interest, that is, lies in the way themes are handled, the way models are used—the story is a piece of "literary creation," in short, in a quite narrowly defined sense.

The essential question, then, is: how serious is Longus? Should we set him beside Xenophon of Ephesus, who is serious to the point of being solemn? Or beside Achilles Tatius, who (in my view) is playing with the genre almost to the point of parody? I shall consider *Daphnis and Chloe* in a number of perspectives: symbolism and religious intentions, realism, literary execution; and also the literary tradition behind the story, the tradition of romance and the Hellenistic literary tradition. Whether he is serious or not, what Longus offers us is a novel, or looks like one; at any rate it is a story. If he has something to say to us, he communicates it to us by means of a δρᾶμα, a "thing done." He does it in his own manner. What is that "thing done," and what is that manner? I shall take each of the two basic interpretations—a serious novel, not a serious novel—using the analyses of H. H. O. Chalk and Rohde as a basis.[4]

First, the nonserious interpretation: *Daphnis and Chloe* has no deep meaning. In that case, the story is more pastoral than novel; in fact it contains little but the pastoral setting. As far as the human story is concerned, all that happens, essentially, is that two young people fall in love; at first they do not know what is happening to them, and they notoriously do not know what to do about it. But they learn what to do about it; and at the end this spiritual good fortune is translated into temporal good fortune as well, and they are enabled to marry. There is the skeleton of the story. The only essential element in the plot, between its beginning and its end, is the children's sexual ignorance. This scarcely credible ignorance is perhaps acceptable in an idyll, a fairyland. But it is the less readily acceptable in that it is made to carry too much weight; the ignorance becomes the action, an action that lasts for practically three books, out of four. It is still less acceptable in view of the way in which the author presents it to us, in that not only does the ignorance carry the weight of the plot, but the author actually emphasizes that ignorance. The explicit lesson of Philetas, at the beginning of book 2, is followed by four chapters which are just as explicit. They begin by underlining the topic—τὸ δὲ τρίτον ὤκνουν φάρμακον ἀποδυθέντες κατακλιθῆναι· θρασύτερον γὰρ οὐ μόνον παρθένων ἀλλὰ καὶ νέων αἰπόλων—"the third remedy—lying together naked—they shrank from trying; for that was too bold a step not just for young girls but for young goatherds too." And finally they very nearly short-circuit the whole story: ἴσως δ'ἄν τι καὶ τῶν ἀληθῶν ἔπραξαν, "perhaps they would really have got down to business," if something else had not happened. The something else—it is the war—keeps us waiting a whole book, and the onset of winter keeps us waiting several more chapters. In the middle of book 3 Daphnis and Chloe resume their experiments; and where other authors might talk vaguely about the birds and the bees, Longus and his characters talk not at all vaguely about sheep and goats. And once more they get nowhere. Immediately afterward, the experienced city-woman Lycaenion takes pity on Daphnis and teaches him what he needs to learn, τὰ ἔργα Ἔρωτος, the deeds of love. But even now the reader has a long time to wait before Longus finishes his story and calls it a day.

That is to say, the ignorance which is so charming at the beginning of the story is so heavily underlined that it becomes the subject of the main plot of the story; for although there are other incidents—Dorcon assaults Chloe in the disguise of a wolf, Daphnis is briefly captured by pirates, Chloe by soldiers—these incidents pale in comparison with Philetas, Lycaenion, and the goats. In any other Greek novel the pirates and so on would have been the principal elements in the action; in this one, they are upstaged by the erotic plot. But no laborious demonstration is really needed to come to the conclusion that there is something in this story that does not quite come off; and the thought comes readily to mind—it came to Rohde's—that this is titillating, a form of pornography. But even a pornographic work has a structure, and here it is the structure of *Daphnis and Chloe* that is in question. In the plot, regarded as a catalogue of "things done," there are only two essential stages: the situation in book 1, the birth of love; and the denouement in book 4, the marriage, which after all comprehends the erotic action (or rather inaction) of books 2 and 3. There is very little "novel" in this because there is very little δρᾶμα, drama, thing done. The incidents that in another story would constitute the drama—pirates, war—are left undeveloped; and the interior drama, the erotic progress, is limited to the discovery of the ὄνομα καὶ ἔργα Ἔρωτος, the name and deeds of love—where in a modern novel there would be, for instance, an altogether fuller psychological development. As a theme, the name and deeds of love are limited. In underlining the erotic progress, Longus has given it a lubricious aspect. Of course, one could accept the sexual experimentation; but let us remember that Longus is inventing, not reporting. Let us remember also that apart from Daphnis and Chloe his characters are not naive, or at least not in that sense. Lycaenion and Gnathon are not; the cowherds Dorcon and Lampis are not; and Chloe has ποικίλαι φωναί aimed at her, insinuations, double-edged remarks. In this respect their world is realistic enough.

Here we are in fact getting near to the crux of the matter. But for the moment let us consider the other interpretation: *Daphnis and Chloe* as a serious novel, Daphnis and Chloe—the characters—as symbols; the story has a message. What is the story talking about? Love; that is what Longus says in the preface: the story is an ἀνάθημα Ἔρωτι, an offering to Love, it will remind him who has loved and instruct him who has not. What Love is, we are told quite explicitly in the exposition of Philetas in 2.7: Love is a god, the god of creation, supreme, fecund, violent. Now if the story is nothing more than a divertissement, an entertainment, then all we have here is a commonplace, a topos: Love makes the world go round, and here it is making Daphnis and Chloe go round. But in Chalk's interpretation Love is much more than that. Love is the very subject of the story—Love, not Daphnis and Chloe; and it is the operation of Love that constitutes the actual body of the story, its plot. For Eros controls everything that happens, all events divine and human. The seasons progress, and Daphnis and Chloe progress with the seasons; and it is Eros who manages all this. If this is correct, the story does have a structure: the passing of the seasons *is* its structure. The erotic progress of the heroes is only one element in that structure; it is a manifestation, a function of the cycle of the seasons. Furthermore, this erotic progress is nothing less than an initiation into the mystery that Love constitutes. The candidates for initiation are at first in a state of innocence, which is ignorance—so their ignorance is necessary. They learn, partly from nature and partly from man, the name and deeds of Love; in so doing, they leave their condition of innocence, to attain, when they are married, the condition of experience; and so they are initiated.

There is drama enough here; continuous drama, things done. The natural setting—the time and place where the things done take place—is not just a setting, it *is* the action. The pastoral mechanism is not just decorative, it is functional. The main difficulty with the entertainment theory is that it does not take enough account of this pastoral mechanism, which is very complex if the story is merely a charming fantasy. If it can be shown that this mechanism is not purposeless, the story immediately becomes dynamic, since the mechanism is dynamic. It becomes, in fact, a novel; a drama, with not only a beginning and an end but a middle as well. In that case, one can see this novel in the same perspective as the novels of Xenophon Ephesius, for instance, or Achilles Tatius: in that the initial movement, the birth, growth, and nature of love—a movement which in Xenophon is brief and simplistic, and in Achilles Tatius is much more complex and profound—becomes, in *Daphnis and Chloe,* the entire story. It is the only thing that does have any importance for the hero and heroine. The rest—the adventures—is relatively unimportant. Longus reduces it, and includes it in the action it contributes to, namely the process whereby Daphnis and Chloe learn what love is; a process which in this case is complete only at the end of the story.

The principal element, then, in the pastoral mechanism is the progression of the seasons. Eros is the motor of this mechanism, an Eros who is older than Time and all-powerful, a primitive Eros who performs the functions of the Magna Mater—or, as Chalk says, of Dionysus. When the second autumn arrives, the "Manifestation of Dionysus," Dionysophanes, arrives with it. I cannot accept the attempt to assimilate practically every element in the story to elements of Dionysiac mystery-ritual; many of them have a much more natural explanation.[5] All the same, many of them do in fact have Dionysiac associations: pines, birds, springs, plants, music, things that occur on every page. Of course, it is hardly surprising to find things of that kind in a country story; but the associations are there, and are only reinforced by the name of Dionysophanes as the deus ex machina. These elements have not been given enough weight. They contribute, and are meant to contribute, to an impression that the story is impregnated with a theology, an "erotic theology" in the sense of a theology of Eros-Dionysus. It is Eros who makes shepherds of Daphnis and Chloe, who reunites them, who authorizes their marriage. Whether in his own person or through Pan and the Nymphs, Eros watches over everything they do, and sometimes he actually guides them. Eros sets in motion and controls the progress of Daphnis and Chloe as he sets in motion and controls the progress of the natural world that they are part of. It *is* initiation into his mysteries that we are concerned with, even if this is a metaphor. This religious vocabulary unquestionably does figure in the common imagination of the period.

The essential thing, then, is this conjunction of heroes and settings. The mechanism is not decorative; it is functional. This is Chalk's thesis. So far, one can agree. But this is where the problem arises: in this very action, this plot, this subject. It is not enough to say, as Longus does, that one is going to be symbolic, to write a symbolic story; one also has to do it successfully, to bring it off. If the subject of the story is Eros, Love, it ought not to be. The subject ought to be people, human beings. This remark calls for some elaboration.

What exactly is it that Longus is saying about Love? That Love is a cosmic force. Perhaps that had to be said. People do say it from time to time: Euripides did, and D. H. Lawrence. Love is not pretty, it is violent, it is not cozy; something of that kind. Perhaps it was particularly necessary to say it to novel-readers, or *romance*-readers, in the second century; even Chariton's Callirhoe, who knows very well that love is not cozy, wishes it were. Longus, let us say, is showing us Love as it really is. So, this is a lesson which applies to everybody: this is how Love is. Only it is hard to see how this lesson, in the form Longus gives it, can apply to any world other than the pastoral, exotic, unique world of this story, or even, within this pastoral world, to anybody but the children Daphnis and Chloe themselves. It is an entirely special case.

Does this special case instruct us? τὸν οὐκ ἐρασθέντα παιδεύσει, says Longus, "it will instruct him who has not loved." If he means that "this story, which does not claim to apply to everybody, will nonetheless recall to you what Love is—τὸν ἐρασθέντα ἀναμνήσει"—or, as the case may be, "will give you an initial lesson," that reduces its effect quite seriously. Perhaps that is the measure of the story: more than charming, but less than profound. Yet Longus uses ambitious terms: Eros, Dionysus, the natural world. Perhaps it is not an initial lesson, but a basic lesson? Love is sexual, fecund, energetic, it expresses itself in deeds and not just words or social conventions, it is not "respectable." In that case, *Daphnis and Chloe* is a treatise: Longus's treatise *On Love*. Certainly it is not really a representation, a mimesis, of people acting thus and thus in life, a μίμησις πράξεως—however serious, however σπουδαῖος, its subject may be. It is difficult to be moved by Daphnis and Chloe, the characters Daphnis and Chloe. They are really a bit insipid; they do not really display much character—much προαίρεσις, or human choice of action, to continue with Aristotelian vocabulary. They *are* children, when all is said and done; charming, yes, but only occasionally *sympathiques,* moving; when Chloe omits to tell Daphnis she has kissed his rival Dorcon might be one such occasion; another might be when Daphnis, after his lesson from Lycaenion, tells Chloe a white lie about saving the goose from the eagle. But we have seen that Daphnis and Chloe are not the real subject; the real subject is Love. Now, in a story in which there is a human action, a πρᾶξις, a drama, it surely is not natural for the main interest to lie anywhere other than in the action and in the human beings. That is the point of saying that the subject ought to be not Eros but people.

Of course, the reader's interest may lie in the adventures, if they are adventures that happen to people; and in this story they are. But if Love is a cosmic adventure, the human beings Daphnis and Chloe are not the only creatures to know Love, and they are not necessary to Love; the seasons would go on revolving, and the birds and the bees and the flowers and the sheep and the goats would go on doing what it is Eros makes them do, without Daphnis and Chloe. That is the whole point, one may say: it is a *cosmic* process; human beings are not all that matters, for nature. But can one tell stories about natural forces? Some myths do, certainly. But myths are usually peopled by superhuman characters. The dramatis personae of Longus's story are human; and the proper study of mankind is man.

At this point one may argue that this is symbolism; realism is not to be expected in the characters in a symbolic story. The element of plot, μῦθος, is slim, the element of ἦθος, character, is weak; but the element that matters is the thought; διάνοια, perhaps, in Aristotle, but here the abstract thought. But other characters in this story are real people. In fact all the other characters are; only Daphnis and Chloe are not. And we return here to the crux of the problem, the mixture of levels: the ideal side by side with the real. Daphnis and Chloe are the figures in an allegory, or perhaps, rather, the actors in a parable; but the rest, who provide them with their context, are presented realistically.

Is this simply a literary manner? A delicate manner, attractive, the opposite of solemn; a light touch? Longus's apologist Chalk, for instance, suggests that it is a matter of tension between real and ideal: "A tension is set up between real and ideal, which gives rise to a legitimate irony."[6] To be quite accurate, he is talking about the contrast between the town and the country, but the analysis will serve for the purpose here too. And as far as the two levels are concerned, we can think of *The Magic Flute*.

Explained in this way, the mixture works for much of the story. Dorcon's assault on Chloe, for example, can take place on two levels at once, Dorcon's and Daphnis's, because there is no conflict between the two interpretations of the incident. It can have one meaning for Dorcon and a different meaning for Daphnis, without the two interpretations clashing, without disturbing the attitude of either participant; and in that case the mixture does just create irony. Or the episode in which Chloe is carried off by the Methymneans: if we accept, as we may, that a second-century reader could have found Pan's intervention credible, then the incidents surrounding Chloe's escape—mysterious noises, anchors sticking fast, oars breaking, sheep howling like wolves, Pan's pipe—can appear perfectly natural to Chloe, wrapped as she is in the cocoon of divine protection, and utterly inexplicable to the Methymneans; and again, there is no conflict between these two reactions, the incidents become merely comic. There are minor incidents where the same happens. When in book 3 Daphnis finds the purse of money that enables him to become a formal suitor for Chloe, the realism of the stench of the dead dolphin near which he finds it highlights the naiveté that makes Daphnis thank the sea, without its being indispensable that we choose between the two interpretations. Again, in 1.23, describing the idyllic life that his heroes lead in the country, Longus suddenly brings in the flies that stop Chloe from curdling her goats' milk; but what that does is to let us measure the distance between idyll and reality—Longus does that quite often.

In all these cases, nothing depends on the relationship between the two levels. They can coexist without clashing, and without doing any harm to the plot, the action. But when it comes to the erotic episodes that are central to the action, the case is different. In these episodes there *is* conflict; the two levels do clash. "Ideal" behavior—idyllic, allegorical, symbolic—can hardly be realistic at the same time, where the principal junctures of the plot are at stake. For the purposes of the religious story, Daphnis and Chloe have to be innocent, and therefore ignorant. We accept that, for the purposes of the symbolism; we tell ourselves that after all, they are only children. But Longus insists on the reality of this ignorance; and he insists on it so much that we begin to look at the matter a little more closely. When we do that, we begin to have doubts. We find ourselves, ultimately, forced to *choose between* the two levels, since the one does, in this case, exclude the other; the story must take one of two paths, it cannot take both as it can in more minor details. It is not the ignorance itself that is hard to swallow; it is the way the author presents it. But he has so to present it if he wants to have any action, any "thing done" at all, on the human level;

because as Rohde said, his story contains little else that can count as action. We find ourselves, thus, back at Rohde's analysis. Rohde did put his finger on the problem after all. It does not disappear in the light of religious interpretation; any story has to have a structure. These episodes are crucial, and they appear to be either lubricious or miscalculated; no other explanation seems possible. To say, as Chalk does, that "when [Longus] is at his most serious he is simultaneously at his most cynically witty" is not an adequate resolution.[7] Mixing serious content and light manner is one thing; wanting to eat your cake and have it too is quite another. It is in this respect that the "serious" interpretation appears to be—not wrong, but inadequate.

But is it adequate to see the erotic episodes as either lubricious or miscalculated? We should look more closely at the element of calculation in *Daphnis and Chloe*. We have to take account, in the first place, of the contribution to the story of pastoral; more broadly, of the literary practice of the period—the period, we will recall, of Lucian and literary mimesis, of literary creation in the sense of recreation from familiar literary materials. We must take into account, in short, the way Longus uses literary, Hellenistic tradition and the tradition of the novel. But there is also Longus's own contribution.

Let us get back to the basic question implied by all of this: what *is Daphnis and Chloe*? Is it a "novel"? Or a "romance"? Or a "pastoral"? This is not quibbling over a label. Different forms have different functions, and at this point it is functions we are concerned with. The story is clearly in some degree both novel and pastoral, but this is not an answer; there can be no "average" between the two, there is no middle ground between them. Questions of form, in the sense of prose or verse, or length, are of no importance here. The essential thing is the function. The specific of pastoral is that it is metaphor: idealizing metaphor, of innocence, or virtue, or utopia, or escapism; or it can serve as a code. Whatever form it takes, pastoral represents a condition in which values are other than what they are in reality. Ideal values are certainly present in *Daphnis and Chloe;* they go together with the rustic setting. But there is more in it than that. There is also drama: the movement from innocence to experience. Pastoral is not propitious to drama, for drama would disturb its ideal world by changing it; Rohde saw that too. On the other hand, drama, action, *is* proper to the novel. Because this spiritual journey seems to me to be the major element in the story, I consider it basically a novel—but a novel with a pastoral, idealizing base.

Longus uses this pastoral base. It allows him to master two major structural elements that in the early Greek novels cause serious problems: the obligatory journey, with its adventures, and divine intervention. The journey becomes a journey in time, motivated and controlled no longer by unpredictable Chance, but by the progression of the seasons; and the gods are no longer external to the action, they are integral in it because they are integral in the country setting. And as a side effect of this pastoral contribution, the birth of love now takes up the entire story, and that offers interesting psychological possibilities. But this is also what embarrasses Longus. The pastoral contribution is not all positive. The writer has to prolong the metaphor, which as we have seen is idealizing, and does not lend itself readily to action, to πρᾶξις. The heroes do nothing. Yet Longus wants innocence to become experience; he wants to teach us what Love is; and Love, he says, is active. In presenting the action to us as the initiation of archetypal figures, he stays in his ideal world. But he cannot remain on that track; since his heroes have to take part in a human action too, the writer has at some point to change to the track proper to the novel.

In his attempt to make his heroes interesting, to make human beings of them—and also to avoid appearing heavy and pretentious, which with such a theme is a real danger—he makes his heroes and his story ambiguous; he adopts the light manner that offended Rohde. That is where the irony, the cynical wit that Chalk talks of, comes in. In fact, under cover of this irony, he leaves the idealizing pastoral track for the realistic novel track; innocence is faced with action. And he conceals his hand by throwing us a challenge: "Interpret that!" What we have here, then, is idealism, but with reservations: a degree of realism is necessitated by the action. What about the rest of the story, the elements that surround and highlight these ideal heroes? Are they realistic?

The setting is in some respects fairly realistic. For instance, the social position of the local aristocrat as represented by Dionysophanes corresponds well enough to the social structure of the area and period. The picture we get of his estate reflects the picture of land use that can be drawn from contemporary inscriptions; the topography of Lesbos corresponds quite well, although not exactly, to Longus's description of it.[8] All this is realistic enough, at any rate, to be recognizable to the average contemporary reader, although perhaps an inhabitant of the island could have picked holes in it. But if the setting is passably realistic, the action is less so; rather, what we are offered is the standard catalogue of conventional action in the novel—pirates, travels, war—but in the form of parody. What are the high points of the traditional novel? The birth of love: in Chariton, Xenophon, Heliodorus, it is dramatic and decisive, love at first sight, *le coup de foudre*. In Longus it is a much less dramatic business, and above all it is presented by the author with humor and irony. Or, pirates, and how to escape from them: instead of shipwrecks and scenes of terror, the air alive with melodramatic sentiment, what do we have in Longus? Cows following the music of a flute, "jumping into the sea lowing"—cows can swim, notice; oh yes, "cows never drown, unless their hooves get soft in the water and drop off . . ."[9] Or the travels: these travelers travel a few hundred yards, a mile or two at most. Or the war. Is it Egypt in revolt against Persia, as in Chariton? No; it is a comic-opera war, which breaks out because somebody steals a length of rope. We can call all this "realism" if we will; it is above all the realism of parody. This parody, this mocking, contributes a great deal to the light touch, the ironic, humorous tone that characterizes the whole story—*including its principal action.* Longus pretends not to take his own story seriously, frames it with parody; by doing that, he gets us to accept it the more readily.

It is just the same with the realism of Longus's dramatis personae. What he wants to do is to frame the main elements of his story—Daphnis and Chloe and their mystic progress—rather than to create characters. The standard novel is inhabited for the most part by conventional people: rather colorless young man and young woman, anxious parents, faithful companions, wily slaves, opportunist rivals, shameless women, noble seigneurs; the types of New Comedy. Longus owes even more to New Comedy than the other novel-authors do, and that is true of his characters: Lamon, Dionysophanes, Gnathon, Dorcon, Lycaenion do what they have to do to fit the plot, far more than they display προαίρεσις, choice of action. Menander, of course, could manage both. But Longus does not need thorough realism. In fact, he does not want it; it would militate against his purpose; the central story he is telling is an idealizing story.

So he calculates; he measures out his realism. He needs enough of it to bring out, by contrast, the central action and the central characters. He needs enough of it to point up his parable, to make it interesting and attractive. But not too much, because we do have to stay in an unreal world. Let us recall the examples quoted earlier: Dorcon's assault on Chloe; the seizure of Chloe by the Methymneans; Daphnis and the dolphin; Chloe as milkmaid and the flies. In these cases, we get a mixture of real and ideal in the same incidents. If we look at the narrative line, we find for instance the sequence of events in book 1: idyllic life, with poetic contest; shepherds pasturing their flocks; the growth of love—followed by the relative realism of Dorcon and the pirates. Or in book 2: Philetas's mythic lesson, experiments that almost become realistic, followed by the irruption into this ideal world of the real men of Methymna. Throughout, Longus is calculating. As he calculates the disposition of episodes within given stages of his work, so too does he calculate the overall economy of the story. With the seduction of Daphnis by Lycaenion, halfway through book 3, Longus passes definitively from idyllic track to realistic track, and the content and whole tone change notably. The major action in the hero's individual spiritual progress is over, and from now on the action of the story becomes almost wholly New Comedy (with occasional plaintive reminders of the idyll). The very style is more straightforward; no longer do we find the leisurely, elaborate tricolon structures that characterize earlier, pastoral scenes.[10] It would be interesting to apply to Longus the statistical method that Hägg uses to analyze the narrative technique of Chariton, Xenophon, and Achilles Tatius.[11] It would show a clear difference between the first part of the story and the ending.

The most important realistic element is the city, the city and the people who live in it, or come from it; the natural contrast for the life of the country. Eros, the principal force in the psychological action, manifests himself in the country; but it is the town that is responsible for the events in the social action that lead to the story's happy ending: that is, the exposure of the children, the Methymnean incursion, the contribution made by the city-woman Lycaenion to Daphnis's progress, the arrival on the scene of Dionysophanes, which results in the recognition of the children. That is to say, it is the city that imposes form on the story, form in an Aristotelian sense, that realizes its potential; that realizes, in fact, the ideal. But Dionysophanes, Lycaenion, Gnathon themselves remain types; they are there to contribute to a situation, and it is the situation, a situation created by the author, that dominates.

Realism in Longus, that is, is essentially a literary means of attaining a highly literary end. That end is to highlight the parable, not to represent people in action, μιμεῖσθαι πράττοντας. Realism is one element among others in the story's *mise en oeuvre,* its literary execution. The *mise en oeuvre* is more important in this novel than in others, in that there is less drama in its action than there is in others. Everything hangs on the author's skill. This is the point at which, and the reason for which, one must turn to the *mise en oeuvre,* those elements which Rohde would have called "literary decoration," and which in Chalk's analysis are integral in the story. Chalk pointed out that the text typically proceeds by a series of triptychs: in each triptych Longus sets out a description of the season, the reaction of the lovers to the season, and the events arising from the season; that is, setting, state of mind, and action. This entails description of the pastoral setting, the deployment of bucolic motifs and Dionysiac motifs, the disposition of numerous topoi, the narration of incidents; the *mise en oeuvre,* in short. The literary execution, in *Daphnis and Chloe,* is emphatically not a mere accompaniment of the action, or a substitute for it. It is what situates it and energizes it. The "how" is quite as important as the "what." Longus is after all a contemporary of Lucian, Achilles Tatius, Philostratus.

The case is just the same for the story's main action, the erotic progress. That action really is extremely slender. Longus disguises just how slender it is by creating his setting carefully and linking it to the action; by telling his story unhurriedly; by including in it piquant adventures, picturesque episodes, intrigues, descriptions, myths. But at the end of it all he has sooner or later to turn to the action; he has to dispose it within the story, and narrate it. The truth is that there is little to tell. But the action cannot disappear totally. It has to be seen to be there, however briefly. And since this is so, here too everything hangs on the "how," on the author's attitude. What is that attitude? After all this, is this a serious novel? Is Longus serious?

Yes; after his fashion. One is tempted to call the work a fairy story written by a Nabokov. It is something less than a novel, perhaps; Eros has made a μῦθος of Chloe, a fable—as Longus predicts, in 2.27. In 2.7 he tells us that the children understood Philetas's story, which is their story, as μῦθος οὐ λόγος: a fable, not a rational account; an echo of Plato, of course, as the book is replete with echoes of earlier writers. There are elements in *Daphnis and Chloe* of Cinderella, of Snow White: their innocence, impenetrable to outsiders without innocence; idealism in the principal characters, despite the realism of the ugly sisters and wicked barons. Like Cinderella, Daphnis and Chloe are divinely protected, untouchable, because they are innocent. But for all that, the story does have another dimension. It would tell us what Love is; that is serious enough.

Only, the manner is not. Longus disguises his enthusiasm. He is constantly retreating from pretension, guarded, constantly putting the ball in the reader's court: deconstructing himself. He gave us fair warning in the proem, before he even started on his story: ἡμῖν δὲ ὁ θεὸς παράσχοι σωφρονοῦσι τὰ τῶν ἄλλων γράφειν—"Help me that God," as Thornley puts it, "to write the passions of others; and while I write, keep me in my own right wits." That is what Rohde, with his background, could not understand: that distance, that irony, that ambivalence. We, in the twentieth century, are better fitted to understand. Like Longus, we have seen enough drama. In short, the story will not work on only one level. It limps here and there, but Longus is well aware of that. He does what he can about it; then he withdraws. He has done what he said he would do: τὸν ἐρασθέντα ἀναμνήσει, τὸν οὐκ ἐρασθέντα παιδεύσει: remind him who has loved, and instruct him who has not. He has told us what Love is. We must make what we can of it.

NOTES

1. October 1988–January 1989. See G. Barber, *Daphnis and Chloe: The Markets and Metamorphoses of an Unknown Bestseller,* Panizzi Lectures, British Library (London, 1989).

2. The translation, revised by J. M. Edmonds, is published in the Loeb edition of Longus by Edmonds (London, 1916). Perhaps, in so describing the story in 1659, Thornley had one eye on Puritan sensibilities.

3. E. Rohde, *Der griechische Roman und seine Vorläufer* (Leipzig, 1876). This work dominated scholarship on the Greek novel for a century; it was reedited, with an

important foreword, by W. Schmid in 1914 (3d ed., Leipzig, the original pagination being indicated in the margin), and reissued with an additional preface by K. Kerényi (4th ed., reprint, Hildesheim, 1960; 5th ed., Hildesheim, 1974).

4. H. H. O. Chalk, "Eros and the Lesbian Pastorals of Longos," *Journal of Hellenic Studies* 80 (1960): 32–51. For Longus in general, see particularly R. L. Hunter, *A Study of "Daphnis and Chloe"* (Cambridge, 1983), which gives a useful lead to the quite extensive bibliography. A valuable general study, to which I here acknowledge a substantial debt, is W. E. McCulloh, *Longus,* Twayne's World Authors Series (New York, 1970). The standard text is the Teubner of M. D. Reeve (Leipzig, 1982); there is also a recent Budé edition by J. R. Vieillefond (Paris, 1987). The most recent English translation is by C. Gill in *Collected Ancient Greek Novels,* ed. B. P. Reardon (Berkeley and Los Angeles, 1989).

5. R. Merkelbach, *Roman und Mysterium in der Antike* (Munich, 1962); on this book, see, e.g., the criticisms by R. Turcan, "Le roman 'initiatique': A propos d'un livre récent," *Revue de l'Histoire des Religions* 163 (1963): 149–99 (rejecting the general thesis that almost all the ancient novels are "mystery-texts" based on mystery cults), and A. Geyer, "Roman und Mysterienritual: Zum Problem eines Bezugs zum dionysischen Mysterienritual im Roman des Longos," *Würzburger Jahrbücher für die Altertumswissenschaft,* n.s. 3 (1977): 176–96 (some novels—e.g., Apuleius's *Metamorphoses*—are mystery-texts, but *Daphnis and Chloe* is not). Most recently, Merkelbach has developed the thesis, for *Daphnis and Chloe,* to the point of attempting a reconstruction from the novel of the (Dionysiac) mysteries (in the period of the Roman Empire, when they were substantially different from the cult of Dionysus in the classical period); see his *Die Hirten des Dionysos: Die Dionysos-mysterien der römischen Kaiserzeit und der bukolische Roman des Longus* (Stuttgart, 1988).

6. Chalk, "Eros," 49.

7. Ibid.

8. Social structure and land use: E. L. Bowie, "The Novels and the Real World," in *Erotica Antiqua: Acta of the International Conference on the Ancient Novel,* ed. B. P. Reardon (Bangor, Wales, 1977), 91–96, esp. 93. Topography: H. J. Mason, "Longus and the Topography of Lesbos," *Transactions of the American Philological Association* 109 (1979): 149–63; P. Green, "Longus, Antiphon, and the Topography of Lesbos," *Journal of Hellenic Studies* 102 (1982): 210–14; Bowie, "Novels," 94, and most recently Bowie, "Theocritus' Seventh *Idyll,* Philetas and Longus," *Classical Quarterly* 35 (1985): 67–91. See also, on Longus's "realism," A. M. Scarcella, *La Lesbo di Longo Sofista* (Rome, 1968).

9. Longus 1.30.6; "obviously an interpolation," says Dalmeyda in the old Budé edition (Paris, 1934—now replaced; see n. 4 above). I doubt it.

10. L. Castiglioni, "Stilo e testo del romanzo pastorale di Longo," *Rendiconti del Istituto Lombardo* 61 (1928): 203–23.

11. T. Hägg, *Narrative Technique in Ancient Greek Romances* (Stockholm, 1971).

CHAPTER EIGHT

Gardens of Desire in Longus's *Daphnis and Chloe:* Nature, Art, and Imitation

Froma I. Zeitlin

Aside from, or perhaps because of, its status as our only surviving specimen of pastoral romance, the most striking feature of *Daphnis and Chloe* is its conceptual originality in the fashioning of its erotic tale.[1] That originality lies especially in two disparate features and in the relations between them: the motivation given at the outset for the production of the work, and the subject of the work itself. For the first, the proem tells us that the entire story purports to be an ecphrasis of a painting the author came upon one day in a sacred grove of the Nymphs on the island of Lesbos, which so charmed him by the aesthetics of its graphic beauty and the appeal of its erotic story (the most beautiful sight he had ever seen) that he was seized with desire (*pothos*) to rival it in a narrative. For the second, the work takes as its subject the erotic education of a youthful pastoral pair, who, having fallen into the condition of desire we identify as love, display an unimaginably "natural" innocence with regard to matters of sex. These two unusual elements, situated at the extremes of sophistication and naiveté, are also conjoined under the more extensive theme of mimetic desire. Together they elevate learning and knowing about eros to an all-pervasive influence in the novel—for those within it (the characters) and for those without (both narrator and reader)—and link up in an intricate dialogue with questions of nature and convention, nature and culture, and nature and art.

By taking a painting as a frame and a motive for the romantic tale, the text brings to the fore those traditional associations of pleasure and persuasive charm (*terpsis, thelxis, peithô*) that from Homer on unite eros and art in their mutual aesthetic concern with the beautiful (*to kalon*) and its seductive and mesmerizing effects (*thauma*) on the beholder. In this convergence, the work looks back to what has come before it; yet the value and power it gives to descriptions of works of art, and to the ecphrastic impulse in particular, mark the text as a child of its time, sharing an aesthetic that belongs to the Second Sophistic, whose echoes we find in such authors as the two Philostrati, Callistratus, Lucian, and other writers of romance.

Even so, the shift of the traditional ecphrasis from the auxiliary function it has in romance fiction to the underlying basis of the narrative, and from a short embedded piece to an entire novel,[2] suggests a bolder, more self-conscious experiment conducted on two fronts. Along with its unusual claim to be an authoritative treatise on eros, the text has something important to teach us not only about the imaginative and perceptual components of the experience that the Greeks constructed and represented as love, but also about the role of art and artifice within the larger cultural system during an era in which it was said by some that while visual art imitates nature, nature also imitates art. This reversal of terms is a highly sophistic conceit, but it demonstrates the extent to which the power of pictorial images was felt to enrapture both the eye and the heart. When Longus's narrator declares that his work "will remind [*anamnêsei*] the one who has loved and teach in advance [*propaideusei*] the one who has not," it is because he insists that "no one has ever escaped eros, nor ever will so long as beauty [*kallos*] exists and there are eyes to see." There is no need to specify what the beloved object of the adoring gaze may be; it may be person, painting, or even the entire landscape of the *locus amoenus* itself. All are subsumed under the heading of visual enthrallment and irresistible desire.

Yet because the text purports to rival the painting and the painting is deemed more lovely than the grove in which it is found, the pairing of art and nature, as well as of art and eros, is intersected by yet another relation—that between the plastic arts and literature (or art and art), between the eye and the voice, the image and the word. This is, after all, what instigates the desire of the viewer to tell the tale. The viewer's desire is therefore also a desire for mimesis, and this factor raises yet another set of questions, also current in Longus's day, with regard to the uses of imitation—both as to its status with respect to the "real" and as to its validity as an enterprise that emulates earlier models. What best bridges the two worlds of "nature" and "art" is the double status of imitation—as a natural means of learning, and also as a high display of the sophistic aesthetic.

Any far-ranging exploration of this intricate web of relations is beyond the scope of this chapter. My aim is to examine certain crucial moments in the work where the experimental nature of the text as a theorem of its own underlying premises seems most apparent, starting with the proem. I propose to consider the status of the narrator in the text as a composite and novel figure: a sophist rhetorician who would match the *graphê* of his writing to the *graphê* of the painting he sees, a man of the city who would insinuate himself into the pastoral milieu, a new kind of *praeceptor amoris* borrowed from the world of lyric,[3] and a new kind of erotic rival in the genre of romance. The desire of the author-spectator to imitate the beauties of the erotic painting he sees leads in turn to the problematics of imitation and mimetic theory, the site where art and nature meet.

I will then take up two other significant examples of the narrator's pictorial (and rhetorical) skills: the description in the second book of the garden of eros that belongs to the old herder-gardener-musician-poet Philetas (2.3–7) and that of the grand *paradeisos,* the garden park that is the property of the urban gentleman Dionysophanes, which, introduced at the beginning of the fourth and final book (4.2–4), serves as the theater for the denouement. In these spaces, erotic and aesthetic elements are most closely intertwined: both gardens are precisely situated at crucial moments in the narrative as sequential models of the children's erotic development. These garden descriptions invite the reader to enjoy their horticultural charms as specimens of expert rhetorical display. They may also be read as spatialized models of the text in the two phases of its development: the first, a site of innocent and private play, embedded in a traditional pastoral milieu; the second, a spectacle for others to behold and a comic stage on which may be openly enacted a theatrical version of a city's pastoral desire.

PROEM

"One day while hunting on the island of Lesbos, I chanced upon the most beautiful sight [*theama*] I had ever seen in a grove of the Nymphs." The object that so excited the narrator's admiration was "an image inscribed [*eikonos graphên*], a narrative of desire [*historian erôtos*]." "The grove was also beautiful [*kalon*]," he admits, with its trees, flowers, and nourishing spring. "But the painting was more delightful [*terpnotera*] still," both for its extraordinary artistic skills (*perittên . . . technên*) and its depiction of an erotic story (*tuchên erôtikên*).

The result was that many, even strangers, were lured by the reputation of the place, "suppliants [*hiketai*] of the Nymphs and spectators [*theatai*] of the painted image [*eikonos*]. On it were depicted women giving birth [*tiktousai*] and others dressing the babies in swaddling clothes [*kosmousai*], children exposed [*ekkeimena*], herding animals nourishing them [*trephonta*], herdsmen taking them up [*anairoumenoi*], young ones placed together (or perhaps making a compact [*sunithemenoi*]), incursion of pirates [*katadromê*], assault of enemies [*embolê*]. And many other things I saw," he says, "and everything pertained to eros [*panta erotika*], and as I watched and wondered [*thaumasanta*], a desire [*pothos*] seized me to 'counterscribe the painting' [*antigrapsai têi graphê*]" (*graphê* meaning both writing and painting).

"I searched out an interpreter of the painting [an exegete], I carefully crafted [*exeponêsamên*] four books," those we are about to read. Their purpose: "a dedicatory offering [*anathêma*] to Eros, the Nymphs, and Pan, and also a delightful possession [*ktêma terpnon*] for all humankind. It will heal the [love]sick and comfort the sufferer [in love], remind [*anamnêsei*] the one who has loved and teach in advance [*propaideusei*] the one who has not." Following his declaration about the universality of love ("no one has ever escaped eros"), he concludes: "I pray that the god [Eros] may grant me to write the love story of others and yet remain in possession of my senses and sobriety [*sôphrosunê*]." Such is the power of what he is about to relate that he needs assistance from Eros not to succumb to the spell of overmastering desire in reanimating the desires of others.

The proem is a tantalizing self-reflexive exercise, an extended conceit that blends and reorganizes the rhetorical and romantic conventions of the ecphrasis through displacement and inversion of the typical relations between viewer and viewed. In the genre of romance the spectators who come upon erotic paintings in the midst of a love story are usually themselves lovers, who subjectively react to the themes of the paintings they see as pertinent to their own amorous conditions. Sophistic author-viewers, however, have a different agenda in their contemplation of works of art: mimetic (to compete with the power of pictorial images through verbal means) and didactic (to use description in order to make some moral or aesthetic point).[4] Longus's proem thus displaces the lover's encounter with erotic painting onto that of the rhetorical viewer, in the first instance, and in the second, substitutes a painting for a person as the visual initiator of erotic desire.

Under the sensuous spell of the painting, this spectator does not react by seizing and carrying off the object of his affections, as a character in romance might do. Rather, his infatuation with the painting makes him an aesthetic rival, aroused by a yearning to match and surpass another's *graphêsis* in a contest of word over image. *Zêlosis* is the general technical term in ancient literary theory for the idea of creative rivalry with the model.[5] But in Longus's time the erotic nature of this rivalry is more directly specified as the figurative analogy that informs the aesthetic sensibility of the cultivated person and determines, even requires, his or her worshipful response to visual beauty, as exemplified in Lucian's treatise *De domo*. Lucian's concern is with oratory, and the beauty he confronts is that of a gorgeous house. The speaker will try to "become part of the beauty [*meros tou kallous . . . genesthai*]" by actually performing in it. To go away speechless after merely looking at the splendor of the place "would not be the conduct of a connoisseur [*philokalou*] nor of one in love with the most beautiful things [*peri ta eumorphôtata erôtikou*]."[6] An ordinary visitor (*idiôtês*) gapes and is mute. "But when a man of culture [*pepaideumenos*] beholds beautiful things, he will not be content . . . to harvest their charm [*to terpnon*] with his eyes alone, and will not endure to be a silent spectator [*aphonos theatês*] of their beauty; he will do all he can to linger there and make some return for the spectacle in speech [*logôi ameipsasthai tên thean*]" (1–2; trans. M. Harmon). "Antigraphic" desire thus poses as a form of courtly homage to the beauty of the beloved object, a gift given in exchange for the pleasures of viewing.

The erotic theme of the beautiful painting, however, turns the rhetorician's trope back on itself to confront a literal version of the artist (and the author-connoisseur) as a lover of beauty. One implication of this relation is that the mimetic ambitions of the author must now expose him to critical judgment from the reader, not only on the merits of his erotic tale but also on the aesthetic quality of its representation. A second implication follows from the central notion that this "lover of beauty" takes the painting as the source for his erotodidactic treatise on "the beauty of love." The authority he claims can be referred to the most conventional cultural questions asked about the status of art. Is it superior or inferior to reality? Is it only an imitation, lacking the immediacy of experience, or is it something that transcends experience, essentializes it, and makes the work available as a permanent possession whose power can be disseminated to others and for always? Furthermore, is the boundary between the two domains truly impassable—or are there crossings at certain strategic points where space opens up for experimental play with the usual categories of perception?[7]

The narrator is last in the chain of transmission from what lies behind the story as a lived reality, to the painting as its commemoration, to the local exegete who can tell the tale. As a true history, which the phrase *historia erôtos* itself suggests, along with the Thucydidean echo of *ktêma* (*eis aei*), possession (for all time),[8] the painting is already the stand-in for an eyewitness report, backed up by an exegete who can explain the facts. But the representation is only a mute reminder of something vital that happened in the past. As erotic representations, both the picture and the narrative may be substitutes for the "real thing." However, the story, imitating the painting, that the author is about to tell will itself have a mimetic effect on others. This is the power commonly granted to erotic fiction. It is supported by the narrator's closing plea for *sôphrosunê* in writing his erotic tale of others' loves: "For love stories [*logos erôtikos*]," declares the lovesick narrator in Achilles Tatius (1.5–6), "are the very fuel of desire [*hupekkauma . . . epithumias*]; and however much a man may school himself to continence [*eis sôphrosunên*], by the force of example he is stimulated to imitate it [*tôi paradeigmati pros tên mimesin erethizetai*]" (trans. S. Gaselee). But by representing his story as a paradigmatic "lesson in love" meant for all ("for no one has ever escaped eros, nor ever will") and himself as a species of *praeceptor amoris*,[9] Longus's narrator raises mimesis to another level, since the tale of erotic education is designed as a practical treatise—to remind (*anamnêsei*) the one who has loved and to teach in advance (*propaideusei*) the one who has not.

Here, then, is an important convergence between the narrator's purpose for the reader in the proem and for those inside the text—a process of education, learning, and discovery, either for the first or second time, at whatever level the gap in knowledge may allow between the most sophisticated lover (of persons and texts) and the one as yet untutored. As the narrator imitates the painting, and the narrative works its mimetic effects on its readers, so the premise of the work is that children learn about eros through mimesis. The text shows education as a prolonged and varied set of exercises in imitation that allows one to discover the world, the self, and the other by learning what can and ought to be imitated—and also what cannot.[10]

IMITATION

Aristotle remarks in the *Poetics* that "imitation is natural to us from childhood and we learn first by imitation." At the same time, he declares, "it is also natural for all to delight in works of imitation on the grounds that both experiences are forms of learning which give us pleasure" (*Poetics* 144b. 5–9). Elaborating further in the *Rhetoric* when he speaks of the nature of pleasure, Aristotle includes the experiences of eros and caps his discussion with the assertion that "we gain pleasure from learning things and wondering at things also present. Wondering [*thauma*] implies the desire of learning, so that the object of wonder is an object of desire, while in learning one is brought into one's natural condition . . . Again since learning and wondering are pleasant, it follows that such things as are acts of imitation must be pleasant—for instance, painting, sculpture, poetry, and every product of skillful imitation," not "because the object of imitation is pleasant in itself," but because considering the relation between the original and the copy stimulates the pleasure of inferring (*syllogismos*) (*Rhetoric* 1.11.1370a21–70b23).

In Longus's work, mimesis is not only an innocent and natural way of learning (in the Aristotelian sense), either as an essential activity for the maturation of children or as a source of cultural appreciation for artistic skill. The narrator's desire ushers us immediately into the whole legacy of mimetic theory he has inherited, drawn from rhetorical, philosophical, aesthetic, and educational ideas that were refined and increasingly valorized over the centuries. Two main strands can be disengaged and are applicable both to the education of children and to the production and enjoyment of art: the first is a concept of imitation as a creative enhancement of nature, describing a relationship to a "reality" outside itself. The second, current in Longus's time, insists on looking back for imitation to earlier models whose authority and value have been established in the past.[11] In the first case, the object of imitation is nature; in the second case it is art, the concept that prevailed in Longus's time. What, after all, is the Second Sophistic, that cultural renaissance of Greek letters, if not a renewed creative energy directed toward highly skilled mimetic reorderings and ambitious emulations of classical and Hellenistic types?[12] For example, Longus translated bucolic poetic diction into prose, but even here, his innovation already had an antecedent in the techniques of the fifth-century B.C. sophist, Gorgias, while the simple style of the narrative is the so-called Attic style that has its model in the prose of the same classical period.

The supreme art of Longus consists in a texture and composition that cunningly interweave imitations of many kinds, from many sources, especially Homer, Theocritus, and Sappho.[13] Even here, Longus may be said to be imitating the pastoral genre, which showed itself capable, as one critic remarks, of "absorbing a wide range of previous literary work and of blurring the distinction between creation and imitation. As a form of original creation, the pastoral underlines the fact that all exists with reference to other works of literature, and not as an unmediated representation of reality."[14] The text of Longus is almost entirely mimetic, a hallucinating echo text that is constituted as a secondary or even tertiary signifying system. The pleasures of the text are thereby doubled as the reader is asked to view through two lenses: that of the naive child whose primary learning provides the plot of the story, and that of the sophisticated voyeur who is permitted to participate in both domains of perception.

The delight of recollection refers not only to one who has loved but to one who has loved letters, rekindling a knowledge and sensation both literary and erotic.[15] In fact, the activities are not unrelated: readers will recall subjective associations connected with *their* education in both love and letters. Recognition of this highly conventional system implies more than a "tension between *physis* [nature] and *technê* [art] that is reflected in the very artificial form in which the 'natural' education of the children is described."[16] Rather, the boldness of Longus's experiment suggests that at a certain level of analysis, love and letters are inseparable, that one's only means for apprehending any experience of eros is already entirely shaped and determined by the cultural system of representations, especially stories about love. As the children speak the language that the narrator writes and live in the spatial landscape he creates, the problematic interplay between nature and art comes alive. If, by the premises of the novel, the children are doing what comes naturally, then when they engage in such pastoral activities as comparing each other to berries or myrtles (1.24), pelting each other with apples, wishing to be the panpipe so that the other might play upon the beloved (1.14.3), imitating the nightingale in their singing, or feeling the first pangs of love in the springtime of the flowers, then a curious set of contradictory processes is set in seesaw motion in the mind of the reader, one now gaining, now losing ascendancy: are these conventions possibly rooted in nature, or (quite the reverse) is our perception of nature merely convention?

The second alternative places the emphasis on artifice and cultural rule making in which art and letters shape the figure of the winged Eros, with the result that his personal appearances in the work bring aesthetic and even comic delight to the educated reader, who recognizes him. The first reaction, however, which responds to the psychological astuteness of the text, gives rise to a peculiar sensation that there, at the root of the pastoral ideal, the conventions of language and erotic behavior are renaturalized. Children naturally imitate and naturally invent, their creative powers unhampered by rigid codes and too much knowledge—yet in this case they "naturally" reproduce those codes. Thus even as their eros renews and recreates the world in a romantic haze, what Daphnis and Chloe say and do while innocently playing in the green spaces where they belong regrounds sexuality in nature and also rejuvenates the inherited systems of language and gesture, as well as the arts of music and dance, which they spontaneously improvise, as when they mime the myth of Pan and Syrinx in appropriate dance at the end of book 2 (2.37.1).[17]

The idea of mimesis works at yet another level. The narrator uses stylistic, compositional, and narrative devices that, recognizably skillful though they may be, paradoxically sustain the mimetic illusion of a "natural" world of consonant harmony and organic eros. This happens because the literary and rhetorical conventions of the text are consonant with what the text aims to represent in the construction of its tale. For example, the temporal progression of the plot, as many have pointed out, conforms to the most natural chronological scheme in that it simply "uses the progress of the seasons both as a framework and as a source of forward movement . . . at once a backcloth and a stimulus to the development of eros."[18] That events are causally linked and artfully made to seem natural occurrences, even when highly implausible, contributes to the sense of an organic development that promotes the inexorable advance of eros.[19] The narrative rhythm is made to coincide with the erotic rhythms of the plot "in which," as one critic remarks, "the sexual awakening of the couple establishes itself as the [primary] pattern and must be an object of suspense and curiosity in itself."[20] Satisfaction must wait until the very end of the text, which concludes, as it must, with the sexual consummation of the wedding night.

The structures of the narrative that favor antiphonal movements of the two young lovers, who now meet, now part, and now remain side by side, are echoed at the level of language in a rhetorical style that shows a preference for parallels with variations, assonances, and rhyming pairs, for clauses of equal lengths and other symmetries.[21] The entire style obeys to the letter the rules of rhetorical handbooks, which identify its techniques as proper for conveying sensations of sweetness (*glukutês*), pleasure (*hêdonê*), and delight (*terpsis*).[22] In short, Longus "has chosen a style entirely suited to his subject" in which "his language and phrasing mirror [imitate] the substance of the thought."[23]

In a text in which art imitates nature but allows nature also to imitate art, it would be difficult, if not impossible, to give a theoretical account of the mimetic interplay of content, form, expression, and idea that is activated precisely and only in the activity of reading. If the representation of nature and the natural deploys all the resources of art, up to and including those devices we may openly call literary and rhetorical, this text reaches a point at which art might even be said to imitate art, but it manages to do so also in the name of nature that produces an "effect of the real" even where it might seem most contrived.

Longus's art therefore strives to conceal its artfulness through mimetic means of every kind, so as to create the sense of "a solid ground" of reality for the work on which the young lovers (and love) may stand.[24] Yet it also necessarily makes the "real" a problem, not only taking pleasure at times in openly disclosing its own textual strategies,[25] but also expanding on the mimetic situation described in the proem. The narrative presents itself as an imitation not of life but of a painting; this inevitably raises the issue of verisimilitude in its relation to the "real," which it aims to imitate in art. Yet the challenge to the ecphrasist is whether he can prove adequate (even superior) in his narrative to the painterly model (*antigrapsai têi graphei*), which may claim not only to be prior in this, the present, aesthetic contest (first came the painting, then the story), but also to be prior absolutely, by reason of the more general prestige of visual qualities (what the rhetoricians called *enargeia*), whose values lie in their ability to be more faithful to "reality," to be "more real."[26]

It is essential from both points of view (reality and art) that the text give the work of art (the painting) the pride of position as the locus of desire that provides the point of entry into the *locus amoenus*. The tableau that attracts the narrator-visitor's gaze is "the most *beautiful* spectacle he had ever seen," and its viewing leads him directly to the actual countryside he describes at the beginning of his narrative (the rich man's estate) as the "most beautiful *possession*" (*ktêma*). This phrase follows the narrator's claim that his completed work will be a pleasurable possession (*ktêma*) for all.[27] The *locus amoenus* evokes desire from the stranger, a longing to find a way in, but with the attendant risk that he might violate its sensibilities—its landscape and inhabitants, its ethos and its nature.[28]

Disseminating his work to the outside world, the narrator also adopts the strategy of proclaiming that the book is an offering to Eros, the Nymphs, and Pan. His work is even more intimately linked to the world he is representing if the painting itself, as the text suggests, is the very one that Daphnis and Chloe, long after their marriage, dedicated to the Nymphs (4.39.2).[29] The act of dedicating objects to the local gods is the typical gesture of country folk, marking each time the completion of some task, episode, or stage of life (e.g., 1.32.1, 4.26.2, 4.37.2). Thus, in dedicating his work at the sacred shrine, the narrator aligns himself with the characters whose story he has told and validates the sacred quality of the tale and its participating deities. Simultaneously taking away (publication to all) and putting back (dedication at the shrine), the narrator also respects the "ecological balance" of the pastoral site whose beauty had so excited his admiration and where his own work (the book) can exist side by side with the model (painting) he had intended to rival.

Other "real" dangers remain; indeed, they are indispensable to the conduct of this erotic story (or any erotic story) and the special setting in which it takes place. Some far more fundamental ambiguities attend the desire of the city people to maintain their ownership of a beautiful place they only visit at their pleasure and for their pleasure. This is especially true when their arrival coincides, as it does in the fourth book, with the erotic maturation of the pastoral pair, who are now ready for marriage. The danger is further increased if we remember that the lovers too are a "pleasurable possession," since they, together with their foster parents, also belong to the master whose *ktêma* (landed estate) they tend (cf. 4.2).[30] At the same time, these dangers highlight the tensions, not only between city and country, but between romance and pastoral, in that the first must somehow inexorably lead its couple to the nuptial chamber and that the second, for all its erotic allure, also needs to protect the idealized innocence of its *locus amoenus*.[31]

Let us turn, then, to this critical encounter between city and country, which appropriately takes place in that garden park, the pastoral showpiece of city folk where aesthetic and erotic interests (as well as art and nature) are more deeply intertwined, and where we meet a third literary genre—New Comedy—the bourgeois drama of the city, which in its orientation toward marriage can be invoked as a compromise between the other two.[32]

GARDENS OF DESIRE

From the outset of the fourth book there are intimations of risk when the symbolic resources of art and nature are used to delight the voyeuristic city folks. By postponing their arrival, the owners may miss the actual spectacle of the vintners hard at work on their various tasks. But no matter; a bunch of beautiful grapes still attached to its branch is thoughtfully saved for them so they may have the "image [*eikôn*] and 'pleasure' [*hêdonê*] of the vintage" (4.5.2). Daphnis entertains them as though in a theater, when he exhibits his musical goats, who prance through their repertory of responses to his piped commands (4.15). Most to the point, however, is the elaborate description of the splendid garden park, the *paradeisos* fit for royalty, that belongs to the master of the place, Dionysophanes, in whose power it lies to consent to or refuse the nuptial union of Daphnis and Chloe.

Here is the grandest ecphrasis of all. It reveals the inherent tensions between city and country in eros and art without reaching a resolution for either. In its perfection, the *paradeisos* seems to blossom as a microcosm of the pastoral world at harmony with the larger environment. Unlike the private closed garden of the old herder, Philetas, where Eros makes an epiphany to him and him alone, this *paradeisos* has a view looking out to the city, the plain, and the sea. Worked for the master by Lamon, Daphnis's foster father, the garden park is not cultivated for any practical function like the tasks Lamon performs in the field or the vineyard but rather for its conspicuous beauty (*pankolon . . . chrêma,* 4.2.1; *kallos,* 4.13.4).[33] The garden's salient features are its size, its situation on high ground, its variety of vegetation, both cultivated and wild, "the vine vying in rivalry with the apples and pears for its fruits . . . the large dark ivy berries imitating clusters of grapes." The *paradeisos* was arranged according to a precise pattern, and the trunks of trees were spaced at regular intervals. "But overhead the branches joined one another and their foliage intertwined; nature [*physis*] itself seemed a work of art [*technê*]. There were beds of flowers, too, some put forth by earth unaided, others wrought by human skill [*technê*] (roses, hyacinths, and lilies planted by the hand; violets, narcissus, and pimpernel through the gift of earth). There was shade for summer, flowers for spring, fruit for autumn, and luscious delight in every season" (4.2–3).

Such garden descriptions are known elsewhere, but Longus has integrated their lush lasciviousness into his well-structured play between the aesthetic and the erotic. At the center of the garden was a temple and altar of Dionysus, the first formal ceremonial structure in the pastoral landscape. Inside the temple were paintings of traditional nonrustic Dionysiac themes, among them Semele giving birth, Ariadne sleeping, Lycurgus fettered, Pentheus torn to pieces. Capping it all was a representation in sculpted relief of the pastoral Dionysiac entourage of the countryside: satyrs treading, bacchants dancing. "Nor was Pan omitted: he was shown sitting on a rock and piping as if he were providing a melody" (4.3.1–2). Lamon was putting the estate thoroughly in order, cleansing and purifying it, and tending to the *paradeisos* (4.1.3); he trimmed, pruned, and propped the vines there, crowning the god Dionysus with garlands and irrigating the flowers (4.4.1).

Meticulously laid out with an eye to every detail, the garden park invites the spectator to enjoy its beauties and relish its skillful design. It also invites the reader to consider the rhetorical and symbolic values of that ornamental scheme. How best to interpret this topological wonder that opens the last book in the vintage season of the second year? In situ, we might say, and in two ways: first, in the broader context of the work as the second garden ecphrasis in the novel, which we may compare with its earlier analogue (2.3–7)—the garden of Philetas, the old herder—who describes it to Daphnis and Chloe after the first vintage when the children had passed through a spring and summer of lovesickness but did not even know the name of their curious ailment nor the means to alleviate it. In situ also, now in its present place in the text, as the stage where events will occur that are finally to bring about the nuptial union toward which the entire narrative has been heading.

Erotics

The social and sexual messages of the garden park seem clear enough, starting from familiar analogies—first, between maiden and garden, and second, between agriculture and matrimony.[34] Daphnis has shown himself a master of the pastoral arts. But he needs another sign of prowess as a cultivator who is adept at putting (or helping put) gardens in order—not only to please his patron so as to win consent for his marriage to Chloe but to show he is symbolically ready to embark upon the social order of matrimony and to tend his own garden (4.4.1–2).

The sexual connotations are still more obvious if we know that Lampis, a disappointed rustic suitor for Chloe's hand, will vandalize the garden out of spite before the arrival of the master so as to spoil Daphnis's chances with Chloe (4.7). Given the prenuptial context, Lampis's violence against the flowers might suggest the impending loss of Chloe's virginity. But while Daphnis and his father first lament the flowers' ruin, they turn in a moment to lament themselves, in fear that their own bodies will be delivered up for punishment to the angry master. Indeed, Chloe herself gives voice to her grief and concern, imagining the worst that might befall her beloved Daphnis (4.8.4–9.1). Thus it is more than implied that the tender garden represents not only the maiden Chloe but also (and even more overtly) the beautiful Daphnis.

This inference is indeed later fulfilled: the temple of Dionysus will be the scene where Gnathon, the greedy parasite from the city, will press his pederastic suit for Daphnis, smitten as he is at first sight with the boy's exemplary beauty (4.11.2). There he will importune his young patron Astylus to intercede for him in order to bring Daphnis into the city and—under Gnathon's expert tutelage—educate the boy into city ways (4.16–17.1; cf. 1.91). The garden, therefore, serves as the site for the symbolic violation of both Daphnis and Chloe, and mirrors what happens outside the garden park in the pastoral world where Gnathon makes a prior physical attempt at raping Daphnis (4.12), and Lampis, in turn, later abducts Chloe and actually carries her off (4.28).

Even though the gardens share some features, especially in the choice of flowers, plants, and trees, the erotic dimensions of Philetas's garden are very different. There the mischievous little figure of Eros waters the plants and flowers with glistening drops from his bath (2.5.4–5); he has the run of the place, skimming with light and nimble steps over myrtle and pomegranate without bruising a single bud or leaf (2.4.2; cf. 2.5.5), or darting like a bird to perch on the branch of a tree (2.6.1; cf. 2.4.3, 5.1). Philetas, herder and lover of Amaryllis in his youthful days, has left his pastures for the quieter task of tending his garden at an age when he is too old to ask the agile Eros for anything more than a *philêma,* a kiss (2.3.3; 2.4.4). Philetas's age is still more relevant. Named for the poet of long ago who first invented the pastoral genre, he is the *praeceptor amoris,* handing down the mythic tradition of eros to the children at the precise moment in their erotic development when they are ready to receive it (2.7–8.1).[35]

The passion of Eros, as yet unnamed, rises spontaneously in the spring and burns hot in the summer out there in the free expanses of the slopes where the flocks wander, while the treading of the grapes in that first fall hints at a sexual consummation in the company of the lusty vintners that could not but be crude and premature. As an erotic domain, the tender horticulture of Philetas's garden could be said to fall between pasturage and vintage. It is thus an appropriate site from which to teach the first social lessons about love (indeed, at Eros's behest), both its mythic ideology and its blunter physiology—the latter, however, only up to a certain point. For Philetas, in prescribing to Daphnis and Chloe the cure for eros, names only three items: kisses, embraces, and lying down together naked (2.7.7).

The reader might imagine that the next essential step would follow "naturally," but Philetas's reticence matches the erotic yet playful quality of Eros himself when he dallies in the beautiful garden and, as a little child, makes laughing sport with the aging Philetas. Like his Eros, Philetas's precepts suggest a preliminary stage that anticipates but is not yet ready (or in the case of Philetas, is no longer ready) for phallic consummation. Although Philetas in his speech recalls the solemn mythic and philosophical foundation of love's irresistible power in nature and the cosmos (2.7), the message of the garden implies that it is not yet the right time for Daphnis and Chloe. Nor will it be the time until the last line of the narrative is written in the fourth book and after a whole winter, spring, and summer have intervened, with the second autumn already well under way. Much has to happen in the meantime: the power of the goatish Pan must be revealed and the god formally installed in worship as a necessary prelude to Daphnis's first explicit lesson in the "works of love" (*ta erôtos erga*, 3.17.2), which introduces him to the long-awaited pleasures of "real sex," but also to its potential dangers when it comes to Chloe and "for the first time."

In the fourth book, Daphnis, already an accomplished musician and herder, also turns from grassy slopes to a tended garden, although its cultivation is of a different sort. Philetas, like his *hortus conclusus*, belongs fully to the pastoral world. Daphnis, his apprenticeship to Philetas (and to Lycaenion) now over, must confront, if only briefly, that other elaborate and enigmatic garden park where city and country intersect, where dangers to the pastoral dream lurk on every side, and where social ideas and theories of art and nature complicate one another to signal a new and essential stage of maturing. The setting may hint at a divine epiphany of the god Dionysus,[36] but it is in this theatrical space that another revelation takes place, that Daphnis's own identity is disclosed, and he passes from his rustic father, Lamon, the skilled gardener, to his true father, Dionysophanes. A place of work, a place of refuge, a place of schematic order as well as of elaborated beauty, it is also social, violent, and sexual—and dramatically speaking, it is comic.

Aesthetics

What of the aesthetics, those theories of art and nature? Here the problem is far more intricate. The *paradeisos* as the epitome of the *locus amoenus* might seem the idealized image of the entire novel. This garden may even serve as the allegory of the whole: it is quartered and four meters in size, corresponding to the four books of the work. In the organization of its plantings it displays the parallelisms and formal symmetries that are favorite rhetorical techniques of the text; it represents the two elements of nature (*physis*) and art (*technê*) as harmoniously intertwined, and its reference to the grapes *vying* (*proserizousa*) with the fruit trees and the ivy *imitating* (*emimêto*) the dark clusters of the grapes seems to echo directly the motivation of the narrator in the proem, who, struck with wonder at the beauty of the painting, longed to *rival* the painting in his *imitation* of it.[37]

As an ecphrastic exercise, the beauty of the style and what it describes might stand as the summit of the narrator's seductive powers. But standing back, as this *paradeisos* does, raised higher than the surrounding terrain, formally arranged in symmetrical patterns according to the patterns of Eastern royalty,[38] with the temple building at its dead center, the garden park also has passed from a living dynamic into a static symbol of art—a *theôria,* something to behold, to contemplate, to theorize about. The garden park is worked by Lamon and Daphnis, not for their own enjoyment, but rather so that "it might be seen" to be beautiful.[39] Moreover, the paintings of Dionysiac scenes are highly conventional in theme and formal in their arrangement (two depictions of females, two of males, two of groups) and given a pastoral decor in the sculpted reliefs that ornament them. If the mention of these paintings on the temple walls also summons up the memory of the painting in the proem that originated the narrator's desire to narrate, the recall of a pictorial surface suggests not so much an idea of *ut pictura poesis*—a proportion between the arts—but rather the limitations of that comparison in favor of a musical analogy that orchestrates the sensations of this world (sight, sound, touch, odor) and, like the music of Pan derived from Echo, can imitate everything.[40]

In the Dionysiac temple of the *paradeisos* Pan is depicted as sitting on a rock, only pretending, of course, to play, and imitating in sculpted relief what goes on in the real world of the narrative.[41] What is more, there is no music of any kind in this grand garden park. No birds are described as singing there, and no song tradition might be associated with it. By contrast, Philetas's garden is the site par excellence of birds that sing and where the musical voice of Eros himself is heard as he flits like a small bird from branch to branch, ready to pass on both music and love to the next generation. Neither Pan nor Dionysus is present in it. Indeed, the epiphany of Eros to Philetas directly follows as an antidote to the Dionysiac buffoonery of the vintage and precedes the revelation of Pan's powers that rounds out the activities of the season.

The formal perfection of the great *paradeisos* is an intrusion into the pastoral world. It is too much for the pastoral fiction of the rustic world and its simpler prenuptial eros, being the stage now for the bourgeois drama of the city that marries off its couples—that species of theater we call New Comedy. The scattered references to Dionysus throughout the work might hint at the idea of a veiled scenario of his mysteries. But the place of the god, for the most part, is reserved in the text for open social occasions of collective work (vintage), play (rustic festivities), or at the meeting of city and country. Given the overt references to theater and acting we find in the *paradeisos* (e.g., 4.17.2–3; cf. 4.15.2), Dionysus might also lay claim to his role as lord of the theater, whether of tragedy (as depicted in the tragic myths in the temple) or of comedy (the genre here being enacted). Imitation, as represented in the garden park, therefore, is imitation (and spectacle) raised to a higher degree.

The narrator, himself a voyeur from the city, may represent the work of his book in the allegory of the *paradeisos* and construct a viewing space that exemplifies the essential categories of nature and art to be used in the service of consummating his erotic plot. Yet he more explicitly claims Philetas's territory as the site of writing, linking his authorial labors (in the proem) with the gardener's task through their joint use of the verb *ekponeomai,* and he aligns the didactic role of his erotic work (e.g., *propaideusei*) with that of the old poet-gardener's instructive (and traditional) role of *praeceptor amoris* (or *erôtodidaskalos;* cf. *paideusas,* 2.8.1).[42] In this way, he identifies himself with Philetas and even more with Eros himself, who, at all the crucial moments of the story, is made to write the plot from within the text. Yet Eros too must become more sophisticated as the plot advances, and as he does so, he becomes more openly sophistic in turn. In an earlier encounter of city and country, Lycaenion must invent the fiction of Eros's authority to teach Daphnis the path to desire's fulfillment. But to include Chloe in the story the plot requires the services of a would-be sophist, whose response to the sight of erotic beauty contrasts with the narrator's transference of mimetic yearning to a work of art and yet confirms the mimetic power of eros he has claimed for his text.

RHETORICS OF EROS

The narrator finds his caricatured counterpart in the *paradeisos* in the figure of Gnathon—the bad lover, the bad teacher, and the bad rhetorician.[43] In the marriage-oriented world of romance (not pastoral), Gnathon is said to be a lover of boys by nature (*physei paiderastês,* 4.11.2)[44] and one, moreover, who only wants Daphnis for crude pleasure (4.19.5). He is also a bad "votary of Dionysus," we might add, in that his drunkenness, gluttony, and debauchery are negative signs of the symposium that celebrates a proper conviviality. Thus he is also a bad *mystagôgos,* who would initiate Daphnis not into the mysteries of eros and Dionysus but into the libertine revels of the city.[45] It is finally Gnathon's rhetoric that suggests a distinction between the way in which the narrator's subtle textual erotics are designed to embellish the tradition and the stilted and ludicrous schoolboy imitation of what we are by now supposed to recognize as the "real thing."

Even the occasion for Gnathon's performance is given a histrionic setting. Astylus has already promised to ask his father for Daphnis so as to hand him over to Gnathon, but "wishing to bring Gnathon into a more cheerful mood, he smilingly asked whether he was not ashamed of his love for a son of Lamon and of his eagerness to lie down with a lad who kept goats; and as he said this, he acted out [*hypekrinato*] disgust at the goatish aroma" (with a pun on "goatish," *tragikos,* as "tragic"). Gnathon, the text tells us, "well-schooled [*pepaideumenos*] in the love stories of legend [*pasan erotikên muthologian*] at the wanton symposia he attended, delivered a discourse appropriate to the situation of himself and Daphnis":

> "No real lover, my master, is fastidious in these matters. In whatever body it may be discovered, he is captivated by beauty. Hence some have fallen in love with a tree, a river, a beast. And yet who would not pity a lover who must fear his beloved? It is a slave's body I love, but a free man's beauty. See how like hyacinth his hair is, how his eyes sparkle beneath his brows like a gem in a golden setting; his face is filled with a ruddy glow, his mouth with teeth white as ivory. From it what true lover would not pray to receive sweet kisses? If it is a shepherd I love, I only imitate the example of the gods. A cowherd was Anchises and yet captivated Aphrodite. Branchos kept goats, and yet Apollo loved him. Ganymede was a shepherd, yet the king of all eloped with him. Let us not despise a lad whose very goats we see yielding a lover's obedience. And let us be grateful to Zeus' eagles for allowing such beauty to abide on earth." Astylus laughed heartily at this fine discourse, and remarked that Eros produced great sophists. (4.7.2–18.1)

This absurd speech is carefully framed as an occasion for parodic amusement and translates eros into an incongruous rhetorical exercise in which the idea of mimesis is represented by a sophist's outworn cliché about gods as lovers. The rhetoric matches the erotics. The sophist narrator had prayed to the god Eros for *sôphrosunê* in writing a book that will recount the passions of others. He asks for strength in his resolve not to come under the spell of what he is composing to the extent of falling in love with its characters so as to wish to abduct them and install them at banquets in the city. This *sôphrosunê* may be construed as prudence, sobriety, self-control—and certainly as the sublimating defense of a loving yet tactful aesthetic distance. Gnathon, on the other hand, is all vulgar appetite; his desire, aroused at the first sight of Daphnis, that boy of surpassing beauty (4.11.2), recalls the first response of that other viewer who was so taken by "the most beautiful sight *he* had ever seen" (proem, 1). By this shift from painting to person and by literally fulfilling the dictum of the proem ("no one has ever escaped eros, nor ever will so long as beauty exists and there are eyes to see"), Gnathon can therefore only atrociously (and comically) imitate what the entire narrative had already discreetly imitated.

The stately *paradeisos* furnishes the appropriate stagy setting for Gnathon's histrionics. It also provides the proper New Comedy backdrop for the recognitions and reconciliations that take place there as preludes demanded by bourgeois society for legitimating eros before it may be consummated in marriage. But this ornate garden can never serve as the *locus amoenus* where the nuptial celebration is held. Once ratified by culture, eros must return to nature, not the private garden of Philetas, but rather the source of it all—the grassy meadow before the cave of the Nymphs where Chloe as a baby was exposed and given into their safekeeping, the same space where long afterward the children deposited their *eikones* or paintings as their tribute to the Nymphs, who, invoked at various critical moments in the text, now lend their pastoral auspices to round off the circle of Chloe's maturation. Their presence also guarantees an air of primitive innocence to the wedding scene, where the celebration in fact may be "too rustic and too georgic" to delight "urban taste" (4.38.3–4).

In the concluding lines, the site shifts once again, when in conformity with the social ethos of eros they are conducted at nightfall into the wedding chamber. "Daphnis and Chloe lay down naked together, embraced and kissed; they stayed awake all night and had even less sleep that night than owls do. And Daphnis did some of the things Lycaenion had taught him, and then for the first time Chloe learned that what they had done in the woods had been mere pastoral play [*poimenôn paignia*]" (4.40.3). The woods, if not the site for furtive and dangerous matings, is only the pleasant playground for youthful love. Sex, on the other hand, especially procreative and marital sex, is a serious if pleasurable activity to be conducted decorously in the privacy of the bedchamber and over whose potentially traumatic enactment the text finally casts a discreet and romantic veil.[46] Yet the use of the term *paignion* remystifies the narrator's association with Eros and with the young lovers themselves, while still leaving the trace of a last significant literary allusion. For the narrative too is a species of erotic (fore)play that has its analogue within the text in the little figure of Eros, who plays in Philetas's garden (2.4.1) and is the internal "author" of the plot, as we have seen. But *paignion* also refers to the fifth-century sophist Gorgias, who ends his defense of Helen by claiming it an encomium for her but a *paignion* for him.

In the three gardens of desire I have examined in some detail (the grove in the proem, the garden of Philetas, and the *paradeisos* of Dionysophanes), my contention has been that in these pictorial spaces, the narrative thematized its poetics of eros as self-conscious variations on the theme of desire, each time involving spectators, sophistics, and forms of visual display in the interests of probing the relations among art (artifice), nature, and imitation. On the level of content, a more culturally constructed text about the conventional workings of eros would be difficult to find. But it can equally be said that there is no other ancient work that more provocatively confronts those conventions and does so through a sustained and extensive dialogue that, from first to last, underwrites the entire narrative design—including and especially the figure of Eros himself.

NOTES

This chapter is an abbreviated and revised version of "The Poetics of *Erôs:* Nature, Art, and Imitation in Longus' *Daphnis and Chloe,*" in *Before Sexuality: The Construction of Erotic Experience in the Ancient Greek World,* ed. D. M. Halperin, J. J. Winkler, and F. I. Zeitlin (Princeton, 1990), 417–64.

1. The text of Longus will generally be cited from M. Reeve's Teubner edition (Leipzig, 1981).

2. On ecphrasis as pictorial description in general, with special application to works of art, see the comprehensive work of P. Friedländer, *Johannes von Gaza und Paulus Silentiarius* (Leipzig, 1912), and J. Palm, "Bemerkungen zur Ekphrase in der griechischen Literatur," *Kungliga Humanistiska vetenskapssamfundet* 1 (1965): 108–211, along with the useful summary in J. H. Hagstrum, *The Sister Arts* (Chicago, 1958), 3–36. For pictorialism in literature and its development, see G. Zanker, "Enargeia in the Ancient Criticism of Poetry," *Rheinisches Museum für Philologie* 124 (1981): 297–311, and Zanker, *Realism in Alexandrian Poetry* (London, 1987), chaps. 1–3. For the use of ecphrases in romances, see O. Schissel von Fleschenberg, "Die Technik des Bildein-satzes," *Philologus* 72 (1913): 83–114; E. C. Harlan, "The Description of Paintings as a Literary Device and Its Application in Achilles Tatius" (Ph.D. diss., Columbia University, 1965); and S. Bartsch, *Decoding the Ancient Novel: The Reader and the Role of Description in Heliodorus and Achilles Tatius* (Princeton, 1989). For more theoretical views of description, cf. M. Beaujour, "Some Paradoxes of Description," *Yale French Studies* 61 (1981): 27–59, and P. Hamon, "Rhetorical Status of the Descriptive," *Yale French Studies* 61 (1981): 1–26. For the proem itself, see J. Kestner, "Ekphrasis as Frame in Longus' *Daphnis and Chloe,*" *Classical World* 67 (1973): 166–71; T. Pandiri, "*Daphnis and Chloe:* The Art of Pastoral Play," *Ramus* 14 (1985): 116–41; and the useful discussion of R. L. Hunter, *A Study of "Daphnis and Chloe"* (Cambridge, 1983), 38–51.

3. On the *praeceptor amoris,* erotic teaching in Latin elegy, and debts to Greek sources (early and late), see A. L. Wheeler, "Erotic Teaching in Roman Elegy and the Greek Sources," part 1, *Classical Philology* 5 (1910): 440–50, and part 2, *Classical Philology* 6 (1911): 56–77.

4. E.g., the works of Philostratus the Elder, Philostratus the Younger, and Callistratus, and in a more openly philosophical vein, Pseudo-Cebes, *Pinax.* Cf. Schissel von Fleschenburg, "Die technik des Bildeinsatzes," Harlan, "Description of Paintings," 52–74, and G. Anderson, *Philostratus: Biography and Belles Lettres in the Third Century* A.D. (London, 1986), 259–68.

5. E.g., Pseudo-Longinus, *On the Sublime* 13.2 (who speaks of both *zêlos* and *mimêsis*), and Dionysius Halicarnassensis, frag. 3 (vol. 6 = *opusc.* 2, p. 2, 200 U-R); J. Bompaire, *Lucien écrivain: Imitation et création* (Paris, 1958), 63–78, and D. A. Russell, "De imitatione," in *Creative Imitation and Latin Literature,* ed. D. West and T. Woodman (Cambridge, 1979), 1–16, 201–2.

6. See also the analogy of the beautiful hall to a gorgeously dressed woman, 7–9, 15–16, 21. This work, which theorizes the relative merits of image and word, and gives actual ecphrases of paintings, is directly relevant to the concerns of Longus and the motivations of *his* narrator; cf. Bompaire, *Lucien écrivain,* 713–21.

7. Cf. J. J. Pollitt, *Art and Experience in Classical Greece* (Cambridge, 1972), 31–64; M. Barasch, *Theories of Art from Plato to Winckelmann* (New York, 1985), 1–44; and Bartsch, *Decoding the Ancient Novel.*

8. Many have noted the echo/reversal of Thucydides here, including Hunter, *Study,* 47–50, and Pandiri, *"Daphnis and Chloe,"* 117–18 and n. 9.

9. The *praeceptor amoris* can promise value to both the experienced and the unschooled (cf. Propertius 2.34, 82: *rudis sive peritus*). Philostratus, *Epistulae* 68 Benner-Forbes, remarks on the value of literary reminiscence: "The erotic poets are pleasant learning even for men who are past the age; for they lead them to thoughts of love and, as it were, make them renew their youth. So do not think yourself too old to hear them; communion with such poets will either keep you from forgetting sexual pleasures or will recall them to you." On the *praeceptor amoris,* see Wheeler, "Erotic Teaching."

10. There are many references to different kinds of mimesis in the text (e.g., 1.3.1, 1.9.2, 1.11.2, 2.25.3,, 2.35.4, 2.37.1, 3.14.5, 3.16.1, 3.21.4, 3.23.4, 4.2.3, 4.17.6). The text's special fondness for comparatives and brief similes also contributes to the mimetic sense of learning through resemblance and comparison. Cf. A. Scobie, "Similes in the Greek Romances," in *More Essays on the Ancient Romance and Its Heritage* (Meisenheim am Glan, 1973), 18.

11. Cf. Russell, "De imitatione," 4; H. Flashar, "Die klassizistische theorie der Mimesis," in *Le classicisme à Rome aux I^{ers} siècles avant et après J.-C.,* Fondation Hardt Entretiens, no. 25 (Geneva, 1979), 59–97; and Hunter, *Study,* 45.

12. The fullest account remains that of Bompaire, *Lucien écrivain,* 1–154; cf. B. P. Reardon, *Courants littéraires des IIe et IIIe siècles après J.-C.* (Paris, 1971), 3–9; Russell, "De imitatione"; Flashar, "Die klassizistische Theorie"; I. M. DuQuesnay, "From Polyphemus to Corydon: Virgil, *Eclogue 2,* and the *Idylls* of Theocritus," in West and Woodman, *Creative Imitation,* 35–69, 206–20; and P. Hadot, *Leçon inaugurale, 18 février 1983,* Collège de France, Chaire d'Histoire de la Pensée Hellenistique et Romaine (Paris, 1983).

13. See esp. G. Valley, *Über den Sprachgebrauch des Longus* (Uppsala, 1926); V. E. Vacarello, "L'eredità della poesia bucolica nel romanzo di Longo," *Il mondo classico* 5 (1935): 307–25; A. Scarcella, "La tecnica dell'imitazione in Longo sofista," *Giornale italiano de filologia classica* 23 (1971): 34–59; L. R. Cresci, "Il romanzo di Longo sofista e la tradizione bucolica," *Atene e Roma,* n.s. 26 (1981): 1–25; O. Schönberger, *Longos: Hirtengeschichten von Daphnis und Chloe,* 3d ed. (Berlin, 1980); and Hunter, *Study,* 59–83 and 116–17 nn. 1 and 5, with bibliography.

14. C. Segal, *Poetry and Myth in Ancient Pastoral* (Princeton, 1981), 3–4.

15. An excellent example of this effect is the narrativizing of the Sapphic apple, "which the pickers left at the top of the tree because they could not reach it" (3.33–34). Cf. W. E. McCulloh, *Longus* (New York, 1970), 74–77, and Hunter, *Study,* 73–76.

16. Hunter, *Study,* 45.

17. H. H. O. Chalk, "Eros and the Lesbian Pastorals of Longos," *Journal of Hellenic Studies* 80 (1960): 32–51, addressing the symbolic and theological valences of Eros, amplifies the sense of a cultural system. Reardon, *Courants littéraires,* disagrees (381).

18. E. L. Bowie, "The Greek Novel," in *The Cambridge History of Classical Literature,* vol. 1, *Greek Literature,* ed. P. E. Easterling and B. M. W. Knox (Cambridge, 1985), 697. See also McCulloh, *Longus,* 68–69; and Reardon, *Courants littéraires,* 377.

19. On causal connections in the plot, see, for example, G. Anderson, *Ancient Fiction: The Novel in the Graeco-Roman World* (London, 1984), 138–40.

20. Ibid., 138.

21. See, for example, E. Rohde, *Der griechische Roman und seine Vorläufer,* 3d ed. (Leipzig, 1914), 550–54; L. Castiglione, "Stile e testo del romanzo pastorale di Longo," *Rendiconti del reale Istituto Lombardo di scienze e lettere,* ser. 2, no. 61 (1928): 203–23; G. Rohde, "Longus und die Bukolik," *Rheinisches Museum für Philologie* 86 (1937): 23–49 (reprinted in *Studien und Interpretationen* [Berlin, 1963], 91–116; here, 96); Schönberger, *Longos,* 37–40, and Hunter, *Study,* 86–92. McCulloh, *Longus,* 63, points to the parallel pairs: Pan/Nymphs, Daphnis/Chloe, goats/sheep, two sets of foster parents. For dou-

blets and repetitions in the plot, see Longus, *Pastorales,* ed. J.-R. Vieillefond (Paris, 1987), ccv–ccviii.

22. The "sweet" style (and its cognates) is identified among the rhetoricians with simplicity of diction and metrical arrangements of words. For discussion of the ancient evidence, see, e.g., Schönberger, *Longus,* 35–36, and Hunter, *Study,* 92–98.

23. Hunter, *Study,* 98.

24. The rusticity of peasant life reflected in its varied activities and practical attitudes further "authenticate" the sense of reality in the work. But these "realities" are already highly stylized elements of the text, continuing the tradition of the "realistic" genres developed first in the Hellenistic period (pace J. J. Winkler, "The Education of Chloe: Hidden Injuries of Sex," in *The Constraints of Desire: The Anthropology of Sex and Gender in Ancient Greece,* 101–26 [New York, 1990], who insists on their anthropological veracity). On realism and its uses in ancient texts, see Zanker, *Realism,* 1–29.

25. For example, the innocent story Lycaenion invents to get Daphnis's attention is actually borrowed from Penelope's erotic dream of the eagle and the geese in *Odyssey* 19 (geese = suitors, eagle = Odysseus).

26. As Palm notes ("Bemerkungen," 210) (and Bartsch quotes [*Decoding the Ancient Novel,* 166–67]): "Literature [of this period] saw that the painter's art could reproduce reality accurately and aptly; since it desired this itself, it developed the feeling that it had to compete with the other art . . . And it became customary to see reality with the eye of the graphic artist and even to regard reality as an art work to be portrayed through the painter's art." For the Hellenistic background, see Zanker, "Enargeia," and *Realism,* chaps. 1–3.

27. Pandiri, *"Daphnis and Chloe,"* 118 and n. 14, also points to the punning use of *ktêma* as both literary work and country estate.

28. Cf. M. E. Blanchard, *Description: Sign, Self, Desire* (The Hague, 1980), on the *locus amoenus:* "The borders of the pastoral world are ill-defined, because it is but a juxtaposition. Its charm is that, kept away from the bustle of civilization, but close enough to the real world to be threatened by it, it is maintained in a constant position of vulnerability . . . The original quality of pastoral literature is in direct relation to the magnitude of the threat and the subsequent triumph of its purity, its virginity" (271). On the containment and simplicity of the pastoral world, see also A. V. Ettin, *Literature and the Pastoral* (New Haven, 1984), 12.

29. See also Hunter, *Study,* 42–43.

30. Pandiri, *"Daphnis and Chloe,"* 130–33, claims the tragic tales of Syrinx and Echo are "introduced to remind the reader of alternative modes, of the version the author has chosen not to follow" (132). But their status is more ambiguous: Chloe takes innocent delight in storytelling, while the reader immediately grasps the tales' psychological power and veiled message. Pandiri wants to "exclude" violence "from Longus' pastoral comedy," but the threat of violence is intrinsic to the representation of eros (especially of defloration—"for the first time") as well as to the narrative dynamics of the plot. I also disagree with Winkler's emphasis on sexual violence as a sign of phallocracy: "If he thinks about it, Daphnis must recognize that Chloe's pain is inextricable from his own desire: he has to acknowledge his desire as, *inter alia,* a desire to hurt her" ("Education of Chloe," 122). But the text shows him doing just the opposite. Reversing the situation, as Winkler suggests ("If one of them has to be taught by an outsider before the other, why should Chloe not have been taught by Dorkon how to make love to Daphnis?" [121]), does nothing to alter the brute fact that a girl's sexual anatomy is different from that of a boy. It is that irreducible difference that so puzzles men and leads them to misinterpret the physiology of virgins as Daphnis does.

31. See the thoughtful and elegant analyses of erotic preoccupations in the pastoral

world by T. G. Rosenmeyer, *The Green Cabinet: Theocritus and the European Pastoral Lyric* (Berkeley and Los Angeles, 1969), 77–85; D. Halperin, *Before Pastoral: Theocritus and the Ancient Tradition of Bucolic Poetry* (New Haven, 1983), 64, 130–31, 178, 242–43; W. Berg, *Early Virgil* (London, 1974), 20–22; and F. Cairns, *Tibullus: A Hellenistic Poet at Rome* (Cambridge, 1979), 21–24. More generally, see R. Poggioli, *The Oaten Flute* (Cambridge, Mass., 1974), 149–52, on the contradictory nature of pastoral desire.

32. On elements of New Comedy in Longus, see Schönberger, *Longos*, 15 (e.g., a peripeteia in the action, 4.19f., the two recognition scenes with their birth tokens). Three figures are borrowed from the comic theater: Gnathon the parasite, Lycaenion the city-woman and courtesan type, and Astylus the young man from the city. See also the discussion in M. Berti, "Sulla interpretazione mistica del romanzo di Longo," *Studi classici e orientali* 16 (1967): 343–58; C. Corbato, "Da Menandro a Caritone: Studi sulla genesi del romanzo greco e i suoi rapporti con la commedia nuova (I)," *Quaderni Triestini sul teatro antico* 1 (1968): 5–44; and Hunter, *Study*, 67–70, together with the fuller bibliography in Pandiri, *"Daphnis and Chloe,"* 139 n. 32.

33. The text semantically emphasizes the special beauty of the place, by calling it *pankalon*, "all beautiful" (used only here) and by its use of the abstract noun *kallos* (beauty), normally reserved for describing beautiful persons, not places or things. (*Kallos* used of the two children [1.7.1], of Daphnis [1.13.2, 4; 1.24.1; 2.2.1; 4.11.2; 4.17.4, 5, 7; 4.18.1; 4.33.1], of Chloe [1.32.1, 4; 4.30.4; 4.32.1; 4.33.4], of the Nymph Echo [3.23.3], of beauty contests [*eris*, 1.15.4, *athlon* (Aphrodite), 3.34.2], and more generally that which Eros pursues [2.7.1].)

34. See A. R. Littlewood, "Romantic Paradises: The Role of the Garden in the Byzantine Romance," *Byzantine and Modern Greek Studies* 5 (1979): 107; Chalk, "Eros," 46–47, and also the remarks of Hunter, *Study*, 97.

35. The text here may echo the actual poetry of Philetas. See J. Hubaux, "Le dieu amour chez Properce et chez Longus," *Bulletin de l'Académie Royale de Belgique, Classe des Lettres*, ser. 5, no. 39 (1953): 263–70 (on Propertius), DuQuesnay, "From Polyphemus to Corydon," 60 (on Vergil), Cairns, *Tibullus*, 25–27 (on Tibullus), and E. L. Bowie, "Theocritus' Seventh *Idyll*, Philetas and Longus," *Classical Quarterly* 35 (1985): 67–91 (on Theocritus). On the figure of Philetas, see also Hunter, *Study*, 76–83.

36. K. Kerényi, *Die griechisch-orientalische Romanliteratur in religionsgeschichtlicher Beleuchtung* (Tübingen, 1927), and R. Merkelbach, "Daphnis und Chloe: Roman und Mysterium," *Antaios* 1 (1960): 47–60, *Roman und Mysterium in der Antike* (Munich, 1962), 192–224, and *Die Hirten des Dionysos* (Stuttgart, 1988) argue for a scenario of Dionysiac mysteries in Longus. Against the view of Merkelbach, see the critiques of R. Turcan, "Le roman 'initiatique': A propos d'un livre récent," *Revue de l'histoire des religions* 163 (1963): 149–99; Berti, "Interpretazione"; B. P. Reardon, "The Greek Novel," *Phoenix* 23 (1969): 305; and A. Geyer, "Roman und Mysterienritual," *Würzburger Jahrbücher für die Altertumswissenschaft*, n.s. 3 (1977): 179–96. Schönberger, *Longos*, 24–28, gives a good summary, but see esp. Hunter, *Study*, 31–38.

37. On the idea that the work (or poem) may have been identified with its setting, see Rosenmeyer, *Green Cabinet*, 200, and Berg, *Early Virgil*, 22–25.

38. On the *paradeisos*, see the discussion of P. Grimal, "Le jardin de Lamon à Lesbos," *Revue archéologique* 49 (1957): 211–14, and the remarks of Vieillefond, *Pastorales*, cxcii, and W. Elliger, *Die Darstellung der Landschaft in der griechischen Dichtung* (Berlin, 1975), 415.

39. There is a strong emphasis on acts of seeing, viewing, and beholding, starting with the patron coming from the city to survey his holdings after the incursion of the Methymneans. But the spectators are now included in the scene and we "see" them "seeing." Thus all is being made ready for the pleasures of the master's viewing (*eis*

pasan theas hêdonên, 4.1.1; cf. 4.13.4–5), including the garden, so it would look well (*hos ophtheie kalos,* 4.1.3), and so too for the goats (4.4.2). The *paradeisos* itself has a view over the plain, pastures, and sea (*euoptos, horân,* etc., 4.3.1), a place from which one might see all.

40. On the importance of music in the work, see, for example, Chalk, "Eros," 37 n. 37 (its erotic mystic aspects), Schönberger, *Longos,* 192, and Pandiri, "*Daphnis and Chloe,*" 132.

41. For a different reading, see Pandiri, "*Daphnis and Chloe,*" 139 n. 25.

42. See also ibid., 118 and 132.

43. J. Bompaire, "A propos de *Daphnis et Chloé* de Longus," *L'information littéraire* 25 (1973): 118, speaks of a "countereducation" to the true *technê erôtikê,* that of the debauched (*asôtoi,* 4.17).

44. Given the crucial role of *physis* (or nature) in the conceptual framing of the work, the characterization of Gnathon's sexual preference as predicated on *physis* cannot be insignificant. But what does it mean? Does it suggest a contest between two kinds of *physis,* since Daphnis unequivocally rejects Gnathon's advances on the basis of his observations about *physis* in the animal world ("billy goats don't mount billy goats" 4.12.3–4)? Yet the animal world itself is not sufficient as an example to humans of sexual practice, since, as Chloe earlier points out to Daphnis, animals adopt a standing position (whereas Philetas bade them lie down together; 3.14). However, that Gnathon is made to pose the greatest threat to the union of Daphnis and Chloe suggests that his kind of *physis* is unacceptable to the ruling ideology of eros. That he is also negatively represented with other vices of appetite and with a disregard for decorum is predicated on his sexual orientation, rather than vice versa (which is what Winkler would claim). To insist on Gnathon's offense as an "innocent" and "innocuous" lack of restraint is to miss the real ideological construct that, from Aristophanes on, impugns a man's sexuality as the basis for more general social (or political) condemnation and satire. Moreover, Gnathon's explicit attempt at sexual violence against Daphnis cannot be ignored. It is crucial to the plot both as the final test of Daphnis's suitability as a husband for Chloe and as a way of equalizing the threat of violence that menaces both Daphnis and Chloe throughout the work. Gnathon's ultimate "redemption," we might note, reaffirms the heterosexual rule, since its price is his rescue of Chloe from her would-be rapist in order to return her to Daphnis's embrace.

45. The name Gnathon (jaws) attests to his status as a parasite at the rich man's table, describing his appetites, and indeed representing the entire man: "Being nothing else than a pair of jaws [*gnathos*] and a belly [*gastêr*] and that which is below the belly [*ta hupo gastera*]" (4.11.2).

46. On the Gorgianic allusion, see Schönberger, *Longos,* ad loc., and Hunter, *Study,* 106. Given that the *Helen* explores the power of language as well as the force of seduction, the echo at the end of *Daphnis and Chloe* is precise and to the point.

PART IV

Romance at
a Critical Distance

CHAPTER NINE

Apollonius, King of Tyre
and the Greek Novel

David Konstan

For all their differences, the surviving Greek erotic novels exhibit a broad affinity in the structure of their plots. All revolve about a relationship, invariably heterosexual, between a primary couple; the relationship is subjected to, and survives, a series of stresses and obstacles that involve the protagonists in a more or less conventional sequence of adventures.[1] Isolde Stark explains that the underlying theme that finds expression in this pattern "is the motif of unchanging, eternal love and fidelity. But if love and fidelity are to be confirmed as unchanging, then they must necessarily be subjected to trials. The result is a continual sequence of trial situations."[2] This is a perceptive description, but such an elementary formula, ultimately reducible to the bare triad of encounter, separation, and reunion, fails to single out the characteristics that set the Greek novels decisively apart from a work like *The History of Apollonius, King of Tyre*. My purpose is to show how this anonymous Latin work, which is frequently taken to be a close relative of the Greek novels (by Chariton, Xenophon of Ephesus, Longus, Heliodorus, and Achilles Tatius), in fact marks a radical departure from their characteristic pattern.[3]

To begin with, in the Greek novel both protagonists are invariably young and nearly the same age. They are equal, moreover, not only in age, but in status: they are either citizens of the same community, as in the novels by Xenophon and Chariton, or young people of comparable social standing. They fall in love with each other at the beginning of the narrative, and are equally passionate, though they are shy of expressing their love openly. Thus, the love is reciprocal, and between equals. In the course of their adventures, both the male and the female partner are subjected to temptations and violence from would-be lovers or rivals. The young people resist such advances, on the whole more passively than actively, since they are usually at the mercy of men or women in positions of power, such as bandits, pirates, satraps, or kings. The protagonists are thus in similar positions, and in order, perhaps, to preserve this symmetry, there seems to be a rule in the Greek novels that the male is not represented as coming to the rescue of the female like a knight in shining armor. Just as both partners find themselves at the mercy of their captors, so they display an equal vigor and resourcefulness in the preservation of their faith, and in their attempts to be reunited.[4]

On the basis of the preceding description, it is easy to see that *Apollonius* is cut to an entirely different pattern from that which informs the Greek romantic novel.[5] To begin with, it represents an unequal relationship between an older, or at all events a more experienced and independent, man and a younger woman residing in the house of her father, though she is mature enough to feel the pangs of passion (cf. *iam adulta virgo,* 15.11.14).[6] Apollonius has arrived shipwrecked and destitute on the shores of Cyrene, in an effort to escape the wrath of the king of Antioch, for the hand of whose daughter he had sued. He is welcomed by the local king, Archistrates, and invited to his palace. In the course of dinner, after a musical performance by the king's daughter, Apollonius demonstrates his superior talent in singing and performing. "Meanwhile, as the king's daughter watched the young man excelling in every art and skill, she was gripped by the cruel fire of a wound: she fell [infinitely] in love" (*incidit in amorem* [*infinitum*]).[7] With the permission of her father, she bestows generous gifts on him. As Apollonius prepares to depart, she bids her father entertain him at his home, "in fear that she would be tormented if she could not look upon her beloved" (17.13.12). There is no indication, however, that Apollonius is under the spell of a comparable passion. He looks rather, it would seem, to practical advantage and the debt of gratitude he owes to Archistrates when he consents to wed the girl: "If it is your wish, let it be fulfilled," he declares to the king (22.16.16). Thus, the symmetrical or reciprocal enamorment that is the mainspring of the Greek novel is displaced here by an asymmetrical attachment.

After the marriage between Apollonius and the daughter of Archistrates, the couple depart by ship for Tyre, since news has reached Apollonius that the king of Antioch is dead, having been struck by lightning. During the voyage, Apollonius's wife dies, to all appearances, in childbirth, and is set adrift at sea in a coffin, which floats ashore at Ephesus. There she is revived, and dedicates herself to the virgin Diana. To be sure, Apollonius will be reunited with her in the end, when, on the advice of a dream (48.40.2–7), he visits the temple of Diana at Ephesus. But to all intents and purposes, the drama of their separation and reunion is suspended for the larger part of the novel. In his grief, Apollonius takes up the trade of merchant and wanders for fourteen years, entirely oblivious of his wife's circumstances. The narrative is blank about his experiences during this period. We are not informed of any tests or attempts on his fidelity, any more than on hers. Rather, the focus of the story shifts to the fate of Tarsia, the daughter of Apollonius and his wife, who is born at sea.

The infant Tarsia is given over to the custody of Stranguillio and Dionysias, the king and queen of Tarsus (for which the girl is named), who had earlier been the beneficiaries of Apollonius's munificence, and they are commissioned to see to her liberal education during Apollonius's absence at sea. But the queen grows jealous when Tarsia begins to outshine her own daughter, and hands her over to a slave to be executed. In the nick of time, Tarsia is taken captive by pirates, and sold in turn to a brothel-keeper in Mytilene (33.25.1–26.10). Upon the return of Apollonius, Dionysias fabricates a story of the death of Tarsia, while the hapless Stranguillio, who had learned too late of his wife's plan, allows himself to be drawn into complicity. Apollonius, shattered by his double loss, secludes himself in the hold of his ship. As luck would have it, his ship is driven by a storm to Mytilene, and there Athenagoras, a sympathetic nobleman who has taken Tarsia's case to heart, solicits her to apply her arts to consoling Apollonius. This leads to the recognition.

The fictitious story of the death of Apollonius's daughter Tarsia is clearly analogous to the apparent death of his wife in its effect on Apollonius. Though the former is an instance of deliberate deception, both times Apollonius is separated from a dear one in the belief that she is no longer alive. In neither case, accordingly, does Apollonius have immediate reason to resort to action; instead, he suffers passively. In this he resembles the heroes of the Greek novels, who are given to lamentation and suicidal urges when faced with the loss of their beloveds. But the torment Apollonius endures at the false news of his daughter's fate has nothing to do with the passion or infatuation that unites the protagonists in the romantic Greek tales. Correspondingly, there is no role for rivals in the form of pirates or princes, whose promises of security and prosperity test the commitment of the heroes. Tarsia's captivity in a brothel (which has a parallel in Xenophon of Ephesus's novel) represents violence to her person, not a trial of her faithfulness. There is no question of rival lovers.

Athenagoras of Mytilene, indeed, initially takes a carnal interest in the girl, and bids for her against the brothel-keeper who finally succeeds in buying her; Athenagoras concedes defeat at the auction with the cynical reflection that he can have her at less cost by presenting himself as her first customer (33.26.7–10). The result of this encounter is that Athenagoras is softened to the point of feeling genuine affection for the girl (39.30.17), and after she has been reunited with her father, he accepts her hand in marriage at the invitation of Apollonius himself (47.39.27–28). Nothing is said of Tarsia's own feelings in the matter; gratitude may have been among her motives, conceivably even love, but this is evidently a matter of indifference to the narrator. Tarsia as a romantic figure has nothing in common with the enamored young women of the Greek novels.

The iterative series of adventures to test fidelity, so characteristic of the Greek novel, is unnecessary to the representation of the character of Tarsia. This is natural enough with respect to Apollonius, since the bond between father and daughter is not normally defined by the kinds of tests that try the loyalty of a betrothed or married couple. But neither is it pertinent to the characterization of Tarsia's relationship with Athenagoras: once united, the two are never subject to trials and separations.

Neither are there tests of the fidelity between Apollonius and his wife, apart from the separation caused by her apparent death at sea. To be sure, both partners—Apollonius, it would seem, as well as his wife—commit themselves to a life of permanent celibacy in the absence of the other, but this choice is simply taken for granted in the tale, and not presented as a problem. Apollonius's grief-stricken decision to take up the itinerant life of a merchant would seem to have been inspired as much by a sense of responsibility toward Archistrates as by strictly amatory sensibilities: "Dear wife and only daughter of the king," he exclaims, "what has happened to you? What shall I answer in your behalf, what shall I announce about you to your father, who took me in when I was poor and in need?" (25.18.16–18).

This is not to say that the author or redactor of our text ascribes to Apollonius no sentiment whatever for Archistrates' daughter; at their wedding, we are told that "there was a great love between the spouses, a wonderful feeling, an incomparable affection, an unheard-of joy, which was encompassed in an eternal devotion" (*ingens amor fit inter coniuges, mirus affectus, incomparabilis dilectio, inaudita laetitia, quae perpetua caritate complectitur*, 23.16.29–31). But *amor* here is evidently being qualified as a properly conjugal emotion, as opposed to the passionate infatuation that unites the young lovers in the Greek novels. We have already remarked that Apollonius seems not to have been moved in the first instance by this latter type of *amor* or erotic passion for the daughter of the king, though it is very much the feeling that she entertains for him. Despite the girl's active prompting of her father, however, her union with Apollonius remains an arranged marriage negotiated between the groom and Archistrates, just like that between Tarsia and Athenagoras.

The one-sided passion of Archistrates' daughter, so different from the reciprocal eros of the Greek romantic novels, is reminiscent of the quite different amatory paradigm characteristic of classic epic. Apollonius's arrival, destitute, on the shores of Cyrene, where a young, nubile princess intercedes with her father on his behalf, calls to mind Odysseus's arrival in Phaeacia, where he is introduced by the princess Nausicaa to the king and queen, who shower him with gifts and assist him in his return to Ithaca.

The latent marriage tale of the princess and the stranger in the *Odyssey* is developed explicitly in later epic.[8] In the *Argonautica* by Apollonius of Rhodes, Medea falls in love with Jason, who has reached the shores of Colchis in more or less helpless straits, assists him in completing the tasks set by her father, and elopes with him for Greece. Catullus, in poem 64, modeled his narrative of Theseus and Ariadne closely on Apollonius's version of the Medea story, and Vergil, in turn, drew on both for his account of the relationship between Dido and Aeneas. The author of *Apollonius* saw the analogy with the epic pattern, since he sprinkles his description of the young woman's love for Apollonius with apposite quotations from the *Aeneid* relating to Dido's passion (18.13.19–21). The restraint with which Apollonius meets the passion of the young princess recalls the detached and instrumental attitude that characterizes each of the epic heroes mentioned.

The adoration of the young princess for the accomplished Apollonius, under whose authority she is placed in order to be tutored in the liberal arts, suggests an unequal relationship that has affinities with a paternal or patriarchal bond. This is not altogether surprising in the context of conventional ideas of marriage in classical antiquity, where an older and more experienced man was imagined as supervising the training of the still immature bride whom he has taken under his roof.[9] The considerable difference in age between husband and wife that was usual in ancient Greece and Rome facilitated this assimilation of wife to daughter. In this respect, Apollonius's initial relationship with his wife bears a certain resemblance to that with his daughter Tarsia. And it is precisely for this reason, I should like to suggest, that the loss of Tarsia is able to stand in for the separation between husband and wife as the primary focus of the narrative. The separations are represented as involving a similar kind of grief, and the effect on Apollonius is manifested each time as a form of withdrawal. The central narrative of *Apollonius* seems tailored to highlight the vicissitudes of an unequal and parental relationship, in which a father figure is rendered distraught at the loss of a loved one, as opposed to the Greek novel with its concentration on reciprocal passion between equals.

At the beginning of the novel, Apollonius is seen as a wealthy and independent young man who has entered the lists of suitors for the hand of the daughter of Antiochus, the king of Antioch. He is thus, we may note in passing, a man of some worldly experience by the time he accepts Archistrates' daughter in marriage. Antiochus poses a riddle to each of the suitors, and proclaims that failure to solve it means death. The riddle contains Antiochus's real reason for placing difficulties in the way of a match for his daughter, since, as we learn, he has raped her and continues to enjoy her as a wife. Hence he determines to do away with Apollonius, even though Apollonius has in fact divined the meaning of the puzzle.

Antiochus is reported later to have died by a stroke of lightning; the fate of his daughter is left moot, since this initial episode is designed chiefly to motivate Apollonius's exile. Paradigmatically, however, Antiochus's perversion of the father-daughter relationship may be understood as a negative example of the proper association between husband and wife. We have seen that Apollonius's relationship with Archistrates' daughter is in some respects modeled on the bond between parent and child. Eros, at least on the part of Apollonius, has effectively been sublimated in the marriage relation. In the case of Antiochus, to the contrary, the father falls in love (*incidit in amorem*, 1.1.8) with his daughter, the very reverse of the situation between Apollonius and Archistrates' daughter, where the passion is all on the side of the younger and female partner. Antiochus thus converts the paternal relationship into a conjugal bond by acting from the motive of passionate *amor* or eros, exactly the opposite of Apollonius's reduction of courtship and marriage to a relationship of tutelage. Common to the relationships, however, is the premise of an asymmetrical or patriarchal association between husband and wife, which is why Antiochus can serve as the antitype to Apollonius.

If the Greek novel exalts a relationship of mutual love between equals as the basis for a marriage that can endure adversity and separation, the conjugal ideal in *Apollonius* looks to a different model. Here, passionate love is seen as something essentially feminine and immature, understandable in the case of Archistrates' young daughter, but inappropriate to a wise and moderate figure like Apollonius. While Athenagoras the Mytilenean, who will become the husband of Tarsia, was moved by a sexual desire for her, he is later overcome by sympathy for her plight, in part, he explains, because he has a virgin daughter of the same age and is capable of fearing a comparable misfortune in her case (34.27.2; nothing further is said about the girl, or about a previous marriage on Athenagoras's part). Thus, Athenagoras's initial lust is converted into a paternal solicitude. Even while Tarsia is still in the power of the brothel-keeper, Athenagoras begins to look after her as though she were an only daughter of his (*ita eam custodiebat ac si unicam suam filiam*, 36.28.18); indeed, according to the text of an alternative redaction of the novel (B), Athenagoras is said to love her as though she were his daughter (36.69.21). The word is *diligebat* (cf. redaction A, 39.30.17), rather than *amabat,* and is particularly appropriate to fatherly feelings.[10]

The centrality of the father-daughter relationship in *Apollonius* may be illustrated by the description of each of the five kings or princes who play a significant role in the text—Apollonius himself (almost to the end of the story), Archistrates, Athenagoras, Antiochus, and Stranguillio—as having exactly one child, and in every case it is a female child.[11] The narrative may be seen as exploring the right relations between father and daughter and husband and wife, in a social milieu in which a man commonly gave his daughter in marriage to a groom considerably older than herself, and likely closer in age to her father.[12] In these circumstances, the affection between husband and wife, at least in the beginning, no doubt had much of the character of a parental relationship, and the resulting ambiguities, or potential ambiguities, seem to have given rise to a narrative pattern that sorted out the roles of father and husband, and emphasized the self-control that must govern eros on such unequal terms.

Antiochus fails to discriminate between the passion suitable to the wooing of a lover and the appropriate feelings toward a daughter. Archistrates is the example of the good father, whose affection for his child is manifested in his willingness to accede to her choice of a partner. Indeed, in a scene that reads like a takeoff on the test imposed by Antiochus on the suitors, Archistrates is beset by three young scholars who have long sought his daughter in matrimony. Archistrates leaves the choice to her, and she replies by letter as follows: "Excellent king and best of fathers, since you allow me, by the grace of your kindness, I shall speak: I want him as my husband, who was defrauded of his patrimony by shipwreck" (20.15.3–5). The reference to Apollonius would seem unmistakable, but the king fails to catch on, and poses the question to the three young men. Apollonius, however, deciphers the riddle, and the king approves his daughter's preference. The three suitors play no further role in the text.[13]

Riddles occur again in the episode in which Tarsia attempts, at Athenagoras's instigation, to draw Apollonius out of his despair by distracting him with versified conundrums. Tarsia is still in the service of the brothel-keeper, except that she has been given the liberty to earn money as an entertainer, exploiting the benefits of her liberal education (36.28.11–19) in which she, like her mother, excelled (cf. 29.21.21–23). There are thus overtones of a seduction, albeit modestly deployed as a contest of wits, and again Apollonius proves equal to the task. Tarsia is filled with admiration, and is described at one point as "on fire with the cleverness of his solutions" (*inflammata prudentia solutionum,* 42.35.6). Apollonius himself, however, is unmoved, and angrily asserts his right to grieve. Thus the unwitting seduction of the father by the daughter is contained, despite the erotic undertones, by the chastity of the girl, on which she insists when first presenting herself to Apollonius (40.32.15–18), and by Apollonius's own invulnerability to frivolous attractions. The same qualities that earned him a wife protect him from the charms of his unrecognized daughter.

At the conclusion of the novel, we are informed that Apollonius, now secure in his power and reigning over Antioch and Pentapolis as well as Tyre, at last produces a son by his wife (51.43.27). This shift to the male heir closes the narrative that is generated by the tension between the relationships of father-daughter and husband-wife. Apollonius installs his son in the place of the now deceased Archistrates as king of Pentapolis, and it is tempting to see here a resolution of the problem of succession that arises in the absence of a male heir: the realms of Antiochus and Archistrates pass to Apollonius's line.[14] But the primary focus of the narrative is not on dynastic tensions but rather on love and marriage. *Apollonius, King of Tyre* appropriates the general form of the Greek novel, involving the separation and reunion of a primary couple, in the service of a distinct problematic in which conjugal love is de-eroticized and passionate infatuation or eros is charged with anxiety over incest.

When erotic desire asserts itself in an adult male like Antiochus, it is the sign of a profound lack of self-control, and the results are both perverse and destructive. Stranguillio's deference to Dionysias's jealousy in her daughter's behalf proves him unable to disentangle himself from a corrupt passion that is implicitly identified as feminine. Apollonius's young wife herself matures into a woman who chooses chastity in the service of Diana rather than love in any form, and when she is reunited with her husband, her joy is modest: "I am your wife, the daughter of King Archistrates . . . You are my Apollonius of Tyre, you are the master who taught me, you are the one who received me from my father Archistrates, you are the one whom I loved not out of erotic passion [*tu es quem adamavi non libidinis causa*], but as a guide to wisdom" (49.41.11–15).[15] Athenagoras too, for all that he is moved to take the virginity of a well-bred, clever, and pretty girl in a brothel (cf. 33.26.1–2, 9–10), is never described as motivated by *amor*. The emotion that is valorized in the novel as the basis for all relationships within the family is a general affection on the model of that which is supposed to exist naturally between father and daughter. Rather than the passionate eros that unites the protagonists in the Greek novel, *Apollonius* celebrates a filial love or affection of the kind that the Romans called *dilectio* and the Greeks *storgê*. The consequences of this ideal are a certain infantilization of the wife—her reduction to the status of protégée—and the transformation of the daughter into a potential seducer, as illustrated not only by Antiochus's incestuous desire, but also by Tarsia's guise as courtesan when she attempts to draw Apollonius out of his sorrow.[16]

In the preface to his edition of *Apollonius*, Gareth Schmeling sides with those who believe that the work was composed originally in Latin as opposed to an adaptation or translation of a Greek model.[17] Schmeling remarks: "The original *Historia* was produced in the third century, with roots in other novels; it is written in Latin, but related to the Greek novels."[18] For the most part, the argument over the provenance of *Apollonius* has been carried on in terms of coin denominations and prices, and possible reflections of topical or social circumstances.[19] Whatever the truth may be about its relation to a Greek original, *The History of Apollonius, King of Tyre* is in its theme and structure entirely different from the erotic pattern

that informs the surviving Greek novels. In the absence of a Greek analogue for such a type, it is economical to treat *Apollonius* as a distinctly
Latin narrative.

NOTES

A longer version of the materials in this chapter will appear in chapter 3 of D. Konstan, *Sexual Symmetry: Love in the Ancient Novel and Related Genres* (Princeton, 1993).

1. Cf. I. Stark, "Strukturen des griechischen Abenteuer- und Liebesromans," in *Der
Antike Roman: Untersuchungen zur literarischen Kommunikations und Gattungsgeschichte,* ed.
H. Kuch (Berlin, 1989), 82–83; P. G. Walsh, *The Roman Novel: The "Satyricon" of
Petronius and the "Metamorphoses" of Apuleius* (Cambridge, 1970), 7–8; M. Coffey, *Ro-
man Satire* (London, 1976), 183.

2. Stark, "Strukturen," 83.

3. Thus, Walsh, *Roman Novel,* 1, omits discussion of *Apollonius* on the grounds that
"it is better regarded as ideal Greek fiction composed in Latin." But see E. Archibald,
"Fathers and Kings in *Apollonius of Tyre,*" in *Images of Authority: Papers Presented to Joyce
Reynolds on the Occasion of Her Seventieth Birthday,* ed. M. M. Mackenzie and C. Roueché, Cambridge Philological Society, supp. vol. 16 (1989): 25: "*HA* differs considerably
from the Hellenistic romances with which it is often discussed."

4. See D. Konstan, "La rappresentazione dei rapporti erotici nel romanzo greco,"
Materiali e discussioni per l' analisi dei testi classici 19 (1987): 9–27, and "Love and the Greek
Novel," *Differences* 2 (1990): 186–205.

5. See Archibald, "Fathers and Kings," 25: "Two of the most significant differences
[from the Greek novels] are that Apollonius is a king rather than a private citizen, and
that he is a father as well as a lover/husband."

6. At the presumed death of his wife, Apollonius is said to "have clipped the first
tender whiskers of his youth" (*primas suae adulescentiae discerp⟨s⟩it barbulas,* 25.18.14), but
this may mean only that this was the first time he had ever shaved off his beard, and not
that his beard at this time was still the first youthful down. Apollonius addresses
Archistrates' daughter as *nondum mulier,* "not yet a woman" (20.14.25–26), and she is
described as *puella* and even as *puellula,* or "little girl," after she is married and pregnant
(24.17.1, 3).

7. The text is that of G. Schmeling, ed., *Historia Apollonii regis Tyri* (Leipzig, 1988),
17.12.27–28.

8. See R. H. Hague, "Ancient Greek Wedding Songs: The Tradition of Praise,"
Journal of Folklore Research 20 (1983): 131–43, esp. 136–38.

9. Cf. Xenophon's *Oeconomicus* on Ischomachus's education of his young wife; also
Pliny's relationship with his young wife Calpurnia, *Epistles* 4.19, and 5.16.2–3 on the
education of young girls.

10. See 1.1.8–9 of Antiochus: "Coepit eam aliter diligere quam patrem oportebat,"
and cf. Catullus 72.3–4: "Dilexi tum te non tantum ut vulgus amicam / sed pater ut
gnatos diligat et generos"; I am grateful to Elizabeth Archibald for calling my attention
to the parallel passage in redaction B.

11. Cf. Archibald, "Fathers and Kings," 26: "Every significant male character has an
only daughter; the 'basic experience' of the story could be seen as variations on the
theme of father-daughter relations."

12. See P. Garnsey and R. Saller, *The Roman Empire: Economy, Society, and Culture*
(Berkeley and Los Angeles, 1987), 131: "The conventional difference in ages at marriage

for men and women must have encouraged a psychological subordination of wife to husband."

13. The inverse connection between the episodes involving Antiochus's daughter and the daughter of Archistrates is signaled by verbal echoes such as *incidit in amorem* of Antiochus and Archistrates' daughter, or the expression *irrumpit cubiculum* (1.1.12) of Antiochus's assault on his daughter's chamber, which is picked up at 18.13.22, where Archistrates' daughter, overcome with love for Apollonius, bursts into her father's bedroom.

14. See esp. Archibald, "Fathers and Kings," 33.

15. In the B redaction, Apollonius is said to repel his wife when she attempts to embrace him, but this is before she has revealed her identity to him (49.80.20–21).

16. Pliny supervises the education of his young wife, Calpurnia, as though she were a child (*Epistles* 4.19), though in another context he can write to her in terms reminiscent of lovers' complaints (*Epistles* 7.5).

17. Greek model: G. A. A. Kortekaas, *Historia Apollonii regis Tyri,* Medievalia Groningana 3 (Groningen, 1984), 106–14, 118–20; cf. E. Rohde, *Der griechische Roman und seine Vorläufer,* 3d ed. (Leipzig, 1914), 435–53. Latin original: E. Klebs, *Die Erzählung von Apollonius aus Tyrus* (Berlin, 1899). Two bits of papyrus that appear to describe a banquet scene at which a character named Apollonius is present have been taken as fragments of the Greek source of our Latin text, but the identification is exceedingly insecure.

18. Schmeling, *Historia Apollonii regis Tyri,* vi.

19. See especially R. Duncan-Jones, *The Economy of the Roman Empire: Quantitative Studies,* 2d ed. (Cambridge, 1982), 251–56.

CHAPTER TEN

Telling the True Story of the Trojan War: The Eyewitness Account of Dictys of Crete

Stefan Merkle

Finding out the truth about the Trojan War was a task that a wide array of Greek writers set themselves quite early in antiquity. It was not the historicity of the war that was doubted, but the authenticity and reliability of the accounts offered by the poets, especially by Homer himself.

In the sixth and fifth centuries B.C., various authors made serious "scientific" efforts to build up a plausible reconstruction of the events. These include philosophers like Xenophanes, who harshly rejected Homer's representation of the gods, genealogists like Hecataeus of Miletus, and historians: Herodotus tells the "true story" of the rape of Helen in his second book (2.113–20), and Thucydides offers what he thinks is reasonable information about the Trojan War in his *Archaeologia* (1.9–11). Authors who worked on the Trojan War from a historical point of view found themselves confronted with a special dilemma: they did not trust the poets' accounts, yet these accounts necessarily had to be their primary sources. The passages in Herodotus and Thucydides show how historians tried to solve this problem: they resorted to alternative sources,[1] sometimes quite dubious; they tried to find traces of "the truth" in Homer's account (Herodotus 2.116; Thucydides 1.9.3; cf. 10.4); and they offered rationalistic explanations and constructions of their own (Herodotus 2.120; Thucydides 1.11.2). Although historians continued to discuss Homer's reliability for centuries, they made no significant progress in method.

At the other end of the spectrum we find two works, both written in imperial times,[2] whose authors deliberately crossed the border into fiction: the *Ephemeris belli Troiani* of Dictys Cretensis (hereafter, *Ephemeris*) and the *Acta diurna belli Troiani* of Dares Phrygius (hereafter, *Acta*). These writers pretended to offer a solution to the historian's dilemma: they claimed that they were eyewitnesses of the Trojan War and could therefore tell the truth about its events. Dictys, we are told, participated in the war on the Greek side; Dares was a Trojan.[3] Their texts have much in common: both present plausible, rationalistic accounts, in which the gods do not appear personally and the archaic superhuman heroism is reduced to human scale. Each text is preserved in sober Latin prose, prefaced with a dedicatory letter that informs the reader that he or she has a translation from the Greek in hand.[4] The translator of the *Ephemeris* calls himself Septimius, and the Dares translator pretends to be Cornelius Nepos, but in neither case can we identify the translator or the author of the Greek original. Furthermore, both Latin texts exerted great influence on later writers: not Homer, nor Vergil, but Dictys and Dares were used as the ancient sources for the numerous adaptations of the Trojan saga in medieval times. Hans Sachs and even Goethe still used Dictys, while the Greek *Ephemeris* was the basis for the Trojan passages in Byzantine world-chronicles from Johannes Malalas (sixth century) to Johannes Tzetzes (twelfth century).

For the last century it has been a tradition among scholars to put forward two general statements about these texts: (1) Dictys, according to his mask as a Cretan, favors the Greeks; Dares, as a Trojan, the Trojans; (2) both texts are of rather poor literary quality, and Dares' account is even worse than Dictys's "dreary chronicle." That a large-scale review or modification of these opinions has never taken place is due mainly to the peculiar history of scholarship on the two texts. When the first Dictys papyrus was published in 1907, the "Diktys-Frage"—the question of whether a Greek original had ever really existed—was answered in the affirmative. By analogy to Dictys, a Greek original was assumed for Dares, too,[5] and thereby the most interesting problem about the works seemed to be solved. As there was complete agreement on the poor literary quality of the texts, it was not considered worthwhile to examine them from a literary point of view. For a long time, even the growing interest in the ancient novel brought about no change. Although the label "Troy Romances," already attributed to the texts in the last century, had helped Dictys and Dares find their place in most monographs on the ancient novel, scholars usually confined themselves to summarizing their contents and repeating the abovementioned statements. It was not until the beginning of the 1970s that somewhat more intensive research began on one of the works, Dictys's *Ephemeris*,[6] but nonetheless the basic attitude toward the text has hardly changed. I will examine how much can still be held true about these received opinions on the *Ephemeris*.

A first glance at the text seems to confirm the judgment of the poor literary quality of the work. As already mentioned, the *Ephemeris* is written in an unpretentious, simple prose style, more reminiscent of a documentary report than of elaborate *Kunstprosa*. But if we take a closer look at the text itself and recall the specific conditions under which it was written, it becomes clear that Dictys had good reasons to adopt such a style; in the first or second century A.D. he was claiming to present an eyewitness account of the Trojan War, a record no one had ever heard of before. And what he had to tell was not just a slightly modified version of Homer and the epic cycle, but a very special, new, rational version of the events: the "true story" of the Trojan War.

In order to make his claim believable, the author felt it necessary to construct an elaborate *Beglaubigungsapparat,* that is, a collection of credentials. He did this in a way that surpassed everything other ancient authors had achieved in this field.

On the one hand, he invented a complicated story of the discovery of the text. In a prologue, the reader is informed that "Dictys" had a copy of his work buried in his grave near Cnossus, where it had lain hidden from the time of the Trojan War on, until in the thirteenth year of Nero's reign (A.D. 66) an earthquake opened the grave and shepherds found the text.[7] They took it to their master, a certain Eupraxides, who passed it on to the *consularis Cretae,* or governor of Crete, who then sent Eupraxides with the find to Rome to present it to the emperor himself. Excited by the discovery, Nero ordered his specialists to render it from the ancient Phoenician language and letters Dictys had used into Greek, and to store it in the Greek library. A comparison with similar passages in other historical or fictitious texts shows that Dictys made use of almost all motifs that had been developed for such purposes in antiquity.[8]

On the other hand—and this is most important for the final shape of the work—Dictys styled himself a reliable historian. Twice, in a kind of "delayed prologue" (1.13) and in a *sphragis* (5.17), he avers his reliability as a historian and comments on his "method," referring (according to historiographical practice) both to his αὐτοψία and to the questioning of eyewitnesses. During the description of the events in which the chronicler himself does not appear, we find him using further formulas taken from historiography, such as providing numerous details about time, battle formations, and strategic actions, or offering alternative explanations for certain events, thus leading the reader to accept his account as the product of conscientious treatment of highly reliable sources.

But most importantly, Dictys made himself the official war-chronicler of the Cretan king Idomeneus. Consequently he chose the genre *ephemeris* for his work, that is, a *commentarius* (the terms were used as synonyms), a military record written in simple prose style. Therefore, an unpretentious description of events was an essential part of the *Beglaubigungsapparat* of the *Ephemeris* and not the consequence of the author's insufficiency. Scholars who stigmatize the text as *Machwerk,* "dreary chronicle," "artless and abrupt," or call it—more jovially—"eine alberne Erzählung aus dem Troischen Kriege," have not paid sufficient attention to this fact.[9]

As the choice of style forced the author to dispense with rhetorical embroidery, it was necessary for him to concentrate on the use of structural techniques and on a consistent construction of his new story. Dictys had considerable talents in this respect, and they are most in evidence in his representation of the figure of Achilles. He skillfully combines archaic material, later motifs, and inventions of his own in order to create a convincing character as well as an original version of the whole story.

The *Ephemeris* is handed down to us in an abridged Latin translation consisting of six books. Only the abovementioned two papyrus fragments remain from the nine books of the Greek original. Close comparison of the Latin text and the Greek fragments shows that in books 1 through 5, which contain the events of the war from the rape of Helen to the sack of Troy, the translator on the whole maintained the structure and contents of the original, but he improved it stylistically. Book 6 of the Latin version is an epitome of four books, which contained the *Nostoi* of the Greeks. From these facts we draw two conclusions: (1) a survey of narrative techniques in the *Ephemeris* must be based on books 1–5 of the Latin translation; (2) in all probability the observed techniques had close equivalents in the Greek text.

As in the *Iliad*, Achilles is the leading character of the account. He dominates events in the center of the story, he is the "best of the Achaeans," he kills Hector and thus brings about the military outcome of the war. But Dictys tells us something else about Achilles, something Homer never mentions: Achilles falls in love with Polyxena, the beautiful daughter of the Trojan king. Although there is no certain evidence, it is commonly assumed that the story of Achilles' love for Polyxena has its origin in Hellenistic times. It probably was invented to explain why Achilles' ghost demands the sacrifice of Polyxena, as we know for example from Euripides' *Hecuba*. Be that as it may, in the *Ephemeris* this love is not just an episode; rather, placed in the center of the account, it is an essential part of the whole story and perfectly integrated into the new construction of events.

Dictys does not tell a "love story," as the authors of Greek romances would have done. We hear nothing about Polyxena's feelings, and the lovers meet only twice. Dictys is interested in Achilles' reactions; he uses the love motif to change the traditional story significantly and to make his innovations plausible. For this purpose he closely connects Achilles' love for Polyxena with the decisive period of the war. It marks the turning point in Achilles' fate as well as in the course of events.

Nevertheless, Achilles' falling in love with Polyxena reads remarkably like the primal scene of a Greek romance. At the beginning of book 3, he sees Polyxena beautifully adorned as a priestess of Apollo and immediately falls in love with her. From the moment he is smitten with Polyxena, he is beside himself with desire; he wanders, aimless and distracted; his behavior and his attitude toward the war change remarkably. Achilles—who up to this point had appeared as the preeminent Greek warrior, admired and beloved by the Greek army—now, out of his deep affection, offers Hector his own withdrawal from the war in exchange for Polyxena's hand. Brusquely snubbed and rejected by the son of Priam, he vows horrible vengeance.

From now on he is painfully torn by his passion for Polyxena, his hatred for Hector and the Trojans, and his sense of duty. These starkly contrasted psychological states are mirrored in his unpredictable behavior. On the one hand, he rages brutally through the Trojan ranks, showing no sign of mercy or humanity. This is the dominating aspect of the account in book 3 and in the first half of book 4; in his extreme severity Achilles causes the defeat of the Trojans. Only in two short but significant passages does the author remind the reader of the reason for Achilles' relentless behavior: we see him bursting into tears as he meets Polyxena the second time; he sends her back to Troy generously provided with precious gifts (3.24, 27). Finally, we hear that Alexander (Paris) and Deiphobus are able to kill him deceitfully in an ambush, because he carelessly meets his enemies unarmed and unprotected in order to negotiate for Polyxena (4.10–11).

Through his increasingly erratic and brutal behavior, Achilles distances himself from the more controlled and civilized conduct toward the Trojans that the Greeks had exhibited up to this point in the piece. In their previous confrontations with the enemy, the Greeks proved themselves far superior, both militarily and ethically. Attacking and killing the enemy deceitfully and underhandedly, making assaults during armistice and funerals—in short, behaving barbarously—is the Trojan method of warfare in the *Ephemeris;* the Greeks fight bravely and honorably. Achilles steadily loses this moral superiority to the Trojans, and the more he loses it, the more he becomes estranged from the Greeks and isolates himself. Dictys makes this process absolutely clear, as two examples will illustrate.

1. Dictys's version of Hector's death shows that Achilles is no longer a brave and honorable hero. In the *Ephemeris,* Achilles kills Hector not in an open fight, but deceitfully in an ambush; moreover, he cuts off the hands of a captured son of Priam before sending him back to Troy with the message of Hector's death (3.15).

2. Afterward, telling the "true story" of the return of Hector's body, Dictys uses the new constellations to create a most impressive and unconventional passage (3.20–27). He turns Homer's famous account on its head: Priam, in Dictys's version a totally wrecked, pitiable old

187

man, arrives with a large entourage, at daylight. He is cordially welcomed by the Greek rulers, but meets a severe and completely unmoved Achilles. In this situation Achilles' isolation within the Greek army becomes evident: in sharp contrast to Homer's version, in the *Ephemeris* the son of Peleus must be induced by the merciful Greek rulers to return Hector's body. He stands all alone in his severity.

Is Dictys's Achilles nothing more than a cross between two traditions, carelessly combined by a clumsy author, as has been argued? The opposite seems true: Dictys obviously was well aware of what he was doing, and tried to make sure that the reader could accept his Achilles as a consistent character. When Achilles first appears in the text (1.14), the author sets him apart through a specific characterization, which explicitly stresses the gulf between his unique *virtus* and his extreme emotionality:

> Hic in primis adulescentiae annis, procerus, decora facie, studio rerum bellicarum omnes iam tum virtute atque gloria superabat, neque tamen aberat ab eo vis quaedam inconsulta et effera morum impatientia. (1.14)

> He in his early adolescence, tall, a fine figure of a man, even then with his dedication to soldiering surpassed all others in virtue and glory, whereas he was not free from a certain urge to behave rashly and with fierce impatience.

This passage is repeated almost verbatim as Ajax finds the son of Peleus mortally wounded. In a kind of eulogy, Ajax says:

> Fuit confirmatum ac verum per mortales nullum hominum existere potuisse, qui te vera virtute superaret, sed, ut palam est, tua te inconsulta temeritas prodidit. (4.15)

> It has been considered as absolutely true among mortals that no human being could exist, who would surpass you in real virtue, but evidently your own rashness had led you to disaster.

The first characterization and the eulogy frame Achilles' inconsistent behavior and his changeable fate. Indeed, this description of Achilles' character recalls Homer's Achilles, but it also fits perfectly in Dictys's account. The author deliberately picked up the tension within Achilles and gave it a new function within his new context. Achilles' passion and his increasing violence is therefore not an inconsistency in his character, but rather the gradual revelation of a characteristic feature, which is part of his personality from the beginning of the story. There can be no doubt that Dictys conceived his Achilles carefully and made every effort to create a convincing character.

This representation of Achilles, however, is not only an impressive depiction of a problematic character; still more, it is an essential part of the conception of the whole work. Achilles' increasing severity corresponds to a gradual change in the attitudes of the Greeks during the course of the story. The contrast between the beginning of the account and its end shows the extent of this development. The *Ephemeris* starts with the description of a peaceful meeting of Greek rulers on Crete. They receive a warm welcome on the island; a great celebration is held in their honor, with a solemn sacrifice and a splendid banquet. Like a bolt from the blue the message of the rape of Helen breaks into this harmonious, almost idyllic world (1.3). The Greeks react calmly and circumspectly and in complete solidarity. Immediately they organize a meeting at Sparta and decide unanimously to send a delegation to Troy to solve the problem peacefully (1.4). Not until these legates return empty-handed, derided and nearly assassinated by the sons of Priam, do they decide to start preparations for the campaign. Thus at the beginning of the account the author presents the Greeks as a peaceful nation living together in harmony and completely irreproachable in their conduct toward foreign nations.

Diametrically opposite to this picture is the Greeks' behavior ten years later, at the end of the war. The description of the sack of Troy (5.12f.) shows the reader that the Greeks have to a large extent lost their moral superiority over the Trojans, which they had maintained for most of the account. The author does not refrain from describing the cruelties found in the traditional versions, including the deliberate massacre of Trojans, who begged for their lives at the city's altars.

But the climax of this development is not reached until the description of the events following the sack of Troy. Only here does the author report the famous quarrel between Odysseus and Ajax that results in Ajax's death (5.14f). And by placing the episode at the end of the account, the author can allow tensions to erupt that had arisen within the Greek army in the course of the story, and construct an impressive finale. To this end Dictys not only changes the traditional position of the episode, he also significantly alters the traditional course of events. The morning after the dispute the Greeks find Ajax *ferro interfectum* (killed by a sword). The Atrides and Odysseus are held to be guilty of his assassination and have to leave the camp disgraced and dishonored. Murder and strife, cruelty and violence now prevail among the Greeks. Transported to the end of the story, the episode is a kind of "epilogue" to the Trojan War, and thus corresponds to the beginning of the account, the "prologue" on Crete and in Sparta. Dictys has deliberately related these two different pictures of the Greeks: the harmony at the beginning and the violence and discord at the end. Within the tale the change in Greek conduct proceeds step by step. In this process Dictys's representation of Achilles has an important function. In the center of his work the author represents the decline of the Greeks through Achilles; the son of Peleus acts on behalf of the Greeks, and prefigures their later conduct.

As we have seen, the author makes this development in Achilles plausible, both by his initial characterization of the hero and by Ajax's eulogy—or, to put it another way, by his adaptation of Homeric material and by his careful use of structural devices. On closer examination of the way Dictys integrates the Achilles-Polyxena story into the course of events, we find him using similar techniques. Two examples will suffice:

1. The preparation of the "love story": in order to prepare for Achilles' dominant role in the center of the account, as well as for his growing isolation within the Greek army, Dictys places the Chryseis-Briseis episode[10]—slightly but significantly changed—toward the end of the second book (2.28–34). In the *Ephemeris,* Achilles first fights for the lives of the soldiers, who die—as in the *Iliad*—of a horrible epidemic, he gives up Hippodamia for love of his fellow warriors, and consequently he is as disappointed about their lack of support as he is furious with Agamemnon (2.33). Unlike in the *Iliad,* Achilles is reconciled shortly afterward, but here again, in Dictys's version of the πρεσβεία (2.50–52), Achilles bitterly complains of the Greeks' attitude toward himself; not Agamemnon alone, he says, but the other Greeks in particular were to blame (2.51). Now Achilles is right in the center of events and has taken up his special position in the Greek army; the first indications of his conduct in book 3 are established. The Chryseis episode simply marks the first alienation between Achilles and the Greek soldiers, whose entire admiration and dedication the hero had enjoyed until then; Dictys therefore adapted the heart of the *Iliad* and subordinated it as a kind of prelude to the center of his account.

2. The disposition of the "love story": since we find no trace of the love story about Achilles and Polyxena before the Greek *Ephemeris* (one of the Dictys papyri contains a part of it), it is hardly possible to determine Dictys's own contributions to his version definitely. But there are at least two important aspects in Dictys's account that do not appear in any other extant version of the story.[11] First, the arrangement of the love story in three parts (3.2: first encounter; 3.24, 27: second encounter at the Lytra; 4.13: Achilles' assassination); as a consequence the Achilles-Polyxena story is located in the beginning, the center, and the end of the crucial phase of the war, which gives a remarkable unity to the account. Second, Hector's involvement in the love story, through which Achilles' love becomes the main motivation for his fierce attacks against Hector and the Trojans that determine the military outcome of the war.

The love story fits perfectly into the conception of the whole work and enables the author to emphasize his main themes in its central passage. On the one hand, the moral decline of the Greeks is foreshadowed by Achilles. On the other hand, the antiheroic tendencies of the work are further developed; in the *Ephemeris,* Achilles' heroic decision for a short but glorious life and his longing to avenge Patroclus's death are replaced by nonheroic lovesickness, Homer's spectacular single combat between Achilles and Hector is changed into an ambush, and finally there is no need for a god to kill Achilles in the *Ephemeris*—only another ambush, a deceitful offer of negotiations about Polyxena. Moreover, the representation of love and passion as a dangerous and destructive power, as shown in the Achilles-Polyxena story, becomes a major motif in the *Ephemeris,* appearing in prominent places in the account: at the beginning, as established by tradition, with the story of Helen and Paris; in the center, where Dictys locates the Achilles-Polyxena story; and at the end, again due to Dictys's arrangement, when Menelaus's love for Helen causes the death of Ajax (5.14f.).[12]

Last but not least, the moral inferiority of the Trojans, emphasized throughout the account, culminates with Achilles' assassination in the temple of Apollo, and so the end of the Achilles-Polyxena story initiates the final stages of the *Ephemeris.* From this point on the atmosphere of the tale changes remarkably. By accumulating ominous events and relevant comments in speeches, the author makes it possible for the reader to conclude that because of their heinous deed, divine wrath overcomes the Trojans.

In sum, generalizations about both the poor literary quality of the text and Dictys's favoring the Greeks are highly doubtful. Within the self-imposed limits of an eyewitness account, the author handled his material with considerable skill. The label "pro-Greek" applies to only one aspect of the text.[13] It is true that the Trojans are presented in a negative way, but in addition we notice an ethical decline among the Greeks. Thus the *Ephemeris* presents two main facets of the Trojan War:

1. The Trojan War is a campaign of a highly cultivated and peaceful nation that had suffered great injustice at the hands of completely unscrupulous barbarians.
2. It is the story of the moral decline of the victors. The Greeks may have won the war, but they are no longer as they had been at the beginning. They have paid for their victory with the loss of their moral integrity.

Is this work, as we often read, nothing more than mere entertainment, *Unterhaltungsliteratur,* conceived only to please educated readers with a surprisingly new version of the Trojan War? This question must be answered separately for the Greek original and the Latin translation.

Paradoxically, an estimation of the completely preserved Latin version is more difficult than that of the original, which is for the most part lost. We cannot clearly determine the time of origin of the translation, nor can we be absolutely sure whether the translator could see through the fictitiousness of the eyewitness construction. The translator's literary ambitions at least leave no doubt: he made an effort to improve the original account stylistically, especially by using Sallustian expressions, and he added moralizing remarks and psychological explanations.

The dating of the Latin version is controversial. The arguments behind the *communis opinio,* ascribing it to the fourth century A.D., have been weakened by recent studies that prefer to date the work to the second or third century and think that the translator should be placed among Latin archaists like Gellius and Fronto.[14] There is no clear evidence for either of these hypotheses, but in my opinion the following considerations make the dating to the fourth century—despite these studies—more likely. It is true that the literati of the second and early third centuries who were mainly interested in antiquarian details had an excellent knowledge of Homer, but they were concerned almost exclusively with details or problems of style, language, and prosody, whereas there was a remarkable lack of interest in the content of his works. Moreover, we have not a single Latin translation of a Greek text that compares to the *Ephemeris* in content and style. The Latin literature of this time does not suggest a readership interested in a Latin version of an eyewitness record like the *Ephemeris.*

On the other hand, in the fourth century we come across a great number of Latin works and translations from Greek into Latin that seem to respond to an intense and widespread interest in historical questions. Examples include the rather novelistic adaptations of the Alexander material, representations of the whole of Roman history, reaching back even to the prehistory of Rome, such as the *Breviaria* of Festus and Eutropius, and the *Corpus Aurelianum,* which contains heterogeneous works of literature. Like the translator of the *Ephemeris,* numerous writers of this period show strong affinities to Sallust's style. In my view a translation of the *Ephemeris* would fit well in this context. As a narrative in the form of a historical source, it would correspond to the interest in history before the foundation of Rome. If these assumptions are correct, the Latin *Ephemeris* must be seen as a kind of didactic *Unterhaltungsliteratur.*

But what about the Greek original? Here at least we can be sure of the time of origin: the Greek *Ephemeris* was written between A.D. 66 and A.D. 200, as the year 66 is mentioned in the prologue, and the older papyrus is dated to about 200. We know, too, that it was the Greek author who deliberately created an anti-Trojan and pessimistic description of the Trojan War. How does this account fit with the Greek literature of this period? That literature is characterized by two basic and divergent tendencies.

Most of the Greek authors of that time reacted to the political predominance of Rome by concentrating on the Greeks' glorious past while ignoring the Romans completely. Others, such as Dio Chrysostom, Appian, and Cassius Dio, dealt primarily with the Romans, their empire, and its past. As we do not know Dictys's positions from other works, a comparison with closely related texts might give us some indication of how to understand the *Ephemeris*. From this period three works are preserved that contain pseudoeyewitness records of the Trojan War: the Τρωικὸς Λόγος (*Orationes* 11) of Dio Chrysostom, a passage in Lucian's *Cock,* and Philostratus's dialogue *Heroicus.*

Among these texts, only Lucian's account (*Cock* 17) can be considered a pure literary game. The cock claims that in a former life he had participated in the Trojan War as the Trojan Euphorbus, and he denies Homer's competence to describe the war; Homer, he says, was at that time a camel in Bactria. The cock's short report about the real facts looks like a compressed parody of eyewitness records like the *Ephemeris.* Such a literary game is far from Dictys's intention: we find no parodic features in the *Ephemeris.*

In Dio's speech, however, and more obviously in Philostratus's dialogue, we clearly recognize extraliterary implications in addition to the authors' literary ambitions. In his Τρωικὸς Λόγος, written about the beginning of the second century A.D., Dio Chrysostom states that Troy had never been sacked by the Greeks. Just the opposite: it was the Greeks who lost the war after they had attacked Troy arbitrarily and without cause. As his source, Dio names the chronicles of Egyptian priests that were based on a report of Menelaus himself. Naturally, this work is above all a splendid, spirited epideictic speech, but it is most probable that with the pro-Trojan conception of the text, Dio expressed his sympathy for the heirs of the Trojans, the Romans.

Even more obvious is Rome's influence in the dialogue *Heroicus* of Philostratus, written shortly after A.D. 200. Here a Thracian vintner, who is in contact with the ghost of the hero Protesilaus, convinces a skeptical Phoenician of the existence and power of the old heroes in his own time. Here, too, a positive picture of the Trojans is drawn. It has long been recognized that there is a strong connection between this dialogue and the religious policy of the imperial family, which had as one of its goals the revival of the ancient hero cults. Philostratus, who lived at the court of Caracalla and his mother Julia Domna, wrote his dialogue in order to support and justify Caracalla's most extravagant worship of the heroes.

The *Heroicus* is of great relevance for the *Ephemeris,* insofar as there are two passages in the dialogue that are most probably to be considered direct polemics against the *Ephemeris.* First, Protesilaus declares that Idomeneus did not take part in the Trojan War (*Heroicus* 30); then we read (*Heroicus*

26.10) that the use of writing was unknown at that time. Thus Philostratus most subtly and elegantly destroys the basis of the *Ephemeris's* claim to authority: Dictys maintained that he wrote his work in Phoenician letters and as Idomeneus's official chronicler. Philostratus had every reason to attack the *Ephemeris:* with its rationalistic, nonheroic conception it is diametrically opposed to Philostratus's aims.

As we can see, these three texts represent a remarkably broad spectrum of literary forms and authorial intentions, all connected by Greek authors in this period with pseudoeyewitness accounts of the Trojan War. But despite the variety of these texts, there are three points in which the *Ephemeris* differs fundamentally from all of them: (1) its strong anti-Trojan tendencies, (2) the choice of the genre of military record, which limited the possibilities of literary shaping, but laid claim to the highest credibility, and (3) the description of the moral decline of the victors.

Thus I offer the following hypothesis. In their highly literary rhetorical works, both Dio and Philostratus express a clear sympathy for Rome. In similar fashion, in the course of an entertaining narrative, Dictys expresses his antipathy to Rome, the heir of Troy, but he does this without a complete moral rehabilitation of the Greeks,[15] and that may indicate that he had an ethical purpose: to reveal the disastrous effects of war on human character.

NOTES

1. Herodotus refers to accounts of Egyptian priests (2.113, 116, 120); Thucydides names well-informed Peloponnesians as his source for one detail (1.9.2).

2. For the dating of the *Ephemeris,* see the discussion that follows. The Latin *Acta* are dated to the fifth century A.D. (see W. Schetter, "Dares und Dracontius über die Vorgeschichte des Trojanischen Krieges," *Hermes* 115 [1987]: 211–31).

3. Dictys and Dares usually are regarded as the authors of the only extant works of a genre called "Troy Romances," which consisted of comparable pseudepigrapha or works based on fictitious sources. The traces that remain of such works before the *Ephemeris,* however, are somewhat faint. With reasonable certainty we can say only that about 200 B.C. a Hegesianax wrote a pseudepigraphon on the Trojan War using the pseudonym Cephalon of Gergithion (Athenaeus 9.393D = F. Jacoby, ed., *Die Fragmente der griechischen Historiker,* vol. 1, *Genealogie und Mythographie,* 3d ed. [Leiden, 1957], 45T7; hereafter cited as *FGrHist*).

4. In the case of Dictys this claim was confirmed by two papyri, the first published in 1907, the second in 1966; both are added to W. Eisenhut's edition: *Dictys Cretensis ephemeridos belli Troiani libri a Lucio Septimio ex Graeco in Latinum sermonem translati, accedunt papyri Dictys Graeci in Aegypto inventae,* 2d ed. (Leipzig, 1973). For the existence of a Greek Dares, however, we have no clear evidence; the often-quoted passages of Ptolemaeus Chennus (*FGrHist* 51T5) and Aelian (*Varia historia* 11.2), where a "Phrygian Iliad" of a Dares is quoted, cannot refer to our Dares (cf. *FGrHist,* 532). Apart from certain disparities in content between the fragments of this "Iliad" and the *Acta,* it is highly probable that Ptolemaeus and Aelian talk about an epos.

5. Most scholars still tend to assume the existence of a Greek Dares. For a detailed discussion of the problem, see A. Beschorner, *Untersuchungen zu Dares Phrygius,* Classica Monacensia, 4 (Tübingen, 1992), 231–43.

6. Translation and commentary: H. J. Marblestone, "Dictys Cretensis: A Study of the 'Ephemeris belli Troiani' as a Cretan Pseudepigraphon" (Ph.D. diss., Brandeis University, 1970). Cf. the translation of R. M. Frazer, *The Trojan War: The Chronicles of Dictys of Crete and Dares the Phrygian* (Bloomington, Ind., 1966). On Dictys and Homer: G. F. Gianotti, "Le metamorfosi di Omero: Il romanzo di Troia dalla specializzazione delle scholae ad un pubblico di non specialisti," *Sigma* 12, no. 1 (1979): 15–32, and P. Venini, "Ditti Cretese e Omero," *Memorie dell' Istituto Lombardo* 37 (1981–82): 161–98. On the dating of the Latin *Ephemeris,* see n. 14 below. On aspects of narrative technique: A. M. Milazzo, "Achille e Polissena in Ditti Cretese: un romanzo nel romanzo?" *Le forme e la storia* 5 (1984): 3–24, and S. Timpanaro, "Sulla composizione e la tecnica narrativa dell'*Ephemeris* di Ditti-Settimio," in *Filologia e forme letterarie: Studi offerti a F. Della Corte* (Urbino, 1987), 4:169–215. On various aspects: W. Eisenhut, "Spätantike Troja-Erzählungen—mit einem Ausblick auf die mittelalterliche Troja-Literatur," *Mittellateinisches Jahrbuch* 18 (1983): 1–28. This chapter is an abstract of S. Merkle, *Die Ephemeris belli Troiani des Diktys von Kreta,* Studien zur klassischen Philologie, 44 (Frankfurt am Main, 1989). For Dares, see: Schetter, "Dares und Dracontius"; Schetter, "Beobachtungen zum Dares Latinus," *Hermes* 116 (1988): 94–109; Eisenhut, "Spätantike Troja-Erzählungen"; Merkle, "*Troiani belli verior textus*: Die Trojaberichte des Dictys und Dares," in *Die deutsche Trojaliteratur des Mittelalters und der Frühen Neuzeit,* ed. H. Brunner (Wiesbaden, 1990), 491–522; Beschorner, *Untersuchungen.*

7. The Latin translator replaced the prologue by his dedicatory letter in which he integrated the story in a slightly altered version. In all probability the Greek πρόλογος was translated and added to the text afterward (cf. Eisenhut, "Spätantike Troja-Erzählungen," 18–22).

8. See, e.g., the report of the discovery of Hercules' plea for peace in Alcmenes' grave in Plutarch, *De genio Socratis* 5.577E f. and 7.578F f., the story of the discovery of Pythagorean texts in the grave of King Numa in Pliny, *Naturalis historia* 13.84–87, Livy 40.29.3–14, and Plutarch, *Numa* 22, the highly complicated construction of Antonius Diogenes, or the later Christian report about the gospel of Matthew in Barnabas's grave. Cf. W. Speyer, *Die literarische Fälschung im heidnischen und christlichen Altertum: Ein Versuch ihrer Deutung,* Handbuch der Altertumswissenschaft, 1.2 (Munich, 1971).

9. See, e.g., R. Helm, *Der antike Roman* (Berlin, 1948), 21; R. T. Bruère, review of *The Trojan War* by R. M. Frazer, *Classical Philology* 61 (1966): 216; Marblestone, *Dictys Cretensis,* 370; W. Aly, *Geschichte der griechischen Literatur* (Leipzig, 1925), 315.

10. Chryseis is called Astynome; Briseis is Hippodamia.

11. See Hyginus, *Fabulae* 110; Philostratus, *Heroicus* 51.1–6; Servius ad Vergil, *Aeneid* 6.57 and 2.321; Scholia ad Lycophron, *Cassandra* 269; Dares 27 and 34.

12. In the *Ephemeris,* the Atrides' motive for their fatal decision in the quarrel between Odysseus and Ajax (5.14f.) is Menelaus's love for Helen. Meeting the approval of *multi boni,* Ajax plans to kill Helen after the sack of Troy. But with the help of Odysseus, Menelaus, *amorem coniugii etiam tunc retinens,* manages to save her life (5.14). As a reward, the Atrides decide in favor of Odysseus. Ajax vows vengeance, his fellow warriors violently revile the Atrides, *quippe quis magis libido desideriumque in femina quam summa militiae potiora forent* (5.15). The following morning, Ajax is found killed.

13. In the case of Dares, too, the label "pro-Trojan" describes only one facet of the account. Not only is Dares' picture of the Trojans much more positive than that of Dictys: the Greeks, too, come off better. Dares rigorously removed the problematic actions of the Greek that "pro-Greek" Dictys does describe, e.g., Iphigenia's sacrifice, Palamedes' assassination, and Ajax's death (cf. also the Greeks' honorable conduct after

the sack of Troy, *Acta* 52). The "Trojan" Dares does not disparage the "enemies," as Dictys does. In general, Dares' and Dictys's accounts are not at all like mirror images, as the fictitious identities of the authors might suggest. The relations between the texts still await study.

14. A. Cameron, "Poetae Novelli," *Harvard Studies in Classical Philology* 84 (1980): 172–75, and E. Champlin, "Serenus Sammonicus," *Harvard Studies in Classical Philology* 85 (1981): 189–212. On the dating, see also Eisenhut, "Spätantike Troja-Erzählungen," 26–28, and Merkle, *Die Ephemeris belli Troiani,* 263–83.

15. See, e.g., Aelian, *Varia historia* 3.12; Dio Chrysostom, *Orationes* 11.150–54.

PART V

The Real World

CHAPTER ELEVEN

Longus, Natural History, and Realism

W. Geoffrey Arnott

I

It is widely recognized that Longus's attitude to the realistic portrayal of scenes and events is an important element in the interpretation of his novel *Daphnis and Chloe.* Was Longus familiar with Lesbos, the scene of his novel, and so able to describe its landscape, pasturage, agriculture, and daily life from observation at first hand, or was the island's name chosen merely as an adventitious symbol for a pastoral Utopia, described from imagination and written sources, not from personal experience?[1] This question is made more difficult by at least two complicating factors. First, there is the need to take account of a tendency in ancient writers to mingle fact and fiction in their records even of allegedly historical events.[2] Second, like many other writers of his period, Longus incorporates into his narrative motifs, ideas, and phrases from earlier writers, developing the borrowed material with a series of variations and additions until the resultant passage conveys a paradoxical double boast—of its author's knowledge of great predecessors revealed by the imitation, and of his own originality revealed by the creative development of borrowed material.[3] In this essay, I examine the question posed above from the angle of natural history, selecting that angle partly because it has been neglected by most classicists, who lack the required specialist interest in wildlife, and partly also because the introduction to Vieillefond's recently published edition of Longus contains a detailed analysis of the novelist's two most extended incursions into the fields of natural history and horticulture (Daphnis's bird-catching expedition, 3.3–11; Dionysophanes' park, 4.2–4), and argues for substantial inaccuracies of detail that can, in the editor's opinion, be explained only by Longus's personal ignorance of subjects such as natural history, horticulture, and hunting.[4] The only way to test the validity of these criticisms (particularly those concerned with natural history) is to submit the relevant passages of Longus to a stringent reexamination in light of what was already known in the time of Longus, and of what has subsequently been discovered by modern specialists.

Before the analysis of individual passages begins, however, a few general points need to be made. Throughout most of *Daphnis and Chloe* specificity is blurred; in its idealization the world is presented with a minimum of identifying detail.[5] We are not usually offered the proliferation of precise information about landscape and natural history that we find, for instance, in Theocritus, who loads the narrative frame of his seventh idyll with names of people, places, geographical features, and allusions to the plants and wildlife of the eastern Mediterranean, and thus creates such an illusion of reality that it is still possible to follow the movements of the people mentioned in the idyll and to see what they saw in the places where they saw them.[6] Such specificity is generally absent from Longus. The pastures where Daphnis and Chloe tend their sheep and goats, for instance, are never described in detail. Three trees that grow there are repeatedly mentioned: a pine (πίτυς) sacred to Pan (2.23.4, 24.2, 31.2, 3, 39.1; 3.12.2; 4.39.2), an evergreen oak (φηγός) under which the lovers sat (2.21.3, 30.2; 4.13.2), and a deciduous oak (δρῦς) where they also sat (1.12.5, 13.4; 2.11.1, 38.3; 3.12.2, 16.1). These trees, however, are never described in detail, and their positions relative to each other and to their pastoral landscape are never clarified.[7]

This common lack of individualizing detail may be illustrated in another way. Longus seems to prefer, in much of his narrative, references to unspecified birds and plants. Thus the general term ἄνθος (flower) occurs twenty-seven or twenty-eight times (there is some doubt over the text at 1.32.2), φυτόν (plant) thirteen times, and ὄρνις (bird) twenth-three times.

Against this pervasive background of an unparticularized landscape, however, Longus chooses to insert from time to time in vivid contrast passages where specific, eye-catching, and memorable details from wildlife are precisely focused. Such passages may be elaborate and extensive, like the three major descriptive pieces interlarded at roughly equal intervals in *Daphnis and Chloe* (Philetas's garden, where Eros was encountered, 2.3–7; Daphnis's bird-catching expedition, directly preceded by a pictorial description of winter and directly followed by an equally pictorial description of the arrival of spring, 3.3–12; Dionysophanes' park and its vandalizing, 4.2–10), where trees, birds, and flowers are specifically named, precisely placed, and sometimes described in loving detail. Or the passages may be no more than individual sentences or phrases, adding by their relatively infrequent insertion a graphic particularity to an otherwise generalized background. Taken together, however, these passages provide enough material for us to test Longus's knowledge of natural history, and so to decide whether his usual preference for the general and nonspecific springs from artistic choice or from ignorance of the natural world.

At the same time, an examination of these encapsulated passages will reveal that sometimes a realistic detail of natural history in Longus is not original to him but derived rather from an identifiable source, such as Theocritus or Homer. This use of borrowed material does not make an investigation of the accuracy of any statement contained therein about wildlife at all less necessary—we are seeking to establish Longus's reliability in this area, not his originality—but it does inevitably complicate issues concerned with Longus's reliability. We shall never be certain that a correctly observed phenomenon in Longus that is unparalleled in extant ancient literature is the fruit of his own observation, since it could always have been taken by such a writer from some lost source.

II

1.26.1–3. Longus's three other references to the τέττιξ—the general term for any cicada, of which there are several species in modern Greece, both large (e.g., *Tibicen plebejus, T. haematodes, Cicada orni*) and small (e.g., *Cicadetta montana, C. atra, C. tibialis, Pagiphora annulata*)[8]—are wholly conventional, emphasizing the attractiveness (1.23.1) and the uninterrupted loudness (1.25.3; cf. 3.24.2) of the noise these insects make.[9] At 1.26.1–3, the same conventional elements can still be found (ἐξήχησεν, "it sounded forth," 2; μηδὲ ἐν τῇ δεξιᾷ σιωπῶντα, "not even silent in the hand," 3; λαλοῦντα, "chattering," 3),[10] but now they are embedded in a narrative that is made to rise above mere conventionality by a series of imaginative touches. A cicada, pursued by a χελιδών, takes refuge under the garment that covers Chloe's breasts. The pursuing bird is thus unable to capture its intended prey, but with its wings it brushes Chloe's cheek as it flies past. The cicada continues its chirring in its hiding place, and does not stop even when Daphnis plunges his hands between Chloe's breasts to retrieve it. The incident charmingly explores the inchoate sexuality of the naive lovers, but how plausible is the story in terms of natural history?

Very plausible indeed, despite the protest of Norman Douglas that no swallow in its senses would dream of capturing a cicada to feed its young.[11] The term χελιδών in Greek covers all five species of hirundine that regularly breed there: Barn Swallow (*Hirundo rustica*), Red-rumped Swallow (*H. daurica*), Sand Martin (*Riparia riparia*), Crag Martin (*Ptyonoprogne rupestris*), and House Martin (*Delichon urbica*).[12] All are insectivorous, and even the relatively tiny House Martin when feeding its young brings insects up to 20 mm long to the nest.[13] Nestlings of the Red-rumped Swallow are reported to have been fed on cicadas—in Uzbekistan.[14] The other details in Longus's account need only summary treatment. The experience of having birds such as swallows, martins, and swifts brush past the head as they hunt fast after insects is one shared by many bird-watchers. A bird's potential prey will accept any hiding place that provides security from capture, and the cleavage of a girl's breasts, covered by a garment, would offer the same prospect of security as a densely foliaged tree-branch. Fear of imminent capture by a bird would easily override the lesser and uncertain danger of coming into contact with a human being. The cicada's chirring from under Chloe's garment and later in Daphnis's hand should cause no surprise. Hidden beneath Chloe's clothes, the insect would find both safety and shade, and such conditions are ideal for its continuous chirring.[15] Certainly human proximity is no barrier to this; I have heard one producing its music unremittingly when placed in a jar held by the hands in a Peking garden.

Longus's account of the χελιδών and the cicada may then be judged as scientifically accurate, but we are not in a position to state whether that accuracy derives from personal observation or from the use of oral or written sources. Stories of swallows or martins feeding their young on cicadas occur elsewhere in Greek literature (Aelian, NA 8.6, Euenus in Anth. Pal. 9.122 = Garland of Philip 2318ff., Plutarch, Mor. 727e),[16] and it may be that here Longus's fellow writers are presenting as a general practice something that originated in one person's isolated observation of an unusual occurrence, in the same way perhaps that the familiar legend of the song of the dying swan may have arisen.[17]

1.27.1, 4. In winter snow (cf. 3.3.1–11.3 and my discussion below of that passage), the φάττα (Woodpigeon, Columba palumbus) is a lowland bird feeding on ivy berries near Dryas's farm buildings, but here at the end of the spring and the beginning of summer (cf. 1.23.1) ἔτερψεν αὐτούς ποτε φάττα βουκολικὸν ἐκ τῆς ὕλης φθεγγομένη, "a Woodpigeon once pleased them [sc., Daphnis and Chloe] singing a pastoral song from the wood" (1.27.1), and when Daphnis tells his story about a maiden meta-morphosed by the gods into a Woodpigeon, the bird is described as ὄρειον ὥσπερ ἡ παρθένος (so Courier: ὄριον ἡ F, ὄρειον ὡς παρθένον V),[18] "of the mountains, like the girl."

Here the ornithological details are absolutely accurate. Although Longus does not specify at this point that Daphnis and Chloe are tending their sheep and goats in the mountains at this time of year, he does so elsewhere (explicitly 2.16.2, 4.6.2; implicitly 1.9.1, 1.11.3, if one prefers F's ὀρῶν to V's ἀγρῶν, 1.15.3; cf. Philetas at 2.5.3). Woodpigeons would be nesting at the end of spring, and in Greece and Turkey they habitually breed in mountain woodlands.[19]

2.12.3–4. On their visit to the countryside around Mytilene at the time of the vintage the young men of Methymne go wildfowling: ἤδη δὲ καὶ ὀρνίθων ἄγρας ἐμέλησεν αὐτοῖς καὶ ἔλαβον βρόχοις χῆνας ἀγρίους καὶ νήττας καὶ ὠτίδας, ὥστε ἡ τέρψις αὐτοῖς καὶ τραπέζης ὠφέλειαν παρεῖχεν, "and now also they occupied themselves with hunting birds, and with snares they caught wild geese and ducks and bustards, with the result that their pleasure also brought benefit for the table." This passage lacks the descriptive detail that so enlivens the later account of Daphnis's bird-catching expedition near Dryas's farmhouse (3.3.1–11.3; see below), but its baldness contains no biological inaccuracies. Large numbers of birds migrate south through Greece and the islands in late summer and early autumn, and some overwinter. The three birds Longus names here either fell or fall into this category.

Χῆνας ἀγρίους (wild geese). Two species of wild goose occur regularly today as passage migrants (in spring and late summer-autumn) and winter visitors, especially in the delta areas of northern Greece and western Anatolia: the Graylag (*Anser anser*) and the Whitefront (*A. albifrons*); a third species, the Bean Goose (*A. fabalis*), appears to have been equally common from autumn to spring up to the end of the last century in at least the modern Greek areas mentioned above.[20] Bones of the Whitefront have been identified on a Bronze Age site near Volos in Thessaly.[21]

Νήττας (ducks). Modern data from the northern Aegean islands are lacking, but at least nine species of wild duck can still be seen regularly in northern Greece at some time between autumn and spring. Kanellis gives the following information about status (C = common, R = regular, P = passage migrant, W = winter visitor).[22]

Shelduck (*Tadorna tadorna*)	CW
Mallard (*Anas platyrhynchus*)	CPW
Teal (*A. crecca*)	CPW
Gadwall (*A. strepera*)	RPW
Wigeon (*A. penelope*)	CPW
Pintail (*A. acuta*)	CPW
Garganey (*A. querquedula*)	PW (probably R)
Shoveller (*A. clypeata*)	RPW
Pochard (*Aythya ferina*)	CPW

Three other species occur further south in mainland Greece:

Ferruginous Duck (*Aythya nyroca*)	RPW
Tufted Duck (*A. fuligula*)	RPW
Red-breasted Merganser (*Mergus serrator*)	RPW

Reports from the Thracian and Anatolian coasts of Turkey are broadly similar, except for the relative scarcity of Merganser, the absence of Garganey, and the presence of Ferruginous Duck (along with Red-crested Pochard, *Netta rufina*) only on the Anatolian coast.[23]

Ὠτίδας (bustards). The accounts attributed to Aristotle seem to imply that both the Great (*Otis tarda*) and Little (*Tetrax tetrax*) Bustards are covered by this term; *Historia animalium* 563a27 and 619b13, mentioning the bird's great size, must refer to the former (102 cm from bill to tail), while Aristotle frag. 293 Rose (quoted by Athenaeus 9.390f), giving the bird the size of a large domestic cock, suggests the Little Bustard (43cm).[24] Bones of both species have been identified on the Bronze Age site near Volos (twelve of Great, thirty-six of Little),[25] and it is clear from such finds and from the numerous mentions in classical literature that the two birds were far more widespread in the ancient Greek world than they are today.[26] The great decline, due to hunting and loss of suitable habitat, began in the late nineteenth century and continues today. The Great Bustard bred in mainland Greece up to the 1860s and was a winter visitor to the Aegean islands, but is now very rarely seen in the eastern Mediterranean.[27] The Little Bustard similarly was a former breeder, passage migrant, and winter visitor in Greece, but since 1950 has virtually disappeared from Greece and the coasts of western Turkey, being seen now very rarely on passage and during the winter.[28] There is no way of deciding which species Longus had in mind at 2.12.3–4.[29]

3.3.1–11.3. Daphnis's bird-catching expedition is a carefully written set piece, and its vivid realism has often been praised. The episode is introduced with a succinct and selectively detailed account of an unusually harsh winter in Lesbos, with snow obliterating the roads, ice everywhere, the trees crushed by the weight of snow, and only the rushing torrents and springs unfrozen (3.3.1–2). Longus's portrayal of the arbor at the side of Dryas's farmyard, where ivy heavy with clusters of berries clothed and interlinked two myrtle trees that grew near each other, has a pictorially full specificity that seems largely confined to these set pieces. The description of the birds that came to feed on the ivy, and of the ways in which they were snared, seems at first sight as accurate as it is precise. But just how accurate are the details in reality?

In the stimulating and provocative introduction to his recently published edition of Longus, Vieillefond submits the passage to a stringent analysis and argues for four substantial inaccuracies that allegedly can be explained only by Longus's personal ignorance about birds and bird-catching.[30] Vieillefond's attacks are powerfully presented but they are not always accurately directed. At least two of his allegations are faulty and need refutation.

First, the birds feeding on the ivy berries and caught by Daphnis are named as κόψιχοι (3.5.2, 8.1, 10.3: Blackbirds, *Turdus merula*), κίχλαι (3.5.2, 11.2: Thrushes, *Turdus* sp.), φάτται (3.5.2, 8.1, 11.2: Wood-pigeons, *Columba palumbus*), and ψᾶρες (3.5.2: Starlings, *Sturnus vulgaris*). Vieillefond claims that Longus goes astray by having Woodpigeons and Thrushes together, because their "passages ne se produisent pas à le même saison."[31] Here, however, it is Vieillefond, not Longus, whose facts are incorrect. Modern observations have confirmed that although Wood-pigeons, Mistle Thrushes (*Turdus viscivorus*), and Song Thrushes (*T. philo-melos*) breed today in the mountains of northern Greece, the only species of these three that nests all over the country (including the island of Lesbos) is the Mistle Thrush.[32] What makes the Woodpigeon and four species of Thrush (Redwing, *T. iliacus,* and Fieldfare, *T. pilaris,* in addition to Mistle and Song Thrushes) familiar birds all over mainland Greece, the islands, and the Turkish coast, however, is the winter influxes from the north, especially massive in the case of Mistle Thrushes and Fieldfares. These birds remain then until the end of winter; they do not have distinct "sea-sons," as Vieillefond alleges.

Second, Vieillefond accuses Longus of three further "implausibilities" in this section, all concerned with the ancient techniques and practicalities of bird-snaring. In his expedition Daphnis is described as using two sorts of trap: ἰξός (birdlime) smeared on rods (3.5.3, 6.1, 8.1, 10.2), and βρόχοι (snares with running nooses and drawstrings: 3.5.3, 6.1, 8.1, 10.2). Daphnis set up his traps in the arbor by Dryas's farmyard, and on both days when trapping took place the hunters apparently stayed in the vicinity of the birds during the fowling. Vieillefond alleges that birds could not have been caught in the ways described by Longus unless the hunters had kept a considerable distance between themselves and their prey, and that in any event a farmyard could never be a suitable location for a bird-catching expedition, because of the habitual disturbance caused to feeding birds by the movements of farm animals and human workers.[33] This objection is invalid for several reasons. First, it is not borne out by the evidence we have about bird-catching in ancient art, where the motif of the bird-catcher with limed rods is not uncommon in mosaic pictures, on sarcophagi re-liefs, and as a decorative feature on lamps and gems.[34] The *piccola caccia* mosaic at Piazza Armerina,[35] for example, dating to the first half of the fourth century A.D., shows a pair of bird-catchers standing with a collec-tion of rods directly under a cherry (or cherry plum) tree and gazing at the two large birds perched in it. The size, position, shape, coloration, and spotted breasts of these birds make their identification as Mistle Thrushes virtually certain. Second, Vieillefond has forgotten that on the occasion of Daphnis's expedition snow covered the earth and all outside work on Dryas's farm had been suspended. Neither man nor domestic animal was creating any disturbance to the birds feeding in the arbor until Daphnis himself came along. Third, as any bird-watcher can confirm, when snow blankets the earth and makes the search for food by predominantly ground-feeding birds difficult or impossible, birds congregate in large numbers at any available source of food (such as berries and seeds) with little or no regard for its nearness to human habitation; in such conditions even Redwings and Fieldfares, normally the wariest of Thrush species in winter, will visit suburban gardens if a supply of food is provided there.

Vieillefond's two final allegations of implausibility concern ancient techniques of fowling. Daphnis set up his limed rods and snares at the point where an ivy plant with heavy clusters of berries climbed up and, with its horizontal stems, linked two myrtle trees growing side by side (3.5.1, 6.1, 10.2). Vieillefond acutely observes that snares with running nooses and drawstrings can be used effectively only when attached to (or threaded through) the bare branches of deciduous trees in winter, while the evergreen leaves of myrtle and ivy and the clusters of ivy berries would hamper the free movement of a drawstring.[36] There can be little doubt that here Vieillefond's allegation is justified.

The last objection is directed against Daphnis's use of birdlime in apparently subzero temperatures (3.3.2, 10.1). In ancient times birdlime was prepared from the pulp of mistletoe berries that had been dried, pounded, stored in water, and finally kneaded with olive oil (cf. Pliny, *HN* 16.248, 24.11), and fowlers smeared it on their rods so that, when these rods had been set up in the vicinity of feeding places or used manually (often with extensions that allowed fowlers to reach high into the branches), any bird that came into contact with the lime would stick fast to the rod and be unable to escape. Relying on information supplied by a mid-nineteenth-century revision of an old French handbook on hunting, Vieillefond claims that Longus must have been personally ignorant of the methods of bird-catching most appropriate to freezing weather, since birdlime itself then freezes and loses its stickiness.[37] Here too Vieillefond appears to be correct; the reports of the old hunters, founded presumably on their own day-to-day experience, are to some extent conformed by the researches of modern chemists and biologists. Although Pliny's recipe for birdlime produces a complicated mixture of organic substances (cf. especially the analysis of the chemical substances in mistletoe by Baudino and Sallé),[38] it is likely that birdlime would freeze in the subzero temperatures implied by Longus.[39]

Evidently Longus's two blunders were due to lack of practical knowledge about bird-catching, just as elsewhere in *Daphnis and Chloe* (1.11.2) he shows a parallel ignorance of one detail of wolf-trapping, when he describes how the local villagers dug a pit four ὀργυῖαι (7.2 meters!) deep in order to trap a she-wolf rearing young.[40] Nevertheless, the presence in Longus of errors in the details of fowling and trapping ought not to blind us to the unvaried excellence of his observations about natural history. To the evidence from this passage that I have already discussed in support of this view of the novelist, one point remains to be added. The four named birds were attracted to the arbor near Dryas's farmyard by the abundant supply there of ivy berries (3.5.1–2). All these birds are known to feed on berries in autumn and winter, and ivy berries are specifically recorded as part of the diet of Woodpigeons, Blackbirds, and Mistle Thrushes at that time.[41]

3.12.2. The novel abounds in references to flowers, but apart from the two set pieces describing Philetas's garden (2.3) and Dionysophanes' πα-ράδεισος (park, 4.2–3), where the plants are carefully tended by gardeners and not left to grow wild, the flowers tend either to be generalized and unspecific, designated simply as ἄνθη or φυτά (see above), or when individualized to be selected from a few of the most popular (but not always precisely identifiable) blooms in classical literature, mentioned en passant often as vehicles for comparison (e.g., 3.20.2–3, Daphnis wears a στεφα-νίσκον ἴων, "a garland of violets/stocks," but Chloe τὴν κόμην ἐφίλησεν ὡς τῶν ἴων κρείττονα, "kissed his hair, as better than the violets/stocks"; or 4.17.5, again about Daphnis's hair, ὑακίνθῳ μὲν τὴν κόμην ὁμοίαν ἔχει, "he has hair like a [?] hyacinth"). Unusually, however, in 3.12.2 three spring flowers are named as part of a delightful but succinct description of spring's arrival, a description that thus balances neatly the similarly selective account of the onset of harsh winter weather (3.3–4; see above) shortly before. Spring brings Daphnis and Chloe back to the pastures, where they wish to offer garlands of spring flowers to the Nymphs, and in their search εὑρέθη καὶ ἴα καὶ νάρκισσος καὶ ἀναγαλλὶς καὶ ὅσα ἦρος πρωτοφορήματα, "violets, narcissi, and pimpernels were found and all the earliest flowers of spring," quickened by the zephyr and a warm sun. Two things should be noted in this list. First, although two of the flowers mentioned (ἴα, νάρκισσος) are common standbys in ancient lyrical evocations of spring, the third one (ἀναγαλλίς) is a literary rarity; it occurs only once else-where,[42] to the best of my knowledge, in extant poetry or evocative prose. If Longus here was dependent on some literary source or sources, it is or they are no longer extant. Secondly, the flowers listed seem to have been accurately chosen as among the earliest spring blooms visible in a Greek landscape.

As Longus himself remarks (2.3.4; cf., e.g., Theophrastus, HP 6.6.7), ἴα can denote at least two different sorts of flower, distinguished from each other in Greek by the labels τὸ μέλαν (black) ἴον and λευκόιον or τὸ λευκὸν (white) ἴον. The former has been identified as the purple-flowered species of the Violaceae (especially Viola odorata, V. fragrans, violet-flowered examples of V. alba) and the latter as various stocks (especially Matthiola incana, M. sinuata, M. tricuspidata),[43] where the blooms even in one single species show a remarkable range of color, from white and pale rose-lilac to darkish shades of violet and reddish purple (cf. Theophrastus, HP 6.6.3, τὸ μέλαν ἴον does not vary in color, unlike τὸ λευκόν· ἐμφανὴς γὰρ ἡ τούτων χροία διαλλάττουσα, "for the color of these latter is clearly varied"). Here

Longus presumably has τὸ λευκὸν ἴον in mind, for although both violets and stocks have an attractive scent that made them equally sought after for garlands (cf., e.g., Longus 3.20.2–3, 22.4; Theophrastus, *HP* 6.6.1–2; Dioscorides medicus 4.121; Hicesius in Athenaeus 15.681c–d), it was τὸ λευκὸν ἴον that was known to be the earlier bloomer; according to Theophrastus, τῶν δ' ἀνθῶν τὸ μὲν πρῶτον ἐκφαίνεται τὸ λευκόιον, ὅπου μὲν ὁ ἀὴρ μαλακώτερος εὐθὺς τοῦ χειμῶνος, ὅπου δὲ σκληρότερος ὕστερον, ἐνιαχοῦ τοῦ ἦρος, "of the flowers the first to appear is the white ἴον; where the air is milder, it appears at the beginning of winter, but where the climate is more severe, it comes later, sometimes in spring (*HP* 6.8.1).[44] Species of *Matthiola* in Greece today regularly flower from early March onward.[45]

The term νάρκισσος covers all the native eastern Mediterranean species of narcissus, of which the earliest bloomer, *Narcissus tazetta*, the Polyanthus Narcissus or Rose of Sharon (flowering December to March), is extremely common throughout Greece in fields and damp places.[46]

Dioscorides medicus (2.178) states that there are two forms of ἀναγαλλίς, one producing a dark blue (κυανεόν) flower, the other crimson (φοινικοῦν). The identification with Scarlet Pimpernel, *Anagallis arvensis,* seems certain, for the nominate species usually has red flowers, but sometimes pink, lilac, or even blue, while the subspecies *A. a. foemina* (if this is not a separate species; taxonomists differ) always has blue flowers. Flowering in Greece begins during March.[47]

3.16.2. Lycaenion's fiction, that an eagle (ἀετός) has seized the finest of her twenty geese, but being unable because of the weight of its prey to lift it and fly up to its usual high crag, it had disappeared with the goose into a low thicket, is an interesting example of the way in which Longus uses identifiable source material. There can be no doubt that here Longus was inspired by Homer's account of Penelope's dream in *Odyssey* 19.596ff. about an eagle killing all her twenty geese, but the novelist has attractively varied and developed his source. Only one goose has now been taken. The story has been given an ironic twist by Longus's substitution of a wanton for a faithful wife in the person of the narrator.[48] And Longus has decked out his version of the story with a number of new details that show a greater knowledge of eagle behavior than one might expect.

In ancient Greece, ἀετός was a general word for eagle, and not confined to any one species. The author of *Historia animalium* realized that several species of eagle (and other eagle-like large predators) were to be found in Greece, but was not able to identify differences in size, shape, color, behavior, and habitat in a way meaningful to modern taxonomy (618b18ff.).[49] This is hardly surprising; plumage variations in individual species make their identification in the field difficult even for birdwatchers today armed with binoculars and detailed handbooks. It will accordingly be preferable here to assess the accuracy of Longus's remarks at 3.16.2 by considering them in light of the known behavior of all species of large eagle in Greece today. There are five of these: Bonelli's Eagle (*Hieraeetus fasciatus*), Spotted Eagle (*Aquila clanga,* a rarish winter visitor and passage migrant in Greece),[50] Imperial Eagle (*A. heliaca*), Golden Eagle (*A. chrysaetus*), and White-tailed Eagle (*Haliaeetus albicilla*).

White-tailed, Imperial, and Bonelli's Eagles have all been observed to prey on geese.[51]

The lifting power of the larger eagles has been much discussed.[52] Wind conditions have a great effect; on a windless day little more than one kilogram can be carried into the air, but against a heavy wind as much as seven kilograms are possible. A full-grown male goose weighs between 2.5 and 4.5 kilograms, a full-grown female between 2 and 4. On a calm day, therefore, the finest of Lycaenion's geese would really be too heavy for even the strongest eagle to lift into the air.

Several species of eagle use high crags as roosting places and day perches, White-tailed, Imperial, and especially Golden Eagles habitually choose high places with a distant prospect where they will remain immobile for hours at a time.[53]

The favored habitat of the Imperial Eagle is the kind of landscape that Lycaenion describes: woods and copses adjoining open grassland.[54]

From where did Longus derive his accurate ornithological information? From personal observation, at first or second hand, or from some literary or scientific source? We can no longer tell. Some of the details of behavior that Longus mentions can be found in a section of *Historia animalium* devoted to eagles: the difficulty of lifting heavy prey (619a32ff., cf. 6ff.), and the eagles' use of inaccessible cliff ledges for nest sites (619a25ff.), but if this passage is a partial source for Longus here—which I rather doubt— it has been used intelligently and without any overt signs of copying.

III

The above discussions by no means cover all the passages in Longus dealing with wildlife; they are simply the ones calling for extensive treatment. Even so, they may also be taken as an exemplary selection illustrating Longus's accuracy of detail in this area. It may be useful finally to confirm this impression of reliability with a much briefer listing of five other passages where one or more aspects of natural history are accurately recorded.

2.4.2. In Philetas's story, Eros is described as easily escaping pursuit by darting under flowering plants, ποτὲ μὲν ταῖς ῥοδωνίαις ὑποτρέχων, ποτὲ δὲ ταῖς μήκωσιν ὑποκρυπτόμενος, ὥσπερ πέρδικος νεοττός, "sometimes running under the rose bushes, sometimes hiding under the poppies, like a fledgling partridge." Although the novel itself is confined to Lesbos, its author's own home is unknown and his imagination in any event not so bounded in a comparison; his πέρδιξ accordingly could be either a Rock Partridge (*Alectoris graeca*), which breeds predominantly in mainland Greece, or a Chukar (*A. chukar*), which breeds in the islands, including Lesbos.[55] In either case Longus's allusion to the fledgling running for cover when pursued produces an image as accurately focused as his comparison just a little later—still in Philetas's tale—of Eros leaping up: ἀνήλατο, καθάπερ ἀηδόνος νεοττός, ἐπὶ τὰς μυρρίνας καὶ κλάδον ἀμείβων ἐκ κλάδου διὰ τῶν φύλλων ἀνεῖρπεν εἰς ἄκρον, "he darted up into the myrtles like a young Nightingale, and moving from branch to branch he crept up through the leaves to the top" (2.6.1), where both language and concepts betray a clear debt to Theocritus 15.120ff.[56] Is there a similar sort of debt, now unidentified or unidentifiable, in the partridge comparison?

2.17.3. The local residents attack the young men of Methymne ὡσεὶ ψᾶρες ἢ κολοιοί, "like Starlings or Jackdaws." This vivid little comparison, which stirs the imagination of anyone who has observed the massed flights of Starlings just before they settle down to roost, or the aerial acrobatics of hundreds of Jackdaws (*Corvus monedula*), loses none of its effect from being secondhand, borrowed originally from Homer (*Iliad* 17.755, where the Achaeans are the object of comparison).[57]

3.12.4. Daphnis and Chloe play their panpipes, καθάπερ τὰς ἀηδόνας ἐς τὴν μουσικὴν ἐρεθίζοντες, αἱ δὲ ὑπεφθέγγοντο ἐν ταῖς λοχμαῖς καὶ τὸν Ἴτυν κατ' ὀλίγον ἠκρίβουν ὥσπερ ἀναμιμνησκόμεναι τῆς ᾠδῆς ἐκ μακρᾶς σιωπῆς, "just as if challenging the Nightingales in music, and they responded quietly in the thickets and perfected gradually their dirge for Itys just as if remembering the song after a long silence." Here three details deserve to be noted. The Nightingales (*Luscinia megarhynchos*) sing from thickets, their most favored habitat.[58] During spring and early summer they sing clearly by day as well as by night (as the author of *HA* 632b21ff. first noted), although the day song differs slightly from the nocturnal one.[59] And the Nightingale's song suddenly reappears in late March or early April.[60]

3.20.4. Chloe gives Daphnis pieces of bread to eat, and while he is chewing she snatches them from his mouth and eats them herself ὥσπερ νεοττὸς ὄρνιθος, "like a young bird." Even though no species is singled out, the detail is ultimately based on (someone's) accurate observation of the way young birds in the nest are often fed by parents who allow food, sometimes regurgitated, to be snatched from their beaks by their offspring.

4.40.3. On their wedding night Daphnis and Chloe do not sleep, ἀγρυπνήσαντες τῆς νυκτὸς ὅσον οὐδὲ γλαῦκες, "keeping awake during the night more than even Little Owls." Little Owls (*Athene noctua*) hunt mainly from dusk to midnight, and then after a pause of about two hours resume their hunting until dawn.[61]

IV

The evidence in these discussions of individual passages from *Daphnis and Chloe* clearly supports the view that in the field of natural history Longus wrote from accurate knowledge, although the errors that have been detected in his descriptions of trapping techniques suggest that this knowledge was not backed up by personal experience of fowling and hunting. We shall never be able to know how far he relied on his own eyes, how far on the observation and writings of others in the field, but the repeated correctness of his own remarks about natural history implies that he was essentially a countryman and not confined within the walls of a library. If all his material about birds and plants had been taken at second hand from books without his possessing the knowledge to verify the facts, is it reasonable to believe that these would have been so consistently reliable in their accuracy? Unfortunately, the birds, flowers, and trees that appear in Longus's novel belong to the fauna and flora of the eastern Mediterranean—mainland Greece, the islands, the Turkish coast—as a whole, and not specifically to any small identifiable area such as Lesbos. Accordingly they provide no help toward finding a solution to the disputed questions about Longus's place of origin and residence.

NOTES

1. For opposing answers to this question, see, e.g., H. J. Mason, "Longus and the Topography of Lesbos," *Transactions of the American Philological Association* 109 (1970): 149–63 (*Daphnis and Chloe* a realistic portrayal of Lesbos), and A. M. Scarcella, "Realtà e letteratura nel paesaggio sociale ed economico del romanzo di Longo Sofista," *Maia* 22 (1970): 107–31 (the novel distanced from reality). Cf. P. M. Green, "Longus, Antiphon, and the Topography of Lesbos," *Journal of Hellenic Studies* 102 (1982): 210ff., and R. L. Hunter, *A Study of "Daphnis and Chloe"* (Cambridge, 1983), 2f.

2. See E. L. Bowie, "The Novels and the Real World," in *Erotica Antiqua: Proceedings of the International Conference on the Ancient Novel,* ed. B. P. Reardon (Bangor, Wales, 1977), 94f.

3. The best general studies are A. M. Scarcella, "La tecnica dell'imitazione in Longo Sofista," *Giornale italiano di filologia classica,* n.s. 2 (1976), 34ff., and Hunter, *Study,* 59ff.; on Longus's debt to Theocritus, see G. Rohde, "Longus und die Bukolik," *Rheinisches Museum für Philologie* 86 (1937): 23ff. (reprinted in *Studien und Interpretationen* [Berlin, 1963], 91–116), and M. Mittelstadt, "Bucolic-Lyric Motifs and Dramatic Narrative in Longus," *Rheinisches Museum für Philologie* 113 (1970): 211ff.; cf. also B. Effe, "Longus: Zur Funktionsgeschichte der Bukolik in der römischen Kaiserzeit," *Hermes* 110 (1982): 65ff.

4. J.-R. Vieillefond, ed., *Pastorales (Daphnis et Chloe)* (Paris, 1987), clxxxii–clxxxiv, cxci–cxcv.

5. Cf. Hunter, *Study,* 21.

6. On the contrast here between Theocritus and Longus, see esp. Scarcella, "Realtà e letteratura," 122ff., and Hunter, *Study,* 21; on this aspect of Theocritus 7, see W. G. Arnott, "Lycidas and Double Perspectives," *Estudios Clasicos* 87 (1984): 335ff.

7. Cf. Vieillefond, *Pastorales,* clxxxix and n. 2.

8. The large species go up to 38 mm in length, the small ones up to 19 mm. The identification in *HA* 556b14ff. of only two kinds of cicada, one big and one small, suggests that the author had not gone beyond size in distinguishing individual species. Cf. C. J. Sundevall, *Die Thierarten des Aristoteles* (Stockholm, 1863), 201, and I. C. Beavis, *Insects and Other Invertebrates in Classical Antiquity* (Exeter, 1988), 92.

9. See esp. Steier, in *Real-Encyclopaedie der classischen Altertumswissenschaft,* ed. A. Pauly and G. Wissowa (Stuttgart, 1894–1963) (hereafter cited as *RE*), 2.9 (1934), s.v. "Tettix," 1115f.; M. Davies and J. Kathirithamby, *Greek Insects* (London, 1986), 113ff., and Beavis, *Insects,* 92ff. Davies and Kathirithamby list passages in which the attractiveness of the sound made by cicadas is praised (e.g., Aristophanes, *Pax* 1160, Apollonius in *Anth. Pal.* 9.264 = *Garland of Philip* 1225, Pamphilus in *Anth. Pal.* 7.201 = *Hellenistic Epigrams* 2840), and others in which verbs like ἠχῶ are used for the production of the sound (e.g., Alcaeus, frag. 347.3, Theocritus 16.96; cf. Gow on Theocritus 1.148). The use of such verbs (in preference to, e.g., ἀείδω) may indicate a realization that the sound did not come from the mouth of the cicada, without any secure knowledge of the true source. *HA* 532b15ff. and 535b17ff. show a rough (though not totally accurate: cf. Beavis, *Insects,* 100f.) idea of the facts; cicadas have a pair of membranes ("tymbals") in resonating cavities on each side of the base of the abdomen, which under muscular control vibrate rapidly.

10. The very presence of chirring cicadas is a conventional feature of descriptions, in prose or verse, of the *locus amoenus;* see G. Schönbeck, *Der locus amoenus von Homer bis Horaz* (Ph.D. diss., Heidelberg University, 1962), 59f.

11. N. Douglas, *Birds and Beasts of the Greek Anthology* (London, 1928), 194.

12. Cf. Sundevall, *Die Thierarten des Aristoteles,* 122f.; W. G. Arnott, "Some Bird Notes in Aristophanes' *Birds,*" in *Tria Lustra: Essays Presented to the Editor of Liverpool Classical Monthly,* ed. H. D. Jocelyn (Liverpool, 1993).

13. S. Cramp et al., *The Birds of the Western Palaearctic,* 6 vols. to date (Oxford, 1977–), 5:290.

14. Ibid. 5:281.

15. Cf. Davies and Kathirithamby, *Greek Insects,* 115f. The experiments of F. Ossianilsson, *Insect Drummers, Opuscula entomologica,* supp. 10 (Lund, 1949), 119ff., have shown that warmth (a temperature of 30 degrees Celsius or more) is a greater stimulus to chirring than exposure to bright sunlight.

16. Cf. Davies and Kathirithamby, *Greek Insects,* 127.

17. Cf. W. G. Arnott, "Swan Songs," *Greece and Rome* 24 (1977): 152f.

18. M. D. Reeve also records, in the apparatus to his edition of *Daphnis and Chloe* by Longus (Leipzig, 1983), Wyttenbach's conjecture ὡραίαν, but that term seems ill suited to a bird with a disproportionately small head, very plump body, and no great distinction of color in its plumage.

19. Steier, *RE* 2.8 (1932), s.v. "Taube," 2455.18ff.; A. Kanellis, *Catalogus faunae Graeciae,* part 2, *Aves,* ed. W. Bauer et al. (Thessalonike, 1969), 80f.; Ornithological Society of Turkey (hereafter cited as OST), *Bird Reports* (1970–73): 144, "generally in the drier coniferous forest areas, mainly in uplands." H. H. O. Chalk, "Eros and the Lesbian Pastorals of Longus," *Journal of Hellenic Studies* 80 (1960): 40, and R. Mer-

kelbach, *Die Hirten des Dionysos* (Stuttgart, 1988), 160 n. 11, suggest that Longus's reference to a φάττα here may have been inspired (at least partly) by reasons of religion, but even if their suggestion is correct, it does not alter the ornithological facts.

20. Kanellis, *Catalogus*, 34f.; OST (1968–69): 18ff.; (1970–73): 43ff.; (1974–75): 30.

21. G. Hinz, *Neue Tierknockenfunde aus der Magula Perkakia in Thessalien*, vol. 1, *Die Nichtwiederkäuer* (Ph.D. diss., University of Munich, 1979), 91.

22. Kanellis, *Catalogus*, 36–40.

23. OST (1968–69): 23–40; (1970–73): 47–60; (1974–75): 32–41.

24. D. W. Thompson, *A Glossary of Greek Birds*, 2d ed. (London, 1936), 338f. (s.v. ὠτίς) presents the ancient evidence clearly, but his primary identification (Great or Houbara Bustard) is slightly misleading (see note 29 below).

25. Hinz, *Neue Tierknockenfunde*, 93f.

26. Cf. Thompson, *Glossary*, 338f.

27. Kanellis, *Catalogus*, 59, 153; Cramp et al., *Birds* 2:659ff.; M. Beaman, "Turkey: Bird Report, 1976–1981," *Sandgrouse* 8 (1986): 18.

28. Kanellis, *Catalogus*, 59; Cramp et al., *Birds* 2:638ff.; Beaman, "Turkey," 18.

29. A third species, the Houbara Bustard (*Chlamydotis undulata*), was known to some classical writers (e.g., Athenaeus 9.390d–e, citing a fragment of Plutarch, presumably the Chaeronean, which discusses the bird and its hunting in north Africa; Oppian, *Cyn.* 2.407, referring to its shaggy ear-tufts), but since its home is the arid deserts of north Africa and the Middle East (only one Greek sighting has been reported over a period of two hundred years: Kanellis, *Catalogus*, 59f.), it may safely be eliminated from any interpretation of the Longus passage.

30. Vieillefond, *Pastorales*, clxxxii–clxxxiv.

31. Ibid., clxxxiii.

32. Here Thompson's comments (s.vv. ἰλιάς, κίχλη) on the distribution of these birds in modern Greece are inaccurate. See Cramp et al., *Birds* 4:311ff.; 5:977ff., 989ff., 1000ff., 1011ff.; Kanellis, *Catalogus*, 80f., 129ff., 156; A. Lambert, "A Specific Check-list of the Birds of Greece," *Ibis* 99 (1957): 60, 87; H. Löhrl, "Zur Vogelwelt der griechischen Insel Lesbos (Mytilene)," *Vogelwelt* 86 (1965): 109; OST (1968–69): 160ff.; (1970–73): 232ff.; (1974–75): 1182ff.; O. Steinfatt, "Vogelkundliche Beobachtungen in Attika," *Journal für Ornithologie* 95 (1954): 28f.; 96 (1955): 92. On the spring and summer habitat of Woodpigeons, see also my discussion of Longus 1.27.1 and 4.

33. Vieillefond, *Pastorals*, clxxxiv.

34. The instances of this motif are listed, illustrated, and fully discussed by K. Lindner, *Beiträge zu Vogelfang und Falknerei im Altertum*, Quellen und Studien zur Geschichte des Jagd, no. 12 (Berlin, 1974), 29ff.

35. See esp. A. Carandini, "Ricerche sullo stile e la cronologia dei mosaici della villa di Piazza Armerina," in *Seminario di archeologia e storia dell' arte greca e romana dell' università di Roma*, Studi miscellanei, no. 7 (Rome, 1964); G. V. Gentili, "I mosaici della villa romana del Casale di Piazza Armerina," *Bolletino d' arte* (1952): 33–46; Gentili, *La Villa Erculia di Piazza Amerina: I mosaici figurati* (Rome, 1959); Gentili, *La villa imperiale di Piazza Armerina* (Rome, 1969); B. Pace, *I mosaici di Piazza Armerina* (Rome, 1955); Lindner, *Beiträge*, 29ff. and plate 1.

36. Vieillefond, *Pastorales*, clxxxiii.

37. N.-J.-B. Boyard and [?] de Marsan, *Nouveau manuel complet du chasseur ou les secrets et les ruses dévoilés mis à la partée de tout le monde* (Paris, 1845), 134; Vieillefond, *Pastorales*, clxxxiii.

38. S. Baudino and G. Sallé, "Les substances actives du gui," *Annales de sciences naturelles: Botanique et biologie vegetale* 8 (1987): 45ff.

39. At Alciphron 2.27, we have a similar description of a man using birdlime to trap

Blackbirds and Thrushes in the branches of trees during a hard winter when snow covered the ground, but here Longus's error is skillfully avoided; the bird-catcher keeps his birdlime in a pot indoors, the trees he smears are just outside his door, and the birds are caught immediately (before the lime has had time to solidify). It may be that Longus here used Alciphron inaccurately as a source, but speculations on these lines are hazardous so long as the dates of both Alciphron and Longus are uncertain.

40. The absurdity of making the pit so deep is well brought out by Vieillefond, *Pastorales,* clxxxivf.

41. Cramp et al., *Birds* 4:316; 5:954, 1004.

42. That other passage is in fact Longus 4.2.6, where the three flowers listed together at 3.12.2 are described as growing wild in Dionysophanes' park.

43. T. G. Tutin et al., *Flora europaea,* vols. 1–6 (Cambridge, 1964–83), 2:272, 277; 1:280.

44. This passage has led some scholars (e.g., J. André, *Lexique des termes de botanique en latin* [Paris, 1956], s.v. "uiola," 330f., Gow on Theocritus 7.64 and on the epigrammatist Nicias 7.3f. = *HE* 2781f., and Page on Meleager 11.56 = *HE* 3981) to assume that λευκόιον may also be the Snowdrop, *Galanthus nivalis.* This identification ignores three facts: (1) the total difference in flower and leaf shapes between the Snowdrop and the stocks; (2) Theophrastus's further statement that the blooms of the white ἴον vary in color; and (3) the reputation of both forms (λευκόν and μέλαν) of ἴον for strong fragrance, altogether lacking in the Snowdrop. The passage of Theophrastus quoted and its continuation pose more problems than they solve. The claim that the white ἴον is the first bloom of spring, appearing even at the beginning of winter in favored places, does not square with the facts about the Snowdrop, which flowers during the autumn (October to December: A. Huxley and W. Taylor, *Flowers of Greece and the Aegean* [London, 1977], 62) in Greece, never in spring. Theophrastus's statement, however, cannot be used to clinch the identification of white ἴον as stock, for he goes on to say that the blooms of the νάρκισσος *follow* those of the white ἴον, but in reality throughout Greece the Polyanthus Narcissus comes into flower *before* any of the stocks.

45. Huxley and Taylor, *Flowers,* 85; O. Polunin and A. Huxley, *Flowers of the Mediterranean* (London, 1965), 79f.

46. Tutin et al., *Flora europaea* 5:79f.; Huxley and Taylor, *Flowers,* 153; K. Lembach, *Die Pflanzen bei Theokrit* (Heidelberg, 1970), 86ff.

47. Tutin et al., *Flora europaea* 3:28; Huxley and Taylor, *Flowers,* 114; cf. Wagler, *RE* 1.1 (1894), s.v. "Anagallis," 2021.9ff.

48. Cf. Hunter, *Study,* 61.

49. Cf., e.g., Thompson, *Glossary,* s.v. ἀετός, 2ff., although his information about the species of eagle to be found in modern Greece is as unreliable as his binomials; see also J. Pollard, *Birds in Greek Life and Myth* (London, 1977), 76ff.

50. Kanellis, *Catalogus,* 46.

51. Cramp et al., *Birds* 2:52f., 237, 260.

52. H. F. Witherby et al., *The Handbook of British Birds,* vols. 1–5 (London, 1940–41), 3:39; L. Brown, *British Birds of Prey* (London, 1976), 182.

53. Cramp et al., *Birds* 2:49ff., 226, 234ff.; Witherby et al., *Handbook* 3:39.

54. Cramp et al., *Birds* 2:226.

55. Cf., e.g., Thompson, *Glossary,* 234ff.; Löhrl, "Zur Vogelwelt der Lesbos," 106; W. G. Arnott, "Some Peripatetic Birds," *Classical Quarterly* 27 (1977): 336f.

56. Cf. Hunter, *Study,* 60.

57. Ibid., 61.

58. "In the Nightingale's habitat the ground zone under the shrub layer is generally rich in brambles, wild roses, nettles and umbellifers growing in rather damp conditions" (E. Simms, *British Thrushes* [London, 1978], 243; cf. Cramp et al., *Birds* 5:623f.).

59. Cramp et al., *Birds* 5:634.

60. In Attica, Steinfatt reported his first Nightingale on 1 April and a colleague's on 25 March ("Vogelkundliche Beobachtungen in Attika" [1954]: 31). I have heard one myself in full voice in Ioannina by 12 April.

61. Cramp et al., *Birds* 4:517. I cannot resist quoting what in this context may seem an ironic comment by an ornithologist in Delphi: "La veille c'était une Chevêche . . . , peu de nocturnes donc, mais j'ai peut-être le sommeil trop profond" (P. Géroudet, "Notes d'ornithologie grecque: Delphes," *Nos oiseaux* 26 [1962]: 173).

CHAPTER TWELVE

The City in
the Greek Novel

Suzanne Saïd

"The ancient city underwent many changes in its appearance and role, its image and the way in which its inhabitants perceived it." Some of these changes have already been explored. J. E. Stambaugh, in the seminal article I have just quoted,[1] concentrated on Athens and on three passages that describe it over the centuries, from Thucydides' report of the funeral oration of Pericles delivered in 431 B.C. to a Hellenistic sketch by Heraclides of Crete of the third century B.C. and Pausanias's description in the second century A.D. Other scholars have investigated the changing views of the city in various literary genres such as epic and lyric poetry,[2] epigrams,[3] and descriptions and praises of the cities from the archaic age to the Byzantine and medieval periods.[4] I wish to address here the views of the city in Greek novel. This question cannot be separated from the consideration of the images of the city at the time of the Roman Empire.

These views are indeed varied. For Pausanias, a city is first and foremost a physical reality and a collection of monuments: in 10.4.1, he denies the very name of "city" (πόλις) to "any built-up area that does not include 'public buildings' [ἀρχεῖα], gymnasium [γυμνάσιον], theater [θέατρον], marketplace [ἀγορὰν], water conducted to a fountain [ὕδωρ κατερχόμενον ἐς κρήνην]." In 3.4.13, Strabo holds that it is but a synonym of civilization: a genuine "city" (πόλις) cannot exist in Celtiberia on account of the country's uncivilized character (τὸ ἀνήμερον). According to Dio of Prusa, it is a genuine political and moral entity: "city" (τὴν πόλιν) means "people dwelling in the same place and governed by laws" (πλῆθος ἀνθρώπων ἐν ταὐτῷ κατοικούντων ὑπὸ νόμου διοικούμενον) (19.20).

The same diversity characterizes the more limited field of the Greek novel. For Chariton as well as for Thucydides, from whom the novelist borrowed the character of Hermocrates, Athens is a collection of busybodies (1.11.6): the Athenians are characterized by their "inquisitiveness" (τὴν πολυπραγμοσύνην τῶν Ἀθηναίων) and their love of gossip and lawsuits (δῆμός ἐστι λάλος καὶ φιλόδικος). For Heliodorus as well as for

Pausanias, it is instead a museum, a collection of buildings that remind the reader of its past grandeur and cultural glory (1.9.1–18.1). Even within the same novel, one can waver between two views of the city. In *Chaereas and Callirhoe,* Chariton first identifies Tyre with its inhabitants: "The Tyrians are by nature a very warlike people who desire a reputation for courage" (Τύριοι δὲ φύσει γένος ἐστὶ μαχιμώτατον καὶ κλέος ἐπ' ἀνδρείᾳ θέλουσι κεκτῆσθαι, 7.2.7). Then he views it as a site: "The city is built in the sea; a narrow causeway joins it to the land and keeps it from being an island" (ἡ μὲν γὰρ πόλις ἐν θαλάσσῃ κατῴκισται, λεπτὴ δὲ εἴσοδος αὐτὴν συνάπτουσα τῇ γῇ κωλύει τὸ μὴ νῆσον εἶναι, 7.2.8).

I shall limit myself here to "the visible city of streets and buildings" in "the five love-and-adventure romances that have come to be regarded as constituting the canon in this form: those of Chariton, Xenophon of Ephesus, Achilles Tatius, Longus and Heliodorus."[5]

CITIES IN TIME AND SPACE

At first glance the subject matter seems to lack unity, because Greek novels are set in different times and places. From Chariton to Heliodorus, the Greek novels extend over two or perhaps five centuries. The oldest surviving novel, *Chaereas and Callirhoe,* must be placed at least before A.D. 150 (because of the recently discovered papyrus fragments) and, as noted by T. Hägg,[6] "there are good reasons for dating it as far back as late Hellenistic times, in the first century B.C." As for the last one, the *Aethiopica,* scholars have opted for various dates between the third and the late fourth century A.D.: the third being the century of the sun-worshipping Roman emperors, Elagabalus and Aurelian; the late fourth because of the striking similarities between the siege of Syene and the Emperor Julian's description of the siege of the Mesopotamian Nisibis by Sapor in A.D. 350.[7] Again, these novels take place either in a remote past or at the present time. *Chaereas and Callirhoe,* the *Aethiopica,* and even *Daphnis and Chloe* are historical novels. Chariton's heroine is the daughter of Hermocrates, a historical figure who played a major role in the defense of Syracuse against the Athenian naval expedition in 415–413 B.C., according to Thucydides.[8] Heliodorus's novel takes place at the time when Egypt stood under Persian dominion, that is, sometime between 585 and 330 B.C. In *Daphnis and Chloe,* the cities of Lesbos keep enough autonomy to fight fratricidal wars. But the *Ephesiaca* as well as *Leucippe and Clitophon* are contemporary novels. Alexandria is the capital of Egypt in Achilles Tatius's novel,[9] and Xenophon's heroes pass through Alexandria and Antioch, which were founded during the Hellenistic period, and they face Roman magistrates such as the prefect of Egypt and the eirenarch of Cilicia.[10] Moreover, the cities of Greek novels are located in a wide geographical area extending, from west to east, from Sicily to Babylon, and, from north to south, from Byzantium to Meroe.

But the same exclusions and preferences are found everywhere. Rome is never mentioned in any Greek novel, and Athens is definitely kept in the background. In Chariton, it is named only to be put aside: it is the city to which Theron will *not* go in order to sell Callirhoe (1.11.4–7). In Heliodorus,[11] it provides a setting for the adventures of a secondary character (Cnemon) told in a secondary narrative (by Cnemon, and not by the author). In Achilles Tatius (5.5.2), it has turned into mere scenery for a painting that represents the adventures of Philomela and Procne. In Xenophon and Longus, it is not even mentioned. By contrast, the heroes are almost never allowed to miss Egypt or Asia Minor (except for Daphnis and Chloe, who never leave the island of Lesbos). If they do not travel to Egypt, like Chariton's heroes, Egypt comes to them with the Egyptian revolt (8.8.1). If they do not pass through Asia Minor, like Heliodorus's heroes, they pretend to be natives of this country and to come from Ephesus (1.22.2).

CITIES AS LANDMARKS

In Greek novels, the cities are above all landmarks that allow for rooting the heroes' travels in the real world. As J. R. Morgan put it in his excellent paper on Heliodorus, "of the seventy-nine place-names (including nationalities) . . . all are authentic,"[12] but some of them are not used accurately: the locations of Chemmis and Bessa in Heliodorus cannot be squared with known towns of that name. The Chemmis of Herodotus is a floating island, and the Bessa of Photius, which was renamed Antinopolis by Hadrian, is situated on the southern boundary of Egypt. In the *Aethiopica,* one can "walk" or "ride" from Syene to Elephantine, which are in fact islands located on the Nile.[13] To these exceptions already pointed out by Morgan, one can add the case of Katadoupoi. This name applies to the Nile falls in Herodotus and Philostratus.[14] It can also refer, again in Philostratus (*VAT* 8.23), to the mountains from which they come. But Heliodorus applies it to a genuine city, which is located near the Nile falls,[15] with a temple of Isis and a palace (2.30.1, 2.32.1). A sentence of Herodotus gives the clue to this strange mistake and illuminates the technique of Heliodorus, who was naming cities from his reading (or rather, misreading) of Herodotus. He might indeed easily deduce from Herodotus's expression Αἴγυπτον πᾶσαν ἀρξαμένην ἀπὸ Καταδούπων τε καὶ Ἐλεφαντίνης πόλιος (2.17) that Katadoupoi, like Elephantine, is a city.

From time to time, these city names are enriched by conventional epithets that can be found in archaic poetry as well as in accounts of journeys like Xenophon's *Anabasis*. These are more ornamental than really descriptive. For example, some cities are said to be "large" (μεγάλη),[16] "very large" (Miletus: Chariton 4.4.3) (μεγίστη) or "small" (Priene: Chariton 4.5.4) (μικρά), "prosperous" (Athens: Chariton 1.11.5; Chemmis: Heliodorus 2.18.15) (εὐδαίμων), "powerful" (Tyre: Chariton 7.4.4) (δυνατωτάτη), "crowded" (Chemmis: Heliodorus 2.18.15) (πολυάνθρωπος), "beautiful" (Rhodes: X.E. 1.11.6; Mazacus: X.E. 5.1.1; Syracuse: X.E. 5.1.1) (καλή), "famous" (Perinthus: X.E. 3.2.1; Tyre: A.T. 8.3.1) (ἔνδοξος, οὐκ ἄσημος) or "holy" (ἱερή), when they are dedicated to a god, as are Ephesus, Delphi, and Memphis.[17]

CITIES' BUILDINGS

The towns are also evoked by the very places that represent the proper setting for urban life according to the Greeks of the imperial age,[18] those for which a city is commended according to Dio, Aelius, Aristides, Quintilian, or Menander the Rhetor, because they are its "adorning" and "confer upon it some beauty" (Menander 2.386.29: κόσμος; 429.1: ὡραίζεται μὲν γὰρ ἡ πόλις κάλλεσιν ἱερῶν καὶ στοῶν καὶ λουτρῶν μεγέθεσιν): the walls,[19] the harbors (Menander 2.386.22, 2.431.3, 2.433.15), the temples (Dio 32.41; Aelius Aristides, *Panath.* 354; Menander 2.362, 2.382.15, 2.386.22, 2.429.16, 2.431.3; Quintilian 3.7.27), the baths (Dio 33.18; Aelius Aristides, *Panath.* 354; Menander 2.386.22, 2.429.16), the gymnasia (Aelius Aristides, *Panath.* 354; Menander 2.382.15), the theaters (Menander 2.382.15, 2.429.16, 2.431.3), the squares bordered by porticoes and the colonnaded streets (Dio 33.18; Aelius Aristides, *Panath.* 354; Menander 2.386.22, 2.429.16, 2.431.3, 2.433.15), the number and the beauty of the private houses (Dio 33.18, 40.10, 47.15). Accordingly, when Calasiris celebrates Delphi, he praises "the streets, the squares and the fountains" ('Επαινέσας οὖν τῶν τε δρόμων καὶ ἀγορῶν καὶ κρηνῶν τὸ ἄστυ, 2.26.4).[20] This is standard praise: in Apuleius's *Golden Ass*, when an eminent female citizen of Hypata boasts of the amenities of her native city, she also says that it excels all other cities "in temples, baths and public works."[21]

Walls, Harbors, Temples, and Gymnasia

The walls are such a characteristic part of the urban landscape in the Hellenistic and imperial periods that cities are always symbolized by their walls on mosaics and their statues are given turret-crowns. Accordingly, in *Leucippe and Clitophon*, a place that has some sort of houses and walls may be called "a rough imitation of a city," though in this instance the "houses" are only "huts" and the "walls" are the marshes of the Nile Delta (4.12.7: εἰσὶ δὲ τῶν νήσων τινὲς καλύβας ἔχουσαι, καὶ αὐτοσχέδιον μεμί-μηνται πόλιν, ταῖς λίμναις τετειχισμέναι; see also 4.12.6, 4.13.6, 4.18.1). Heliodorus enlarges on this description of the islands where the so-called herders dwell by comparing the water that encircles their entire settlement to a "wall," the vast quantity of reeds growing in the marsh to a "palisade" (1.6.1: τῷ μὲν ὕδατι πάντες ὅσα τείχει χρώμενοι, τὸν δὲ πολὺν κατὰ τὸ ἕλος κάλαμον ἀντὶ χαρακώματος προβεβλημένοι), and the whole place to a "secure stronghold" (ibid., φρούριον ἰσχυρόν).

The walls are usually mentioned when a city (Tyre in Chariton, or Memphis, Philae, or Syene in Heliodorus) is besieged. Chariton is content with allusions to the "walls" (τείχη) and the "gates" (πύλαι) of a city that is "solidly built" (ὀχυρῶς ᾠκοδομημένης τῆς πόλεως) (7.2.9, 7.4.2, 3, 4, 6, 8, 9). But Heliodorus abounds in details when he describes the siege of Syene, which is a kind of anthology of all the extraordinary devices used to attack or defend a city. He alludes to the "battlement" (τῶν ἐπάλξεων), "the section of the wall between two turrets" (μεταπύργιον), "the cracks between the planks in the city gates [τῶν κατὰ τὰς πύλας σανιδωμάτων] which they pack with oakum and pitch," and "the fissures that the heat of summer has caused to open up in the black and fertile soil" (διὰ τῶν ἀραιωμάτων τῆς γῆς, οἷς μέλαινα καὶ εὔγειος οὖσα πρὸς τῆς θερινῆς ὥρας κατέσχιστο).[22]

But the walls are also liable to be transformed into a tribune in the *Aethiopica*. In book 7, Arsace gives orders for a pavilion to be erected beneath a canopy of purple embroidered with gold, from which she calls on the enemy's leaders and watches the battle between Thyamis and Petosiris (7.3.2). In book 8, she looks at Chariclea's punishment from the wall (8.9.10), for the execution takes place, as was usual in Greek cities, outside the wall.

The harbors are frequently alluded to in Greek novels, but are never described. We are only given from time to time their number (some cities, such as Miletus and Syracuse, have more than one: Chariton 2.1.6, 3.3.18), and their excellence may be stressed: Miletus has, according to Chariton, "a fine natural harbor" (εἰς ὅρμον . . . εὐφυέστατον εἰς ὑποδο-χήν 1.11.8).

The temples are an important element of the urban landscape in Greek novels. Their appearance is no doubt connected with the importance of religious festivals, which regularly provide the background for love at first sight.[23] It is also near or in a temple that the heroes are married or reunited in the novels of Chariton, Xenophon of Ephesus, and Achilles Tatius,[24] and the heroines usually run to the temples when they are in danger of being raped.[25] Even apart from such occasions, the temples are at the center of an intense social life. The heroes never stop going there to pray,[26] perform sacrifices,[27] deposit offerings,[28] and consult oracles.[29] In the *Ae-thiopica*, temples also provide housing for the Egyptian priests of Memphis as well as for the gymnosophists of Meroe.[30] As usual, these temples are poorly depicted. Paradoxically, the most precisely visualized temple is the temple of Isis at Memphis that appears in the dream of Thyamis (Helio-dorus 1.18.4). But the details given here, "the torchlights," "the altars and sacred hearths drenched with the blood of all kinds of animals," "the gates and the colonnades teeming with people," and "the shrine itself," have nothing peculiar; they are typical of any temple.

Gymnasia are also alluded to in Greek novels, for their heroes are usually young Greeks belonging to the urban elite. Chariton's Chaereas has been "brought up in the gymnasium" (γυμνασίοις ἐντραφεὶς, 1.2.6) and is sup-posed to have spent most of his time there (1.1.9). As a matter of fact, he is coming from the gymnasium when he first meets Callirhoe (1.1.5). The hero of the *Aethiopica* is also cursorily presented as "a lifelong devotee of the gymnasium" (γυμνασίων ἀνὴρ . . . ἐκ νέων ἀσκητὴς, 10.31.5). All this does not amount to much. The remarkable obliteration of the gymnasi-um, one of the most conspicuous features of the Greek urban landscape, is no doubt due to the systematic downplaying of homosexuality in the Greek novel.[31] Indeed, the gymnasium is the regular setting for homosex-ual love affairs, as demonstrated by the two novels that are concerned with homosexuality. In the *Ephesiaca*, Hippothous tells the heroes how he met Hyperanthes and fell in love with him at the gymnasium ('Ηράσθην δὲ τὰ πρῶτα ἐν γυμνασίοις, 3.2.2) and in *Leucippe and Clitophon*, the priest who attacks the sexual integrity of Thersander recalls how "in the gymnasi-um . . . in wrestling with the boys, he always clung more tightly with the ones who were more manly" (8.9.4).

Theater, Agora, and Palace: From Early to Later Empire

The theater remains a hallmark of urban life. It continues to be used for performances: Achilles Tatius mentions recitals where dressed-up actors would give dramatic readings from Homer.[32] But most of the allusions to "theater" are found in metaphors. They sometimes describe an audience seated in a theaterlike shape (Longus 4.15.2; Heliodorus 5.14.3). More often, they refer to tragic performances more akin to Hellenistic melodra-mas with their lavish settings and pathetic scenes than to classical tragedy. According to Chariton, when Chaereas entered the court, "it was like being in a theater packed with pathetic scenes, with emotions tumbling over each other—weeping and rejoicing, astonishment and pity, disbelief and prayers" (ἔδοξας ἂν ἐν θεάτρῳ παρεῖναι μυρίων παθῶν πλήρει· πάντα ἦν ὁμοῦ, δάκρυα, χαρά, θάμβος, ἔλεος, ἀπιστία, εὐχαί, 5.8.2). Achilles Tatius compares to a "theater" the gorgeous display of a peacock's tail

(1.16.2). Heliodorus, who is the most theatrical of the novelists and uses metaphorically a large number of stage terms,[33] displays the same taste for a "theater" packed with various spectacles. The narrative opens with a bewildering tableau combining the most extreme opposites, a mass of dead bodies and the remains of a banquet. It goes on with a lavish pageant at Delphi, a fatal duel fought by two brothers, and the pitiful pantomime of the Syenians begging for their lives (1.1.6, 7.6.4, 9.5.3). But in Greek novels as well as in Greek cities of the Hellenistic and imperial period, the theater also became a regular meeting place for assemblies,[34] so Chariton uses χειροτονία δὲ ἦν ὡς ἐν θεάτρῳ (5.3.4) metaphorically to mean that a vote was taken as in a civic assembly,[35] and Heliodorus compares the Ethiopians addressing from their boats the besieged Persians and Syenians to orators addressing a "theater" from an assembly (τότε δὴ καὶ οἱ Αἰθίοπες πλησιάσαντες ὥσπερ ἀπ' ἐκκλησίας τῶν πορθμείων πρὸς τὸ πολιορκούμενον θέατρον τοιάδε ἔλεγον, 9.6.1). In these two novels, civic assemblies take place in the theater. In Chariton, the regular assembly that asks for the wedding of the two heroes, the extraordinary one that inquires after Callirhoe's tomb robbers and decides to send an embassy for her, and the final one, summoned by the Syracusans who want to see the heroes and hear from Chaereas the whole story of his journey, meet in the theater (1.1.12, 3.4.4, 3.4.7, 8.7.1, 8.7.3, 8.8.15). In the *Aethiopica,* the special session of the assembly that ratifies the proposal of an expedition against Theagenes to revenge Chariclea's abduction is also held by night in the theater of Delphi (4.19.4, 4.21.2). But in Heliodorus this is part and parcel of the archaizing decor of Delphi, together with the procession and the Pythian games.[36] It does not mirror a contemporary reality, as it did in Chariton, but rather echoes Demosthenes' *On the Crown* (169–70) and the famous description of the Athenians' reactions when they were informed that Philip had seized Elateia.

The agora is not only replaced by the theater as the assembly's meeting place; it is also progressively deprived of its other functions and obliterated by the palace from Chariton to Heliodorus.

Chariton reflects the early Roman Empire during which the agora was still the city's nerve center: when he wants to stress the cosmopolitan character of Athens thronged with visitors from all over the world, he compares it to an agora where one can see everyone (1.11.5: ὥσπερ γὰρ ἐν ἀγορᾷ τοὺς ἄνδρας οὕτως ἐν Ἀθήναις τὰς πόλεις ἔστιν ἰδεῖν). People usually stroll there, as does Hermocrates (8.6.3), when the ships of Chaereas reach Syracuse. The agora also serves as a political and juridical center. At Syracuse, Chaereas's trial is supposed to take place in the agora (1.5.3), and at Aradus, "the building where the town council usually transacted its business" is situated on the agora.[37] Finally it is a market: at Miletus one sells and buys slaves there.[38] In rich cities like Aradus, which was an active commercial center, it is large and enclosed with porticoes (7.6.3: Κἀκεῖνοι τοὺς μὲν εὐνούχους καὶ θεραπαινίδας καὶ πάντα τὰ εὐωνότερα σώματα συνήθροισαν εἰς τὴν ἀγοράν, αὕτη γὰρ εὐρυχωρίαν εἶχε. τοσοῦτο δὲ ἦν τὸ πλῆθος, ὥστε οὐ μόνον ἐν ταῖς στοαῖς, ἀλλὰ καὶ ὑπαίθριοι διενυκτέ-ρευσαν). This detail is obviously anachronistic in a novel that is supposed to take place during the early fourth century B.C.: the description of Chariton fits better the Ionian agora of the early Roman Empire, when it was increasingly treated as a closed, colonnaded court.[39]

Xenophon and Achilles Tatius offer comparable images of the agora. In the *Ephesiaca* (5.9.4), it is mentioned once and is nothing but a market at Tarentum, where the brothel-keeper brings Anthia to exhibit her to prospective buyers. But in *Leucippe and Clitophon,* the agora is far more conspicuous: it is a center for social life and a meeting place in all the cities of the Greek world. At Alexandria, Clitophon is taking a stroll in the agora when he meets Clinias (5.8.2). At Byzantium, Callisthenes acts as the escort of Sostratus in the agora (8.17.8). At Ephesus, the agora is crowded all night long by drunken people during the Artemis festival (6.3.2).

With Heliodorus, one enters the world of late antiquity where, as archeologists of the proto-Byzantine period have pointed out,[40] the agora is no more the living center of the city. The ἀγοραί (a noteworthy plural) are mentioned only in association with "the streets and the fountains" (2.26.4) or "the temples and the streets" (2.33.3) of Delphi. This is one more sign of the backward-looking image of Delphi in the *Aethiopica.* A similar antiquarian bias may be detected in another occurrence of agora: "at the time when the marketplace is full" (καὶ περὶ πλήθουσαν ἀγορὰν, 4.7.10). This set expression borrowed from the classical historians Herodotus and Xenophon (Herodotus 2.173, 4.181, 7.223; Xenophon, *Anabasis* 2.1.7) is a fairly standard way of indicating the hours before midday. The last occurrence of the word is even more telling: ἀγορά in 2.30.2 has lost any connection to a place; it refers to a "deal" that takes place in a temple.

In the *Aethiopica,* the agora is superseded by the palace. Here again, one has to emphasize the gap between Heliodorus and his predecessors, Xenophon, Achilles Tatius,[41] and Longus. The palace is conspicuously absent from their novels, which are set in a more or less contemporary world. There the most significant buildings (except porticoes and temples) are the rich houses of the urban elite, such as the large and wealthy house of Clitophon's father at Tyre with its beautiful park (1.15.1), the house of Melitte at Ephesus, which is "one of the best of the city" (5.17.1), and the house of Dionysophanes, where he gives a banquet attended by the best of the Mytileneans (4.34.2).

The world represented in Chariton's novel is more complex. On the one hand, Miletus belongs to the contemporary reality. As usual in the Greek cities of Asia Minor during the early empire, its most conspicuous building is the splendid house of Dionysius that surprises Theron by its size and its luxury (1.13.1). On the other hand, the royal palace, as part of the historical fiction, is assigned to the Persian Empire. It is cursorily alluded to at Tyre (8.5.7), but it becomes the center of action at Babylon in books 5 and 6: crowds keep pouring around it (5.5.7, 6.2.1), and the trial takes place in an unusually big and beautiful room (this rather abstract description is typical of Chariton's style) designated as a law court, with the king's throne in the middle (5.4.5). As a result, Callirhoe is separated from her husband and brought into the palace to be entrusted to the queen, whereas Dionysius and his son are left outside (5.10.5, 6.2.5; see also 6.3.9, 6.4.9, 7.1.1, 7.1.6).

By contrast, the entire action of the *Aethiopica* (except for flashbacks to Athens and Delphi) takes place within a monarchical universe: Egypt is ruled by the Persians and Meroe is a kindgom. The royal palace is therefore preeminent. At Meroe, it is the place where all the king's treasures have been piled up,[42] and the center of intellectual life. When Calasiris tells Chariclea about his meeting with the queen of Ethiopia, he says that "the royal court is ever the home of wise men" (οἰκειοῦται γὰρ ἀεὶ τὸ σοφῶν γένος ἡ βασίλειος αὐλή, 4.12.1), a passing indication perfectly in harmony with the third century of the Empress Julia Domna and her gathering of an intellectual elite around her. In the Egyptian cities under Persian dominion such as Memphis and Katadoupoi, there is also a "royal palace" (βασίλεια,) (7.1.4, 7.9.1, 8.1.7), which is the residence of the satrap in the king's absence, whence its name, σατραπεῖα (7.12.3, 8.3.5, 8.12.2, 8.12.3, 8.14.1). This palace is exceptional for its sumptuousness: it has "an imposing gateway of a grandeur far exceeding that of a private dwelling" (προπυλαίοις . . . ὑπερόγκοις καὶ πλέον ἢ κατὰ ἰδιωτικὴν οἴκησιν ἐξηρμένοις, 7.12.3). This preeminence of the palace is not, as in Chariton's Babylon, a mere consequence of the historical setting. It mirrors a significant change from civic to monarchic ideology. The agora, which was the showcase of Greek civic pride and wealth in the novels of the early empire, has been replaced by the palace, the visible demonstration of the emperor's power in an empire that was becoming increasingly centralized.

THREE VIEWS OF THE CITY: FUNCTIONAL SETTING, ARCHAIZING SCENERY, TOURIST ATTRACTIONS

There is also a significant evolution in the evocation of the various cities, from a purely functional and abstract representation to a more or less touristic image that provides some cities with an easily recognizable identity thanks to a few symbolic monuments well known to everyone.

If one looks at the towns that serve as decor for Chariton's novel, one is led to conclude that the setting of the action is abstract and idealized. Chariton, who models himself on Thucydides, is content with the details required by the plot, and rigorously discards any picturesque particulars. He limits the description of the minor cities to a few relevant details. Priene is a place where Hyginus leaves his attendants without supervision, so it is reduced to the inn where they live luxuriously (4.5.5) until their arrest. Tyre is besieged by the Egpytians. Accordingly, Chariton, who wants to glorify Chaereas's success in capturing it, is content to emphasize its strong position and to allude to its walls and gates (7.2.8, 7.2.9, 7.4.3, 7.4.6). The harbor of Paphos is characterized by the shrine of Aphrodite that belongs in fact to Old Paphos, some miles inland,[43] not only because this monument was famous, but also because Aphrodite is thematically linked to the heroine. Aradus is hardly better dealt with: it is restricted to an old shrine of Aphrodite (7.5.1; the goddess has to be present at the denouement of a plot she controlled from the beginning) and to the agora's colonnades and council building, which are large enough to hold the prisoners of Chaereas (7.6.3–4).

The three towns that serve as a setting for the major part of Chariton's novel—Syracuse, Miletus, and Babylon—present much the same picture. Chariton's Syracuse is first and foremost a typical Hellenistic town,[44] with streets (1.1.6, 1.5.1), houses (1.3.6, 1.4.10), agora (1.5.3), gymnasium (1.1.5, 1.1.10), palestra (1.4.3), theater (1.1.12, 1.3.4, 1.3.7, 8.7.1, 8.7.3, 8.8.15), and a harbor with brothels and taverns (1.7.3). But the focal point of the town is the sumptuous tomb of Callirhoe (1.6.5), which is itself fictitious. As for the shrine of Aphrodite (1.1.4, 8.8.15), it is far from being the most important temple in a town famous for the temples of Apollo, Athena, and Zeus Olympius.[45] The only detail that points to a specific Syracusan reality is quite unobtrusive: three times (3.3.18, 3.4.2, 8.6.3), Chariton refers to the harbors, which were notorious in antiquity for their quality (see Pseudo-Scylax 13 and Strabo 6.2.4).

The allusions to Babylon are also significant. One cannot find in the novel the slightest allusion to the two marvels of this city, its famous walls broad enough to allow the meeting of two carts on their top (Strabo 16.30 and AP 9.58), and the suspended gardens of Semiramis (Dio 6.37 and AP 7.740, 9.58). Chariton's Babylon is limited to the royal palace (5.4.5, 5.5.8, 5.10.9, 6.2.1, 6.3.9, 6.4.10, 7.1.1, 7.1.6), the houses where the satraps are lodged (5.2.2), the narrow and crowded streets (5.5.8, 6.1.1, 6.2.4), and the altars by which the king sets magnificent sacrifices (6.2.4).

The case of Miletus is even more illuminating. Many details suggest that Chariton was well acquainted with the town and its topography. He knows the existence of several harbors (2.1.6), but he hardly describes them (he merely mentions the banks [2.1.6] there). He locates the house of Dionysius "near the so-called famous harbor" (μέχρι τῆς οἰκίας ἥτις ἦν ἐπ' αὐτοῦ τοῦ λιμένος τοῦ δοκίμου γεγομένου, 3.2.11). This is probably a periphrasis for the famous Bay of Lions near which archaeologists have found traces of a residential area.[46] But Chariton carefully avoids the proper name "Bay of Lions," and he does not allude to the famous Didymeion, which, as Dio (40.8) reminds us, was to Miletus what the Parthenon was to Athens or the temple of Artemis was to Ephesus. In the novel, this temple dedicated to Apollo is totally superseded, in the city, by the temple of Homonoia (3.2.16) and, in the countryside, by the shrine of Aphrodite (2.2.7, 2.3.5–10, 2.5.1–12, 3.2.12, 3.6.3–5, 3.8.3–9.3, 4.1.4–5), which plays an important role in the novel's plot. As a matter of fact, Miletus, with its sanctuary dedicated to Aphrodite and the tomb of Chaereas, which "was like her own [Callirhoe's] tomb in Syracuse in all respects— shape, size, costliness" (4.1.6), is made into a mirror image of Syracuse, in spite of its actual topography. Thus, Chariton creates an economical setting for a novel located in the past by a process of abstraction, discarding any allusion to well-known contemporary monuments.

There are obvious similarities between Chariton's historical novel and the contemporary novel of Xenophon. His *Ephesiaca* usually provides us with a highly selective view of cities. The description of Tarsus in Cilicia includes only some generic places where the action is set: the prison where the eirenarch of Cilicia puts the robbers, the house where he receives Anthia, and the cemetery near the city where he buries her (2.13.6, 3.7.4). Alexandria is but a prison (4.3.1), Perinthus a gymnasium (3.2.2). Mazacus is restricted to the gates near which the hero finds lodging (3.1.3). This "realistic" detail is all the more interesting, because we know for sure that it is false. Strabo tells us that this city, which was the μητρόπολις τοῦ ἔθνους, was "unfortified: by nature and left without walls, because of the neglect of the prefects or perhaps intentionally so" (ἀνώχυρος διὰ τὴν ὀλιγωρίαν τῶν ἡγεμόνων καὶ ἀτείχιστος, τάχα δὲ καὶ ἐπίτηδες, 12.2.7). In fact, Xenophon reshapes Mazacus according to the idea he forms of the polis (and we have seen that, for the Greeks of the Hellenistic and Roman ages, a polis was defined by its walls), without any regard for its actual appearance. In the same way, the images of Byzantium, Syracuse, and Lesbos are limited to fictitious locations such as the houses of Aristomachus and Aegialeus or the tomb of Hyperanthes (3.2.11, 5.1.2, 5.15.4).

But, contrary to Chariton, Xenophon does not totally discard the most famous buildings of the cities he mentions. At Ephesus, the Artemision, one of the seven wonders of the world (*AP* 9.58), provides a setting for the beginning as well as the end of the novel (1.2.1, 1.5.3, 5.12.2). Xenophon is even able sometimes to achieve a kind of compromise between the demands of his plot and a desire to portray some of the major tourist attractions. At Rhodes, for example, there is not only the famous temple of Helios (1.12.2, 5.11.3–6, 5.12.1, 5.12.3), which the two heroes enter many times, but also a temple of Isis near which they meet at the end (5.13.2), because of the role played by Isis in the novel. The case of Memphis is even more illuminating, for the actual Memphis, like Xenophon's Memphis, had two temples dedicated to Isis and Apis. The temple of Isis had been in existence since the fifth century B.C. (according to Herodotus, it was "large and worth being looked at," 2.176), but it had become far less important under the Roman Empire. Nevertheless it plays a major role in Xenophon's novel, because Isis takes over the role of protector for the heroine when the action reaches Egypt. On the contrary, the temple of Apis was the major attraction of the city, according to Strabo,[47] and it is alluded to in the novel because it was "the most illustrious shrine in Egypt" (5.4.8). And the heroine Anthia is there given an oracle, as expected from a god who was well known for his fortunetelling, according to the testimonies of Dio (32.13) and Pausanias (7.22.2–4).

Compared with Xenophon, Achilles Tatius and Heliodorus have a decidedly more archaizing taste. Achilles Tatius, who uses the Artemision as a setting for his novel (mainly in books 7 and 8), is more lavish: he enriches the picture of Xenophon by including "the grove at the back of the temple" and "the cave forbidden to women except those who enter as pure virgins" (8.6.1), and by dwelling at great length—as Pausanias usually does—on the myth connected to the place, the story of Pan and Syrinx (8.6.1–15). Heliodorus is more selective. His presentation of Memphis is characterized by a markedly antiquarian bias: he excludes the "modern" temple of Apis and is content with the temple of Isis (1.18.4, 2.25.2, 7.2.2, 7.8.5–7, 7.9.1, 7.11.1) praised by Herodotus. This is a deliberate choice, as demonstrated by his portraits of Athens and Delphi, which reflect the same archaizing taste. This point has been convincingly demonstrated about Delphi in three recent papers by J. Pouilloux and G. Rougemont.[48] Their work enables me to concentrate on Athens.[49]

Heliodorus's Athens is a montage of political and cultural references that reflect his interest in antiquities. His aim is to recall the days of Athenian greatness and create a fifth-century atmosphere, but his picture is not devoid of anachronistic details. For instance, the Prytanaeum becomes a place where the members of the Areopagus dine during the festival of the Great Panathenaia (1.9.1, 10.2), whereas in classical Athens, the Prytaneis, who served as the executive committee of the Council, would have their meals in the *tholos* and the σίτησις at the Prytaneion would be a privilege granted by the city to its benefactors.[50] The confusion is not difficult to understand: it was easy to assimilate to the "presidents" of the Council the members of the Areopagus, which became the most important council in the Roman Empire, and it was tempting to connect these Prytaneis with the Prytanaeum, all the more so since in other cities the Prytanaeum was a building where meals were served to the magistrates.[51] The mention of the βάραθρον into which many people voted to hurl the parricide Cnemon is also inaccurate: classical Greek texts would reserve this punishment for "those who have done wrong to the People of Athens," as said by the Cannonus's decree quoted by Xenophon in the *Hellenica* (1.7.20).[52]

The cultural references are more accurate, for they call on places familiar to any educated Greek having some training in philosophy. Thisbe arranges an appointment for Aristippus in "the garden where the Monument of the Epicureans is" (1.16.5), and Demainete commits suicide in the Academia: she hurls herself into the pit "where the polemarch performs the traditional sacrifice to the heroes" (1.17.5). Pausanias provides confirmation for the accuracy of the setting. According to him, a funeral monument existed near the Academia, erected in honor of all the Athenians who died in battle, alongside the burial place of the tyrannicides Harmodius and Aristogiton (1.29.4, 1.29.15). And, as well pointed out by J. R. Morgan,[53] the function Heliodorus gives to the polemarch is consistent with the *Constitution of the Athenians,* which reports that "the polemarch made offerings to the dead at war and to Harmodius and Aristogiton" (58.1). There is obviously a great irony in choosing a place dedicated to wisdom and filled with glorious memories as the setting for a rather squalid love story and a suicide that is far from heroic, all the more so when one knows that there existed, precisely within the walls of the Academia, two altars dedicated to Eros and Anteros in order to mark the very spot from which, according to Pausanias (1.30.1), two lovers were supposed to have thrown themselves.

Greek novelists from Xenophon onward were also interested in exotic travels and tried to satisfy the taste of their audience for tourist attractions. In the *Ephesiaca,* this interest does not amount to much. Indeed, Xenophon reports that Anthia and Habrocomes, once landed at Rhodes, "tour the whole city" (Οἱ δὲ τήν τε πόλιν ἅπασαν ἐξιστόρησαν, 1.12.2). But tourism is eclipsed by religion: Xenophon does not go into the details of this tour, whereas he insists on the offerings they give to the temple of Helios (καὶ ἀνέθεσαν εἰς τὸ τοῦ Ἡλίου ἱερὸν πανοπλίαν χρυσῆν καὶ ἐπέγραψαν εἰς ὑπόμνημα ἐπίγραμμα τῶν ἀναθέντων, 1.12.2). He also portrays an Indian king who comes to Alexandria "to see the city and do business" (κατὰ θέαν τῆς πόλεως καὶ κατὰ χρείαν ἐμπορίας, 3.11.2). But he is only interested in his business, that is, the purchase of Anthia (3.11.3). He mentions that Hippothous and his band came to Laodice of Syria "and took up lodgings there not as pirates this time, but posing as tourists" (κἀνταῦθα ἐπεδήμουν οὐκέτι ὡς λησταί, ἀλλ' ὡς κατὰ θέαν τῆς πόλεως ἥκοντες, 4.1.1). But this detail is quickly dismissed.

Achilles Tatius is more concerned with tourism. The novel begins with a description of Sidon, where the narrator presents himself as a tourist:

arriving at Sidon after a violent storm, he offers a sacrifice to Astarte and then "tours the rest of the city to see its memorial offerings" (περιϊὼν οὖν καὶ τὴν ἄλλην πόλιν καὶ περισκοπῶν τὰ ἀναθήματα, 1.1.2). He is imitated by the heroes, who, after a shipwreck at Pelousion, are told that Zeus Casius can be consulted as an oracle and, after praying, "visit the temple" (περιήειμεν τὸν νεών, 3.6.2).

All the same, the prologue of *Daphnis and Chloe* opens by mentioning a narrator who is a tourist as well as a hunter and sees, in a grove that was sacred to the Nymphs, the most beautiful sight he has ever seen ('Εν Λέσβῳ θηρῶν ἐν ἄλσει Νυμφῶν θέαμα εἶδον κάλλιστον ὧν εἶδον), and the novel itself begins with a rather accurate description of Mytilene.[54]

Heliodorus also turns his characters into tourists. Charicles, who "steals away from the land of his birth and flees from his wretched house . . . wanders through many lands" until he comes to Egypt and Katadoupoi "to find out about the cataracts of the Nile."[55] Moreover, the king of Ethiopia, after winning a decisive victory over the Persians and entering Syene, becomes a mere tourist interested, like Pausanias, in old rites and famous sites: "He inquired of the priests what the origin of the Neiloa was and whether there were any curiosities in the city that they could show him."[56] This behavior is most unlikely, since Ethiopia is, in many ways, a kind of super-Egypt. Predictably, the king is not at all amazed by what he has been told, and replies to the priests: "But all the things of which you speak so proudly belong not to Egypt, but to Ethiopia" (9.22.7). Nevertheless, he has to be a tourist, so that the readers might visit with him the two wonders of Syene, the Nilometer and "the sundials that cast no shadow at noon," the description of which is borrowed almost word for word from Strabo or his source.[57]

Such tourist's curiosity is likely to inspire descriptions of every amazing site. For instance, at the beginning of *Daphnis and Chloe,* we are given a highly selective description of Mytilene, which is worth admiring: it is "big and beautiful" (μεγάλη καὶ καλή) and, above all, it has "canals through which the sea flows gently" (διείληπται γὰρ εὐρίποις ὑπεισρεούσης τῆς θαλάσσης), and "bridges of white polished stone, which are its adorning" (καὶ κεκόσμηται γεφύραις ξεστοῦ καὶ λευκοῦ λίθου). This feature of Mytilenean landscape is so remarkable that it is used elsewhere as a reference: when Pausanias describes Megalopolis, a town of Arcadia cut in two by a river, he draws a comparison not only with Cnide, but also with Mytilene.[58] The final sentence gives the reason for this ecphrasis: "You would think you were looking at an island, not a city" (νομίσαις οὐ πόλιν ὁρᾶν ἀλλὰ νῆσον). What appeals to Longus and his sophisticated audience is the paradoxical character of a town that is an island, the more so if this town is itself located within an island.

This delight in paradoxical sights that afford many opportunities for elaborate style and highly artificial expression also explains why Achilles Tatius chooses to describe Sidon and Tyre. Sidon has a "broad double harbor" (δίδυμος λιμήν): "where the bay curves round on the right, a second entrance has been channeled, a further inlet for the tidewater" (ἧ γὰρ ὁ κόλπος κατὰ πλευρὰν ἐπὶ δεξιὰ κοιλαίνεται, στόμα δεύτερον ὀρώρυκται, καὶ τὸ ὕδωρ αὖθις εἰσρεῖ).[59] The last sentence summarizes the extraordinary character of this "harbor within a harbor" (καὶ γίνεται τοῦ λιμένος ἄλλος λιμήν). Tyre is also an exceptional site: "it is claimed by land and sea and belongs to both . . . a narrow neck joins her to the mainland, like the island's throat. But she has no foundation in the sea, and the water flows freely under her. Below the isthmus lies the channel crossing" (2.14.2–4: ἐρίζει δὲ περὶ ταύτης γῆ καὶ θάλασσα. ἕλκει μὲν ἡ θάλασσα, ἕλκει δὲ ἡ γῆ, ἡ δὲ εἰς ἀμφότερα αὐτὴν ἥρμοσε. καὶ γὰρ ἐν θαλάσσῃ κάθηται καὶ οὐκ ἀφῆκε τὴν γῆν· συνδεῖ γὰρ αὐτὴν πρὸς τὴν ἤπειρον στενὸς αὐχήν, καὶ ἔστιν ὥσπερ τῆς νήσου τράχηλος. οὐκ ἐρρίζωται δὲ κατὰ τῆς θαλάσσης, ἀλλὰ τὸ ὕδωρ ὑπορρεῖ κάτωθεν. Ὑπόκειται δὲ πορθμὸς κάτωθεν ἰσθμῷ), and the description ends by focusing on the puzzling character of a reality that turns the reader's expectations upside down: "It is a novel sight: a sea-city and a mainland island" (καὶ γίνεται τὸ θέαμα καινόν, πόλις ἐν θαλάσσῃ καὶ νῆσος ἐν γῇ). All the same, the swamps of the Nile Delta and the "cities" of the "Herders" are outstanding natural curiosities that become baroque showpieces. First, the narrator insists on "the competing claims of water and sea" and their unexpected settlement: "the water turning so much land into a sea, the land in turn absorbing so great and sweet a sea their victories show perfect equality—neither is ever the loser" (4.12.3: ἔστι δὲ ἰδεῖν ποταμοῦ καὶ γῆς φιλονεικίαν. ἐρίζετον ἀλλήλοις ἑκάτερος, τὸ μὲν ὕδωρ τοσαύτην γῆν πελαγῶσαι, ἡ δὲ γῆ τοσαύτην χωρῆσαι γλυκεῖαν θάλασσαν. καὶ νικῶσι μὲν τὴν ἴσην νίκην οἱ δύο, οὐδαμοῦ δὲ φαίνεται τὸ νικώμενον·). Then he underlines the paradox of an artifact produced by nature itself: some of the islands that are protected by marshes in place of walls are imitations of cities provided by nature (αὐτοσχέδιον μεμίμηνται πόλιν, ταῖς λίμναις τετειχισμέναι, 4.12.7).

The lengthy description of Alexandris (5.1.1–6) obeys the same logic. Achilles Tatius is less concerned with evoking precisely the largest city of Roman Egypt than with piling up the unusual and paradoxical. He refers briefly to "the temple of Zeus Celestial" (τὸν Διὸς Οὐρανίον νεών, 5.2.2), which is unmistakenly the Serapeum.[60] The hero himself points out that "the high god whose Greek name is Zeus is known as Serapis in Egypt" (5.2.1). He mentions cursorily "the quarter named for Alexander himself" (τὸν ἐπώνυμον Ἀλεξάνδρου τόπον, 5.1.3),[61] and the gates of the Sun and Moon (ἐκ τῶν Ἡλίου πυλῶν ἐς τὰς Σελήνης πύλας, 5.1.2).[62] But he insists on the lighthouse of the Pharos, which ranked among the seven marvels of the world: Chaereas exposes to the heroes and the readers this paradoxical feat of engineering genius (δείκνυσι τὴν κατασκευὴν . . . θαυμασίαν τινὰ καὶ παράλογον, 5.6.2) that succeeds in connecting the water to the clouds (5.6.3: ὄρος ἦν ἐν μέσῃ τῇ θαλάσσῃ κείμενον, ψαῦον αὐτῶν τῶν νεφῶν. ὑπέρρει δὲ ὕδωρ κάτωθεν αὐτοῦ τοῦ ποιήματος). Above all, Achilles Tatius is struck by the size of the city, the number of its inhabitants, and the beauty of its buildings, and conveys his admiration by an elaborate sentence that emphasizes the paradoxical conjunction of opposites: "I saw two new and unheard of sights: the city's very largeness challenged its loveliness and the populace vied with the city for size. Both won contests" (εἶδον δὲ δύο καινὰ καὶ παράλογα, μεγέθους πρὸς κάλλος ἅμιλλαν καὶ δήμου πρὸς πόλιν φιλονεικίαν καὶ ἀμφότερα νικῶντα, 5.1.6). As for the splendid beauty (τῆς πόλεως ἀστράπτον τὸ κάλλος, 5.1.1), it consists mainly in colonnaded streets. Clitophon draws attention first to the line of columns that, on each side, led straight across the entire city from the entrance of the Sun to the opposite entrance of the Moon (5.1.2: στάθμη μὲν κιόνων ὄρθιος ἑκατέρωθεν ἐκ τῶν Ἡλίου πυλῶν ἐς τὰς Σελήνης πύλας), and then to the two rows of columns that intersected at right angles in the center (5.1.4: ὅσος γὰρ κιόνων ὄρχατος εἰς τὴν εὐθυωρίαν, τοσοῦτος ἕτερος εἰς τὰ ἐγκάρσια). However, these colonnaded streets that "may have originated in late Hellenistic coastal Syria,"[63] and "became particularly widespread throughout the cities of the eastern provinces of the Roman Empire,"[64] do not seem to be characteristic of the Alexandrian urban landscape, at least at the time of Diodorus and Strabo.[65] What is depicted by Achilles Tatius is the idea of the city, not its concrete, individualized form: with its regular layout and its monumental structures, Alexandria embodies the wonders of the modern city, which stand in utter contrast to the disorder of "old" cities like Athens.[66]

Greek novels paid much attention to the city perceived in terms of its monuments and physical structure, but as far as the city is concerned, this is only one side of the coin. It would be necessary to complement this investigation by examining the city as a community and portraying the social world of the Greek novel. Nevertheless, it is my hope that this essay, which makes no claim to completeness, will illustrate, as noted by E. Bowie,[67] and brilliantly demonstrated by P. Veyne and F. Millar for the Roman novel,[68] that "the novels merit treatment as evidence for Greco-Roman society" and will contribute to a better understanding of the evolution of the cities.

From Chariton to Heliodorus, the novels seem to reflect faithfully the city's landscape. They allude to all the elements that had become the hallmarks of urban life: walls, temples, gymnasia, theaters, agorai, and palaces. They also give expression to some of the major changes the town had undergone from early to late empire. The growth of centralization is mirrored by the preeminence of the palace in the *Aethiopica,* whereas the importance of the agora, which is the town's social center in Chariton, Xenophon of Ephesus, and Achilles Tatius, witnesses the city's political and administrative role even at the height of the Roman Empire. But the novels are by no means exact copies of the real world. They are highly selective, as demonstrated by the treatment of the gymnasium, which assumed an important social role in the cities of the Greek world, but is scarcely alluded to by Chariton and Heliodorus, who pay no attention to homosexual relationships.

These different views of the city may also help illuminate the development of the novel as a genre. In *Chaereas and Callirhoe,* the description of the geographical setting is strictly subordinated to the necessities of the plot, and the classical atmosphere is mostly created through abstraction: Chariton does not mention the most famous monuments of Syracuse, Miletus, and Babylon, and he focuses on fictitious locations. The narrative strategy of the *Aethiopica* is totally different. Instead of discarding contemporary details, Heliodorus creates a historical decor by patching together more or less accurate details borrowed from prestigious sources, and his descriptions of classical sites such as Athens and Delphi are characterized by a markedly antiquarian bias. As for Achilles Tatius, he is mainly concerned with tourist attractions, extraordinary sites that allow the display of every kind of rhetorical device: *mise en abîme* (Sidon, which has a harbor within the harbor), conjunction of opposites (the island of the Herders is a city, that is, a human artifact, improvised by nature) or paradoxical formulas (Alexandria challenges a continent by its size and a nation by the number of its inhabitants). There is only one description of a city, Mytilene, in *Daphnis and Chloe,* but it is enough to demonstrate that Longus shared some of the aesthetic choices of Achilles Tatius. Compared to the other novels, the *Ephesiaca* looks like a compromise: Xenophon sometimes shares the interest of Achilles Tatius in major tourist attractions, but most of the time, he is content with a highly selective view of the city, as is Chariton. However, the city in Greek novels remains a stereotype and its individuation is limited to place names and abstract, paradoxical features.

Notes

1. J. E. Stambaugh, "The Idea of the City: Three Views of Athens," *Classical Journal* 69 (1974–75): 309.

2. E. Kienzle, *Der Lobpreis von Städten und Ländern in der älteren griechischen Dichtung* (Ph.D. diss., University of Basel, 1932); S. Scully, *Homer and the Sacred City* (Ithaca, N.Y., 1990).

3. K. Hartigan, *The Poets and Their Cities: Selections from the Anthology about Greek Cities,* Beiträge zur klassische Philologie, no. 87 (1979).

4. C. J. Classen, *Die Stadt im Spiegel der Descriptiones und Laudes Urbium in der antiken*

und mittelalterlichen Literatur bis zum Ende des zwölfen Jahrhunderts, Beiträge zur Altertumswissenschaft, no. 2 (1980).

5. B. Pike, *The Image of the City in Modern Literature* (Princeton, 1981), 4; B. P. Reardon, ed., *Collected Ancient Greek Novels* (Berkeley and Los Angeles, 1989), 2.

6. T. Hägg, *The Novel in Antiquity* (Oxford, 1983), 59.

7. Ibid., 5–6.

8. On *Chaereas and Callirhoe* as a historical novel, see T. Hägg, "Callirhoe and Parthenope: The Beginnings of the Historical Novel," *Classical Antiquity* 6 (1987): 194–98, and A. Billault, "De l'histoire au roman: Hermocrate de Syracuse," *Revue des etudes grecques* 102 (1989): 540–48.

9. This novel mentions a "satrap" of Egypt (4.11.1, 4.13.4), but "this does not necessarily refer to the Persian magistrate; it may be an atticist way of saying prefect (cf. Philostratus, *VS* 1.22.3)" (Hägg, "Callirhoe and Parthenope," 199).

10. Prefect: cf. 3.12.6, 4.2.1, 4.2.9, 5.3.1, 5.5.2. Hägg, "Callirhoe and Parthenope," 200: "This mention . . . makes the novel post-hellenistic." Eirenarch: cf. 2.13.3. Reardon, *Collected Ancient Greek Novels,* 146 n. 13: "This mention . . . is one of the few indications of Xenophon's date: the office is first mentioned, as far as is known, in an inscription of A.D. 116–117 found not very far from Ephesus."

11. Cf. 1.9–17. See J. R. Morgan, "The Story of Cnemon in Heliodorus' *Aithiopike,*" *Journal of Hellenic Studies* 109 (1989): 99–113.

12. J. R. Morgan, "Historical Romance and Realism," *Classical Antiquity* 1 (1982): 247.

13. Cf. 9.7.3, 9.11.2, 10.1.2. See Morgan, "Historical Romance and Realism," 249.

14. Herodotus 2.17 and Philostratus, *VAT* 3.20, 6.1, 6.17.

15. Cf. 2.29.5: Charicles visits Katadoupoi "to find out about the cataracts of the Nile."

16. E.g., Athens: Chariton 1.11.5; Alexandria: A.T. 2.31.6; Syracuse: X.E. 5.1.1; Rhodes: X.E. 1.11.6; Mazacus in Cappadocia: X.E. 3.1.1; Thebes: Heliodorus 2.25.6.

17. E.g., Ephesus is sacred (X.E. 1.12.2), because Artemis is "the ancestral goddess of the city (τὴν πάτριον ἡμῖν θεόν, τὴν μεγάλην Ἐφεσίων Ἄρτεμιν, X.E. 1.11.5, 2.11.8, 3.3.5); Memphis is "sacred to Isis" (Μέμφιν τὴν ἱερὰν τῆς Ἴσιδος, X.E. 4.1.3) and Delphi is "sacred to Apollo but a holy place for the other gods too" (ἱερὰν μὲν Ἀπόλλωνος θεῶν δὲ τῶν ἄλλων τέμενος, Heliodorus 2.26.1).

18. On Greek cities under the Roman Empire, see A. H. M. Jones, *The Greek City from Alexander to Justinian* (Oxford, 1940). On city planning, see R. Martin, *L'urbanisme dans la Grèce antique* (Paris, 1956), and E. J. Owens, *The City in the Greek and Roman World* (London, 1991).

19. Aelius Aristides, *Panath.* 351; Menander 2.431.3; Quintilian 3.2.27. See Owens, *City,* 151: "Town walls did not only have a military function . . . They were also a sign of independence and, in the imperial period, a mark of status and privilege. City walls and their gates were important public monuments."

20. For Heliodorus, these places summarize the city, as demonstrated by 2.33.3: when Charicles says that Chariclea is so beautiful that she draws all eyes and attentions to herself wherever she appears in the temples, colonnades, and agorai (ὅπου δὴ φαινομένη ναῶν ἢ δρόμων ἢ ἀγορῶν καθάπερ ἀρχέτυπον ἄγαλμα πᾶσαν ὄψιν καὶ δάνοιαν ἐφ' ἑαυτὴν ἐπιστρέφει), he means of course everywhere.

21. See F. Millar, "The World of *The Golden Ass,*" *Journal of Roman Studies* 71 (1981): 72.

22. Cf. 9.3.2, 9.3.7, 9.4.3, 9.5.1. Morgan, "Historical Romance and Realism," 244, draws attention to the technical character of ἀραιωμάτων that is applied elsewhere to the fissures of the ground near the Nile.

23. Chariton 1.1.4: "A public festival of Aphrodite took place" when Chareas first met Callirhoe; X.E. 1.2.2: "The local festival of Artemis was in progress" when Habrocomes saw Anthia for the first time; Heliodorus 2.34.1–3.6: the Pythian games, which happen to coincide with the sacrifice and the sacred mission the Aenianes send to Neoptolemus at Delphi, are the setting for the first meeting of Theagenes and Chariclea, 1.10.1: "It was during the festival of the Great Panathenaia" that De-mainete's passion for Cnemon becomes blatant, and 7.2.2: "while Thyamis was per-forming public sacrifices" in the temple of Isis at Memphis, Arsace "cast on him eyes of lust." These festivals are not the only ones mentioned in Greek novels. See also X.E. 5.11.2: "A magnificent public festival was being celebrated by the whole popula-tion of Rhodes in honor of Helios," and A.T. 6.3.2: "It was the festival of Artemis in Ephesus."

24. In Chariton 3.2.16, Dionysus receives Callirhoe as his bride in the temple of the Concord at Miletus. In Xenophon 5.13.2, Habrocomes and Anthia meet again "near the temple of Isis" in Rhodes, and Leucippe and Clitophon at the temple of Artemis in Ephesus (A.T. 7.16).

25. X.E. 5.4.6: the temple of Isis in Memphis; A.T. 7.13.2: the temple of Artemis in Ephesus.

26. S.E. 4.3.2: the temple of Isis in Memphis; Heliodorus 2.26.4–5: the temple of Apollo in Delphi.

27. A.T. 1.1.2: the temple of Astarte in Sidon; Heliodorus 2.25.1: the temple of Memphis; 3.5.2: the altar of Neoptolemus in Delphi; 5.13.2: the temple of Hermes in Chemmis.

28. X.E. 1.12.2: the temple of Helios at Rhodes; Heliodorus 7.11.2: the temple of Isis in Memphis.

29. X.E. 1.6.1: the oracle of Colophon; 4.4.8: the temple of Apis in Memphis; A.T. 3.6.2: the temple of Zeus Casius in Pelousion; Heliodorus 2.26.5, 2.35.5: the oracle of Delphi.

30. Heliodorus 7.9.1, 10.4.1. In Delphi, Calasiris is allowed to "make his home into the temple precinct" (2.27.1).

31. Hägg, *Novel in Antiquity,* 44–45.

32. 3.20.4, 3.20.7. Reardon, *Collected Ancient Greek Novels,* 218 n. 52: "Such perform-ers are mentioned by Achilles' contemporaries Athenaios (*Deipnosophistai* 14.620b) and Artemidorus (*Oneirokritika* 4.2)."

33. See J. H. W. Walden, "Stage Terms in Heliodorus's *Aethiopica,*" *Harvard Studies in Classical Philology* 5 (1894): 1–43.

34. For political meetings taking place in theaters, see W. A. MacDonald, *The Meet-ing Places of the Greeks* (Baltimore, 1943). In Athens the Pnyx had been completely superseded by the theater by the second century B.C. A passage often quoted from Acts 19:23–41 indicates also that, at Ephesus, the theater has replaced the agora as a regular meeting place by the first century A.D. All the same, in *The Golden Ass* (3.2–9), the trial of Lucius at Hypata takes place in the theater (see Millar, "World," 70 n. 44).

35. Reardon, *Collected Ancient Greek Novels,* 78 n. 78.

36. See J. Pouilloux, "Delphes dans les *Ethiopiques* d'Héliodore: La réalité dans la fiction," *Journal des Savants* (1983): 259–86; Pouilloux, "Roman grec et réalité: Un épisode delphique des *Ethiopiques* d'Héliodore," in *Hommages à L. Lerat* (Paris, 1984), 691–702.

37. 7.6.4: εἰς οἴκημα τῆς ἀγορᾶς . . . , ἐν ᾧ συνήθως οἱ ἄρχοντες ἐχρημάτιζον. This is in agreement with the town planning of Greek cities of the Hellenistic and imperial period (see R. Martin, *Recherches sur l' agora grecque* [Paris, 1952], 292–93).

38. 1.13.6, 2.1.6.

39. On the contrast between the "old manner" agora and the Ionian one, see

Pausanias 6.24.2. On this evolution, see Martin, *Recherches,* and more summarily, Martin, *L'urbanisme,* 266–75, and Owens, *City,* 153. On the so-called Ionian agora, see M. Waelkens, "Hellenistic and Romance Influences in the Imperial Architecture of Asia Minor," in *The Greek Renaissance in the Roman Empire,* ed. S. Walker and A. Cameron, *Bulletin of the Institute of Classical Studies,* supp. 55 (1989): 81–82.

40. For instance, in Thessalonike (see J. M. Spieser, "Les villes en Grèce du IIIᵉ au VIIᵉ s.," in *Villes et peuplement dans l'Illyricum protobyzantin* [Rome, 1984], 318–21) the colonnaded porticoes that were destroyed by an earthquake during the first half of the seventh century A.D. were not rebuilt. All the same, in Athens, the ruined agora was nearly deserted at the end of the third century A.D. For a tentative explanation of "the collapse of urban ideology," see J. M. Spieser, "L'évolution de la ville byzantine de l'époque paléochrétienne à l'iconoclasme," in *Hommes et richesses dans l'Empire byzantin: t.1 IVᵉ-VIIᵉ. siècle* (Paris, 1989), 97–106.

41. ἡ σατραπεία is mentioned once in *Leucippe and Clitophon* (4.13.4). But this residence of the "satrap" of Egypt (an atticist way of saying "prefect"; see note 9) is not described.

42. 9.24.1. In Egypt also, the most beautiful things—for instance, a prisoner as handsome as Theagenes—are sent to the "royal court" (5.9.2).

43. 8.2.7. See Reardon, *Collected Ancient Greek Novels,* 113 n.2.

44. J. Bompaire, "Le décor sicilien dans le roman grec et la littérature contemporaine," *Revue des etudes grecques* 90 (1977): 60.

45. See "Syracuse" in *Real-Encyclopaedie der classischen Altertumswissenschaft,* ed. A. Pauly and G. Wissowa (Stuttgart, 1894–1963), and in R. Stillwell, ed., *The Princeton Encyclopedia of Classical Sites* (Princeton, 1976).

46. On Miletus's topography during the Roman Empire, see M. Leglay, *Villes, temples, et sanctuaires de l'Orient Romain* (Paris, 1986), 179–200, and G. Kleiner, *Das Römische Milet* (Wiesbaden, 1970).

47. 17.31–32. On the value of the systematic description of Strabo, see D. J. Thompson, *Memphis under the Ptolemies* (Princeton, 1988), 9–31.

48. See Pouilloux, "Delphes," 263–70; "Roman grec et réalité," 691–92, and G. Rougemont, "Delphes chez Héliodore," in *Le monde du roman grec,* ed. M. F. Baslez, P. Hoffman, and M. Trédé (Paris, 1992), 93–99.

49. See E. Oudot, "Images d'Athènes dans les romans grecs," in *Le monde du roman grec,* 101–11.

50. See G. Miller, *The Prytaneion* (Berkeley and Los Angeles, 1978), 4–11.

51. Ibid., 24.

52. See L. Gernet, "Sur l'exécution capitale," in *Anthropologie de la Grèce antique* (Paris, 1968), 308–11.

53. Reardon, *Collected Ancient Greek Novels,* 368 n. 21 (to J. R. Morgan's translation of Heliodorus, 1.17).

54. 1.1.1. See H. J. Mason, "Longus and the Topography of Lesbos," *Transactions of the American Philological Association* 109 (1979): 149–63; P. Green, "Longus, Antiphon, and the Topography of Lesbos," *Journal of Hellenic Studies* 102 (1982): 210–14; and E. L. Bowie, "Theocritus' Seventh *Idyll,* Philetas and Longus," *Classical Quarterly* 35 (1985), 73–74. As emphasized by C. Gill (Reardon, *Collected Ancient Greek Novels,* 289 n. 3), "these scholars agree that Longus' picture of the topography of Lesbos is generally accurate."

55. 2.29.5: ὑπεξάγω δὲ τῆς ἐνεγκούσης καὶ τὴν ἐρημίαν τῆς οἰκίας ἀποδιδράσκω . . . καὶ πολλοῖς ἐμπλανηθεὶς τόποις ἦλθον δὴ καὶ εἰς τὴν σὴν Αἴγυπτον καὶ Καταδούπους αὐτοὺς καθ' ἱστορίαν τῶν καταρρακτῶν τοῦ Νείλου.

56. 9.22.2: τῶν τε Νειλῴων ἥτις γένεσις παρὰ τῶν ἱερέων ἐκπυνθανόμενος καὶ εἴ τι θαύματος ἢ θεάματος ἄξιον κατὰ τὴν πόλιν ἐπιδεικνύναι ἔχουσιν.

57. 17.1.48. See the commentary of J. Morgan (Reardon, *Collected Ancient Greek Novels*, 553 n. 221).

58. 8.30.20. This characteristic feature of Mytilene's topography is also emphasized by Strabo (13.2.2) and Diodorus (13.79.5–6).

59. Strabo (16.2.22), who emphasizes the quality of Sidon's harbor, is far less precise. But the *Descriptio terrae sanctae* of Johannes Phocas (see E. Vilborg, ed., *Achilles Tatius, Leucippe and Clitophon* [Stockholm, 1955], Testimonia, 10), praises this description for its accuracy and vividness.

60. As pointed out by P. M. Fraser, *Ptolemaic Alexandria* (Oxford, 1972), 248 and 804, the cult of Serapis was developed at Alexandria during the Roman Empire, and the Roman Serapeum that replaced the Ptolemaic temple was erected by Trajan or Hadrian and destroyed in A.D. 391.

61. It may be the quarter located around the tomb of Alexander, which Xenobius also locates "in the middle of the city." But Strabo, who is an eyewitness, places the burial place of Alexander in the area of the palaces (17.1.8: μέρος δὲ τῶν βασιλείων ἐστὶ καὶ τὸ καλούμενον Σῆμα, ὃ περίβολος ἦν ἐν ᾧ αἱ τῶν βασιλέων ταφαὶ καὶ ἡ 'Αλεξάνδρου), that is, near the coast (see Fraser, *Ptolemaic Alexandria*, 36 n. 85).

62. These gates are also alluded to by a fourth-century papyrus and by the Byzantine historian John Malalas (see K. Plepelits, trans., *Achilles Tatius Leukippe und Kleitophon* [Stuttgart, 1980], 14–16). But Strabo only refers to a gate called Canobian (17.1.10: τῆς πύλης τῆς Κανωβικῆς). In order to reconcile the two traditions, Plepelits, relying on John Malalas, who tells about a visit of Antoninus Pius to Alexandria, suggests that the gates were given a new name to honor the emperor, who is indeed figured as the sun god, with his wife Faustina as moon goddess on some coins from Alexandria from 141 and 151–52.

63. See Waelkens, "Hellenistic and Romance Influences," 81 n. 39, for the bibliography concerning the origins of colonnaded streets.

64. Owens, *City*, 140.

65. Diodorus (17.52.3–4) praises the wealthy temples, the rich houses, and the sumptuous palace, but does not allude to any colonnaded street, and Strabo (17.1.7) only refers to the width of the two streets that intersect at right angles and to the size of the porticoes that surround the gymnasium.

66. When Philostratus (*VAT* 2.23) describes the Indian city of Taxila, he says that it was built "without any order, as in Athens" (ἀτάκτως καὶ ἀττικῶς). On the irregularity that characterizes the old towns that have grown up over a long period of time, see Owens, *City*, 11–12.

67. See E. L. Bowie, "The Novels and the Real World," in *Erotica Antiqua: Acta of the International Conference on the Ancient Novel*, ed. B. Reardon (Bangor, Wales, 1977), 93.

68. See Millar, "World," and P. Veyne, "Vie de Trimalcion," in *La société romaine* (Paris, 1990), 13–56.

CHAPTER THIRTEEN

Trimalchio's Underworld

John Bodel

Trimalchio, the freedman hero of Petronius's *Satyricon,* is preoccupied with death. To be precise, he is obsessed with the idea that one must live life to the fullest, since death marks the end of all pleasures. Early in the banquet episode, a silver skeleton brought into the dining room and cast on the table into a variety of postures inspires the host to produce a poetic commentary on the theme of mortality.

> Eheu nos miseros, quam totus homuncio nil est!
> Sic erimus cuncti, postquam nos auferet Orcus.
> Ergo vivamus, dum licet esse bene.
>
> (Petronius 34.10)[1]

Alas for us poor wretches, how insignificant a thing man is— virtually nothing. Thus shall we all be after Death carries us off. Therefore let's live while we can be (or eat) well.

Trimalchio's doggerel captures the essence of his philosophy. For Trimalchio the joys of life revolve around physical pleasures, particularly (though not exclusively) those of the table, so here the typically atrocious pun on "eating" and "being" in the final phrase (*esse* < *sum* and *edo*) articulates one of his fundamental concerns: for Trimalchio, living is eating.[2]

Images of death recur so frequently at Trimalchio's banquet that some have seen the theme as a controlling metaphor for the entire episode;[3] others have found in the same insistent association of dining and dying nothing more than the traditional techniques of parody and caricature.[4] Realism and symbolism here diverge: one leads along a dark and somber path to a view of Petronius as a moralist condemning the vices of his age; the other traverses a more scenic route that offers entertainment as the ultimate goal. Lacking clear bearings in both the literary and the historical landscape, the cautious reader may well feel uncertain which road to follow.

A recent attempt to skirt this critical dilemma encourages us to abandon the conventional search for meaning in a work primarily concerned with the process, ultimately futile, of attempting to make sense of events that turn out to be uninterpretable.[5] Central to this view of the work as a protracted exercise in aporia is the concept of the repertoire, the package of literary and cultural knowledge that any reader brings to a text, and when it comes to our repertoire, we modern readers must inevitably feel that we are traveling uncomfortably light. For it is clear that Petronius expected his readers' bags to be fully packed, not only with the accoutrements of literary learning but with a full complement of experience of the contemporary world. This of course we cannot gain;[6] and yet if we are to replicate the responses Petronius meant to elicit in his original readers, we must learn to distinguish the social realities he faithfully mirrors from the cultural conventions he purposefully distorts, much as we have learned to distinguish the generic models that broadly inform his narrative from the specific literary topoi he subverts through travesty and burlesque. Thematic coherence in the *Cena* is achieved through a synthesis of the traditionally "high" culture of literary allusion and the conventionally "low" medium of popular artistic expression, and depends for its cogency on a sensitive reception of both.[7] Properly read, the visual language of Trimalchio's household decor combines with the verbal imagery of Petronius's narrative to suggest that Trimalchio's obsession with death must be seen within the context of a broader allegorical representation of Encolpius's experience at the banquet as a trip to the underworld; that this *Katabasismotiv* is inextricably linked to Petronius's conception of the ambivalent nature of an ex-slave's position in society; and that, when viewed in this light, Trimalchio's vulgar hedonism emerges as a natural byproduct of his status as a freedman.[8]

I

Late in the *Cena* episode, Encolpius and his companions attempt to flee the banquet but are thwarted by an officious butler and a ferocious watchdog (72.7–73.1). Petronius here casts his heroes in the unlikely roles of Aeneas and the sibyl in a Vergilian underworld: the ornamental fishpond into which Ascyltus falls becomes, in Encolpius's mind, a Stygian whirlpool (*gurges*) (72.7); the Cerberus-like hound is bought off with scraps from the dinner table (72.9: cf. *Aen.* 6.417–23); and the butler's solemn admonition that guests of Trimalchio are never permitted to leave by the same route by which they arrived (72.10) recalls the sibyl's famous description of the downward slope to the underworld—easy in the descent but difficult to climb (*Aen.* 6.126–29). Encolpius and his companions are, as he says, "trapped in a new kind of labyrinth" (*novi generis labyrintho inclusi*, 73.1).

Aeneas, it will be remembered, had paused before embarking on his tour with the sibyl to admire the depiction of the Minoan labyrinth fashioned by Daedalus on the doors of the temple of Apollo at Cumae (*Aen.* 6.23–30). Vergil's phrase *inextricabilis error* (*Aen.* 6.27) there recalls Varro's description of the legendary tomb of Lars Porsena as *labyrinthum inextricabile* (ap. Pliny, *HN* 36.91) and foreshadows Aeneas's journey into a labyrinthine land of the dead.[9] In the *Satyricon* a link between the underworld imagery and the prevalent theme of trickery and illusion is forged in the figure of Trimalchio's cook, Daedalus, whose name is revealed only in the immediately preceding scene (70.2). Designer of the temple doors at Cumae and builder of the Minoan labyrinth, Daedalus in Trimalchio's home turns food into art and thus becomes the architect of a feast from which there is no escape.[10] It seems clear that Petronius here exploited the common ancient association of labyrinths, tombs, and the underworld to suggest that Trimalchio's home is in some sense to be regarded as a house of the dead.[11] The setting of the *Cena* in a "Greek city" (81.3) (probably Puteoli) on the Campanian coast no doubt facilitated the idea: nearby in the territory of Cumae, where Trimalchio and Aeneas consulted their very different sibyls (48.8), lay Lake Avernus with its ancient cult of the dead and legendary entrance to the underworld.[12]

Where did Petronius get the idea of deploying an allusion to Hades to make a satiric point? From Plato, it has been plausibly suggested, who in his *Protagoras* neatly condemned the sophists assembled at Callias's house by twice putting words from Homer's *Nekyia* into Socrates' mouth.[13] It is perhaps worth noting, however, that the conceit did not go unnoticed by the devotees of rival schools. The Cynic Crates of Thebes followed Plato closely, employing the same technique (and even borrowing the same Homeric verse) in order to attack his old teacher, Stilpo of Megara; and Crates' younger contemporary, the Skeptic Timon of Phlius, made use of the same device in a somewhat different fashion in two of his *Silloi*.[14] Whether Crates and Timon merely alluded in passing to Homer's *Nekyia* or whether they developed the theme in detail, setting entire scenes in Hades, is uncertain, but full-scale visits to the underworld had enjoyed a long history in satiric and comic (or seriocomic) writing ever since Aristophanes sent Dionysus to Hades in search of Euripides.[15] Indeed, by the middle years of the first century B.C. the conceit had gained such wide currency that a Roman gentleman could summon up a host of pejorative associations simply by referring to the entourage of a leading man as a *nekyia*.[16]

What is more, the device of a burlesque visit to Hades seems to have been especially characteristic of the literary form with which Petronius's *Satyricon* shares as many similarities as any other, Menippean satire.[17] Menippus himself had written a *Nekyia* (Diogenes Laertius 6.101), and it seems that the underworld may have held a peculiar fascination for him.[18] That, at any rate, is the impression to be gained from the works of Menippus's most prominent imitator, Lucian. To what extent Menippus's satires can be reconstructed on the basis of Lucian's later adaptations is a matter of controversy, but Lucian's debt to his predecessor in three of his essays (*Dialogues of the Dead, Necyomantia* [or *Menippus*], and *Cataplus*) is widely recognized.[19] Within the Roman tradition of Menippean satire, the fragmentary remnants of Varro's *Saturae Menippeae* allow few inferences about either the original models or Varro's distinctly romanized versions, but one of Varro's poems seems to have involved a conversation with various spirits of the dead on the topic of suicide and was probably set in the underworld.[20] Seneca's *Apocolocyntosis,* no doubt the most conspicuous specimen of the form in Petronius's day, concludes with a comic descent to Hades (13–15) in which several striking parallels with Lucian's *Cataplus* seem to point to a common source, generally identified as the *Nekyia* of Menippus.[21]

Recognizing that earlier (and later) writers of Menippean satire cast whole scenes, or major sections of longer works, in an actual Hades may lead us to wonder whether Petronius developed the theme of a comic catabasis on a grander scale than the concentration of Vergilian allusions near the end of the *Cena* alone would indicate. When we recall that banquets of the blessed had been a standard feature of comic *nekyiai* since the time of Aristophanes,[22] the suspicion arises that Trimalchio's feast may have been intended in part as a travesty of this topos, in which Petronius signaled his intention to portray Trimalchio's home as an underworld earlier in the episode. Consideration of the elaborate ring structure of the *Cena* confirms that he did indeed establish the catabasis motif at the outset.[23] The deliberate pairing of the Cerberus-like watchdog (*canis catenarius*) encountered during the abortive escape attempt (72.7) with a chained watchdog (*canis ingens catena vinctus*) painted in trompe l'oeil in Trimalchio's vestibule (29.1) establishes a connection between the Vergilian interlude late in the banquet and the description of the appointments of Trimalchio's home at the beginning of the episode.[24] In the latter passage Encolpius goes on to inspect the mural in Trimalchio's portico (29.2–6), much as Aeneas had paused before entering the precinct of Apollo at Cumae to admire the decoration fashioned by Daedalus on the temple doors (*Aen.* 6.20–34).[25] Just as the depiction there of the Minoan labyrinth foreshadows Aeneas's descent into the underworld, so in the *Satyricon* the scenes painted on Trimalchio's wall, which trace his rise from slavery to social prominence as a wealthy freedman, suggest that Encolpius is entering a house of the dead. In order to understand the significance of this autobiographical frieze, we need to know how such a visual narrative would have been read. What were the cultural conventions of biographical art in Petronius's day? Where were such representations found and what purposes did they serve?

II

We know from the elder Pliny that historical scenes were introduced into Roman painting in the third century B.C. and were occasionally thereafter used by successful generals to advertise their military exploits; painted panels depicting conquered cities and successful battles were paraded in a Roman triumph and were subsequently hung on temple walls, in the forum, or, on rare occasions, in the home of the *triumphator* for temporary public display.[26] The latest instance of this practice we hear of, however, belongs to the end of the second century B.C., and the only surviving remnants of the tradition derive from monumental tombs discovered in the Esquiline burial ground in Rome and dating from the middle republican period.[27]

Elsewhere Pliny mentions a painting said by Sulla to have been commissioned for his Tusculan villa showing his troops awarding him a grass crown during the Social War; but Cicero, who later owned the villa, makes no mention of such a depiction, and Pliny is inclined to doubt the truth of the report.[28] In the fictional world of Apuleius's *Metamorphoses,* the hapless Charite vows to dedicate a painted panel in her atrium commemorating her escape with Lucius from the robbers' den; unfortunately we have no way of knowing whether the author conceived of this memorial as a plausible specimen of historical art or rather, as Charite's following words (*accedes antiquis et ipse miraculis,* "you yourself will join the ancient tales of marvels") suggest, as part of her fantasy likening Lucius to the fabled beast-saviors of classical mythology, themselves popular subjects of ancient scene painting.[29]

According to a late imperial biography, the emperor Gordian I displayed in the famous *domus rostrata* of Pompey a painting of a gladiatorial exhibition sponsored during his aedileship (SHA, *Gord.* 3.6–7), and we find a similar scene of an animal hunt (*venatio*) portrayed in a mosaic pavement from a late Roman villa in Tunisia, in this case with an accompanying inscription identifying the proprietor of the villa as the sponsor of the show.[30] Closer in spirit and virtually contemporary in date to Trimalchio's mural is a well-known painting from the tablinum of a modest private house north of the forum at Pompeii depicting a public distribution of bread.[31] All three representations illustrate singular acts of munificence on the part of the house owners as a means of demonstrating their honorific positions in their communities. Unlike Trimalchio's mural, which centers on the private and personal accomplishments of the individual, these panels, by focusing on emblematic acts of civic euergetism, schematically represent the stature of their subjects as public benefactors. The scenes are biographical in the sense that they depict specific incidents in the lives of the men they commemorate, but the episodes selected for representation are chosen not so much for their intrinsic importance as for their symbolic value as general indicators of status. They are, moreover, isolated scenes commemorating individual events, and in this respect they differ fundamentally from Trimalchio's mural, which comprises a series of images arranged sequentially to present a coherent account of his life. Pictorial narratives of the sort envisioned by Petronius are not found in a domestic setting before the late empire, a period when the social conventions of household decoration had radically transformed the parameters of personal commemoration operative during the classical period.[32]

Large-figure painted friezes ("megalographies") such as the Dionysiac cycle from the Villa of the Mysteries at Pompeii or the mythological frescoes from the villa of P. Fannius Synistor at Boscoreale give us some idea of the monumental scale Trimalchio's memorial might have assumed, but none of the few surviving specimens of the genre provides a precedent for its autobiographical subject.[33] The closest parallels we find for the compositional technique and commemorative purpose of Trimalchio's mural derive from funerary monuments such as the so-called Tomb of Fabius on the Esquiline, which exhibits a series of biographical scenes in four superimposed registers, or the late republican–early Augustan tomb of the baker M. Vergilius Eurysaces outside the Porta Maggiore at Rome, around three sides of which runs a sculpted frieze depicting various operations associated with the making and distribution of bread.[34] We do not happen to find complete biographical cycles from infancy through adulthood depicted on Roman funerary monuments (or elsewhere) before the end of the first century A.D., and the style seems to have flourished primarily during the second and third centuries, when the fashion of burying the dead in sculpted sarcophagi provided an artistic medium well suited for detailed commemoration of the individual.[35] Monuments such as the tomb of C. Vestorius Priscus at Pompeii remind us, however, that Romans of Petronius's day knew of similar tomb paintings that no longer survive.[36] Indeed, what is most striking about the history of biographical narratives in Roman art of the republic and early empire is the absence of evidence for such representations in domestic contexts and the close association of this form of artistic expression with commemoration of the dead. If biographical cycles were painted in private homes in Petronius's day, we do not hear of the practice and none has survived. Such parallels as exist for the style and composition of Trimalchio's mural derive exclusively from funerary art.

Precisely how Petronius's original readers would have responded to this sepulchral imagery is difficult to say, but we can perhaps be guided by imagining our own reactions if presented with the house of a Gatsby-like figure with a hearse parked in the drive and the initials R.I.P. emblazoned on the doormat.[37] It is in any case clear that the half-allegorical, half-realistic depiction of Trimalchio's career adorning the portico would have struck Petronius's original readers as decidedly incongruous, even macabre, in a domestic setting, for no contemporary Roman could have failed to recognize that Trimalchio's house is decorated in the manner of a Roman tomb. These funereal associations, though unsettling, may not have been entirely unexpected: the extravagant procession from the public baths that precedes the banquet (28.4–5) resembles nothing so much as a Roman cortege, with Trimalchio cast in the role of the deceased.[38] Where else could such a procession lead but to the grave?

The implication for our interpretation of the *Cena* seems obvious: Trimalchio's house is a mausoleum, a home of the dead.[39] Hence the irony underlying the host's apologetic explanation later in the banquet for the fastidious attention he devotes to the appointments of his tomb: "Valde enim falsum est vivo quidem domos cultas esse, non curari eas, ubi diutius nobis habitandum est" (It is very wrong to decorate our houses for our lifetimes and not to take care of those where we must live for a longer time, 71.7). In one respect Trimalchio here merely gives voice to a widespread popular conception of the tomb as a home for the deceased. It is, however, typical of Trimalchio's failure to distinguish between the artistic conventions of life and death that he not only decorates his tomb like a house but decorates his house like a tomb.[40] As uninvited guests, Encolpius and his companions come to the banquet as *umbrae,* shadows, of the rhetorician Agamemnon, only to enter a house filled with shadows of a very different sort: the shades of the dead.[41] An outsider to the cultural milieu of Trimalchio and his friends, Encolpius enters their world as if on a catabasis. The nature of the shades he will encounter is made clear by the content of Trimalchio's biographical mural, a passage that we must now consider in detail.

III

Erat autem venalicium ⟨cum⟩ titulis pictum, et ipse Trimalchio capillatus caduceum tenebat Minervaque ducente Romam intrabat. Hinc quemadmodum ratiocinari didicisset deinque dispensator factus esset, omnia diligenter curiosus pictor cum inscriptione reddiderat. In deficiente vero iam porticu levatum mento in tribunal excelsum Mercurius rapiebat. Praesto erat Fortuna ⟨cum⟩ cornu abundanti [copiosa] et tres Parcae aurea pensa torquentes. (Petr. 29.3–6)

There was, moreover, a painted scene of a slave market with the slaves carrying placards, and Trimalchio himself as a long-haired boy holding Mercury's staff was entering Rome with Minerva leading the way. Here was shown how he had learned to keep accounts and had then been made chief steward in his master's household—everything the painstaking artist had carefully rendered with captions. At the very end of the portico Mercury was snatching Trimalchio up by the chin and raising him onto a lofty tribunal; Fortune with her overflowing horn of plenty was standing nearby, and the three Fates twisting their golden threads.

The painting depicts five scenes from Trimalchio's life, arranged chronologically: (1) his sale as a boy on the slave auction block; (2) Trimalchio as a pampered youth (*capillatus*: cf. 63.3) in the guise of Mercury (with caduceus) entering Rome in the company of Minerva; (3) Trimalchio learning to do accounts, and (4) Trimalchio being promoted to the chief position of administrative responsibility in his master's household; and finally, set off from the other scenes, (5) Trimalchio transported by Mercury onto a tribunal, where he is attended by symbols of prosperity.

The most striking feature of the composition, as has often been remarked, is its peculiar blend of realism and allegory: in some scenes Trimalchio is represented as an ordinary slave (nos. 1, 3, and 4), while in others he appears as a deity (2) or in the company of divine or semidivine beings (2, 5). Like any good ecphrasis, this one operates on several levels, and the disconcerting mixture of realism and fantasy here serves at least two purposes. On one level, it foreshadows the deceptions to come and alerts us to a presentation of Trimalchio's banquet that is to be both literal and metaphorical; on another it enables Petronius to sketch in deftly the social background against which Trimalchio is to be viewed.

The first scene—Trimalchio's sale on the slave market—establishes the two main themes at the outset. We have only two certain examples of *venalicia* represented in Roman art; both are on the tombstones of freedmen (fig. 1).[42] Opinions differ as to how the scenes, which are essentially similar, should be interpreted. According to one view, they allude to the profession of the honorands as slave dealers and therefore belong to a well-established tradition of funerary reliefs representing the occupation of the deceased;[43] according to the other, the iconography of the scenes, which highlights the slave being sold rather than the buyer or seller, suggests that the *venalicia* represent a critical moment in the life of the men commemorated in the epitaphs—the transactions that brought them into their patrons' households.[44] Trimalchio's *venalicium* scene, which appears first in the series both sequentially and chronologically, supports the latter interpretation (although Trimalchio too trafficked in slaves: cf. 76.6), but with

Fig. 1. Scene of a slave sale from the funerary relief of a freedman at Arlon, as represented in a drawing of the seventeenth century (first or second century A.D.; after Kolendo, "Eléments," 177, fig. 4).

the present state of our knowledge we cannot be certain which view is correct, if indeed the same explanation applies in both cases. What is certain is that the first panel in Trimalchio's frieze shows him to be, on the one hand, a man unashamed of his servile origins and, on the other, a man whose aesthetic sensibilities do not discriminate between houses of the living and houses of the dead.

The second scene introduces a new element of pretension into Trimalchio's self-portrait and sharpens the focus on his social background. The image of the pampered slave boy entering Rome (or possibly his "colony") in stately procession with Minerva has about it the air of an emperor's triumphal *adventus* and was no doubt intended in part to suggest Trimalchio's preposterously inflated opinion of his own accomplishments.[45] At another level, the picture of an unprepossessing young man escorted by a divine female protector into a city evokes a narrative motif familiar from the fabled accounts of legendary heroes, and thus implicitly elevates Trimalchio's biography to the same heroic status:[46] in place of the mythological and epic cycles favored by many of his contemporaries as subjects for their wall paintings, Trimalchio presents the story of his own life as a kind of epic saga.[47] In another respect, Trimalchio's autobiographical mural, prominently displayed in a public area near the front of his house, occupies a position reserved in the homes of the Roman nobility for the honorific display of ancestral portraits and painted family trees.[48] As an ex-slave, a self-made man "born of himself" (*ex se natus*),[49] Trimalchio has no ancestors and no family history, hence no ancestral masks (*imagines*) to decorate his atrium, only a depiction of his own career adorning the portico and, with his household gods, a true likeness (*veram imaginem*) of himself (60.9).

Trimalchio's appearance with an attribute of Mercury (the caduceus), on the other hand, places the scene squarely in the center of a nascent but already distinctive tradition of self-representation in Roman popular art. This type of allegorical assimilation, in which a private person is directly identified with a particular deity, first appears in the western provinces in the funerary art of the late Julio-Claudian era in the neighborhood of Rome, and for the next eighty years is found predominantly on the monuments of slaves and freedmen of eastern extraction. Throughout this period the most frequently represented god is Mercury, whose prominence is plausibly explained by the desire of many ex-slaves to commemorate their successful careers in commerce. What is perhaps most striking about this phenomenon is the lack of any direct precedent for private deifications in popular art of the Hellenistic and earlier Roman periods. In other words, the form of funerary expression that Trimalchio translates onto his house walls seems to have been the invention of well-to-do freedmen from the Greek East who had come to the Italian peninsula as slaves.[50] This is precisely the social category to which Trimalchio belongs. Trimalchio's identification with Mercury thus would have reminded Petronius's contemporaries unmistakably of the type of sculpted relief that had recently begun to appear on the funerary monuments of slaves and freedmen with backgrounds very similar to that of Trimalchio.[51] Like his counterparts in the real world, Trimalchio borrowed his iconographic symbolism from the pictorial language of the imperial regime, adapting images such as that found on a sculpted altar of late Augustan date showing a Mercury-Augustus figure being led by Roma or Minerva (fig. 2) and transforming their official public messages into more personal statements of individual success.[52] In this respect, Trimalchio's self-representation as Mercury is fully in step with a popular artistic fashion of his day; his eccentricity lies in projecting a motif normally associated with posthumous commemoration onto the walls of his house.

The third and fourth scenes, depicting Trimalchio's training as an accountant and subsequent promotion to the post of dispensator, seem to convey the same funereal associations, though less dramatically: what parallels we have for representations of Romans computing accounts or engaged in financial occupations derive from funerary monuments, particularly those of slaves and freedmen.[53] The main purpose of these penultimate episodes, however, in sketching the outlines of Trimalchio's rapid ascent to the pinnacle of a domestic slave's career, is to set the stage for the fifth and final scene, which is marked off from the others visually by its

Fig. 2. Side panel of the Bologna altar showing Minerva-Roma leading
Mercury-Augustus (ca. 10 B.C.–A.D. 15; Bologna, Museo Civico inv. Pal. 1632;
Deutsches Archäologisches Institut Rom neg. no. 7264).

position at the end of the portico (*in deficiente . . . porticu*) and syntactically, within the composition of the ecphrasis, by Encolpius's parenthetic remark about the picture captions. This structural separation of the final scene signals a corresponding distinction in content; whereas the first four panels depict Trimalchio's career as a slave, the final scene alludes to his status as a freedman. As has long been recognized, the tribunal to which Mercury escorts Trimalchio is the privileged seat in the theater or amphitheater reserved for the sponsors of public shows, a position Trimalchio once held by virtue of his appointment to the local board of Augustales (30.1, 71.12; cf. 71.9). It thus represents emblematically, in a manner similar to the gladiatorial scenes discussed above, Trimalchio's prestigious position as *princeps libertinorum*, "first of the freedmen," in his community.[54]

Once this basic compositional dichotomy is recognized, the image of Trimalchio borne aloft by Mercury can be seen to encapsulate the principal themes established in the earlier episodes. Trimalchio himself assumes the guise of Mercury in his arrival scene—and there can be no doubt that he regarded the god of commerce as his patron deity (cf. 67.7, 77.4)—but in the present context Mercury clearly appears as the Psychopompus, the guide of souls, who conducts dead spirits from this world to the next. This is apparent not only from the picture suggested by the participle *levatum* (raised up) but also from the verb *rapiebat* (snatched), which is the standard term used in Latin funerary inscriptions to describe the sudden removal of a soul from life. Traditionally, Hermes, the messenger of Persephone, leads the departed to an afterlife in the underworld; in Trimalchio's mural, however, the presence of the Fates and Fortuna points to an entirely different realm—the heavenly abode of the immortals.[55] Trimalchio represents his elevation from slavery to freedom as an apotheosis, a transition from life to a blessed afterlife. From the perspective of the reader, however, who has been shown a house that is like a tomb, the same scene conveys quite a different impression. One man's heaven may be another man's hell, and Mercury's ambivalent role as vehicle of apotheosis and escort to Hades neatly signals the ambiguity of the presentation.[56]

The closest parallels to Trimalchio's apotheosis scene derive, fittingly, from the biographical narratives on Roman sarcophagi, where, however, the motif is restricted to the commemoration of children. Indeed, the overall structure of Trimalchio's mural, with its detailed exposition of his early years as a slave and its chronological telescoping of his career as a freedman (later recounted at length: 76.2–77.5) into a single emblematic scene, more closely resembles the narrative patterns found on the sarcophagi of adolescents than on those of adults. Whereas the latter devote primary attention to the symbolic expression of the cardinal virtues of aristocratic male life, the narrative scenes on children's sarcophagi necessarily focus instead on precocious talents and the promise of an excellence never fulfilled: the bathing of the infant (recalling the epiphanic baths of gods and heroes), often under the watchful eye of the Fates; the education of the young child in the company of the Muses; and the final blessing bestowed on those who die young—apotheosis.[57]

A well-known sarcophagus front now in the Villa Doria Pamphili in Rome provides a typical and, for our purposes, particularly apt illustration of the type (fig. 3).[58] From left to right the relief panel shows, first, the standard bathing scene with a nurse lifting the infant from a tub into the lap of the mother, here accompanied by the three Fates and a fourth female figure, possibly Nemesis or Fortuna, holding a scepter; next, at the center of the panel, a nursing scene, followed by a vignette of the young boy at school reading to his teacher while Hermes, as god of eloquence, and Melpomene and Thalia, the Muses of tragedy and comedy, look on; finally, the deceased, now a youth, reclining on the wings of an eagle in flight and being transported aloft in a chariot led by Mercury.[59] We find here the same odd mixture of realism and allegory that characterizes Trimalchio's mural, and we note the similar symbolic functions served by many of the same figures. Less apparent, perhaps, though no less striking, is the close structural similarity between the sequence of scenes on Trimalchio's wall and the arrangement of episodes, each one conventional, on the Doria Pamphili sarcophagus: in place of the warm domestic bath scene Trimalchio shows the harsh realities of the slave market; for the mother suckling her babe, he has the privileged slave's version of a nurturing environment—a protecting goddess leading the way to commercial prosperity; instead of an aristocratic training in the liberal arts, Trimalchio undergoes a practical course in accounting; and finally, in place of the heroic translation to a divine afterlife, Trimalchio represents his manumission as an apotheosis. It is as if his life as a slave is equivalent to that of a child, his promotion to the ranks of freedmen a transcendant metamorphosis presupposing a metaphorical death.

The picture of Trimalchio "raised up by the chin" (*levatum mento*) crystallizes this allegorical synthesis in a single polyvalent image. Educated Romans of Petronius's day were well aware that Alexander the Great, in imitation of the god-kings of the Near East, had himself represented by Lysippus (and others) with his face turned toward the heavens in order to suggest his heroic stature on earth and his claim to a divine afterlife, and it is possible that the image of Trimalchio with head uplifted would have been recognized as making a similar claim.[60] More certainly Mercury's gesture would have reminded contemporary Romans of a homoerotic motif familiar to us primarily from Greek vase painting in which an older

Fig. 3. Sarcophagus relief now in the Villa Doria Pamphili, Rome, showing narrative scenes of a child's life, culminating in his apotheosis A.D. 175–200; Deutsches Archäologisches Institut Rom neg. no. 8332).

lover (ἐραστής) caresses the chin of a beloved youth (ἐρώμενος) between thumb and uplifted palm.[61] In grasping Trimalchio by the chin, Mercury the Psychopomp slides imperceptibly into his earlier manifestation as Patron of Commerce; Trimalchio emerges as the fortunate object of his affection; and the transportation scene itself forecasts the theme of financial prosperity suggested by the three Fates and Fortuna.[62]

It is not images, however, but words that show how the concepts of apotheosis and manumission converge in the picture of Trimalchio being raised up by the chin. In defending the transmitted text *levatum mento*, P. B. Corbett aptly compares the expression *supponere manum* (or *digitum* or *bracchia*) *mento*, "to place a hand (or finger or arm) under the chin," used once literally by Propertius and twice metaphorically by Ovid to describe the gesture of assistance offered to a drowning man; the image of Trimalchio lifted by the chin, he concludes, suggests a figurative deliverance from difficulties and alludes specifically to the rescue of a man at sea.[63] The metaphor of shipwreck was, of course, commonplace in Roman popular expression, but the particular image chosen by Trimalchio to represent his emergence from slavery has an appropriateness in context that no contemporary Roman could have missed. The lexicographer Nonius Marcellus tells us that newly freed slaves shaved their heads "because they seemed to be escaping the storm of servitude, just as those freed from shipwreck are wont to do,"[64] and we have unimpeachable evidence that Petronius's readers were expected to be familiar with the conceptual universe from which this explanation derived. Later in the banquet one of the freedmen guests, after describing the difficulties he faced as an ambitious slave in a competitive household, goes on to say that eventually, thanks to his master's goodwill, he "swam out" (*enatavi*, 57.10). The idea of "swimming out" of troubles was by no means restricted to the concept of escaping slavery (cf. Cicero, *Tusc.* 5.87), but Nonius's testimony leaves little doubt that Trimalchio's apotheosis scene is deliberately couched in terms—and images—designed to appeal to a popular perception of manumission as a figurative deliverance from a hostile sea.

In linking Trimalchio's vision of a divine transformation to the mundane reality of manumission, the central image of the culminating scene in Trimalchio's pictorial autobiography represents in microcosm the complex thematic consistency of the whole: visual image and verbal description coincide to characterize Trimalchio's world as an underworld of ex-slaves. Encolpius and his companions, posing as freeborn *scholastici*, declamation buffs (10.6), or, in Giton's case, a slave, are outsiders to this cultural milieu. That is why Petronius can represent their visit to Trimalchio's home as a catabasis: the underworld into which they have stumbled is an underworld defined by civil status, an underworld of freedmen.

John Bodel

IV

Thirty years ago Paul Veyne, in a justly celebrated essay, elucidated the social realities of the early imperial age on which Petronius founded his portrait of a boorish host: widespread enfranchisement of newly manumitted slaves, unprecedented opportunities for the acquisition of wealth through trade, and a cultural ideology dominated by an idle, landed elite; above all, a social universe structured around juridical status. Barred by law and custom from entry into the elite circles to which he aspires, Trimalchio, as an ex-slave, lives in a world apart, separate and unequal.[65] The ways in which this basic cultural fact informs Petronius's literary aims in the *Cena* are manifold and complex; I have tried to illuminate one facet of his presentation by showing how Petronius links Trimalchio's civil status at the outset to a depiction of his house as a social underworld. Recognizing this association does not explain the many variations on the theme of death that appear throughout the banquet, but it does suggest that Petronius's manipulation of death imagery in the *Cena* must be seen in the context of his depiction of a freedman's society, that Trimalchio's obsession with death is somehow connected with his status as an ex-slave.

Cast in this light, Trimalchio's crude *carpe diem* philosophy may appear as neither undiluted realism nor overt symbolism, but rather something in between. Like the freedmen's frequent assertions that they are indeed human beings—*homines inter homines* (39.4, 57.4–5, 74.13)—Trimalchio's ostentatious hedonism has about it a certain tendentiousness, the source of which is not hard to find. Roman slaves were treated in law, and often in practice, as less than human, the equivalent, in many ways, of animals.[66] A passage elsewhere in the *Satyricon* illustrates the point nicely: on the road to Croton the hired man Corax complains about the load he is made to carry: "Iumentum me putatis esse aut lapidariam navem? Hominis operas locavi, non caballi. Nec minus liber sum quam vos" (Do you think I'm a pack animal or a barge for hauling stones? I hired out to do the work of a human being, not a horse, I'm no less a free man than you, 117.12). The implication is that if Corax were a slave he could expect to be treated like a beast of burden.

The position of the freedman in Roman society was a peculiar one, and the behavior of the ex-slave was often seen to reflect his former condition of servitude. Having been deprived of many of the simple pleasures of human existence, the slave, once freed, naturally tended to indulge his appetites—for physical pleasures, of course, but also for respectability. The loosening of restraints at manumission let forth a flood of pent-up human desires, not always well directed or well formed, that resulted in a variety of excesses—or so, at any rate, many of our surviving literary authorities believed.[67] For many freeborn Romans, in short, the slave was seen as father to the freedman. Acknowledging this widespread perception among the Roman slaveholding classes helps us view Petronius's portrait of a wealthy freedman in perspective.

It has been suggested that the logical extension of the labyrinth motif established late in the banquet is to regard Trimalchio as a sort of Minotaur who figuratively devours his guests by subjecting them to his domineering personality.[68] Like the Cretan monster, half man, half beast, Trimalchio is a mongrel: as a freedman he has the status of a human being, but as an ex-slave he bears the indelible marks of his former servitude, when he possessed no more rights than an animal. Both creatures live in a world of their own, shut off from the rest of society. Furthermore, like the disembodied spirits that inhabit the underworld, who have the form but not the substance of humans, Trimalchio is a free man in appearance only: he lacks the essential quality of *ingenuitas,* free birth. Hence the mood of melancholy many have felt pervades the determined merriment at Trimalchio's table; hence also Trimalchio's preoccupation with death, the final emancipation. Once property, now propertied, he and his fellow freedmen live against the clock, desperately striving to compensate for a past that can be neither redeemed nor effaced. This, for Petronius, is the defining characteristic of a freedman's mentality, the prevailing ethos of Trimalchio's underworld.

NOTES

1. Here and throughout I give the text of K. Müller's third edition, in K. Müller and W. Ehlers, *Petronius Satyrica: Schelmenszenen* (Munich, 1983).

2. Petronius plays on a much-quoted Socratic aphorism to the effect that "one should eat to live rather than live to eat": see B. Baldwin, "Petronius 34.10," *Maia* 31 (1979): 145.

3. Notably, W. Arrowsmith, "Luxury and Death in the *Satyricon,*" *Arion* 5 (1966): 304–31; cf. H. Bacon, "The Sibyl in the Bottle," *Virginia Quarterly Review* 34 (1958): 262–76; C. Saylor, "Funeral Games: The Significance of Games in the *Cena Trimalchionis,*" *Latomus* 46 (1987): 593–602; and R. Herzog, "Fest, Terror und Tod in Petrons *Satyrica,*" in *Das Fest,* ed. W. Haug and R. Warning (Munich, 1989), 120–50.

4. E.g., J. P. Sullivan, "Petronius and His Modern Critics," *Bucknell Review* 19 (1971): 123f. (parody); P. G. Walsh, "Was Petronius a Moralist?" *Greece and Rome* 21 (1974): 187f. (satire). For the *Realien,* see K. M. D. Dunbabin, "*Sic Erimus Cuncti* . . . The Skeleton in Graeco-Roman Art," *Jahrbuch des Deutschen Archäologischen Instituts* 101 (1986): 185–255, esp. 191–212.

5. N. Slater, *Reading Petronius* (Baltimore, 1990), esp. 235–51; note also Herzog, "Fest, Terror und Tod," 148f., and, for a different view of Petronius's literary aims in frustrating the reader's expectations, G. Schmeling, "The *Satyricon:* The Sense of an Ending," *Rheinisches Museum für Philologie* 134 (1991): 352–77.

6. For Slater, *Reading Petronius,* 20f. (cf. 17), the social norms of the Neronian age can be extrapolated from "the reader created by the text itself."

7. A strong element of what Bakhtin called the "carnivalesque" runs throughout the *Satyricon*, but whether in Petronius's hands the characteristic inversions of high and low function more as a literary mode (as Bakhtin principally conceived of them in his well-known study of Rabelais and his world) or as a social construct (see the helpful reformulation by P. Stallybrass and A. White, *The Politics and Poetics of Transgression* [Ithaca, N.Y., 1986], esp. 6–26), remains unclear. Herzog's attempt ("Fest, Terror und Tod") to penetrate the gloom by applying Iser's conceptual triad "reality–fictionality–the imaginary" does not shed as much light as one might hope.

8. For underworld themes elsewhere in the novel, see D. Blickman, "The Romance of Encolpius and Circe," *Atene e Roma* 33 (1988): 7–16, and F. I. Zeitlin, "Romanus Petronius: A Study of the *Troiae Halosis* and the *Bellum Civile*," *Latomus* 30 (1971): 67–73, on the episode at Croton (116–41). Note also the similar structural functions served by the "deaths" of Trimalchio (78.5–6), Lichas (115.7–20), and Eumolpus (141.2–11) in closing major sections of the narrative.

9. P. J. Enk, "De labyrinthi imagine in foribus templi Cumani insculpta," *Mnemosyne* 11 (1958): 325–28.

10. For Petronius's travesty of Vergil in this episode, see A. Collignon, *Etude sur Pétrone* (Paris, 1892), 119f.; A. D. Leeman, "Morte e scambio nel romanzo picaresco di Petronio," *Giornale italiano di filologia classica* 20 (1967): 155; Averil Cameron, "Myth and Meaning: Some Modern Comparisons," *Latomus* 29 (1970): 405f.; M.-C. Minazio, "La maison-piège de Trimalcion," in *Mélanges Esther Bréguet* (Geneva, 1975), 21–27; F. Dupont, *Le plaisir et la loi* (Paris, 1977), 147–51; P. Fedeli, "Petronio: Il viaggio, il labirintho," *Materiali e discussioni per l'analisi dei testi classici* 6 (1981): 102–9, 113–15, and note R. M. Newton, "Trimalchio's Hellish Bath," *Classical Journal* 77 (1982): 315–19, on the scene in Trimalchio's baths (73.2–5) as a parody of Vergil's Elysian Fields.

11. For labyrinths as entrances to the underworld, cf., e.g., K. Kerényi, *Labyrinth-Studien*, 2d ed. (Zurich, 1950), 17–20, 31–33.

12. Cf. M. W. Frederiksen, *Campania*, ed. N. Purcell (Rome, 1984), 75–77.

13. So E. Courtney, "Petronius and the Underworld," *American Journal of Philology* 108 (1987): 408–10, citing Plato, *Protagoras* 315b (≈ *Od.* 11.601: Sisyphus) and 315c (≈ *Od.* 11.582); for both passages, see G. Calogero, *Platone: Il Protagoro*, 3d ed. (Florence, 1958), 25 ad loc. In the preceding paragraph (315a), Protagoras himself is likened to Orpheus.

14. Crates: H. Lloyd-Jones and P. Parsons, *Supplementum Hellenisticum* (Berlin, 1983), no. 347 (= Diogenes Laertius 2.118), adapting *Od.* 11.582; cf. no. 349 (= Plutarch, *Mor.* 830c). Timon: *Suppl. Hell.,* 368 and nos. 783 (= A. A. Long and D. N. Sedley, *The Hellenistic Philosophers* [Cambridge, 1987], no. 2B) and 812 (= Long and Sedley, no. 3F; cf. *Od.* 11.568–71). See A. A. Long, "Timon of Phlius: Pyrrhonist and Satirist," *Proceedings of the Cambridge Philological Society*, n.s. 24 (1978): 75, 81.

15. See, above all, G. Ettig, "Acheruntica," *Leipziger Studien zur classischen Philologie* 13 (1890): 251–410, esp. 389f.; also P. Lejay, *Q. Horati Flacci Satirae* (Paris, 1911), 475–77, and R. Seaford, *Euripides' Cyclops* (Oxford, 1988), 37f.

16. So Atticus to Cicero on Caesar's supporters in March of 49: cf. Cicero, *Att.* 9.10.7, 9.11.2, 9.18.2.

17. The term is a modern invention (probably Lipsius's) usefully applied to a distinct type of seriocomic essay in mixed prose and verse; see J. C. Relihan, "On the Origins of 'Menippean Satire' as the Name of a Literary Genre," *Classical Philology* 79 (1984): 226–29. Parody and literary allusion are characteristic of the form: E. Courtney, "Parody and Literary Allusion in Menippean Satire," *Philologus* 106 (1962): 86–100. For metaphoric descents to the underworld in the ancient novel, cf., e.g., Xenophon Ephesius 4.6.6–7 (the sopping of Cerberus); Apuleius, *Met.* 6.16.3–20.6 (Psyche's catabasis).

18. See G.Crönert, *Kolotes und Menedemos* (Leipzig, 1906), 1, on Diogenes Laertius 6.102.

19. Cf. B. P. McCarthy, "Lucian and Menippus," *Yale ClassicalStudies* 4 (1934): 3–58, esp. 31–50; J. Hall, *Lucian's Satire* (New York, 1981), 64–150; and R. Pratesi, "Timone, Luciano e Menippo: Rapporti nell'ambito di un genere letterario," *Prometheus* 11 (1985): 40–68; 12 (1986): 39–56, 123–38.

20. According to Cicero, *Acad.* 1.8, Varro adapted rather than translated his Menippean models. For the Περὶ 'Εξαγωγῆς (*On Suicide*) (frag. 405–10 Bücheler), see J. Vahlen, *Coniectanea in M. Terentii Varronis Saturarum Menippearum Reliquias* (Leipzig, 1858), 208f., and Lejay, *Satirae,* 476.

21. Cf., e.g., O. Weinreich, *Senecas Apocolocyntosis* (Berlin, 1923), 121–24; Hall, *Lucian's Satire,* 106–8.

22. Cf. Aristophanes, *Ran.* 337–39, 504ff., frag. 488; Pherecrates, *Metalles* frag. 108; further, F. Graf, *Eleusis und die orphische Dichtung Athens in vorhellenistischer Zeit* (Berlin, 1974), 82f., 98–103.

23. See T. K. Hubbard, "The Narrative Architecture of Petronius' *Satyricon*," *L'antiquité classique* 55 (1986): 190–212.

24. Cf. L. Callebat, "Structures narratives et modes de représentation dans le *Satyricon* de Pétrone," *Revue des études latines* 52 (1974): 301. Encolpius's reaction to the painted watchdog (for which see P. Veyne, "Cave canem," *Mélanges de l'Ecole Française de Rome, Antiquité* 75 [1963]: 59–66)—*paene resupinatus crura mea fregi* (29.1)—parallels Ascyltus's response to its live counterpart: *in piscinam cecid*[*it*] (72.7).

25. Fedeli, "Petronio," 114 compares Aeneas's inspection of the temple doors (*Aen.* 6.33–34) with Encolpius's amazement at Trimalchio's entourage (28.6) and at his doorkeeper and magpie (29.1), but oddly overlooks the most striking similarity between the two passages—the two ecphrases on historical art.

26. Pliny, *HN* 35.22–23. On historical art during the republic, see in general G. Zinserling, "Studien zu den Historiendarstellungen der römischen Republik," *Wissenschaftliche Zeitschrift der Friedrich-Schiller-Universität Jena* 9 (1959–60): 403–48, and T. Hölscher, "Die Anfänge römischer Repräsentationskunst," *Mitteilungen des Deutschen Archäologischen Instituts, Römische Abteilung* 85 (1978): 315–57.

27. See Zinserling, "Studien," 417f.; B. M. Felletti Maj, *La tradizione italica nell'arte romana* (Rome, 1977), 59–65; and, for the Esquiline tomb paintings, F. Coarelli, "Frammento di affresco dall'Esquilino con scena storica," in *Affreschi romani dalle raccolte dell'Antiquarium Comunale* (Rome, 1976), 13–28.

28. Pliny, *HN* 22.12; cf. Zinserling, "Studien," 410f.

29. Apuleius, *Met.* 6.29.2–3. Votive tablets depicting escapes from danger (especially shipwrecks) were normally dedicated in temples (e.g., Cicero, *Verr.* 4.122; Horace, *Carm.* 1.5.13–16; Plutarch, *Mar.* 40.1, with Zinserling, "Studien," 411). We do not hear of other examples in private houses.

30. See A. Beschaouch, "La mosaïque de chasse découverte à Smirat en Tunisie," *Comptes rendus des séances de l'Académie des Inscriptions et Belles-lettres* (1966): 134–57; K. M. D. Dunbabin, *The Mosaics of Roman North Africa* (Oxford, 1978), 67–69 (69–76 for similar mosaic scenes); and, more generally on the commemorative and symbolic functions such autobiographical mosaics served, Y. Thébert, in *A History of Private Life from Pagan Rome to Byzantium,* ed. P. Veyne, trans. A. Goldhammer (Cambridge, Mass., 1987), 397–409.

31. Museo Archeologico Nazionale di Napoli (hereafter, MNN) inv. no. 9071; cf. T. Fröhlich, *Lararien- und Fassadenbilder in den Vesuvstädten* (Mainz, 1991), 236–41 and plate 23.1.

32. Cf. Sidonius Apollinaris, *Ep.* 22.158–68, with D. and R. Rebuffat, "De Sidoine

Apollinaire à la Tombe François," *Latomus* 37 (1978): 88–104 (whose arguments for a long tradition of biographical wall painting in Roman homes, however, are unpersuasive).

33. Cf. R. Ling, *Roman Painting* (Cambridge, 1991), 101–7; further, C. Parslow, "The 'Forum Frieze' of Pompeii in Its Archaeological Context" (forthcoming).

34. The Esquiline tomb conventionally attributed to one of the patrician Fabii (but more plausibly assigned to a common soldier, M. Fanius: E. La Rocca, "Fabio o Fannio: l'affresco medio-repubblicano dell'Esquilino come riflesso dell'arte 'rappresentiva' e come espressione di mobilitá sociale," *Dialoghi di archeologia,* ser. 3.2 [1984]: 31–53), illustrates a comparable medium (painted scenes with accompanying text) and seems to show the essential element of a continuous narrative (the repeated appearance of the central figure in consecutive scenes). The tomb of Eurysaces presents a series of scenes from the life of the deceased organized into a coherent sequence: see P. Giancio Rossetto, *Il sepolcro del fornaio M. Virgilio Eurisace* (Rome, 1973).

35. Cf. N. Kampen, "Biographical Narration and Roman Funerary Art," *American Journal of Archaeology* 85 (1981): 47–58. The chronological arrangement of Trimalchio's mural is consistent with the earliest phase of iconographic developments during this period.

36. See J. M. Dentzer, "La tombe de C. Vestorius dans la tradition de la peinture italique," *Mélanges de l'Ecole Française de Rome, Antiquité* 74 (1962): 533–94.

37. F. Scott Fitzgerald's intention to write Trimalchio into the title character of *The Great Gatsby* (a work originally to have been entitled *Trimalchio at West Egg*) is openly acknowledged (chap. 7 init.) and widely recognized: cf. P. L. MacKendrick, "The Great Gatsby and Trimalchio," *Classical Journal* 45 (1950): 307–14.

38. So D. Gagliardi, "Il corteo di Trimalchione," *Rivista di filologia e di istruzione classica* 112 (1984): 285–87. Trimalchio's funereal entrance corresponds, structurally and thematically, with his mock funeral in the banquet's climactic final scene (78).

39. The funerary character of the decoration in Trimalchio's portico is generally noted by G. Bagnani, "The House of Trimalchio," *American Journal of Philology* 75 (1954): 23, and M. Grondona, *La religione e la superstizione nella Cena Trimalchionis* (Brussels, 1980), 13f., though neither remarks its thematic significance. Herzog, "Fest, Terror und Tod," 125–30, sees the image of Trimalchio's house as a tomb as part of a systematic blending of fiction and reality throughout the work. For E. Schlant, "Petronius: Our Contemporary," *Helios* 18 (1991): 54–66, underworld imagery in the *Cena* is subsumed within a broader frame of mythological allegory.

40. Not surprisingly, the structures exhibit many of the same decorative features: a clock (26.9, 71.11); Trimalchio on a tribunal (29.5, 72.9); gladiatorial games (29.9, 72.6); emblems of Trimalchio's maritime ventures (30.2, 71.9). The representation of Fortunata as Venus on Trimalchio's tomb (71.11: cf. Grondona, *La religione,* 49 and n. 146) recalls the marble statuette of Venus (representing Fortunata: P. Veyne, "La Vénus de Trimalcion," *Latomus* 23 [1964]: 802–6) housed with Trimalchio's *lares* (29.8). The minute concern shown by Roman freedmen for their funerary monuments is discussed by G. Fabre, *Libertus* (Rome, 1981), 142–62, and copiously illustrated in several recent art historical studies (for which see D. E. E. Kleiner, "Roman Funerary Art and Architecture: Observations on the Significance of Recent Studies," *Journal of Roman Archaeology* 1 [1988]: 115–19).

41. The poignancy of the double entendre inherent in *umbra*—"uninvited guest" (cf. Horace, *Sat.* 2.8.22, *Ep.* 1.5.28) and "ghost" (e.g., Petronius 122 v. 124)—would not have escaped an author writing a satiric "banquet" with Horace's *Cena Nasidieni* (*Sat.* 2.8) very much in mind: the "shadows" of Maecenas in Horace's satire (2.8.21f.) find their counterparts in the *Satyricon* in Encolpius and his friends, disdainful guests at the

banquet of a freedman whose pretentious nomenclature (71.12) proclaims an association with Maecenas himself.

42. For the earlier of the two, erected at Capua in the late republic or Augustan period, see Frederiksen, *Campania,* plate 8, and *Corpus inscriptionum Latinarum* (hereafter, *CIL*), 10.8222. The second, known only from the drawing reproduced in figure 1, was dedicated at Arlon sometime in the first or second century A.D. (*CIL* 13.3986). One of the scenes in the so-called forum frieze from the Praedia of Julia Felix has sometimes been taken to represent the sale of a young slave girl at Pompeii (MNN 9067); other interpretations, however, are possible, and the function of the vignette as a generic scene of daily life is in any case different from the commemorative purpose served by the slave sales depicted in Trimalchio's mural and the two funerary reliefs: see Parslow, "Forum Frieze."

43. See Frederiksen, *Campania,* 302. For the type, cf. G. Zimmer, *Römische Berufsdarstellungen* (Berlin, 1982), 6–16, and note the funerary relief of an avowed "fleshpeddler" (σωματέμπορος) from Amphipolis (also a freedman) showing a chained gang of slaves being led to market: H. Duchène, "Sur la stéle d'Aulus Caprilius Timotheos, *sômatemporos,*" *Bulletin de correspondance hellénique* 110 (1986): 513–30, esp. 528ff.

44. J. Kolendo, "Eléments pour une enquête sur l'iconographie des esclaves dans l'art hellénistique et romain," in *Schiavitù, manomissione e classi dipendenti nel mondo antico* (Rome, 1979), 161–74, at 162, 164f.

45. F. Magi, "L'*Adventus* di Trimalchione e il freggio A della Cancelleria," *Archeologia classica* 23 (1971): 88–92.

46. Cf., e.g., Herodotus 1.60.3–5; Livy 1.24.8–10, with A. Borghini, ". . . Minervaque ducente Romam intrabat: Nota a Petr. Sat. XXIX 3," *Aufidus* 6 (1988): 50–53.

47. Bagnani, "House of Trimalchio," 23, credits Maiuri with this observation and coins the happy term "Trimalchioneia" to describe the piece. For mythological and epic scene painting in friezes (a style that largely fell out of fashion after the early years of Augustus) and panel pictures (the preferred form in Trimalchio's day), see Ling, *Roman Painting,* 107–41.

48. Cf., e.g., Pliny, *HN* 35.6–7; Polybius 6.53.4–10; Sallust, *Jug.* 4.5–6; Valerius Maximus 5.8.3.

49. Cf. Tacitus, *Ann.* 11.21.3; Cicero, *Phil.* 6.17.

50. See H. Wrede, *Consecratio in Formam Deorum* (Mainz, 1981), esp. 67f., 93–105. For a similar combination of realistic elements, gods (Mercury and Minerva), and mythical allegory in a single composition (the facade painting of a Pompeian carpenters' shop), see Fröhlich, *Lararien- und Fassadenbilder,* 62f., 319f. Conceptually Trimalchio's mural has much in common with this sort of street art.

51. The elder Pliny provides a fair indication of how Petronius's well-bred contemporaries might have responded to this artistic innovation in reporting the fate of one Arellius, highly esteemed as a painter in late republican Rome, until he debased his art (*ni flagitio insigni corrupisset artem*) by painting portraits of his mistresses as goddesses (*HN* 35.119).

52. Cf. B. Combet-Farnoux, *Mercure Romain* (Rome, 1980), 445–47, 463–65, plate 8; Wrede, *Consecratio,* 280 (cf. 68); and, on the "internalization" (*Verinnerlichung*) in private life of the official images of empire, P. Zanker, "*Bilderzwang:* Augustan Political Symbolism in the Private Sphere," in *Image and Mystery in the Roman World,* ed. J. Huskinson, M. Beard, and J. Reynolds (Gloucester, 1988), 1–13.

53. Regrettably, Zimmer, *Römische Berufsdarstellungen,* 2, excluded financial professions from his survey of pictorial representations of Roman occupations, but we may note a slave with an abacus computing accounts (or bequests) at his master's bedside on a sarcophagus of the Flavian period (H. Stuart Jones, *Sculptures of the Museo Capitolino*

[Oxford, 1912], 138) and a freedman banker who portrayed his occupation on his funerary altar, datable to the 60s A.D. (D. E. E. Kleiner, *Roman Imperial Funerary Altars with Portraits* [Rome, 1987], 121–23, no. 16 [plates 11.1–2]). How Trimalchio's elevation to the position of chief household accountant may have been depicted we cannot say; perhaps he was shown assigning tasks to other slaves or, like the procurator in his own dining room (30.1), receiving accounts (cf. *CIL* 6.4885).

54. For the phrase, cf. *CIL* 4.117 (= *Inscriptiones Latinae selectae* 6419g) with M. I. Rostovtzeff, *The Social and Economic History of the Roman Empire*, 2d ed., rev. P. M. Fraser (Oxford, 1957), 96. Membership in a municipal college of Augustales was an honor associated particularly with freedmen: cf. R. Duthoy, "La fonction sociale de l'Augustalité," *Epigraphica* 36 (1974): 134–41.

55. It seems that Hermes-Mercury is not generally imagined as leading his charges up to the heavens before the first century A.D.: cf. F. Cumont, *Lux Perpetua* (Paris, 1949), 300f.

56. A similar ambiguity inspired the pointedly misapplied quotation of Catullus 3.13 at *Apocolocyntosis* 11.6 (cf. P. T. Eden, *Seneca: Apocolocyntosis* [Cambridge, 1984], 127f.) and is implicit in Apuleius's description of Mercury as "that go-between god of those up above and those below" (*deus iste superum et inferum commeator*, *Apol.* 64; cf. *Met.* 11.11.1).

57. See Kampen, "Biographical Narration," 51–55.

58. As briefly remarked by Grondona, *La religione*, 10f.

59. See F. Cumont, *Recherches sur le symbolisme funéraire des Romains* (Paris, 1942), 336f.

60. So E. Campanile, "Interpretazioni petroniane," *Studi e saggi linguistici* 4 (1964): 123–25, and R. Stefanini, "Da Gilgames a Petronio," *Paideia* 22 (1967): 293–95; cf. R. R. R. Smith, *Hellenistic Royal Portraits* (Oxford, 1988), 47. The three Fates spinning golden thread for Trimalchio recall the Fates who spin a Golden Age for Nero in Seneca's Menippean satire: cf. *Apoc.* 4.1 v. 9 with Eden, *Seneca*, 76f.

61. See J. R. Clarke, "The Decor of the House of Jupiter and Ganymede at Ostia Antica: Private Residence Turned Gay Hotel?" in *Roman Art in the Private Sphere*, ed. E. K. Gazda (Ann Arbor, Mich. 1991), 96f. and fig. 4 = 10, for a convincing reconstruction of this gesture in a domestic panel painting of the late second century A.D. (aa. 184–192) from Ostia.

62. Trimalchio set great store by his actual service as master's pet: cf. 75.10–11 with J. Bodel, "Trimalchio and the Candelabrum," *Classical Philology* 84 (1989): 224–31, and Bodel, "Trimalchio's Coming of Age," *Phoenix* 43 (1989): 72–74.

63. P. B. Corbett, "Petroniana," *Classical Philology* 62 (1967): 260–61, and Corbett, "In Defense of the Honest Scribe of H," in *Miscellanea codicologica F. Masai dicata*, ed. P. Cockshaw, M.-C. Garand, and P. Jodogne (Ghent, 1979), 2.390, adducing Propertius 3.7.69, Ovid, *Pont.* 2.3.39 and 2.6.14, and comparing Petronius 43.4, *et quod illius mentum sustulit, hereditatem accepit* (and what really lifted his chin up, he came into an inheritance). The trope belongs to the same sphere as our figure of "keeping one's head above water."

64. W. M. Lindsay, ed., *Nonius Marcellus* (Leipzig, 1903), 848: "Qui liberi fiebant ea causa calvi erant, quod tempestatem servitutis videbantur effugere, ut naufragio liberati solent."

65. P. Veyne, "Vie de Trimalcion," *Annales ESC* 16 (1961): 213–47.

66. See, e.g., M. I. Finley, *Ancient Slavery and Modern Ideology* (London, 1980), 73–75; K. R. Bradley, *Slaves and Masters in the Roman Empire* (Brussels, 1984), 113–37; and, for a more nuanced view of the peculiar legal status of slaves as human property, A. Watson, *Roman Slave Law* (Baltimore, 1987), 46–66.

67. See G. Boulvert, *Domestique et fonctionnaire sous le Haut-Empire romain* (Paris, 1974), 231f., for a collection of evidence. Aristotle had remarked a similar phenomenon in the pathology of the nouveaux riches: "The difference between the newly rich and those who have had wealth a long time is that the newly rich have more and worse bad habits. For to be newly rich is to be, as it were, uneducated in wealth" (*Rhet.* 2.1391a).

68. Cf. Minazio, "Maison-piège," 24–26; Fedeli, "Petronio," 107. Etched on a pillar in the sumptuous house of M. Lucretius at Pompeii (IX.3.5) is a depiction of a maze with the following caption: *Labyrinthus. Hic habitat Minotaurus.* (The labyrinth. Here lives the Minotaur. *CIL* 4.2331; plate 38, fig. 1). Who wrote it and with what purpose no one can say.

CHAPTER FOURTEEN

Women and Marriage in the Greek Novels: The Boundaries of Romance

Brigitte Egger

In the five extant Greek novels of the so-called ideal type (attributed to Chariton, Xenophon of Ephesus, Achilles Tatius, Longus, and Helio-dorus) seventeen couples get married; twenty-three times a conjugal union is unsuccessfully aspired to, and at least forty times matrimony is mentioned of couples already wedded. This astonishing total of eighty occurrences amounts to an average, roughly, of one marriage for every ten Teubner pages, or one for every seven pages of the recent omnibus edition of English translations.[1]

Such statistical niceties aside, marriage is the social backbone of the romances and the focus of the love plots. Its flip side, ardent desire out of wedlock, often depicted in salacious detail and highly rhetorical mono-logues of erotic suffering, may offer the reader much piquancy or sus-pense, but even where ambivalent seduction, threatened rape, and the erotic fantasy of female victimization are most prominent, such untamed forms of desire are always eventually suppressed, and often punished, in favor of legalized heterosexuality. Despite the tensions played out between these conflicting forms of eroticism, marriage finally proceeds with all propriety and with the adequate social decorum of respectability. The paradigm of the couple, generally on the rise in the history of mentality of the first few centuries A.D.,[2] in the novels is that of married lovers. Achilles Tatius's Clitophon, for instance, may toy with the idea of having a stormy affair with his cousin Leucippe, while going through with the wedding that has been arranged by his father, but by the beginning of book 4, when Leucippe, after eloping with him, rather suddenly convinces him that she must remain a conventional romance heroine (that is, a virgin) until prop-erly wedded, we know what to expect. Similarly, the other reformed rake of this novel, Callisthenes, after kidnapping the young woman he desires from her home, is at last ready to do the right thing and ask her father for her hand (8.18.3). In Chariton, an entire polis assembly has little else to do but act as matchmaker for the leading couple, and then follow the fates of that union with avid interest, while the populace of Babylon discusses the pros and cons of the heroine's two marriages (1.1.11ff., 6.1.1ff.) and the Great King himself is viewed in the role of protector of matrimony (5.6.4). In Heliodorus, even Egyptian brigands acknowledge the conventions of the Greek marital system (1.19f., 5.20–29).

Marriage is constantly on the novelists' minds. To them, the whole world is married (as most people, we may presume, actually were, a point not usually noted in ancient literature). Not only the central *Liebespaar,* but also the backstage before which the story of great love and loyalty is played out, is suited to this theme: the many married couples among the supporting cast of the world of romance contribute to setting the tone—not only such obvious cases as Xenophon's husband and mummified wife (5.1.6ff.) or Chariton's royal Persian couple, but also details less conspicuous in the fabric of the narrative, such as Chaereas's conviction that only unmarried Egyptians will want to follow him to Syracuse (Ch. 8.2.14), an exiled doctor's longing to return to his wife and children (X 3.4.4), or the regular cooperation of wives and husbands, both free and slave, in family decisions in Longus.

As for the protagonist couples themselves, the romances have individual propriety standards for their heroines' many encounters with men, but the idea of matrimony looms large in each of them. "Marriage," as the metaphor for the legitimized sexuality that the romances endorse, is often also a respectable cover for menacing rape (a major theme of the novels), since even forced sex tends to be couched in the notion of a long-term, socially sanctioned relationship: only few of the many lustful pursuers of the heroines' chastity, although in a position to dispose of them as their slaves or captives, have less than "marriage" in mind. None of Chariclea's admirers, for instance, dares to wish to possess her in less than honorable wedlock.[3] Another example is the importance that Chariton lends to the status of Callirhoe's union with Dionysius, making clear from the beginning that it is respectable marriage to his slave, not concubinage, that the master wants (παλλακήν vs. γαμετὴν κατὰ νόμους, 3.1.6; cf. 3.2 and 2.6.3). Only the most disreputable barbarians or brigands (such as the Indian Psammis or the robber Anchialus in Xenophon) fail to raise the female protagonist from slavery to the prospects of a proper wife before exerting their sexual rights (ἐξουσία). The use of the terms γάμος, γαμεῖν, and cognates, which occur over three hundred times throughout the texts,[4] corroborates this: hardly any of these instances have the general meaning of "sexual union,"[5] but nearly always the connotation is unequivocally that of "marriage,"[6] which is specified as "according to the laws" only in critical circumstances.[7]

For the protagonists, the connection of passionate love and sexuality with marriage (and vice versa) is almost inevitable. This combination of passion with the social institution of matrimony is one of the criteria that distinguish the "ideal" Greek novels from other types of ancient erotic literature, as well as from other ancient prose fiction.[8] As Chariton puts it in his well-known programmatic statement at the beginning of book 8: Enough now of all the adventures—back to legitimate love and legal marriage; I trust that my readers will appreciate this most.[9]

Marriage is central to the Greek romances in a number of ways. It works as a structural, organizing principle: since a wedding or reunion of the couple necessarily belongs to the happy ending and their reestablishment in their hometowns, the entire course of intervening events may be viewed as oriented toward that goal. Matrimony is not only the sentimental focus and locus of sexuality for the central couples, but also the core of their moral integrity and identity. Emotionally, it stands for safety, belonging, homecoming—the only security left in the world of the Hellenistic individual isolated from political community and meaning, who has been identified as the intended romance reader.[10] Loyalty to the lover or spouse comes to mean the equivalent of self-possession, autonomy, and sense of identity.[11] As Xenophon's Abrocomes aptly puts it, to whom his wife is "the purpose for his whole life": "They [may] rule over my body, but I am keeping the freedom over my soul." By this he means "I would never agree out of my free will to betray my wife!"[12]

Since matrimony is at the core of the narratives, it is worthwhile to take a closer look at its workings and ideological implications. All of our five extant novels are historically vague to a certain extent, yet their representations of the world are not all set within purely imaginary boundaries. In the constructed reality of romantic fiction, some operational elements are better defined than others according to their local, social, and temporal coordinates. One of them is marriage as an institution of private law.

After several decades of literary theory, it would be more than naive to assume that the relationship between "fiction" and "reality" is anything like straightfoward or that external referents for narrative construction can be simply pinpointed. The special discourse of romance, frequently termed "illusionist" or "escapist," complicates the problem. The Greek novels (like most fiction) certainly do not offer—and do not strive to offer—images directly representational of their contemporary environments. Social questions and the relationship of the genre to the "real world" have been discussed to a certain extent in romance scholarship.[13] I do not aim to discuss here the complex issues of what myths and realia of late Hellenism may be reflected in the romances, and in what ways they build their narratives with elements thereof. I will concentrate instead on two specific points. The first is the social institution of marriage, particularly in its implications for women; the second is the question of reader-ship. The importance of marriage for women is implied by the romances themselves. In patriarchal societies such as those in which the Greek novels were written and read, where femininity is largely defined by sexual and marital status, marital concerns have particular relevance for women. I will look at the institution, then, from the female, and specifically the female readers', point of view.

Certain parts of the fictional discourse must be recognizable and plausi-ble to an audience to make successful communication possible. In the drama surrounding Callirhoe's unborn baby (Ch 2.9ff.), for instance, readers should know that according to classical and post-classical Greek law, the child of a female slave always had servile status; otherwise they need a commentary to grasp the whole force of Callirhoe's predicament. Likewise, in the question of why she leaves her small son with Dionysius (an act of apparent bad mothering that has puzzled and dismayed many a scholar), familiarity with ancient family law is implied: since he was the official father, there was no legal way for her or Chaereas to claim the child at all. In the fight between her two husbands about who has the better right to keep her as his wife (Ch 5.8ff.), readers must understand the underlying arguments about the contraction of marriage in order to fully appreciate the debate. Another example is Melite's impending divorce from Ther-sander, in which the issue of her dowry comes up (A 8.8ff). To compre-hend the whole meaning of the lawsuit fought by the cuckolded husband, readers should probably be aware that in Hellenistic law only a woman who was found guilty of adultery by a public trial (κριθεῖσα) could be fined in regard to the repayment of her dowry in case of separation (στερέσθαι τῆς φερνῆς).

Legal assumptions are part of the wider question of the novels' construc-tion of gender. My second issue, which I will approach through the first, is a very old one: the question of women readers. The existence of this female audience for the ancient romances has been asserted by critics since the seventeenth century.[14] After general, if often cautious, acceptance of this reader group, especially in the 1970s and early 1980s (some critics even went so far as to suggest the possibility of female authorship for the novels),[15] recent contributions tend to downplay this audience group. Numerous problems of women's literacy, level of education, and access to books are involved. Generally, research in social history and in papyrology has established that there was a constant increase in educational oppor-tunities for Greek women from the third century B.C. onward.[16] Docu-mentation is best for Greek women living in Ptolemaic and Roman Egypt, an area with the added advantage that some of the novels were actually read there.

Papyri show Greek women in Egypt as active and visible participants in the economic and social life of their households and communities: as landowners and -lessors, taxpayers, signers of contracts, and participants in legal transactions and business dealings. [17] They were legally able to own property of every kind in their own right, to inherit, and to make wills. Marriage did not make them subject to their husbands. In total, they owned almost as much land as men, and they were involved in many kinds of trade and business. [18] They even held public office, as they did elsewhere in the Hellenized parts of the Roman Empire (which may have chiefly meant fulfilling liturgies and providing money to the community), though they had, of course, no political rights proper in the modern sense.

Generally, women's literacy is connected with their improved economic and legal standing. A number of Egyptian documents supply evidence of their education. [19] Though a minority of daughters can be shown to have acquired an education, it is difficult to estimate just what proportion of the female population of Greco-Roman Egypt could actually read and write. Not only socioeconomic class, but historical time and geographical place, helped determine whether a girl would be educated. Further testimony from the fields of art and epigraphy, [20] as well as from post-classical literature, strengthens the conclusion that the Egyptian development, at least in tendency, may be assumed for other Hellenized regions as well. Of foremost importance is the question not only whether women were simply literate (able to sign their names on legal documents or compose letters), but also whether they had enough education to engage in, and enjoy, leisure-time reading. Such a level of proficiency was still limited to the prosperous classes; within these, a certain number of women (but fewer than men) had literary skills.

Turning to the Greek novels, their main female characters read and write as a matter of course, and with ease (though for practical reasons, not for enjoyment or entertainment), an indication that the authors did not view this as beyond actual contemporary women's reach. One woman was actually the dedicatee of a novel: Antonius Diogenes' sister, Isidora, [21] who, I would venture, read such books. Furthermore, women are explicitly included among the internal audiences of the novels who follow the development of the love plot with great interest and involvement. To simplify matters, I propose to include women also as aural readers (listeners), in order to concentrate on the second argument within the discussion of a female audience, that of content and the rendering of women and of "female interest" within the romances—features that invite female identification. The character and amount of this internal evidence certainly varies among the five individual authors, [22] but female identification is implied in all of them. I will disregard these distinctions here in order to contribute to the discussion of the female reader by examining one detail:

the literary presentation of women in marital law, which I take as symptomatic of the fantasy of women in the Greek romances in general.

How do marriages work in our texts? Several layers of imagination, drawn from various repertoires, collude to shape this key romance theme. The first impression may be that the central lovers find each other in a fairy-tale manner, especially where the narrators deal with the situation quickly: the heroes meet at a religious festival, there is mutual love at first sight, but also shyness, parental dissent, or the threat of other suitors; after these obstacles and numerous further trials of separation, rivals, shipwreck, and robbers are overcome, they are reunited and live happily ever after. Traces of a folk-tale pattern are at work in the Greek novels, as several studies have shown.[23] Callirhoe in Chariton has numerous high-ranking suitors, but she loves a commoner; he succeeds in gaining her father's approval, though not by valiant deeds, but by means somewhat more passive, Tyche, and the help of others, in accordance with the genre's specific ideal of masculinity. However, he displays greater heroism later, when he wins her back from his competitors. In Longus, a pauper, the young man preferred by the heroine, finds a treasure; now the richest of all the marriage candidates, he becomes eligible. In the other novels, too, elements of fairy tale or folk tale come to mind readily: the unrecognized princess who proves her true status by ordeals and her lover who asserts his worth by heroic feats (Chariclea and Theagenes in Heliodorus) are finally wed.

On another plane, a variety of allusions from the post-classical mythical and literary imaginary come into play: in Xenophon, for example, we have a version of Hippolytan hubris that ends well in the hero's acceptance of Eros and nuptials (1.1ff.); in Heliodorus, an encounter between Nausicaa and a traveling stranger, which, this time, has a romantic conclusion (Cnemon and Nausiclea, 6.8); in Longus, the children of two couples are exposed and miraculously rediscovered fifteen years later; in Chariton, the heroine's bigamous story is clearly modeled on the paradigm of Helen of Troy. Furthermore, readers (ancient and modern) who prefer a symbolic reading of the novels as *Mysterientexte* will find added meaning in the religious metaphor of the *hieros gamos* and the ordeals of the lovers.

But the fantasy of marriage operates on more than these levels of folk tale, myth, allegory, and intertextuality. Underneath the overriding sentimental interest and the narrators' penchant for literary imitation and engagement of classical subtexts, marital matters also have a practical dimension. All the novelists display certain assumptions not only about the emotional and social value of marriage, but also about its legal aspects. They do so both as members of their own societies, with their specific cultural experiences, and as learned writers of antiquarian and rhetorical literary interests, who are also aware of generic conventions. The novelists are not fantasizing out of the blue, but with an image of the past on their minds: for at least two of them, Chariton and Heliodorus, this is explicitly a Hellenic past that they considered classical; for the others more vaguely so. This nostalgic outlook, a turning back to the age before the Roman occupation, and an avoidance of contemporary concerns, has been explained as characteristic of the literature of the Second Sophistic and its political and cultural background.[24]

As is now generally accepted, the novelists were well-read, educated men of literary aspirations—theories of juvenile, trivial, uncultivated, or frivolous writers (and readers) have become obsolete,[25] and recent studies, quite to the contrary, underline the literaricity and poetic self-awareness of the novels. Within their striving for a sophisticated discourse, we have to recognize a certain nostalgic, archaizing interest that is typical of their period. One symptom of this attitude is a regression to historical legal conventions, as the novelists obviously knew them from their literary experience and rhetorical training.[26] But this is only one side of the coin. Though the romances are not primarily concerned with the operational aspects of marriage, these attitudes do surface now and then in the sentimental discourse, complementing as well as disrupting the romantic notions.

Did the novelists know, and apply, classical—which means to us, Attic—Greek law, rather than portraying legal conditions of their own times? This has been assumed by the scholars who have examined the subject of marriage law in our texts—an expectation based on their historical setting.[27] However, one of the major social changes from the times of the classical polis (particularly of the Athenian orientation) to that of the romances occurred in the status of women. Attic law, with its elaborations of personal and property rights, gives us a clear picture of a citizen woman's juridical situation.[28] She was under the legal control of her husband or a male relative all her life. The overriding patriarchal political and private interests of the οἶκος put her into an absolutely dependent position. The legal contraction of a marriage viewed her entirely as an object: it was a deal between her κύριος (legal guardian)—usually her father, if she was the average marriage age, that is, in her early teens—and her groom. The dowry was entirely at her husband's disposal as long as the marriage lasted, and afterward had to be returned to her male relatives. She certainly had no right of choice; her consent either to marriage or to divorce was unnecessary. The two standard parts of the proceedings were ἐγγύη or ἐγγύησις (betrothal) and ἔκδοσις (ekdosis was the "handing out" of the bride from one household, οἶκος, to another), both inevitably at the hands of her κύριος. If she was an ἐπίκληρος, an heiress in the absence of a male successor to the line, she was passed to her closest surviving male relative even if already living in matrimony, in order to preserve the family property, since she could neither inherit nor possess assets in her own name. Without asking now to what extent the Athenian legal discourse may be truly representative of women's actual living conditions, one thing is certain: as far as the discourse of law went, things could only get better for upper- and middle-class women after the end of the classical era.

Hellenistic and imperial Greek private law is widely attested by papyrus findings from Egypt, specifically by numerous marriage contracts and divorce deeds, which specify the legal conditions involved.[29] Significant developments from Attic legal conventions occurred in regard to women's status.[30] The Greek woman was now the subject of marriage contracts; she could even sign them herself (with the assistance not exclusively of her κύριος, but of any family member, usually the one that had helped financially—even her mother—to guarantee her monetary obligations). In pre-Roman times, she was sometimes explicitly granted influence concerning her husband's dealings with her dowry (κοινῇ κυριεύουσα; φερνή or προίξ); documents from the Roman era did not even mention this anymore, since it was probably implied as a matter of course.[31] In addition to this possible influence on her marital assets, she held various kinds of property in her own right (παράφερνα, προσφορά). If she was divorced or widowed, the dowry was usually returned directly to her, not to her male agnates. Diverse stipulations regulated fines for her husband if he wronged her. Only Ptolemaic contracts, however, mention financial sanctions against the wife, the loss of her dowry (στερέσθαι τῆς φερνῆς), in case she broke the agreement; for the imperial era, there is no documentation of such a custom.[32]

The institutions of the ἐγγύη and of the *epiclerate* disappeared altogether, and the ἔκδοσις became a mere formality; it came to be replaced by a nuptial contract (ὁμολογία or συγγραφὴ συνοικεσίου; συγχώρησις), and was now an agreement between the two spouses rather than a business transaction between the κύριοι of the two households. The office of legal guardianship for women in general was reduced to a largely formal significance.[33] Another sign of women's improved status was the *autoekdosis* ("self-handing-out"): their capacity to give themselves in marriage, with a family member as a witness, but by their own authority. All this shows that paternal and male control was visibly diminished, compared to classical Attic norms. Greco-Egyptian marital law was definitely comparatively *frauenfreundlich*.[34]

There are indeed a number of reflections of the new legal thinking in our romances. A conspicuous case is Callirhoe's *autoekdotic* marriage to Dionysius, in "which she gave herself" (ἐκδομένην ἑαυτήν, 3.2.9), which Chariton explicitly treats in its legal dimension (3.2.8, 5.8.5).[35] Also, Melite, who chooses Clitophon as a husband, "gives herself and all her

Brigitte Egger

possessions" (δίδωσιν ἑαυτὴν καὶ πᾶσαν ἑαυτῆς οὐσίαν, 5.11.6). Heiresses are at times expected by their fathers and obviously compelled by economic dependence and emotional pressure into marrying close relatives, presumably to keep the money in the family (though this is not explicitly stated), but are by no means *legally* obliged to: for example, Calligone to her stepbrother, Leucippe to her cousin (A 1.11.2f., 2.11.1f.), Chariclea to a paternal cousin, twice (H 2.33.4ff., 10.24.1). All heroines of romance, in fact, seem to be *epikleroi* by classical standards, since they have no brothers. Neither this term itself not its application is ever mentioned; this shows the novelists' awareness of the changed contemporary practice. Although paternal potestas (over daughters as well as sons) looms large in the background, it seems to be more a matter of economic and social pressure than an expression of legal control.

A legal guardian of an adult woman in the classical sense does not occur in the romances.[36] Achilles' Melite contracts a marriage, disposes of her property (5.11, 5.14), administers her economic affairs (διοικήσασα δέ τινα τῶν κατὰ τοὺς ἀγρούς, 5.17.10), and goes to court (8.8ff.), apparently without the assistance or permission of a tutor.[37] Indications of shared matrimonial property are found in several couples' agreements, usually in favor of the bride.[38] In an ironic perversion of the usual marriage arrangements, both of the father's acceptance of a proposal (H 5.28) and of conventions regarding property rights, the pirate chief Trachinus promises to make Chariclea, once he has captured her, the "joint mistress" of the seized booty, δέσποινα σὺν ἡμῖν τῶν ἁπάντων (H 5.26.1), and arranges a proper wedding festival to show his serious intentions.

On the other hand, however, an analysis of the novels' underlying juridical assumptions reveals many traits that seem to come straight from the authors' classical library.[39] The marriage of daughters is almost always at the exclusive discretion of the father, the mother is usually not consulted, either. The consent of the couple to be married appears legally unnecessary: the girl's opinion is not sought, most strikingly so at Callirhoe's first wedding (when her parents bring the bridegroom into her room, she does not even know who he is; Ch 1.1.5) or in Leucippe's engagement (her father affiances her by letter; A 5.10.3). This patriarchal power of deciding family connections sometimes opposes the ideal of the love match, establishing the first in a long line of obstacles to threaten the relationship, and may turn into a major source of generational conflict and even motivate the young couple's flight from the parental home—yet ultimately, it is never fundamentally questioned.[40]

That the heroines eventually do get to marry the men with whom they happen to be in love anyway is part of the inevitable happy ending, a hopeful generic convention. From the girls' legal point of view, it is a lucky coincidence that they cannot influence.[41] The one notable exception

268

to this rule is Heliodorus's Chariclea, who decides to take her marital fate in her own hands and presents two fathers, each of whom has already selected a son-in-law, with her refusal and her own choice. Elsewhere, the problem of patriarchal authority is neutralized in line with the generic ideology of harmonizing contradictions within social relations: the good romance father just happens to give, by his exclusive decision, to his daughter the husband whom she would select herself if she could—that is, if she is a positive female figure who deserves poetic happiness.

Other women, who are not the heroines, are not so fortunate: Chaereas affiances his sister to his friend Polycharmus as a reward of socioeconomic advancement for his loyal help; her perspective is not even mentioned (Ch 8.8.12). Xenophon's Manto, who hoped that she would be allowed her own choice, is given without any ado to a groom whom her father brings back from a business trip (2.5.6); his Thelxinoe, who has eloped with her lover to escape a union forced on her by her parents, cannot return home and must live in poverty (5.1). And Chariton's Callirhoe, who has obtained the love match of her preference herself, advises Dionysius to give his own daughter to her presumed half-brother once both children have grown up (8.4.6).

On closer inspection, it is only in marriages in foreign parts and in the absence of parents that we find *autoekdosis* of the bride—for instance, Callirhoe's in Miletus (Ch 3.2), or Anthia's in Tarsus (X 2.13.8, 3.6.1)—but both are forced into this alliance by physical and mental exigencies. These emergency marriages, in which the father did not give away his daughter, are inevitably doomed to fail. Though legally perfectly valid, they are not up to standard according to the ethos of the novels.[42] It is for the same sentimental and moral reason that Melite's *autoekdotic* (and, unknown to her, bigamous) union with Clitophon, also contracted abroad (5.14.2), takes second place to his relationship with Leucippe (which is finally condoned by both fathers' consent). As these examples indicate, women's legal conditions in the Greek novels lag behind the reality of their contemporary readers. The lack of legal self-determination and independence is in line with the more general social limitation that is characteristic of the situation of women in the novels. Both are a regression to a largely obsolete historical state. The real-life women readers of these books were far more emancipated than their protagonists.

But it is not the conventions of straightforward classical Attic law that the novelists portray, either. They commit significant anachronistic mistakes when referring to women's legal situation in the past. Heliodorus, for instance, uses the Attic term (κατ)ἐγγυᾶν, the all-powerful father's act of betrothing a daughter to a groom chosen by him, several times. In the cases of two minor characters, Nausiclea and Charicles' unnamed genuine child, the procedure is indeed "classical": it is a deal exclusively between father and groom (6.8.1f., 2.29.3).[43] But if one thinks that Charicles' later attempt to make his other daughter, the female protagonist, accept the man of his dreams (2.33ff.) is also an indication of strictly Attic legal norms, one is mistaken. They entailed no need for the bride's consent (ἐπινεύειν), nor the right on a daughter's part to resist a father's decision (which the heroine claims with two fathers) and to propose her own candidate (as she does with the second).[44] Charicles, her Athenian father, who admits that it is only partly up to him to choose a son-in-law (ὅσα γε εἰς βούλησιν ἥκει τὴν ἐμήν, 4.7.9), finally despairs of her refusal so much that he sees no way of making her agree to marriage other than to resort to Egyptian sorcery (2.33.6), while Hydaspes, her Ethiopian father, once he realizes her wishes, is easily persuaded by his wife to agree (10.38.2). In the scenario presented in the novel, Chariclea, however difficult it may be for her to insist on or even pronounce her own preference, cannot simply be forced.[45]

On the one hand, then, Heliodorus cites Attic conventions when it suits him; further incidents include allusions to the classical formula of "marriage for the sake of procreating legitimate children" (1.19.7, 10.40.2). On the other hand, he suddenly not only introduces a daughter's right to choose a husband by herself but also refers to an ethical legal principle:[46] "If it is a case of marriage, both spouses' consent is necessary" (εἰ δὲ γάμος τὸ γινόμενον, τὸ παρ' ἀμφοτέρων βούλημα συννεύειν ἀναγκαῖον, 1.21.2), the prophet-bandit Thyamis says to Chariclea, asking her alone to accept his proposal, in the presence of her alleged brother—who, if this were classical law, would definitely act as her κύριος and decide the matter. More historical imprecision occurs in the case of the ἕδνα, the bridal gifts that Chariclea receives from her groom (4.15.2): entirely lacking in Attic, Hellenistic, and early imperial Greek law, they may count among the novel's ubiquitous Homeric allusions, but possibly they are also a reference to historical reality, where the term and practice are in use again in papyri from the early fourth century onward.[47] And sometimes, Heliodorus is even more *frauenfeindlich* than Attic law: with his notion that even female adulterers have to face the death penalty—which, in this form, did not exist even there.[48]

Similarly, Achilles first makes as much as do the other novelists of the exclusive paternal control (by his time obsolete) in marital decisions (1.7.4f., 1.11.1f., 2.11–12), but then he shows an awareness of the contemporary custom of grooms acknowledging the receipt of fake dowries, a measure meant to ensure the economic security of the bride (in the Calligone subplot, 8.17.4), and of a widow's ability to confer her possessions on a new husband by her own choice and to fight a lawsuit, both without a guardian (7.7ff., 5.14.2, 7.7.5). His handling of this divorce case further demonstrates the amalgam of legal suppositions with which we are presented: Melite's opponent claims that she must lose her dowry if proven an adulterer (ἀφεῖσθαι τῆς προικός, 8.8.13), while her lover faces death. As noted above, such punishment for the wife is not attested in legal papyri of Achilles' period; here he opts for a conservative version again, for dramatic reasons.

As these few examples show, many of the legal conventions connected to marriage are a mixture of the nostalgic and the contemporary. The same applies to the other three novels. The use of the Attic legal term *ekdosis,* originally the handing over of the bride to her groom by her *kyrios,* is symptomatic of this development. In the novels, the term has lost its strict legal meaning of exclusive paternal prerogative: the agent of this operation is usually the father, but may also be a woman (e.g., Arsace, H 7.23.5, 7.24.4), a mother together with the father (Persinna, H 10.21.3; the πατέρες in X 5.1.6; cf. 1.7.7; the parents in Longus), or a brother (Ch 8.8.12);[49] the bride may give herself (Callirhoe, Anthia, Melite; but also Chariclea, who waits for her father's official permission, yet has made her own decision: ὡς ἀνδρὶ συνθεμένη . . . ἐμαυτὴν ἐπέδωκα, H 1.25.4). Finally, the "handed-over" spouse may also be a son (e.g., A 1.7.4, 1.11.2). What we actually find, then, is a combination of old and new legal assumptions, literary allusions and contemporary practice. Historical consistency is apparently no great concern of the novelists. They seem to have employed legal features just as they happened to need them for their plot-related, dramatic, and sentimental purposes. However, the archaizing (if historically imprecise) traits generally predominate.

This vague employment of archaizing legal conditions is an integral aspect of the novels' conservative discourse and nostalgic interest. However, there is a specific side to it that concerns the romances' female images, and this is my final and main point: whenever the texts archaize, they impose on their women limitations and incapacities that did not exist in the same degree for their approximately contemporary readers. For Egypt, where some of the romances were definitely read (as well as possibly also produced) and enjoyed relative popularity, this is certain; for other Hellenized regions of the Greek-speaking East of the Roman Empire, a similar relationship may be assumed.[50] The fabrication of femininity, as endorsed by the texts, is conventional and archaizing as compared to contemporary reality; I have tried to demonstrate one concrete aspect of this in the example of marital law.

This limited and nostalgic view of women's legal possibilities is typical of the romances' more general confirmation of restricted female roles, and a characteristic feature of the type of reading that the texts imply. But this social disablement of women is not conspicuous. For centuries, critics of the Greek novel have felt the heroines to be "powerful" and "dominating" characters (whether they liked them for that or not), who sadly outclass their male partners, and have underlined their superiority or at least their equality as a noteworthy phenomenon within Greek literature and a surprising development of post-classical thought.

These readings were not simply biased or wrong, but reactions to other effective signals of the texts. The spotlight of the narratives is indeed focused on the heroines in various ways, and the more interesting among them tend to outshine their male counterparts. Some of the female protagonists, above all Chariton's Callirhoe and Heliodorus's Chariclea, not only possess more beauty and a higher social standing than their spouses, but also demonstrate greater passive survival skills, intelligence, and generally a higher degree of what we might call practical common sense. Yet in the last analysis it is only the woman's erotic radiance and emotional strength, aided at times by her cunning, that actually lend her "predominance," power over others, primarily to manipulate the men who actually have authority. This is the main means by which she influences the world around her—rather than by any clearly improved status and freedom of choice or movement within the social setting constructed by this type of fiction. Socially and operationally, the women remain constrained. Legal considerations are just one aspect of this archaizing handicap; the fictional women's incapacity to act can be found in other realms as well. Female power may be described best as informal or passive.[51]

This is true even for the genre's most assertive and active heroine, Heliodorus's Chariclea, characterized as σοφὴ καὶ καλή (3.4.1; cf. 5.26.2), who possesses the skills of rhetoric, archery, and a very quick wit, as well as an iron will and divine protection. She, like all the other romance heroines, escapes from the majority of her predicaments (rape threats) by the force of her attraction (for instance, in her manipulation of Thyamis and Trachinus, 1.21.3ff., 5.26). Other prominent examples of such an apparent reversal of power are Callirhoe outmaneuvering Dionysius (with some help by Plangon, Ch 2.11ff.), and Calligone turning her captor into her "slave" (A 8.16). Although otherwise disabled, the heroine rules supreme in the one province of the text of which she is ambivalently and passively in charge: the erotic. The narratives concentrate constantly on the attractiveness and emotions of their women protagonists, and in this sense are gynocentric, but the world of romance is dominated in every other aspect by its men. The novels work with the principle of emotional gynocentrism, but factual androcentrism.[52]

What are the implications of these findings for the female romance audience? This question is particularly important since these texts offer themselves to female identification, especially in Chariton and Heliodorus. How would women readers be involved in this construct? How could they be attracted to female characters portrayed in the way that I have described—so immensely emotionally powerful and erotically ravishing, but at the same time so restricted and disempowered? This is, of course, an age-old male fantasy that we find as early as in the Homeric epics. Helen in the *Iliad* and Penelope in the *Odyssey* possess the same combination of attributes: both exercise great erotic power over men, but are incapable of taking direct action. Chariton, incidentally, who integrates numerous Homeric quotations into his narrative, alludes to these two epic women in connection with his heroine, thus putting her in the literary tradition of such a configuration of the female ideal (5.5.9; cf. 2.6.1, 5.2.8). But whereas in the epic context this female role is only one of many themes, in Chariton it is absolutely central, even to the point of structuring the plot. This indicates a focus of interest on female eroticism. The price paid for women's erotic centrality is their social containment in the realms of law and marriage, among others.

That this hoary patriarchal fantasy is one of the few male constructions of the female still highly appealing to women themselves is attested by the more than twenty million female readers of the "Harlequin" type of contemporary popular romantic fiction (in the United States alone), women of all social and educational backgrounds and age groups.[53] I am not proposing a simple equation; the institutional and market conditions of the two cannot be compared, nor can the entire range of gender fantasies in modern pop fiction be found in the Greek romances. Yet one leading notion, the strong narcissistic fantasy of women's emotional and erotic omnipotence, linked with their actual powerlessness and often archaizing social and legal limitations, is characteristic of both. Sociopsychological studies indicate that it is exactly this outlook of gender roles, a constantly repeated image, that attracts today's women even to the point of addictive reading.[54] I am far from claiming a similarly far-reaching effect for the ancient Greek romances, but the same strategies of gender construction are at work in them, even if these strategies are often not so visible next to other, more obvious themes and voices. The same kind of comfort that is entailed in traditionally restricted but secure gender roles may have been one of the attractions of the Greek novels, too.

Let us, in conclusion, return to the marriages that I have discussed as examples. Legal realia (as attested in a multitude of papyri) are not primary concerns of our love stories. Typically, burning passion, the beauty of the bride, oaths of fidelity, and assertions of unending love are described— hardly ever a real marital contract. The novelists indulge in ecphrases of wedding festivals; rarely do they broach the question of dowry. The protagonists' carefree wealth is a given; the specific economic conditions of conjugal agreements go unmentioned. But while the emotional, erotic, and dramatic aspects of the protagonists' relationships always prevail, the effect of the factually debilitated image of women is insidiously potent. It works subtly, subconsciously, hidden under sentimental dreams and fantasies of the erotically powerful female on whom all eyes are focused. Love covers everything. The love ideal is, to a certain extent, a liberating and egalitarian force, but its containment in archaizing legal norms, in marriage nostalgically viewed as socially constraining to women, undermines this impression of equality. What is readily noticed is women's emotional omnipotence, their enormous sexual sway over men, their strong characters. Yet this image is deconstructed by other, often less covert messages, which reaffirm women's legal limitations and their inability to act. That they are also enclosed in one of the genre's key structural and emotional themes, marriage, makes them even more effective.

Legal regulations are only one expression of a society's view of gender relations. Often, the law tends to be more conservative than other aspects of reality and expressions of mentality; but in the case of women in late Hellenistic society, it is not so conservative and constraining a discourse as that of Greek romance.

NOTES

1. These statistics are based on the 800 pages of Hercher's edition of the *erotici scriptores* (outdated, but chosen here for statistical standardization), and ca. 550 pages of translations of the "Big Five" in B. P. Reardon, ed., *Collected Ancient Greek Novels* (Berkeley and Los Angeles, 1989). The five novels are cited here as Ch(ariton), X(enophon), A(chilles Tatius), L(ongus), and He(liodorus). I have not considered the fragments, nor those homosexual unions that are intended to be lifelong. All translations are mine.

2. Cf. P. Veyne, "La famille et l'amour sous le haut-empire romaine," *Annales ESC* 33 (1978): 35–63, and P. Veyne, ed., *A History of Private Life*, vol. 1, *From Pagan Rome to Byzantium* (Cambridge, Mass, 1987).

3. These admirers are Theagenes; her two cousins, Alcamenes and Meroebus; the Phoenician merchant; the brigand prophet Thyamis; the pirate Trachinus; and the Persian slave, Achaemenes. The only exceptions might be Oroondates, the satrap, and the pirate Pelorus—but they never get a chance to make up their minds. More typically, Thyamis wants Chariclea as a proper wife "for the procreation of heirs rather than for sexual pleasure" (οὐ τῆς καθ' ἡδονὴν χρείας ἀλλὰ τῆς εἰς διαδοχὴν σπορᾶς, 1.19.7), and alleges that he plans marriage (γάμος, 1.20.2f.), rather than raping a captive woman (βιάζεσθαι, 1.21.2). Trachinus, another brigand chief, also intends τὸν γάμον τῆς κόρης (5.20.8).

4. Chariton: eighty-one times; Xenophon: thirty-five times; Achilles: eighty-three times; Longus: thirty-two times; Heliodorus: ninety times (numbers thanks to the disk count of the *Thesaurus Linguae Graecae*).

5. Callirhoe's imagined cohabitation with Zeus (Ch 6.7.12) is ambivalent; Achilles' "union of plants and rivers" (γάμος φυτῶν, γάμος ὑδάτων, 1.18), stresses the sexual aspect (Clitophon is trying to get Leucippe interested in a fling with him, not in a wedding). In the drawn-out drama of Melite's unconsummated marriage to Clitophon, the spicier, sexual connotation of the term is clearly in the foreground (e.g., A 5.15.–16); see also her pun on κενογάμιον (5.14.4). Heliodorus distinguishes between "marriage" and "sexual experience": γάμον καὶ ἀνδρὸς ὁμιλίας ἀπείρατον κόρην (10.33.2); cf. γάμου ἀγνήν (X 5.2.5, 2.13.8).

6. συνοικεῖν, συνοικίζειν, συνεῖναι, συνουσιάζειν, and related terms are sometimes employed as equivalents (e.g., A 8.18.4; H. 1.21.2, 1.22.6, 10.21.2), but can also be applied in a less specific sense (e.g., Manto's desired association with Abrocomes, X 2.5.2; Anthia's living with the goatherd, X 2.9, or Psammis's rape attempt, X 3.11.4).

7. E.g., Callirhoe's problematical second marriage: γαμετὴ κατὰ νόμους (Ch 3.1.6), κατὰ νόμους ἔγημα (3.2.8); παίδων ἐπ' ἀρότῳ κατὰ νόμους Ἑλληνικούς (3.2.2); a brigand's (hardly believable) promise to Anthia: γάμον νόμιμον (X 1.6.7); cf. γάμον ἔνθεσμον (H 1.25.2).

8. The "ideal" Greek novels are distinguished, in particular, from the Latin novel and the remains of "realistic" Greek fiction (such as the Onos, Lollianus's Phoenicica, Iamblichus's Babyloniaca, Antonius Diogenes' Wonders beyond Thule, and, probably, Iolaus). Achilles Tatius is a borderline case: he plays with the generic conventions of both types, but finally settles for the "ideal" brand.

9. The narrator says νομίζω δὲ καὶ τὸ τελευταῖον τοῦτο σύγγραμμα τοῖς ἀναγινώσκουσιν ἥδιστον γενήσεσθαι· καθάρσιον γάρ ἐστι τῶν ἐν τοῖς πρώτοις σκυθρωπῶν. οὐκέτι λῃστεία καὶ δουλεία καὶ δίκη καὶ μάχη καὶ ἀποκαρτέρησις καὶ πόλεμος καὶ ἅλωσις, ἀλλὰ ἔρωτες δίκαιοι ἐν τούτῳ ⟨καὶ⟩ νόμιμοι γάμοι (8.1.4): "I believe that this final book will be the most pleasing to my readers; for it is a relief from the grim events in the former books: there is no more piracy, slavery, lawsuits, fighting, attempted suicide, war, and capture in it, but legitimate love(s) and legal marriages." This happy ending indeed includes one new and two restored "legitimate" marriages (while only the hapless Dionysius has to remain with mere memories of a spouse).

10. Cf. B. P. Reardon, "The Greek Novel," Phoenix 23 (1969): 291–309, and Reardon, The Form of Greek Romance (Princeton, 1991), 172f.

11. For the female protagonist especially this is frequently identical with escaping rape by men whom she has not chosen; only in Heliodorus is this ideal exaggerated into the principle of virginity per se. For his Chariclea marriage is really an antidote against ἐπιθυμίας αἰσχρὸς ὄνομα (4.10.6), or an abatement of the wickedness of physical desire, for herself and for her fiancé.

12. αὕτη ἦν γὰρ αὐτῷ τοῦ βίου παντὸς . . . ἡ ὑπόθεσις (5.8.2); ἔχουσιν ἐξουσίαν μου τοῦ σώματος, τὴν ψυχὴν δὲ ἐλευθέραν ἔχω . . . οὐ γὰρ ἄν ποτε πεισθείην ἑκὼν Ἀνθίαν ἀδικῆσαι (2.4.4). Such rhetoric of chastity by female as well as male protagonists, often characterized by high pathos, abounds in the novels. Losing sexual self-determination and relinquishing the ideal of faithful couplehood is worse to them than death—though the standards tend to be more relaxed for men than for women.

13. See, for instance, E. L. Bowie, "Greeks and Their Past in the Second Sophistic," Past and Present 46 (1970): 3–41; E. L. Bowie, "The Novels and the Real World," in Erotica Antiqua, ed. B. P. Reardon (Bangor, Wales, 1977), 91–99; M. Futre Pinheiro, "Aspects de la problématique sociale et économique dans le roman d'Héliodore," and C. Ruiz-Montero, "Cariton de Afrodisias y el mondo real," in Piccolo mondo antico: Le donne, gli amori, i costumi, il mondo reale nel romanzo antico, ed. P. Liviabella Furiani and A. Scarcella (Perugia, 1989), 15–42 and 107–49; K. Treu, "Der Realitätsgehalt des antiken Romans," in Der antike Roman: Untersuchungen zur literarischen Kommunikation und Gattungsgeschichte, ed. H. Kuch et al. (Berlin, 1989), 107–25; A. Scarcella, "Realtà e litteratura nel paesaggio sociale ed economico del romanzo di Longo sofista," Maia 22 (1970): 103–31; A. Scarcella, "Les structures socio-économiques du roman de Xénophon d'Éphese," Revue des études grecques 90 (1977): 249–62. F. Zimmerman, "Kallirhoes Verkauf durch Theron: Eine juristisch-philologische Betrachtung," Aus der byzantinischen Arbeit der DDR 1 (1957): 72–81.

14. Cf. B. Egger, "Zu den Frauenrollen im griechischen Roman: Die Frau als Heldin und Leserin," Groningen Colloquia on the Novel 1 (1988): 33–66.

15. T. Hägg, *The Novel in Antiquity* (Berkeley and Los Angeles, 1983), 95f.; N. Holzberg, *Der antike Roman: Eine Einführung* (Munich, 1986), 42.

16. Cf. S. Pomeroy, "Technikai kai Mousikai: The Education of Women in the Fourth Century and in the Hellenistic Period," *American Journal of Ancient History* 2 (1977): 51–68; S. G. Cole, "Could Greek Women Read and Write?" and S. Pomeroy, "Women in Roman Egypt: A Preliminary Study Based on Papyri," in *Reflections of Women in Antiquity,* ed. H. Foley (London, 1981), 219–45 and 303–22; S. Pomeroy, *Women in Hellenistic Egypt from Alexander to Cleopatra* (New York, 1985); W. Harris, *Ancient Literacy* (Cambridge, Mass., 1989), 127ff., 239ff., 248ff.

17. For the economic, social, and legal position of women living in Greco-Roman Egypt, see H. J. Wolff, "Die Grundlagen des griechischen Eherechts," *Tijdschrift voor Rechtsgeschiedenis* 20 (1952): 1–29 and 157–80; R. Taubenschlag, *The Law of Greco-Roman Egypt in the Light of the Papyri (332 BC–640 AD)* (Warsaw, 1955); C. Preaux, "Le statut de la femme à l'époque hellénistique, principalement en Egypte," *La femme: Recueils de la Société Jean Bodin* 11 (1959): 127–75; G. Häge, *Ehegüterrechtliche verhältnisse in den griechischen Payri Ägyptens bis Diokletian,* Gräzistische Abhandlungen, no. 3 (Cologne, 1968); J. Modrzejewski, "Zum hellenistischen Ehegüterrecht im griechischen und römischen Ägypten," *Zeitschrift der Savigny-Stiftung für Rechtsgeschichte (Römische Abteilung)* 87 (1970): 50–84; C. Vatin, *Recherches sur le mariage et la condition de la femme mariée a l'époque hellénistique,* Bibliothèque des Ecoles Françaises d'Athènes et de Rome, no. 216 (Paris, 1970); H. J. Wolff, "Hellenistisches Privatrecht," *Zeitschrift der Savigny-Stiftung für Rechtsgeschichte (Römische Abteilung)* 90 (1973): 63–90; J. Modrzejewski, "La structure juridique du mariage grec," in *Scritti in onore di O. Montevecchi,* ed. E. Bresciani et al. (Bologna, 1981), 231–68; D. Hobson, "Women as Property Owners in Roman Egypt," *Transactions of the American Philological Association* 113 (1983): 311–21; D. Hobson, "The Role of Women in the Economic Life of Roman Egypt: A Case Study from First-Century Tebtunis," *Echos du monde classique* 28, n.s. 3 (1984): 373–90; and Pomeroy, "Women in Roman Egypt" and *Women in Hellenistic Egypt.*

18. Cf. Hobson, "Women as Property Owners" and "Role of Women"; Pomeroy, "Women in Roman Egypt."

19. Cf. Pomeroy, "Technikai kai Mousikai" and "Women in Roman Egypt"; Cole, "Could Greek Women Read and Write?"; Harris, *Ancient Literacy.*

20. There is evidence in the form of Hellenistic terra-cotta statuettes, depicting young girls with book rolls on their knees, and portraits showing women in erudite poses (discussed, e.g., in Pomeroy, "Technikai kai Mousikai," 52; Cole, "Could Greek Women Read and Write?" 321ff.; Harris, *Ancient Literacy,* 263ff.

For inscriptions referring to the schooling of girls, see Pomeroy, "Technikai kai Mousikai," 53f.; Cole, "Could Greek Women Read and Write?" 232f.; Harris, *Ancient Literacy,* 244. Several epigraphical texts concerning the social position of women are collected in H. W. Pleket, ed., *Epigraphica II: Texts on the Social History of the Greek World,* Textus minores, no. 41 (Leiden, 1969). For a critical analysis of women's public roles and office holding, see R. Van Bremen, "Women and Wealth," in *Images of Women in Antiquity,* ed. A. Cameron and A. Kuhrt (London, 1981), 223–41.

21. Photius, *Bibliotheca,* 111a–b.

22. Especially in Longus; I am not always sure whether he should be grouped with the others in one genre, but he will be included here.

23. See I. Nolting-Hauff, "Märchenromane mit leidendem Helden," *Poetica* 6 (1974): 129–78 and 418–55; C. Ruiz-Montero, "The Structural Pattern of the Ancient Greek Romances and the Morphology of the Folktale of V. Propp," *Fabula* 22 (1981): 228–38; N. Frye, *The Secular Scripture: A Study of the Structure of Romance* (Cambridge, Mass., 1976).

24. Cf. B. van Groningen, "General Literary Tendencies in the Second Century A.D.," *Mnemosyne* 18 (1965): 41–56; B. P. Reardon, "The Second Sophistic and the Novel," in *Approaches to the Second Sophistic: Papers Presented at the 105th Meeting of the American Philological Association,* ed. G. Bowersock (University Park, Pa., 1974), 23–29; Bowie, "Novels in the Real World."

25. The age-old rating of these trivial readers and texts as not really worthy of scholarly attention resulted, at least in part, from a reluctance on the part of classical scholars to imagine that serious, sophisticated men in classical antiquity could have read for entertainment in general, and for romantic interest in particular. For recent discussions of audience, se B. Wesseling, "The Audience of the Ancient Novel," *Groningen Colloquia on the Novel* 1 (1988): 67–79; K. Treu, "Der antike Roman und sein Publikum," in Kuch et al., *Der antike Roman,* 178–97; and R. I. Pervo, *Profit with Delight: The Literary Genre of the Acts of the Apostles* (Philadelphia, 1987).

26. Chariton, by his own definition a lawyer's secretary (1.1.1), and the later, "Sophistic" authors are certainly interested in legal details, at times even juridical niceties, such as the former's court hearings at Babylon (5.4ff.), or Melite's and Clitophon's adultery trial in Achilles (7.7ff).

27. A. Calderini, "La ἐγγύησις matrimoniale nei romanzieri greci e nei papiri," *Aegyptus* 39 (1959): 29–39; P. Liviabella Furiani, "Gamos e kenogamion nel romanzo di Achille Tazio," *Euphrosyne* 16 (1988): 271–80; A. Scarcella, "Aspetti del diritto e del costume matrimoniali nel romanzo di Eliodoro," *Materiali e contributi per la storia della narrativa greco-latina* 1 (1976): 59–95. The latter even suggested using a novel, Heliodoro's *Chariclea,* for a better understanding of Attic law itself—a somewhat problematic undertaking, given the temporal, societal, and generic differences between the two. Scarcella concedes that changes from Attic practice have occurred, but attributes them exclusively to a different moral (not legal) outlook. Similarly, P. Liviabella Furiani, who thinks that "Achilles Tatius is describing the marital law and customs of his own time, but puts them side by side with the classical tradition, which is generally confirmed" (271), analyzes the matrimonial evidence within this novel in regard to classical Attic conventions. E. Karabelias, "Le roman de Chariton d'Aphrodisias et le droit: Renversements de situation et exploitation des ambiguités juridiques," in *Symposion 1988: Vorträge zur griechischen und hellenistischen Rechtsgeschichte (Sienna-Pisa, 6.–8. Juni 1988),* ed. G. Nenci and G. Thür (Cologne, 1990), 369–96, also examines family law in Chariton in terms of the Attic model.

28. Cf., e.g., A. Harrison, *The Law of Athens,* 2 vols. (Oxford, 1976–81); R. Garner, *Law and Society in Classical Athens* (London, 1987).

29. A list of marriage documents on papyrus is found in O. Montevecchi, "Ricerche di sociologia nei documenti dell' Egitto greco-romano," *Aegyptus* 16 (1936): 3–83; and Montevecchi, *La Papirologia* (Turin, 1973), 204ff. They are discussed in Modrzejewski, "La structure juridique," 248ff.; Taubenschlag, *Law,* 120ff.; Vatin, *Recherches,* 165ff., 200ff.; Häge, *Ehegüterrechtliche Verhältnisse,* 24 ff., 132ff.; and Preaux, "Le statut de la femme," 147f. H. Maehler, "La posizione giuridica della donna nell' Egitto tolemaico," *Quaderni di storia* 30 (1989): 5–24, stresses the social and legal limitations of Greek women living in Ptolemaic Egypt in contrast to the still far better status of their female Egyptian contemporaries.

30. I am basing my discussion of Greco-Egyptian marriage law on the studies mentioned above in n. 17. This field has met with wide scholarly interest, though there is no modern standard textbook yet on the private law of this era; the late H. J. Wolff's work for the *Handbuch der Altertumswissenschaften* is currently being completed by J. Modrzejewski.

31. This is assumed by H. J. Wolff, *Written and Unwritten Marriages in Hellenistic and*

Brigitte Egger

Postclassical Roman Law, Philological Monographs Published by the American Philological Association, no. 9 (Haverford, Pa., 1939), 55; Häge, *Ehegüterrechtliche Verhältnisse,* 147ff. takes a more cautious view.

32. Lacking evidence of legal papyri, some scholars of Greek law take a passage from Achilles Tatius as evidence for this practice in the second century A.D.; cf. H. J. Wolff, s.v. προίξ in *Real-Encyclopaedie der classischen Altertumswissenschaft,* ed. A. Pauly and G. Wissowa (Stuttgart, 1894–1963), 23.1 (45 Halbband [1957], 133–70); W. Erdmann, *Die Ehe im alten Griechenland,* Münchner Beiträge zur Papyrusforschung, no. 20 (Munich, 1934), 330. They may be disregarding the specific literary character of this text and its complex construction of social reality, which is my topic here. Romance discourse is less straightforward than that of legal papyri.

33. A woman needed the assistance and signature of a legal guardian (often, but not necessarily, her husband or a relative) only for official contracts, not for any sort of private commercial transaction. His power had a purely formal character: the woman made contracts μετὰ κυρίον, no longer διὰ κυρίου. The new Hellenistic situation of Greek women is summed up by H. J. Wolff as *unbeschränkt vermögens- und verfügungsfähig* ("Hellenistisches Privatrecht," 67).

34. Conditions in non-Attic poleis of the fifth and fourth centuries are likely to have been more liberal in regard to women, but are, outside Sparta, hard to pin down. Historical distinctions are necessary, but may not contribute much to my point: the novelists read the Attic texts (mainly the orators) for their legal history, as we do.

35. It is sometimes mentioned in the scholarship of legal history as providing an early example of *autoekdosis;* cf. Modrzejewski, "La structure juridique," 57ff., and Karabelias, "Le roman de Chariton," 376.

36. A possible exception is Ch 6.2.6, where Dionysius claims that in Miletus he was the *kyrios,* and able to prevent Callirhoe even from receiving a letter: this occurrence might have classical legal implications. A point in question is also a shepherd's vague statement, οὐδενός εἰμι τῶν ἐμῶν κύριος (I am not master of my own [house], 3.31.3)—this might include his (lacking) right to determine his daughter's marriage. Both statements, however, are inconclusive.

37. ῥήτορες and συνήγοροι are mentioned as her advocates and defense counsel in her adultery trial, but no guardian is named. She is clearly a person *sui iuris.*

38. Callirhoe and Dionysius: πάντων παρεχώρησε τῇ γυναικὶ δέσποιναννν αὐτὴν ἀπέδειξε τῆς οἰκίας (Ch 3.7.7); Anthia and Perilaus: πάντων γὰρ ἐξουσίαν εἶχε τῶν Περιλάου (X 3.5.9); Calligone and Callisthenes: (A 8.17.3f.); Clitophon and Melite (the opposite situation in accordance with this novel's reversed gender roles: πάντων ἀποφῆναι δεσπότην [A 5.14.2; cf. 5.11.6]). In each of these cases, economic terms are specified for the security of the prospective spouse who is far away from home and the protection of his or her family.

39. Cf. Calderini, "La ἐγγύησις matrimoniale," Scarcella, "Aspetti del diritto," and Liviabella Furiani, "Gamos e kenogamion," for more details of "classical" marital conventions in the novels.

40. Every successful marriage is sanctioned by paternal consent. Chariclea in Heliodorus travels through half the world to obtain it, and even Achilles' Clitophon, the most adventurous of the male romance protagonists, finally states οὐκ ἠθέλομεν ἀπάτορα γενέσθαι τὸν γάμον (we did not want our marriage to happen without our fathers) (8.5.8).

41. They may try by more indirect means to obtain their choice: Callirhoe asks the goddess to "give" her the man she has just seen (Ch 1.1.7), Anthia pines away until her parents notice that there is something wrong (X 1.5.5), Chariclea is physically lovesick to avoid an unwanted marriage (H 3.7.1), Leucippe runs away from home after an ugly

scene with her mother (A 2.29f.)—but none of the heroines before Chariclea dares to confide in her father. The sons are also passive, but less so: Chaereas and Daphnis at least tell their parents of their wishes.

42. Furthermore, each of the four weddings with *autoekdosis* that occur in the romances is the bride's second marriage (the fourth instance is Chariclea, H 1.21: she is already "married" in intention, if not in fact).

43. Similarly, in H 5.19.1 and 5.21.2 (agreement between Calasiris, Chariclea's alleged father, and the Phoenician merchant) or 5.28f. (Trachinus and Calasiris).

44. ἀπηγόρευται γὰρ αὐτῇ γάμος (H 2.33.4).

45. The fact that she is Charicles' adopted child may again be a moral factor, but not a legal one, since she later induces her birth father, who has also already picked out a son-in-law (10.24), to agree to the man of her choice. The necessity of her consent is stressed several times (e.g., 4.13.3, 4.15.3).

46. *Ethisches Rechtsprinzip* in legal literature refers to the concept of both parties' assent as necessary to marriage.

47. The only other occurrence of ἕδνα in the romances is a sarcastic use in the myth of Procne and Philomela (A 5.5.4). Cf. L 3.25 for wooing presents given to the bride's father.

48. Demaenete, an Athenian woman (1.11.4, 1.17.5); the identical fate is imagined for the Ethiopian and Persian adulterers Persinna (4.8.6) and Arsace (8.15.2). Nowhere did Greek law provide for capital punishment for the wives in adultery cases; it occurs only in rhetorical exercises of the Roman period. The case of Demaenete's relatives, who sue Aristippus for murder and charge that adultery was only a πρόκάλυμμα τοῦ φόνου (H 2.9.2), illustrates this: it is an allusion to Lysias's *First Oration,* the classical adultery trial, where the death of the male adulterer is the point in question, but we hear nothing about the wife's fate.

49. Chaereas acts as the bride's *kyrios* though their father is alive and present, assigning her a dowry from his war loot, so I would not explain this incident as evincing the traditional modalities of Attic *eggye* and *ekdosis* (as does Karabelias, "Le roman de Chariton," 375); that this is another romantic adaption of a conventional motif (which still entails female objectification) is indicated by the public character of this betrothal.

50. Modrzejewski, "Zum hellenistischen Ehegüterrecht," 79ff., and other scholars argue for a legal Koine for most of the Hellenized regions within the Hellenistic areas. In Egypt, there is no influence of Egyptian enchoric or Roman law on Greek customs; even after the *Constitution Antoniana,* separate legal systems were enforced for the different parts of the population.

51. If a woman oversteps these boundaries and has actual power, she is inevitably a negative character and punished eventually.

52. For another interpretation, see S. Wiersma, "The Ancient Greek Novel and Its Heroines: A Female Paradox," *Mnemosyne* 63 (1990): 109–23.

53. Cf. A. Snitow, "Mass Market Romance: Pornography for Women Is Different," *Radical History Review* 20 (Spring-Summer 1979): 141–61; T. Modleski, *Loving with a Vengeance: Mass-produced Fantasies for Women* (New York, 1982); A. Radway, *Reading the Romance: Women, Patriarchy, and Popular Literature* (Chapel Hill, N.C., 1984); M. Jensen, *Love's $weet Return: The Harlequin Story* (Toronto, 1984). For an application of feminist theory of romance and pornography to ancient novels, see H. Elsom, "Callirhoe: Displaying the Phallic Woman"; H. Montague, "Sweet and Pleasant Passion: Female and Male Fantasy in Ancient Romance Novels," in *Pornography and Representation in Greece and Rome,* ed. A. Richlin (New York, 1992), 212–30 and 231–49; and chap. 21 below.

54. One explanation states that in times of changing gender roles, when strictly

circumscribed models of femininity (as well as of masculinity) are relaxed, fantasies about the security of traditional, more limited gender identities tend to increase, even if or just because they are socially more or less obsolete. For contemporary recreational reading this is certainly true: since the late 1960s, paperback romance sales have soared. Possible parallels for Greco-Roman Egypt leisure-time reading may be suggested by these similar consolations of gender, but of course cannot be historically verified. I explore these questions further in my forthcoming book on the subject.

PART VI

Fictions Sacred and Profane

CHAPTER FIFTEEN

Novel and Aretalogy

Reinhold Merkelbach

An aretalogy is a statement (-λογία) about the αρετή of a god, that is, about a mighty deed in which the god demonstrates his power. In this context the word ἀρετή almost means "success." An aretalogy was regarded as proof that a god—be he Asklepios, Sarapis, or a city-god—is actively at work here on earth, and frequently persons who witness the great deed are mentioned by name.

Three extracts from aretalogies should serve as examples.

The first two passages are from an Oxyrhynchus papyrus. The title of the book is *The Great Deed* [ἀρετή] *of Zeus-Helios-Sarapis Concerning the Helmsman Syrion*.[1] The story about the event is not preserved on the papyrus, though one may reasonably suppose that it deals with the rescue of Syrion from a storm at sea. Holy water is apparently mentioned, but for our purposes only the final sentence is significant: "The miraculous deed [of the god] is registered in the libraries of Mercurius. Let all present say: 'There is but one god, [and he is] Zeus-Sarapis.'"[2]

The following three observations can be made on the basis of this text:

1. The report about the successful intervention of Sarapis was registered in a temple.
2. Apparently it was read before a congregation of Sarapis devotees.
3. Those present responded with a ritual cry of praise (an acclamation) for the god.

The next text, another aretalogy of Sarapis, was inscribed on a stone on the island of Delos. One Apollonius, a priest of Sarapis, reports that the Delians at first wanted to forbid the new cult. The priest was accused and had to defend himself in court. But when the proceedings began, his opponents were unable to make an accusation. Apollonius here couches his report in an address to Sarapis: "There you with your wife [Isis] caused that great amazement [θάμβος] among the people; for you hindered those wicked men in their attempted accusation by causing the tongues in their jaws to be inaudible, as a result of which no one heard a single word and there was no written speech supporting the accusation. They [those who were present] declared with religious fervor [θείως] that the prosecutors resembled god-struck statues or stones."[3] And then we read in lines 90–91: "The entire people were amazed on that day at your miraculous power." Here witnesses are put forward who saw and were amazed at the great event. The astonishment of the witnesses is a part of many aretalogies.[4]

4. This amazement of a crowd of witnesses may be regarded as a fourth characteristic of aretalogies.

The third text I would like to discuss is an inscription from Lydia. It is a report of a woman, and one can also call it a confession: "I, Antonia, daughter of Antonius [have dedicated this stele] to Apollo Bozenos, because I went to the round-dance in a dirty dress. After I was punished I confessed and made this dedication in praise of the god, because I became healthy again."[5]

Here too a god is praised, and here too the inscription is erected in a temple precinct so that all the god's devotees can read it there and recognize his power. Such confessional inscriptions have been found in great numbers in the temple precincts of various local gods in Lydia. To date we know of about ninety, and each year the number increases. They always begin or conclude with praise of the god; one sometimes also finds "Great is the god so and so."[6]

Two more observations may be made on the basis of the inscription of Antonia:

5. The god proves his power by healing the sick.
6. Aretalogies can be couched in the form of a confession. The god is praised by a person who publicly acknowledges a transgression and thanks the god for pardoning him or her and leading him or her back to the right path.

There used to be lengthy books about the miracle healings on the part of Sarapis. The ancients considered miracle healing a demonstration of the power of a god, and therefore such wonders are referred to in aretalogies. Many such reports were inscribed on the walls of the temples of Asklepios in Epidaurus and in Rome.[7]

This practice was taken over by the Christians. At the bidding of Saint Augustine, reports (libelli) were collected in Hippo Regius about miracle healings by means of the relics of the first martyr, Stephanus. Augustine's friends Possidius and Evodius made similar collections of reports. Those who had been healed put a report of the illness and the therapy on the protocol, and frequently the libellus was signed by witnesses. These reports were read before the congregation and kept in the archives of the church.[8]

The confessional inscriptions from Lydia have sometimes been compared to Augustine's *Confessions*. Augustine, just like the Lydians in their confessions, reports his transgressions, the change in his way of life, and the grace of God. From the Christian East we possess long books on the healing miracles performed by saints: those by Cosmas and Damianus at Constantinople,[9] by Cyrus and Johannes at Menuthis,[10] by Thecla at Seleucia in Cilicia,[11] by Demetrius at Thessalonike,[12] and by others.[13] These books belong to the tradition of the pagan aretalogies.

Let us now turn to the ancient novels. We find in them all six characteristics of the aretalogies.

1. Storage in temple. Aretalogies could be read on inscriptions in the temple precincts or on the walls of temples, or they could be kept on record in temple libraries; the reports of miracle healings by the relics of Stephanus were kept in the cathedral archives by Augustine and his friends.

Similarly, we read in the novel of Xenophon of Ephesus and in the *Historia Apollonii* that each of these books was deposited in the temple of Artemis of Ephesus.[14]

2. Public recitation. The story about the helmsman Syrion was read before a congregation of Sarapis devotees. The Delian Sarapis aretalogy and the confessional inscriptions from Lydia could be read by the public in the temple precincts. The *libelli* collected by Augustine were read before the congregation.[15]

One finds something similar in the novel of Clement. Here we read that on a Sunday in the presence of the congregation, Peter baptizes Faustinianus (the father of the family). In the sermon that follows, Peter relates the history of the family:[16] "[Petrus] die dominica baptizavit eum [sc., Faustinianum] atque in medio populi ex conversione eius materiam sumens omnes casus eius exposuit" (Peter baptized him on Sunday and standing in the midst of the people he made Faustinianus's conversion his theme, relating all the events of his life).

The Christian miracles were read in the churches, on the anniversaries of the saints and on other occasions. The word "legend" is derived from this lecture.

3. Acclamations. Upon hearing the story about the helmsman Syrion, the congregation cried out in acclamation: "There is but one god, Zeus-Sarapis." Augustine's reports about the miracle healings with the relics of Stephanus several times end with the congregation breaking out in praise of God.[17]

One finds similar acclamations in the novel of Clement; in the penultimate chapter of the *Recognitiones* we read: "Tantam itaque sanctus spiritus in illa die gratiam suae virtutis (= ἀρετῆς) ostendit, ut omnes a minimo usque ad maximum una voce confiterentur deum" (On that day the Holy

Ghost showed that his grace had so much power, that everyone, young and old, cried out with one voice a confession of their faith in God, 10.71.1, p. 370, 23).

In the novel of Xenophon of Ephesus, Anthia and Habrockomes meet after a long separation in front of the temple of Isis on Rhodes, and then we read: ὁ δὲ δῆμος ὁ Ῥοδίων ἀνευφήμησέ τε καὶ ἀνωλόλυξε, μεγάλην θεὸν ἀνακαλοῦντες τὴν Ἶσιν (the populace of the Rhodians broke out in cries of joy and praise, calling Isis the great goddess, 5.13.3). The actual wording of this ritual acclamation is known from other sources: "Great is the mistress Isis," μεγάλη Ἶσις ἡ κυρία.[18]

Achilles Tatius's heroine Leucippe is acquitted of all guilt by divine judgment, whereupon all persons present shout out in praise and joy: πᾶς . . . ὁ δῆμος ἐξεβόησεν ὑφ᾽ ἡδονῆς.[19]

Christian texts abound in acclamations.[20]

4. The amazement of the crowd of witnesses. When Appuleius has Lucius changed back from a donkey into a human being, we read *populi mirantur* (the people are amazed).[21]

The *Historia Apollonii* contains a scene in which Tarsia, whom everyone had thought was dead, is shown to be alive (chap. 50): *mirantur cives* (the citizens are amazed).

Longus relates how pirates abducted Chloe, and then released her because Pan appeared to their leader in a dream. Chloe and her animals are set on land and the animals form a circle about her. Chloe is wreathed with a sprig from a pine tree, and one hears the sound of a syrinx. And then Longus writes: θαύματι δὲ πάντων ἐχομένων καὶ τὸν Πᾶνα ἀνευφημούντων (Everyone was seized with amazement and they praised Pan, 2.29.2).

There are similar passages from Xenophon, Heliodorus, and the Clementine novel,[22] and of course in the Christian miracle books.[23]

5. Healings. Healings play a prominent role in aretalogies and Christian miracle collections. We find them also in the ancient novels, especially in the novel of Clement. Peter heals the crippled hand of Mattidia; he also heals her sick hostess, and many others.[24]

6. Confessions. I now come to the last and most important characteristic common to aretalogies and the ancient novels: confession and the account of one's former life.

It was customary in many cults that candidates for admisson had to render an account of their past. Often this took the form of a general, all-encompassing confession. The candidates who openly confessed their former errors (the word generally used is ἐξαγορεύειν) were then absolved through the grace of a god. A new life began for the initiates.

The heroes of the novels too report on their earlier lives, and these reports nearly always take place in a temple.

Appuleius's Lucius prepares for initiation into the mysteries of Isis and he rents a room in the temple precincts. There he receives members of his family and tells us: "After addressing each of them individually as was thought proper, I related my earlier misfortunes and present joys" (*adfatis itaque ex officio singulis narratisque meis propere et pristinis aerumnis et praesentibus gaudiis*, 11.19.1). In other words, Lucius describes his life, and since his past was not without its flaws, we can say that he confesses.

In the novel of Achilles Tatius, the two heroes, Clitophon and Leucippe, relate the vicissitudes of their lives to a priest of Artemis in a side chamber of the temple.[25]

In the *Historia Apollonii*, an apparition called an "angel" appears to Apollonius, telling him to travel to Ephesus in order to relate his past errors (chap. 48, *omnes casus tuos . . . expone per ordinem*). He acts accordingly: "He begs to be admitted into the sanctuary so that he can relate all his misfortunes in the presence of Diana" (*Rogat sibi aperiri sacrarium, ut in conspectu Dianae omnes casus suos exponeret*). His wife, who has been separated from him for a long time and whom Apollonius believes to be dead, is the chief priestess in the temple of Artemis. It is to her that he tells the story of his life. The recognition scene follows, and a happy ending.

Nearly every character in the Clementine novel relates the course of his life to Peter.[26] The Christian miracle books contain a wealth of such reports.[27]

Finally, there are two texts that parody the love novel, namely the *Satyrica* of Petronius and the Iolaus fragment preserved by an Oxyrhynchus papyrus. Both texts contain parodies of confessions. Encolpius confesses that he was unable to take advantage of an opportunity that a beautiful woman offered him. In the Iolaus fragment, a eunuch is given the role of confessor; the eunuch relates a whole series of shameful deeds that Iolaus has to admit. If confession scenes are part of the stock in trade of parodistic novels, they must have been characteristic of the ancient love novel.[28]

One should also consider the testimonies for votive pictures and picture series in temples and churches. They were intended to provide informaton about the power of the gods, and as such they too are aretalogies.[29]

To illustrate how the traditions of the aretalogy were continued in the Greek novel, I shall now consider briefly the last book of the *Aethiopica*; first, a recap of the basic plot of the work, without going into its symbolic meaning.[30]

Hydaspes and Persinna, the king and queen of the Ethiopians, had a single daughter named Chariclea. Astonishingly, the color of the child's skin was white, and because the queen feared that she would be suspected of infidelity, she ordered that the child be exposed, but equipped with tokens so that she could be recognized again. Various apparently fortuitous circumstances led to the child's being brought to Delphi in faraway Greece, where she was then reared by Charicles, a priest of Apollo-Helios.

At the age of seventeen, on the occasion of a ceremony connected with the Pythian games, she falls in love with the Thessalian youth Theagenes, and an Egyptian priest present at the ceremony recognizes from Chariclea's recognition tokens that she is a daughter of the royal family of Ethiopia. He reveals this to the girl, and a divine oracle instructs her to go back to her native country. Theagenes and Chariclea take flight to return to Ethiopia, the land of the sun god. The lovers vow to maintain their chastity until they marry, and they pretend to be brother and sister.

When in Egypt, they fall into the hands of the Persians, who happen to be ruling the country at the time. The Ethiopians, however, have declared war against the Persians, and Theagenes and Chariclea are taken captive by an Ethiopian patrol. They are brought as booty to King Hydaspes, Chariclea's father, who of course knows nothing about this. The Ethiopians had the custom of sacrificing their first prisoners of war to Helios in a ceremony of triumph, and this is what now appears to be the fate of Theagenes and Chariclea.

The Ethiopians defeat the Persians, peace is made, and the Ethiopians celebrate their victory festival. The description of this festival is replete with aretalogical motifs. Those to be sacrificed are divided into two groups. Virginal men and women are to be sacrificed to Helios and Selene, all others to Dionysus. The victims have to walk across a glowing-hot grate endowed with a special force: only those men and women who had never had a sexual experience could endure its heat. When Theagenes steps onto the grate, it is clear that he is pure: "Everyone was astounded that so handsome a man had not experienced the (gifts of) Aphrodite."[31] Next Chariclea steps onto the grate, and she remains unharmed by the fire though standing there for a long time. Her beauty made a strong impression on everyone: "At the same time amazement seized everyone, and they shouted out a single cry which did not consist of articulated words, but which expressed their astonishment."[32]

Chariclea then jumps down from the burning grate and accuses the king. She claims that his intention to sacrificed her is illegal; that only foreigners, not Ethiopians, can be sacrificed, and that she is an Ethiopian. Hydaspes is amazed and does not believe her.[33] Chariclea continues: she explains that he, Hydaspes, is in fact her father. They resort to legal proceedings.[34] Chariclea produces as evidence her recognition tokens. In astonishment,[35] Chariclea's mother recognizes her to be her true daughter; and a priest bears witness to the exposure of the child.[36] All who are present applaud and shout; everyone is surprised, and even Hydaspes is convinced and seized with amazement.[37] The people raise a din that reaches up to the heavens.[38]

Hydaspes silences the masses and addresses: "you who are present";[39] he also refers to them as witnesses of the marvelous recognition of his daughter. He says that the gods, through their miraculous workings,[40] brought his daughter back from Greece to her native country, but now that she has been consecrated as a victim for Helios, he must remain true to his promise and sacrifice her. "But the masses of the Ethiopians were shaken, . . . and they cried out in a single voice 'Save the girl.'"[41]

There follows a series of acclamations (ἐκβοήσεις) such as are especially characteristic of the Roman imperial period.[42] They were cried out in the senate, circus, theater, courts of law, town councils, guilds, and public assemblies—in other words, just about everywhere. The public was trained to take up the acclamations uttered by their leading speakers, and to divide up into groups of alternating choruses, which competed against each other in the intensity of their shouts. Heliodorus reports the choruses' shout (10.17.1–2):

σῶζε τὸ βασίλειον αἷμα,
—σῶζε τὴν ὑπὸ θεῶν σωθεῖσαν.
ἔχομεν τὴν χάριν,
—πεπλήρωται ἡμῖν τὸ νόμιμον.
ἐγνωρίσαμεν σὲ ὡς βασιλέα,
—γνώριζε καὶ σὺ σαυτὸν ὡς πατέρα.
ἱλήκοιεν οἱ θεοὶ τῆς δοκούσης παρανομίας,
—πλέον παρανομήσομεν ἀνθιστάμενοι τοῖς ἐκείνων
    βουλήμασιν.
μηδεὶς ἀναιρείτω τὴν ὑπ' ἐκείνων περισωθεῖσαν,
—ὁ τοῦ δήμου πατὴρ γίνου καὶ κατ' οἶκον πατήρ.

Save the royal blood,
—save the woman who has been saved by the gods.
We are thankful [for your offer],
—our traditional customs have been satisfied.
We have recognized you as a [true] king,
—and you, recognize yourself as a [true] father.
May the gods look kindly on this seeming transgression,
—[but] we would commit a greater transgression, if we
    opposed their will.
No one may kill those who have been saved by them [the gods],
—be not only father of your people, but father in your household.

Hydaspes is only too happy to give way to the will of the people, and he is delighted when he sees "how the groups of the people indulged almost too long in shouting out acclamations to each, and how they accompanied their cries of well-wishing by skipping around with almost too much revelry."[43] So it is decided that Chariclea is not to be sacrificed; it was often assumed that the masses were divinely inspired when they shouted out acclamations.[44]

The girl withdraws with her mother, queen Persinna, into a tent; her mother wants to enjoy hearing a "story about her [the daughter's] fate."[45] This would amount to a confession,[46] and so Charicle is at first unwilling, but finally she decides to give "those reports for which the time was ripe."[47] She says: "I am now compelled to proceed to a naked and undisguised accusation against myself," and she is prepared "to reveal the facts."[48] She admits that Theagenes is not her brother, but her spouse, although the two have maintained their chastity.

Meanwhile there is great excitement outside at the triumphal festivities. One of the bulls that was to be sacrificed gets loose, and Theagenes recaptures it. The people cry out in admiration and amazement.[49] Then a wrestling match is arranged between Theagenes and a gigantic Ethiopian athlete. Theagenes is victorious, and again the people break out into cries of amazement.[50]

Next, Chariclea's foster father from Delphi, Charicles, makes an unexpected appearance on the scene. He had tracked down the fugitive pair, and he recognizes the winner of the wrestling match as the abductor of his foster daughter. The people are dismayed as he accuses Theagenes,[51] and the latter admits the truth of the accusation.[52] Chariclea rushes forth out of the tent, and a happy ending follows. As the people view the denouement, they accompany their shouts of well-wishing with dancing.[53] A priest demands that they recognize the miraculous workings of the god,[54] and that the Ethiopians not only spare Theagenes from sacrifice, but that from now on they put an end to the entire practice of human sacrifice.

The king agrees and he addresses the people: "You who are present,[55] since these things have come about by the will of the gods, to oppose them would be unjust; let them [the gods] be witnesses, they who have arranged these things, and you too, who have shown yourselves to be in agreement with them,"[56] and he betroths Chariclea and Theagenes. The people respond with shouts of joy and applause.[57]

One could almost say that the last book of the *Aethiopica* is a long, elaborate aretalogy about the miraculous workings of the sun god.

It strikes me as evident that religious aretalogies played a significant role in the development of the new literary genre of the novel, and that this applies especially to the accounts about one's past life and earlier errors that we encounter in many different cults. Such reports about one's earlier, sinful ways and one's present happiness were of necessity at the same time reports about the power and the mercy of a divinity. Reports of this kind, deposited in a temple library, would easily be copied and circulated; witness the book of Heraclitus deposited in the temple of Artemis at Ephesus. An interesting text circulating would be imitated, and the result might be almost a novel.

I do not wish to suggest that the novel arose *only* from the aretalogies; many other factors had an influence. But how easily a confession can be transformed into a literary work is clear if one considers similar phenomena in modern times.

There existed among the German Pietists and the English Puritans a widespread genre of edifying literature, in which the authors related their earlier lives, the temptations to which they were exposed, their sinful errors, and their final salvation. Thus John Bunyan, the author of *The Pilgrim's Progress,* wrote a book of memoirs in which he related (that is, confessed) that he had earlier committed most awful sins that actually were unpardonable: he had cursed and, yet worse, he had sworn. But he was saved by the grace of God. The title of the book is *Grace Abounding to the Chief of Sinners.*

One of the most important works of German literature is *Wilhelm Meisters Lehrjahre,* or *Wilhelm Meister's Apprenticeship,* by Goethe. This long novel is divided into several books, one of which contains the life story of a devout lady told by herself; it is entitled *Bekenntnisse einer schönen Seele,* "Confessions of a Beautiful Soul."

Wilhelm Meisters Lehrjahre also refers to depositing a life's story in a temple library. In this novel, Goethe describes a ceremony of initiation into a guild of Freemasons, and in the course of this Wilhelm is allowed to see a book. In this book, Wilhelm's guild brothers had kept a record of his activities during the past years. The book in the Freemasons' library had the title *Wilhelm Meisters Lehrjahre,* the same title as Goethe's novel. The book must have had the same contents, just as the confessions in the ancient novels must have had the same contents as the novels themselves. It would seem that the Freemasons had books similar to the edifying literature of the Pietists and Puritans.

NOTES

1. *POxy.* 11, no. 1382 = M. Totti, *Ausgewählte Texte der Isis- und Sarapisreligion* (Hildesheim, 1985), no. 13, title, subscribed below the text: Διὸς Ἡλίου μεγάλου Cαράπιδος ἀρετὴ ἡ περὶ Cυρίωνα τὸν κυβερνήτην.

2. καὶ καταχωρίζεται ἡ ἀρετὴ ἐν ταῖς Μερκουρίου βιβλιοθήκαις. οἱ παρόντες εἴπατε· Εἷς Ζεὺς Cάραπις.

3. *IG* 11.4, no. 1299 = H. Engelmann, *The Delian Aretalogy of Sarapis* (Leiden, 1975) = M. Totti, *Ausgewählte Texte,* no. 11, verses 84–91:

Reinhold Merkelbach

ἔνθα cὺ κεῖνο πέλωρον ἐν ἀνδράcι θάμβοc ἔτευξαc
cῇ τ'ἄλοχοc· φῶταc γὰρ ἀλιτρονόουc ἐπέδηcαc
οἵ ῥα δίκην πόρcυνον, ἐνὶ γναθμοῖc ὑπανύccαc
γλῶccαν ἀναύδητον, τῆc οὔτ' ὄπιν ἔκλεεν οὐθείc
οὔτε γράμμα δίκηc ἐπιτάρροθον· ἀλλ' ἄρα θείωc
cτεῦντο θεοπλήγεccιν ἐοικόταc εἰδώλοιcιν
ἔμμεναι ἢ λάεccιν· ἅπαc δ' ἄρα λαὸc ἐκείνωι
cὴν ἀρετὴν θάμβηcεν ἐν ἤματι (κτλ.)

4. Some examples: *Acta Alexandrinorum,* ed. H. Musurillo (Leipzig, 1961), 8.51–53 (p. 34) from *POxy.* 1242. ἡ τοῦ Cαράπιδοc προτομή, ἣν ἐβάcταζον οἱ πρέcβειc, αἰφνίδιον ἵδρωcεν, θεαcάμενοc δὲ Τραιανὸc ἀπεθαύμαcεν. Augustine, *De civitate Dei* 22.8.10 (p. 574, 27 Dombart), *Stupentibus qui aderant.* Ibid. §13 (p. 575, 29), *admirantibus atque gaudentibus omnibus. Acta apostolorum* 3.10–11, ἐπλήcθηcαν θάμβουc καὶ ἐκcτάcεωc . . . cυνέδραμεν πᾶc ὁ λαὸc . . . ἔκθαμβοι. Cf. E. Peterson, ΕΙΣ ΘΕΟΣ (Göttingen, 1926), 193–95.

5. *Tituli Asiae Minoris* 5.1, no. 238 (from Kula; ed. P. Herrmann, spelling normalized): 'Αντωνία 'Αντωνίου 'Απόλλωνι θεῷ Βοζηνῷ διὰ τὸ ἀναβεβηκέναι με ἐπὶ τὸν χορὸν ἐν ῥυπαρῷ ἐπενδύτῃ· κολαcθεῖcα δὲ ἐξωμολογηcάμην καὶ ἀνέθηκα εὐλογίαν, ὅτι ἐγενόμην ὁλόκληροc.

6. Cf. *Tit. As. Min.* 5.1, 179a, Μέγαc Ζεὺc ἐκ διδύμων δρυῶν κατεκτιcμένοc καὶ αἱ δυνάμειc (= ἀρεταί) αὐτοῦ. No. 179b. 525, 1–3, Μέγαc Μεὶc (Lunus) 'Αρτεμιδώρου 'Αξίοττα κατέχων καὶ ἡ δύναμιc αὐτοῦ. No. 318, lines 2 and 23–24.

7. For examples from inscriptions, see G. Dittenberger, *Sylloge inscriptionum Graecarum* (Leipzig, 1920), nos. 1168–70 (Epidaurus) and 1173 (Rome); R. Herzog, *Die Wunderheilungen von Epidauros* (Leipzig, 1931); M. Guarducci, *Epigrafia Greca* (Rome, 1978), 4:147–66. Books on healing miracles of Sarapis: *Artemidorus* 2.44 (ed. Pack, p. 179); cf. Strabon 17.1.17, p. 801C (Canopus); Aelius Aristides 45.29 (p. 361, 2 Keil).

8. Augustine, *De civitate Dei* 22.8.20 (ed. Dombart, p. 577, 20), *libelli . . . qui recitarentur in populis.* Cf. §21 (pp. 578, 7, and 579, 10), §22 (pp. 580, 32; 581, 2 and 8); *De miraculis S. Stephani protomartyris* (J.-P. Migne, *Patrologia Latina* 41, 833–54). Cf. P. Brown, *Augustine of Hippo* (Berkeley and Los Angeles, 1967), 413–18; F. van der Meer, *Augustine the Bishop* (London, 1961), 527–57.

9. *Kosmas und Damian, Texte und Einleitung,* ed. L. Deubner (Leipzig, 1907); *Cosmae et Damiani sanctorum medicorum vitam et miracula e codice Londinensi,* ed. E. Rupprecht (Berlin, 1935). Cosmas and Damianus supplanted the Dioscuri.

10. By Sophronius: N. Fernandez Marcos, *Los thaumata de Sofronio* (Madrid, 1975). Cyrus and Johannes succeeded to the healing powers of Isis and Sarapis.

11. G. Dagron, *Vie et miracles de Sainte Thècle* (Paris, 1978). Thecla supplanted the heathen healing hero Sarpedon.

12. P. Lemerle, *Les plus anciens recueils des miracles de Saint Démétrius* (Paris, 1979).

13. H. Delehaye, "Les recueils antiques des miracles des saints," *Analecta Bollandiana* 43 (1925): 5–85 and 305–25 (on Latin miracle books).

14. Xen. Eph. 5.15.2 (Habrocomes and Anthia), ἐπὶ τὸ ἱερὸν τῆc 'Αρτέμιδοc ᾔεcαν . . . καὶ τὴν γραφὴν τῇ θεῷ ἀνέθεcαν πάντα ὅcα τε ἔπαθον καὶ ὅcα ἔδραcαν. *Historia Apollonii regis Tyri* 51 (end of chapter, recension RB), "Casus suos suorumque ipse [sc., Apollonius] descripsit et duo volumina fecit; unum Dianae in templo Ephesiorum, aliud in bibliotheca sua exposuit."

15. See above, note 8.

16. "Clemens," *Recognitiones* 10.72.5 (p. 371 Rehm).

17. Augustine, *De civitate Dei* 22.8.3 (p. 571, 16; a woman reports how she was healed), "Illis audientibus multumque mirantibus et glorificantibus deum." Section 22 (p. 580, 20), "Procedimus ad populum, plena erat ecclesia, personabat vocibus gaudiorum: 'Deo gratias, deo laudes!' nemine tacente hinc atque inde clamantium"; (p. 581, 20) *admirationis clamor exortus est.*

18. K. Preisendanz, *Papyri Graecae magicae,* vol. 2 (Leipzig, 1931), no. XXIVa, p. 151; *Inscriptiones Graecae* 14.2413.3n; O. Weinreich, *Ausgewählte Schriften* (Amsterdam, 1969), 1:431.

19. Act. Tat. 8.14.2 (p. 157, 3 Vilborg). Cf. also 7.16.1 (p. 139, 11), οἱ δὲ παρόντες . . . εὐφήμουν . . . τὴν Ἄρτεμιν.

20. E. Peterson, ΕΙΣ ΘΕΟΣ, 182–222.

21. Appuleius, *Metam.* 11.3.6, "Populi mirantur, religiosi venerantur tam evidentem maximi numinis potentiam (= δύναμιν) . . . claraque et consona voce, caelo manus adtendentes, testantur tam inlustre deae beneficium."

22. Xen. Eph. 4.2.9, θαῦμα δὲ τὸ γενόμενον τοῖς παροῦσιν ἦν (§10). (ὁ ἄρχων) ἐθαύμασεν; Heliodorus 8.9.15, ἡ πόλις . . . "καθαρὸν τὸ γύναιον" ἀνεβόα;8.9.16, ὡς τὴν μὲν πόλιν ὑπὸ χαρᾶς ἅμα καὶ ἐκπλήξεως μέγα τι καὶ σύμφωνον ἐκβοῆςαι καὶ μεγάλους τοὺς θεοὺς ἐπικαλεῖςθαι; "Clemens," *Homiliae* 12.23.8 (p. 186, 1), οἱ ἀκούcαντες κατεπλάγηcαν. *Recognitiones* 7.23.8 (p. 208, 7), *ut etiam turbae adstantes mirarentur;* 9.35.5 (p. 320, 26), *populus quidem admiratione ipse obstupefactus est.*

23. Cf. the following two examples from the miracles of Cosmas and Damianus. In *Mir.* 9.68 (p. 116 Deubner), a man reports having been cured by the saints "with the result that many of those who listened to him were amazed at what he related to them" (ὥστε πολλοὺς τῶν ἀκουσάντων θαυμάσαι . . . ἐπὶ τοῖς ἀπαγγελθεῖσιν αὐτοῖς). The author of one of the miracle collections introduces his book as follows (179 D): "I have heard how the great miracles of the . . . saints . . . Kosmas and Damianos . . . were read in this temple [i.e., church], and I hear about the miracle-healings that were performed not just daily, but hourly, both from those who were healed themselves and from the witnesses and the attendents of the healed" (τάς μεγάλας τῶν . . . ἁγίων . . . Κοcμᾶ καὶ Δαμανοῦ θαυματουργίας . . . ἐν τῷ ἁγίῳ τούτων ναῷ ἀναγινωcκομένας ἀκούcας, καὶ τὰς καθ' ἑκάστην ἡμέραν τε καὶ ὥραν γινομένας ἰάceιc ἀκούω, τὰς μέν παρ αὐτῶν τῶν ἰαθέντων, τὰς δὲ παρὰ τῶν αὐτοπτῶν καὶ ὑπηρετῶν γενομένων τῶν θεραπευθέντων).

On the anniversaries of these saints, individuals who had been healed in earlier years presented themselves and gave public testimony (*Mir.* 41.30–33, p. 200 D).

24. "Clemens," *Homiliae* 12.23.6–8 (pp. 185, 18–186, 3) = *Recognitiones* 7.23.5–7 (pp. 207, 24–208); *Recognitiones* 10.68–72 (pp. 369–71).

25. Ach. Tat. 8.5.1, κἀγὼ πάντα τὰ κατὰ τὴν ἀποδημίαν τὴν ἀπὸ Τύρου διηγοῦμαι κτλ; 15.3, ἡ Λευκίππη δὲ . . . τὰ cυμβάντα μετὰ ἡδονῆς διηγεῖτο.

26. "Clemens," *Homiliae* 12.8–10 (pp. 177, 21–179, 15); cf. *Recognitiones* 7.8–10 (pp. 200, 26–202, 9); *Homiliae,* 12.15–18 (pp. 181, 8–183, 12, Mattidia); cf. *Recognitiones* 7.15–18 (pp. 203, 23–205, 23); *Homiliae* 13.7–8 (pp. 196, 13–197, 18, Niketes-Faustinus); cf. *Recognitiones* 7.32–33 (pp. 212, 19–213, 15); *Homiliae* 14.7 (pp. 207, 19–208, 16, Faustus); cf. *Recognitiones* 9.33 (p. 319, 18–29).

27. An example pertaining to the confession: in the encomium for Saint Therapon, "one conducted [a woman] to Saint Therapon, and she acknowledged her transgression and repented" (προcήνεγκαν τῷ ἁγίῳ Θεράποντι ἐξομολογουμένην τὸ πλημμελὲς καὶ ἀναγορεύουcαν), and the saint healed her (L. Deubner, *De incubatione capita quattor* [Leipzig, 1900], 131). The title of the Jewish novel about Joseph and Aseneth is ἐξομολόγηcιc καὶ μετάνοια Ἀcενεθ.

28. Parodistic confessions: see *POxy.* 3010 (Iolaus romance) and Petronius 130 and

Reinhold Merkelbach

132, with the remarks of O. Raith, "Unschuldsbeteuerung und Sündenbekenntnis im Gebet des Enkolp an Priap," *Studii clasice* 13 (1971): 109–25.

29. For paintings and painted cycles in temples and churches, see Longus, *Daphnis and Chloe;* Prudentius, *Peristephanon* 9; Tibullus 1.3.27f. (the poet asks for divine help): "Nunc dea nunc succurre mihi; nam posse mederi / picta docet templis multa tabella tuis." Juvenal 12.25–28 on shipwreck: "Cetera sortis / eiusdem pars dira quidem, sed cognita multis / et quam votiva testantur fana tabella / plurima: Pictores quis nescit ab iside pasci?" Cf. Schol. ad loc. "Tabella": "Quam naufragio liberati ponunt. antiquitus enim solebant qui naufragio liberati essent pro voto pingere tabellas et in templi Isidis ponere." At Amasea (Pontus), there was a picture cycle referring to the martyrdom of Saint Euphemia; see the oration by Asterius of Amasea, *Euphémie de Chalcédoine,* ed. F. Halkin (Brussels, 1965), 1–8.

30. See R. Merkelbach, *Roman und Mysterium in der Antike* (Munich, 1962), 234–98.

31. 10.9.1, θαυμασθεὶς πρὸς ἁπάντων . . . ὅτι περ οὕτως ἀκμαῖος ἀνὴρ ἀπείρατος εἴη τῶν Ἀφροδίτης.

32. 10.9.4, θάμβος γοῦν ἅμα πάντας κατέσχε, καὶ βοὴν μίαν ἄσημον μὲν καὶ ἄναρθρον, δηλωτικὴν δὲ τοῦ θαύματος ἐπήχησαν.

33. 10.12.1, τοῦ δὲ θαυμάζοντος κτλ.

34. See also the Sarapis aretalogy about legal proceedings, discussed above.

35. 10.13.1, θάμβος.

36. 10.18.1, ὁ σοφὸς Cιcιμίθρης ἐμαρτύρησεν (with reference to the preceding 10.14).

37. 10.15.1, κρότον καὶ θόρυβον, . . . (πάντων) ἐκπλαγέντων . . . τὸν Ὑδάσπην . . . θαύματος ἐχόμενον.

38. 10.16.3 (τὸν δῆμον) ἠχήν τέ τινα θεσπεσίαν ἄχρις αἰθέρος αἴροντας.

39. 10.16.4, ὦ παρόντες. Cf. above, οἱ παρόντες in the aretalogy of the helmsman Syrion.

40. 10.16.6, θαυματουργοῦντες. The θαυματουργία of Cosmas and Damianus is often mentioned in the collections of miracles worked by these saints; cf. no. 1.64 (p. 101 Deubner), 3.3 (p. 104), 9.77 (p. 117).

41. 10.17.1, τὸ δὲ πλῆθος τῶν Αἰθιόπων ἐσείσθη πρὸς τὰ εἰρημένα, καὶ . . . μέγα τι καὶ ἀθρόον ἐξέκραγεν "σῶζε τὴν κόεην" ἀναβοῶντες κτλ.

42. See the references in E. Peterson, ΕΙΣ ΘΕΟΣ, 141–45, and T. Klauser, *Reallexikon für Antike und Christentum* (Stuttgart, 1950), 216–33.

43. 10.17.3, τοὺς δήμους ἐπαλλήλοις ταῖς ἐκβοήσεσι χρονιώτερον ἐντρυφῶντας καὶ ταῖς εὐφημίαις ἀγερωχότερον ἐπισκιρτῶνας.

44. Cassius Dio concludes a description of an acclamation at the horse races in the Roman circus with the following words: "From some divine influence they were enthusiastically infused by a god; otherwise it would not have been possible that so many thousands of people could begin to shout out the same words simultaneously as though they were a trained choir, and that they could pronounce these words all without any mistake as if they had learned them before" (75.4.6, p. 342 Boissevain, οὐ γὰρ ἂν ἄλλως τοσαῦται μυριάδες ἀνθρώπων οὔτε ἤρξαντο τὰ αὐτὰ ἅμα ἀναβοᾶν ὥσπερ τις ἀκριβῶς χορὸς δεδιδαγμένος οὔτ᾽ εἶπον αὐτὰ ἀπταίστως ὡς καὶ μεμελετημένα).

45. 10.18.3, τοῖς κατὰ σαυτὴν διηγήμασι.

46. 10.29.4 (Persinna to Chariclea): ἐξαγόρευε; 33.4, εἴ μοι . . . ἐξαγορεύειν βούλοιο. Cf. 18.2 (Theagenes is supposed to confess). In 38.2, Chariclea has already confessed everything to her mother (ἄρτι μοι . . . ἐκείνης . . . ἐξαγορευσάσης).

47. 10.33.4, πρὸς τὰ καιριώτερα τῶν διηγημάτων ὥρμησεν.

48. 10.29.5, πρὸς γυμνὴν δὲ λοιπὸν καὶ ἀπαρακάλυπτον χωρεῖν τὴν ἐμαυτῆς κατηγορίαν ἀναγκάζομαι; 10.30.1, τὰ ὄντα ἀνακαλύπτειν.

49. 10.30.5, ἡ τοῦ δήμου βοὴ . . . τὸ θαῦμα ἐξεφώνει.
50. 10.32.3, μιᾶς δὴ οὖν βοῆς . . . ὑπὸ τοῦ πλήθους ἀρθείσης.
51. 10.35.2, θαυμάζοντες; 10.36.1, ἐξετίθετο, he narrates.
52. 10.37.1, ἀληθῆ . . . τὰ κατηγορηθέντα.
53. 10.38.3, ὁ δῆμος . . . cὺν εὐφήμοις ταῖς βοαῖς ἐξεχόρευε.
54. 10.39.3, αἰcθανώμεθα τοῦ θείου θαυματουργήματος. Mention was made of the miraculous workings of the gods in 10.16.6.
55. ὦ παρόντες, as in 10.16.4.
56. 10.40.1, θεῶν νεύματι τούτων οὕτω διαπεπραγμένων τὸ ἀντιβαίνειν ἀθέμιτον, ὥστε ὑπὸ μάρτυσιν αὐτοῖς τε τοῖς ταῦτα ἐπικλώcαcι καὶ ὑμῖν ἀκόλουθα ἐκείνοις φρονεῖν ἐνδεικνυμένοις.
57. 10.41.1, ἐπευφήμηcεν ὁ cτρατός, καὶ τῶν χειρῶν . . . ἐπεκτύπηcαν. Cf. the description of the marriage shortly thereafter (10.41.3): cὺν εὐφημίαιc καὶ κρότοιc καὶ χοροῖc . . . παρεπέμποντο.

CHAPTER SIXTEEN

The Social World of the *Acts of Peter*

Judith Perkins

Societies are characterized by competing relations of power, but, distanced by history, cultures often appear univocal. Either only the discourse produced by the dominant culture is left or, dulled by time, our ears are not keen enough to overhear the competing strains. Such a situation adversely affects the understanding and tracing of social change over time. It is by good fortune, therefore, that, from the social body known as the Roman Empire, narratives remain that embody the voices—the values and passions—of alienated groups at the brink of momentous change.

I maintain that in the so-called *Apocryphal Acts of the Apostles,* signs and strategies of an emerging representational and social challenge are preserved. These texts, the *Acts of John, Peter, Paul, Andrew,* and *Thomas,* were composed over a range of geographical locations in Greece, Asia Minor, and Syria in the second and early third centuries.[1] Each exhibits a similar plot line, tracing the adventures, preaching, and death of a particular apostle. Their content may well reflect oral material circulating widely among early Christian communities. And their form, as has been noted, recalls the ancient novel, for the prose narratives of the *Acts* and the novel share an emphasis on adventures and trials, on travel, on the marvelous.[2] The connection may be more substantive than these coincidences of plot. Studies of the ancient novel have explained the emergence and popularity of these fictive prose narratives by pointing to new and changed social needs; for example, a new rootlessness in the Hellenistic world, or the rise of the individual, or a new search for meaning.[3] Recently Averil Cameron has discussed the *Apocryphal Acts* in related terms as narratives that build and maintain group structures.[4] There is growing recognition that, notwithstanding the similar or separate origins or influences traced for the ancient novel and the *Acts,* the stories people choose to tell about themselves work to construct and define both their being and their being in the world.[5]

Thus, the *Apocryphal Acts* ought to provide evidence for the mental categories and sense-making efforts of communities in the early empire. But until recently the *Acts* have been largely ignored, by religious scholars because of their fictiveness (and heresy, in some cases) and by literary historians because of their Christian content.[6] It is now time to integrate their testimony into a less artificially partitioned picture of the early empire. Their witness becomes increasingly important as the recognition grows that the ancient novel was not, as earlier scholars had claimed, written by and for the unsophisticated.[7] The *Apocryphal Acts* preserve rare access to examples of a popular narrative voice.

This study will concentrate on the *Acts of Peter,* a text very likely written in Asia Minor in the late second century.[8] The plot of this narrative is simple. The apostle Paul departs from Rome, leaving his flock vulnerable to his rival, Simon, who calls himself "the great Power of God" (48.22). Nearly the whole congregation apostatizes; only a few believers and the housebound sick remain true (49.16). Finally Peter arrives, promising to reclaim the converts through his "deeds and marvelous powers" (54.26–27). Peter challenges Simon to a contest in raising the dead. Stands are erected and a fee charged (69.32, 70.28), and, in front of a great crowd, Peter performs three resurrections. Simon betrays himself to be a sorcerer; he does kill one man with a whisper, but is only able to invest a single corpse with the merest traces of life—a raised head and blinking eyes (76.1–2). The defeated Simon finally flies away but falls from the sky as a result of Peter's prayers and breaks his leg in three places. One of Simon's followers provides the moral for the action: "Simon, if the Power of God is broken, shall not the God himself, whose power you are, be proven an illusion?" (84.1–2). Peter quickly gains converts, and the text concludes with his condemnation by officials annoyed at losing their sexual partners because of his preaching on continence, his crucifixion, burial, and return in two dream visitations.

The *Acts* is not a simple religious text, focused on Christian morality, or hopes for immortality, or some other such homiletic orthodoxy, but rather a text with an implicit social agenda. Even as the *Acts* affirms the superior healing prowess of the Christian community and shows suffering as profitable, it challenges the power and routes to power inhering in the surrounding culture. In the early empire, religion and politics often shared the same discourse.[9]

Readers of the *Acts* live in an upside-down world—a world of reversed values and forms. Peter's explanation of his desire for an upside-down crucifixion defines this world.[10] He wishes to die upside-down because Adam's birth "established the whole of this cosmic system . . . and changed all the signs of their nature, so as to consider fair those things that were not fair, and take those that were really evil to be good. Concerning this the Lord says in a mystery, 'Unless you make what is on the right hand as what is on the left . . . and what is above as what is below and what is behind as what is before, you will not recognize the kingdom'" (94.5–15). This is a message with obvious radical social overtones if taken in a "this world" sense; other textual elements suggest that taking it so in this text would not be a misreading.

The *Acts* plainly represents that the wrong leaders are on top in this world. In a work so emphatically centered on mercy and multiple forgiveness, Nero is portrayed quite harshly.[11] Early in the text, he is called (on good authority, a voice from heaven), a "godless and wicked man" (46.9). He exposes his wicked nature again after Peter's martyrdom when he is angry because "he would have liked to punish him [Peter] more cruelly and with extra severity" (100.17–18). But Nero is no match for a Peter perfected by death. The apostle appears to the emperor in a dream, scourges him, and says: "Nero, you cannot now persecute or destroy the servants of Christ. Keep your hands from them!" (102.2–3). This dream embodies a powerfully subversive image—the emperor enduring a servile punishment as well as an inversion of reality: martyrs on occasion were tortured and put to death at imperial festivals.[12] Peter's triumph over the emperor could not be clearer: "And so Nero, being greatly alarmed because of this vision, kept away from the disciples from the time that Peter departed this life" (102.4–6).

In this way, Peter decisively removes Nero as a threat to his community. It is a bold move. The person of the emperor and his imperial cult were critical in articulating power relations in the Greek East. And yet even earlier than this in the *Acts,* a statue of the emperor is destroyed, kicked to pieces by a demon exorcised by Peter. Marcellus, a senator and the owner of the statue, is terrified, and with good reason. There is evidence that a citizen was executed merely for urinating near an imperial statue; Dio of Prusa was harassed for burying his wife and son in the courtyard of a building that contained an imperial statue.[13] In the *Acts,* Peter calms Marcellus, telling him that if he really believes in Christ he can restore the statue by sprinkling it with water. "And Marcellus did not doubt," the narrator says, "but believed with his whole heart," and in this way successfully reformed the statue, averting harm from himself (59.19). Simon Price has demonstrated how the imperial cult reinforced the charisma of the emperor and his government.[14] Yet the action of this scene deflates the constitutive power surrounding the cult; it displays that with belief in the Lord and trust in his leaders, the imperial statue is in reality just "stones" (*lapides istos,* 59.23).

Moreover, a redundant complex of images in both these scenes hints at what is understood to be deficient in the imperial power. Marcellus's hands are repeatedly referred to throughout the statue scene: "Marcellus also was uplifted in spirit, because this first miracle was done by his hands" (59.39). Throughout the text, the healing or helping hand of the Christian community is emphasized. When Peter meets a blind widow he gives her his hand and tells her, "Jesus gives you his right hand . . . and he says to you through me, 'Open your eyes and see and walk on your own.' And at once the widow saw Peter laying his hand on her" (66.18–25). Peter himself had experienced this helping hand; when he was struck down and blinded at the Transfiguration, the Lord gave him his hand and lifted him up (*et dans mihi manum elevavit me*, 67.16–17). This complex of images woven throughout the *Acts* suggests that help was not seen to be provided by the hostile hands of the emperor or the rule he embodied. In its depiction of the emperor, the *Acts* projects one aspect of the world that is upside down (what is above that should not be) and at the same time strikes out at two central supports of any political culture—deference to superior authority and the state religion.

The fiction of the *Acts* allows its audience to imagine the function of the senatorial class in its community—not a likely scenario in this period.[15] Once again, what is above should not be. The high birth of Marcellus, the Christian senator, makes it harder, not easier, for him to help his community. Save that his conversion and reconversion affect many dependents, Marcellus is not an untypical convert. First he was converted by Paul, only to be seduced away by Simon; then, like others, he was reconverted by Peter's signs and wonders, in his case a talking dog sent by the apostle to castigate Simon.[16] But the text underlines an inherent weakness in the senator.[17] On the night before Peter's decisive contest with Simon, Marcellus has a dream. In this he sees Peter and before him a woman, "all black, . . . dancing, with an iron collar around her neck and chains on her hands and feet. When you saw her you said aloud to me, 'Marcellus, the whole power of Simon and of his god is in this dancer; take off her head!' But I said to you, 'Brother Peter, I am a senator of noble family, and I have never stained my hands, nor killed even a sparrow at any time'" (70.9–15).

A likeness of Peter has to do the deed. The text clearly locates Marcellus's weakness and his inability to protect the community from Satan in his class consciousness. Marcellus errs again later in the *Acts* and, again, it is his status that betrays him. After Peter dies, Marcellus takes him down from the cross: "He washed him in milk and wine; and he ground up seven pounds of mastic, and also fifty pounds of myrrh and aloe and spice and embalmed his body, and filled a trough of stone of great value with Attic honey and laid it in his own burial vault" (100.1–5). Yet Marcellus gets no praise for his devotion and expense. Instead, Peter returns from the beyond to reprimand him: "Marcellus, you heard the Lord saying, 'Let the dead be buried by the dead?'" (100.6–7). He rejects Marcellus's actions;

actions, it should be noted, that include the most typical of his class—the ostentatious display of his wealth.[18] Peter reminds us that the Lord's words now direct Marcellus even with respect to how he spends his wealth. The source of Marcellus's error is clearly articulated: he acted without "taking anyone's advice, since it was not allowed" (98.16). The text repeats its basic point, that the requisites of Marcellus's high position disabled him and prevented his acquiring the knowledge he needed to act correctly.

The same message about the detriment of high birth reappears in the characterization of another highborn character, Agrippa. Before his crucifixion, Peter begs his followers not to be angry at Agrippa, "for he is the servant of his father's influence (90.16–17). Vouaux thought this phrase (*patrikês energeias*) referred to Satan, but the Latin translator who explains *traditionis illius* understood it better. Agrippa is constrained from seeing his error by his lineage and his tradition. Through Marcellus, who cannot act to kill Satan, and Agrippa, who acts badly in killing Peter, the *Acts* reveals leaders who must be rejected for the same reasons the surrounding pagan political culture must admire them. The phrase "like his ancestors" can be found in numerous honorific inscriptions throughout the Greek East.[19] In the surrounding pagan culture, high birth helped ensure leadership.

The dream reproach Peter issues to Marcellus, his assumption that Marcellus's actions, even his expenditures, are under the control of the Lord's word, has important implications, especially linked as it is in the *Acts* to a more radical redirection of patronage. In feudal societies, it has been suggested, power functioned essentially through signs and levies;[20] in the early Roman Empire power functioned through signs (such as the rites and ceremonies of the imperial cult) and through the public patronage of the upper classes. Individuals spent lavishly in their quest for *philotimia,* for honor and prestige. The importance of this kind of expenditure cannot be overstated. Cities prospered through the expenditures of the wealthy; money, buildings, entertainment, supplies, and services were all donated by wealthy individuals. Cities responded with public testimonials of thanks. Such patronage is, as Paul Veyne has noted, at base a sign of an unequal distribution of power—"I give because you cannot."[21] When a group consistently displayed its superiority by such means, it acted as a political class.[22] Patronage should be recognized as a political act. Veyne shows how the numerous honors voted by cities to their benefactors (in the empire, most conspicuously the emperor, the governor, and other notables) proclaimed for all to see what the established order was.[23] Patronage was one of the means by which those on top manifested their power and dominance, and it is in this context that the repetitious emphasis on patronage in the *Acts* needs to be considered.

Robert Stoops has examined the operation and importance of patronage in the *Acts;*[24] I would like to link his conclusions to the themes of power I see in the text. Stoops notes the repeated occasions of patronage shown in the text. Both the resurrected senator and his mother, for example, are patrons: "She came to Marcellus' house bringing Peter two thousand pieces of gold and saying to Peter, 'Divide these among the virgins of Christ who serve him.' But when the boy who had risen from the dead saw that he had given nothing to anyone, he went home and opened his chest and himself brought four thousand gold pieces" (79.8–13). Such large amounts of money, in fact, may not be so inflated for a cure. Galen received the very substantial sum of forty thousand sesterces for his cure of Boethus's wife, and there is evidence that a doctor "would have been rich for life if he had made a particularly successful cure."[25] Eubula also acts as a patron after her stolen goods are restored: "But Eubula having recovered all her property gave it for the care of the poor . . . and despising and renouncing the world she gave [alms] to the widows and orphans and clothed the poor" (65.19–23). Peter even accepts the donation of a notoriously rich and adulterous woman, Chryse, rejecting the advice that he not accept such money: "But Peter, when he heard this, laughed and said to the brethren, I do not know what this woman is as regards her usual way of life; in taking her money I did not take it without reason; for she was bringing it as a debtor to Christ, and is giving it to Christ's servants; for he himself has provided for them" (80.10–14).

Patronage is an important theme in the *Acts,* where Christ is offered as the ultimate source of all blessings. No longer are wealthy human patrons honored for their largess. This narrative enterprise depriving patrons of their honor ought to be understood as a political act, just as bestowing honors on benefactors was. If, as Veyne maintains, the honors shown benefactors publicly project the established order, redirecting such recognition to another entity not only destabilizes the established order, but erects a competing order in its place. The characterization of patronage in the *Acts* supports the narrative's critique of the surrounding political culture.

In this way the *Acts* replaces prevailing pagan social institutions with a Christian community. When "the only person explicitly called a patron in the *Acts,*"[26] Marcellus, buried Peter, he acted as a typical member of his class; he demonstrated his wealth by his display of his riches. The text's specificity (seven pounds of mastic, fifty pounds of myrrh) reflects the culture's avid interest in accounting for such details. It surprises us at first that Marcellus's action, seemingly harmless and done out of love, is serious enough to warrant Peter's return from the beyond. That it does alerts us to the importance of the apostle's message: wealth is no longer in the control of the wealthy, but susceptible to Christ's word and control. Stoops interprets this scene as showing that "the wealth of believers is to be used to benefit others. The honor it brings belongs to Christ."[27] In the

Roman world, honor shows power, and our text is quite explicit about who this Christ is to whom honor is due. Peter experienced Christ at the Transfiguration and describes him—he "who is both great and little, beautiful and ugly, young and old, . . . beauteous [*speciosum*], yet appearing among us poor and ugly [*humilem*]" (69.18–19). Similarly the widows see the Lord in many forms, *quomodo alias et alias dominum viderint* (69.18–19).[28]

These descriptions suggest that the "polymorphic" Christ embodies in himself a utopian community, a mingling of classes diverging almost totally from the reality of the second century where status was being increasingly delineated in law, and contempt for the vulgus by the well-born was nearly universal.[29]

Some of the vocabulary used to describe Christ, in fact, belongs to the socially stratifying vocabulary of the period.[30] One can almost hear in the depiction of Christ as both *speciosum* and *humilem* the defiance and desire for recognition of those who, like this Christ, may appear low and base to those, in this world of reversed values, on top, but who value themselves as somehow beautiful—*speciosum*. By presenting this Christ, who is a hypostatized and utopian image of the community, the *Acts* betrays its sense that the community itself as well as its Lord deserves power and honor.

The text's repeated financial references also suggest that the *Acts* issued from a community interested in constructing an alternative social structure. Attention to finances seems almost obsessive in the *Acts;* few scenes have no financial references. Some of these perform a narrative function. In the Coptic fragment, for example, Ptolemy, saved from his lust by the fortuitous paralysis of Peter's daughter, leaves her a bequest. This scene serves to depict Peter, a church leader, as a good money manager and trusty dispenser of charity: "He bequeathed a piece of land in the name of my daughter . . . But I being given this trust, executed it with care . . . I sold the land, and kept back none of the price of the land but gave all the money to the poor" (P.8502). Similarly, the Chryse episode (where Peter accepts a contribution from a notorious woman) establishes that money may be accepted from any benefactor, if it is used for the community's good.

But the reader also learns a number of seemingly gratuitous financial details; that, for example, the converted ship captain had to stay and sell his cargo before following Peter to Rome (53.11–12), that a fee was charged to see the contest between Peter and Simon (70.28), that the widows received a gold piece for gathering at Marcellus's house (66.15). The value of Eubula's stolen property is precisely described (63.18–20). We are told of Nero's anger at Marcellus for planning to use his money to help Christians, and Marcellus is himself depicted as angry that he wasted his money on Christians after his conversion by Simon, and so on throughout the text (55.5–18). The *Acts* is thick with references to money. Like the references to the emperor and patronage, this emphasis on money is also part of the social web of meaning in the text. There are no more powerful signifiers for social networks than sexuality and property. With respect to the former, Peter Brown recently has demonstrated the strong social significance of the Church's call for continence in the early empire. By ending sexual congress, Christians displayed their hopes for ending the contemporary society.[31] The emphasis on continence is not so pervasive in the *Acts of Peter* as it is in many of the other *Apocryphal Acts,* but it was the effect of Peter's preaching on continence—"many other women besides fell in love with the doctrine of purity and separated from their husbands, and men too ceased to sleep with their wives" (86.8–11)—that resulted in his martyrdom.

Sharing with other Christian groups the goal of ending contemporary society, the community of the *Acts of Peter,* through its repeated emphasis on money and property, also envisions the construction of an alternate society in its place. Property as a social or literary signifier acts to represent an extension of the social body; by its nature property allows the body to be extended into social space through accumulation and exchange and through the social and economic interaction involved in such accumulation and exchange.[32] By suffusing the text with financial references, the *Acts* insists on this Christian community's substance, on its determination to have a material existence. When he triumphs over Simon, raising the dead and healing the sick, Peter exhibits Christ's and the community's power; when he transfers control over and the honor due money from the wealthy to Christ (the control being under the direction of Christian leaders), he exhibits a changed social reality to control this power. For centuries the wealthy had manifested their substance and power through patronage. The *Acts* projects a community that by its possession of money and dispensing of it similarly displays its substantive nature and framework for power.[33]

It is difficult to define the actual composition of the community to whom the *Acts* was directed. If one subtracts the senators as unlikely converts, the text mentions the kinds of people other sources have led us to expect—wealthy women, a prison official and his wife, a shipper, an innkeeper, a goldsmith.[34] There is one anomalous social indicator in the text; it contains what Dimitris Kyrtatas has called "the strongest statement in favor of manumission in Christian literature."[35] Before he will resurrect the young senator, Peter persuades the young man's mother to allow the slaves she manumitted on his death to remain free. She agrees and even guarantees to continue to supply their support (77.13–15). Peter explains his request: "For I know that some will feel injured on seeing your son restored to life, because these men will become his slaves once again" (77.8–10). "Some" (*quorundam*)—freedmen, perhaps, who would be able to identify with the blow of being freed and then having freedom snatched back. The detailed description of the revenge that Marcellus's slaves worked on Simon similarly shows a sympathy for the sensibilities of slaves. This sympathy for the underclasses seems fitting in a text that affirms its belief in a "carpenter and son of a carpenter" (71.24–25); as Peter insists, "none of you should expect another [saviour] than him who was despised and mocked by the Jews" (54.28–29).

The *Acts of Peter* seems to reflect a group that would have little difficulty feeling allegiance with a craftsman, a carpenter. By its rejection of the emperor, his cult, and the natural leadership of the upper classes, and through its revised notion of patronage, the *Acts* reflects an estrangement from the surrounding political and social culture that devalued classes other than the wealthy and the wellborn. The *Acts* seems written for a community that connected religion with a social and political agenda. In the *Acts of Peter* we overhear, I suggest, a group that proves the validity of the anachronistic warning Dio Cassius puts into the mouth of Maecenas: "Do not, therefore, permit anyone to be an atheist or a sorcerer . . . For such men, by speaking the truth sometimes, but greatly falsehood, often encourage a great many to attempt revolutions" (52.36).[36] If not revolution, at least change. The *Acts* displays an ease with the notion of forms broken, being reformed, and existing anew—a statue shattered and re-fashioned; a dried fish revivified, swimming again; three dead men resurrected. Such repeated images not only represent but make conceivable the possibility of radical change—embodying a promise of reformation and restructuring after what appeared to be destruction. The social and political implications are plain.

There is evidence for an audience ready for such a message in Asia Minor, the most likely location for the *Acts'* genesis.[37] The *Orations* of Dio of Prusa, for example, testify to social and political unrest and factionalism throughout the region, unrest precisely among those groups receiving attention in the *Acts of Peter*—artisans and tradespeople.[38] Rioting as a form of collective action manifests strains in a society and a challenge to existing social and political systems.[39] Thus the rioting that contemporary sources testify to corroborates the existence of the social strains we have seen articulated in the *Acts,* and these pressures perhaps explain the challenge to the contemporary operating systems of power that are implicit in the *Acts*.

The *Acts* is very much a radical document. It works to construct a new site of power in the culture—the Christian community—whose superior healing powers manifest its strength. The *Acts* then displays a Christian community intent to separate out and constitute new categories of people for social attention: the poor, the sick, the suffering. These new categories call forth new social structures to contain and deliver Christian power. (It is around just such categories that Christianity's later social and political power would grow.) Such a message plainly contests the prevailing systems of power.

For the *Acts of Peter* to be both a religious tract and a social and political text is not a particularly unusual occurrence in the context of the early empire. Political subversion rather routinely operated under the guise of pagan religiosity in the provinces, as G. W. Bowersock has shown,[40] and Simon Price has established the close connection between the exercise of political power and the operation of the imperial cult. Fictive prose narratives may have been particularly amenable to combining within themselves such various levels of signification. Reinhold Merkelbach has suggested that many of the ancient novels, apparently entertaining secular texts, may, in fact, embody the ritual concerns of contemporary mystery religions.[41] My reading of the *Acts of Peter* would seem to lend support to Merkelbach's supposition, demonstrating that related prose narratives likewise join the religious and the secular. As Merkelbach reads the ancient novels as religious texts, so I have contended that the *Acts of Peter,* a religious text, should be read as projecting a social and political agenda. It is part of the rhetoric of Christianity to separate the religious and the political, but in the early Roman Empire this rhetoric had not yet prevailed, and its assumptions should not be allowed to constrict our reading of the prose narratives of the period.

NOTES

1. E. Hennecke, *New Testament Apocrypha,* ed. W. Schneemelcher, trans. R. M. Wilson, vol. 2 (Philadelphia, 1965), has a discussion of dating and location of composition. See also S. L. Davies, *The Revolt of the Widows* (Carbondale, Ill., 1980), 3–10.

2. R. Söder, *Die apokryphen Apostelgeschichten und der romanhafte Literatur der Antike* (Stuttgart, 1932). R. Pervo, *Profit with Delight: The Literary Genre of the Acts of the Apostles* (Philadelphia, 1987), 86–135, examines the relationship between the forms of the ancient novel and the *Acts,* both canonical and apocryphal. Cf. A. Cameron, *Christianity and the Rhetoric of Empire* (Berkeley and Los Angeles, 1991), 117–18.

3. B. Reardon, *Courants littéraires grecs des IIe et IIIe siècles* (Paris, 1971); T. Hägg, *The Novel in Antiquity* (Berkeley and Los Angeles, 1983). For a valuable discussion of the ancient novel, see E. L. Bowie, "The Greek Novel," in *The Cambridge History of Classical Literature,* vol. 1, Greek Literature, ed. P. E. Easterling and B. M. W. Knox (Cambridge, 1985), 683–99.

4. Cameron, *Christianity,* 116.

5. V. Turner, "Social Dramas and Stories about Them," *Critical Inquiry* 7 (1980): 141–68; F. Kermode, *The Genesis of Secrecy: On the Interpretation of Narrative* (Cambridge, Mass., 1979).

6. J. D. Kaestli, "Les principales orientations de la recherche sur les actes apocryphes des Apôtres," in *Les actes apocryphes des Apôtres*, ed. F. Bovon, Publication de la faculté de théologie de l'université de Genève no. 4 (Geneva, 1981), 49–67.

7. D. Levin, "To Whom Did the Ancient Novelists Address Themselves?" *Rivista studios classicos* 25 (1977): 18–29; B. P. Reardon, "The Second Sophistic and the Novel," in *Approaches to the Second Sophistic,* ed. G. W. Bowersock (University Park, Pa., 1974), 23–29.

8. *Acta apostolorum apocrypha,* ed. R. Lipsius and M. Bonnet (Leipzig, 1891–1903; reprint, Darmstadt, 1959). Translations are from Hennecke and Schneemelcher, *New Testament Apocrypha.* Text references are to the edition of Lipsius and Bonnet by page and line number. Cf. Leon Vouaux, *Les Actes de Pierre: Introduction, textes, traduction et commentaire* (Paris, 1922); R. Stoops, Jr., "Miracle Stories and Vision Reports in the *Acts of Peter*" (Ph.D. diss., Harvard University, 1982); Stoops, "Patronage in the *Acts of Peter,*" *Semeia* 38 (1986): 91–100; Stoops, "Christ as Patron in the *Acts of Peter,*" *Semeia* 56 (1992), appeared too late to be included in my discussion. For place and date, see G. Ficker, *Die Petrusakten* (Leipzig, 1903), 37–40, and Vouaux, *Les Actes de Pierre,* 200–214. For discussion of the Latin text, see C. H. Turner, "The Latin Acts of Peter," *Journal of Theological Studies* 32 (1931): 118–33.

9. S. Price, *Rituals and Power: The Roman Imperial Cult in Asia Minor* (Cambridge, 1984), 235.

10. J. Smith, "Birth Upside Down or Right Side Up!" *History of Religions* 9 (1969–70): 281–303. P. Brown, *The Body and Society* (New York, 1988), 106, discusses this type of cosmic dimension.

11. For the emphasis on multiple forgiveness, see 47.20–23, 54.5–6, 58.6–8.

12. For degradation of corporal punishment, see P. Garnsey, *Social Status and Legal Privilege in the Roman Empire* (Oxford, 1970), 104, 136, 138, 139; see Price, *Rituals and Power,* 124, for imperial festivals.

13. For urination, see Price, *Rituals and Power,* 195, citing *Historia Augusta, Caracalla* 5.7; for Dio, see Pliny, *Ep.* 10.81, and C. P. Jones, *The Roman World of Dio Chrysostom* (Cambridge, Mass., 1978), 114. Celsus accuses Christians of destroying statues of divinities to show their powerlessness (Origen, *Contra Celsum* 8.38).

14. Price, *Rituals and Power,* 191–206.

15. A. H. M. Jones, "The Social Background of the Struggle between Paganism and Christianity," in *The Conflict between Paganism and Christianity,* ed. A. Momigliano (Oxford, 1973), 17.

16. Stoops, "Patronage," 97. Stoops's discussion of Marcellus is quite complete; I have only one addition. Stoops faults Marcellus's supposed belief that he can buy salvation through money. I do not find this disapproved of in the text. Rather, the text seems to share Clement of Alexander's suggestion that dispensing money is a good way of finding divine favor: "O excellent tradings! O divine merchandise. One purchases immortality for money, and by giving perishing things of the world, receives in exchange for these an eternal mansion" (*Quis dives salvetur* 32).

17. Stoops, "Patronage," 98.

18. Vouaux, *Les Actes de Pierre,* 461 n. 3, believes this scene primarily reflects the text's distaste for the corporeal.

19. R. MacMullen, *Roman Social Relations* (New Haven, 1974), 101; see also Garnsey, *Social Status,* 229.

20. M. Foucault, "Truth and Power," in *The Foucault Reader,* ed. Paul Rabinow (New York, 1984), 66.

21. P. Veyne, *Bread and Circuses,* trans. B. Pearce, (London, 1990), xiv.

22. Ibid., 105.

23. Ibid., 125.

24. Stoops articulates an overview of patronage in the *Acts* and also at least suggests the existence of an incipient social structure underlying the action ("Miracle Stories," 317).

25. *On Prognosis,* ed. and trans. V. Nutton, *Corpus mediocorum Graecorum* 5.8.1 (Berlin, 1979), 180. The sums of money expressed, however, seem more likely to be round numbers, to convey a general sense of large amounts of money, as is often the case in Latin novels. Cf. R. Duncan-Jones, *The Economy of the Roman Empire* (Cambridge, 1974), 238–59.

26. Stoops, "Patronage," 96 (*Acts* 55.4).

27. Ibid., 98.

28. D. R. Cartlidge, "Transfigurations of Metamorphosis Traditions in the *Acts of John, Thomas, Peter,*" *Semeia* 38 (1986): 53–66. He calls attention to the "sense of inclusiveness in the polymorphic Christology of the APt." (63).

29. For widespread contempt for the lowly, see MacMullen, *Roman Social Relations.* Cf. Celsus's attitude in Origen (*Contra Celsum* 3.52–55). Dio Chrysostom's comments in *Or.* 7.115 and 65.7 reflect this contempt.

30. MacMullen, *Roman Social Relations* 109; Garnsey, *Social Status,* 221–33.

31. Brown, *Body and Society,* 64, and J. Perkins, "The Apocryphal Acts of the Apostles and Early Christian Martyrdom," *Arethusa* 15 (1985): 211–30.

32. D. Chidester, *Salvation and Suicide* (Bloomington, Ind., 1988), 97.

33. Stoops, "Miracle Stories," 317.

34. W. Meeks, *The First Urban Christians* (New Haven, 1983), 51–73; D. Kyrtatas, *The Social Structure of Early Christian Communities* (London, 1987), 183.

35. Kyrtatas, *Social Structure,* 66; for Christian attitudes toward slaves and freedmen, 25–74.

36. Cf. A. Momigliano, "The Disadvantage of Monotheism for a Universal State," *Classical Philology* 81 (1986): 285–97. For the relevance of this speech to Dio's time, cf. F. Millar, *A Study of Cassius Dio* (Oxford, 1964), 104.

37. D. Magie, *Roman Rule in Asia Minor to the End of the Third Century after Christ,* 2 vols. (Princeton, 1950), 1:600, 635; S. Dickey, "Some Economic Conditions of Asia Minor Affecting the Expansion of Christianity," in *Studies in Early Christianity,* ed. S. J. Case (New York, 1928), 402–15. For the idea that Christians could be seen as belonging to such alienated groups, see *Contra Celsum* 1.1.

38. Dio of Prusa 34.16ff., 19ff.

39. N. J. Smelser, *Theory of Collective Behavior* (New York, 1963).

40. G. W. Bowersock, "The Mechanics of Subversion in the Roman Provinces," in *Opposition et résistances a l'empire d'Auguste à Trajan,* ed. A. Giovannini (Geneva, 1987), 291–317.

41. R. Merkelbach, *Roman und Mysterium in der Antike* (Munich, 1962). Merkelbach's views have been much contested, but the place of religion in the ancient novel is clearly an important one.

CHAPTER SEVENTEEN

Ancient and Contemporary in Byzantine Novels

Suzanne MacAlister

A total of nine novels or romances[1]—in complete or fragmentary form—survive from the Greek world of the Middle Ages. These were composed during the period dating from the first half of the 1100s to around 1453 (when Constantinople fell to the Ottoman Turks). Eleventh-century Constantinople had heralded the beginning of a climate of intellectual and creative activity, and in the twelfth century we see a learned revival of the novel in literary language,[2] together with the appearance of the Byzantine epic, *Digenis Acritas*.[3] The twelfth-century novels were followed in the thirteenth and fourteenth centuries by others written in the vernacular.[4] Like the novels of the ancient Greek world, the Byzantine examples are concerned with love and adventure; unlike the ancient novels, all but one are in verse.[5]

The works I consider in this chapter are the three complete novels from the learned revival of the genre in the twelfth century, namely, Eustathius Macrembolites' *Hysmine and Hysminias,* Theodore Prodromus's *Rhodanthe and Dosicles,* and Nicetas Eugenianus's *Drosilla and Charicles*[6]—probably all written in the thirties or forties of the century.[7] I attempt to demonstrate that the Byzantine novelists, alienated by time and Christianity from their Hellenic predecessors, adopted the discourse of the ancient pagan novel and, through this, made their own special statements. The discussion focuses on the ways in which these twelfth-century writers used the ancient novelists' conventions relating to nonhuman guidance and relevation and the ways in which they also deployed and manipulated the voices of other diverse alien discourses of their heritage in their appropriation of the genre of the ancient novel. Throughout all these considerations, Bakhtin's concept of "alien speech"—discourse shaped by the perspectives, systems of concepts and values, and language of another[8]—will prove a useful tool for understanding the layers of intertextuality that emerge, and will assist our hearing of these new novels' utterances. I conclude that, while there seem to be strong similarities between the ancient and the revival novels, the revival novels ultimately reflect certain contemporary attitudes rather than the attitudes of antiquity.

The novels of both periods share the theme of love between a young couple who face a prolonged series of trials and adventures, and whose story invariably has a happy ending. These novels express the human and spiritual experience of the ordinary person of the age in which the genre was created.[9] This late-Hellenistic world was one in which isolated private individuals were struggling for control over their lives. People were experiencing themselves as potential victims of chance, and were seeking security and identity either in other human beings or in one or several gods of personal religion.[10] For the Greeks of this early era, then, the novel expressed familiar fears and aspirations.

In the twelfth century the ancient novel was at a peak of popularity it had not enjoyed since its *floruit*.[11] But its new readers' view of the world would have been vastly different than that held by its original readers. The twelfth-century Byzantine could only conceive the late-Hellenistic world of the ancient novel from the contemporary perspective of an "enlightened" Christianity, which provided both social identity and security in the face of the incomprehensible. In twelfth-century Byzantium, the ancient novel was confronting a different consciousness from that of the particular historical moment and socially specific environment in which it had first taken shape and meaning.[12] Some of its elements were in harmony with its new environment (or, with allegorization, could be made so),[13] but others were in dissonance.

The novels of the Byzantine revival take from the ancient novels entire episodes; their writers uproot and insert into their own works passages or phrases from their predecessors and echo their descriptions. Given the renewed popularity of the ancient novel, the novels of the revival would have found readers, many of whom were already familiar with the works of the original genre and would have readily recognized the appropriation. But the Byzantine exercise is not a case of simple mimesis. Simple mimesis takes the object of imitation seriously, makes it its own, and assimilates it.[14] Yet, although the resulting discourse in these new works might appear to be a self-conscious appropriation and reproduction of the ancient novel and its conventions, analysis reveals a shaping and an inversion of the original that are sometimes so subtle that they can only be discerned through close historical and literary commentary.

The Byzantine writers of the genre's revival employ the alien discourse of the earlier novels and direct their own statements toward responses deriving from the specific expectations of their twelfth-century audience. They implant their own intentions in the novels' discourse to make it serve their new aims, and construct their own utterances in the face of their contemporary audience's assumptions. The use of the discourse of the ancient novel in this way provides an ideal example of what Bakhtin would later term "alien speech polemic." With this device, Bakhtin said, "it is not the object that serves as the arena for the encounter, but rather the subjective belief system of the listener."[15]

The challenges produced in the new novels can be both overt and hidden, and a comprehension of the separateness of the two—although the separateness is sometimes difficult to discern—is essential for a more complete understanding of the new novelists' intentions. Here again Bakhtin's conceptual framework proves useful. Bakhtin sees overt polemic (which can still be subtle) as focusing on the alien speech act being refuted; that is, the object of challenge is simply the action being referred to. Hidden polemic, on the other hand, is usually directed at a particular concept or general idea that is denoted or expressed by the alien speech—and only strikes at the alien speech act indirectly, clashing with it on the grounds of what it might symbolize.[16]

One way in which the revival novels confronted both the expectations and the conceptual frameworks of their contemporary audience was by reformulating the ancient novels' use of nonhuman revelation and its effects. In the new novels, as in their ancient predecessors, some nonhuman force—chance, villains, a pagan god—is introduced to randomly disrupt the flow of everyday events. In the ancient novel, dreams provided a foreknowledge or understanding of the working of nonhuman forces; in the Byzantine revival, dreams are also introduced, apparently to provide foreknowledge and understanding. But in the revival works, such supernaturally presented information is constantly made irrelevant. Information provided by nonhuman means either emerges as redundant, is negated somehow by human action, or is rendered as a secondary consideration in the face of human reason or initiative.

Most episodes in the Byzantine novels that relate to the notion of nonhuman understanding or foreknowledge involve a dream or dreaming. Many draw on, or allude to, particular episodes that can be isolated in the ancient novels; others appropriate the ancient genre's conventions. All involve some form of polemic, either overt or hidden.

An example of overt polemic can be isolated in Prodromus's and Eugenianus's adaptation of an episode found in Achilles Tatius's *Leucippe and Clitophon*. There Leucippe had rejected the hero's attempt on her virginity by stating that she had experienced a dream wherein the goddess Artemis had promised her salvation but had ordered her to remain a virgin until their eventual marriage (4.1.4). In Prodromus's and Eugenianus's novels, the women similarly reject the men's attempts on their virginity by arguing that they wished to wait, as their dreams had given them confidence that their trials in foreign lands would eventually come to an end, and that their marriages would take place in their homelands (*RD* 3.66–75; *DC* 8.151–60). Eugenianus's protagonist supplies the additional argument that she could not even conceive of doing such a thing in a foreign land (8.161–62). Both Prodromus's and Eugenianus's dreams fail to include their model's order from the deity that the girl remain a virgin. In the ancient novel, the deity's command had dictated the action immediately following, since it was in obedience to the command that the young man had abandoned his amorous intentions. By substituting human factors and reasons for a pagan god's intervention, Eugenianus and Prodromus refute the alien speech act of Achilles Tatius.

In contrast to this example, where the ancient novel's act itself is the object of variance, most of the episodes contain a hidden polemic that *obliquely* strikes at the act, colliding with it on the basis of what it symbolizes. For example, in Eugenianus's *Drosilla and Charicles,* during a period of separation brought about by chance, as is usual in the ancient novel, the heroes enjoy dreams that provide information of each other's whereabouts (Drosilla: 6.243–57; Charicles: 6.663–67). However, human intervention prevents Drosilla finding Charicles with the guidance given in her dream; and human agency, rather than Charicles' dream of Drosilla's whereabouts, brings about the couple's reunion. After Drosilla had dreamed that Charicles is staying in a nearby inn, her hostess escorts her there. On arrival, however, her mission is thwarted by the innkeeper's son, Callidemus, who, desiring Drosilla for himself, denies Charicles' presence at the inn (6.277f.). Drosilla returns to her hostess's house, while Charicles, back at the inn, dreams of her whereabouts (6.663–67). In obedience to his dream, Charicles sets off to find Drosilla (7.11). At this time Drosilla's hostess is questioning the weeping girl about Charicles. Charicles' companion, Cleandrus, who happens at that very time to be standing on a nearby road, overhears and bears the news of Drosilla's whereabouts to Charicles (7.25ff.)

To an audience familiar with the conventions of the ancient novel, the revelation in Drosilla's dream would have provided a tense anticipation of the couple's imminent reunion. Then, following this, the anticipation provided by the revelation in Charicles' parallel dream would be threatened by the news that the revelation to Drosilla of Charicles' whereabouts has been thwarted by Callidemus's interference. Eugenianus thus contributes to his narrative even more than the expected suspense: the audience has now been led to fear another stumbling block. In this way the ancient novel's convention of using the dream as an anticipatory device is made more subtle.

Later on in Eugenianus's *Drosilla and Charicles,* it is the traveling merchant, Gnathon, rather than the divine guidance provided in the dreams of the youngsters' fathers, who finds the missing couple (8.263ff.). The youngsters are, furthermore, located in a town other than the one the dreams had indicated, while at the same time the fathers, unsuccessful in their mission, wait in the town to which they had been guided, as the narrator says, "trusting in the god" (8.295). The episode was likely adapted from Achilles Tatius's *Leucippe and Clitophon*. There, the father of Leucippe had located the lost Clitophon and his daughter in Ephesus after traveling there in accordance with a god's guidance provided in a dream (7.12.4). Achilles Tatius's dream is the only one in the extant works of the genre—both in its early period and in its revival—to provide precisely this kind of guidance, and it could well have been Eugenianus's model.

In the subplot of his novel, Eugenianus has Calligone reciprocate Cleandrus's love as a result of her dream of the god Eros uniting them in marriage (3.2–7). This is the same theme we find in Hysminias's first dream in Macrembolites' *Hysmine and Hysminias*. But whereas the conventions of the ancient novel dictated that such dream predictions were eventually fulfilled, the revelation in Calligone's dream is rendered false by the couple's premature deaths (8.184, 310ff.): Calligone is killed at the hands of bandits (8.184), and Cleandrus's death is brought about by his own human will (8.310ff.). Eugenianus may be manipulating the conventions of the ancient novel to his own ends. The revelation in Calligone's dream could even be regarded as being paradoxically fulfilled: the couple does, after all, become united in death. In all these examples, supernatural guidance and revelation become undermined, or somehow rendered superfluous or false, by human action or by human initiative.

In *Rhodanthe and Dosicles*, Prodromus follows the conventions of the ancient novel and concentrates a cluster of three dream episodes around the beginning of the narrative segment that contains the couple's trials and separations, that is, at the commencement of the novel's main chronotope. ("Chronotope" is Bakhtin's term for a unit of analysis for studying texts according to the ratio and nature of the temporal and spatial categories represented.[17] "The chronotope is the place where the knots of the narrative are tied and untied. It can be said without qualification that to them belongs the meaning that shapes narrative."[18] Bakhtin uses the term to refer both to the points "where the knots of the narrative are tied and untied" and to that which lies between these points.)[19] Analysis of the ancient novels shows that it is at, or in connection with, such pivotal moments that most dreams are encountered.[20] As chance plays such a large part in the ancient novel genre and chance events cannot be predicted by such human activities as forethought, experience, or analysis, an alternative means of foreknowledge or understanding—such as the dream—was brought into play.[21] Not only did the dream serve as an accompanying, apparently nonhuman means of understanding chance events; it also served, itself, as the intrusive chance. Hence it is usual in the ancient novel for the dream motif to accompany or refer to the plot's pivotal points, and in many cases, structurally, for clusters to appear at these points. Prodromus's adoption of the convention is, however, striking: two of the three dreams he introduces in his cluster are merely conjectured ones. (The third is Rhodanthe's dream of returning to her homeland, which she uses to protect her virginity.)

The first conjectured dream is introduced abruptly into the narrative at the point immediately preceding the description of the pirate attack—that is, at the pivotal chance event that triggers the novel's main chronotope. This is precisely the place in the narrative where an audience versed in the conventions of the ancient novel would anticipate a dream to provide a foreshadowing of future events. The audience's assumptions are assaulted, however, by the unexpected nature of the dream episode. The hero conjectures from his sleeping companion's leg movements, and from being seen to be swallowing saliva in his sleep, that he is dreaming of the dance he had performed while awake, and of drinking wine:

> Even though he was asleep at the time, Nausicrates nevertheless seemed to be dreaming of drinking wine. He was drawing his right hand towards his mouth just as if his hand was deftly stretching out a drinking vessel, although in reality he was only gulping down his saliva. He was probably dreaming that he was gulping down wine and—I imagine—that he saw in his sleep an image of wine and of the brimming bowl. It was as if the visions themselves of wine and drunkenness were not spared Nausicrates even in sleep. And though he was lying right there on his bed, he was playing at wrapping his legs about and bending them, and from his movements you could see that he was rendering in his sleep the form of a dance he had been performing while he was awake. (*RD* 3.19–32)

Here, yet another alien voice has been made to intrude on the discourse of the ancient novel to strike another oblique blow, not only at what a dream's conventional uses might denote but, as well, at notions of what dreams represented and assumptions about the supernatural. Prodromus clearly appropriates the physiological theories on dreaming that were expounded by Aristotle (who denied any notion of the dream's prophetic qualities) in his treatises on sleep and dreaming in the *Parva naturalia*.[22] Most significant among these for the moment is Aristotle's theory of elements of dreams being part of a concurrent reality: people can dream of enjoying sweet drinks when it is phlegm they have trickling down their throats (*PN* 463a).

Prodromus's other conjectured dream alerts the hero to action that prevents the rape of the heroine,[23] in a manner that recalls Leucippe's mother's dream in Achilles Tatius's *Leucippe and Clitophon*. There Clitophon describes how Panthea, alerted by a dream, had rushed to her daughter's bedchamber and prevented his and Leucippe's prearranged union:

> When I heard the sound of the door opening, I jumped up straight-away but she was already there by the bed. Then, when I realized the strife I was in, I sprang away and rushed through the doors at a pace . . . First of all Panthea went into a swoon and fell to the ground. When she had taken hold of herself she . . . yelled out to her daughter, saying "You have ruined my hopes, Leucippe . . . alas, I never expected to see this sort of marriage for you . . . If only you had suffered this outrage through the norms of war, if only it had been some victorious Thracian who had committed the outrage upon you. But now, you wretched girl, your reputation is ruined as well as your happiness. Even the visions of my dreams have deceived me, the dream I had was not one that showed the real truth of what was happening . . . and I didn't even see the man who was ravishing you, and haven't a clue about how the horrible business happened . . ." When it was clear to Leucippe that I had got away, she plucked up her courage and said, "Don't abuse me for the loss of my virginity, Mother, nothing has happened to give any validity to what you're saying. I don't even know who it was who was here—whether it was some god, some hero, or a robber. I was lying there terrified and I couldn't even scream out because of my fear. Terror freezes a person's speech." (*LC* 2.23–25)

Yet in Prodromus's *Rhodanthe and Dosicles,* no dream in fact takes place in the episode; instead, when Rhodanthe cries out against Gobryas, her pirate attacker, Dosicles assumes she is dreaming, and it is the commotion the hero makes in his act of accusing her of dreaming and of reassuring her that dreams are illusions anyway that drives away the attacker:

> Gobryas . . . drew near to Rhodanthe who was lying down and said, "Greetings, oh wife of Gobryas, don't be disturbed at my presence but embrace me as your bridegroom . . ." He spoke thus and bent down towards her and proceeded to kiss her on the mouth. But the girl . . . ran across to Dosicles as fast as she could and standing by him with sheer terror in her heart she said, "Save me, Dosicles, from this tyrant of a barbarian, save me, your beloved virgin, get me away from the power of this robber. I am ruined, hurry, truly I am done for." By that time sleep had barely taken hold of Dosicles but, alerted by the maiden's shouts, it flew from him with the greatest of speed. He opened his eyes, stood up from his lowly bed . . . and, fully stirred to action, addressed the girl, "Alas, Rhodanthe, what is terri-

fying you? Would you please tell me! would you please tell me! Look, here I am, your Dosicles, let me know of your strife. I can assure you that you've been asleep and all you saw were just the traces of dreams that take on strange images of monsters. Night is frequently wont to transform in its dreams all sorts of impressions into different forms. You have been terrified out of your wits by some physically repulsive invention. Are you frightened at the sight of a bogey like infants are? What is this? Stop it . . ." As Dosicles was saying these things to the suffering girl, Gobryas . . . having failed in his attempt . . . crept away in silence to his own quarters. (*RD* 3.271–322)

With his two conjectured dreams, then, Prodromus not only refutes the alien speech act but also focuses his polemic on general notions that the alien speech of the novel signifies. In the first case, although the dream is a reality to the dreamer, in the waking reality it is mere illusion. With his second conjectured dream, Prodromus inverts the alien speech act even further: he manages to create a "nondream" episode wherein the "nondream" actually serves the ancient novelists' device of a revelatory dream—precisely because it is not a dream.

Prodromus uses another dream to reject notions of dream interpretation. Dream interpretation—the encouragement or despondency it provides, the actions it motivates, and the irony it creates—is a frequently used device in the ancient novel.[24] When, at the beginning of *Rhodanthe and Dosicles,* the lovesick Dosicles dreams of the unattainable Rhodanthe smiling (2.335–41), he responds to the smile in ancient novel terms and interprets it as an encouraging allegorical sign that he would win the young woman. But Prodromus renders this encouragement a fleeting illusion: it endures only so long as the dream endures. On waking, Dosicles rejects the dream—and the encouragement it contained—as illusory, and it is his reasoned rejection of the dream, rather than the alien speech encouragement it provided, that motivates his actions. Here Prodromus appropriates the ancient voice of Aristotelian theory in order to have Dosicles reject the phenomenon as a mere remnant of sensory perception and reflection of a daytime preoccupation (2.322–33; cf. Aristotle, *PN* 459b–461a)[25] as a means of indirectly striking at what the dream act symbolizes. Prodromus challenges assumptions about notions of dream interpretation by again rendering the dream itself an illusion.

Dosicles' dream of Rhodanthe smiling and his response may represent a deliberate inversion on Prodromus's part of a dream and its consequences in Heliodorus's *Aethiopica.* There the bandit chief, Thyamis, had experienced a dream of the goddess Isis handing him the heroine Chariclea (1.18.3–4), which, on waking, he interpreted to suit his own desire as allegorically conveying to him the message that he would win the young woman (1.18.5, 1.19.1). Prodromus seems to be twisting Heliodorus's two elements of the dream and the dreamer's interpretation to his own purpose. He has Dosicles interpret the dream to suit his similar desire but, in contrast to his model, has the dreamer's favorable interpretation contained *within the dream itself* (2.340–43). In the *Aethiopica* it turned out that Thyamis's dream had presented patently objective pictures of what was indeed to happen,[26] but its several interpretations as allegorical were false, and it was Thyamis's misinterpretations that inadvertently brought about the true fulfillment of the dream in the subsequent narrative. In Prodromus's adaptation, both the allegorical revelation and the interpretation within the dream are fulfilled, but it is Dosicles' reasoned rejection of the dream that brings about this fulfillment.[27]

In *Hysmine and Hysminias,* Macrembolites adopts the ancient novel convention of the couple falling in love before the commencement of their trials and adventures. In the typical ancient novel, the couple's love is instant, and is brought about through the intrusion of a nonhuman force (a god or chance). But in Macrembolites' discourse an oneiric appearance of Eros (3.1) only triggers in the reluctant Hysminias a sexual awareness of Hysmine. This awareness is then transformed into love by way of another dream, which occurs on the same night and which has a specifically physical and erotic content (3.5–7). This part of the second dream's content clearly reflects the preoccupations of Hysminias as he lay awake after his first dream.[28] The psychological element that occurs as a result of the first dream, then, generates the second, and it is the physical element apparent in the second, rather than the alien speech intrusion of Eros—the nonhuman force—that provides the impulse for Hysminias's love.

Both Hysminias's dream and its contents are adapted from an episode in Achilles Tatius's *Leucippe and Clitophon.* There Clitophon had described waking situations with Leucippe; the contents of Hysminias's dream leading up to its physical climax reflect elements of Clitophon's waking situations.[29] Clitophon had continued his narrative with a reference to a dream he had enjoyed of eating, conversing, and sporting with the young woman, and to the annoyance he had felt at being awakened from it—ἀπολέσας ὄνειρον οὕτω γλυκύν (1.6.5). The termination of Clitophon's brief account of his dream is appropriated by Macrembolites when he has Hysminias end the long account of his dream by stating that he was annoyed at abruptly waking and losing such a delightful dream—οὕτω καλὸν ἀπολέσας ὄνειρον (3.7). In Achilles Tatius's novel, Clitophon's dream and his statement of annoyance at waking from it merely provided an illustration of his obsession with Leucippe. In Macrembolites' novel, the appropriated statement is made to serve as the main turning point in the narrative: Hysminias states that he then sought to experience again what he had experienced in his dream (3.7). His earlier reluctance to reciprocate Hysmine's love is abandoned, and he too falls in love.[30]

Macrembolites' use of Achilles Tatius plays with his audience's assumptions that the function of Hysminias's dream is to foreshadow the couple's eventual marriage. This assumption is, however, subtly challenged by his shaping of the alien speech of Aristotelian theory to the alien speech of the ancient novel. Aristotle, in discussing the circumstances under which dreams can sometimes appear predictive, had said that dream experiences are often the first cause of waking actions because the way has been paved in the dream for the intention to perform the action (PN 463a), and Macrembolites has Hysminias express quite clearly that it was the experience in his dream that aroused his desire.

Macrembolites' adoption of Aristotle's theory and insertion of it into his novel is not the only instance where he has used Aristotle for his own purposes; several other exclusively Aristotelian theories can be found in *Hysmine and Hysminias* and, as with Prodromus, all the theories he voices derive from the same treatises in the *Parva naturalia*.[31] In some cases, the novelists voice different aspects of the same theory; significantly here is the theory that elements in dreams are actually part of a concurrent reality. Aristotle had explained that, to people in sleep, faint sounds can appear loud, and phlegm slipping down the throat can appear as sweet flavors (PN 463a). Prodromus voiced this when one of his characters was seen to be swallowing saliva in his sleep. Macrembolites voices Aristotle's other example when he has Hysminias experience a terrifying dream of Hysmine's mother shouting and calling on a mob of women to pursue him: Hysminias's companion presents the rational explanation that the noise in the dream was a real one, a part of concurrent reality, since at that moment Hysminias was being called from a distance (5.5).

In these various ways, then, the Byzantine novelists adopted the ancient novel's conventions relating to the intervention of nonhuman forces in human affairs. At times their representations rely on their contemporary audience's tacit knowledge of dreams as prophetic or revelatory. But their object here is to shatter the assumptions of the audience by inverting or twisting the alien speech act, or through the introduction of elements that negate or question the truth of such assumptions. In other instances, nonhuman intervention would at first appear to produce consequences that conform to the conventions of the ancient novel, yet here again active human elements take precedence over the nonhuman or supernatural ones. At all times the alien speech is subordinated to the actions or motivations of human agents or to scientific explanation, and in some cases, to both.

The underlying discourse I have isolated in the alien speech of these revival novels surely reflected contemporary social conditions. This was an intensely Christian society, and any affirmation of supernatural guidance from pagan forces would have had to be denied. What we find, and this was most obvious in the example of overt polemic, is a rejection of both the veracity and the existence of pagan gods. Such a rejection reflects not only general Byzantine attitudes, but a particular mood that seems to have been current among certain of the contemporary intelligentsia.[32] For example, the twelfth-century polymath Tzetzes, in his explication of ancient dietites, allegorized the pagan gods either as elements of the universe, as emotions or intellectual forces, or as originally human beings.[33] In his scholarly treatment of Homer's *Iliad,* he dismissed any notion of the Olympian gods' intervention in the story of the judgment of Paris as untrue and nonsense.[34] There is evidence that this attitude may have been shared by others: Manasses, the writer of the novel *Aristandrus and Kallithea,* which exists in fragmentary form only, also wrote a chronicle from which he totally omitted the judgment, despite its inclusion in the sources he had used for it.[35]

But we can also argue that the revival novels' more hidden polemic represented a response to a contemporary political situation. In the Byzantine culture of the twelfth century, a climate of scientific inquiry was intensifying. This mood had started to emerge alongside the scholarly activity of the eleventh century, as is particularly evident in the works of Psellus and Italus. Around the turn of the century, and continuing into the twelfth century, scholarly commentaries on certain works of Aristotle started to be compiled for the first time since late antiquity. This exercise was being carried out, as evidence suggests, mainly by two men— Eustratius, the Metropolitan of Nicaea, and Michael of Ephesus—under the possible aegis of the imperial Anna Comnena, and can be dated mainly to a period of her banishment to a monastery between the years 1118 and 1138.[36]

It has been shown, however, that the serious study of works of the Hellenic heritage presented threats both to entrenched power and to scholars who were engaging in such inquiry.[37] In the case of entrenched power, any revival of a heritage that encouraged analysis, criticism, and reason posed a danger to imperial control and orthodox doctrines; in the case of scholars, safeguards had to be taken against condemnation for heresy. Such a condemnation was actually faced by Eustratius of Nicaea, one of the two main figures involved in the exegesis of the Aristotelian texts. Eustratius was charged with heresy and was probably suspended for life from his career in the Church in 1117 under Alexius I Comnenus,[38] only one or two decades prior to the suggested date for the composition of the revival novels. Among the charges brought against him was one that claimed he had advanced a view that "Christ reasoned in the manner of Aristotle."[39]

The study of ancient philosophy nevertheless did continue in the twelfth century, but to read it seriously was dangerous. Those who did engage in it tended to focus on the exegesis of the safer works of Aristotle, for example the biological works, certain books of the *Nicomachean Ethics,* the *Politics,* the *Rhetoric,* sections of the *Organon,* and the *Parva naturalia,*[40] that is, the single work of Aristotle that contains all the scientific and rational explanations that were voiced in the revival novels.

The writers of the genre's revival were experimenting in a potentially dangerous area; the ancient novel world involved paganism, which had to be rejected and denied, and matters of sexuality, which constituted threats to Christian ideals and values. As one means of remaining orthodox, or nonheretical, the novelists subjected their works to the sorts of compromising changes I have attempted to isolate. Where novel convention called for the intrusion of pagan gods, the Byzantine Christian writers distorted it, inverted it, or rejected it outright. Sex—a vital part of the novel—was removed from "reality" and confined within dreams. And, in turn, within the narrow context of the dream, the writers turned to their Hellenic heritage and appropriated the alien voice of Aristotle to deny the reality of supernatural revelation and to render it and what it depicted as illusion. Even this may have been moving in the direction of heresy: revelation and prophecy had been an integral part of Christian belief since biblical times. Reviving the ancient novel was laden with risks and dangers. Those writers who attempted to revive it sought to make their activity safe through the highly sophisticated use of what Bakhtin would later term alien speech. If charges of heresy were brought against them, their defenses were ready-made.

NOTES

1. That is, works of fiction whose subject is love and adventure. Whether to describe these works as novels or romances has emerged as a question among Byzantinists as it has among scholars of the ancient novel. See, for example, the discussion by T. Hägg, who prefers "novel" as the more unmarked term, "less liable to implant prejudices as to the nature of the genre"; T. Hägg, *The Novel in Antiquity* (Oxford, 1983), 4. Because all but one of the nine Byzantine works are written in verse, R. Beaton says in his introduction to *The Medieval Greek Romance* that "it is for this reason, as well as to emphasise the links between most of them and similar literature in the west, that I have adopted the generic term 'romance' rather than 'novel'" (R. Beaton, *The Medieval Greek Romance* [Cambridge, 1989], 1). The term "novel" is chosen for this chapter because the specific works it will consider are conscious revivals of the early genre. To follow Beaton and deviate from the term "novel" for a chapter in this collection could, from the outset,

"implant prejudices" and serve to create an impression that the Byzantine works and the earlier novels are more different in content and convention than they actually are.

2. Four novels are extant from this group: three complete (Macrembolites' *Hysmine and Hysminias*, Prodromus's *Rhodanthe and Dosicles*, and Eugenianus's *Drosilla and Charicles*) and one in fragmentary form (Manasses' *Aristandrus and Callithea*). See H. Hunger, *Die hochsprachliche profane Literatur der Byzantiner II* (Munich, 1978), for a bibliography of scholarship and discussion, and, most recently, Beaton, *Medieval Greek Romance*, 49–86.

3. This work has been the subject of a great deal of scholarly attention; see Beaton, *Medieval Greek Romance*, 27–48, for discussion and bibliography.

4. Five works survive from this group (the anonymous *Tale of Achilles*, *Callimachus and Chrysorrhoe*, *Belthandrus and Chrysantza*, *Libistrus and Rhodamne*, and *The Tale of Troy*). For discussion and bibliography of texts in the vernacular, see H.-G. Beck, *Geschichte der byzantinischen Volksliteratur* (Munich, 1971), and Beaton, *Medieval Greek Romance*, 98–131. To this group of vernacular texts may be added the six works translated or adapted from Western originals; ibid., 132–42.

5. Of the twelfth-century novels, Macrembolites' *Hysmine and Hysminias* was written in prose, Prodromus's *Rhodanthe and Dosicles* and Eugenianus's *Drosilla and Charicles* in the Byzantine twelve-syllable accentual meter, and Manasses' *Aristandrus and Callithea* in the popular fifteen-syllable "political" verse. The later vernacular works were all written in political verse.

6. *Hysmine and Hysminias*, in *Erotici scriptores*, ed. G. Hirschig (Paris, 1856), 533–97; *Rhodanthe and Dosicles*, in *Erotici scriptores Graeci*, ed. R. Hercher (Leipzig, 1859), 289–434; *Drosilla and Charicles*, in Hirschig, *Erotici scriptores*, 1–69. I will not consider the fourth work of this group (Manasses' *Aristandrus and Callithea*), which, because it exists in fragments only, does not lend itself to the sort of analysis used here.

7. See S. MacAlister, "Byzantine Twelfth-Century Romances: A Relative Chronology," *Byzantine and Modern Greek Studies* 15 (1991): 175–210. There an attempt has been made to demonstrate that, contrary to prevailing opinion, which sees Macerembolites' *Hysmine and Hysminias* as the last of the series of revival works written in the latter part of the century, it was in fact the first and was probably written during the thirties or forties of the twelfth century. The article argues that all the revival novels were part of the same milieu, and were written about the same time.

8. M. M. Bakhtin, "Discourse in the Novel," in *The Dialogic Imagination*, ed. M. Holquist (Austin, Tex., 1981), 256–422 (first published in Russian as *Voprosy literatury i estetiki*, Moscow, 1975); "Discourse Typology in Prose," in *Twentieth-Century Literary Theory*, ed. V. Lambropoulos and D. N. Miller (New York, 1987), 285–303 (first published in Russian in *Problemy tvorcesta Dostoevskogo* [Leningrad, 1929]).

9. B. P. Reardon, "The Greek Novel," *Phoenix* 23 (1969): 293; *Courants littéraires grecs des IIe et IIIe siècles après J.-C.* (Paris, 1971), 341ff.; "Aspects of the Greek Novel," *Greece and Rome* 23 (1976): 121; "Theme, Structure, and Narrative in Chariton," *Yale Classical Studies* 27 (1982): 6.

10. Reardon, "The Greek Novel," 294; "Theme, Structure, and Narrative in Chariton," 6.

11. Evidence suggests that the novels (those of Achilles Tatius and Heliodorus at any rate) continued to be known and read to some degree during the years following the genre's death. Interest seems to have intensified with the "renaissance" in the ninth century, after which references to the works steadily increase over the next few centuries prior to the learned revival of the genre in the twelfth century. In the twelfth century, apart from frequent literary reminiscences (of Achilles Tatius in particular) scattered throughout contemporary writing, Achilles Tatius is referred to by Gregory of Corinth

and by Ioannes Phocas; Eustathius of Thessalonike alludes to him, although without mentioning his name, and the first medieval codex of his novel was copied in the Greek areas of southern Italy. See A. Dyck, ed., *Michael Psellus— The Essays on Euripides and George of Pisidia and on Heliodorus and Achilles Tatius* (Vienna, 1986), 86 and n. 31.

12. For a general discussion of the importance of this to the concept of alien speech, see Bakhtin, "Discourse in the Novel," esp. 276–77.

13. The novels, with their descriptions of lovers striving and suffering toward their goal, could be interpreted as allegorical descriptions of the soul's aspiration toward salvation (see S. V. Poljakova, *Iz istorii vizandijskogo romans* [Moscow, 1979], 43–53). Evidence suggests that the first such allegorical interpretation of an ancient novel made its appearance in the twelfth century with a defense of Heliodorus' *Aethiopica* by a certain Philip-Philagathus of Cerami in Sicily (see Poljakova, *Iz istorii*, 44–48, and N. G. Wilson, *Scholars of Byzantium* [Baltimore, 1983], 216–17 and 216 n. 1).

14. Bakhtin, "Discourse Typology in Prose," 290.

15. Bakhtin, "Discourse in the Novel," 282.

16. Ibid.

17. M. M. Bakhtin, "Forms of Time and the Chronotope in the Novel," in *The Dialogic Imagination,* 84–258.

18. Ibid., 250.

19. Ibid., 252.

20. The observation has been made that a dream will occur at a crisis in the narrative in other literary genres; for example, Homeric epic and historiography (see W. S. Messer, *The Dream in Homer and Greek Tragedy* [New York, 1918], 8, 11, 25, 29, 31, 48–49 n. 200), in the Old Testament (where dreams or visions tend to occur at junctures marked by a disorientation of the collective will of God's chosen people; see R. H. Bloch, *A Study of the Dream Motif in the Old French Narrative* [Ph.D. diss., Stanford University, 1970], 13), and in Christian hagiography (where conversions are often instigated by dreams or visions, and just prior to death or martyrdom a future saint or martyr will often experience a dream or vision of paradise). Among all genres the ancient novel does tend to stand out as the one where this phenomenon is to be found most, particularly with regard to dream clustering.

21. For a link between the intrusion of chance events and such phenomena as omens, dreams, and fortunetelling, see Bakhtin, "Forms of Time and Chronotope in the Novel," 95.

22. The revival novels' use of Aristotle is the subject of a separate article, S. MacAlister, "Aristotle on the Dream: A Twelfth-Century Romance Revival," *Byzantion* (1990): 195–212.

23. Dreams are not infrequently used to protect the heroine's virginity: see, for example, dreams in Achilles Tatius's *Leucippe and Clitophon* (4.1.4), also used by Eugenianus and Prodromus, discussed above.

24. See discussions in, for example, Shadi Bartsch, *Decoding the Ancient Novel: The Reader and the Role of Description in Heliodorus and Achilles Tatius* (Princeton, 1989), chap. 3; S. MacAlister, "Oneirocriticism and the Ancient Greek Novel," in *The Ancient Novel: Classical Paradigms and Modern Perspectives,* ed. J. Tatum and G. Vernazza (Hanover, N.H., 1990), 68, and MacAlister, *Dreams and Suicides: The Greek Novel in Antiquity and the Byzantine Empire* (London, forthcoming).

25. These theories were reasonably widespread in the ancient world, but clearly brought together by Aristotle in his treatise *De insomniis.* Macrembolites is also unmistakably using the theory of waking preoccupation in the next dream to be discussed here.

26. Eventually, on the death of his father Calasiris, Thyamis was entrusted with

aspects of his father's role, including that of protector of Chariclea (8.3.7). Another part of Thyamis's dream, which had depicted the temple of Isis in his hometown of Memphis being filled with clamoring crowds, lighted torches, and altars flowing with sacrifices, was presenting a patently objective picture of the scene that takes place on the death of Calasiris (7.8.5).

27. The suggestion that Prodromus is appropriating and inverting Heliodorus's statement could be strengthened by further parallels: both dreamers had lain awake in disturbed states of mind until sleep had come over them at the time of the cockcrow (in Dosicles' case, ᾠδὰς ἐς αὐτὰς δευτέρας ἀλεκτόρων [2.320], and in Thyamis's case, Καθ ὃν γὰρ καιρὸν ἀλεκτρυόνες ᾄδουσιν [1.18.3]).

28. Hysminias had been fantasizing about making love to the girl (3.4). Macrembolites exploits this Aristotelian theory elsewhere in his novel (5.1, cf. 4.10; 5.3, cf. 4.23; 5.3, cf. 4.24; 7.18–19, cf. 2.7–10; 7.18, cf. 6.18 and 7.9).

29. Prior to his dream, Clitophon had described his feelings about a meal at which Leucippe had been present; Clitophon felt like a person in a dream (1.5.3). Macrembolites transfers this episode from Clitophon's waking reality to Hysminias's dream—part of which depicts a meal with Hysmine. Clitophon had retired to bed after the meal at which he had become sated with gazing at Leucippe (1.6.1); Hysminias describes his dream meal with Hysmine in similar terms (3.5). Prior to Clitophon's description of the meal, he had described Leucippe's beauty (1.4.3); Hysminias describes Hysmine's beauty within the dream, with a significant number of similarities to Clitophon's description (3.6). Clitophon consults his cousin Clineas, who gives him advice about a maiden's resistance in lovemaking (1.10.5–6); it seems that this advice is being directly followed in Hysminias's dream (3.7).

30. This dream and Macrembolites' possible appropriation of the alien speech of spirituality in addition to that of the novel are considered in MacAlister, "Byzantine Twelfth-Century Romances," 202.

31. That is, those that relate to sleep and dreaming: De somno et vigilia, De insomniis, and De divinatione per somnia.

32. For this attitude, see E. M. Jeffreys, "The Judgement of Paris in Later Byzantine Literature," Byzantion 48 (1978): 112–31.

33. See H. Hunger, "Allegorische Mythendeutung in der Antike und bei Johannes Tzetzes," Jahrbuch der österreichischen Byzantinistike 3 (1954): 46.

34. J. Boissonade, ed., Tzetzae Allegoriae in Homeri Iliadem (Paris, 1851; reprint, Hildesheim, 1976), 214–333. For discussion, see Jeffreys, "Judgement of Paris."

35. For discussion, see Jeffreys, "Judgement of Paris," 126–28.

36. R. Browning, "An Unpublished Funeral Oration on Anna Comnena," Proceedings of the Cambridge Philological Society 118, no. 8 (1962): 6–7.

37. R. Browning, "Enlightenment and Repression in Byzantium in the Eleventh and Twelfth Centuries," Past and Present 69 (1975): 3–23.

38. Browning, "Unpublished Funeral Oration," 6.

39. See P. Joannou, "Eustrate de Nicée: Trois pièces inédites de son procès (1117)," Revue des études Byzantines 10 (1943); cf. M. Angold, The Byzantine Empire, 1025–1204 (London, 1984), 151.

40. For a discussion of the twelfth-century commentaries on Aristotle, see A. Preus, Aristotle and Michael of Ephesus: On the Movement and Progression of Animals (New York, 1981).

CHAPTER EIGHTEEN

A Legacy of the *Alexander Romance* in Arab Writings: Al-Iskandar, Founder of Alexandria

Faustina C. W. Doufikar-Aerts

In antiquity Alexander the Great was already supposed to have been the founder of the Egyptian city named after him. The story relating the foundation of Alexandria was immortalized long after his death in a legendary account now called "the *Alexander Romance* of Pseudo-Callisthenes,"[1] which was composed, it is generally assumed, by a native of Alexandria.

In the tenth century A.D., at least 650 years later, the legends of the foundation of this city, which had become part of the Arab world since its conquest by the Arabs in the year A.D. 641, were recorded again by an author called Abû 'l-Ḥasan al-Mas'ûdî. This Arabic version is the subject of this chapter, which considers the questions of origin, relationship with antiquity, and the form and substance of that text.

The story of Alexander's founding of Alexandria is a product of Arab authorship, reflecting the new cultural surroundings and presenting a reinterpretation of the ancient literary data, whereas the earlier anonymous *Alexander Romance*, known as "the Pseudo-Callisthenes," reflects its author's Hellenistic conception of Alexander.[2] As has long been recognized, the Pseudo-Callisthenes has been responsible for the widespread fame of its hero Alexander; it was the source for many a post-Hellenistic and medieval romance and, indeed, the cause of the renown of Alexandria itself.[3]

I

The Arab author al-Masʿûdî was born circa A.D. 896 in Baghdad. Having spent part of his life traveling to such remote places as Madagascar and Ceylon, he settled in Fustat (Egypt), where he died in the year A.D. 956. He was the author of numerous works, which can be classified by subject: works on religion, philosophy, science, history, and geography. At least thirty-six books and epistles of his are known;[4] unfortunately, only two works from the entire oeuvre of this prolific writer have survived complete. Al-Masʿûdî has been much esteemed by European scholars, who have honored him as "the Herodotus of the Arabs" and "the Muslim Pliny," and described him as "the forerunner of modern reporters and globetrotters."[5] Arab historians had already shown appreciation for his work,[6] especially for one of the surviving works: *Murûj ad-Dhahab wa Maʿâdin al-Jawhar* (Meadows of gold and mines of gems);[7] this work was completed in A.D. 947 and later revised by its author, but the revision has not survived.

The *Murûj* is roughly divided into two parts: a section on Islamic history, and a preceding section providing diverse information on various regions of the world and on non-Muslim peoples, including history, geography, ethnography, and religion. In this first part he dedicates three more or less substantial episodes to Alexander the Great. The first time, Alexander figures against the background of Greek history (§664–79). The second time, he appears in a chapter concerned exclusively with his adventures in India (§680–98). Finally, he is found in a chapter on the history of Alexandria (§827–43), the contents of which are the subject of this chapter.

Among stories about some buildings in Alexandria and noteworthy events in the city's history, a wondrous account is given of the city's foundation by "Al-Iskandar," as Alexander was called in Arabic. The story runs as follows:

> And Al-Iskandar instructed the laborers and the craftsmen to take positions on spots around the site for the city-wall. On each parcel of ground he put an upright pale; from each pale to the next he attached ropes that were interconnected. He joined them all to a marble pillar that stood in front of his tent. On top of the pillar he hung a huge melodious bell. He told his men and the guardian to command the craftsmen, the builders, and the workers to start laying the foundations of the whole city all at once, exactly at the same time that they heard the bell ring and at the moment that the ropes, to which on all parts small bells were attached, started to move. Al-Iskandar preferred that this should take place at a certain time that he would choose under a fortunate constellation. But, [finally] on the day that Al-

Iskandar was expecting the auspicious moment under the right constellation, he started to nod off and fell sleep. Then there came a raven
that alighted on the rope of the large bell on top of the pillar and set it
in motion. This caused the bell to ring, the connected ropes to move,
and all the little bells to shake—this [construction] being the result of
philosophical planning and mechanical inventiveness.[8] Thereupon,
when the craftsmen saw the stirring of the ropes and heard the
sounds, they placed the foundations all at one time, and the noise of
praising and glorifying exclamations ascended. Then Al-Iskandar
awoke from his sleep and asked what had happened and they told him
and he was amazed. Then he spoke: "I wanted a thing to happen, but
God the Supreme wanted it differently; God forbids unless it is His
will. I wished an eternal city, but God the Lofty One wills its early
perdition and its desolation and a confusion of kings ruling over it.[9]

Al-Masʿûdî does not fail to fascinate his reader. But he may also offer us
an important insight into the ways a Muslim-Arabic literary creation could
be inspired by ancient Greek literature. At first sight the contents seem
far remote from the "original" city-founding story in the *Alexander Romance*. On reflection, however, the story is not altogether alien to the
antique traditions concerning the foundation of Alexandria: in the Pseudo-
Callisthenes Romance one comes on a similar legendary account. There it
was told that Alexander ordered that the outline of the planned city should
be marked. The workers marked it with a track of meal. When birds came
down to pick up the meal and thus obliterated the marks, Alexander was,
just as in the later narrative, amazed by the event, and saw in it an omen
with respect to his city.[10]

The parallel between the two accounts suggests that the stories are
indeed related. This suggestion becomes more convincing after one re-
views the contexts of the accounts. In al-Masʿûdî's story the passage translated above is preceded by a statement about the environment where Alexander intends to build the city:

And he [Al-Iskandar] found in this place the remnants of a huge
edifice and a great number of marble pillars; in the center there was a
large column which had on it an inscription in Musnad script—that
is, the earliest script of Ḥimyar and the kings of ʿĀd:[11]

> I am Shaddâd Ben ʿĀd Ben Shaddâd Ben ʿĀd;
> I have strengthened with my own hands this land
> I have cut out the largest column
> from towering mountains
> I have built the "Many-columned Iram"
> whose creation never has been equaled in the land

I have wished to build here [a city] like Iram
that I might bring to it every person
of brave character and noble nature
from all the tribes and nations
since there is no fear nor decrepitude
no solicitude nor illness
but then He, who rushed me and made me turn
from what I'd wished to do, struck me
by events that made endless my distress and sorrow
that diminished my sleep and made me restless
then I left my house under protection
not on account of the power of a tyrannical king
nor for fear of a tremendous army
neither frightened for terror or disgrace
but because the measured (life)time is completed
and the leaving of traces is interrupted
through the power of the Almighty the Omnipotent[12]
So whoever sees the remnants I left
and gets to know my history
my long lifespan, my perspicacity
and my severe alertness
let him not be misled by the world after me
because it is delusive: it takes from you what it gave
and takes back what it brought close

and a long speech demonstrating the vanity of the world and cautioning against being deluded by it or relying too much on it. (*Murûj*,
§827)

Al-Mas'ûdî continues his account by telling how Al-Iskandar ponders
these words and thereupon decides to build his eternal city.

In the *Alexander Romance* a corresponding account is found in the
description of an old temple of Zeus in the same plain in which Alexander
plotted the city; he sees here "two tablets [in the *Vita Alexandri* they are
referred to as 'obelisks'] of red marble, which were very beautiful, fixed
under a statue, and upon them was engraved a legend in hieroglyphs ['in
letters of the priests'], which ran thus: 'After that I, Sesonchosis, the ruler
of the world, was first recognized as lord upon earth, I erected this statue in
honour of the great god the Sun, the equal of Serapis, in gratitude for the
benefits which I received from him.'"[13] In a second meeting between
Alexander and Sesonchosis in the cave of the gods, the ancient king speaks
to him: "I am Sesonchosis, the world-conquering king who has joined the
ranks of the gods. But I was not so fortunate as you, for you will have an
immortal name even after death.' And I [Alexander] asked, 'How is that,

my lord?' He replied: 'For although I conquered the whole world and subjugated so many peoples, nobody knows my name. But you shall have great renown for building in Egypt the city of Sk'andria, which is dear to the gods.'"[14] These two encounters with Sesonchosis show in combination a number of elements common to the admonishing speech of the ancient king Shaddâd.[15] This king seems to figure as the counterpart of Sesonchosis:[16] he is also an ancient world conqueror who expresses his commitment to God, although he is referred to as a Himyarite king.

Apart from these fragments, there is another act that occurs in both foundation accounts: Alexander places an inscription, after having finished the building of the city. In the Pseudo-Callisthenes this inscription consists of the first five letters of the Greek alphabet: A, B, Γ, Δ, E. These letters stand for the sentence: Alexander ('Αλέξανδρος) the greatest King (Βασιλεύς) of the Lineage (Γένος) of Zeus (Διός) Founded ("Εκτισεν) this incomparable city (*Vita Alexandri* 1.32.4; Syr. 1.32, p. 110; Arm. cap. 87, p. 51; C 1.32, p. 110), while in the account of al-Mas'ûdî it is a lengthy inscription concerning Alexander's purpose in founding the city.

The examples quoted above suggest that an ancient version in some way lies at the root of the new one. The resemblance in content is less distinct, but in the entourage, the similarities are too conspicuous to be mere coincidence. Unfortunately there is no decisive answer to the question of what kind of *Vorlage* or source material al-Mas'ûdî may have had at his disposal. He does not mention his sources except for a vague reference to "a group of scholars" (*Murûj*, §827). Whatever form this material had when it reached him, he presented it in a way obviously in agreement with his own assumptions about Alexander, ones reflecting an Arab–Muslim interpretation of antiquity.[17]

II

Al-Mas'ûdî's cultural and literary environment must be responsible for some of the peculiarities found in his account. Its most obvious innovations are the altered purpose of the story, and the Islamization of its hero Alexander. A closer look at these changes will be illuminating.

First, Al-Iskandar's observations concerning the future of Alexandria contrast with the predictions for the city in the antique romance. In the earlier one, the omen of the birds picking up the meal was explained as bringing prosperity and fortune to the inhabitants of Alexandria; it is said, "This city which has been built shall feed the entire world, and men born in it shall be everywhere; like birds they shall travel through the entire world."[18]

Another event mentioned in the account of Pseudo-Callisthenes, Alexander's offer to the god Serapis, which is interrupted by an eagle,[19] has a favorable effect, as it results in Alexander's receiving an auspicious prediction for Alexandria. In a dream he is told by the god Serapis that the city shall bear his name forever: "And the city that has been built shall remain strong forever. It shall cast light upon the fire and illuminate the infernal regions.[20] And it shall make the south wind quail when it breathes its harmful breath, so that the terrible doings of the evil spirits shall be of no avail against this city. For earthquake is to grip but a short while, and likewise, plague and famine; so, too, shall there be war, but it shall not present great danger; rather, like a dream, it shall quickly pass through the city."[21] In al-Masʿûdî's narrative, however, the untimely foundation as the result of an exceptional event, also caused by a bird, forecasts a less favorable future: Al-Iskandar regretfully admits that Alexandria will never become the fortunate, prosperous, eternal metropolis he meant it to be. This is emphasized by Al-Iskandar's words presented in the lengthy inscription mentioned above (*Murûj*, §832). This prediction is conspicuous because there does not seem to be any compelling reason for the author to misrepresent the old data. On the contrary: Alexandria had been flourishing already in al-Masʿûdî's days for more than a thousand years, as he undoubtedly was aware.

This curious change in the prospects of the city signifies a complete departure from the ancient Greek romance's favorable account of the entrance into Egypt and the foundation of Alexandria, as well as its account of Alexander's meeting with the Carthaginians, his recognition as the son of Ammon, and his acceptance by the Egyptians. Al-Masʿûdî diverts this tendency thoroughly. He speaks of "the early perdition" and "the desolation" of the city, and "a confusion of kings ruling over it."[22] He even goes so far as to append to the foundation record a story in which clear signs of the imminent decay of the city are already manifest: he reports the immediate attack on Alexandria by creatures crawling out of the sea by night. They destroy and corrupt night after night what has been built by day. Al-Iskandar, still according to al-Masʿûdî's account, sees in this attack a sign of the fulfillment of God's will. Nevertheless, he is annoyed with the situation and he tries to solve the problem in a spectacular manner. He constructs a kind of "submarine" in which he descends to the bottom of the sea, accompanied by two drafters. There he discovers the demonic creatures that had distressed him for so long. The drafters make sketches of the demons in all their different guises with animal heads and carrying diverse implements. These drawings permit Al-Iskandar, after his return from the expedition, to produce duplicates of the creatures in copper and stone. He then tricks the demons by placing the copies on pillars along the coast; at the mere sight of their own images the sea monsters are so frightened that they instantly disappear into the sea, never to return (*Murûj*, §830–31).[23]

Al-Mas'ûdî, showing here once more his predilection for "juicy" narratives, appears to have attached the submarine theme, which is known from a different context in the Romance (*Vita Alexandri* 2.38; C 2.38, pp. 301, 303), to the legends about Alexandria. This suggests he is deliberately stressing unfavorable signs. The addition of the submarine theme, combined here with the monster motif, could serve no other purpose, since, so far as we know, this theme had never before been connected with the foundation story. Besides, al-Mas'ûdî affirms this intention with the words spoken by Al-Iskandar when he perceives the attack: "This is the beginning of the ruination of its structure and the fulfillment of the will of the Creator to extinguish it" (*Murûj*, §830). The altered tendency in the Arabic story is underlined by a later passage in the text, which has already been mentioned: the passage in which Al-Iskandar places an inscription on the town gate, in which he formulates his intentions for the city: "This is Al-Iskandarîyya [Alexandria], I wanted to build it for prosperity and success, for fortune and happiness, for pleasure and steadiness in eternity; but the Creator—the Sublime and Mighty One—King of the heavens and the earth and the Annihilator of nations, did not will us to build it this way" (*Murûj*, §832). Thereby al-Mas'ûdî expresses Al-Iskandar's acquiescence in the divine interference, and at the same time his abandonment of his ambition to create the ideal city.

In this connection it is also worth noting that the curious change of prospects for the city was caused by Al-Iskandar's failure to execute the planned foundation under the right constellation. This lack of luck in bending the stars to his will is in itself a significant departure from the antique tradition, for astrology, where it occurs in the Pseudo-Callisthenes, is applied successfully and generally in favor of Alexander. An obvious example is the famous astrological practice applied by Nektanebo: at the moment of Alexander's birth the stars were observed and the delivery was delayed in order to have the child's birth fall under the right constellation. In this case the venture was successful: a *cosmocrator* was born (*Vita Alexandri* 1.12; Syr. 1.12, pp. 11–12; C 1.12, p. 30; Arm. cap. 25–26, p. 32).

These repeated departures of the Arabic text from the classical tradition's presentation of Alexander's image raise inevitable questions concerning the reason for these changes: the unfortunate prospects for the city, the Islamic features of Alexander, and the generally unfavorable atmosphere of the story. Can these characteristics of al-Mas'ûdî's story be explained in light of an (Arabic) tradition? Do they form part of a development traceable in Alexander material in Arabic literature? Before exploring this point, we should turn first to religious aspects of the Arabic account: the Islamization of the image of Alexander.

This Islamic image is clearly perceptible in the way al-Mas'ûdî portrays Al-Iskandar: as a servant of God in a particularly Muslim fashion. This is witnessed by the use of such exclamations as "God forbids unless it is His will." He means to demonstrate the overwhelming will of God, this being one of the major principles of Islam.[24] In this respect it must be observed that the astrological practice of awaiting a fortunate constellation to initiate such an important thing as the founding of a city was felt to be perfectly legitimate. Indeed, al-Masʿûdî does not seem to question the rightness of this method at all, nor whether the predictions for the city will come true. This is not surprising: using astrology for this purpose was a widespread practice in the medieval Muslim world.[25] Perhaps al-Masʿûdî was even aware that the method, according to the system of *ikhtiyârât* (in Latin, *electiones*), was a system that had been taken over from the Greeks: καθαρ-χαί.[26] In any case, al-Masʿûdî's report gives no reason to assume a negative attitude toward astrology on his behalf, based on a dislike of the practice. So the lack of success associated with astrology does not seem to be an indication of the writer's disapproval of the method, on either philosophical or religious grounds.[27]

More surprising, however, is the eagerness shown by Al-Iskandar in the same passage to interpret the unexpected occurrence as an interference of God, thus leaving the final decision about whether the city was to become eternal explicitly in his hands. Al-Masʿûdî here lets Al-Iskandar accept ostentatiously the divine action, in evident conformity with the Islamic principle of dedication to God's will. This religious attitude of Al-Iskandar presented by al-Masʿûdî is remarkable. Not so much the phenomenon itself, which is not unique; much post-classical literature tended to Judaize or to Christianize the image of Alexander.[28] The implicit Islamic features are striking, since the author does not seem to have been ignorant of Alexander's background; on the contrary, al-Masʿûdî shows a great interest in and familiarity with (translated) Greek literature of all kinds.[29] Additionally he confirms that Alexander lived in a period before Christ,[30] which would have prevented him logically from having been either a Muslim or a Christian, though not necessarily from having been a monotheist. Thus the author carefully avoids having Al-Iskandar express any religious formula—albeit Islamic in nature—that makes reference either to the prophet Muhammed or to Christ. It is notable, however, that al-Masʿûdî does not dwell on the religious behavior of Al-Iskandar in the other parts of this book that deal with the hero's exploits.

As for the Islamization of the story, it may be the element responsible for the two features mentioned above, the reversed prospects for the city and the diverted tendency of the account in general. Since Al-Iskandar was portrayed as a religious person, his confident, determined character had to be softened in order to bring his deeds into agreement with an Islamic image. But that does not account for all the peculiarities noted, nor does it explain the religious element itself.

III

The Arabic Alexander story must be regarded against its background and the most important fields of influence. First, al-Mas'ûdî's composition is unique as a piece of Alexander literature: it did not form part of any earlier (Arabic) Alexander text. It is beyond the scope of this chapter to go deeply into the work of predecessors and contemporaries of al-Mas'ûdî. However, in order to give an idea of the material extant in the author's time that may have been familiar to him, a brief mention should be made of the works of the prominent historians Dînawarî,[31] Ya'qûbî,[32] and Tabarî;[33] their works comprise histories of "Al-Iskandar" that are linked with the Pseudo-Callisthenes.[34] Further, there is the history of the Christian chronicler Eutychius, whom he knew in person.[35] Al-Mas'ûdî may also have known the work of the geographer al-Hamadhâni,[36] which manifests traces of the *Alexander Romance* on several occasions (Alexander's founding of Alexandria and encounters with the Brahmans and Nektanebo). Al-Hamadhânî even reports a foundation story for Alexandria, which runs as follows:

And when Al-Iskandar meant to build her [Alexandria], he entered a huge temple of the Greeks and sacrificed there many sacrificial animals. And he asked the priests to show him what would happen to the city: would the building be completed and what would it be like? And he saw in his sleep as if the wall of that temple spoke to him saying: "You will build a city whose renown shall pass into all regions of the world and innumerable people shall live in it. And agreeable winds shall mingle in its air. The wisdom of its people shall be established. The vehemence of sandstorms and severe warmth shall be averted from it. The harshness of severe coldness and frost shall rush from it. Evil shall depart from it so that no diabolical confusion will strike it. And if kings and nations shall bring their armies and besiege it, no damage shall come over it."[37]

This record is clearly based on Pseudo-Callisthenes, to judge from the striking similarity with the passage in the romance quoted above. In none of the works mentioned, however, can a foundation story of Alexandria be found similar to that of al-Mas'ûdî. Furthermore, it is difficult to say whether al-Mas'ûdî actually saw or read the Arabic version of the Pseudo-Callisthenes, which is believed to have been made in the ninth century A.D. on the basis of the Syriac version.[38] If he did, it does not seem likely that he used it directly as a source for his writings on Alexandria. The Syriac *Alexander Romance* lacks precisely the details with regard to the foundation of Alexandria, such as the track of meal obliterated by birds and the sacrifice disturbed by an eagle. Therefore it is not appropriate to consider the Arabic translation of it the source for al-Masʿûdî's foundation story.

It is more likely that another recension served as a model for al-Masʿûdî's reports on Alexandria. In this respect the Γ-type recension, or a version close to it, must be considered, for a number of reasons: first, the Γ-type recension contains the aforementioned elements, besides other common aspects. In addition, it has a submarine adventure, which is also wanting in the Syriac version. And yet another argument seems to point in the same direction: the Γ-recension includes an interpolation that gives an exceptional foundation story, referring apparently to Alexandria.

IV

The Γ-recension is preserved in three manuscripts,[39] and derived its material from two earlier recensions, the B-type and the E-type. The E-type recension is represented by a single manuscript, discovered only recently. It has been identified as a Christian-Byzantine composition from the beginning of the eighth century A.D.[40] The (anonymous) composer of E created a completely rearranged version of the Romance based on the B-type recension, and using material from other sources: Palladius, Pseudo-Methodius, and an Alexandrian world chronicle.[41] The discovery of E has thrown a new light on the character and date of creation of Γ.[42]

Returning to the interpolation in Γ: it can be stated with certainty now that this episode, 2.23–44,[43] was derived from E 20–35.[44] Of particular interest here is the passage on Alexandria (2.28 is E 24). One of the peculiarities in this episode is Alexander committing himself to the one true God, declaring all other gods worthless. He also builds a high tower in which he fixes plaques with his own portrait and those of the future rulers of the realm. The resemblance of this episode to al-Masʿûdî's account is threefold: first, the commitment to God in the monotheistic sense in connection with the foundation of Alexandria;[45] second, the building of a high tower[46]—Alexander is famous in Arabic literature for having constructed the renowned lighthouse of Alexandria, which is mentioned also by al-Masʿûdî (*Murûj*, §836–41); and finally, the matter of the plaques finds its counterpart in "drawings" said to have been made by Al-Iskandar under the inscription mentioned above, showing the city's future (*Murûj*, §832).

In the course of his analysis of the passage (24–28) of interpolation 2.23–44 in manuscript C of the Pseudo-Callisthenes, which belongs to recension Γ, Pfister paid special attention to 2.28.[47] He concluded that this interpolation originally belonged to the *Gedankenkreis* of the Jewish community of Alexandria in the first century A.D. This hypothesis has been put in a different light by the discovery of manuscript E. Nevertheless, except for Pfister's hypothesis about the character of the interpolation in Γ, much of his line of thought is still valid. He suggested the existence of a connection between the interpolation and a story which does not form part of it, but is a pseudepigraphical work ascribed to Epiphanius, bishop of Salamis.[48] In this story is related how Alexander transported the bones of the prophet Jeremiah to Alexandria in order to avert the danger of poisonous snakes.

A comparison of this legend with the story of the monsters attacking Alexandria yields the following resemblances. In al-Mas'ûdî, Alexandria is attacked by monsters from the sea, while in Pseudo-Epiphanius attacks are made by poisonous snakes and crocodiles from the river. Another similarity is the way in which Alexander tries to scare them off; in both cases his strategy is "to expel evil by showing it its own face." In Pseudo-Epiphanius, Alexander transports snakes, which are ὀφιομάχοι, from Argos to Alexandria. In al-Mas'ûdî he copies the monsters and scares them with their own images. Finally, as the trick of the snakes is not completely successful, the bones of Jeremiah are placed on different spots around the city, according to Pseudo-Epiphanius. In al-Mas'ûdî, however, Alexander's trick is reported as successful. In this case the parallel is to be found in the placing of the copies at different spots along the coast. Besides, al-Mas'ûdî mentions a second attack from the sea as well, which seems incompatible with his earlier statements; anyhow, these attacks are parried by stationing talismans on pillars (obelisks) along the coast (*Murûj*, §834). The similarity between the episodes is more than a faint reflection, so the idea of a connection between them seems to make sense. Pfister linked this story to the abovementioned interpolation, considering both episodes to belong to an early Jewish Alexander tradition, along with a third episode, that of Alexander's entrance into Jerusalem (C 2.23–24, E 20), which is also part of the interpolation. Apart from the alleged Jewish character of the episode in Γ, which appears now in fact to be Christian, the idea of a related group of traditions still stands up.[49] In another review of the same episodes, Simon, who already deemed C to be of Christian origin, suggested that the installment of the bones of Jeremiah in Alexandria was nothing but a replacement, on religious grounds, of the protective function of the (heathen) Agathodaimon.[50] This sanctuary had been built, according to the Pseudo-Callisthenes (*Vita Alexandri* 1.32), on the remnants of an enormous serpent that had been killed at the building site by the laborers. During the construction of the shrine, many snakes emerged from the place and settled in the houses, where they stayed and where they were kept to safeguard against poisonous snakes. They were honored as ἀγαθοὶ δαίμονες. The episodes found in Pseudo-Epiphanius's and al-Mas'ûdî's versions of the monsters both find their counterparts in this antique version.[51]

It seems plausible that there was a group of local traditions, among which could be reckoned the Hebrew Alexander Romance, which is clearly of Egyptian origin from pre-Islamic times.[52] The common element in these traditions is that they are colored by religious motives, either Christian or Jewish. The appearance of both episodes in one story, as in al-Mas'ûdî, sustains this view and is an additional argument in favor of the existence of a common source. Consequently, the origins of the account given by al-Mas'ûdî could be sought in the same source. This group of traditions took shape roughly between the sixth and eighth centuries; some legends that go back to this tradition may still have been current in certain circles of tenth-century Egypt (Alexandria). Al-Mas'ûdî refers at least twice in his report on Alexandria to opinions of "the Alexandrians and Egyptians." The possibility must therefore seriously be entertained that al-Mas'ûdî indeed derived the theme from a local legend. Another indication of this is the curious fact that a story similar to that told by al-Mas'ûdî is related by another author in connection with the foundation of the city of Cairo (A.D. 969), which took place fourteen years after al-Mas'ûdî's death.[53] In this story, however, no reference is made to Alexander. It is impossible to determine whether al-Mas'ûdî's story is to be considered the source for this account, which dates only from the fifteenth century; it is conceivable that the stories have a common source, a local legend, for instance, which could either have originated in the local Alexander tradition or have been incorporated in it, or which could even have existed independently.

V

Having thrown some light on the background and origin of the Arabic story, we turn now to some points in the form and substance of its text.

Al-Mas'ûdî's account shows signs that it emanated from a conception of Alexander that had developed in the area previously and was still current at that time. Two important fields of influence left their traces: on the one hand, religious literature; on the other hand, the broad domain of the so-called Wisdom Literature. The impact of Islamic literature on the Arab writer's conception of Alexander appears to be considerable. This development is due to the question of the identification of Alexander in the Islamic region: it was suggested by exegetes of Islam that a prophetic person mentioned in the Qur'ân (S. 18.82–98) was to be identified with Alexander the Great. The person in question is referred to in the Qur'ân as "Dhû 'l-Qarnayn," which means "the Two-horned." The Two-horned appears in the Qur'ân as a messenger of God in early times, who built the wall to enclose the horrible peoples of Gog and Magog. He was sent to convert the nations of the world. Muslim exegetes of the Qur'ân have wrestled from early times to this day with the identification of Dhû 'l-Qarnayn with Alexander.[54] Al-Mas'ûdî was well aware of the controversial nature of this topic, about which there was no consensus among scholars and theologians. However, he did not openly dispute the identification. The question, though unsettled, has greatly affected the image of Alexander as conceived by Muslims.

This religious image acted on literature through two different channels, primarily by way of a romance handed down by the ninth-century historian Ibn Hishâm,[55] in which the protagonist is the aforementioned Dhû 'l-Qarnayn. This romance, entitled *Kitâb at-Tijân* (Book of the crowns), reaches back to an eighth-century work ascribed to Wahb Ibn Munabbih.[56] This work was entitled *Kitâb al-Mulûk al-Mutawwaja* (Book of the crowned kings).[57] It has been convincingly demonstrated that this latter book came into existence within a century after the conquest of Egypt, significantly enough in Alexandria.[58] Even though the protagonist of the Dhû 'l-Qarnayn Romance is referred to in the book as a Himyarite king, his exploits are to a certain extent recognizable as the exploits of Alexander, especially those typical of the local Jewish Alexander tradition.[59] (The appearance of the Himyarite king Shaddâd in al-Mas'ûdî's story can hardly be a coincidence.) But of even more significance here is Dhû 'l-Qarnayn's display of great missionary activity. His religious attitude seems to be a mixture of features rooted either in the Jewish tradition (consider, for example, the visit to Jerusalem) or in the Qur'ân.[60] Apart from this Dhû 'l-Qarnayn Romance, there existed from early Islamic times a group of Dhû 'l-Qarnayn texts, similar in scheme but somewhat different in detail. In these texts the identification of Dhû 'l-Qarnayn with Al-Iskandar was more clearly made, and the main point of the stories was Al-Iskandar's quest for the Water of Life in company with the mythic saint al-Khidhr.[61] The important thing is that in these texts Dhû 'l-Qarnayn is always the pious servant of God, seeking to convert strange people in the most extreme parts of the world.

The second channel through which the effect could be imposed was Islamic religious literature, in particular the commentaries on the Qur'ân and collections of Traditions (al-Hadîth). The result of this influence was that, even though there was no decisive answer about the identification of the Two-horned with Alexander, it happened that the Arabic Al-Iskandar "inherited" the image and thus the pious characteristics of the Two-horned messenger. This development can be observed already in the work of al-Mas'ûdî's predecessor Dînawarî.[62]

The other field of influence that must be reviewed is the Arabic literary genre known as Wisdom Literature.[63] There are strong indications of the extent of this influence in al-Mas'ûdî's text. The genre, which was already extremely popular long before the author's time, was originally based on compilations of maxims and proverbs ascribed to Arab sages from the pre-Islamic period. It developed into a genre, or rather a common manner to transmit (collections of) wise sayings, maxims, proverbs, anecdotes, and admonitions of wise men and philosophers. Eventually a main component of this literature came to consist of translated Greek and Persian gnomic material.[64] In the era previous to that of al-Mas'ûdî,[65] the personality of Al-Iskandar had become closely associated with this type of Arabic literature; wise sayings, exemplary behavior, and contemplative visions were attributed to Al-Iskandar, who was sometimes transformed in these compilations into a philosopher himself.[66]

Also based on this type of literature are the elegiac speeches of ancient philosophers attending Al-Iskandar's funeral, typical of the Arabic Alexander tradition.[67] Al-Mas'ûdî himself devotes a chapter to these speeches in the Murûj (vol. 2, §676). These speeches are in general of a cynical nature, and they stress the transience and vanity of worldly greatness and power. It is precisely this tendency that can be recognized in al-Mas'ûdî's narrative on Alexandria. It manifests itself in the attitude of Al-Iskandar, in the course of events, and also in the text itself, where the inscription in Musnad script ends with the remark about "a long speech demonstrating the vanity of the world and cautioning against being deluded by it or relying too much on it." Al-Iskandar's failure to execute his project and the changed role of prognostication in the Arabic story fit well in this picture.

Astrology, it seems, was influenced by this trend. The alteration in the story is not necessarily to be attributed to al-Mas'ûdî himself, but is rather the result of the previous developments in the image of Alexander. This supposition can be sustained by the account of Damîrî,[68] another Arab writer, in which astrology plays a role in determining Al-Iskandar's future; in order to condition his destiny, his father (an astrologer!) awaits the right constellation to beget by his wife a child who would have eternal life. In this case, too, the opportunity to seize the propitious moment fails accidentally to be exploited, and so the parents are left with a less promising constellation under which to beget the child, who, because of this failure, was destined to become only a *cosmocrator!*[69]

There is a problem, however, with this account: it dates from the fourteenth century. Yet an earlier version appears in "Qişşat-Al-Iskandar" (The story of Alexander), a story preserved in a manuscript in the British Library (Add. 5928). This story is believed to date from the eighth century.[70] One may conclude that an earlier tradition could be responsible for al-Mas'ûdî's view of the role of astrology, unfavorable to Al-Iskandar, as presented in his story. Returning to al-Mas'ûdî's story now, it is legitimate to make this suggestion about the meaning of al-Mas'ûdî's account in connection with the two other reports, the admonitions of the ancient king Shaddâd and the attack by sea monsters: Al-Iskandar neglected the indications given by Shaddâd, whose speech was evidently meant as a warning against recklessness (hubris). Al-Iskandar, however, interpreted it wrongly as an encouragement to build the eternal city. In consequence he was "punished" by divine interference and plagued by the sea demons, which made him repent. Al-Mas'ûdî portrayed Al-Iskandar in a way that fit in with the image created in Wisdom Literature and that also agreed with the conception developed in religious literature.

VI

From this sketch of the literary context of al-Mas'ûdî's foundation story, it becomes clear that a complex of influential factors decisively affected the image of Alexander and thus the representation of the events associated with his founding of Alexandria. These influences must have been quite strong considering that al-Mas'ûdî, in spite of being a well-informed and not uncritical compiler, portrayed Al-Iskandar as he did, and apparently without reserve.

Set against this background, the peculiar characteristics of this Arabic story seem to make sense. It is less incomprehensible that Alexander, the ancient *cosmocrator,* could become a religious person, a Muslim indeed, and that Alexandria, the city that was supposed to become a center of eternal prosperity, fame, and fortune, could be reduced to a settlement with unfavorable prospects. This example of the legacy of the ancient novel in Arabic literature manifests the marks left on it by the Arab-Muslim environment. The legendary past of Alexandria was brought to life in it again. And Alexander the Great, indissolubly connected with the city, survived through the intermediary al-Mas'ûdî, surprisingly well adapted to the new cultural and literary circumstances. With this account al-Mas'ûdî certainly enriched the Arabic Alexander tradition, and he may also have contributed to the process of integration of the Islamic features of Al-Iskandar with the antique conception. This synthesis was to result, in the course of the eleventh century, in the emergence of the integral Arabic version of Alexander the Great:[71] Al-Iskandar Dhû 'l-Qarnayn.

Notes

1. It was composed in the period between 323 B.C. and the end of the third century A.D.

2. On the origins of the Pseudo-Callisthenes, see R. Merkelbach, *Die Quellen des Griechischen Alexanderromans,* 2d ed. (Munich, 1977).

3. On the Pseudo-Callisthenes in its many versions and derivatives, see G. Cary, *The Medieval Alexander,* ed. D. J. A. Ross (reprint, Cambridge, 1967), 9–59, and W. J. Aerts, J. M. M. Hermans, and E. Visser, eds., *Alexander the Great in the Middle Ages: Ten Studies on the Last Days of Alexander in Literary and Historical Writings* (Nijmegen, the Netherlands, 1978).

4. An informative study of the life and works of al-Mas'ûdî is A. M. H. Shboul, *Al-Mas'ûdî and His World* (London, 1979). Also of interest is T. Khalidi, *Islamic History: The Histories of Mas'ûdî* (Albany, 1975).

5. See Shboul, *Al-Mas'ûdî and this World,* xviii–xix and 55–56.

6. Ibid., xvi and 65.

7. Hereafter cited as *"Murûj."* For this study, the five-volume Arabic edition of C. Pellat (Beirut, 1968–74) was used, as well as the edition of Muḥammad Muḥyî ad-Dîn Abdul Ḥamîd, printed by the Islamic Library of Beirut. See also *Les prairies d'or,* ed. and trans. C. Barbier de Meynard and P. de Courteille, 9 vols. (Paris, 1861–77), and *Meadows of Gold: The Abbasids, by Mas'ûdî,* ed. and trans. P. Lunde and C. Stone (London, 1989).

8. It is difficult to establish whether this remark refers to presumed qualities of Alexander. Evidently the sentence was hard for later readers to interpret; for example, a later historian, Taqî ad-Dîn al-Maqrîzî, who copied al-Mas'ûdî's story in his *Khiṭaṭ,* changed the word "philosophical" to "technical." See T. Maqrîzî, *Kitâb al-Mawâ 'iz wa 'l-l'tibâr bi Dhikr al-Khiṭaṭ wa 'l-'Athâr* ("Chitat"), ed. Bulaq (Cairo, 1853), 149.

9. *Murûj,* §829, 2:100–101. Cf. *Les prairies d'or,* 2:423–25.

10. See H. van Thiel, ed. and trans., *Leben und Taten Alexanders von Makedonien: Der griechische Alexanderroman nach der Handschrift L,* Texte zur Forschung, no. 13 (Darmstadt, 1983), *Vita Alexandri* 1.32.2, 44, 45. See also below, n. 18. Several other recensions of the Pseudo-Callisthenes have been examined. For the Armenian Alexander Romance (A-type recension), see A. M. Wolohojian, trans., *The Romance of Alexander the Great by Pseudo-Callisthenes* (New York, 1969). For German translations, see A. Ausfeld, *Der Griechische Alexanderroman,* ed. W. Kroll (Leipzig, 1907), and F. Pfister, *Der Alexanderroman,* ed. E. Heitsch, R. Merkelbach, and C. Zintzen, Beiträge zur klassischen Philologie, no. 92 (Meisenheim am Glan, 1978). For the Greek manuscript L (B-type recension), see van Thiel, *Leben und Taten.* For the Greek version C (Γ-type recension), see U. von Lauenstein, *Der Griechische Alexanderroman Rezension Γ,* vol. 1, ed. R. Merkelbach, Beiträge zur klassischen Philologie, no. 4 (Meisenheim am Glan, 1962); H. Engelmann, *Der Griechische Alexanderroman Rezension Γ,* vol. 2, ed. R. Merkelbach, Beiträge zur klassischen Philologie, no. 12 (Meisenheim am Glan, 1963); and F. Parthe, *Der Griechische Alexanderroman Rezension Γ,* vol. 3, ed. R. Merkelbach, Beiträge zur klassischen Philologie, no. 33 (Meisenheim am Glan, 1969). For the Syriac version (D-type recension), see E. A. Wallis Budge, *The History of Alexander the Great, Being a Syriac Version, Edited from Five Manuscripts, of the Pseudo-Callisthenes* (1889; reprint, London, 1976). For the Byzantine version (E-type recension), see J. Trumpf, ed., *Anonymi Byzantini vita Alexandri regis Macedonum* (Stuttgart, 1974).

11. 'Âd was an ancient tribe that, according to Islamic tradition, lived in pre-Islamic times in South Arabia. *Encyclopedia of Islam,* 1st ed. (Leiden, 1913–38); 2d ed. (Leiden, 1954–), 1:169.

12. It conveys the impression that this is an allusion to the Qur'ân verses concerning the punishment of the 'Âd; cf. Qur'ân S.41.15–16, S.46.26, S.51.41–42, S.54.19–21, S.69.4, 6–7.

13. Syr. 1.32, ed. Wallis Budge, p. 39. See also *Vita Alexandri* 1.33.7; Arm. cap. 90, ed. Wolohojian, p. 53; C 1.33, ed. von Lauenstein, p. 114.

14. Arm. cap. 247, p. 140. See also *Vita Alexandri* 3.24.2, and Syr. 3.14, pp. 126–27. A somewhat different version is found in C 3.21, pp. 370–71.

15. It is noteworthy that the text of this inscription in the *Murûj* is in rhymed prose. Several passages in the Pseudo-Callisthenes, among which is the corresponding passage, 1.33, were originally composed in choliambi and hexameter. See L. Bergson, ed., *Carmina Preacipue Choliambica apud Pseudo-Callisthenem reperta,* Acta Universitatis Stockholmiensis, Studia Graeca Stockholmiensia, no. 7 (Stockholm, 1989).

16. The phenomenon of the replacement of antique figures by other ones, according to the aim of the reviser, is also encountered elsewhere; cf. *Eine jüdische Gründungsgeschichte Alexandrias mit einem Anhang über den Besuch Alexanders in Jerusalem,* Sitzungsberichte der Heidelberger Akademie der Wissenschaften, Philosophisch-historische Klasse, no. 11 (Heidelberg, 1914), revised under the title "Eine Gründungsgeschichte Alexandrias und Alexanders Besuch in Jerusalem," in *Kleine Schriften zum Alexanderroman,* ed. E. Heitsch, R. Merkelbach, and C. Zintzen, Beiträge zur klassischen Philologie, no. 61 (Meisenheim am Glan, 1976), 84.

17. Shboul puts forward the suggestion that al-Mas'ûdî "may have contributed himself to the enrichment of the literary [Alexander] tradition," or at least that "he exercised a degree of freedom in using his sources, and in presenting his account." This remark alludes to all the Alexander episodes in the *Murûj.* Shboul, *Al-Mas'ûdî and His World,* 118.

18. Cf. *Vita Alexandri* 1.32.2; Arm. cap. 85, p. 51; C 1.32, p. 110. Syr. 1.33, pp. 42–43, has a somewhat different version: the track of meal picked up by birds has been replaced by an admonition on the part of Aristoteles against the huge dimensions of the planned city. Then, although there is no question of birds here, augurs are consulted and they give advice: "O king, begin the building of the city, for it will be great, and renowned, and abounding in revenues, and all the ends of the earth will bring articles of trade to it. Many countries will be fed by it, but it will not be dependent on any country for sustenance; and everything manufactured in it will be esteemed by the rest of the world, and they will carry it to remote lands." Without the allusion to the birds these remarks do not really make sense.

19. *Vita Alexandri* 1.33.4; Arm. cap. 89, p. 52; C 1.33, p. 114; Syr. lacks this passage.

20. It is noteworthy that the "brightness" of Alexandria is made much of in Arabic literature, and also by al-Mas'ûdî, who claims that Alexandria could do without lighting by night on account of the extreme whiteness of its marble. See *Murûj,* §833.

21. Arm. cap. 93, p. 54. See also *Vita Alexandri* 1.33.7–8; C 1.33, pp. 114–15; Syr. 1.32, p. 41. A similar passage is extant in an Arabic version in the geographical work of Ibn al-Faqîh al-Hamadhânî.

22. Even though there is some historical truth in this view of the alternation of Alexandrian rulers, al-Mas'ûdî's primary purpose is evidently to sketch an unfortunate future, very different from the Alexander Romance.

23. F. de Polignac offered an interesting suggestion with respect to the sea monsters: "Il est tentant de reconnaître dans les effigies des monstres marins les représentations des antiques divinités" ("L'image d'Alexandre dans la littérature arabe: L'orient face à l'Hellénisme?" *Arabica* 29 [1982]: 305). The idea reinforces the assumption of local legendary elements in the story.

24. Other testimonies are found in the episode of the inscription.

25. The horoscope of the foundation of the city of Baghdad, for instance, is still in existence. The practice of this type of astrology appears side by side with astronomy. On the role of astrology in the courts of Islamic rulers, see C. A. Nallino, "Sun, Moon, and Stars (Muhammadan)," in *Encyclopaedia of Religion and Ethics,* ed. J. Hastings, vol. 12 (Edinburgh, 1921), 93.

26. *Encyclopedia of Islam,* 1:515, s.v. "astrology."

27. Cf. Nallino, "Sun, Moon, and Stars," 101.

28. On this topic, see Cary, *Medieval Alexander,* esp. part B, chaps. 1–4. On the

Christianized Alexander in the Syriac and Ethiopic Alexander Romances, see Wallis Budge, History, and E. A. Wallis Budge, The Life and Exploits of Alexander the Great: A Series of the Ethiopic Histories of Alexander by the Pseudo-Callisthenes and Other Writers (London, 1896). See also T. Nöldeke, Beiträge zur Geschichte des Alexanderromans, Denkschriften der Kaiserliche Akademie der Wissenschaften, Philosophisch-historische Klasse 38, vol. 5 (Vienna, 1890); F. Pfister, Alexander der Große in den Offenbarungen der Griechen, Juden, Mohammedaner und Christen, Deutsche Akademie der Wissenschaften (Berlin, 1956), reprinted in Heitsch, Merkelbach, and Zintzer, Kleine Schriften, 301–47; A. Abel, Le roman d'Alexandre: Légendaire médiéval (Brussels, 1955); and M. Simon, "Alexandre le Grand, juif et chrétien," Revue d'histoire et de philosophie religieuses 21, no. 1 (1941): 175–91.

29. See Shboul, Al-Mas'ûdî and His World, esp. chap. 4 on pre-Islamic history, 95.

30. See Murûj, §1435. Al-Mas'ûdî mentions that the period from King Al-Iskandar until the birth of the Messiah (Jesus) lasts 369 years, and from the Messiah to the prophet (Mohammed) 521 years. Finally he states that the period between the death of the prophet and Dhû 'l-Qarnayn (!) lasts 935 years.

31. Abû Ḥanîfa Aḥmed Ibn Dâwûd Ibn Wânand ad-Dînawarî † A.D. 895, Al-Akhbâr aṭ-Ṭiwâl (The long histories), ed. W. Guirgass (Leiden, 1888), 31.

32. Aḥmed Ibn Abî Ya'qûb Ibn Wâḍiḥ al-Ya'qûbî † A.D. 897, At-Târîkh (Historiae), ed. M. T. Houtsma, vol. 1 (Leiden, 1883), 161.

33. Abû Ja'far Muḥammed Ibn Jarîr aṭ-Ṭabarî † A.D. 923, Tâ'rîkh ar-Rusul wa 'l-Mulûk (Annales), ed. M. J. de Goeje, ser. 1, vol. 2 (Leiden, 1902), 693.

34. See Nöldeke, Beiträge.

35. Eutychius (Sa'îd Ibn al-Biṭrîq). He was born in Fustat in A.D. 877. He died as patriarch of Alexandria in 940. His historiographical work "Annales" was first published with a Latin translation by Edward Pocock in 1858–59. The history of Alexander is found in a second edition, "Eutychii Patriarchae Alexandrini annales," ed. L. Cheikho, in Corpus scriptorum Christianorum Orientalium, vol. 1 (Beirut, 1906), 77.

36. Ibn al-Faqîh Abû Bakr Aḥmed al-Hamadhânî † circa 903, Kitâb al-Buldân. The compendium of this work has survived: M. J. de Goeje, ed., Mukhtaṣar Kitâb al-Buldân, Bibliotheca geographorum Arabicorum, vol. 5 (Leiden, 1885). See also Shboul, Al-Mas'ûdi and His World, 154, 231, and 265 n. 29.

37. Hamadhânî, Kitâb al-Buldân, 70.

38. The text of the Arabic version of the Pseudo-Callisthenes, which was supposedly translated from the Syriac, has not survived so far as is known. Numerous publications have been dedicated to this subject: Nöldeke, Beiträge; Abel, Le roman d'Alexandre; A. R. Anderson, "Alexander's Horns," American Philological Association Transactions and Proceedings 58 (1927): 100–122; Abû 'l-Wafâ' al-Mubashshir Ibn Fâtik, Mukhtâr al-Ḥikam wa Maḥâsin al-Kalim (Dicts and sayings of the philosophers), ed. A. Badawi (Madrid, 1958); E. E. Bertel's, Roman ob Alexandre i ego glavnye versii na vostoke (Moscow, 1948); Wallis Budge, Life and Exploits and History; I. Friedländer, Die Chadhirlegende und der Alexanderroman (Leipzig, 1913); E. Garcia Gomez, Un texto arabe occidental de la leyenda de Alejandro (Madrid, 1929); P. J. V. van Leeuwen, De Maleische Alexanderroman (Utrecht, 1937); Pfister, Offenbarungen. I have been able to verify the remarks of D. J. A. Ross in Cary, Medieval Alexander, 12, mentioned also by Shboul, Al-Mas'ûdi and His World, 142, concerning an Arabic manuscript, which is assumed to be a sample of the lost Arabic version. This assumption must be rejected. The manuscript in question (Aya Sofya 3003–4) is the original of the Cairo manuscript K22974, mentioned in F. Sezgin, Geschichte des Arabischen Schrifttums (Leiden, 1967), 1:305, which is defined as a photocopy of an unspecified manuscript from Istanbul. The title of this manuscript is Sîrat-Al-Iskandar wa mâ fîhâ min al-'Ajâ' ib wa 'l-Gharâ' ib (The biography of Alexander with its

wonders and marvels). The text does not represent the Arabic translation of the Pseudo-Callisthenes. It is an extensive Islamic Alexander Romance, ascribed (erroneously) to Ka'b al-Aḥbâr, and is dated 1466. My current research has shown that the story is related to the branch of legendary Arabic Alexander traditions, to which also belongs a series of manuscripts catalogued by W. Ahlwardt in *Verzeichnis der Arabischen Manuscripten der Königlichen Bibliothek zu Berlin*, vol. 8 (Berlin, 1896), and the manuscripts Add. 7366–68 of the British Library. The Malaysian translation, examined by van Leeuwen, is based on this tradition.

39. R: cod. Bodleianus Barocc. 20; D: cod. Venetus; and C: cod. Parisinus Gr., supp. 113. C was published by C. Müller (Paris, 1846). A new edition of recension Γ was made by von Lauenstein, Engelmann, and Parthe.

40. See Trumpf in his preface to the edition of E (*Anonymi*). See also Merkelbach, *Die Quellen*, 136–38.

41. *Excerpta Latina barbari;* see Trumpf, *Anonymi*, xvii, and Merkelbach, *Die Quellen*, 136.

42. See Merkelbach, *Die Quellen*, 206. Since the E-recension lacks crucial clues such as the traditional foundation story found in most versions of the Pseudo-Callisthenes (1.30–33), it is not under consideration as the possible direct source for al-Mas'ûdî's story—at least not in the form it has come down to us in Ms. Q: Oxon, Bodl. Baroccianus 17.

43. Engelmann, *Der Griechische Alexanderroman*, 214–329.

44. Trumpf, *Anonymi*, 75–129. See also Merkelbach, *Die Quellen*, 136–38.

45. Pfister pointed out that the god referred to is the God of the Old and New Testaments and that the origin of this episode is to be sought in the institution of the Serapis cult in the Pseudo-Callisthenes. See "Gründungsgeschichte," 84, 86, and 92. In al-Mas'ûdî's story the unification of God is made much of in the inscription: "Praise be to God, the Lord of the inhabitants of the world, there is no God but Him, the Lord of every thing!" These are typical Islamic words spoken by Al-Iskandar: a new (Islamic) version of the replacement of the Serapis cult, it seems.

46. Pfister's suggestion of an allusion to a minaret is interesting since the episode appears now to date from a period after the Islamization of the area. See Pfister, *Offenbarungen*, 324.

47. Pfister, "Gründungsgeschichte," 81–103.

48. Pseudo-Epiphanius, *Marginalien und Materialien,* ed. E. Nestle, vol. 2 (1893), 1–64, reprinted by Pfister under the title "Pseudo-Epiphanius, prophetarum vitae," in Heitsch, Merkelbach, and Zintzen, *Kleine Schriften,* 351–52.

49. E and Γ having appeared to be Christian does not necessarily exclude the tradition's having its roots in a Jewish circle of traditions, which is clear from the incorporation into E of the episode of Jerusalem. The composer of E probably went back for this episode to an Alexandrian world chronicle.

50. Simon, "Alexandre le Grand," 175–91.

51. With respect to the development of legends, it is significant that the names of the two main rivers of Alexandria were Drakon and Agothodaemon.

52. J. Gaster, "An Old Hebrew Romance of Alexander," *Journal of the Royal Asiatic Society* 19 (1892): 485–549.

53. Ibn Taghrîbirdî, *Al-Nujûm aẓ-Ẓâhira fî Mulûk Miṣr wa 'l-Qâhira,* ed. T. G. J. Juynboll, 2 vols. (Leiden, 1855), 2:416. Abû 'l-Maḥâsin Jamâl ad-Dîn Yûsuf Ibn Taghrîbirdî was born ca. A.D. 1410 in Cairo.

54. As early as the eighth century the identification was a matter of debate; witness the enunciation of the littérateur al-Jaḥiẓ in his *Kitâb at-Tarbî' wa 't-Tadwîr* (Book of squareness and roundness), 86–87; see D. M. Dunlop, *Arab Civilization to* A.D. 1500

(Beirut, 1971), 48. And the question is not yet settled, since even a contemporary Qur'ân commentary states that Dhû 'l-Qarnayn should be identified as Cyrus, a theory that was proposed by G. M. Redslob in 1855 but did not find followers among Western scholars. The commentary is M. A. Daryabadi, *Holy Quran Translation and Commentary,* vol. 3 (Lucknow, India, 1981–83). A survey of the question is also presented in Friedländer, *Die Chadhirlegende;* for the Two-horned see also Anderson, "Alexander's Horns," and Abel, *Le roman d'Alexandre.*

55. Abdulmâlik Ibn Hishâm al-Ḥimyarî al-Baṣrî died in A.D. 834.

56. Wahb Ibn Munabbih († 728) was a well-known authority in the field of isrâ'îlîyyât (biblical tradition), to whom the information about this tradition is frequently ascribed.

57. This work has not survived; the *Kitâb at-Tîjân* was published by M. Lidzbarski, "Zu den arabischen Alexandergeschichten," *Zeitschrift für Assyriologie* 3 (1893): 263–312.

58. This theory has been put forward by T. Nagel in *Alexander der Große in der frühislamischen Volksliteratur* (Waldorf-Hessen, Germany, 1978), 76.

59. Ibid., 53

60. The story refers to the Qur'ân-verses S.18.82–98 on several occasions. Apart from that, the whole framework of the story seems to present primarily an elaboration of these verses (with additions).

61. See Friedländer, *Die Chadhirlegende.*

62. Dînawarî, *Al-Akhbâr aṭ-Ṭiwâl,* 31. See also Nöldeke, *Beiträge,* 36–37.

63. See D. Gutas, "Classical Arabic Wisdom Literature: Nature and Scope," *Journal of the American Oriental Society* 101, no. 1 (1981): 49–86.

64. D. Gutas, *Greek Wisdom Literature in Arabic Translation: A Study of the Graeco-Arabic Gnomologia,* American Oriental Series, vol. 60 (New Haven, 1975).

65. As early as the time of Caliph Hishâm Ibn 'Abdulmâlik (reigned A.D. 724–43), a "Romance Cycle" of correspondence between Aristotle and Alexander was composed under the supervision of his secretary, Sâlim Abû 'l-'Alâ'. It was an elaboration of Greek material associated with the literature of "Mirrors for Princes." See Gutas, "Classical Arabic Wisdom Literature," 61. See also the articles of M. Grignaschi: "Les 'Rasâ'il 'Arisṭâṭâlîsa 'ilâ-l-Iskandar' de Sâlim Abû-l-'Alâ' et l'activité culturelle à l'époque Omayyade," *Bulletin d'études orientales* 19 (1965–66): 7–83; "Le roman épistolaire classique conservé dans la version arabe de Sâlim Abû-l-'Alâ'," *Le Muséon* 80 (1967): 211–64.

66. In the ninth century, Ḥunayn Ibn Isḥâq composed a book of proverbs ascribed to philosophers among whom Alexander was reckoned: *Nawâdir al-Falâsifa.* See Cary, *Medieval Alexander,* 23.

67. Except for al-Mas'ûdî's predecessor Ya'qûbî and his contemporary Eutychius, the eleventh-century scholar al-Mubashshir Ibn Fâtik must be considered the representative par excellence of this type. He is the author of *Mukhtâr al-Ḥikam,* a work that was translated into Spanish in 1257, entitled *Bocados de oro.* It was also translated into Latin, Middle French, and Middle English. See above, n. 38. On the dissemination of this work, see Cary, *Medieval Alexander,* 22–23 and 151. See also Pfister, "Eine orientalische Alexandergeschichte in mittelenglischer Prozabearbeitung," *Englische Studien* 47 (1940): 19–60, reprinted in Heitsch, Merkelbach, and Zintzen, *Kleine Schriften,* 206–11.

68. Ibn Mûsa Kamâl ad-Dîn ad-Damîrî was born in Cairo, ca. A.D. 1341.

69. Kamâl ad-Dîn ad-Damîrî, *Ḥayât al-Ḥayawân,* ed. M. T. Houtsma, 2 vols. (Cairo, 1887), 2:18–20.

70. The manuscript was copied ca. 1510. Yet Friedländer (*Die Chadhirlegende,* 129) has convincingly proved, on the basis of the chain of authorities, to which the tradition

is ascribed by the author 'Umâra himself, that the original story dated from the second century of the Islamic era.

71. Meant here is the figure Al-Iskandar Dhû al-Qarnayn as represented in the *Mukhtâr al-Ḥikam* of Mubashshir Ibn Fâtik, and also the protagonist of the Arabic Alexander Romance edited by Garcia Gomez, *Un texto arabe occidental*.

PART VII

Pursuing the Idea
of Ancient Fiction

CHAPTER NINETEEN

From Apuleius's Psyche to Chrétien's Erec and Enide

David Rollo

Intertextual studies of post-Renaissance texts can take a great deal for granted: authorship as an appropriating signature; the book as graphemic artifact inextricably associated with a system of mass production and circulation; the cognitive hegemony of the written word granted by institutional education. Furthermore, as heirs to a historicism of printed literature, such studies avail themselves of the luxury of precise chronology, and are thereby permitted to view influence (anxious or otherwise) as an axiomatic mechanism in the development of literary genealogies. In contrast, the task of analyzing any work of twelfth-century literature in terms of textual filiation can never be an unqualified success. There are simply too many lacunae in our present knowledge. Although aspects of the modern phenomena of authorship, literacy, and textual emulation were already developing in the twelfth century, their precise nature and extent remain to be defined.[1] The literary works at the disposal of a twelfth-century author elude anything but the most approximate identification; moreover, the study of influence as a linear phenomenon is, strictly speaking, only ever rendered possible in cases in which written evidence provides precise dating for the two or more texts in question.[2] Even when chronology itself is not a problem, analysis of intertextual filiation may often be foreclosed by questions of textual dissemination, survival, and accessibility.

Such is the case of Apuleius's *Asinus aureus*.[3] It is certainly true that no material evidence of this work has survived from the Francophone cultures of twelfth-century France and England.[4] Despite its obvious pertinence to Neoplatonic thought, it does not seem to have influenced the Latin works emanating, directly or otherwise, from the School of Chartres. In fact, as far as we know today, the only manuscript of the *Asinus aureus* available to the twelfth-century reader was to be found over a thousand miles away from the English Channel, in the library of the Italian abbey of Monte Cassino.[5] Yet this absence of tangible proof has led to an often belligerent skepticism toward the possibility of a twelfth-century

Francophone readership. As a result, the central issue has degenerated into an ever-frustrated form of cultural archeology, toward an exhuming quest for material evidence that systematically rejects the transformative testimony of literature and explains everything in terms of folklore, that most accommodating rationalization for all and any thematic or structural analogy.[6]

My response to this question is fairly straightforward. First, because cultural fragmentation is an inevitable corollary of the relative localization of twelfth-century literary communities, it is an anachronistic absurdity to presuppose that all medieval authors were acquainted with the same texts (and thus to argue that it is unlikely that anyone in the Francophone North could have known the *Asinus aureus* because, say, writers associated with the School of Chartres do not seem to have been influenced by it). Second, to assume that vernacularity in some way implies "popular" or "folkloric" origins is offensively crude and belletristic, and derives ultimately from a nineteenth-century proclivity to consider the twelfth-century author as spokesperson for the childlike "naturalistic" voice of the people (along, perhaps, with entertaining props such as the graybeard bard strumming a harp and delivering the tales of the "folk" in a fireside recital).[7] Such a view is deliriously inappropriate to early Francophone romances, written by authors schooled in the stylistic and thematic imitation of classical paradigms;[8] the Latin works of twelfth-century humanists undoubtedly represent artifacts of "high" culture—but so too do contemporaneous vernacular works.[9] Third, the scribal text is the most perishable of commodities, and only a fraction of the manuscripts produced during the Middle Ages still exists today; to confuse what has not survived with what was not known is historically jejune. What is more, even if we adhere to the argument that Monte Cassino possessed the only text of the *Asinus aureus* available at the time, we still cannot discount the plausibility of its dissemination among a specifically French-speaking public. Although geographically distant from the Francophone kingdoms of the north, Monte Cassino became culturally central to a northern expansionism that, by the second half of the twelfth century, had led to the creation of a Norman kingdom straddling southern Italy and Sicily.[10] As one of the preeminent centers of learning in this area of increasing northern influence, Monte Cassino had by this time been visited by scholars from elsewhere in Europe for well over one hundred years. Therefore, we must keep an open mind to the strong possibility that the *Asinus aureus* was read and perhaps also copied by visitors from the regions forming the northern axis of French culture. That such copies may have been known only to limited circles is plausible, indeed likely; that they have not survived is fully consistent with the fate of most medieval manuscripts, and would place them in prestigious company.[11] Because the argument demanding material proof is really no argument at all if assessed in the context of a scribal culture, the only cogent evidence that can exist must be derived from the eloquent testimony of contemporaneous literary production.

At precisely the time at which the Normans were definitively consolidating their control over southern Italy, authors working in the northern Francophone regions wrote a number of narratives that bear, with varying emphases and articulations, striking analogies to the Apuleian story of Cupid and Psyche.[12] Of these, I shall concentrate on Chrétien de Troyes's *Erec et Enide* (ca. 1170), which, to my knowledge, has not so far been studied with reference to the Apuleian paradigm. Through an intertextual analysis, I hope to demonstrate that the two works explore tensions of gender in such similar ways that even the commodious *échappatoire* of the folkloric morpheme cannot be stretched wide enough to account for all the themes and structures they hold in common. As a point of departure, a contrastive paraphrase of the respective plots of the two works is in order:

Erec et Enide: Erec (young, handsome, noble [89–90, 650]) marries Enide (young, beautiful beyond words, socially inferior [401–532]); Guenivere supervises Enide's presentation at Arthur's court (1532–1652), where the young man and woman are subsequently married (1870–2249); Erec spends an inordinate amount of time in bed with Enide, preferring the pleasures of the flesh to the responsibilities incumbent on him as a member of a social order (2430–68); after a night of passion, Enide contemplates her sleeping husband and, her tears falling on his chest (2489–91), laments his loss of chivalric identity (2492–2503); her words wake Erec, who is then privy to Enide's revelation (2504–71); the angry husband instructs his wife to rise, dress, and prepare her horse for a journey (2572–79); Enide regrets her foolishness (2585–91), convinced she will be sent into a solitary exile (2592) and will never so much as see her husband again (2593–94); however, contrary to her expectations, Erec joins her in her life of hardship (2715–20), stipulating, nevertheless, that Enide must from now on never speak to him (2764–71; 2912–17; 3003–6); throughout a number of adventures, Enide disobeys her husband's injunction (2841–44; 2979–92) and regains his trust; the couple is finally crowned (6769–6825).[13]

Apuleius's "Cupid and Psyche":[14] Cupid (young, handsome, divine) sequesters Psyche (young,[15] beautiful beyond words,[16] mortal);[17] Cupid visits Psyche only under cover of darkness,[18] specifying that his beloved must obey his stipulation never to attempt to learn his identity;[19] he devotes so much energy to his own amorous concerns that he neglects entirely the duties incumbent on him as god of love;[20] after a night of passion, Psyche, with the aid of a lamp, disobeys her

husband's injunction, contemplating him for the first time and learning his divine identity;[21] Cupid is woken by a drop of oil falling on his
shoulder,[22] and immediately flies out of Psyche's reach;[23] as punishment for her disobedience, he then sends Psyche into a solitary corrective exile;[24] after a number of hardships,[25] Psyche regains Cupid's
trust,[26] and is finally deified.[27]

Although the broad similarities in thematic development (bliss with
beloved, followed by estrangement or exile, leading to final reconciliation)
are indeed common to the folk tales of several continents,[28] I find the
correspondence or analogy of certain details eloquent. These, although
perceptible, cannot be convincing unless analyzed in the context in which
they appear. In the present case, this context is prepared by another Latin
paradigm, Martianus Capella's *De nuptiis Mercurii et Philologiae*.[29] In *Erec et
Enide*, Chrétien attempts through language to render eloquent a hidden
context of inquiry. This context is Enide, a woman who emerges as exemplary of her gender. She, at first a central yet constantly evasive presence,
fulfills a role comparable to that played in *De nuptiis* by Pallas, the textually
inaccessible female figure standing as the consummaton of epistemic apotheosis. The first third of *Erec et Enide* textually reenacts the inadequacies
that *De nuptiis* unveils in its own linguistic constructs—Enide is at first as
inscrutable to language as the supralinguistic universal cognition guaran-
teed by Pallas. The revelation of her wisdom becomes the goal of the
remaining portion of the romance.
De nuptiis breaks off as Philologia and Mercurius are led into the marital
thalamus. The end of the text signals the effacement of language, since the
ineffable conjunction of the two celestial categories, and their eventual
relationship with Pallas, necessarily lies beyond the bounds of mortal
textuality. In *Erec et Enide*, however, the more down-to-earth stress on the
relationship between language and a woman is clearly open to further
elaboration. Accordingly, in terms of thematic correspondence, *Erec et
Enide* passes beyond the point at which the Latin model ends. It does so
precisely through describing events that take place in a marital bedroom, a
space identical to the one Philologia and Mercurius enter as *De nuptiis* ends.
This pivotal bedroom episode sets in motion the drama of masculine
dominion that occupies the latter two thirds of the romance. It is through
this exploration of power and gender that *Erec et Enide* closely corresponds
to certain aspects of the story of Cupid and Psyche, the ultimate tale of an
exile resulting from a bedroom transgression.
Apuleius's story attributes human traits to all its participant categories,
and recounts the soul's travails through recognizable patterns of gender
interaction.[30] The identity of Cupid is nuanced early in the story by a
systematic emphasis on the phallic. According to the Milesian oracle,
Psyche is to marry not a man (or even a god), but a serpent; the jealous

sisters subsequently embellish this prophecy, convincing Psyche that she is the prisoner of a nocturnal creature remarkable for its insatiable appetite and the venom it oozes during its bedroom visitations:

> Pro vero namque comperimus, nec te, sociae scilicet doloris casusque tui, celare possumus, immanem colubrum multinodis voluminibus serpentem, veneno noxio colla sanguinantem hiantemque ingluvie profunda, tecum noctibus latenter acquiescere. (5.17)

> We now know the truth, you see, and since of course we share your pain and plight, we cannot conceal it from you. It is a monstrous snake gliding with many-knotted coils, its bloody neck oozing noxious poison and its deep maw gaping wide, that sleeps beside you hidden in the night.

In short, Psyche is led off to become the explicit victim of a male category figuratively assuming erective attributes, and, hardly surprisingly, she is in due course made pregnant by the venomous bite of her ever-potent bedmate. This association of the male with the erective would in itself be of little consequence, were it not for a number of restrictions the serpent places on his new bride. She is unquestioningly to accept her supine position of obeisance; moreover, she is not to attempt to learn the identity of the power that confines her to passivity. Erotic plaything and blind slave, Psyche is accordingly an object subordinated to male desire and to masculine dominion. Her eventual resolve to behead the serpent is both a rebellion against Cupid's cognitive restrictions and a severance of his phallic potency. Armed with lamp and dagger, Psyche prepares the metaphorical tools for that final gesture of transgressive self-empowerment, emasculation itself, which in turn entails as its corollary Psyche's equally metaphorical shedding of her femininity—on entering the bedchamber, she is said to alter her sex (5.22: *sexum mutatur*). At hand is a transfer of gendered categories.

Although Psyche abandons her resolution to truncate as soon as she contemplates the beauty of her husband, this empowering transfer is nonetheless achieved. The emasculating blade may fall from Psyche's hands, but it is replaced by objects that figuratively serve the same purpose. The conflation of the god of love and genital attributes at this point still obtains, Cupid on this occasion emerging primarily as a rubicund head, a white neck encircled by hair, and a pair of wings. But, archetypally masculine as they are, these attributes are no longer presented in terms of venomous potency. Rather, they are now dormant:

> Videt capitis aurei genialem caesariem ambrosia temulentam, cervices lacteas genasque purpureas pererrantes crinium globos decoriter impeditos, alios antependulos, alios retropendulos, quorum splen-

dore nimio fulgurante iam et ipsum lumen lucernae vacillabat. Per
umeros volatilis dei pinnae roscidae micanti flore candicant, et quam-
vis alis quiescentibus extimae plumulae tenellae ac delicatae tremule
resultantes inquieta lasciviunt. (5.22)

On his golden head she saw the glorious hair drenched with ambrosia:
wandering over his milky neck and rosy cheeks were the neatly shack-
led ringlets of his locks, some prettily hanging in front, others behind;
the lightning of their great brilliance made even the lamp's light flick-
er. Along the shoulders of the winged god white feathers glistened
like flowers in the morning dew; and although his wings were at rest,
soft and delicate little plumes along their edges quivered restlessly in
wanton play.

Phallic attributes are nevertheless still present, transferred through extended hypallage from Cupid to the objects that Psyche manipulates:

Quae dum insatiabili animo Psyche, satis et curiosa, rimatur atque
pertrectat et mariti sui miratur arma, depromit unam de pharetra
sagittam et puncto pollicis extremam aciem periclitabunda trementis
etiam nunc articuli nisu fortiore pupugit altius, ut per summam
cutem roraverint parvulae sanguinis rosei guttae. Sic ignara Psyche
sponte in Amoris incidit amorem. Tunc magis magisque cupidine
flagrans Cupidinis, prona in eum effictim inhians, patulis ac petulan-
tibus saviis festinanter ingestis, de somni mensura metuebat. Sed dum
bono tanto percita saucia mente fluctuat, lucerna illa sive perfidia
pessima sive invidia noxia sive quod tale corpus contingere et quasi
basiare et ipsa gestiebat, evomuit de summa luminis sui stillam fer-
ventis olei super umerum dei dexterum. (5.23)

Insatiably, and with some curiosity, Psyche scrutinised and handled
and marvelled at her husband's arms. She drew one of the arrows
from the quiver and tested the point against the tip of her finger; but
her hand was still trembling and she pushed a little too hard and
pricked too deep, so that tiny drops of rose-red blood moistened the
surface of her skin. Thus without knowing it Psyche of her own
accord fell in love with Love. Then more and more enflamed with
desire for Cupid, she leaned over him, panting desperately for him.
She eagerly covered him with impassioned and impetuous kisses till
she feared about the depth of his slumber. But while her wounded
heart was swirling under the excitement of so much bliss, the lamp—
either from wicked treachery or malicious jealousy or simply because
it too longed to touch and, in its way, kiss such a beautiful body—
sputtered forth from the top of its flame a drop of boiling oil on to the
god's right shoulder.

In fascination, Psyche handles the god's arrows, finally inserting one into herself and drawing blood. The symbol and vehicle of masculine power is appropriated by a woman and employed as the catalyst for her now self-sufficient passage from virgin innocence to experience. From this point on, the blind slave acquires vision, and she at once begins to invert the circumstances of her imprisonment, employing for her own gratification the male under whom she previously existed as an ignorant object of pleasure. This appropriation of metaphorized masculine power reaches its apogee at the moment at which Psyche's lamp, the illuminating impulse for her liberating gestures, achieves its ejaculatory overflowing. While the phallic is divorced from the penis in the successive descriptions of Cupid, it subsequently ceases, through Psyche's actions, to be the sole possession of men and becomes an objectified construct to be manipulated by men and women alike.

But, however objectified and open to manipulation the privilege of knowledge may be, it continues to be configured in masculine terms that necessarily peripheralize the female.[31] This serves to suggest the phallic myth of male exclusivity, through which the physiological appendage that the female other does not have becomes an emblematic concretion of what the female other should not have. But this illicit equation runs the permanent risk of reversal, creating conditions in which the appropriation by the other of self-arrogated male privilege can only be viewed in terms of privation and absence. Women cannot grow penises, and to partake of their superimposed phallic rights implies expropriation, an emasculating loss of potency in the male. The physical sign of this loss is the wound sustained by Cupid at precisely the moment of Psyche's ejaculatory self-consummation. And it is to palliate and heal this stigmatum of lost dominion that Cupid abandons Psyche to hardship.

The analogous scene of *Erec et Enide* introduces no emasculating dagger, no ebullient lamp. It does not even include an explicit prohibition. The preceding third of the romance, however, does introduce a woman, who, if not a slave deprived of sight, is an object textually deprived of voice. Enide's reification in these early scenes is absolute. She never speaks; she is given to Erec by her father, she is stable attendant, domestic lackey, dressing-room aide, last-minute entrant (and winner) of two beauty contests. This supernumerary status in a masculine order is obliquely attested early in the text through an apparent celebration of Enide's beauty:

> Ce fu cele por verité
> qui fu fete por esgarder,
> qu'an se poïst an li mirer
> ausi com an un mireor.
> (438–41)

It was in truth the kind that was made to be looked at,
for in it, one could behold oneself, as in a mirror.

The first person described gazing at Enide is Erec himself, who sees in
her an appropriate mirror for the beauty of his self-fashioning:

> Erec d'autre part s'esbahi,
> quant an li si grant biauté vit.
> (448–49)

Erec, for his part, was astonished when he saw
such great beauty in her.

Enide is thus at first a specular surface that can only reflect signifiers
imposed by an exterior hegemony. This divorce from autonomous signification is further heightened by the text's absolute failure to report any of
her words. She obviously speaks to her parents, to Arthur, to Guenivere,
and to Erec himself, but her words are either rendered by paraphrase or left
as no more than an inference. The systematic nature of this omission draws
attention to the moment at which the text diverges from its previous
trajectory in order to accord Enide a voice for the first time. And it is
precisely this divergence that occurs in the bedroom.

Within this confined space, Psyche first gains vision, understanding,
knowledge, those privileges of the masculine dominion under which she
had lived. However, the comparable episode of *Erec et Enide* exploits no
theme of homicide, and still less, it would seem, of emasculation. Enide
accedes to subjectivity in far less picturesque terms. To paraphrase: Erec
spends so much time in bed with Enide that he neglects his chivalric duties;
this remains hidden from him until one morning:

> Son seignor a mont et a val
> comança tant a regarder;
> le cors vit bel et le vis cler,
> et plora de si grant ravine
> que, plorant, desor la peitrine
> an chieent les lermes sor lui.
> "Lasse," fet ele, "con mar fui!
> De mon païs que ving ça querre?
> Bien me doit essorbir la terre,
> quant toz li miaudres chevaliers,
> li plus hardiz et li plus fiers,
> qui onques fust ne cuens ne rois,
> li plus lëax, li plus cortois,
> a del tot an tot relanquie
> par moi tote chevalerie.

Dons l'ai ge honi tot por voir;
nel volsisse por nul avoir."
Lors li dist: "Amis, con mar fus!"
A tant se tot, si ne dist plus.
Et cil ne dormi pas formant,
la voiz oï tot an dormant;
de la parole s'esveilla
et de ce molt se merveilla
que si formant plorer la vit.
(2486–2509)

Enide began to gaze at her husband from head to foot. Seeing his fine body and his clear face, she wept so much that the tears she cried fell upon his chest. "Alas—what misfortune has come over me! What was I looking for when I left my country to come here? The ground should swallow me up, since the greatest knight of them all, the boldest and most daring ever to be a count or a king, the most loyal and courtly, has completely abandoned chivalry for me. I have truly dishonored him, which I would not have wanted at any price." Then she said: "My friend, what misfortune for you!" Then she fell silent, saying no more. And he was not deeply asleep and heard her voice as he slept. He woke at her voice and was astonished that he should see her so bitterly weeping.

The nature of Enide's transgression may give rise to almost unlimited interpretations, since Chrétien himself offers no authorial commentary to elucidate the motives behind either Enide's words or the reaction they prompt in Erec. In the absence of such authorizing props, the critic is obliged to supplement with his or her own impressionistic response. As a point of departure, let us therefore hypothesize an antimony of gendered power, and place Erec between its polarities as a hesitant category. On one side stands a male collectivity, *barnage,* a ritualized context for male inter-action that demands patterns of conformity from Erec, its favored adher-ent. On the other lies the supine Enide, perpetrator of the worst suspicions of the misogynist; she is siren of the senses, purveyor of lusting caresses, congenital whore, eminently irresponsible and degrading. Both polarities are ridiculously lacking in nuance; but, if only by contrast, they do serve to heighten the complexities Chrétien brings to bear. Although the initial criticism of Erec is indeed made by a group of men, it attaches no blame to Enide for Erec's dereliction. Moreover, as son of a king, and future king himself, Erec has to fill a social role of considerable responsibility that does not in any way presuppose that his wife remain a cipher. Indeed, it is specifically as an appeal to this responsibility that *barnage* first articulates its censure. Erec's former companions do not imply a choice between polarized spheres of society and sex, but a reasoned balance of the two. And Enide, because erotically objectified from the beginning, can only respond to their criticism by blaming herself. At this moment, she still does not understand that it is not *barnage* that debases her, but the role she has been made to play in Erec's hands.

Our hypothesized antinomy becomes directly relevant, however, to the tensions underlying Erec's behavior. He reacts not so much to Enide daring to speak as to what she says. Since her words reflexively reiterate the censures of other men, Erec undergoes the crushing indignity of hearing his wife act as the voice of all the reasoned responsibility he has abandoned. In his eyes, she has empowered herself through his vulnerability, and in the process has displaced him in precisely the role that he knows he should play. He in consequence behaves as though Enide has indeed shown herself to be the misogynist's nightmare: she has spoken out of turn, and must learn only to speak when instructed; she has dragged him into the depravity of the senses, and must be erotically neutralized through hardships that accommodate no sexual contact. Not only does he impose this grotesque parody onto his wife; he simultaneously makes himself into a caricature of the chivalric paragon. Because in his view he has been led astray by a woman and in effect cut off from other men, he behaves as though his masculinity has been excised; in response, he assumes the role of the hyperbolic champion, exhibiting gratuitous heroism to palliate the gendered loss that he and he alone believes himself to have undergone. He has tragically misread his wife, his former companions, and, finally, himself.

In this way, Apuleius and Chrétien employ analogous scenes to analogous ends. Both use the bedroom as an erotic space in which patterns of masculine self-fashioning are perceived to be subverted by a female agent. In both, the woman's apparent transgression precipitates a vindictive exile designed to heal a wounded construct of masculinity and to punish female pride. Both depict a crisis of illusory emasculation, conflating the questioning of prerogative with the expropriation of authority, the male figure in each case seeking to remedy a loss he can only equate with a woman's corresponding gain. The exile sequences of the two texts, nevertheless, seem to diverge in one crucial respect. While Psyche stumbles alone through a journey to forgiveness, Enide is accompanied by Erec in her itinerant life of hardship. But the distinction is finally no more than apparent, and for one reason: as the exile progresses, the precedent of Psyche is followed, in different ways, but with eloquent results, not only by Enide but also by Erec. Therefore, while Apuleius abstracts Cupid from a central role in his narrative, Chrétien correctively effaces Erec's former self through an accelerated process of change, and eventually offers a revisionary alternative configured by a female antecedent.

On a more superficial level, the plots have little in common. But this is hardly an argument against intertexuality. It would show extraordinary literary ingenuousness to argue that direct filiation obtains only in those cases in which two texts exactly correspond in all aspects of their thematic development. The Apuleian paradigm is populated by inimical or indifferent divine powers (Venus, Ceres, Juno), a beneficent troop of ants, an intelligent eagle, a compassionate reed, and a conciliatory tower, these last three endowed with speech. Anthropomorphic props of this kind are alien to the Arthurian world of Chrétien's romances, and the possibility of an intertextual relationship is not weakened because they are absent from *Erec et Enide*. On the contrary: these are precisely the elements of the paradigm that either would be jettisoned altogether or, if retained, would reappear in functionally different garb. For reasons of simple coherence and intelligibility, Chrétien's transpositions of a classical text would necessarily be rendered consistent with the values of the community about and for which he writes. For example, in the many cases in which his romances show the influence of various tales from Ovid's *Metamorphoses,* they do so as selective appropriations of essential thematic tensions; they judiciously restructure, realign, retain, delete.[32] To put it simply: in discussing the possibility of an intertextual relationship linking Apuleius's story and *Erec et Enide,* I am not talking about the literary procedure of precise one-for-one correspondence that we today call "translation."[33]

These procedures of romance realignment are clearly shown in four episodes. In the first of these, Erec and Enide meet a lascivious count. He desires Enide, wishes to marry her, and suggests they murder Erec; Enide feigns acquiescence and subsequently warns her husband; the two escape and, when pursued, Erec defeats the count in combat. Disdainful, brutal, objectifying, the count reflects Erec's own tyrannical egocentrism, and, by circumventing this adversary, Enide helps Erec take the first step in overcoming his insensitivity. Here again, Enide precipitates change in the closed space of the bedroom; here again, she remains awake while Erec sleeps, and rouses him with her words; here again, she transgresses his authority, this time disregarding his command that she should never speak without his permission. Once more, then, motifs common also to the classical paradigm are suggested. In this instance, furthermore, they are complemented by a recurrent and remarkably Apuleian stress on decapitation, which is proposed once by Enide (3386) and twice by the count (3525, 3528) as an appropriate means of killing Erec. In strictly thematic terms, this second episode therefore corresponds to the Apuleian model even more closely than its earlier analogue: like Psyche under the influence of her sisters, a woman here enters the bedroom after conniving with a third party to decapitate her husband. Enide, nevertheless, does not wake her partner in an abandoned act of decapitation; she does so in order to warn him of a stratagem that takes his decapitation as a possible prerequisite for its successful resolution.

In responding positively to Enide's warning, Erec for the first time shows himself capable of respecting his wife as an individual, and begins to abandon the hyperbolically masculine self-fashioning he had adopted in forcing her to join him in exile. Accordingly, a process of emasculation is indeed initiated by a woman's influence—but the masculinity to be excised is of an entirely negative type. Through this second bedroom episode, Enide begins to succeed, both literally and figuratively, where Psyche had failed: she takes the first step toward equality with her partner and begins to truncate the power of the monster she married. The deflation of this male prerogative is amply demonstrated in the episode that immediately follows the defeat of the count. Enide warns Erec of the approach of an armed knight and once again draws his censure (but this will be for the last time). The knight who charges toward them bears the resonant name of Guivret le Petit—"Little Little-Snake." A serpent for the first time makes its explicit appearance in the text and does so in the form of a man whose only function is to wait within his castle to challenge any armed knight who might happen to pass. He will then fight this adversary until one of them is forced to yield:

> [i]l ot veü devant ses lices
> un chevalier armé passer
> a cui se vialt d'armes lasser,
> ou il a lui se lassera
> tant que toz recreanz sera.
> (3676–80)

He has seen pass before his lists an armed knight with whom he wishes to measure himself either to the point of his own exhaustion, or to the point that his adversary will tire and abandon the challenge.

Guivret views the simple fact of accepting defeat in this display of prowess to be the sign of the *recreanz*. Use of this term reflects Erec's misinterpretation of Enide's words: in both cases, fear of being recreant leads to a set of male postures of the most anarchic nature. Erec, like Guivret, has espoused a masculinity that is finally arbitrary and primitive, and stands as the antithesis of the social role he had abandoned in his own *recreantise*. To pursue manhood in this manner reveals a desire to measure one's masculine proportions against others. But Guivret's name, behavior, and tiny size deflate male hyperbole through parodically inverting the patterns of its own self-celebration. Knighthood deprived of social function is here physically projected as an anxiety of the exiguous, as an inade-quacy that can seek to supplement its deficient stature only within a closed system of male ritual. Erec's victory over this representative of vacuous chivalry marks a further stage in his understanding of his flawed appraisal of manhood.[34] Shunning all efforts to heal his body, Erec carries the wounds sustained as the visible sign of contrition. The illusory wound of emasculation suffered by Cupid is answered by the physical wounds through which Erec consciously renders himself vulnerable to change. The subliminal theme of lost manhood begins to be resolved in the gradual erosion of a specific view of masculinity.

This erosion is both dramatized and accelerated in the first task the wounded Erec undertakes. A young woman begs him for help: two giants have captured her companion, stripped him naked, bound him head and foot, and now whip him with scourges as he is led through the forest on horseback. This tableau reflects the social questions raised by the preceding portion of the romance. A masculinity of a physical strength inversely proportionate to its intelligence has forcibly destroyed a heterosexual bond, marginalized the female, and subjected the male to humiliation and captivity. Male hyperbole is here presented as brutal, subhuman, and demeaning, predicated on reducing women to irrelevance and punishing any man who resists its tyrannical stipulations. But the denuding of the knight, the stripping away of all outward indices of chivalry, simply serves to enhance the strength of his fundamentally human stature, which is here set in stark contrast with the grotesque inhumanity of his tormentors. Erec in effect witnesses, figuratively enacted, his own marital history, but with one distinction: the knight resists the forces to which Erec himself had succumbed. In leading his wife into exile, Erec has betrayed both Enide and himself to an exaggerated construction of masculinity as monstrous as the giants who torture the knight. Thus confronted by his own internal drama, Erec at once challenges the values to which he has willingly fallen victim: he overcomes the giants, restores the knight to dignity, reunites the lovers, and, in the process, rehearses the course he will now follow in his relationship with Enide.

The scene is, moreover, unique in its stripping away of formulaic descriptions of knightly prowess and its insistence on more tangible manifestations of suffering. The stark reality of the knight's torture and humiliation is of an urgency that stands far above, and ultimately ridicules, the ritual patterns of struggle common to all of Erec's early encounters with armed combatants. The true violence in the text is located not in the tedious postures of martial conflict, but in the degradation of the individual. In its refusal to mask any longer the reality of victimization, this episode corresponds to the first scene of bodily torture in Apuleius's story. Psyche had emotionally suffered, certainly, on being abandoned by Cupid, but the fairy-tale patina is broken, and the arbitrary misery of the mortal condition revealed, only when she is prisoner of Venus and subjected to Sollicitudo and Tristities:

> Quibus intro vocatis torquendam tradidit eam. At illae sequentes erile praeceptum Psychen misellam flagellis afflictam et ceteris tormentis excruciatam iterum dominae conspectui reddunt. (6.9)

> When they had been summoned in, she handed Psyche over to them for torture. Following their mistress's orders they scourged poor Psyche with whips and tortured her with every other sort of device, and brought her back to Venus' presence.

Psyche's pathetic vulnerability to divine ire is further underscored by references to her pregnant belly, which give way to still more violence, this time at the hands of Venus herself: "His editis involat eam vestemque plurifariam diloricat, capilloque discisso et capite conquassato graviter affligit" (6.10). In a scene emblematic of her entire story, a pregnant girl is dragged by the hair, whipped, and beaten about the head. This exemplary relationship to wider thematic tensions is also found in the corresponding episode of *Erec et Enide,* although with a significant shift of gender. Here, it is the male figure refracting Erec's own plight who is the victim of suffering. For the first time in the romance, therefore, Erec bears analogies, albeit obliquely, not to Cupid, but to Psyche.

Two anthropomorphic agents of torture armed with scourges are therefore introduced in Apuleius's story as a prelude to the tyranny of Venus (which is manifested in the four tasks she sets for Psyche). The equivalent figures in *Erec et Enide,* however, fulfill the opposite function, as an exterior but central signal for the end of Erec's unthinking loyalty to a flawed manhood (which has been manifested in the four chivalric adventures in which he had forbidden Enide to speak). This transformation is completed through the deathlike swoon into which Erec falls as a result of his victory. Enide rushes to him and laments over the body she takes to be dead. This return to the recurrent motif of a woman contemplating her unconscious husband extends the progressive web of intertextual analogy still further. The death of Cupid had been Psyche's original intent (and encouraged by a third party); the death of Erec had been the intent of the count (and strategically encouraged by Enide); but in this third episode, Enide views Erec's death as an accomplished fact, a reality for which she considers herself to be solely responsible:

> "Ha!," fet ele, "dolante Enyde,
> de mon seignor sui omecide;
> par ma folie l'ai ocis:
> ancor fust or mes sires vis,

> se ge, come outrageuse e fole,
> n'eüsse dite la parol
> por coi mes sires ça s'esmut."
>   (4585–91)

"Ah," she said, "grieving Enide! I am the murderer of my husband. I have killed him with my madness. My husband would still be alive now if I had not, like an insolent and crazy woman, said the word that led my husband to this pass."

Enide's lament retrospectively assimilates the words she originally uttered in the bedroom with an act of murder: if she had not spoken then, Erec would never have set in motion the circumstances leading to his death. In short, Enide has unwittingly brought about precisely the result that Psyche had at first sought through her own nocturnal transgression. The two women, moreover, respond to the fact of murder in an identical manner: Psyche recoils in horror at the crime she was about to commit and at once resolves to end her life with a dagger; Enide recoils in horror at the crime she has committed and at once resolves to end her life with a sword.

But Enide is interrupted by the arrival of yet another count, who, like his predecessor, incarnates the values formerly held by Erec. He too, moreover, desires Enide and proclaims that she shall be his wife. The ensuing journey to the count's palace startlingly recalls the marital procession undertaken by Psyche at the beginning of the Apuleian paradigm. Here, the nuptial journey is described as a funeral cortege, and the grieving Psyche as a living corpse to whom marriage and death are one:

> Perfectis igitur feralis thalami cum summo maerore solemnibus, toto prosequente populo vivum producitur funus, et lacrimosa Psyche comitatur non nuptias sed exsequias suas. (4.34)

> Therefore, the ceremonial preparations for this funereal marriage were completed in utmost grief, the living corpse was led from the house accompanied by the entire populace, and a tearful Psyche marched along, not in her wedding procession but in her own funeral cortège.

Psyche is then transported to Cupid's palace. Similarly, the grieving Enide is accompanied by the assembled throng into the palace of the man she is to marry:

> Enyde chevauchoit delez,
> qui de son duel fere ne fine;
> sovant se pasme et chiet sovine;
> li chevalier qui la menoient
> antre lor braz la retenoient

Si la retienent et confortent;
jusqu'a Limors le cors an portent
et mainnent el palés le conte.
Toz le pueples aprés aus monte,
dames, chevalier et borjois.
              (4696–4705)

Enide rode along beside, continuing to give expression to her grief.
She often swoons and falls backward. The knights who accompanied
her held her up in their arms. They continue to support and comfort
her until they reach Limors with the body and take it to the count's
palace. The whole populace comes up behind them—ladies, knights,
and townsfolk.

This nuptial journey is, furthermore, the funeral procession of Erec.
Presumed dead, this living corpse is placed on a makeshift bier and carried
toward the ceremonial burial that the count intends to perform. The count
to Enide:

"Et g'en ferai le cors porter,
s'iert mis an terre a grant enor."
              (4668–69)

A tant se trest li cuens arriere,
et dist: "Feisons tost une biere
sor coi le cors an porterons;
et avoec la dame an manerons
tot droit au chastel de Limors;
la sera anfoïz li cors,
puis voldrai la dame esposer."
              (4677–83)

"And I will have the body brought. It will be buried with great
honor." At which the count stepped back and said: "Let us quickly
make a bier on which to carry the body. And we shall take the lady
with us straight to the castle of Limors. There the body will be buried,
and I then wish to marry the lady."

The marital history of the couple therefore begins anew by reverting to
the trace of Psyche's wedding, with aspects of Psyche's role now shared by
both Enide and Erec, and with the domineering presence of Cupid re-
fracted through the figure of the count. In this case, however, the bride is
unwilling, and, on being physically struck for her insolence, states that she
would rather die than yield. At this moment, Enide wakes Erec with her
words for the third time:

Antre ces diz et ces tançons
revint Erec de pasmeisons,
ausi come hom qui s'esvoille.
S'il s'esbahi, ne fu mervoille,
des genz qui'il vit an viron lui;
mes grant duel a et grant enui,
quant la voiz sa fame entandi.
Del dois a terre descendi,
et trait l'espee isnelemant;
ire li done hardemant,
et l'amors qu'an sa fame avoit.
Cele part cort ou il la voit.
et fiert par mi le chief le conte
si qu'il l'escervele et esfronte
sanz desfiance et sanz parole;
li sans et la cervele an vole.

(4815–30)

In the middle of this dispute, Erec recovered consciousness like a man who awakes from sleep. It was hardly surprising that he was amazed at all the people he saw around him. But he was particularly concerned and troubled when he heard his wife's voice. He got off the dais and quickly drew his sword; his anger and his love for his wife gave him courage. He ran to where he saw her and struck the count squarely on the head, beating out his brains and shattering his forehead without so much as a word of defiance. Blood and brains exploded.

This, the final variation on the paradigm, conjoins elements found in its antecedents. As in the bedroom, Enide wakes Erec with her words; as in her warning, she reacts to the advances of a count; as in her lament, a sword is drawn to kill. But on this occasion Erec awakens to full enlightenment, and immediately protects his wife, rather than the conventional values of manhood that he had sought to defend when woken by her first nocturnal lament. In taking up the sword, he in effect completes the murderous blow rehearsed by Psyche, and thereby consummates his own figurative mutation of gender. Just as Psyche overthrows the conventions of her sex in taking up the dagger, Erec definitively responds to an altered perception of masculinity as he wields the sword. But, unlike Psyche, he does not falter in his resolve, and with one gesture simultaneously decapitates and emasculates the serpent reflecting his former self. Therefore, while Psyche achieves parity with Cupid, it is Erec who finally proves himself the equal of Enide. Through the exemplary selflessness she shows during their exile, he overcomes his egocentrism, and bears as a physical penance the wounds he sustains in defeating Guivret and the giants; by refusing to allow these signs of contrition to heal, he actively precipitates the death of his former self and thereby prepares his definitive awakening. And, by symbolically excising his former tyranny, he effectively begins his second marriage.

If these analogies are taken as intertextually convincing, it is, I feel, safe to posit that they owe their presence to some form of Apuleius's text, and not to the Fulgentian paraphrase. On the most accessible level of thematic correspondence, this account lacks several functionally significant motifs present in both *Erec et Enide* and Apuleius's story. Neither Fulgentius's paraphrase nor his gloss even mentions the nuptial and funereal journey Psyche undertakes as the living corpse; neither presents Psyche's transgression in terms of gender mutation; neither makes reference to Psyche's plan to behead the serpent; neither describes Psyche taking up her dagger to end her life in horror at her husband's death. Accordingly, if we choose to accept the case for textual filiation, we are obliged to acknowledge that it is extremely implausible that Chrétien had access only to Fulgentius's version. To do so would entail the following almost perversely recalcitrant conclusion: that Chrétien's reading of Fulgentius's paraphrase and gloss enabled him to extrapolate a number of details that, by sheer coincidence, happen also to be of functional significance in the Apuleian original. This is not a particularly satisfying hypothesis.[35] If we accept an intertextual relationship as convincing, we must also accept that at least one twelfth-century author knew the story of Cupid and Psyche as written by Apuleius.[36]

None of the above, of course, forecloses the issue of Apuleius's reception in the High Middle Ages. Nonetheless, the argument for a knowledge of the *Asinus aureus* in the Francophone North can only be furthered by sensitive recognition of the validity of textual filiation. The effort must be cumulative: the other texts that have been seen to bear similarities to the story of Cupid and Psyche may yield a great deal, and could productively be studied in terms of the themes they hold in common, both with one another and with the Apuleian paradigm. Many questions arise: why, for example, should Chrétien's *Erec et Enide* and *Chevalier de la Charrete,* Marie de France's *Yonec,* Renaut de Beaujeu's *Bel Inconnu,* and the anonymous *Partonopeu de Blois* all exploit a narrative structure similar to the classical model in order to explore questions of power and gender, in some cases with additional emphases on emasculating razors (*Charrete, Yonec*), gender metamorphosis or reversal performed in the bedroom (*Charrete, Yonec*), and supernatural, serpentine spouses (*Bel Inconnu, Partonopeu*)?[37] If this is to be explained in terms of folklore, why should all these authors not only know the same folk tale but also set out to transform it into the literary text by exploiting a common nexus of symbols, do so with a similar effect, and in all cases show analogies to Apuleius's treatment of these issues? These questions, and a whole host of others, must be negotiated by the proponents of folklore before they can be dismissed, and must be negotiated on their own terms: that is, the folklorists must show themselves to be sensitive and able literary critics (not simply anachronistic statisticians) in order to reject literary evidence.

NOTES

1. For a lucid discussion of these questions and of the alterity of medieval authorship, see D. Hult, *Self-fulfilling Prophecies: Readership and Authority in the First "Roman de la Rose"* (Cambridge, 1986), particularly 10–104.

2. Accordingly, problems arise in any effort to gain intertextual access to two undatable works containing passages that reveal themselves to be practically identical in terms of language or thematic configuration. These problems can only be negotiated in a largely impressionistic manner, entailing, unconsciously or otherwise, a specific choice of textual anteriority on the part of the critic (a choice itself often determined by the precarious criterion of personal taste—the view that stylistic "inferiority" betrays a later work; the hierarchical elaboration of a canon, often manifested in the assumed priority of Latin over the vernacular). That twelfth-century romances are almost always rewritings of preexisting works has been a recognized tenet of medieval studies since the discipline developed in the last century. The past thirty years have seen a vast corpus of works devoted to this phenomenon. For a still relatively recent example, see the special issue of the journal *Littérature,* vol. 41 (February 1981).

3. For early arguments that it was known in twelfth-century France, see M. Kawczynski, "Ist Apuleius im Mittelater bekannt gewesen?" in *Festgabe für A. Mussafia* (Halle, 1905), and J. Reinhold, *"Floire et Blancheflor": Etude de littérature comparée* (Paris, 1906). These were attacked and ridiculed by G. Huet, "Le roman d'Apulée était-il connu au moyen-âge?" *Le Moyen Age* 22 (1909), and J.-Ö. Swahn, *The Tale of Cupid and Psyche: Aarne-Thompson 425 and 428* (Lund, 1955), esp. 397. These, in their turn, were questioned in their findings by D. Fehling, *Amor und Psyche: Die Schöpfung des Apuleius und ihre Einwirkung auf das Märchen, eine Kritik des romantischen Märchentheorie* (Wiesbaden, 1977). Of all the above, Fehling addresses the issue from the most sophisticated theoretical viewpoint, drawing attention to the problems inherent in the methodology of folkloric analysis employed by Swahn.

4. No manuscripts of this work survive in northern Europe. It is not present, furthermore, in any of the medieval library catalogues reproduced by G. Becker in *Catalogi bibliothecarum antiqui* (Bonn, 1885). Let it be stressed, however, that twelfth-century authors had ample evidence at their disposal that Apuleius had written a work of this name; it is mentioned in one of the most widely studied works of the Middle Ages, Saint Augustine's *De civitate Dei* 18.18 ("Sicut Apuleius, in libris quos *Asini Aurei* titulo inscripsit, sibi ipsi refert accidisse, ut accepto veneno, humano animo permanent, asinus fieret"). The late twelfth-century historian and ethnographer Gerald of Wales quotes this passage verbatim in his *Topographia Hibernica* (2.19), and does so specifically in the context of his own tale of an Irishman who retains his cognitive faculties when transformed into a wolf.

5. See D. S. Robertson, "The Manuscripts of the *Metamorphoses* of Apuleius," *Classical Quarterly* 18 (1924): 85–99.

6. Consider, for example, Swahn's characterization (caricature?) of Kawczynski in *Tale of Cupid and Psyche,* 391.

7. R. H. Bloch discusses the survival of this tendency in "New Philology and Old French," *Speculum* 65, no. 1 (1990): 38–58. It is certainly true that Chrétien claims in his prologue that the romance to follow transposes material derived from a *conte d'avanture,* perhaps (although not certainly) of Celtic origin. However, if such a Celtic ("folkloric"?) tale did indeed exist, it has not survived. The most likely Celtic candidate is the Welsh *Gereint;* this, however, exists only in a fourteenth-century manuscript, and largely derives from *Erec et Enide* itself. It also must be borne in mind that Chrétien, like many of his contemporaries, was notoriously evasive in recognizing his sources, frequently citing the most elaborate bibliographical red herrings.

8. John of Salisbury's description of the pedagogy of Bernard of Chartres reveals the importance of classical models to twelfth-century education; see *Metalogicon,* ed. C. Webb (Oxford, 1929), 1:24.

9. D. Kelly has produced several books and articles on this question; the most relevant of these to the works of Chrétien are *Sens and Conjointure in the "Chevalier de la Charrette"* (The Hague, 1966), and "The Source and Meaning of *Conjointure* in Chrétien's *Erec* 14," *Viator: Medieval and Renaissance Studies* 1 (1970): 179–200.

10. For the interrelationship of the northern and southern thrusts of Normal expansion, consult D. C. Douglas, *The Norman Achievement, 1050–1100* (Berkeley and Los Angeles, 1969), and *The Norman Fate: 1100–1154* (Berkeley and Los Angeles, 1976); on Monte Cassino and the Normans, see R. Palmarocchi, *L'abbazia di Monte Cassino e la conquista normannica* (Rome, 1913). Contemporary documentation of the Norman conquest of southern Italy is provided in G. Malaterra, *De Rebus Gestis Rogerii Calabriae et Siciliae Comitis et Roberti Guiscardi Ducis Fratris Eius,* ed. E. Pontieri (Bologna, 1928).

11. Several of the works that Chrétien de Troyes lists under his authorship in the prologue of *Cligés* have not come down to us; we do not even have the original version of *Tristan.* A. Micha provides information about the lost works of Chrétien in the introduction to his edition of *Cligés,* Classiques Français du Moyen Age, no. 84 (Paris, 1975). For observations on the originary *Tristan,* see *Le roman de Tristan par Thomas: Poème du XIIe siècle,* ed. J. Bédier, 2 vols., Société des Anciens Textes Français, no. 44 (Paris, 1902), 2:165.

12. Of these, *Partonopeu de Blois* has received the most attention, although in somewhat cautious terms. In order to sidestep the Apuleian problem, critics have advanced Fulgentius's fifth- or early sixty-century paraphrase of the story as the most plausible paradigm. Bibliographic notes relevant to this question are provided by Fehling, *Amor und Psyche,* 37–46. I shall return to Fulgentius later.

13. All textual references to *Erec et Enide* are consistent with the text of the Guiot manuscript, ed. M. Roques, Classiques Français du Moyen Age, no. 80 (Paris, 1981). The translations are my own and have benefited from cross-referencing with the translation of the Foerster paradigm provided by D. D. R. Owen in *Chrétien de Troyes: Arthurian Romances* (London, 1987).

14. All textual references to the *Asinus aureus* will specify book and paragraph numbers consistent with the edition of J. A. Hanson, *Apuleius, "Metamorphoses"* (Cambridge, Mass., 1989), vol. 1; the translations provided are by Hanson. References to the Fulgentian paraphrase will specify page and line numbers consistent with the Helm edition of Fulgentius's works, *Fabii Planciadis Fulgentii V.C. opera* (Leipzig, 1898).

15. Apuleius: 4.28; Fulgentius: 66.22.

16. Apuleius: 4.28; absent from Fulgentius.

17. Apuleius: 4.28; Fulgentius: 66.21–22.

18. Apuleius: 5.4; Fulgentius: 67.19–21.

19. Apuleius: 5.6; Fulgentius: 67.23–24, 69.14–15 (gloss).

20. Apuleius: 5.28; absent from Fulgentius.

21. Apuleius: 5.22; Fulgentius: 68.9–10.

22. Apuleius: 5.23; Fulgentius: 68.11–12, 69.22 (gloss).

23. Apuleius: 5.23–24; Fulgentius: 68.14.

24. Apuleius: 5.24–25; Fulgentius: 68.13–14, 69.24–25 (gloss).

25. Apuleius: 5.25–6.21; Fulgentius: 68.14–15.

26. Apuleius: 6.22; Fulgentius: 68.15.

27. Apuleius: 6.23–24; Fulgentius, 68.15, simply mentions that she finally marries Cupid with Jupiter's consent.

28. See Swahn, *Tale of Cupid and Psyche.*

29. My reading of *De nuptiis* is largely influenced by J. Préaux, "Jean Scot et Martin de Laon en face du *De nuptiis* de Martianus Capella," in *Jean Scot Erigène et l'histoire de la philosophie,* Colloques Internationaux du Centre National de Recherche Scientifique, no. 561 (Paris, 1977), 161–70. Préaux develops the insights of the ninth-century glossators he mentions in his title by arguing that it is in fact Pallas, and not Mercurius, who stands as the true absolute with which the human intellect endeavors to reach communion. I see in *Erec et Enide* a direct redeployment of these configurations: the writing subject (cf. Philologia) attempts to deploy his linguistic episteme (cf. Mercurius) to convey a given wisdom (cf. Pallas). In this I disagree with K. D. Uitti, "A propos de philologie," *Littérature* 41 (February 1981): 30–46; Uitti, "Vernacularization and Old French Romance Mythopoesis with Emphasis on Chrétien's *Erec et Enide,*" in *The Sower and His Seed: Essays on Chrétien de Troyes,* ed. R. T. Pickens (Lexington, Ky., 1983), 81–115, and S. Musseter, "The Education of Chrétien's Enide," *The Romanic Review* 73 (1982): 147–66, who place Philologia in a one-to-one correspondence with Enide herself.

30. An extremely wide-ranging feminist reading of Psyche has been provided by L. R. Edwards, *Psyche as Hero: Female Heroism and Fictional Form* (Middletown, Conn., 1984), although principally as a paradigm for the female protagonists of various eighteenth- and nineteenth-century novels. The seminal study of patriarchal structures and female rebellion in the Apuleian text remains E. Neumann, *Apuleius: Amor und Psyche, mit einem Kommentar von Erich Neumann: Ein Beitrag zur seelischen Entwicklung des Weiblichen* (Zurich, 1952); even though he devotes little detailed attention to the passages of the text that interest me here, Neumann's reading is complementary to my own. A useful introduction to current critical questions and an unfussy bibliography are provided by E. J. Kenney in his edition, *Apuleius: "Cupid and Psyche,"* Cambridge Greek and Latin Classics (Cambridge, 1990).

31. Apuleius is certainly not the last to (attempt to) split these two signifiers; a fairly recent case is provided in the writing of Lacanian psychoanalysis. J. Gallop provides a rebuttal (lucid and entertainingly written) of Lacan's distinction in "Phallus/Penis: Same Difference," which appears in *Thinking through the Body* (New York, 1988). While on the topic of feminist criticism, I should point out that the early section of *Erec et Enide* explores the male construction of the "feminine" (to the exclusion of the female) along specular lines remarkably similar to those discussed by L. Irigaray in *Speculum de l'autre femme* (Paris, 1974), particularly 165–208; the specular matrix is also of course pertinent to the late classical etiologies of Psyche herself, particularly that furnished by Martianus Capella in *De nuptiis* 1.7, where Psyche, on her birth, is said to have received the mirror of self-contemplation from Urania. (Although now somewhat antiquated, the word *psyche,* incidentally, still means "full-length mirror" in French.) Restrictions of space prevent me here from investigating any further the tripartite relationship of *Erec et Enide, De nuptiis,* and the Apuleian text, but there is still much to be done in this

direction. For example, it may not be coincidental that the articles of clothing that Martianus's Psyche receives at her birth in *De nuptiis* 1.7 correspond to those given to Enide on her arrival in Arthur's court (a crown, *Erec* 1639–41; a band of gold around the hair, *Erec* 1635–36; a purple-red robe, *Erec* 1598–1601; flowers, *Erec* 1639–40; jewelry, *Erec* 1592–93, 1645); this textual/textile "birth" of Psyche in Enide would have particularly cogent implications, since it prepares Chrétien's switch from *De nuptiis* to the Apuleian story as the paradigm for the rest of his romance.

32. As is demonstrated by, for example, J. Dornbush, "Ovid's *Pyramus and Thisbe* and Chrétien's *Le Chevalier de la Charrete*," *Romance Philology* 36 (1982): 34–43.

33. I shall concentrate only on those episodes of *Erec et Enide* that are pertinent to my comparative argument. For nuanced discussion of the journey of the couple and the importance of Enide in bringing it to a successful resolution, see in particular Z. P. Zaddy, *Chrétien Studies: Problems of Form and Meaning in "Erec," "Yvain," "Cligés," and the "Charrette"* (Glasgow, 1973); S. Musseter, "Education"; J. Brumlik, "Chrétien's Enide: Wife, Mistress, and Metaphor," *Kentucky Romance Quarterly* 55 (1988): 401–18; and particularly G. M. Armstrong, "Enide and Solomon's Wife: Figures of Romance *Sapientia*," *French Forum* 14 (1989): 401–18. Although less directly, D. Maddox also provides pertinent comments in his groundbreaking anthropological study *Structure and Sacring: The Systematic Kingdom in Chrétien's "Erec et Enide"* (Lexington, Ky., 1978).

34. Guivret, let us note, later returns and himself implicitly shows his own reappraisal of chivalric valor.

35. This is not to say that Chrétien could not have known the Fulgentian text. But if he did, *Erec et Enide* shows no sign of being influenced by its accompanying gloss. Within the Christianized interpretation Fulgentius offers, Psyche and Cupid are conjoined from the start as the twin attributes of humanity (Cupid, glossed as *cupiditas,* representing first a neutral potentiality of the Edenic soul and subsequently a negative stigma contingent on the Fall). Nevertheless, consistent as this commentary may be with the broad tensions operative within Genesis 2 and 3, it evades strict allegorical cohesion to the Apuleian original. Contrary to the implications of the gloss, Apuleius's story does not fuse Cupid with Psyche; Cupid always remains a fundamentally discrete and divine category. Furthermore, the circumstances of Psyche's communion with a higher power are entirely negative in the original, and carry none of the Edenic resonances subjacent to the gloss Fulgentius furnishes. Ultimately, in fact, Psyche's gaining of vision, which the Fulgentian gloss sees as analogous to eating from the tree of knowledge, is a frustrated and fleeting perception of the possibility of true parity with the divine. This gesture of rebellion against a facile and infantilizing ontology is the soteriological antithesis of Eve's calamitous weakness. The exile of the Apuleian soul, like that of its Christian analogue, may entail expulsion into a life of hardship. But unlike divorce from Eden, this exile is not a radical isolation from a total and unreflecting knowledge bestowed by transcendent communion with a divine power. It is not a fall from divine fullness, since Psyche's existence, not only after her transgression, but also before it, is always predicated on absence. *Erec et Enide,* in its negative presentation of the female figure's life before exile, corresponds far more closely to Apuleius's text than to this Christian interpretation; it also bears closer analogies to the original in presenting masculine and feminine figures who are discrete entities (rather than conjoined categories) and in exploring their relationship through patterns of gender interaction. (It also, let us note, never presents sexuality, the *cupiditas* of the gloss, as a sin.) Accepting an intertextual hypothesis, we could suggest, certainly, that Chrétien may have known Fulgentius's text. But, if he did, he also had at his disposal a more complete account of the story of Cupid and Psyche than the paraphrase, and created in his own

rewriting a text either ignoring or deliberately inverting the exegetical thrust of the gloss.

36. If accepted, this possibility raises the question of Chrétien's knowledge of, and apparent disregard for, the rest of the *Asinus aureus*. As a final open-ended remark, I shall list a series of analogies between *Erec et Enide* and Apuleius's frame narrative (analogies that cannot be drawn with the Fulgentian text, which concentrates only on Cupid and Psyche): Enide, a thinking human being, is deprived by Erec of the use of any discursive powers and forced to ride as an equal among eight horses; her initial role in the itinerant life of hardship is similar to that of Lucius, condemned to walk among the horses as a pack-ass, still capable of thought yet deprived of speech. On a less significant thematic level, the configurations of hospitality (through which Erec first meets Enide, and the conditions for Enide's divorce from language are created) are similar to those obtaining in Apuleius's description of Lucius's arrival at the house of Milo (through which Lucius meets Fotis, and the conditions for his divorce from language are created): Erec/Lucius arrives; Enide/Fotis tends to his horse; Erec/Lucius joins Licoranz/Milo and his wife for a meal, and is served by Enide/Fotis; Erec's sensual reaction to Enide is to see in her body a mirror of beauty, while Lucius's sensual reaction to Fotis is to see in her hair a mirror of beauty; Enide's sexual expertise (after the wedding) is greater than Erec's, while Fotis's sexual expertise (still at the house of Milo) is greater than Lucius's; (later) Erec's enlightenment is symbolically bound up with Enide refusing to eat, while Lucius's is caused by the ass finally having the opportunity to eat. Furthermore, on a more theoretical level, the term *conjointure,* which Chrétien uses in his prologue to designate both the process and the result of his lending of eloquence to the humble *conte,* finds a fascinating analogue in the stress Apuleius lays on the principle of *mutuus nexus* at the beginning of the first book of a work that also deals with an accession to speech. For the question of discourse in the frame-narrative, see J. Tatum, *Apuleius and "The Golden Ass"* (Ithaca, N.Y., 1979), and J. J. Winkler, *Auctor and Actor: A Narratological Reading of Apuleius' "Golden Ass"* (Berkeley and Los Angeles, 1985).

37. Editions: Chrétien de Troyes, *Le Chevalier de la Charrete,* ed. M. Roques, Classiques Français du Moyen Age, no. 86 (Paris, 1983); Marie de France, *Lais,* ed. J. Rychner, Classiques Français du Moyen Age, no. 93 (Paris, 1981); R. de Beaujeu, *Le Bel Inconnu,* ed. G. P. Williams, Classiques Français du Moyen Age, no. 38 (Paris, 1983); *Partonopeu de Blois,* ed. J. Gildea, 2 vols. (Villanova, Pa., 1967–68).

CHAPTER TWENTY

The Reemergence
of Greek Prose Fiction
in the Nineteenth and
Twentieth Centuries

Peter Bien

I

Prose fiction is now an established genre in Greece, although it still has not overshadowed poetry. Among Modern Greek writers with international reputations—Cavafy, Seféris, Rítsos, Elýtis, and Kazantzákis—only the last was a novelist, and he considered his novels secondary to his poetry and drama. Nevertheless, the novel did reemerge. Precisely when is another matter. Aléxandros Kotsiás stated that real novel writing in Greece did not start until the 1930s,[1] that is, until the expulsion of Greeks from Anatolia owing to the Asia Minor disaster of 1922 had led to massive urbanization and had ended the *Megáli Idéa* (great idea) by which Hellas was meant to win back Constantinople and once again become the dominant power in the eastern Mediterranean.

Kotsiás is not alone in dating "real" novel writing from the 1930s. Yórgos Theotokás wrote in his influential manifesto *Eléfthero pnévma* (Free spirit), published in 1929: "As much as we love our poets, we cannot live in the twentieth century by lyricism alone . . . We demand a real discussion of ideas, . . . a real novel."[2] In 1934, in an article entitled "I néa logotehnía" (The new literature), Theotokás argued that the main purpose of the novel was "to replace the ancient epic" as the quintessential expression of Greek reality.[3] In his own most ambitious work, *Argó,* he has his protagonist define what is meant by "a real novel": it is one whose primary goal is characterization, "the creation of people first of all,"[4] by which Theotokás means *individuals.* I emphasize this because it connects the Greek genre with the individualism of the mainstream novel of the West. Theotokás and Kotziás, in talking about so-called real novels instead of what had passed for novels in Greece until that time, are talking about a literary form that adheres to certain generic expectations. In any case, the novel blossomed in the 1930s, producing estimable works by Theotokás himself, Angelos Terzákis, Strátis Myrivílis, Ilías Venézis, Kosmás Polítis, Fótis Kóndoglu, Thrásos Kastanákis, and M. Karagátsis. I repeat that the genre did not eclipse poetry; indeed, poetry experienced its own significant renewal during this decade. But prose fiction truly established itself in Greece in the wake of the Asia Minor disaster.

Traditional histories of Modern Greek literature, however, place the reemergence of prose fiction considerably earlier, although disagreeing precisely when. One view favors the 1880s, the time when, at least according to Marxist analysis, the Greek middle class was establishing itself.[5] This was also the period when the demoticist crusade to replace *katharévusa* ("purified" Greek) was mustering its forces under the leadership of Yánnis Psiháris, who kept preaching that "the crucial time for a nation is the time when it begins to write prose."[6] He favored prose for several reasons. Practically, he argued, it was more likely than poetry to affect all areas of cultural life—law, government, commerce—as well as the arts.[7] Sociologically, he assumed prose to be the bourgeoisie's natural form. He felt that a national culture presupposed a reading public, that a reading public of any size and sophistication presupposed urbanization, and that an urban public desired prose. He was supported in this by Emmanuel Roïdis, whose earlier work *I Pápissa Ioánna* (1866) had ridiculed the then-dominant romantic mode of the historical novel in the interest of encouraging Greek writers to focus on contemporary life, which increasingly meant city life.[8] In 1879, Dimítrios Vikélas published *Lukís Láras*,[9] which, in treating commerce and in presenting a hero devoted to business success, departed from the bucolic subject matter of the romantics. This was widely read.[10] In 1880, a translation of Zola's *Nana,* also widely read, added further stimulation to this tendency. Urban novels came in the 1890s from the pens of Grigórios Xenópulos and Yánnis Kondylákis, but the two most remarkable careers that developed in the decade of the 1880s itself were those of Yeóryios Viziinós and Aléxandros Papadiamándis, writers of stories in which individualized characters are depicted with psychological realism—meeting Theotokás's criterion for the "real novel."[11] Each of these authors has been recently translated;[12] thus Greekless readers can now taste an art that—although influenced by the West (both writers were aware of European currents)—possesses a flavor all its own.

Before the 1880s there were very few novels in the nineteenth century, and none earlier. The first novel (if it can be called that) came in 1834: Panayótis Sútsos's *Léandros,* a wildly romantic fictionalized autobiography in the epistolary style, echoing Ugo Foscolo's *Ultime lettere di Jacopo Ortis* (1798–1802) and Goethe's epistolary novel *Die Leiden des Jungen Werther* (1774). The intense turmoil of the Greek Revolution had concluded only six years earlier, to be followed by the assassination of the new state's first president in 1831 and the imposition of a Bavarian monarch on Greece by the Great Powers in 1832. These facts are relevant because at the precise time of *Léandros,* whose prose was sterile, irrelevant to contemporary reality, and incapable of stimulating the growth of further prose in Greece (Sútsos in any case considering himself primarily a poet), there also emerged the curious phenomenon of General Makriyánnis, an illiterate soldier who at the age of thrity-two arranged to be taught to read and write so that he could record the truth about what had happened. His *Apomnimonévmata* (Memoirs), one of the glories of Modern Greek prose and culture, was composed from 1829 onward in an almost indecipherable hand innocent of punctuation and spelling. This document displays novelistic powers of narration, description, and dialogue. Yet it exercised no influence at all on the development of nineteenth-century Greek prose because it was written in the then-despised demotic rather than in *katharévusa* and because it remained unpublished until 1907, and even then passed largely unnoticed until the period of the Second World War when, ironically, it was a poet, George Seféris, who invited all Greek writers to learn from the "illiterate master."

Still another work that might have influenced later production but never did—because it was not reissued until 1989—was Grigórios Palaiológos's *O Polipathís* (1839). Although self-consciously imitative of Lesage's picaresque *Gil Blas* (1715–35) and Faddey Venediktovich Bulgarin's *Ivan Vyzhigin* (1830; translated into French in 1831 and known as "the Russian Gil Blas"), this neglected work "unfolds a panorama of the customs of its times."[13]

The above catalogue of the meager production of prose fiction in Greece suggests two of the many factors that have set Greek prose apart from the prose of Western Europe: the estimation of poetry as superior to prose, and the *glossikó zítima* (language question) involving a demotic idiom, spoken by the uneducated, versus a "purified" language written, and in some circumstances spoken, by the educated.

Léandros was followed in succeeding decades by a handful of novels that resembled it in escaping contemporary reality. The fashion was now the historical novel in imitation of works by French authors and Sir Walter Scott that were appearing in translation in the Athenian periodical *Pandóra.* An example of the Greek production is Aléxandros Rangavís's *O afthéndis tu Moréos* (The Lord of the Peloponnesus), based on Scott's *Ivanhoe* (1820), and serialized in *Pandóra* in 1850. It introduces us to still another of the facts that distinguish the literary situation in Greece from developments elsewhere, in this case the myth of a unified Greek innocence and purity in relation to Western European depravity. The subject treated is the Greek resistance to the Frankish invaders of the thirteenth century, the Villehardouin. Rangavís, in suggesting that this invasion and all others left the Greeks uninfluenced and untainted, is not only covering up the realities of his own time but is also rebutting the insinuation of Jakob Fallmerayer, promulgated in 1830,[14] that current Peloponnesians were not the descendants of ancient Greeks but the offspring of Slavic invaders. What we see in its infancy here, along with the myth of indigenous innocence, is the further myth of Hellenic continuity from ancient times to the present. All these factors will be encountered again when I explore the conflict in Greece between orality (*foní*) and literacy (*grafí*). Suffice it to say here that Rangavís himself, although the author of many fictional works, dismissed prose fiction, including his own, as secondary to tragedies, poetry, and especially epic poetry—genres still relatively oral in Greek conception—when he wrote his pioneering history of Greek literature in 1877.[15]

But mid-nineteenth-century Greece did produce one genuinely Greek novel in the realistic mode among all these others that mimicked foreign models or escaped contemporary relevance by means of romantic agonies or historical deceptions. This was Pávlos Kalligás's *Thános Vlékas*, serialized in *Pandóra* in 1855 but not reissued in book form until 1891—so, in a way, the exception that proves the rule. Its subject is the brigandage that was sabotaging the legal structure of the new Greek state; it also treats the problem of land distribution—all the woes of the countryside, seen honestly in distinction to what we find in the scores of so-called *ithografiká mithistorímata*,[16] whose portrayal of an idealized village life so distressed Psiháris and Theotokás. Yet even *Thános Vlékas* was a dead end because of the obligatory *katharévusa* language that undermines the novel's realism. Although meant to be an honest portrayal of peasant life, it calls a jug of cool water an *anghíon psihrú ídatos* instead of a *kanáta krío neró*, and it even purifies the villagers' sighs from their natural (and suspiciously Turkish) *ach* to the Attic *aï*.

One can begin to see why Kotsiás's claim that real novel writing in Greece did not begin until the 1930s is perhaps the most accurate assessment.

Be that as it may, what, if anything, did the nineteenth-century prose writers possess as models? I have already mentioned various foreign influences: Zola in the 1880s; Scott, Goethe, and Lesage earlier. One may add Mme de Staël, whose *Corinne* (1807) appeared in Greek translation in 1835. But what about eighteenth-century prose in Greek? And what about the medieval Greek novel or the classical paradigm—the ancient Greek novel? Mario Vitti has examined these questions in an essay whose title, "The Inadequate Tradition," betrays his conclusion. There were no eighteenth-century Greek novels. When Greek prose fiction first reemerged in the mid-nineteenth century it seems to have been "imported wholesale from the West,"[17] whether directly or via Russia. Nevertheless, the extended reemergence that includes the twentieth as well as the late nineteenth century does offer some connections with earlier Greek prose, either indigenous or imported, although never directly with ancient or Byzantine Greek novels, which indeed came to be viewed as foreign and un-Greek.[18]

Research into Greek book production from the late seventeenth century until the outbreak of the revolution shows that religious texts were favored by readers in Greece itself and in the diaspora during this period.[19] "The gospels, epistles, and liturgy, with their incessant reading, constitute perhaps the chief points of a literate culture in the body of oral knowledge."[20] To these texts in *koine* or ecclesiastical Greek we must add the *sinaksária,* popularized saints' lives written in demotic. These circulated in individual pamphlets or in compilations such as *Amartolón sortiría* (Venice, 1641, drawn from Italian originals), *Perí iróon, stratigón, filosófon, agíon ke állon onomastón anthrópon* (Rome, 1659), and *Néon martirolóyion* (Venice, 1794), the last of which has been reprinted down to our own day.[21]

These are particularly important for our consideration since they offer a possible link between ancient Greek novels and modern ones. The death of the ancient Greek novel may have been hastened by relief from the anxieties of the Hellenistic age, relief occasioned by the general acceptance of Christianity in the fourth century. The ancient novel's worries about capricious Fortune seem to have been transferred to the *sinaksári,* which offers a Christian solution. Furthermore, the ancient Greek novel "bears witness to the fascination exercised by the thought of invincible chastity and beautiful young persons facing pain with reckless readiness, features which we find again in hagiographic romance."[22] It may be argued, in short, that "the saints' lives of the Middle Ages were in many respects the natural successor to the novel."[23] In modern times, Níkos Kazantzákis was an avid reader of the *sinaksária* in his boyhood; we know that they stirred his imagination in a novelistic manner.[24] Among his own prose fictions, *O Christós ksanastavrónetai* (Christ recrucified) is in effect an account of the lives of two saints, Manoliós, the young martyred idealist, and Fótis, the mature surviving sufferer. *O teleftaíos pirasmós* (The last temptation) and *O ftohúlis tu Theú* (The poor man of God) may also be viewed in this context. But the best and most surprising example is the novel whose provisional title we know from a letter.[25] It was meant to be called *To sinaksári tu Zorbá* (The saint's life of Zorbás)—appropriately so, because the book's hero, although very pagan, exemplifies a modern way to deal successfully with capricious Fortune.[26]

Among indigenous texts that also must be mentioned are the dialogues of Plato. At least two twentieth-century works that perhaps may be called novels are self-consciously based on this source. These are Kazantzákis's *Simbósion* (Symposium, probably 1924 or 1926) and Kóstas Várnalis's *I alithiní apología tu Sokráti* (The true apology of Socrates, 1933).

An indigenous text that enjoyed prolonged popularity was the *Alex-*

ander Romance, which derives originally from Pseudo-Callisthenes (ca. A.D. 300). The question of whether this is a novel at all, as opposed to a romanticized biography, has been raised by Tomas Hägg. In any case, its truth or historicity is enlived by fantastic elements and compromised by gross liberties of time and place.[27] In a word, it is a *mithistórima* (myth-history or myth-story), the precise term used in Modern Greece for the novel. The *Alexander Romance* remained popular down to the nineteenth century. The prose version includes in its title the word *diíyisis* (tale):[28] *Diíyisis Aleksándru tu Makedónos.*[29] Today the normal word for "tale" or "short story" in Greece is still the same, although its gender in demotic continues the neuter of Byzantine times: *diíyima.* This does not prove any continuity from Pseudo-Callisthenes to Viziinós, but, along with the saints' lives discussed above, it does suggest that the reemergence of Modern Greek prose fiction, although primarily an import from the West, may have been influenced to some degree by indigenous texts.

If we turn now to nonindigenous texts, Rígas Velestinlís in the last decade of the eighteenth century introduced into Greece a translation of some love stories from Nicolas-Edme Rétif de la Bretonne's *Les contemporaines, ou avantures des plus jolies femmes de l'âge présent* (1780) and, inspired by the French Revolution, planned also to translate Montesquieu's *Esprit des lois* in order to bring to his benighted fellow citizens the spirit of the French Enlightenment. Earlier in the century some other translations, always generated by a didactic purpose, circulated.[30]

This survey of the inadequate tradition leads as well to a half-dozen or so extremely popular prose works in demotic that originated in the East. These have been surveyed by George Kehayióglou. I shall confine myself to just two: the stories of Sindbad and Scheherazade. The first, called *Sindípas* in its Greek version, knew two Byzantine forms, one in the learned language, the other in a more popular idiom. Additional versions in demotic appeared after the Fall of Constantinople; at least twenty-five popular editions were printed in Venice, and cheap reprints continue to this day.[31] Sindbad is reflected in Greek folklore, in the Karagiózis puppet theater, and perhaps in the prose of Roïdis and Hatzís. Scheherazade, known as Halimá in Greek, entered the Hellenic written tradition in the eighteenth century through European intermediaries, the *Arabian Nights* being first translated into Greek from the Italian. Issued in 1757–62, this text "was reprinted many times, with enormous success; [*I Halimá*] circulates even today in cheap popular editions."[32] More research is needed on the precise effect of this and other Oriental texts on Modern Greek fiction. What we can say for certain is that a half-dozen or so such texts circulated widely, along with the *Alexander Romance* and the *sinaksária,* for centuries before the Greek novel reemerged in 1834. (Or was it in 1855, or the 1880s, or after 1930?)[33]

For the present, our conclusion must remain Mario Vitti's, that the reemergent Greek novel does not represent "the culmination of a narrative genre which had developed naturally in the Greek world, but rather a sudden change in direction."[34] Such a conclusion is consistent not only with the views of certain Greek theoreticians but also with Ian Watt's theory explaining the novel's emergence in England. Watt's analysis remains probably the most useful for us even though it has been subjected to numerous criticisms.[35] He begins by asking whether the work of Defoe, Richardson, and Fielding was a continuation of ancient Greek fiction or other existing texts. He goes on to show that Fielding and Richardson themselves "viewed their work as involving a break with the old-fashioned romances." In literary history, the difference is normally explained by the dominance of realism.[36] Yet it is not enough, claims Watt, to say that novels are realistic; we must realize that they reflect a different view of the real. For older texts, the real resides in universals; for the novel, it resides in particulars.[37] The novel is atomistic. It reflects "that vast transformation of Western civilization since the Renaissance which has replaced the unified world picture of the Middle Ages with another very different one—one which presents us, essentially, with a developing but unplanned aggregate of particular individuals having particular experiences at particular times and at particular places."[38] Of course, the unified world picture of the Middle Ages did not capitulate entirely to the atomistic view, but continued in various forms that reacted against that view—for example, the organicist model of evolution promulgated in the eighteenth century by Johann Gottfried von Herder, in which individual entities are seen "as components of processes which aggregate into wholes greater than, or qualitatively different from, the sum of their parts."[39] The competition between these two opposing philosophies of the nature of reality, the atomistic and the unified/collective, has continued to our day to exacerbate the rivalry in Greece between prose and poetry; indeed, the organic view manifests itself in a general preference for orality that has inhibited the development of prose fiction.

Watt continues his analysis of Western fiction by showing the specific effects of the post-Renaissance philosophy on plot, characterization, the naming of characters, the treatment of time and place, and the nature of the language employed. In all areas, he sees the new genre as ostentatiously breaking with tradition in order to inaugurate a change of direction.[40]

All this is connected in Watt's analysis with the rise of capitalism and the increasing dominance of the bourgeois class. Urbanization, new degrees and patterns of literacy, the increase in leisure, the appearance of newspapers that ran serializations of novels, authors' financial dependence on booksellers and circulating libraries rather than on aristocratic patrons, money as a motive in authorship—factors such as these, which affected prose much more than verse, were "merely reflections of . . . the great power and self-confidence of the middle class."[41]

The role of women should be emphasized. Urban life freed them from the drudgery of the farm; middle-class women, and also "servant women of the better sort," formed the largest proportion of novel readers.[42] Even the railroad eventually played a part, since long journeys in first-class compartments provided the privacy and leisure needed for the multi-volume novels of Victorian times.

It should be clear that Greece was different from England in many of these respects. It had no vast transformation introducing an atomistic world-view, no industrial revolution, minimal urbanization before the Asia Minor disaster, restricted literacy, no circulating libraries, not even much of a railroad system. And there is no word for "privacy" in the Modern Greek language.

As for the rise of the middle class in Greece, some say that it occurred during the revolutionary period, others—for example, the Marxist historian Yánnis Kordátos—during the 1880s,[43] while still others link it to the bloodless revolution at Gudí in 1909 that brought Elefthérios Venizélos to power, or to the urbanization that accelerated after 1922 owing to the influx of refugees from Anatolia. All four periods—the revolutionary, the demoticist, the pre–First World War, and the post–Asia Minor disaster— have been suggested as starting points for the "real" novel in Greece, confirming the social analysis that is shared by Greek theoreticians who join scholars like Ian Watt in viewing the novel as a sudden change of direction mirroring a shift from traditional assumptions that no longer conformed to economic and social conditions. When Yórgos Theotokás declared in 1929 that Greeks in the twentieth century could not live by poetry alone but needed "a real discussion of ideas, . . . a real novel," he was calling on Greek prose writers, as Peter Mackridge explains, "to move away from the traditional themes of peasant life or of the urban poor, and to write instead about the urban middle class."[44] Similarly, when Psiháris preached from the 1880s onward that "the crucial time for a nation is the time when it begins to write prose," he did so because he assumed prose to be the bourgeoisie's natural form.

II

In examining the delayed reemergence of Greek prose fiction in the nine-teenth and twentieth centuries, and the failure of that genre even today to dominate poetry, it would therefore seem useful to employ the same analy-sis that Ian Watt applied to the rise of the novel in England, agreeing with Mario Vitti's conclusion that prose fiction "found conditions more favour-able to its development and expansion in Western Europe" than in Greece.[45] But we must be careful. Quite aside from the possible inade-quacy of Watt's analysis in explaining the rise of the novel in the West itself, we should remember that Greece is sufficiently different from Western Europe even though it has been subjected to some of the same social and economic forces that have affected the northern nations. The analysis offered by Ian Watt must be supplemented—not replaced—by something else, something more exclusively Greek.

Mary Layoun does this by asking what happens when the modern novel "is transplanted to a society in which there exists neither an indigenous, let alone ascendant, bourgeoisie nor a developed capitalist mode of production." She views the rise of the novel in Greece as tied to Greece's "dependent and underdeveloped social, economic, and cultural position vis-à-vis an expanding and hegemonic West," with earlier Greek novels attempting "to resist the challenge of Western hegemony by calling up the 'traditional,' the 'indigenous,' the 'popular,' or the transcendent," while at the same time they ironically "disdained Greek narrative traditions and folk culture . . . In the absence of an established bourgeois culture and its notions of the 'coherent' and 'orderly' individual and the 'meaningful' details of that individual's life, the early modern Greek novel attempted an 'orderly' narrative purveyance of the 'disorderly' peasant and his or her village life."[46] This useful analysis supplements Watt by applying his categories in a new way. But the work of Dimítris Tzióvas goes further.[47] It introduces two categories absent in Watt, *foní* (voice) and *grafí* (text)—categories that relate to modern Greece in a way quite different from their application to more "advanced" nations. I have already catalogued various indigenous factors that may help explain the delayed reemergence of prose fiction in Greece: the valuation of poetry above prose; the *glossikó zítima;* the myth of Hellenic innocence and purity in relation to Western European depravity; the additional myth of Hellenic continuity from ancient times to the present; collectivity versus atomization; organicism. What Tzióvas does is to subsume these characteristics under the assertion that Greece remains even today—and assuredly was throughout the nineteenth century—a proto-literate society: that is, a society that combines "oral and literate attitudes in a period of transition."[48] The enduring bias toward the oral, toward *foní* as opposed to *grafí,* may help explain the continuing dominance of poetry over prose, for a poem, even if printed, has closer ties to residual orality than does a novel.

Writing is hardly absent from Greece. Indeed, in the nineteenth century it assumed ever-increasing importance as intellectuals such as Adamándios Koraïs attempted to prepare the Greek Revolution; then, after the revolution, when illiterate soldiers like Makriyánnis and Kolokotrónis felt the need to establish, through written memoirs, the truth of what had happened; finally, when Konstandínos Paparrigópulos produced his massive *Istoría tu ellinikú éthnus* (1860–72) in order to demonstrate the organic unity of Hellenism, with Byzantium linking the ancients to the moderns, all as an answer to Fallmerayer's assertion (1830) that Greeks are Slavs in disguise.

What happened as *grafí* increased, however, was paradoxically the ever-stronger sanctioning of *foní*. As the nineteenth century evolved, a series of related phases combined to reinforce this tendency so strongly, and in so many different areas of national life, that the general bias toward orality has continued into the twentieth century in ways that still influence prose fiction.

The first phase involved the ancestor worship inculcated in Modern Greeks before, during, and after the revolution by their own intellectuals and by Western philhellenes. Since the purpose was to stimulate liberation from the tyranny of the Ottomans, the figures most often invoked were Pericles, the later orators, and the dramatists, all connected with orality, as opposed to Plato, who, quite aside from his advocacy of authoritarian government, distrusts poets and himself "plays a decisive role, even though his own discourse retains some of the hallmarks of previous oralism," in the change whereby "language managed acoustically on echo principles is met with competition from language managed visually on architectural principles."[49] The legacy of this early indoctrination persisted until recently in Greek education, with its emphasis on recitation and memorization.

The second phase, stimulated by Fallmerayer's disturbing theory, extended ancestor worship to Byzantine and post-Byzantine Greeks, strengthening orality in new ways because the elements of continuity offered to counteract Fallmerayer's assumption of discontinuity were church ritual and folk song, each of which could be a civilizing force in a barely literate society. Both the historical investigations of Paparrigópulos, already mentioned, and the folklore research carried on principally at first by N. G. Politis elaborated the myth of Hellenic organic continuity. This, in turn, led to the myth of indigenous purity in relation to Western Europe.

In attempting to develop a national culture, late nineteenth-century Greeks were no longer able to invoke a high (written) culture, meant to be enhanced, as opposed to a common or vulgar (oral) culture, meant to be disparaged. Nor could early-twentieth-century Greeks do so, since it was only "after 1920, when urbanization and industrialization manifested themselves intensely in Greece" that "the term *laïkós politismós* (popular civilization) [began to] appear sporadically." "Hence the contrast between high (written) and common (spoken) culture took another form: the conflict between ethnic life and local customs, on the one hand, and the foreign civilization of enlightened Europe on the other."[50] Hellenism was seen as an incorruptible unity that could "never be assimilated or annihilated."[51]

The third phase affixed a still firmer seal of orality to organicism, the

Byzantine link, and even the ancient Greek inheritance. It occurred from roughly 1890 to 1920 with the flowering of demoticism, which viewed the Greek language as the indisputable evidence of Hellenic continuity. Was not that language in its various forms the vehicle of Pericles, Demosthenes, the New Testament, the church liturgy, the folk songs of the Byzantine and Turkish periods, the exemplary prose of Makriyánnis? Was not Homer, in his day, a demotic bard just like the epic singers still circulating in the Greek countryside? In short, the uninterrupted orality of the uninterrupted Greek language was seen as the ultimate guarantee of the uninterrupted continuity of Greek culture, a culture necessarily favoring *foní* over *grafí*.

It should be evident how strongly these factors in Greece clash with factors advanced by Ian Watt, and by Greek theoreticians such as Theotokás and Psiháris, as preconditions for the rise of prose fiction. Not only did Greek culture lack the stimuli that encouraged atomistic and mechanistic views in the West; it imported from the West the organicism and romanticism that were reacting there to the alleged sterility of such views. In sum, clinging to tradition, Greece developed the collectivist, supraatomistic myths I have described.

These, in turn, favored poetry because of the assumed equations "poetry = speech" and "speech = community."[52] That poetry was now largely written could be overlooked, given the orality surviving in poetic drama, the emphasis on recitation in schools, the declamation at public events (for example, Angelos Sikelianós's sensational poem on freedom shouted into the faces of the Nazi occupying forces at Kostís Palamás's funeral in 1943—a poem now known by most Greek schoolchildren). In modern Greece to some extent, as in ancient Greece, "to understand . . . poetry we must understand the festivals and the rituals of conviviality which gave poetry its functional setting."[53] Even when verse was not actually declaimed or performed, it was considered the modern continuation of an oral tradition. The *dimotiká tragúdia* (folk songs) were seen on the one hand as direct descendants of the choruses of ancient Greek tragedy owing to the supposed derivation of the word *tragúdi* from *tragodía*,[54] while on the other hand they were seen as signifying "the continuity of the Homeric epics which on the whole represented the 'unity of the Greek race.'"[55] The normal colloquial term for a poem today in Greece is not *píima* but *tragúdi*, even though the poem is more likely to be read in a book than recited on a platform, much less sung. The term means more than a particular "song"; it connotes an organically unified, uninterrupted tradition involving the medieval *dimotiká tragúdia* plus ancient drama and Homeric epic.

Prose, evoking not an indigenous tradition but rather a foreign importation, was generally excluded from this vision of a unified national literary expression. Kostís Palamás, the dominant figure in poetry from roughly 1890 to 1910, worried about the incursions of prose's realistic bias on poetry. "The more prose expands and trespasses into the domain of verse," he declared in his 1906 prologue to *O dodekálogos tu yíftu* (The twelve words of the gypsy), "the more will verse take refuge on the highest peaks of dream, inaccessible to prose."[56] What he preached—and practiced—was a "national poetry" that would be "chiefly epic." This poetry would "echo the uninterrupted struggles and the great idea of the race, against the fearful enemy, the man of different religion and race, today's plunderer, tomorrow's conquerer. The national consciousness needs an image."[57] What we see here in the fulsome language of Greek romanticism is the vision of unified Hellenic purity in contrast to everything imported, the vision of a nation that can never be assimilated or annihilated, of a collectivity based on *foní,* not *grafí.*

No wonder that prose in Greece was forced so much on the defensive. It was trapped in contradiction since on the one hand it, too, strove to form the national consciousness, this time by means of a departure from poetic tradition, while on the other hand its own driving stimuli of *dimotikismós* (demoticism) and *ethnismós* ("nationism")[58] were forces aligned against it and in favor of poetry. The results are predictable, at least in hindsight. In formulations of the novelist's challenge, we find that writers of prose are urged to achieve the status of poets.[59] Kazantzákis, the most celebrated novelist Greece has produced, set out in *O Kapetán Mihális* (Captain Michael) to write the "epic novel of Crete,"[60] by which he meant, quite aside from the "nationistic" vision articulated in the passage from Palamás just cited, the amalgamation of realism and fantasy.[61] Furthermore, in an age in which epic is no longer considered a viable form in verse, Kazantzákis devoted most of his energies for a decade, starting in 1925, to the composition of a huge sequel to Homer's *Odyssey,* and he planned, but never executed, a second epic of equal length based on the medieval hero Akrítas, the border guard defending Byzantium against people of a different religion and race. Most curious of all, even when he had achieved international renown as a novelist, he denigrated the novelistic genre as secondary on the grounds that it strives for a merely realistic portrayal of phenomena, neglecting the essence behind them.[62] Insofar as he did at times accept his work in this genre, he did so because of his conviction that he had discovered ways to make the novel "poetic," for example by recording in *The Saint's Life of Zorbás* the virtues of a hero of orality as opposed to a despised, unvital, and un-Greek penpusher who, until he meets Zorbás, is misled by the West.

III

Kazantzákis offers an extreme example of orality's insinuation into a Greek novelist's career. The emphasis on orality did not eliminate prose's development, even though it clearly inhibited that development. Prose fiction did reemerge in the nineteenth and twentieth centuries. Greek novelists and short-story writers did produce a notable body of work, at least from the 1880s onward, and especially after 1930. Nonetheless, there is something strangely unsatisfying about Greek prose fiction considered from a Western perspective. Greece has produced world-class poets but no novelist to stand beside a Jane Austen, a Dickens, a Balzac, a Tolstoy, or a Dostoevski. Viewed from the Western perspective that expects the realistic, nineteenth-century conventions of plotting, causality, characterization, specificity of time and place, and elimination of linguistic ornateness, the Greek novel seems defective (although from another perspective its alleged defects may constitute its charm).

I have suggested that the cause is the bias toward orality in Greek culture. As Tzióvas has written, "The art of literary composition in Greece has its roots in the oral mode of narration . . . The principal oral narrative genre is the epic . . . If we consider climactic linearity to be the prime characteristic of plot, we can then argue that the epic does not have a plot. Examining the Greek novel from this point of view, we find that one of its features is the lack of plot. This is evident in many twentieth-century novels, for example *Argó, I zoí en táfo, To tríto stefáni,* and *To dipló vivlío,* all of which use a mainly episodic structure rather than a tight and intricately organized plot . . . The episodic structure persists as a remnant of orality."[63]

Regarding language, many Western readers are annoyed by what they consider the overwriting in Greek prose (although, once again, from a different perspective this can constitute its charm). Especially during the demoticist period, novelists were eager to demonstrate demotic Greek's versatility as a literary medium; thus they employed a richness of diction that readers now denigrate as precisely that ornateness which the novelistic genre is meant to eschew. Most basically, however, this tendency may be ascribed not so much to demoticism *per se* as to the primacy in Greece of oral expression, which "is not compositive but, rather, accumulative, filled with epithets and redundancies[,] . . . voluble laxity, and not the tightly constructed intensity of textuality."[64]

The *foní-grafí* conflict is sometimes the very subject matter of Greek prose fiction. In Kazantzákis, for example, it determines the major conflict not only between Zorbás and the Boss in *Víos ke politía tu Aléksi Zorbá,* as already noted, but also between Mihális and Kosmás in *O Kapetán Mihális.* In Pandelís Prevelákis's work, "a similar opposition is personified in *O ílios tu thanátu* by Aunt Rusáki (popular tradition) and Loïzos Damolínos (Western intellectualism)," the latter emphasizing "the deadlock Prevelákis himself experienced as a European-educated intellectual in a nation where culture continues to be oral."[65] The *foní-grafí* conflict may be seen as well in the characterization of the two brothers in Karkavítsas's *O arheológos,* where "the pen and its products . . . , personified in the firstborn son Aristódimos, assume priority . . . whereas speech . . . , personified in the secondborn son Dimitrákis, is marginalised and devalued." In this case, the conflict is expressed "*inside* the ethnic boundaries . . . , rather than with the 'other'"; the pen is "associated with the classical, pagan inheritance, the voice with the Byzantine, Christian inheritance." As might be expected, "sterility and the death–wish . . . characterise the first, while Eros and the living force . . . attach to the second."[66]

Perhaps the most subtle pressure of orality on Modern Greek prose involves the insinuation of attitudes that affect technique. This phenomenon has been studied recently in relation to Viziinós, Psiháris, and Karkavítsas. Regarding the first, Mihális Chryssanthópoulos notes the perceptive comment by Palamás in 1896 that Viziinós is a "short-story-writing poet" guided by the "philosophical art of the poet."[67] Chryssanthópoulos characterizes the tension in Viziinós as between the stories' "metaphorical and their referential aspect," caused, in turn, by the author's "endeavour to put together memory and imagination, in order to create a literary space that on the one hand can be interpreted as autobiography and on the other as fantasy."[68] In other words, Viziinós is reluctant to favor realism over romance. In technique, this works itself out through the narrative strategies that Chryssanthópoulos analyzes, strategies that enable Viziinós first to use "verifiable historical data to give the reader an impression of verisimilitude, and then, by shifting the point of view, [to substitute] fictional data for them, presented as though they were historically accurate."[69]

Since Viziinós "was already an established poet when he published his stories,"[70] the intrusion of poetic—that is, in a Greek context, of oral—elements into his prose technique is not surprising. When we turn to Psiháris, however, we are dealing with a figure who campaigned for prose and a consequent break with the past, and whose own writings are exclusively in that genre. How curious, then, to find his work, too, affected by poetic rather than prosaic practices and theories. This has been demonstrated by Roderick Beaton in relation to the novel *To taksídi mu* (My journey, 1888) and by David Holton in relation to the short stories. In both cases there is a self-conscious "relationship with the *paramíthi* [tale, fable], which could be called the opposite extreme to realism."[71] In *To taksídi mu* the narrator, instead of projecting the atomistic view that energizes realistic fiction, is identified with a "collective 'Homeric' *voice* that may be considered to emerge directly 'from the *mouth* of the people'"[72]—to project the myth, founded on orality, of an organic, unified, indestructible Hellenism. Finally, in Karkavítsas's *O arheológos,* written in 1904, we encounter a text with the agenda of restoring its characters to a world-view favored by prose fiction as practiced in the West. Yet that agenda undermines itself, since middle-class historical consciousness in Greece is "marked by a contradiction: at the class level it conceives of history as a process admitting of radical break, change and development; at the nation-alist level, however, it dreams of the race as unchanging, persisting through time thanks to permanent historical factors."[73] Because the "mode of narration chosen by Karkavítsas is the folk tale which . . . overprivileges orality and the collective, anonymous culture of the folk, thus indirectly underprivileging fictional writing," the subject is "kept imprisoned within the rhythms of . . . continuity and cannot attain to difference and the acquisition of an historical identity."[74]

Políti exposes a further contradiction that bears on my overall discussion of the conflicts in Greece between poetry and prose, orality and literacy. It is that the imposition of folk tale, and consequently of orality, "turns out to be a 'trick'. The absence of . . . history is simply 'make believe'." When all is said and done, *foní* in this text, as well as in the larger cultural situation, "cannot stand on its own. To be operative, it needs the sanction of learned authority, that is, of . . . *grafí*."[75]

IV

These are some of the factors that distinguish Greece from Western Europe in the development of prose fiction. I have emphasized Greece's lack of a massive Western-style Renaissance; its delayed industrial revolution, ur-banization, and formation of a middle class; the different role of women; the lack of libraries and of a desire for privacy; the myths of Hellenic innocence, continuity, organicism, and collectivity. As a possible source for all the rest, I have suggested the residual orality that characterized protoliterate Greek society in the nineteenth century and has left its mark on the content and technique of Modern Greek prose in the twentieth.

It should be clear from these perspectives on Greek prose that the re-emergent genre owes little to classical paradigms; the possible linkage through the *sinaksária*, although an attractive hypothesis, is much too thin a thread from which to hang a theory of continuity. Modern Greek ances-tor worship, mediated by the West, saw the early Greek novel, and Helle-nistic art in general, as symptomatic of decline, and therefore not to be emulated. On the other hand, although it is fair to agree in some ways with Roderick Beaton that the "Greek novel when it reappears after 1834 is imported wholesale from the West," it is also imperative, when discussing this reemergence, to understand the indigenous factors, especially the Greeks' obsession with their glorious past, that have made the novel in Greece develop in ways interestingly different from its counterpart in Western Europe.

NOTES

1. Kotsiás's remark was made at the 1986 international symposium on the Greek novel, A.D. 1–1985, organized at King's College, London, by Roderick Beaton.

2. Y. Theotokás, *Eléfthero pnévma* (Athens, 1929), cited in T. Doulis, *Disaster and Fiction* (Berkeley and Los Angeles, 1977), 167. In fact, Theotokás was inveighing less against poetry than against the traditional *ithografikó* novel that ignored urban life and concentrated on the Greek village.

3. Y. Theotokás, "I néa logotehnía," *Idéa* 3, no. 13 (January 1934), cited in D. Tzióvas, "George Theotokás and the Art of Fiction," in *The Greek Novel, A.D. 1–1985*, ed. R. Beaton (London, 1988), 71. Compare Angelos Terzákis, who stated his belief in 1933 that the novel was "the preeminent expressive literary form of the age" (cited in M. Vitti, *Istoría tis neoellinikís logotehnías* [Athens, 1978], 330). Similarly, Kléon Paráschos declared in 1937, "The strong advance that the writing of novels exhibits in Greece today . . . reflects . . . our intellectual and social realities . . . No other form but the novel can express this complex world" (K. Paráschos, "I néa ellinikí pezografía," *To Néon Krátos* [September 1937]: 69, cited in Doulis, *Disaster and Fiction*, 169).

4. Cited in Tzióvas, "George Theotokas," 72.

5. Y. Kordátos, *Istoría tis neoellinikís logotehnías*, 2 vols. in 1 (Athens, 1962), 338. Precisely when the Greek middle class established itself is a vexed question. In the view of some commentators, the time should be advanced to the 1910s, when Elefthérios Venizélos came to power owing to the Gudí "revolution" of 1909. For a brief discussion of problems raised by this view, see N. Mouzélis, "Piós píre ti Vastílli," *To Víma*, 25–26 March 1989, 39. He notes the Marxist argument that even if the Gudí revolution itself was not clearly bourgeois in nature, its effects were, because the Venizelist ideology "brought about changes that aided the development of industrial capitalism in the 1920s and 1930s." On Gudí in general, see S. V. Papacosma, *The Military in Greek Politics: The 1909 Coup d'Etat* (Kent, Ohio, 1977).

6. K. Th. Dimarás, *Istoría tis neoellinikís logotehnías*, 3d ed. (Athens, 1964), 376, citing Y. Psiháris, *Róda ke míla*, vol. 4 (Athens, 1907), 254.

7. Vitti, *Istoría*, 258.

8. Kordátos, *Istoría*, 279–80.

9. *Lukís Láras* was reissued in 1991 by Ermís Publishers, Athens, with a preface by Mariánna Dítsa. See M. Dítsa, "O 'Lukís Láras' tu Dimitríu Vikéla," *To Víma*, 22 December 1991, B5.

10. Vitti, *Istoría*, 236–37.

11. For aspects of Viziinós's art that resist psychological realism, see section 3 below. Regarding Papadiamándis, M. N. Layoun (*Travels of a Genre: The Modern Novel and Ideology* [Princeton, 1990], 21–55) offers a revisionist reading of *I Fónissa* (The murderess) in which she concludes that, precisely because of the structure of the novel itself, the author "cannot quite be the vehement enemy of all things 'Frankish' [i.e., western European] as his critics have suggested" (53).

12. A. Papadiamantis, *Tales from a Greek Island*, trans. E. Constantinides (Baltimore, 1987); Papadiamantes, *The Murderess*, trans. P. Levi (London, 1983); G. M. Vizyenos, *My Mother's Sin and Other Stories*, trans. W. F. Wyatt, Jr. (Hanover, N.H., 1988).

13. N. Vayenás, "Enas simantikós pezográfos," *To Víma*, 3 December 1989, 62.

14. J. P. Fallmerayer, *Geschichte der Halbinsel Morea während des Mittelalters*, 2 vols. (Stuttgart, 1830).

15. M. Vitti, "The Inadequate Tradition: Prose Narrative during the First Half of the Nineteenth Century," in Beaton, *Greek Novel*, 4; A. R. Rangabé, *Histoire littéraire de la Grèce moderne*, 2 vols. (Paris, 1877); Rangabé, *Précis d' une histoire de la littérature néo-hellénique* (Berlin, 1877).

16. The term derives from the French *roman de moeurs* (Vitti, *Istoría*, 230).

17. Beaton, *Greek Novel*, viii.

18. Witness the view of the historian Paparrigópulos, writing in 1877, that *Erotókritos* is to be preferred to the Byzantine novels because the Cretan romance, although presenting feudal jousts, nevertheless "neither beguiles us into foreign lands nor imposes on us foreign-speaking characters, as do . . . those other poems" (S. Alexíou, "Eisagoyí," in V. Kornáros, *Erotókritos*, critical edition (Athens, 1980), civ, citing Paparrigópulos's *Istoría tu ellinikú éthnus*, 4th ed. [Athens, 1877], 5:636).

19. G. Veloudís, *Das griechische Druck- und Verlagshaus "Glikis" in Venedig (1670–1854): Das griechische Buch zur Zeit der Türkenherrschaft* (Wiesbaden, 1974). See the chapter called "Verzeichnis der Glikis-Ausgaben" (93–127), which lists 1,052 individual titles from 1670 to 1820 from this one house alone. Total book production for the same period was 4,054 titles (85). From 1700 to 1825, 59.28 percent of the books produced were religious. Grammatical titles accounted for 8.28 percent, while "other" made up 32.28 percent. The last category increased from a low of 15.8 percent in 1700–1725 to a high of 76.5 percent in 1801–25, while the religious category decreased from a high of 77.6 percent in 1726–50 to a low of 21.5 percent in 1801–25 (86).

20. A. Polítis, "To vivlío méso paragoyís tis proforikís gnósis," in *To vivlió stis proviomihanikés kinoníes*, Praktiká, A´ Diethnús Simposíu tu Kéntru Neoellinikón Erevnón (Athens, 1982), 279.

21. Vitti, *Istoría*, 77–78; "Inadequate Tradition," 5, 9 n. 5.

22. A. D. Nock, *Conversion* (London, 1933), 200.

23. Beaton, *Greek Novel*, viii.

24. "Selling all my toys to my friends, I purchased the lives of the saints in popular, pamphlet-sized editions. Each evening I sat [in] our courtyard and read out loud all the various ordeals the saints had endured . . . Distant seas unfolded in my childish imagination, boats cast off furtively, monasteries glittered among rocky crags, lions carried water to the ascetics" (N. Kazantzákis, *Report to Greco* [New York, 1965], 71–72).

25. H. Kazantzakis, *Nikos Kazantzakis: A Biography* (New York, 1968), 401.

26. The definitive title as well—*Víos ke politía tu Aléksi Zorbá*—begins with a formula commonly used in the titles of saints' lives.

27. T. Hägg, "The Beginnings of the Historical Novel," in Beaton, *Greek Novel*, 174.

28. "A rhymed version in vernacular Greek printed in Venice in 1529" may have been used by Kornáros in his *Erotókritos* (D. Holton, "*Erotókritos* and Greek Tradition," in Beaton, *Greek Novel*, 150; Holton, *Diíyisi tu Aleksándru* [The tale of Alexander: The rhymed version] [Thessalonike, 1974]). A prose version in demotic, first printed in Venice in 1699 as a pamphlet, circulated widely in the late eighteenth and early nineteenth centuries in connection with the revolutionary ferment of those years (Vitti, *Istoría*, 78; "Inadequate Tradition," 9 n. 4). *Erotókritos* itself, although in verse, should also be mentioned if only because of its extremely wide dissemination (occasionally in prose adaptations) among both the common people within Greece and the intelligentsia of the diaspora (who preferred to read it in a *katharévusa* translation). Stylianós Alexíou gives details (c–ciii), but concludes (cviii) that as far as content is concerned the poem's influence on nineteenth-century Greek literature was "necessarily small, because the shock of 1789 and the Napoleonic wars definitively dissolved the passé idealism of the ancient aristocratic societies of the Middle Ages and the Renaissance . . . Literature now expressed the life of the rising bourgeoisie, as well as the emotions of the isolated individual in their midst. Thus in the new period of [Greek] literature . . . it was natural for Kornáros to exert influence that was chiefly formal, that is, influence relating to linguistic and poetic sensibility." On the other hand, to the extent that "*Erotókritos*, and many other fictional texts that can be linked to the Byzantine and post-Byzantine

romances, . . . passed into oral tradition in the form of extended stories, legends, and songs, . . . they thereby played an indirect but important and formative role in the emergence of modern prose fiction" through novelists such as Viziinós, Papadiamándis, Myrivílis, and Venézis, who self-consciously draw on this oral tradition (private communicaton of Margaret Alexiou to the author, 1990).

29. Vitti, "Inadequate Tradition," 5, 9 n. 4, 10.

30. Kordátos, Istoría, 104.

31. G. Kehayióglou, "Translations of Eastern 'Novels' and Their Influence on Late Byzantine and Modern Greek Fiction (11th–18th Centuries)," in Beaton, Greek Novel, 160.

32. Ibid., 157, 161, 162.

33. Disagreement over the date when prose reemerged is hardly surprising once we realize that even greater disagreement exists over the date when Modern Greek literature itself began. An entire conference was devoted to this problem in November 1991 at the Greek Institute of Byzantine and Post-Byzantine Studies in Venice, with Mario Vitti favoring the early nineteenth century, Stylianós Alexíou opting for the seventeenth-century Cretan renaissance, George Savídis choosing 1519 because of the appearance then of Bergadís's Apókopos, the first printed text in demotic, Hans Eideneier favoring the poems of Theódoros Protopródromos in the twelfth century, and others going as far back as the end of the tenth or beginning of the eleventh century, the time of Diyenís Akrítas. See S. Bakoyannopúlu, "Anástasi sti Venetía," To Víma, 27 October 1991, B9.

34. Vitti, "Inadequate Tradition," 9.

35. I. Watt, The Rise of the Novel: Studies in Defoe, Richardson, and Fielding (Berkeley and Los Angeles, 1957). Criticisms of Watt come from various directions. T. Lovell (Consuming Ficton [London, 1987], 22) questions the three major phenomena that form Watt's thesis, "all directly or indirectly themselves a function of the development of capitalism: the conventions of formal realism . . . ; the values and mental attitudes of the rising bourgeoisie . . . ; and the shift in literary production to the commodity form, produced for an anonymous middle-class readership." Lovell's rebuttal, "while acknowledging the significance of Ian Watt's location of coherent, rational, and orderly individualism and realism in the rise of the English novel, astutely critiques that position for its disregard of the simultaneously dominant presence of the gothic, of the less-than-rational, and the desirous. Lovell's analysis also offers a crucial corrective to Watt's exclusion of the women who dominated not only the consumption of the early novel but also, until the mid-nineteenth century and the novel's entry into the fields of high literature, its production. [Lovell] pays rather more careful attention to the initial status of the novel as a 'debased,' 'debasing,' and just barely literary form . . . [I]t is only later that the novel comes to occupy a stable and exalted role in bourgeois literary culture" (Layoun, Travels of a Genre, 5–6). D. Spender (Mothers of the Novel: One Hundred Good Women Writers before Jane Austen [London, 1986]) provides a feminist corrective to Watt. E. D. Ermarth (Realism and Consensus in the English Novel [Princeton, 1983]) exposes the conventions underlying the "realism" supposedly governing the novelistic genre. M. M. Bakhtin ("Forms of Time and Chronotope in the Novel," in The Dialogic Imagination: Four Essays [Austin, 1981], 86–110) traces the novel back to the ancient Greek romances, focusing on the various narrative "voices" in the novel and on the extent to which novels express national character and culture. M. McKeon (Origins of the English Novel, 1600–1740 [Baltimore, 1987], 4–10), citing Lévi-Strauss and Frye, elaborates on the archetypalist criticism of Watt, commenting (10) that this approach "tends to over-emphasize continuity and identity" in opposition to Watt's evolutionist position and his assertion that the novel is superior to earlier forms. A useful survey of various

approaches may be found in L. J. Davis, *Factual Fictions: The Origins of the English Novel* (New York, 1983). When all is said and done, however, Lovell concludes: "Yet finally Watt is surely right. For the primary parenting of the novel was performed neither by its literary mothers nor its founding fathers, but by capitalism . . . This is the kernel of Watt's thesis, and so far it remains unchallenged" (45). Similarly, Layoun, despite her questioning of Watt's assumptions as they apply to Greece, acknowledges that "the rise of the novel in West Europe was tied to the rise of a particular ascendant and soon-to-be hegemonic class and to the dominant ideology of that class" (33).

36. Watt, *Rise of the Novel,* 9–10. The term *réalisme* was first used in 1835 in relation to Rembrandt's *verité humaine,* in contradistinction to the *idéalité poétique* of neoclassic art (10). The term was subsequently applied to authors such as Flaubert and then, by extension, to the novelistic genre per se.

37. Ibid., 12. See R. Williams, *Keywords: A Vocabulary of Culture and Society,* rev. ed. (New York, 1985), 257–62, for an extensive discussion of the problems arising from the term "realism" as that term is used in philosophy, painting, and literature.

38. Watt, *Rise of the Novel,* 31.

39. H. White, *Metahistory* (Baltimore, 1973), 15, cited in D. Tzióvas, *The Nationism of the Demoticists and Its Impact on Their Literary Theory (1888–1930)* (Amsterdam, 1986), 61.

40. Thus "Defoe and Richardson are the first great writers in [English] literature who did not take their plots from mythology, history, legend or previous literature" since they, unlike older writers, rejected the "premise . . . that, since Nature is essentially complete and unchanging, its records, whether scriptural, legendary or historical, constitute a definitive repertoire of human experience" (Watt, *Rise of the Novel,* 14). Plots are now "acted out by particular people in particular circumstances, rather than . . . by general human types" (15). Time in novels resists anachronism. Furthermore, in the new genre "a causal connection operating through time replaces the reliance of earlier narratives on disguises and coincidences" (22). Place, instead of being vague or general, as in Shakespeare's plays, takes on the specificity of a guidebook. As for language, Watt notes (28) that the new genre rejected "the tradition of linguisitic ornateness" established in the Greek romances by Heliodorus's *Aethiopica* and continuing in John Lyly's *Euphues* (1578–80). The eighteenth-century novelists' "basically realistic intentions . . . required something very different from the accepted modes of literary prose" (29).

41. Watt, *Rise of the Novel,* 59.

42. Ibid., 43, citing Fanny Burney's *Diary* for 26 March 1778.

43. Kordátos, *Istoría,* 338.

44. P. Mackridge, "European Influences on the Greek Novel during the 1930s," *Journal of Modern Greek Studies* 3 (1985): 5.

45. Vitti, "Inadequate Tradition," 4.

46. Layoun, *Travels of a Genre,* 32, 33, 250, 32.

47. D. Tzióvas, "Residual Orality and Belated Textuality in Greek Literature and Culture," *Journal of Modern Greek Studies* 7 (1989): 321–35.

48. O. Murray, review of *The Interface between the Written and the Oral,* by Jack Goody, *Times Literary Supplement,* 16–22 June 1989, 656. Further investigation is needed concerning the relation between protoliterate societies and the viability of prose fiction. Nineteenth-century Russia, for example, was protoliterate, yet produced superb novels more or less in the realistic mode. South America has produced novels, like Greece's, that tend not to be in that mode. Ireland, another protoliterate society in the nineteenth and early twentieth centuries, produced mainly poets and dramatists (except for James Joyce). Ideally, the case of Greece should be examined comparatively with these and

other examples in mind. In addition, one must be careful not to assume that the production of novels in Greece in the 1920s and thereafter automatically suggests a transition to a literate society. In 1927, according to one source, 35 percent of men and 66 percent of women were still illiterate in Greece (*Anayénnisi* 1, no. 8 [April 1927]: 573).

49. E. A. Havelock, *The Literate Revolution in Greece and Its Cultural Consequences* (Princeton, 1982), 9. Compare W. V. Harris, *Ancient Literacy* (Cambridge, Mass., 1989), 91, who notes the criticism of writing that Plato puts in the mouth of Socrates in the *Phaedrus* (274c–277a), but who then remarks (92) that Plato and his contemporaries who expressed hostility toward certain uses of writing "were needless to say creatures of a partly literate culture and heavily dependent on writing. Their eventual acceptance of the written word was inevitable. In the end Plato came to recommend universal education"—in his last work, the *Laws* (7.809e–810b).

50. Tzióvas, "Residual Orality," 324.

51. J. Políti, "The Tongue and the Pen: A Reading of Karkavítsas' *O Arheológos*," in Beaton, *Greek Novel*, 42.

52. Certain theoretical bases for the second equation are presented by Tzióvas (*Nationism*, 102–6; 435 nn. 53–56, 62; 436 nn. 63–64), drawing on the work of Gadamer, Derrida, Heidegger, Ong, and Herder.

53. Murray, Review of *Interface*, 656.

54. S. P. Kyriakídis, *Ai istorikaí arhaí tis dimódus neoellinikís piíseos* (Thessalonike, 1934).

55. Tzióvas, *Nationism*, 238, drawing on statements by the demoticist Aléxandros Delmúzos.

56. K. Palamás, *The Twelve Words of the Gypsy* (Memphis, 1975), xxxi.

57. Tzióvas, *Nationism*, 47, citing K. Palamás, *Apanda*, 16 vols. (Athens, 1960–69), 6:495.

58. The coinage "nationism" is used by Tzióvas, *Nationism*, to distinguish *ethnismós* from *ethnikismós* (nationalism). *Ethnismós* is normally translated "patriotism" or "nationality."

59. Vitti, *Istoría*, 341, citing Y. Theotokás, "I téhni tu mithistorímatos," *Epohés*, no. 20 (1964): 9.

60. P. Bien, "*O Kapetán Mihális*, an Epic (Romance?) Manqué," *Journal of Modern Greek Studies* 5 (1987): 154, citing N. Kazantzákis, "Déka epistolés tu Kazantzáki ston Hurmúzio," *Tetrádia "Efthínis"* 3 (1977): 192.

61. Fielding, too, thought of his novels as epics in prose, substituting coincidence for fantasy. See Watt, *Rise of the Novel*, 239, 251–53. Regarding *O Kapetán Mihális*, Bien argues ("*O Kapetán Mihális*") that Kazantzákis's attempt to amalgamate the epic and novelistic genres is artistically unsuccessful.

62. See P. Bien, "Kazantzákis' Attitude towards Prose Fiction," in Beaton, *Greek Novel*, 81–89.

63. Tzióvas, "Residual Orality," 327–28.

64. Ibid., 328.

65. Ibid., 331, summarizing P. Mackridge, "Popular Tradition and Individual Creativity: Pandelis Prevelakis (1909–86)," *Modern Greek Studies Yearbook* 2 (1986): 147–49.

66. Políti, "Tongue and the Pen," 47.

67. M. Chryssanthópoulos, "Reality and Imagination: The Use of History in the Short Stories of Yeóryios Viziinós," in Beaton, *Greek Novel*, 11–12, citing Palamás, *Apanda* 15:157, 159.

68. Ibid., 12.

69. Ibid., 13.

70. Ibid., 11.

71. D. Holton, "Psycharis and the Short Story," *Mandatoforos*, no. 28 (1988): 67.

72. R. Beaton, ed., "Aporíes diavázondas ton Psihári: Afiyimatiká ke idologiká provlímata sto *Taksídi*," *Mandatoforos*, no. 28 (1988): 49; italics added.

73. Políti, "Tongue and the Pen," 42.

74. Ibid., 46. Compare Kazantzákis's opinion written in a 1909 review of this novel, where he says in the language of his day what Políti says in the idiom of Bakhtin, Jameson, Said, and Derrida. Kazantzákis calls Karkavítsas a "mediocre allegorist in his *Archeologist*, in which . . . he attempts . . . to elevate his characters, so full of blood and life, into dead, . . . bloodless symbols" (*Néa Zoí*, October–November 1909, reprinted in M. Yalurákis, *O kritikós N. Kazantzákis* [Athens, 1973], 14).

75. Políti, "Tongue and the Pen," 47, 51–52. Further problems are introduced by A. Polítis, "To vivlío," who shows the extent to which supposedly oral materials were originally written ones.

CHAPTER TWENTY-ONE

From *Interlude in Arcady* to *Daphnis and Chloe:* Two Thousand Years of Erotic Fantasy

Holly W. Montague

> On a rock sat a girl, a creature of such indescribable beauty that one might have taken her for a goddess. Despite her great distress at her plight, she had an air of courage and nobility. On her head she wore a crown of laurel; from her shoulders hung a quiver; her left arm leaned on the bow, the hand hanging relaxed at the wrist. . . Her head was bowed, and she gazed steadily at a young man lying at her feet.

Thus Heliodorus introduces Chariclea, the engaging heroine of his *Aethiopica*.[1] The ancient romances in general are populated by beautiful and vigorous young female characters. These figures are vividly described; at times, their inner lives are depicted with an intensity that strikingly anticipates the work of much later writers. In what follows I will examine some of the parallels between ancient and modern romance novels, with particular regard to their heroines. My discussion will be informed by recent criticism of contemporary fiction.[2] More specifically, I will refer to studies of those popular novels known generically as "Harlequins."[3] Critics of Harlequins not only have continued the now-familiar project of rediscovering and analyzing images and treatments of women in fiction but also have brought to bear more recently developed theories concerning "women's" reading and writing.[4] These various studies have yielded remarkable insights about the multiple ways in which readers enjoy Harlequins: not only as entertaining fantasy, but as explorations of women's experiences.[5] Ancient romances lend themselves to similar readings; in fact, some feminist approaches to the erotic novel apply better to ancient works than to contemporary ones.

The anachronistic nature of this project must be acknowledged at the outset. Harlequins are written for an audience (almost exclusively female) that is carefully identified, and whose preferences are intensively analyzed, by the publishers.[6] Literary critics have been able to conduct their own, rather differently oriented surveys of readers.[7] Thus there is available a wealth of data about the contemporary reception of Harlequins. No comparable information exists for ancient romance. The questions of how ancient novels came to be written, and who was originally meant to read them, are indeed vexed ones; however, no one has conclusively argued for a preponderance of women—or of any other group—among the original audiences.[8] It is also likely that some contemporary ways of reading (above all the deep personal engagement with characters common among audiences today) would have appeared bizarre in antiquity. Criticism of Harlequins, then, must be used only to suggest ways in which romances from different periods may be read and reread; no argument about the ancient texts can be grounded in a discussion of the practices of specific readers.[9]

Once one places questions of original contexts and readerships to the side, ancient romance turns out to prefigure mass market fiction in a number of ways. I will focus on two famous Greek romances: Longus's *Daphnis and Chloe* (A.D. 200?) and Achilles Tatius's *Leucippe and Clitophon* (late second century A.D.?).[10] Both works concern pairs of young lovers whose attempts to marry are repeatedly thwarted by a variety of disasters. *Leucippe and Clitophon* is full of travel and exotic adventure; *Daphnis and Chloe,* though it takes place in an idealized rural setting, also features kidnapping by pirates and other colorful distractions. All these elements of plot and setting are familiar enough to readers of supermarket romances. A typical Harlequin of the late 1960s is entitled *Interlude in Arcady* (Margery Hilton, 1969). Like *Daphnis and Chloe, Arcady* takes place against a lovely rural background. Such is often the case in modern romance; otherwise, the setting tends to be exotic. In any event, it is important in Harlequins of most periods that connections to the everyday world be tenuous.[11] The story line of *Arcady* also resembles that of *Daphnis and Chloe* in its broad scheme. We see countless ingeniously contrived romantic opportunities being narrowly missed. Needham and Utter, the authors of a compendious study of romantic heroines, describe this common narrative structure as an "obstacle course."[12] In pursuit of this effect, *Arcady* displays some elaborate logic. The two main characters are living together in a remote house and pretending to have a love affair so that the man may write a play unhindered by the hordes of women who would otherwise harass him. (In much the same way, would-be suitors—and rapists—plague ancient heroines and, to a lesser extent, heroes.) For the two characters in *Arcady* actually to have an affair would, as it were, destroy the pretense. Yet the possibility of consummation is always enjoyably present. For instance, early in the story the characters are compelled to share a bedroom. (A critic of Harlequins has claimed that this sort of postponed gratification is especially appealing to a female audience because women's sexuality thrives on passivity and waiting.[13] On the other hand, delayed resolution is important to all kinds of romance—not to say all kinds of fiction.) Further obvious parallels between ancient and contemporary romances include fantasies of class mobility. Daphnis and Chloe are both upper-class but disguised throughout most of the story as shepherds. Along with marriage comes social elevation for both of them. Harlequin heroines often marry men of higher social status.[14]

Both ancient and modern romances also take place within a sensuous atmosphere. The reader is encouraged to visualize all sorts of pleasurable or otherwise stirring scenes, often of a sexual nature. The means of encouragement are varied. The ancient novels contain many ecphrases, or detailed descriptions of artworks. A notable ecphrasis opens Longus's work. The speaker describes a visit he once paid to a beautiful grove, where he saw "a painting that told a story of love." The picture showed "women giving birth, others dressing the babies, babies exposed, animals suckling them, shepherds adopting them, young people pledging love, a pirate's raid, an enemy attack—and more, much more, all of it romantic." The entire narrative that follows presents itself as an interpretation of the picture. Achilles Tatius describes a number of mythical tableaux full of sometimes barely sublimated, sometimes explicit sexuality.[15] The first is, once more, the ecphrasis that opens the novel. This time the subject is not the novel's story but the mythical tale of Europa's abduction by Zeus in the form of a bull.[16] Europa is shown dressed in garments that reveal her body: the narrator describes her belly, waist, hips, and breasts. Europa's companions can be seen on the shore, their skirts drawn up to reveal their legs, their hair loose. These ecphrases prompt the reader to visualize the action that follows; the events of both novels are told with much bright graphic detail.

Contemporary narratives, too, offer an abundance of visual pleasure. Here, in addition to lavish descriptions, we have elaborate covers.[17] Designs have changed dramatically in the past few decades. The cover of Hilton's *Arcady* is more or less typical of the late 1960s. A young woman's face occupies much of the picture. She smiles dreamily, lifting to her face a sketchy hand on which a ring is visible. In the next decades, however, cover designs began to make a great display of the heroine. The cover of *Tomorrow—Come Soon* (Jessica Steele, 1984), for instance, shows a man, whose features are partly hidden, embracing a woman. She wears a pink dress with a revealing neckline. Her expression is ambiguous; she appears troubled. Her emotional experience, however, is not the main point of the composition, which emphasizes the appearance of her body, and particularly her breasts. If the reader is invited to identify with the heroine, she is also encouraged, even before opening the book, to regard her as a desirable object. Works like *Tomorrow* are difficult to fit into any argument for the feminist impact of Harlequins. *Tomorrow*'s back-cover blurb summarizes its premise: "When her father suddenly announced he had enough money to pay for the expensive operation that would end her years as a cripple, Devon was overjoyed. The joy turned to horror when he confessed he had embezzled the money from Grant Harrington, his boss. Grant demanded the debt be repaid. And Devon's horror deepened when she realized payment in cash wasn't what he had in mind." Similarly, in *See Only Me* (Shirley Larson, 1986) the heroine is blind, but the hero helps her find a cure. Such temporary physical disabilities may be a means of restoring an element of female dependency that could more easily be assumed in Harlequins written during past decades. A modern romance need not, however, have a story line of this kind to merit a cover that displays the woman as an object of desire.[18]

It is hardly a surprise, with respect to the tradition of romance in general, that an appeal should be made to seemingly divergent, even opposing, erotic tastes. As Utter and Needham remarked, *Pamela* seemed likely to appeal equally to the "ladies" who flaunted copies in public and to "rakes" who presumably would find much to enjoy in the detailed description of a girl's inner life.[19] Such bivalent appeal would seem less to be expected in a genre supposedly created for (and to a large extent by) women. Readers of Harlequins, it would seem, derive pleasure from seeing women as objects of intense male desire.[20]

The question, however, is not merely one of "male" or "female" identification, of gazing or being gazed upon. In romances of all periods, we find not only the erotic display of women's bodies, but violence, and threats of violence, graphically described. Characters are repeatedly exposed to extreme dangers, which are often described in a titillating or prurient way. Cutting and stabbing form a major motif in *Leucippe and Clitophon*. Achilles Tatius quickly establishes the sexual associations of this theme through a dream narrated near the beginning of the story. The narrator dreams that he and his half-sister Calligone (in fact promised in marriage to one another) share one body below the waist.[21] A horrible woman appears and cuts them apart with a sickle.[22] Once Clitophon has fallen in love with Leucippe, another dream reinforces the connection. As the lovers go to bed together, Leucippe's mother has a nightmare in which a robber slashes her daughter's belly from her "modest spot" upward.[23] Achilles Tatius continues to embroider on this motif, sometimes describing the cutting instruments in great detail. In the most extravagant instance, Leucippe becomes the object of a pretended sacrifice, fitted out with a false belly and stabbed with a trick knife.[24]

Longus uses erotic imagery somewhat differently than does Achilles Tatius. Achilles Tatius often puts his heroine in a position much like that of the characters in modern "slasher" films. The impression these exaggerated incidents give is to some extent reinforced by statements so misogynistic as to be humorous, which are made by minor characters. (Near the beginning of the story, a cousin of Clitophon's delivers a mannered speech against marriage, including many well-known literary references to the evils of women.)[25] Longus, in contrast, treats Daphnis and Chloe in a parallel fashion during much of the tale.[26] Both are kidnapped in similar incidents.[27] Daphnis, toward the end of the novel, is approached by a man who tries to rape him, much as a cowherd has earlier tried to rape Chloe.[28] Throughout this novel, however, there are indications that women especially tend to be the targets of sexual violence. Most arresting, perhaps, are stories told by various characters. The tale of Pan and Syrinx and the story of Echo both involve sexual aggression or violence.[29] Finally, while Daphnis is initiated uneventfully into the joys of lovemaking by a neighbor woman named Lycaenion, Chloe must wait for the traditional wedding night. As Lycaenion has told Daphnis, this promises to be a painful experience: "She will cry out and weep and lie there, bleeding heavily."[30] When the bridal night arrives, the narrator describes it as follows: "Daphnis did some of the things Lycaenion had taught him; and then, for the first time, Chloe found out that what they had done in the woods had been nothing but shepherds' games."[31]

Students of Harlequins also point out violence and threats, the appeal of which, since the audience is assumed to identify with the female object, has been viewed as sadomasochistic.[32] Even the characters seem aware of what would be the popular psychological interpretation of many events, as we see for instance in *Love's Sweet Revenge,* where the hero says "I would like to beat you," and the heroine replies, "I bet you would, too. Is that how you get your kicks?"[33] It has been suggested that even incidents in which the relations between men and women become abusive can be read in a feminist way.[34] The reader can use them consciously as an opportunity to examine problems that exist between the sexes. Radway indeed suggests that readers engage in such critical examination even as they enjoy the narratives in a more simply pleasurable manner.[35]

Radway's approach, which takes into account the possibility that readers may experience novels in various ways (sometimes even in contradictory ways), seems to me especially promising as a basis for the feminist interpretation of ancient novels. One may more readily find feminist inspiration in ancient novels than in Harlequins. Criticism of Harlequins necessarily has consisted in large part of rehabilitation, since the novels have drawn fire from a number of quarters.[36] The negative views are understandable: contemporary fictions show a tendency to make female inferiority seem acceptable, if not desirable, in the final analysis. This characteristic may be obvious even from the examples I have cited. The heroines learn to love men who have all too often threatened them with physical violence: the resolution or, better, the capitulation is accomplished with no visible irony. On the contrary, it is made to seem reasonable.[37] A feminist reading of Harlequins, then, must to some extent be accomplished "against" the text.

Ancient romance does not require recuperation of the type performed on Harlequins. The reputation of the works is not in question.[38] Nor, for that matter, is there a line of antifeminist propaganda to be traced from one novel to the next. Readers are not encouraged to rationalize victimization. Rather, events are narrated from varying perspectives, but often in such a way as to permit, even at times to suggest, critical views of the social configurations presented. Perhaps the best example is *Daphnis and Chloe,* particularly as it has been reconsidered by Winkler.[39] Longus presents the sometimes violent treatment of the female disturbingly, often pathetically, and in such a manner as to encourage consideration of sexual inequalities. The two characters start out nearly as equals. Gender actually becomes a theme as Chloe begins to lose her autonomy relative to Daphnis. Unlike the Harlequins, *Daphnis and Chloe* contains no implicit argument for submission; rather, from the beginning to the ambivalent ending we have a strong sense of the pain of a young woman's experience of courtship and marriage.

It must be admitted that *Daphnis and Chloe* is a particularly ironic and emotionally subtle romance. *Leucippe and Clitophon* lacks by definition the ambiguities of Longus's omniscient narrative. The narrator is a young man who seems obsessed with uncanny sexual fear. Other characters are strongly and vocally misogynistic.[40] A feminist interpretation might indeed include criticism of the attitudes thus displayed, transparent as they may be. However, *Leucippe and Clitophon* also, along with the rest of the ancient romances, offers a basis for a more optimistic rereading; namely, the powerful depiction of the heroine.

Studies of female characters are a familiar element of feminist criticism. Critics have often taken fictional characters as useful models for the understanding of female modes of existence. Proponents range chronologically from de Beauvoir (1953) through Ellmann (1968) to Heilbrun (1979) and beyond.[41] Some heroines of ancient romance fit obviously into such projects. Longus's Chloe, for example, can readily be compared to Colette's Claudine or to others among Colette's young female figures. Colette, of course, was important to de Beauvoir's arguments, perhaps because so many of her characters are poised between active subjectivity and the most abandoned passivity. Chloe is a similar character, in her eager pursuit of Daphnis, in her occasional uncertainty, and in her eventual submersion in a female role.

There are other ancient characters whose awareness of themselves and of their situations would be impressive in novels of much later periods.

One heroine perhaps more "liberated" in a modern sense than Leucippe, or even Chloe, is Heliodorus's Chariclea. In Chariclea I find the answer I would offer to those who say that the feminist project of identifying positive figures for role models in literature is at best superannuated, at worst regressively romantic. Heliodorus's heroine is a fit object for just such a rescue mission as Fetterley, for example, has made on behalf of characters in modern novels.[42] At one perilous juncture Chariclea's mother advises her to take refuge in her status as a female, since "a mother's natural love can keep her daughter's lapse secret, a woman's fellow feeling can mask another woman's sin." Chariclea responds: "This is my greatest misfortune . . . even people of intelligence find my words unintelligible and are deaf when I speak of my misfortune."[43] This statement epitomizes the heroism of female characters in romance. Often subjected to far greater danger than most male figures, Chariclea nevertheless constantly forgoes any advantage she might be able to derive from a presumption of weakness. I cite Chariclea's remark, however, as a metaphor for the condition of many heroines in ancient literature. These characters are not granted their full importance; too often we assume, like Chariclea's mother, that we have "made allowances for" their sex, yet we fail to register their heroic qualities. Surely the time is not over for restoring to these characters the recognition that their own words demand.

NOTES

1. For dating, see the general introduction to B. P. Reardon, ed., *Collected Ancient Greek Novels* (Berkeley and Los Angeles, 1989), 5, and J. R. Morgan's introduction (ibid., 352) to his translation of Heliodorus. Morgan's translation is quoted (with minor orthographical changes) in the present citation (354) and throughout this chapter. Also quoted are translations by J. Winkler of Achilles Tatius and by C. Gill of Longus, also in *Collected Ancient Greek Novels.*

2. I am mainly indebted to the following: T. Modleski, *Loving with a Vengeance: Mass-produced Fantasies for Women* (New York, 1982); J. Radway, *Reading the Romance: Women, Patriarchy, and Popular Literature* (Chapel Hill, N.C., 1984); A. Snitow, "Mass Market Romance: Pornography for Women Is Different," in *Powers of Desire: The Politics of Sexuality,* ed. A. Snitow, C. Stansell, and S. Thompson (New York, 1983); and C. Thurston, *The Romance Revolution: Erotic Novels for Women and the Quest for a New Sexual Identity* (Urbana, Ill., 1987). See now also T. Modleski, "Some Functions of Feminist Criticism," *October* 49 (1989): 3–24.

3. Several other series exist most notably "Silhouette"; I will use "Harlequin" to refer to romances published in all such lines. All romances cited are published by Harlequin unless otherwise indicated.

4. For the latter project, I refer especially to Modleski, *Loving with a Vengeance;* she develops the argument further in her discussion of "soap operas" (85–109, 110–14) than in her treatment of Harlequins. For criticism of various approaches, see further below, nn. 9, 32, 25.

5. The term "exploration" is important in Radway's arguments (*Reading the Romance,* e.g., 74, 75, 168). She also refers to romances as "experiments" in sexual relations (168).

6. On market research, see Radway, *Reading the Romance,* 40–45. Thurston both discusses and conducts surveys (*Romance Revolution,* 113–38). She mentions among others (115) a study published by Mills and Boon, the British arm of Harlequin. Thurston's sample of readers is derived from polls conducted by romance publishers. Thurston's surveys, in turn, were used by the publishers, presumably for marketing purposes (135 n. 1).

7. The arguments of Thurston, *Romance Revolution,* and Radway, *Reading the Romance,* are based largely on surveys. Thurston's method (outlined on 113–38) is wide-ranging, while Radway examines a particular community (see 46–58).

8. On a possible "middle-class" and female readership of the ancient novels, see T. Hägg, *The Novel in Antiquity* (Berkeley and Los Angeles, 1983), 89–91. He cites B. Perry, *The Ancient Romances* (Berkeley and Los Angeles, 1967). (Hägg gives no particular page, but see esp. 56, 63.) Such speculations have been challenged: see E. L. Bowie, "Who Read the Greek Novels?" in *The Ancient Novel: Classical Paradigms and Modern Perspectives,* ed. J. Tatum and G. Vernazza (Hanover, N.H., 1990), 150–51.

9. The survey approach to understanding the ways in which novels are read may in any case be questioned. For a general critique of the "ethnographic" method as exemplified by Radway, see Modleski, "Some Functions of Feminist Criticism." An alternative is suggested by R. Brownstein in *Becoming a Heroine* (New York, 1982). This study of women in modern romances (not those of mass market literature, but those found in such authors as Eliot, Brontë, and James) discusses the activity of reading in great detail, drawing on Brownstein's own experience and (to a lesser extent) that of her friends and students. Brownstein provides examples of the intense personal engagement with characters to which I have just referred.

10. For these dates, see Reardon, *Collected Ancient Greek Novels,* 5.

11. This and the following generalizations are most specifically supported by Snitow, "Mass Market Romance," who cites publishers' advice to authors (248, 250, 252). See also the instruction sheets printed by Thurston, *Romance Revolution,* 52–55 (excerpts), 223–26. Snitow explains the advantages of foreign places and hospitals as settings: "[They] offer removal from the household, highlighted emotional states, and a supply of strangers" ("Mass Market Romance," 248). A setting that is emphatically "elsewhere" also promotes the exercise of fantasy on a larger scale. As Radway has commented, "Romance functions always as a utopian wish-fulfillment fantasy through which women try to imagine themselves as they often are not in day-to-day existence" (*Reading the Romance,* 151). In another context, Radway contrasts the "utopian" and fantastic romance plot with what she sees as a high degree of accuracy in the descriptions of foreign places (109). It is, however, not necessary to view the two as so strongly contradictory, since the very sense of being elsewhere than in one's everyday life could be seen to promote fantasy, questions of accuracy aside.

Some aspects of popular romance appear to have changed in recent years. In 1993 the shelves of new and used bookstores, as well as supermarkets, contain numerous novels whose circumstances are realistic in comparison to those I have described. Often the setting is an ordinary city or suburban one. However, even as novels situated in the present appear to become more realistic, specialized lines have developed, devoted to travel or history. (Lines of both these types are advertised inside the covers of *A Woman's Place* [1990; paperback, 1991], which is itself more or less contemporary and realistic.) Such works continue to have exotic locations. In addition, much space on shelves is devoted to historical and exotic romances outside series.

12. R. Utter and G. Needham, *Pamela's Daughters* (New York, 1936), 19.

13. Snitow, "Mass Market Romance," 250; cf. Modleski, *Loving with a Vengeance*, 98ff., on soap operas.

14. See, e.g., Modleski, 48. This characteristic, like the prevalence of exotic locations, appears to have changed in recent years. Heroines may now be lawyers or journalists; some own businesses. Nevertheless there are clear continuities with earlier technique. In *It All Depends on Love* (1990; paperback, 1991), a surgeon, working in London, is driven by exhaustion to take a vacation in the country. Here she improbably spends her time working incognito at a low-level job in the computer business owned by her eventual husband. In addition to being unaware of her skills, he thinks she is much younger than she is. In this way the relationship is established with the woman at an artificial disadvantage. Here again there is great variation from one subcategory to another, and the importance of historical romance (which allows more traditional plots) may be noted.

15. Longus: Reardon, *Collected Ancient Greek Novels*, 288–89. On visual description in *Leucippe and Clitophon*, see S. Bartsch, *Decoding the Ancient Novel: The Reader and the Role of Description in Heliodorus and Achilles Tatius* (Princeton, 1989). The opening ecphrasis is discussed on pages 40–44 and 48–55. Early in the novel, Achilles Tatius suggests the proper reaction to his erotic descriptions when he shows Clitophon's response to a rendition of the story of Apollo and Daphne: "This lyrical interlude fanned higher the fire in my soul, for stories of love stir feelings of lust" (Reardon, *Collected Ancient Greek Novels*, 180).

16. Reardon, *Collected Ancient Greek Novels*, 176–77.

17. These covers, it should be noted, are not chosen by the writers. Radway, *Reading the Romance*, discusses readers' negative reaction to overly erotic covers (104, 166–67, the latter in connection with objectionably pornographic "garbage dump" romances).

18. When I sought permission to reprint the covers, Harlequin denied it. In a letter of 20 May 1992, Harlequin's lawyer informed me: "Harlequin does not wish to associate itself with articles that do not reflect well on its product . . . I think you will agree that [yours] is not a favourable article from our point of view." I am returned, in this sense, to the publishing conditions of the Second Sophistic, where an ecphrasis of a work of art, rather than an on-site inspection of the work of art itself, was the norm. I regret that words do not suffice to do justice to the erotic effects of Harlequin's illustrations.

19. Utter and Needham, *Pamela's Daughters*, 4–6.

20. Cf. Modleski, *Loving with a Vengeance*, 52–54; she cites J. Berger's classic statement on this subject in *Ways of Seeing* (New York, 1973), 47.

21. See Bartsch, *Decoding the Ancient Novel*, 85–89.

22. Reardon, *Collected Ancient Greek Novels*, 178.

23. Ibid., 201; see Bartsch, *Decoding the Ancient Novel*, 88.

24. Reardon, *Collected Ancient Greek Novels*, 216–18; Bartsch (*Decoding the Ancient Novel*, 88) relates the pretended disembowelment to the dream of Leucippe's mother. See also the diptych of Prometheus and Andromeda described in 3.6. Perseus's sword is described at length: half of the blade is curved like a sickle; half is pointed, so that it can both cut and pierce its victim (Reardon, *Collected Ancient Greek Novels*, 211). The diptych is discussed by Bartsch, *Decoding the Ancient Novel*, 55–59.

25. Reardon, *Collected Ancient Greek Novels*, 181–84. On the extensive background of this speech, see Winkler's note ad loc. Another character, Menelaus, makes a somewhat similar speech (205–7). His arguments, however, are rebutted by Clitophon.

26. On the similarity, and then the emerging differences, between Daphnis and Chloe, see J. Winkler, "The Education of Chloe," in *Constraints of Desire: The Anthropology of Sex and Gender in Ancient Greece* (New York, 1990), 101–26. As he puts it, "Daphnis, to be sure, experiences some of this violence but Longus has made Chloe the

silent center of the plot . . . it is she whose body is discovered to be 'essentially' (that is, conventionally) vulnerable to sexual intercourse" (117). The parallel between Daphnis and Chloe is not equaled in any of the other ancient romances; nevertheless, most occasionally show males as objects of desire. My epigraph shows Chariclea regarding Theagenes, who in what follows is described in detail: "He had a radiant, manly beauty, and his cheek appeared more gleaming white because of the red streak of blood running down it" (Reardon, *Collected Ancient Greek Novels*, 354). *Leucippe and Clitophon* contains arguments for the superiority of young males as love objects (see the previous note). The death of Charicles (lover of the misogynistic Cleinias), which recalls that of Hippolytus, is a rare instance of erotic mutilation of a male in Achilles Tatius.

27. Daphnis: Reardon, *Collected Ancient Greek Novels*, 309–10; Chloe: 311–12.

28. Ibid., 297–98, 337–38.

29. Ibid., 316–17, 327.

30. Ibid., 325.

31. Ibid., 348.

32. For an account and criticism of this view, see Modleski, *Loving with a Vengeance*, 29–30 and 37–38. See also Snitow, "Mass Market Romance," 256.

33. M. Wibberley, *Love's Sweet Revenge* (Toronto, 1979), 106.

34. See Modleski, *Loving with a Vengeance*, 37–38, for women's active rather than passive use of romantic fantasy. For an extensive feminist rereading of blatantly pornographic material, see L. Williams, *Hard Core: Power, Pleasure, and the "Frenzy of the Visible"* (Berkeley and Los Angeles, 1989).

35. Radway sometimes speaks of the romances themselves as containing social criticism. For instance, she describes romance as "an exploration of the meaning of patriarchy for women" (*Reading the Romance*, 75; cf. 168–69). Readers in her sample also claim to have themselves developed more critical attitudes about patriarchy as a result of romance reading (101–2). However, she acknowledges that romance reading often serves as a form of escape (87–93) or compensatory nurturing (94–97). It will always remain a question, in any individual case, whether reading is a liberating activity or reinforces contentment with things as they are (cf. Modleski, *Loving with a Vengeance*, 36–37). Modleski has recently criticized the entire notion of studying popular texts through "ethnographies," or surveys of readers who supposedly read in a different way than do literary critics ("Some Functions of Feminist Criticism," 8–13, with reference to Radway). Indeed, Radway's recuperation of romance seems based on her own judgment of the texts as well as on what the readers say.

36. For a typically negative view of Harlequins, and a condescending opinion of their readers, see Thurston, *Romance Revolution*, 114–15, citing T. Henighan's radio interview in "Love at First Sight: Romance Novels and the Romantic Fantasy," ed. C. Harrison (CBS Radio series transcript, 1984). Few critics today, no matter how sympathetic, are unreservedly enthusiastic about Harlequins. Snitow, admitting some of the limitations of the form, occupies a middle ground, attempting neither to vindicate Harlequins as art nor to condemn them entirely ("Mass Market Romance," 246–47).

37. Radway concedes this point, referring to "romance's conservative countermessages" (*Reading the Romance*, 217). Cf. Modleski, *Loving with a Vengeance*, e.g., 43, 52, 54, 57. My opinion on this matter is based on my own reading of romances dating from the 1960s up to the present. When one looks for direct feminist statements in Harlequins the results are comparatively unsatisfying. Such statements seem merely fashionable. One novel that might appear to display awareness is A. Sellers's *Male Chauvinist* (New York, 1985; cited by Thurston, *Romance Revolution*, 162–63 as a feminist work). The title character's up-to-date politics prompts him to say things like this:

"A lot of men think that women have a rape fantasy, and it's just not true. And if last night gave you that idea about me, well, it shouldn't have."

38. But see Perry, *Ancient Romances,* 4–8, for deprecatory views of the novel in general during antiquity (Perry endorses these views).

39. Winkler, "Education of Chloe"; see n. 26 above.

40. I refer to the speeches of Cleinias and Menelaus; see n. 25 above.

41. S. de Beauvoir, *The Second Sex* (Paris, 1953; trans. Harmondsworth, 1972); M. Ellmann, *Thinking about Women* (New York, 1968); C. Heilbrun, *Reinventing Womanhood* (New York, 1979). Criticism of literary images of women has recently been subjected to scrutiny by T. Moi in *Sexual/Textual Politics: Feminist Literary Theory* (London, 1985; reprint, London, 1990), 42–49. It should be noted that Moi discusses only works that are geared toward finding, or deploring the lack of, positive images of women. She does not include in this category more complex efforts such as those just named.

42. J. Fetterley, *The Resisting Reader* (Bloomington, Ind., 1978).

43. Reardon, *Collected Ancient Greek Novels,* 579.

How Antiquity Read
Its Novels

CHAPTER TWENTY-TWO

Who Read Ancient Novels?

Susan A. Stephens

Those who write about the ancient novel make assumptions, often implicit and often unconscious, about its intended audience and its relationship to those texts perceived to belong to the ancient high culture. From these assumptions they frequently draw conclusions about the novel's origins, its cultural impact, and its ultimate significance as a literary artifact. Answers to the question "Who read ancient novels?" have tended to take a common form. Novel readers are somehow perceived to have been *qualitatively* different from the readers of other ancient books: they have been identified as the newly literate, a bourgeois class that supposedly flourished in the imperial period in the eastern Mediterranean, or they have been viewed as the sort of readers who reflect characters within the novels themselves, women or young men approaching adulthood.[1] Indeed, Tomas Hägg combines these categorizing models and adds a third, those in need of religion, when he describes the novel audience as "rootless, at a loss, restlessly searching—the people who needed and welcomed the novel are the same as those who were attracted by mystery religions and Christianity: the people of Alexandria and other big cities around the eastern Mediterranean. But a prerequisite for the genesis and flourishing of this genre, here as in eighteenth-century England, was of course an increased level of literacy in the population . . . The population outside the big cities, the women, people looking for romanticism and idealism—all now had the opportunity to have their wishes fulfilled."[2]

Teasing substance out of the debris of the ancient world is a delicate process. More delicate still is learning to recognize the cultural biases and a priori assumptions that we bring to the project. In attempting to imagine an audience for the ancient novel we need to ask ourselves whether evidence for a widespread and popular readership really exists, or whether the tenacious belief in such a readership results from the instinct, deeply rooted in classical scholarship, that only such fifth- and fourth-century canons and genres as epic, lyric, tragedy, history, and philosophical dialogue (carefully purged of their less-than-distinguished representatives) could have merited attention from intellectuals and the serious readers of the ancient world. Such an ideal ancient reader is one whom we would be hard-pressed to find today—someone who happily reads Gibbon or Nietzsche, but eschews *Lolita* or *Tristram Shandy*. We also need to ask to what extent our notion of the popular audience is dependent on an assessment of the books themselves. It is widely assumed that the development of the ancient novel entailed a linear progression of increasing narrative complexity. The typical paradigm assembles the five extant Greek novels on a continuum with Chariton, who is perceived as simple and straightforward, at its beginning, and the admittedly complex and sophisticated Heliodorus at its end.[3] And for the simple Chariton we assume that there must have been a simple audience.

Central to this vision of a popular audience, as Hägg's remark illustrates, is the insidious model of the rise of the novel in the eighteenth century. While the analogy comes readily enough to mind, closer consideration reveals its inappropriateness for antiquity. The eighteenth-century phenomenon was dependent on the invention of the printing press, which permitted the cheap dissemination of texts, and a growing middle class who came to read privately for entertainment. The development of the latter seems to have been the product of a Protestantism that actively encouraged the private reading of the Bible, as well as a newly industrializing Europe that required a more literate work force.[4] But neither of these phenomena has an ancient analogue.

First, the technology of book production remained laborious and time-consuming; books were costly. Egypt maintained a monopoly on the production and marketing of papyrus from which the majority of the ancient book rolls were made, and though papyrus was likely a cheaper commodity than animal hides, estimates of the price of the blank roll range from one to two days' wages for a common laborer up to as much as that of five or six days.[5] Add to this the cost of a skilled copyist's labor and it is obvious that owning ancient books would have fallen outside the experience of all but the well-to-do. Nor did circulating libraries (which may serve to defray the costs of books for the literate poor in the modern world) or anything remotely similar yet exist. Furthermore, ancient books were normally written without punctuation or word breaks, and private copies are usually found in a crabbed cursive style that must have placed greater demands on a reader's skills. Neither of these circumstances seems consistent with the view that reading was likely to have been a widespread pastime.

Second, the rise of an ancient middle class is a myth. The bulk of the ancient Mediterranean population lived a rural, subsistence-level existence. The urban population consisted mainly of poor people. At the top of the social pyramid would have been Roman senators and knights, estimated at no more than 1 percent of the population;[6] below them were the urban aristocracies of the smaller cities within the empire. The absolute numbers of Greek-reading elites of the empire, as compared to those of fifth-century Athens, were undoubtedly on the increase in the first two centuries A.D., due in no small measure to the greater stability of Roman imperial rule, which permitted local aristocracies to flourish in the service of imperial administration, and increased travel and exchange between urban centers. But such literacy as existed even within elite groups was on the decline by the third century A.D.[7]

In order to understand the nature of ancient readers, it is crucial not to lose sight of the causal link between wealth and education. Aristotle tells us that leisure is necessary for education, and indeed for the ability to lead the good life in general. This is not snobbery so much as practical reality: to acquire enough literacy to read a text of Xenophon the Athenian—about the minimum necessary for anyone who wanted to read novels—would have taken several years. Plato in the *Laws* supposes that three years would be sufficient for schoolboys to read and write at an adequate level.[8] Therefore, it is appropriate to ask how a populace, in the main at subsistence level or slightly above, would acquire sufficient free time for education. This is not to say that the odds were insurmountable for any who truly needed or desired to learn how to read, but without a demonstrable functional need for literacy there can hardly have been incentives for much of the populace to acquire the skill. William Harris, for example, estimates that "the overall level of literacy [during the first through the third centuries A.D.] is likely to have been below 15%."[9]

But is there a qualitatively different reading public, however large or small, to be distinguished either from or within these urban elites? The notion of subsidized and universal elementary education seems to have been in the main the dream of the philosopher, rather than the practical reality of ancient cities.[10] We cannot therefore attribute the putative growth of a new literate class to better public education. Ancient education consisted of the grammar school, which taught the basics of reading and writing, followed by advanced rhetorical training for the few.[11] So Harris's "under 15%," which includes both groups, would in fact be considerably smaller if only those who received the more advanced education were counted, perhaps as few as 5 percent of the total population. In theory this division between grammatical and rhetorical education might account for the two different sets of readers—elite and popular—of which scholars are fond. But this two-tiered system was a stable feature of Greek and later Roman education from its inception and cannot be shown to have produced anything like an identifiably popular readership before it is postulated as a formative influence in the writing of ancient novels. Furthermore, it does appear that the novelists themselves rather expected from their readers the sophistication gained from at least some rhetorical education.[12] In addition to those who received a grammatical or rhetorical education, there would undoubtedly have been some who procured moderate wealth from trade, as well as slaves from well-to-do households who would have learned to read as part of their duties.[13] But, again, there is no evidence either that these latter two groups were very populous or that they could constitute a distinctive class of readers whose sufficiently homogeneous tastes succeeded in shaping the literary marketplace.

Hägg would identify as unique to this period the sort of persons to whom Christianity and the mystery religions appealed. But this is unsatisfactory on a number of grounds. While scholars have identified many of the earliest Christians as urban in origin, ranking well below Roman or municipal aristocracies in social status and often linked to wealth from trade, it has yet to be demonstrated that such people were substantial in number or even identifiable as a discrete segment of the population before the experience of conversion marked them as a separate group. In fact, Christians seem to have consisted of individuals from many different groups. W. Meeks, in *The First Urban Christians,* remarks that "not only was there a mixture of social levels in each congregation; but also, in each individual category that we are able to identify there is evidence of divergent rankings in the different dimensions of status."[14] Indeed, it is this inconsistency, that is, the movement of individuals either above or below the social rank into which they were born, that Meeks and others would point to as *the* characteristic feature of early Christians, the feature that led them to find satisfaction and a sense of belonging in a new communal religious experience. But this trait is psychological; it is an internalized sense of belonging that could not have marked off a segment of the population *before* it manifested itself in an overt action like conversion to Christianity. Those who were potentially Christian were not a sufficiently distinct group for an ancient-novel writer to regard their "visible yearnings and spiritual restlessness" as a target of opportunity. When Christians did become a distinct group, it was well after the first novels would have been written.[15]

Nor were the earliest urban Christians necessarily literate. Those who were could only have received the same education as their non-Christian social equals—the grammatical and the more advanced rhetorical training that flourished in the cities and towns of the empire—access to which was dictated by wealth and class. Certainly Christians, after their conversion, seem not to have constituted much of an audience for anything beyond conversion literature—that is, the books of the Old and New Testament, homilies, and martyr tales—a literature that in technical finesse ranks well below even the least sophisticated of the Greek novels. But even in this respect it is not clear what proportion of the converted could actually read or were read to in community worship.

However, the small size of the ancient population of readers would not preclude ancient novels from being a popular source of entertainment. Novels might have been read aloud to those who could not read them (as Christian texts undoubtedly were read for the benefit of an illiterate congregation). But were they? Ancient sources attest to many kinds of public performance. Rhetoricians declaimed extempore on themes proposed by their audiences; theaters produced tragedies and comedies as well as pantomime and burlesque; festivals provided occasions for poetic competitions as well as the recitation of Homer, and authors so desiring might give public readings of their works. But nothing is said of novel readings, and even the shortest surviving novels are too long for convenient public recitation. Lucian mentions female impersonators in soft garments who dance or mime the stories of love-stricken women—Phaedra, Parthenope, and Rhodope (*De saltatione* 2)—and, in another dialogue, he mentions those who take the roles of Metiochus or Ninus or Achilles (*Pseudologista* 25). But although it is possible for street performers or mime artists to have popularized novel characters or plot lines, what such performances could have transmitted was an exciting story, not the novels themselves. Therefore, it is scarcely credible that these opportunities to excerpt and condense complex stories would have served as an impetus for the emergence of the genre or sustained its growth.

I have been arguing, in a general way, that the most popular and most persistent view of the readership for ancient novels is not really tenable, given what we know about the social structure of the ancient world. I would now like to descend from that theoretical high road to examine the physical remains of ancient novels themselves to see what, if anything, they tell us about their ancient owners.

The discoveries of fragments of Greek novels on papyrus, some extending to several columns, began in 1896 with the publication of *Ninus*. Currently, we have, in addition to the five complete Greek novels, tantalizing glimpses of at least seven others (*Ninus, Metiochus and Parthenope, Calligone, Anthia, Chione, Sesonchosis,* and Lollianus's *Phoenicica*), two to four fragments of Antonius Diogenes, and scraps of a number of others that look to us like novels, although of these too little has survived for certitude. Novel fragments range in date—assigned on the basis of handwriting and format—from the first century A.D. (*Ninus*) to the early sixth century A.D. (Heliodorus).

All of them are now in very fragmentary condition; they were discovered in the refuse heaps and abandoned foundations of the larger towns and urban centers of Greco-Roman Egypt, where thanks to the aridity of the climate, more than five thousand fragmentary rolls and codices of Greek literature have survived in the sands. Finds are not distributed evenly over the eight hundred years of Greco-Roman occupation: most of these literary fragments were copied between the second and fourth centuries A.D. and were excavated from only a limited number of sites. About 75 percent of the novel fragments whose provenance is known have come from Oxyrhynchus, and most of the remainder from the Faiyum. Though they are now only a tiny sample of what the whole must have been,[16] these papyrus fragments of abandoned or worn-out books, thus preserved, may in their sheer numbers serve as a kind of laboratory to study ancient literary tastes before the winnowing effects of time, taste, and classical scholarship. Relative numbers of surviving authors give some hint, however crude, of their overall significance (or popularity), and an examination of the physical presentation of ancient manuscripts may provide useful clues about the social milieu of their owners.

When the number of fragments of discrete manuscripts of narrative fiction is compared to the number of those of other authors or genres, an interesting picture emerges. Taken in the aggregate, the number of fragments of this allegedly popular material is surprisingly small. I count forty-two discrete manuscripts of ancient novels. This includes the twenty-eight fragments (ten of which are very dubious) included in *Ancient Greek Novels: The Fragments,*[17] four of Chariton, six of Achilles Tatius, two of Dictys of Crete, one of Heliodorus, and a scrap from Lucian's *Asinus.* No papyri of Xenophon of Ephesus or of Longus, nor of the Latin novels, have as yet been found. Because all these novel fragments were copied between the first and sixth centuries A.D., I have limited my *comparanda* to manuscripts of other authors that were copied during these same six centuries. Using a disinterested tally by Orsolina Montevecchi in *La papirologia,* published in 1973,[18] which is conveniently broken into fifty-year periods, I find that within this same six-century time frame, there are almost four times as many fragments of lyric (161), three times as many of tragedy (131), and slightly more New Comedy and Menander (56).[19] This is a count only of manuscripts copied during this period; texts of canonical authors that were made in earlier periods and continued to be used would increase the numbers of the actual texts available to read.

Nor does comparison with other types of literature taken in the aggregate suggest that novels were any more popular: there are twenty-nine surviving fragments of the *Acts of the Alexandrians,* which was anti-Roman and often anti-Semitic protest literature, written by Alexandrian Greeks and circulated during the first through the third centuries A.D.; forty-three fragments of anonymous philosophical prose; and thirty-four fragments from grammatical or metrical works. However, texts of the Old and New Testament, now including only those copied in the period from the second to the fourth century A.D., readers of which were, by Hägg's assessment, the same as those to whom romance would have appealed, are considerably more numerous (172). A comparison of individual works produces a similar pattern—Montevecchi lists four manuscripts of Chariton, but eighteen of the *Aetia* of Callimachus, not including the scholia, fifteen of Hermas's *Shepherd* (a second-century Christian homilitic), thirty-seven of Thucydides, and eighty-eight fragments of Demosthenes. A table of further comparisons appears below.

Comparison with the number of fragments of Homer's *Iliad* and *Odyssey* provides an even more dramatic contrast. Montevecchi lists 432 texts for the *Iliad* and 122 for the *Odyssey* (and by 1993 the numbers for both were considerably higher). Since both the *Iliad* and the *Odyssey* were employed in schools in the earliest stages of reading, they come as close to popular literature as any ancient text can. However, the survival patterns for manuscripts, even for the *Iliad,* provide an interesting insight into readers' habits. Conventionally one book of the *Iliad* would have been copied onto one papyrus roll. Therefore, if a reader possessed the whole of the *Iliad,* he would have twenty-four discrete rolls. Yet there are twice as many fragments of books 1 and 2 surviving than of books 3 and 4, and the numbers of fragments of the remaining books diminish consistently— fragments from book 24 are one-sixth the total for book 1. This suggests that large numbers of copies of books 1 and 2 owe their existence to their use as school texts, and that the bulk of such readers did not go on to purchase, have copied, or copy for themselves the entire poem.

If I update Montevecchi's data to the present writing, the disparity in number becomes even greater; there are now over 1,000 fragments of Homer published, 120 fragments of Demosthenes, and 77 of Thucydides. With this last author the fiction of popularity is difficult to maintain— Thucydides' Greek can never have been easy to read, nor was he, as Homer was, studied and copied in the grammar schools, which served to increase the number of copies of an ancient author in circulation; yet on a statistical basis, Thucydides seems to have been among the most widely read prose writers in the ancient world. It is unlikely that the number of his manuscripts is this large only because it reflects a desire to own or display a manuscript with overtly intellectual connotations for purposes of status enhancement. Thucydides began to enjoy a certain vogue from the first century B.C., and his influence among the literary elite can be observed during the Second Sophistic. It is evident in an anonymous rhetorical exercise as early as the first century A.D.,[20] in the extant Greek novelists themselves, and in a writer as late as Procopius. Further, the number of rhetorical themes based on material from his history indicates that he was familiar to the rhetorical theorists and compilers of handbooks, if not to their students in general.[21]

Disparate as the numbers of fragments of novelists and texts of Homer, Demosthenes, and Thucydides are, continuing papyrological publication is likely to increase the gap, because there has been a tendency in all collections to stockpile the fragments of known authors who have well-established texts and are well represented by published fragments for students' dissertations or for collective publication (as the numbers below demonstrate), while editors tend to publish more promptly new and unusual material that expands our understanding of the dimensions of ancient literature. This is not to say that all fragments of ancient novels have already been published, or even correctly identified, but rather to emphasize that they do not exist in current collections in sufficient quantities to alter radically the picture I have set out above. In fact, the relative proportion of novel fragments to those of the canonical writers of antiquity is likely to shrink. A graphic illustration of this can be seen in the *Oxyrhynchus Papyri,* which have published respectively seven fragments of Theocritus (vol. 50), twelve of Plato (vol. 52), eight of Euripides (vol. 53), ten of Demosthenes (vol. 55), and twenty-one of Thucydides (vol. 57). During this same period, only one new manuscript of Achilles Tatius (or indeed any other novel fragment) has appeared (vol. 55).

It is possible to interpret the statistics I have set out above in a somewhat different way, to argue that they demonstrate that the novels were *more* popular than any other nonreligious or school texts written during or after the period of the Second Sophistic. There are six fragments of Achilles Tatius in total; only four published fragments of Plutarch, although each is from a different work; only two of Strabo, one of Lucian, and one of Libanius. But with such a low statistical sample (1–2–4–6), are we justified in concluding that Achilles Tatius was six times as popular as Lucian, or only that neither Achilles Tatius nor Lucian was much read in comparison to Plato, Demosthenes, or Thucydides?[22] Looking at the material in the aggregate tends to suggest the latter assumption: there are after all about the same number of fragments of philosophical prose (43) as there are of novels (42).

Besides considering the sheer number of manuscripts, it may be possible to conjecture something about the social milieu of owners of ancient manuscripts by examining the formats and writing styles of the novel fragments, and comparing them with material from three distinctly recognizable groups: (1) standard works of the high culture, tragedy, comedy, history, and their commentaries, (2) writings that can be identified as Christian, and (3) works of the not-quite-literate, or the inexperienced, writer. The handwriting of the first group varies from elegant and carefully executed calligraphy to competent but not necessarily attractive writing, to—for commentaries especially—rapidly formed and idiosyncratic cursives. For the second group, C. H. Roberts, in analyzing manuscripts of the Old and New Testaments, has argued cogently that Christian manuscripts do look rather different in style and format from the works of classical literature. He dubbed the Christian writing style "reform documentary," linking it in type to documentary recordkeeping, rather than an elite education or training in the schools of professional copyists.[23] Those who wrote it seem to have adapted a documentary style to literary texts, and sometimes betray their origins with certain linguistic and technical features, the most significant of which is that Christians preferred the codex form to the roll. Often these texts have lettering slightly larger than is usual in non-Christian books, one supposes either to facilitate public reading or to aid those not quite so skilled in private reading. In addition to these, there is a third readily identifiable class—semiliterate productions that have been carelessly copied, full of spelling and other errors. A good number of these are thought to have been the work of schoolboys— writing exercises, word lists, copies of a few lines of Homer; others may have been the exercises of those learning in the scribal schools, or those who wrote inexpertly and therefore, one assumes, infrequently. Inexperienced writers, however, might be able to read quite easily, and if novels were truly popular, we should expect such people occasionally to have copied lines, or even whole texts, from novels. Just as the trade-educated Christians copied sacred books, and schoolboys wrote Homeric word lists, at least a few novel readers should have left a few manuscripts (though by no means the majority) that would betray their origins.

However, in style and layout novel fragments in the aggregate look different both from the early New Testament material and from unskilled productions. I find them to be indistinguishable from rolls or codices of classical authors such as Sappho, Thucydides, Demosthenes, and Plato, not written in the semidocumentary or indeed in the semiliterate style one might expect. A few of the texts have the look of coffee-table books, handsomely set-out rolls with wide margins written in graceful and calligraphic hands, which might suggest the well-to-do buying the latest literary fad for its social cachet, not necessarily for its intellectual content. But then a number of manuscripts of Homer or Hesiod or the lyric poets could also fall into this class. A few have the look of scholarly books, like commentaries or the *Constitution of Athens*,[24] that could have been copied by individuals for their own use. But most fall between; they appear to have been competent, professionally copied books, indistinguishable from a run-of-the-mill copy of Demosthenes or Plato. All but a few have been corrected, and apart from such familiar errors in the long tradition of hand copying of manuscripts as haplography, dittography, omission, or miscopying of the exemplar, novel texts are in remarkably good shape.

Some, to be sure, were copied on the backs of previously used rolls, either other literary texts or documents, but this practice is found also in texts we regularly assume to have been the possessions of an intellectual elite; for example, the *Constitution of Athens* was written on the back of a document; Didymus's *Commentary on Demosthenes* was written on one side of a roll,[25] Hierocles' *Stoic Elements* on the other[26]—three texts no one would link with a popular reader or a bourgeois audience. Unfortunately, the habit of recycling allows us to make no deductions about the intellectual or social milieu of the reader.[27] The practice may indicate nothing beyond ancient habits of thrift. Or it may mean that such texts were difficult to acquire from a local bookseller and that interested parties were forced to have private copies made. A letter from the third century A.D. from Oxyrhynchus gives us a glimpse into this process in which one man asks another to procure for him a copy of Hypsicrates's *Kômôdoumenoi* (Those who are subjects for comedy), indicating its probable location in another man's library.[28] If this inference is correct for novels, then they may have actually been difficult to procure, rather than popular.

That some of the novel fragments are written in the codex, which is a form patently preferred, if not popularized, by Christian copyists, seems to me of little consequence in forging a link between audience and text, although others have tried to do so.[29] While certainly the vast majority of New Testament manuscripts and other Christian literature was written in the codex form as early as the second century A.D., by the fourth century A.D. 90 percent of all books, even those of non-Christian high culture, are found to have been copied in codices. At issue are only those written in the second and third centuries A.D. Thirty-four novel fragments fall between these dates. Of these, only three are in the codex form, or about 9 percent. Seven percent is reported as the average for the non-Christian codices copied during this period,[30] and a variation of 2 percent is surely too small to be deemed significant.

The conclusion seems to me inescapable that the novels were not popular with the denizens of Greco-Roman Egypt—Christian or otherwise. It is possible to dismiss this statistical sampling as atypical, on the ground that reading patterns in the big cities would have been vastly different from the smaller urban centers of the Egyptian countryside. But perhaps this is unwise. Surely Greek towns like Oxyrhynchus would have contained fewer intellectuals than the big cities like Alexandria, and a rather higher percentage of the sort of readers who may be characterized as members of a bourgeois or popular audience. Further, there is a surprising lack of testimony about novels and novel writers in other ancient sources, and apart from a small number of references to books whose contents might be considered salacious, such as Achilles Tatius, Apuleius, Petronius, or the *Milesiaca,* little is said about novel reading. Christian polemicists, for example, do not caution their flocks against the evils of novel reading, and while Julian can admonish his priests in Asia Minor not to read "love stories" (*erôtikas hypotheseis*), the tenor of his letter (*Epistulae* 89b) does not allow us to infer that "love stories" were any more commonly circulated than texts of high culture, like the plays of Aristophanes, which he also interdicts. The novelists themselves, unlike their eighteenth- and nineteenth-century counterparts, do not show their own characters reading novels. On balance, it does not appear that novels attracted much attention, so in fact Egypt may be quite typical.

While statistics cannot tell us who read novels, they do suggest that Greco-Egyptian readers owned novels with considerably less frequency than they owned copies of Homer, Demosthenes, or Thucydides. Ancient readers of the latter authors we now think of as belonging to "high culture," and they were at least an existing reading public—a public that in education and in inclination and ability to read and write matches well with the authors of novels themselves, a public for which their contemporaries were writing. No evidence currently available allows us to construct another set of readers for ancient novels. The need to create a different audience for stories we perceive as romantic or fanciful may simply reflect our own cultural prejudices.

Table of Comparisons

The list includes the number of fragments of individual manuscripts (papyrus or parchment) found in Egypt that can be assigned to the period between the first and sixth centuries A.D., unless otherwise noted. "+" means that the figure given is based on incomplete information, and is in all probability higher (though not lower).

Texts taken in the aggregate:

Acts of the Alexandrians	29+
Grammatical/metrical treatises	34+
All novel fragments	42 (10 of which are doubtful)
Anonymous philosophical prose	43+
New Comedy	63+
Tragedy	131+
Lyric	161+
OT + NT (2–4 only)	172+

Individual authors or texts (including a number of authors from the classical and Hellenistic periods, a representative sample of Christian texts, and a number of writers, such as Oppian and Strabo, whose *floruit* coincides with that of the novelists):

Favorinus	1
Lucian, *Asinus*	1
Oppian	2
Strabo	2
Lycophron	3

Philo	3
Aristoxenus	3
Chariton	4
Plutarch	4
Life of Aesop	5
Aratus	5
Achilles Tatius	6
Euripides, *Medea*	6
Gospel of John (2–4 only)	12
Euripides, *Orestes*	13
Genesis	14
Hermas, *Shepherd*	14
Acts of the Apostles	15
Callimachus, *Aetia*	18
Psalms	30+
Herodotus	41+
Thucydides	75+
Demosthenes	120+
Homer, *Iliad*	600+

NOTES

1. Proponents of this view include B. Egger, T. Hägg, B. E. Perry, and G. L. Schmeling, though recently there has been some movement away from the notion of a popular audience, e.g., E. L. Bowie's assessment in "The Greek Novel," in *The Cambridge History of Classical Literature,* vol. 1, *Greek Literature,* ed. P. E. Easterling and B. M. W. Knox (Cambridge, 1985), 683–99, or B. Wesseling, "The Audience of the Ancient Novels," in *Groningen Colloquia on the Novel,* vol. 1, ed. H. Hofman (Groningen, 1988). See also W. V. Harris's remarks in *Ancient Literacy* (Cambridge, Mass., 1989), 228–29.

2. T. Hägg, *The Novel in Antiquity* (Berkeley and Los Angeles, 1983), 90. While Hägg acknowledges that increased literacy did not mean "the general ability to read and write," he does believe the "stratum of Greek or Hellenized citizens" within the empire required a different kind of reading material than its literate predecessors.

3. See, for example, B. Reardon's introduction to *Collected Ancient Greek Novels* (Berkeley and Los Angeles, 1989), 9, or Bowie, "Greek Novel," 688ff.

4. L. Stone, "Literacy and Education in England, 1640–1900," *Past and Present* 42 (1969): 69–139. Even if the rise of Christianity can be shown to have similarly encouraged the reading of the New Testament, this cannot have taken place early enough to have stimulated the development and growth of the novel.

5. N. Lewis, *Papyrus in Classical Antiquity,* 2d ed. (Brussels, 1974), 133. See also Lewis's update, *Papyrus in Classical Antiquity: A Supplement,* Papyrologica Bruxelensia, no. 23 (Brussels, 1989): 40–41.

6. R. MacMullen, *Roman Social Relations* (New Haven, 1974), 89.

7. R. A. Kaster, *Guardians of Language: The Grammarians and Society in Late Antiquity* (Berkeley and Los Angeles, 1988), 35–50.

8. *Laws* 7.809e–810b. Plato's discussion is instructive. He couples learning letters

with learning how to play the lyre as two essential features of education. "For a ten-year-old child three years is appropriate for letters, and for lyre playing it is appropriate to start at thirteen and continue for three years . . . They must work at letters sufficiently to be able to write and read." A little further on in this passage, however, it is clear that the bulk of ancient literary learning still consisted not of reading but of memorization (810e–811a).

9. Harris, *Ancient Literacy*, 267.

10. Ibid., 129–39.

11. Kaster, *Guardians of Language*, 35–50.

12. See, for example, S. Bartsch's compelling demonstration in *Decoding the Ancient Novel: The Reader and the Role of Description in Heliodorus and Achilles Tatius* (Princeton, 1989) of the way in which the novelists often adapt techniques of description learned in the schools to the exigencies of narrative, or the more technical analysis of M. Reeve, "Hiatus in the Greek Novelists," *Classical Quarterly*, n.s. 21 (1971): 514–39.

13. For a discussion of the literacy of slaves in this period, see Harris, *Ancient Literacy*, 255–59.

14. W. Meeks, *The First Urban Christians: The Social World of the Apostle Paul* (New Haven, 1983), 73.

15. R. MacMullen argues in *Christianizing the Roman Empire* (New Haven, 1984) that the major impetus for conversion was Constantine's example, supported by his preference for Christians in positions of responsibility. Before Constantine their numbers were indeed quite small. See esp. 102ff.

16. An estimate of the number of Greek books in circulation in Greco-Roman Egypt is impossible to make: unknown variables include the percentage of the population who would own books and the average number of books owned. Even estimates of the total population of Egypt and the number of those who could read Greek vary widely.

17. S. A. Stephens and J. J. Winkler, eds., *Ancient Greek Novels: The Fragments* (Princeton, 1993).

18. O. Montevecchi, *La papirologia* (Milan, 1973), 360–63. Because the most recent edition of *La papirologia* does not include an updated version of these tables, I have relied on the 1973 edition.

19. My totals for the fragments of ancient novels are actually higher than Montevecchi's 1973 count of this material (ibid.), but since the higher number would tend to work against my thesis, not reinforce it, I have let the disparity stand.

20. S. A. Stephens, *Yale Papyri in the Beinecke Rare Book and Manuscript Library*, 2 vols., American Society of Papyrologists Monograph Series, no. 24 (Chico, Calif., 1985), vol. 2, no. 105.

21. See R. Kohl, *De scholasticarum declamationum argumentis ex historia petitis*, Rhetorische Studien, no. 4 (Paderborne, Germany, 1915), 26–45, and the index to C. Walz, *Rhetores Graeci* [1832–36], vol. 9 (reprint, Osnabrück, Germany, 1968).

22. It is also possible to speculate from these statistics that Heliodorus and Longus being less well represented than Chariton or Achilles Tatius indicates an unsophisticated readership. But again the numbers are so small (6–4–1–0) that, e.g., the discovery of two fragments of Heliodorus could radically alter the conclusion.

23. C. H. Roberts, *Manuscript, Society, and Belief* (London, 1977), 14.

24. H. J. M. Milne, *Catalogue of Literary Papyri in the British Museum*, 1st ed. (London, 1927), no. 108.

25. *Berliner Klassikertexte herausgegeben von der Generalverwaltung der Königlichen Museen in Berlin*, 1st ed., vol. 1, ed. H. Diels and W. Schubart (Berlin, 1904).

26. *Berliner Klassikertexte herausgegeben von der Generalverwaltung der Königlichen Museen in Berlin*, 1st ed., vol. 4, ed. W. Schubart and H. von Arnim (Berlin, 1908).

27. For the novel fragments, there are twenty-two with backs blank, eight codices, and twelve written on the backs of other texts or subsequently reused for other texts. I was able to check the formats of thirty-eight manuscripts of Thucydides as a control, and found twenty-six have backs blank, eight are codices, and four are copied onto recycled paper or themselves reused. The larger number of novel fragments on recycled material may mean that novels, relatively speaking, were harder to acquire, or intrinsically less valuable (which is not the same as being "popular"), or it may mean nothing at all.

28. *POxy,* vol. 18, no. 2192. The letter has been dated to ca. A.D. 170.

29. For example, Hägg, *Novel in Antiquity,* 95.

30. C. H. Roberts and T. C. Skeat, *The Birth of the Codex* (Oxford, 1983), 37.

CHAPTER TWENTY-THREE

The Roman Audience
of *The Golden Ass*

Ken Dowden

Was Apuleius's *Metamorphoses* (the so-called *Golden Ass*) written not at the end of his career, but early—perhaps around A.D. 155, rather than around A.D. 170? Was it written not at Carthage, but in Rome? In either case, even if true, these might not seem adjustments of much interest except to those who write encyclopedias of literature. But in fact they change the associations and significance of the work, and our understanding of the *Metamorphoses* is the richer for this new place. In the context of Apuleius's oeuvre, it becomes a piece defining his ideas of style and of himself and establishing his quality for the arbiters of taste of that era. It is an inaugural work. By restoring it to Rome and Roman audiences, we realign the work so that it fits better into the history and profile of Latin literature, where it at present stands in too much danger of being an oddity. My arguments will vary in strength and appeal, but I hope that they are usefully suggestive and present at the minimum a hypothesis worth entertaining. Perhaps we can make some sense of this extraordinary work by making it a little more "intraordinary."

ROME—WHERE ELSE?

There is no doubt that the *Metamorphoses* is a distinctive work compared to the Latin literature students and readers normally encounter. Its date is well after the end of "Silver Latin." Its style is extravagant beyond the bounds within which classical authors generally allowed themselves to work. And in genre it is held with a single other work, Petronius's *Satyricon,* to constitute the "Roman Novel." We cannot be sure there were any "novels" in the first two centuries A.D. beyond these, making it a little misleading to describe it as "the one Latin romance to have survived complete from the classical period," as though there had been a whole genre-full of them.[1] The works of Petronius and Apuleius are in fact *hors de genre.* The *Metamorphoses* is an alien in the pages of Latin literature, in need of some contextual space to live in. How did it come to be written? For what audience was it intended? After all, for its original audience, it had its context.

One approach might be to exile the work from Latin culture, to regard it as a singular outcrop of Greek culture into a Latin world, only accidentally written in Latin. If only it were written in Greek, it might then fall into place—with the Greek novels. Some of these extended narratives are contemporary with Apuleius, and like some of their authors, Apuleius can be described as a sophist, a public speaker performing before admiring crowds, rather a Greek stance itself. Yet the literary texture of Apuleius's novel and the social presuppositions of any work written in Latin undermine this simple association with the Greek novels. The work maintains a dialogue with literature and styles of all periods, even down to the choice of vocabulary.[2] Its social presuppositions are perhaps illuminated when one is confronted by Hägg's suggestion that some of the Greek novels might have been read out by scribes to their townsfolk—something unimaginable for the *Metamorphoses* in the Latin West, because of the enormous gulf between the high circles for which Latin literature was written and the majority of the population. It is hard, too, to believe that the *Metamorphoses* could ever have become the subject for a dining-room mosaic, as the novel of Metiochus and Parthenope did at Antioch.[3] Even the label "sophist," which has some explanatory force in drawing together the Greek works of Achilles, Longus, and Iamblichus and associating them with the remarkable and widespread performances of the Greek Second Sophistic, only adds to the oddity and marginality of Apuleius in the Latin West.

Though it is possible to view Apuleius, like Cicero before him or Boethius after him, as transposing Greek learning into Latin, there remains a problem in understanding the Latin audience for the *Metamorphoses:* as a work of entertainment (at least at first sight), it forfeits the license given to Greek learning to be re-presented in Latin dress. If one excludes Latin poetic innovation from Greece, which clearly stands on a cultural plateau despite any disclaimers poets include in their work ("mere trifles"), there has been nothing like the *Metamorphoses* since Plautus—an intertext that Apuleius is keen to activate in his prologue.

The epicenter of the problem is clear: the *Metamorphoses* is part of the history of Latin literature, however unusual it may be and however much this may tempt us to generate explanatory frameworks that exclude it and explain it away—by association with the non-Latin world (Greek), by confinement to the chronological margins (post-classical, decadent), or by removal to the geographical margins (African).

CARTHAGE AND ROME:
SETTINGS, AUDIENCES, AND MARKET

The audience envisaged by Apuleius was one of
highly educated Romans.
—P. G. Walsh, "Apuleius"

Apuleius has been closely associated with North Africa in the minds of writers. After all, he came originally from Madaura, and later, in the late 150s and early 160s, he had extraordinary success at Carthage as an orator in the sophistic mode. But he was also one of a number of writers, such as Fronto and Tertullian, who hailed from Africa and exhibited a taste for an exotic, nonclassical style. At the beginning of this century (and occasionally since then) this was accounted for on the supposition that what they wrote was, in some regional sense, "African Latin"—with the racialist subtext that that is the sort of Latin that Africans might be expected to write.[4] This view had the effect of marginalizing such writing and removing the difficulty and interest posed by such renovation of the style in which Latin was written. But it has long since been recognized that "African" Latin was the artistic language of an era, not the spoken language of a region, and that provincialism was despised in Latin style.[5]

If his style cannot be declared African and marginalized, perhaps Apuleius's audience should not be either, and we should pause to think about audiences and writing in Rome and in the provinces. In Rome, writers wrote for the Roman audiences seen, for instance, in Pliny's letters. Persons of provincial origin also went to Rome to contribute to this literature of high society. The Senecas and Lucan, and Martial too, came from Spain. Fronto came from Africa. All this is merged in a passage of Brock's otherwise meticulous study when she characterizes the times of Apuleius and Fronto as follows: "Roman and Italian literature was for the time exhausted, the Spanish school of the first century A.D. had come to an end with Martial, and the day of Gaul had not yet dawned. Literature was almost exclusively in the hands of Africans."[6] The Latin literature of Rome continued after Pliny, Juvenal, and Suetonius: the overpowering wave of the Greek Second Sophistic did not drive all Western writers to write in Greek, even if it overwhelmed the likes of Favorinus and Marcus Aurelius.[7] We hear, for instance, of the scarcely African "new poets" (*poetae novelli*), even if we do not have their works to read. Such work must have flourished at recitals attended by the literati of the city, even if no Pliny was there to record their occurrence. So there was no end to literature by Romans and Italians, nor—as Fronto shows us—to literature written at Rome and in Italy.

Meanwhile, despite the reasonable expectation that the provinces might now themselves become prime audiences for provincial Latin literature, there is little evidence of anything but literature for the elite of Rome and for the imperial circles. The principal exceptions are Apuleius's own *Apologia* and *Florida*—for which I suggest a different explanation below—and Christian literature, which sometimes had other audiences in mind. Surviving and reported pagan Latin authors usually wrote at Rome, addressed Rome, adopted its perspective, and intended their work to be released and spread ("published") from Rome. This naturally reflects the honor and status that is sought by writing and that is awarded most fully at the center of society, where power lies. There was no court or political power to create a centripetal effect in the Greek East. There honor, status, and culture were more evenly spread—until, much later, Constantinople became the Rome of the East.

In the West, Apuleius does not herald a new wave of decentralized literature. If he had been primarily addressing provincial audiences in his published works, he would be practically unique: how, in the light of Latin literary history, can the *Metamorphoses*—or indeed any of his works—have been written principally for the North African market?[8] This invites us to take a different view of the *Florida* and the *Apologia,* works ostensibly delivered to North African audiences. Admittedly, the *Florida* is based on speeches he made in North Africa, consisting above all of their colorful and engaging preambles, which the Greeks called *prolaliai* (preliminary chats). Indeed, they would have been read eagerly in the provinces, just as we know the works of Pliny were in the Italian *municipia*. Equally, there was obviously literary activity in the provinces; apart from Apuleius himself, we know for instance of his friend Clemens, who was writing an epic on Alexander (*Florida* §7). But did the *Florida* and *Apologia* perhaps have the Roman market in their sights?

We know something of the Carthaginian audience from the pages of Apuleius. Although he speaks in theaters before large audiences, his eyes are usually fixed on the class that matters, the proud and self-conscious literati. He praises their Carthage and flatters them—above all through association with Rome, the ultimate source of status. Their Curia (senate-house) is *sanctissima* (very sacred, 29.23), like the Roman senate, and it follows the proposal of *consularis sui* (its own consular, 29.27) like the senate following the lead of its consuls and consulars; their decision is a very *senatus consultum* (29.22). As members of the Carthaginian Curia, they are *principes Africae viri* (foremost men of Africa), a term full of emotional association with the leaders of Rome. And the panegyrics that Apuleius regularly pronounces for the proconsul (and even his promising son, 15.4) represent the panegyrics for the emperor at Rome, whose emanation he is. But most Roman of all is the level of culture of which the Carthaginian elite can boast. It has so many *eruditionis amicos* (friends of culture, 33.25); it is a place where *tota civitas eruditissimi estis* (as a whole state you are utterly cultured, 41.16). This is the *pulcherrimus coetus* (most beautiful gathering, 10.5) that Apuleius finds in a city so great (10.6)[9] that it requires a philosopher to praise it (27.1), and so learned that it becomes the very *Camena togatorum* (The muse of those that wear the toga, 41.20).

Apuleius, then, paints his Carthaginian audience in Roman colors. But the process is double-edged. On the one hand, Carthage is elevated by the portrait and becomes another Rome, a parallel Rome; on the other hand, it becomes a derivative Rome, a microcosm, dependent on somewhere else, more real, for its value. It is evident that any writer interested in fame and immortality is not going to restrict his ambitions to Carthaginian distribution and readership. And the tale of the survival of Latin literature simultaneously leads us to the conclusion that the *Florida* must have succeeded at Rome. Indeed, examination of their contents will show that this series of extracts, however much drawn from Apuleius's Carthaginian practice, is of exemplary and broad interest in both style and content; it is not a parochial work, however much it may owe its origins to Apuleius's actual local oratory. Someone sent Apuleius's speeches, or the *Florida* (the "flowers" from them), to Rome. The person with the best motive is Apuleius himself.

A case worth comparing is that of Horace in his *Epistles:* here his life and friends provide the ostensible occasion for writing, and perhaps some will have been pleased to have "received" them. But the target is in fact the literary public at Rome, not a few friends in particular. In Apuleius's case, on this model, the most important target would be the literary Everest, Roman society. The same applies to Apuleius's defense speech, the *Apologia,* where the local market, the bourgeois of Oea, look like small fry beside its towering literary ambitions and beside its destiny to be the sole Latin forensic speech to survive from antiquity by an author other than Cicero.

THE SURVIVAL OF APULEIUS'S WRITINGS AT ROME

Apuleius's works survive because they were copied—in specific places at specific times. One group of manuscripts contains half his works, another the other half. Because, however, the *Florida* is split, most of it at the end of one half, but a few fragments at the head of the second half, we can see that our knowledge of Apuleius's works goes back to a single, wrongly divided manuscript, and that but for this single manuscript none of his work would survive. Where did that manuscript come from? There is a celebrated "subscription," or footnote, following the *Metamorphoses,* in manuscript F, our sole source for one of these traditions: from it we learn that the text was reviewed and emended by a member of the highest Roman society in Rome, and in Byzantium, in A.D. 395–97. It looks as though Apuleius's work survives because it circulated in Rome, and given the enormous literary effort Apuleius put into its construction I think he must be the man who got it there. At some stage, whether 395 or earlier, a box of Apuleian scrolls could be found in Rome to be transcribed to the new format, the codex. Only a few years later Augustine thought Apuleius a name worth conjuring with in his work for the world market, the *Civitas Dei*. At much the same time Macrobius displayed knowledge of Apuleius in his echt-Roman *Saturnalia*. These writers indeed all came from Africa, but it is Rome that links their work.[10]

It would have been extraordinary if Apuleius's work had survived as a result of circulation in North Africa. This is perhaps made clearer by an exceptional case: the so-called *Anthologia Latina* did survive because of provincial circulation. It represents a collection that one Luxorius made of literature written by himself, his friends, and his countrymen. He put it together under Hilderic, the Vandal king of North Africa in A.D. 523–30, and had originally included Apuleius's own *De remediis salutaribus*. Revealingly, however, that work is lost, leaving the Roman tradition as the only tradition for Apuleius's surviving works.[11]

APULEIUS'S ROMAN PERIOD

I have so far supposed that the *Metamorphoses* circulated, and was intended to circulate, in Rome. There may, however, also be a case for supposing that Rome is where it was written. It may be a product of Apuleius's Roman period.

The most revealing passage for Apuleius's Roman period is the *prolalia, Florida* §17, of around A.D. 163. In it Apuleius speaks most highly of the incoming proconsul of Africa, Scipio Orfitus, a man of considerable distinction, who had been *consul ordinarius* as long before as A.D. 149; his father had been consul before him (A.D. 110), and his son would be after him (A.D. 178).[12] Apuleius knows him well and touches sensitively but proudly on their *amicitia* (friendship, association) at an earlier stage in Rome, which he believes Orfitus also valued. At that time, Apuleius reveals, he himself was winning a literary reputation among Orfitus's friends. Here too fits another man, Apuleius's champion in the proposal that he should be honored with a statue at Carthage, Aemilianus Strabo (*Florida* §16).[13] Strabo and Apuleius had been comrades in their cultural pursuits (*commilitium studiorum*), and, whether literally or metaphorically, had had the same masters (*magistri*). Indeed, Strabo deigned to call himself Apuleius's "fellow pupil" (*condiscipulus*), to the latter's great joy. But this man was also consul in A.D. 156, and surely an esteemed member of the Orfitus circle. In 156, Apuleius's Roman period was probably at an end (except if he continued it by correspondence)[14]—he would arrive in Oea that year (*Apologia* §55).

To a period before the trial at Sabratha, and probably to the Roman period, belong Apuleius's apparently Catullan poems, the *Ludicra* (Jocular pieces). One is quoted at *Apologia* §6, and one (frag. 1 Beaujeu) referred to some person's behavior having been different in Athens, showing the Athens-Rome transition to be in Apuleius's mind at the time. Many other works will go back to this period, as we can see from the list of genres he had already attempted (*Florida* §9). At Rome, though he may not quite have learned Latin like his hero Lucius, he may well have learned fashionable Latin, whose signature is the predilection for the vocabulary of preclassical authors so visible in the *Metamorphoses*. He had, it must be remembered, literary ambitions from the earliest age (*ab ineunte aevo, Apology* §5 and *Florida* §17). At Rome he had that ability recognized and authenticated.

WAS THE *METAMORPHOSES* AN EARLY WORK?

A date late in Apuleius's career is usually envisaged for the *Metamorphoses,* but the arguments for it are not irresistible. The overwhelming style is not in itself a good argument for late dating: one has only to compare the youthful exuberance of Richard Strauss's *Don Juan,* written at the age of twenty-four. Arguments from quality are just as treacherous. To view his Platonic philosophical works as early because we do not regard them as adequately original is only an alternative to disputing they are by Apuleius at all: both approaches reflect distaste and set aside the obvious argument for late dating—that the second book, *On Plato,* is addressed to his son Faustinus. The converse may sound reasonable, but has no greater strength: "It is right to treat Apuleius' novel as the climax of his work not because a late date is indisputable . . . but because it is the most original and the most justifiably celebrated of his writings."[15]

Remaining arguments against an early date are only arguments from silence—at his trial, or in lists of his works.[16] Nothing rules out an early date, and in fact there is a contrary argument from silence: the absence of Carthage from the *Metamorphoses.* This is surprising in a work that contains what appear to be a number of autobiographical reflections. Most famous is the wicked association of hero with author by calling him, contrary to the story line, a man "from Madaura," Apuleius's own hometown (11.27). The statement at the same point that he was fairly poor may have some basis in fact, as it was an accusation at his trial too (*Apologia*

§18), though doubtless it was a rich man's poverty. The travel, discovery, and curiosity of Lucius may reflect that of Apuleius in his youth, as he toured the Greek world. And the following period might account for the stress in 1.1 and later in book 11 on the transition from Greece to Rome: he left his studies in Athens and the Greek world to set about the acquisition of Roman culture and status.

Youth may of course be recalled in old age, but other, more general, factors point in this direction. Perhaps the extreme sensitivity to style and to his relationship with his audience is a sign of a writer attempting to establish himself in front of an audience both certain of its values and ready to test other would-be entrants against those values. (It was a test that we can tell Apuleius passed from the way in which he refers to his Roman period in the *Florida*.) Then there is the marked interest in Roman legal institutions, which suggested to Bernhard a dating during Apuleius's Roman period, a sort of *tirocinium fori,* the training in advocacy at Rome, so important for young persons of quality.[17]

There can be no doubt that Apuleius, however much he may have been interested in culture from the cradle, was made into the person he was by those crucial years between about A.D. 145 and 155. For the rest of his life—at least insofar as it is known to us—he would be energized by the dialogue between the Greek and the Latin cultures, which he experienced in succession at this time. Whether or not the reader accepts my view of the *Metamorphoses* as actually written at Rome in the 150s, his hero and his progress from Greece to Rome and the progress of the book from Greek to Latin by *desultoria scientia* (the art of leaping from one horse to another) are underlined as formative. And his (later?) career as philosopher and sophist continued his internal ambivalence between Greek conceptions and Latin linguistic flair. The *Metamorphoses,* however, subjectively seems still very close to the excitement and recognition of that period of cultural transition.

REFLECTIONS OF THE *METAMORPHOSES* IN THE *APOLOGIA*?

Another indication of an early date may be furnished by reflections or echoes of the *Metamorphoses* in the *Apologia* of A.D. 158. I do not suppose that these are deliberate allusions (I cannot see any motive for that); rather, the experience of having written the *Metamorphoses* remained fresh in his imagination and vocabulary.

A simple example is the description of Mercury in the *Apologia* (§64) as *iste superum et inferum commeator* (that commuter between those above and those below) reflected in the description of Anubis in the *Metamorphoses* (11.11) as *ille superum commeator et inferum.* This is lent significance because these are highly idiosyncratic expressions, *commeator* not being found else-where in the whole of Latin. On the same page of the *Apologia,* the creator and first principle of the universe is called *totius rerum naturae causa et ratio et origo initialis, summus animi genitor* (cause, reason and primal origin of the whole universe, supreme begetter of mind)—a phrase that calls to mind two passages of the *Metamorphoses:* the description of Isis herself as *rerum naturae parens . . . saeculorum progenies initialis, summa numinum* (parent of the universe . . . primal offspring of the aeons, supreme amongst divin-ities, 11.5); and the important description of Venus, which clinches the connection with Isis, so asserting the unity and meaning of the novel, *en rerum naturae prisca parens, en elementorum origo initialis* (lo, ancient parent of the universe; lo, primal origin of the elements, 4.30). *Initialis* (primal) is another idiosyncratic word: in this theological sense it scarcely stretches beyond these passages, and the phrase *origo initialis* is clearly one of those stylish Latin neologisms for the rendering of Greek (in this case *arche*) of which Apuleius boasts in the *Apologia* (§38).[18]

These types of expression are, I think, called into existence by theologi-cal concerns, not invented for occasional use in a speech. If we are prepared to think that the *Metamorphoses* has a theological level, then the likely direction of transit of these terms is from *Metamorphoses* to *Apologia.* These are just a few of the possible parallels.[19] But the most powerful one is that between his discussion of the use of a boy for divination in the *Apologia* (50.2) and the depiction of Psyche and her surroundings in the *Meta-morphoses.*

This discussion of divination goes into the detail of daimones and the human soul. Its opening recalls his splendid declamation on the divine sign of Socrates, the *De deo Socratis:* "Platoni credam inter deos atque homines natura et loco medias quasdam divorum potestates intersitas" (I may be-lieve Plato, that between gods and men there are situated certain divine powers intermediate in nature and in position). As the *De deo Socratis* otherwise offers no visible means of dating,[20] one is left to wonder wheth-er this passage shows that it was already written. The continuation of the passage then recalls Psyche at that moment when she arrives from her rock in Cupid's garden and palace. There is significance, as I have argued else-where,[21] in the fact that the susceptible Psyche ("Soul" in Greek) is *simplex* ("simple," almost "tender"), a key motif repeated in the *Apologia,* where Apuleius speaks of an *animum humanum . . . puerilem et simplicem* (a human mind . . . childish and simple, §43). This mind can be put to sleep (as Psyche is), and *paulisper remota corporis memoria* (gradually distancing the memory of its body—as Psyche should by forgetting her sisters) may *redire ad naturam suam quae est immortalis scilicet et divina* (return to its own nature, which is, to be sure, immortal and divine,—as Psyche does, ac-quiring immortality through union with Cupid, her personal daemon). In the *Apologia,* Apuleius is dealing with the use of a boy for divination and speaks of his requisite qualities *ut in eo . . . divina potestas quasi bonis aedibus digne diversetur* (so that a divine power may fitly take up residence in him, as though in a good mansion), recalling the house of Cupid (*Metamorphoses* 5.1), which is visibly *dei cuiuspiam . . . diversorium* (the residence of some god). This, incidentally, clarifies for us that Psyche's visit can be taken as one within the self, within that palace that (if we can forget the world outside) is the residence of a daemon, our own. There is even one more point: this soul must be *expergitus* (awake) and *nulla oblivione saucia* (wounded by no forgetfulness, *Apologia* §43), both failures in Psyche's fourth task.

This whole passage, however we express it, is too close in ideas and vocabulary to the tableaux of Cupid and Psyche for the connection to be merely coincidental. And again it seems that the *Metamorphoses* passages are more systematically motivated and therefore likely to be the source of Apuleius's more occasional presentation in the *Apologia.* If so, the *Metamorphoses* dates before 158 and, I suggest, to the end of his Roman period, around A.D. 154 or 155.

THE PHILOSOPHER SEXTUS

Mention of the philosopher Sextus may also be something that fits the earlier 150s at Rome. In the opening pages of Apuleius's novel (1.2), Lucius claims descent from him: "Thessaly—because it is there that our fame rests upon the basis of our origin on our mother's side, going back to that famous Plutarch and later [*mox*] his nephew, the philosopher Sextus— well, that is the Thessaly I was heading for on business." The dating of Sextus is rather complicated, but in brief it is as follows:[22] once one sets an anecdotal tradition aside, the only real date we have for him is a *floruit* (a key date), the alleged date at which he peaked, in 119—together with an influential philosopher, Agathobulus, for whom this is a reasonable date. But in addition he contributed to Marcus Aurelius's education. Marcus Aurelius and Verus had been listening to Sextus in Rome at the same time as they were listening to Claudius Maximus, the severe Stoic and consul of about 144–45, who later heard the case against Apuleius at Sabratha.[23] This was clearly before Maximus went to Pannonia—by 150. He looks like an elderly and revered man of the 140s. Indeed, men of the 150s at Rome might talk of him, but I suspect from his age, his absence from the pages of Gellius, and even from the fact that he did not become head of the Academy, that he was dead by then.

Mention of Sextus in the *Metamorphoses,* then, is more attuned to the 150s than to the 170s. The interesting word in Apuleius's reference is *mox* (later): in recognizing that Sextus was subsequent to Plutarch, it brings him nearer Apuleius's own time and experience. Like (his older friend?) Gellius,[24] Apuleius must have heard the then head of Plato's Academy, Taurus, during his time at Athens, and like Gellius he must have heard Taurus proudly mention his acquaintance with Plutarch;[25] but Sextus has not quite receded into history like Plutarch and remains a name to conjure with, despite his lesser significance relative to Plutarch. Did Apuleius himself have the remarkable fortune to hear Sextus, nephew of Plutarch, shortly before he died? Apuleius would have been in Athens perhaps around A.D. 145–50. He might just have been in time.

JUSTIN AND THE CHRISTIANS

In a 1989 article, B. Baldwin drew attention to the remarkable thematic coincidences between the story of the Miller's Wife in Apuleius and a particular case in real life at Rome involving a man of dubious morality and his Christian wife who even Justin Martyr admits had formerly "delighted in drunkenness and every vice." "The Christian lady divorces her husband for his sins, he plots and gains vengeance, albeit against her religious instructor rather than herself. In Apuleius (*Metamorphoses* 9.29–30), the husband divorces the wife for her immorality, only to fall victim to her supernatural revenge."[26] The question is how one accounts for the parallel, if one accepts that it goes beyond coincidence. On an Afrocentric view of Apuleius, even if one dismisses the idea that Apuleius "pored over court reports of Christian trials," the information must be gotten to Africa by some means.[27] But what if Apuleius was in Rome when the case occurred?

During his time at Rome, Apuleius must have come across Justin, a man not so different from himself, except that he finally embraced Christianity. Both had begun their lives committed to "seeking the truth" (*studium veri*). Both had turned to the Platonism of the age and clearly drawn it from similar sources (as had their influential contemporary, the Gnostic Valentinus). Even the conversion scene of Justin, after solitary meditation in a place near the sea, curiously mirrors the conversion of Lucius in *Metamorphoses* 11.1.[28]

Justin, too, appears to have been based at Rome during the 150s, though his chronology is far from clear. The work of interest to us is his *Second Apology,* a work complaining to the emperor and senate about the condemnation of certain Christians by Lollius Urbicus, *praefectus urbi* (city prefect), during the 150s. The dating of the work is bedeviled by its association with Justin's martyrdom; indeed, the author foresees his own martyrdom in this work, a prophecy to which authors from Eusebius to the present day have been credulously receptive. An association with the martyrdom forces the work into the 160s, but others think more in terms of the mid-150s.[29]

It would have done Justin little good to challenge the meticulous record of Urbicus, a man of exceptional authority and standing, whom Apuleius mentions with requisite respect in the *Apologia* (not least because he had also in the 150s rejected the claims of Apuleius's later enemy Sicinius Aemilianus).[30] Justin may well have made an enemy of the establishment this way, if indeed he had not done so earlier by continuing to masquerade as a philosopher while having defected from Platonism to Christianity. He had other enemies too, notably a Cynic philosopher he and his pupil Tatian name as Crescens, and of whom we may know nothing more. But an Apuleian link suggests a solution. Crescens is not enough to go on: what was the rest of his name? There are not many Crescentes, but Crescens Calpurnianus is a known and eminent combination (one was *consul suffectus* in A.D. 200), and we do know a Calpurnianus at this time: Apuleius's (Roman) *Ludicra* represents him as seeking toothpaste for his personal appearance in case he should ever smile. That would be a suitable insult for someone as marginal and critical of normal behavior as a Cynic.[31]

If the Roman elite had no liking for Justin, we may begin to understand the virulence of Apuleius's condemnation of the Miller's Wife (*Metamorphoses* 9.14), whose monotheism is a gratuitous and therefore Apuleian feature. The target of Apuleius's criticism in this portrait would then be not Judaism, but the Christianity of the likes of Justin in the Rome of the 150s.[32] If Justin's *Second Apology*, or at least the case it protests, belongs to the mid-150s, Apuleius was in Rome himself at the time of the very case his story so resembles, and his sympathies in the case may be viewed as determined by the circles he frequents. It becomes an interpretation of real life, akin to the way satirists construct exemplary icons out of events in their experience.

THE *DEA SYRIA*

Rome also explains something of Apuleius's attitude to the *Dea Syria*. He has elaborated the picture we find in the Pseudo-Lucianic *Onos*, sharpening its contrast with propriety in general and the Isis religion in particular. The Isis religion is presented as dignified, chaste, and continent, but above all in our context it is presented as established and loyal. Its priesthood has a history going back to the times of Sulla, forming a "most ancient college," *collegium vetustissimum* (11.30, associating it with the *collegia* of the traditional Roman religion). And the ceremony of the new sailing season presented in the last book of the *Metamorphoses,* the *Ploiaphesia,* begins with prayers for "the great emperor, the senate, the knights, and the whole

Roman People" (*principi magno, senatuique et equiti, totoque Romano populo,* 11.17). This loyalty is something to which Christians could never aspire, and which was not possible in the same way for the *Dea Syria,* because it was not an established religion, whereas the cult of Isis had been included in the official Roman calendar since the time of Caligula.[33]

The *Dea Syria* so far appears in general terms a worthy target for an Apuleius attempting to establish his ideological credentials with the Roman elite. But there are more specific points. First, the archaeological evidence, such as it is, supports the importance of the *Dea Syria* in Rome, but not in North Africa. For Apuleius to attack the *Dea Syria* at all implies a Roman perspective. Second, the particular interest of Apuleius in her religion, in ecstasy, and in prophecy contrasts markedly with most ancient writing on the subject, which is solely interested in, and indeed obsessed by, the importance of fish in the authentic Syrian form of the religion. Only two other authors share Apuleius's slant. One is Firmicus Maternus (fourth century A.D.), who I think is following Apuleius. The other is Florus, in an indignant section of his so-called *Epitome.* This work, so close to the imperial court and its interests, is usually put at the end of Hadrian's reign, toward 138, but there is no special reason why it should not be a work of the 140s. In either case, this peculiar and presumably modish work is apparently the source of Apuleius's view—something that would make sense if that view was formed in Rome in the 150s.[34]

CONCLUSION: THE INTERPRETATION OF APULEIUS

Perhaps, then, Apuleius's oeuvre is not to be marginalized to North Africa, but was targeted at the same elite audience that pagan Latin literature always was. Perhaps, too, the *Metamorphoses* was actually written while Apuleius was in Rome, making his literary name in the circle of Orfitus in the early 150s A.D. It would explain some curious details, above all the ways in which the tale of the Miller's Wife recalls aspects of a real trial of Christians of which Justin complains: this turns out to be a remarkable instance of intertextuality with reality.

In turn, this Roman context for the *Metamorphoses* will have implications for the texts that may be admitted for the purposes of interpretation of the novel. An elite, philosophically trained audience, used to hearing Sextus, Taurus, Claudius Maximus, and others, is well placed to situate *Cupid and Psyche* amid Platonic intertexts—meaning not just references to Plato, but the whole digestion, reception, and contemporary understanding or mental picture of Platonism, with its interest in souls and the daemon of Socrates. It also explains clearly what has been a wayward and neglected, but readily perceptible, intertextual relationship, that between *Cupid and*

Psyche and Valentinus's myth of Sophia. The simple fact is that Valentinus himself lectured in Rome in the 140s and 150s, and his theories have their place in contemporary intertextuality.[35]

NOTES

1. The words of P. G. Walsh, "Apuleius," in *The Cambridge History of Classical Literature,* ed. P. E. Easterling and B. M. W. Knox (Cambridge, 1985), 774. Apuleius's lost work, the *Hermagoras,* is often thought to have been a novel, perhaps mixing verse and prose like the *Satyricon,* though it might equally have been a philosophical dialogue: fragments in J. Beaujeu, *Apulée: Opuscules philosophiques et fragments* (Paris, 1973), 171f.; novel according to B. E. Perry, "On Apuleius's *Hermagoras,*" *American Journal of Philology* 48 (1927): 263–66.

2. E.g., Ovid, *Metamorphoses* (see J. K. Krabbe, *The Metamorphoses of Apuleius* [New York, 1989], chap. 2); Vergil, *Aeneid* (e.g., E. Finkelpearl, "Psyche, Aeneas, and an Ass: Apuleius, *Metamorphoses* 6.10–6.21," *Transactions of the American Philological Association* 120 (1990): 333–48; even Gellius (cf. L. Holford-Strevens, *Aulus Gellius* [London, 1988], 17f.).

3. Scribes: T. Hägg, *The Novel in Antiquity* (Oxford, 1983), 93. Parthenope: ibid., 18, 20.

4. M. D. Brock, *Studies in Fronto and His Age* (Cambridge, 1911), 164, traces the theory back to K. Sittl, *Die lokale Verschiedenheiten der lateinischen Sprache* (Erlangen, 1882). The major propagator was P. Monceaux, *Les Africains: Etude sur la littérature latine d'Afrique: Les païens* (Paris, 1894). The theory still leaves its traces: J. G. Griffiths, *Apuleius of Madauros: The Isis-Book (Metamorphoses, Book XI)* (Leiden, 1975), 56f. For the modern perspective on "African Latin": L. Callebat, *Sermo Cotidianus dans les Métamorphoses d'Apulée* (Caen, 1968), 19; Callebat, "La prose des *Métamorphoses:* Génèse et spécificité," in *Aspects of Apuleius's "Golden Ass,"* ed. B. L. Hijmans, Jr., and R. T. van der Paardt (Groningen, 1978), esp. 168.

5. Refutation: Brock, *Studies,* 161–261; E. Norden, *Die antike Kunstprosa,* 2 vols. (Leipzig, 1898), 2:588–98. Despised provincialism: Brock, *Studies,* 175–78; Holford-Strevens, *Aulus Gellius,* 11 n.17.

6. Brock, *Studies,* 163.

7. Romans writing in Greek: P. Steinmetz, *Untersuchungen zur römischen Literatur des zweiten Jahrhunderts nach Christi Geburt,* Palingenesia, vol. 16 (Wiesbaden, 1982), 2f.

8. Callebat thinks of African high society as the target audience: "La prose des *Métamorphoses,*" 167. I am not sure what Walsh means by "Romans" in the epigraph to this section.

9. Carthage may even be *sanctissima*—1.4 surely refers to Carthage and associates it with "sacrosanct" Rome (*Metamorphoses* 11.26).

10. Manuscript tradition: e.g., Beaujeu, *Apulée,* xlvi. Boxes of rolls: M. Haslam, "A Problem in the History of the Transmission of Texts Exemplified in Demosthenes," *Liverpool Classical Monthly* 1 (1976): 9–10. Subscriptions: L. D. Reynolds and N. G. Wilson, *Scribes and Scholars: A Guide to the Transmission of Greek and Latin Literature,* 2d ed. (Oxford, 1974), 35–37.

11. Luxorius: A. Riese, *Anthologia Latina,* part 1, fasc. 1 (Leipzig, 1869), xxv–xxvii, poem 203, apparatus p. 273; F. J. E. Raby, *A History of Secular Latin Poetry in the Middle Ages,* 2d ed. (Oxford, 1957), 1:114.

12. Prosopographical material from *Prosopographia Imperii Romani,* ed. E. Groag and

A. Stein, 2d ed., parts 1–3 (Berlin, 1933), part 4 (Berlin, 1952), part 5 (Berlin, 1970–87) (hereafter cited as *PIR* with entry reference). Orfiti: *PIR*, C1447.

13. Aemilianus: R. Helm, *Apuleii Platonici Madaurensis opera quae supersunt*, vol. 2, part 2, *Florida* (reprint, Leipzig, 1959), xx.

14. The suggestion is made by Holford-Strevens, *Aulus Gellius*, that Gellius and Apuleius continued correspondence.

15. Walsh, "Apuleius," 778.

16. Silence in *Apologia:* Helm, *Florida*, ix; M. Bernhard, *Der Stil des Apuleius von Madaura* (Stuttgart, 1927), 358; Griffiths, *Isis-Book*, 10; A. Scobie, *Apuleius Metamorphoses (Asinus Auerus) I: A Commentary* (Meisenheim am Glan, 1975), 93. Silence in *Florida:* Bernhard, *Stil*, 358, Griffiths, *Isis-Book*, 11. Bernhard nonetheless prefers an early date.

17. Legal references and Rome: Bernhard, *Stil*, 359.

18. Materials from *Thesaurus linguae Latinae* (Leipzig, 1900–). *Commeator* otherwise occurs only by conjecture in a damaged inscription with no contest (. . .]MEATO[. . . , in *Corpus inscriptionum Latinarum* (Berlin, 1863–), 8.22672). The only other theological uses of *initialis* (neither qualifying *origo*) are Varro in Probus on Vergil, *Ecl.* 6.31, and Pseudo-Tertullian, *Execr.* 3.

19. Other reflections of the *Metamorphoses* in the *Apologia:* (1) *Apologia* §56, "Si qui forte adest eorundem sollemnium mihi particeps, signum dato, et audias licet," reflecting the religious scruples at *Metamorphoses* 11.23, including *cognosceres, si liceret audire;* (2) *Apologia* §56, defense of the use of linen (*purissimum . . . velamen*) to wrap his statuette, with appeal to Pythagoras for wool being taboo (cf. *Metamorphoses* 11.1, Pythagoras, for seven as the most appropriate number for religious observances) and its use by Egyptian priests. This reflects not only Herodotus 2.81 but also *Metamorphoses* 11.10 (e.g., *linteae vestis candore puro luminosi*); (3) *Metamorphoses* 1.11: Lucius states, if curiously, where he comes from, and the first place on the list is Hymettus in Attica. This seems to lie behind *Apologia* §24 *fin.* "non elegi illud tuum Atticum Zarat ut in eo nascerer."

20. Beaujeu, *Apulée*, xxxv.

21. K. Dowden, "Psyche on the Rock," *Latomus* 41 (1982): 341f.

22. Anecdotal tradition: Cassius Dio 71.1; Philostratus, *Lives of the Sophists* 557 (copied by Suda, s.v. "Markos"); George Synkellos 665 Dindorf. The tradition adopted here: *Scriptores historiae augustae* (hereafter cited as *SHA*), *Marcus* 3.2 (drawn from Eutropius 8.12 or a common source?); crucially, Marcus Aurelius, *Ad se ipsum* 1.0; George Synkellos, *Chronogr.* 659, 662 Dindorf; Eusebius, *Hieron Chron.*, Olympiad 224.3, 231.8–9.

23. Maximus, *Vir tam austerae sectae* (*Apologia* §19): *PIR* C933 (= 934), *SHA*, *Marcus* 3.2, Marcus Aurelius, *Ad se ipsum* 1.15.

24. Holford-Strevens, *Aulus Gellius*, 17.

25. Taurus: Gellius, *Noctes Atticae* 1.26; J. Dillon, *The Middle Platonists* (London, 1977), 237f., 308.

26. B. Baldwin, "Apuleius and the Christians," *Liverpool Classical Monthly* 14, no. 4 (1989): 55.

27. I do not believe the contention, which Baldwin (ibid., 55 n. 2) draws from H. E. Butler and A. S. Owen, *Apulei Apologia* (Oxford, 1914), that the *Apology* in some way implies the presence of Urbicus at Apuleius's trial.

28. Philosophical quest and conversion: *Dialogue with Trypho* §2–3. Apuleius's and Justin's Platonisms similar: L. W. Barnard, *Justin Martyr: His Life and Thought* (Cambridge, 1967), 35, 96–98; but seed and ineffable god appear also in Valentinus; see B. Layton, *The Gnostic Scriptures* (London, 1987), 14, 235; and Justin is part of a widespread

Ken Dowden

distinctive Middle Platonism; see, e.g., J. Whittaker, "Platonic Philosophy in the Early
Empire," in *Aufstieg und Niedergang der Römischen Welt,* ed. H. Temporini et al. (Berlin,
1987), 2.36.1.81–123, esp. 105, 109, 115, 118 (embracing also Valentinus, 122); cf. P.
Keresztes, "The 'So-Called' Second Apology of Justin," *Latomus* 24 (1965): 826–65.

29. *2 Apol.* addressed to the Senate, e.g., title; to the emperor, §§2, 3; Urbicus, *2
Apol.* §§1–2. Written not long after *1 Apol.:* Barnard, *Justin Martyr,* 19–21, but Urbicus
looks dead at §1 ("in the time of Urbicus"?), and cf. Keresztes, "Second Apology," 867–
69. Date of martyrdom: *Chron. Pasch.,* Migne, *Patrologia Graeca,* vol. 92, col. 629, 258
Dindorf; A.D. 165, for want of better: H. Musurillo, *The Acts of the Christian Martyrs*
(Oxford, 1972), xviii; Barnard, *Justin Martyr,* 5 (under Marcus; also Eusebius, *Historia
ecclesiastica* 4.16).

30. Lollius Urbicus, *PIR* L327; *inter alia,* he built the Antonine Wall in Scotland
(*SHA, Pius* 5.4). Sicinius Aemilianus, *Apologia* §2.

31. Crescens: *2 Apol.* §3, Tatian, *Adv. Graecos* 19.1. Calpurnianus: Apuleius, *Ludicra*
(title: frag. 1, Beaujeu, *Apulée,* 171) in *Apologia* §6. M. Antius Crescens Calpurnianus,
consul suffectus ca. A.D. 200, *PIR* A781.

32. P. G. Walsh has long proposed Christianity, but remains Afrocentric; see *The
Roman Novel: The "Satyricon" of Petronius and the "Metamorphoses" of Apuleius* (Cambridge, 1970), 187f.

33. Contrast with Isis: B. L. Hijmans, Jr., R. T. van der Paardt et al., *Groningen
Commentaries on Apuelius,* book 8 (Groningen, 1977), app. 4 (hereafter cited as *GCA*).
Loyal dedications: L. Vidman, *Sylloge inscriptionum religionis Isiacae et Sarapiacae* (Berlin,
1969), nos. 403–5 (Rome). Atargatis, etc., never part of calendar: J. J. W. Drijvers, "Die
Dea Syria und andere Syrische Gottheiten im Imperium Romanum," in *Die Orientalischen Religionen in Römerreich,* ed. M. J. Vermaseren (Leiden, 1981), 243. Caligula:
e.g., A. D. Nock, *Conversion: The Old and the New in Religion from Alexander the Great to
Augustine of Hippo* (Oxford, 1933), 124; R. E. Witt, *Isis in the Graeco-Roman World*
(London, 1971), 162, 224.

34. Rome and North Africa: Drijvers, "Dea Syria," 245, 246, 249 (Melqart instead),
GCA 286. Sources: P.-L. Van Berg, *Corpus cultus Deae Syriae,* vol. 1, part 1, *Répertoire
des sources grecques et latines* (Leiden, 1972), including: Apuleius, *Metamorphoses* 8.29 (no.
96 Van Berg); Firmicus Maternus, *De errore* 4.2 (no. 115); Florus, *Epitome* 2.7 (no. 94).

35. Platonic contexts and intertexts: Dowden, "Psyche on the Rock." Psyche and
Sophia: see G. Heinrici, "Zur Geschichte der Psyche: Eine religionsgeschichtliche
Skizze," *Preussische Jahrbücher* 90 (1897): 390–417, esp. 409–17, reprinted in *Amor und
Psyche,* ed. G. Binder and R. Merkelbach, Wege der Forschung, no. 126 (Darmstadt,
1968), 56–86, esp. 78–86; and K. Dowden, "Psyche and the Gnostics," in *Symposium
Apuleianum Groninganum* (Groningen, 1981), 157–64.

CHAPTER TWENTY-FOUR

The Readership of Greek Novels in the Ancient World

Ewen Bowie

Widely divergent opinions have been expressed on the readership either envisaged or achieved by ancient novelists for their works—a divergence largely the result of an almost total lack of evidence on the second of these two related issues. In an ideal world, it would be desirable to approach the questions of intended and actual readerships separately, and also to build up evidence and argument for each of the known novels independently, moving from conclusions concerning the readership of each to a general theory about overall readership. But of the arguments about intended and actual readership, more converge than conflict; what might count as evidence for either the intended or the actual readership of any one novel is exiguous; and most arguments that hold for one are applicable to all or many. Accordingly, I shall attempt to discuss the general issue first, and shall only mark out an argument as limited to either intended or actual readership when that limitation is significant.

There remains, of course, a problem in defining the category "novel" and in deciding how that category should be subdivided. I include in the category the five "ideal" novels extant in complete texts (Chariton, Xenophon, Achilles Tatius, Longus, and Heliodorus); related works known from Photius (Iamblichus's *Babyloniaca*), and papyrus fragments (the most important are Lollianus's *Phoenicica, Ninus, Metiochus and Parthenope, Iolaus, Sesonchosis, Chione, Calligone,* and one that may concern a character Herpyllis); and finally fictional works in which sexual relationships play a much less central role, the *Wonders beyond Thule* of Antonius Diogenes and the *Metamorphoses,* which I believe to be by Lucian. Only the accident that we have no Greek text or fragment of *Apollonius, King of Tyre* excludes it from the list. Both Lucian's *Verae historiae* and the Pseudo-Callisthenes *Alexander* seem to me to belong to different, albeit related, genres.

Within the genre one broad division has often been assumed, principally in considering the novels extant in full texts: to wit, between the "first novels" and those that display manifest sophistic influences—Achilles Tatius, Heliodorus, and Longus.[1] It was chiefly on the "first novels" that one of the most dismissive modern verdicts was pronounced by a scholar who has contributed greatly to our understanding of the genre. In his book *The Ancient Romances,* B. E. Perry opines that "the form itself . . . was . . . confined, in Graeco-Roman antiquity, to a narrow range of uses, tending either to become stereotyped as melodrama for the edification of children and the poor-in-spirit, or employed by intellectuals on isolated occasions for the ostensible purpose of satire or parody . . . The novel appears first on a low and disrespectable level of literature, adapted to the taste and understanding of uncultivated or frivolous-minded people."[2] Later in the same work, Perry develops the hypothesis of a juvenile readership with particular reference to Chariton: "It is probable that Chariton's romance was well known in the second century after Christ and that it was read by many people, particularly, we may suspect, by young people of both sexes. There is such a thing as juvenile literature even in our own highly sophisticated age; and in ancient times the ideal novel must have catered to that obscure but far-flung literary market long before it became adapted in some measure to the taste and outlook of mature or educated minds."[3] Perry also confidently asserts a juvenile readership for the *Ninus* romance.[4] Admittedly, Perry also concedes that "in *Daphnis and Chloe* the novel approached the top level of literary quality for its time,"[5] but it is not clear whether in doing so he intends to exempt Longus from his general condemnation.

Assertion of a juvenile or intellectually underdeveloped readership is an old ploy in dealing with literature about whose qualities one has doubts or whose claims to be taken seriously one wishes to undermine. Strabo had tried to explain the mythological content of early poetry as geared to an immature age: later the same lessons could be taught by history or philosophy. In the fifth century A.D., Macrobius dismissed the novels of Petronius and Apuleius as *argumenta fictis casibus referta* and as mere *nutricum cunae.*[6] In modern discussions of the novel, the notion of a young readership seems partly to derive from the age of the typical lovers—a curious argument rapidly scotched by Tomas Hägg[7]—and partly from the sentimentality of the narrative, an equally unsatisfactory consideration to which I return below.

I doubt if there is much more to be said for the view, which goes back at least as far as Rohde, and to which Hägg himself gave some support, that many of the readers—and even some of the authors—were women.[8]

One line of argument asks us to consider the presentation of women in the novels. Hägg notes the strength of characters like Chariton's Callirhoe, by contrast with his Chaereas, and Achilles Tatius's Melite, but on the other hand takes the view that the ideal of womanhood held up is a male product. More recently, Brigitte Egger has argued persuasively that the images of women presented by the novelists are reconcilable with the aspirations of women in the Greco-Roman world.[9] It is also the case, however, that these images correspond to male views of women and their social role in the period. Egger's arguments, therefore, have removed any obstacle that the novels' presentation of women might have constituted to a hypothesis of a female readership, but they do not, I think, render that presentation a testimony to female rather than male readership. To my eye there remain hints that a male rather than female readership was the *primary* constituency envisaged by the novelists. In Longus's work the introductory tale's reference to hunting in Lesbos—which could so easily have been cast differently—sets up a situation that would have been familiar to a male member of the Greek upper classes at first hand, but would not have been so to a female. The sexual forwardness of some experienced Greek women—Achilles Tatius's Melite, and even more, Longus's Lycaenion, who gives Daphnis practical instruction in sex—is hardly what the heads of Greek *oikoi* would be happy to commend to their wives and daughters. It also seems to me more likely that the long debate in Achilles Tatius 2.36–38 on the respective delights *for a male* of homosexual and heterosexual activity was intended more for a male than a female reader, though of course I accept the judgment of a female colleague that it has its fascination for women too.[10]

A prima facie more fruitful area of investigation is the level of women's education. One of our novelists, Antonius Diogenes, is said by Photius (our only evidence) actually to have dedicated his work to his sister Isidora, whom he described as φιλομαθῶς ἐχούσῃ.[11] Can this be taken as evidence that for Diogenes and his readers it was entirely natural to suppose that his work might find female readers φιλομαθῶς ἐχούσας? Unfortunately, even this text is not straightforward. The prefatory letter to Isidora was included in or preceded by another letter addressed to one Faustinus, which raises questions about the immediacy of Isidora's presumed access to literary texts. It then emerges from Photius's account that the letter to Isidora cited another from Balagrus to his wife Phila, daughter of Antipater, telling of the discovery of the tablets bearing the text of the ἄπιστα during Alexander's sack of Tyre. This bogus "authentication" (like the list of authorities prefaced to each book) stands in provocative contradiction to the posture Diogenes took up in the letter to Faustinus himself, that he was a poet of Old Comedy and the fabricator of things false and incredible. It seems, then, that Isidora has a number of functions. She stands for a gullible reader, avid for information, who may accept at face value what Faustinus (admittedly on cue!) is to take as a spoof; her pairing with Faustinus (conceivably her husband?) may have a literary role as a foreshadowing of the wife-husband pair Balagrus and Phila and the brother-sister pair Mantineas and Dercyllis. Doubtless she would not be so used by

Diogenes unless such a class of reader was conceivable. But unfortunately her use cannot tell us how numerous or typical such readers might be.

Evidence from other quarters can at least give some indication of what level of education might be expected for some women in the first three centuries A.D., but it is not a precise indication, and like all aspects of the whole debate on literacy it leaves wide margins of uncertainty.[12] Even on a pessimistic view it is likely that many women achieved some basic literacy (but always in much smaller numbers than men);[13] that would enable them to read the text of a novel.

But for most of the novels it is not simply the ability to read the text that is at issue; indeed, the regular practice of reading aloud by slaves to their owners means that the ability to read is not in itself a condition of "reader-ship" in a broader sense. What is at issue is the ability to pick up the novelists' allusions to earlier literature and to respond to these allusions in the intended direction. It may be that *Ninus, Chione,* and Iamblichus's *Babyloniaca* made as few demands on the reader's educational attainments as Xenophon of Ephesus, although without a complete text it is impossi-ble to tell. But even of the "early" novels it is probable that *Metiochus and Parthenope* (with its allusions to Herodotus and archaic writers like Ibycus and Anaximenes), and certain that Chariton, required a well-read reader to appreciate the force of the quotations and allusions. Those in Chariton's work include Homer, Sappho, Euripides, Herodotus, Thucydides, Xeno-phon, the orators, Menander, Apollonius, and Theocritus.[14] The range of allusion in the three "sophistic" novelists is even wider (I discuss those of Longus below). Moreover, Chariton, like the "sophistic" novelists, has his characters deploy rhetoric in a way he surely expected his readers to ad-mire. What we must ask, therefore, is how many women had an education that familiarized them with a range of texts wider than such central authors as Homer and Euripides, and with the basic moves of rhetoric.

Certainly many women with grammatical (as it were, secondary) and some with rhetorical and even philosophical education are attested at many periods of Greek culture. But the proportion of the female popula-tion educated to these various levels is clearly smaller than that of the male population: we gain the impression that among women, they are very much exceptions, and that if anything, there are fewer in the Roman period than before. At the level of tertiary education the world that we see through Dio, Plutarch, Gellius, Lucian, Aristides, Athenaeus, and Phi-lostratus, the world of sophistic declamations, philosophical lectures, and intellectual *conversazioni,* is almost entirely a male world. All Lucian's targets, all Philostratus's sophists, all the learned acquaintances of Aris-tides and Gellius are men.

There are, indeed, some remarkable exceptions, women who com-posed either prose works or poetry. In the former category stands Pamphile, daughter of a *grammaticus* from Egypt, probably Alexandria, and resident at Epidaurus. The Suda gives her thirty-three books of *historika hypomnemata,* several epitomes, and a work on sex (περὶ ἀφροδισίων). Photius had access to an eight-book edition in whose preface Pamphile claimed that her knowledge derived from conversations with her husband (whose side she had not left in their thirteen years of marriage) and with his many intellectual friends, as well as from her own reading of books. One wonders if the preface to the book on sex was as explicit. It is tempting to suppose that Photius's and the Suda's dating to Nero may derive from the dedication of one of her works.[15] As in the case of some other educated women attested on inscriptions, it is significant that Pamphile is herself from a family in the education industry, and so could receive her schooling in-house.[16]

Our other two prose writers are linked to another religious and cultural center of old Greece, Delphi. Plutarch believed that girls should be educated and had a wife who was: he addressed to her the *consolatio* on the death of their two-year-old daughter Timoxena, and she herself composed a work, *On Love of Self-Adornment,* that she addressed to one Aristylla.[17] Both women would have been expected to read the works dedicated to them. Education was also expected of the Eurydice for whom, along with her bridegroom Pollianus, he composed the *Advice on Marriage,* and of the priestess Clea, dedicatee of both the *Fine Deeds of Women* and (a much more intellectually taxing work) the essay *Isis and Osiris.*[18] It is also from Delphi that we have our only evidence in the high empire of a woman delivering lectures. Early in the second century, perhaps at the Pythia of A.D. 115 and A.D. 119, Aufria, whose ethnic name is unfortunately lost, was honored first by Delphian citizenship and then by the erection of statues for her display of *paideia* in "many fine and very pleasing discourses."[19] More than two centuries later, Sosipatra was sufficiently expert in philosophy (which she taught in her home in Pergamum) to be written up by Eunapius at about the time Hypatia was establishing her reputation in Alexandria. But even Sosipatra proves the rule—her educators, who predicted that she would have a mind οὐ κατὰ γυναῖκα καὶ ἄνθρωπον . . . μόνον, are not human but demons or heroes.[20]

In poetry the *Greek Anthology* offers no imperial successors to the Hellenistic women poets Erinna and Nossis. But the works of three are inscribed on the Memnon Colossus. The most eminent and voluminous is Julia Balbilla, sister of Antiochus Philopappus and granddaughter of the last king of Commagene, who commemorated the visit of Hadrian and Sabina to the colossus in November 130 in four elegiac poems written in pseudo-Sapphic dialect. The colossus also preserves the works of two other (clearly amateur) women poets, Caecilia Trebulla and Damo.[21]

Julia Balbilla clearly moved at the highest social level, and here we may also document more women with serious intellectual interests. These are suggested for Trajan's wife Plotina by her interest in the succession to the headship of the Garden of Epicurus at Athens.[22] The empress Julia Domna notoriously professed an interest in literature of various kinds.[23]

These cases establish only that a number of women in the upper crust of Greco-Roman society were able both to read and to compose literature. They cannot help determine what proportion of women in the upper classes of the Greek cities were potential readers. We are taken further down the social scale by the case of Hermione, who died in Egypt circa A.D. 200, described on her mummy portrait as *grammatike:* but it is not clear whether she is simply being credited with literacy or actually taught *grammata*. Much later, we hear of Eusebius's use for copying of κόραι at a lower social level, perhaps even slaves, but not demonstrably girls who themselves would spend time reading.[24]

Overall, the small tally of women who make a contribution to the literary history of the imperial Greek world seems to me to strengthen the case for doubting that many women received a rhetorical education and were equipped to appreciate Chariton or the sophistic novelists. But it must be conceded that the evidence is desperately short, and that no very confident judgment can be made.

The suggestions of a juvenile or female audience both reflect the reluctance of scholars to concede that novels had the same audience as other literary works. The same reluctance moves Hägg to consider audiences in villages listening to recitations by scribes, or slow readers helped along by pictures. Hägg supports the hypothesis of reading by scribes with the argument that it accounts better for "the wider circulation of the novel than itinerant story-tellers." I do not find the grounds or the conclusion very convincing: it would be more attractive if we had evidence of scribes in the Greco-Roman world acting in this way (presumably for a fee?), but as far as I know we do not, and the furthest that I am happy to go is to endorse Bryan Reardon's suggestion that there may have been "small reading circles" along with the more prevalent habit of individual reading.[25]

The notion of a "wider circulation" also needs examination. It goes together with the view that the novel, at least in its early manifestations, was a "popular" form.[26] But although "popular" is a reasonable label to attach to the earliest quasi-novel, the *Dream of Nectanebus,* translated from Egyptian and attested on a papyrus of the second century B.C., and might just suit the sentimental and clumsy Xenophon of Ephesus (if we could be sure we had a text whose paternity he would acknowledge), it does not seem to me appropriate to Chariton (far less to the three sophistic novelists), unless by "popular" we mean "likely to attract a readership among the educated bourgeoisie."[27] We must also question Hägg's ascription of "wider circulation." Our papyri of novels are vastly outnumbered by those of Homer and Euripides of the same period,[28] and no one novelist is represented by as many papyri from the period as Hesiod or Callimachus.

Hägg also argues that what appears to be an illustrated novel text of the second century A.D. shows that the early novels were intended for readers who found the act of reading difficult. The notion that illustration was to help inexperienced readers is very speculative, and we must remember that we have a fragment of an illustrated Homer, too.[29] I would be ready to give greater weight to Hägg's observation that some novels are in codices, not rolls, but the proportion is very small—four codices against about forty rolls, one of these codices being as late as circa A.D. 550—and does little to support Hägg's suggestions.[30]

There are indeed, overall, a number of points which could support the notion that the readership of the novel may have spilled over from the class of *pepaideumenoi* who read other literary works to reach a slightly wider circle. I am not persuaded, however, that the *typical* reader envisaged by Chariton or Xenophon (far less by the sophistic novelists) was significantly different from the sort that we assume for the *Lives* and *Moralia* of Plutarch, for the historians, or for Lucian, or the sort of people who attended lectures and epideictic performances by philosophers and sophists. The reasons for thinking that they are different are more often left unstated than explicitly presented, but I suspect they are basically four.

First, the theme of love and the sentimentality of its treatment mark off the novels from these other works.[31] Yet this cannot carry the argument very far. Love, and love treated sentimentally, is a central motif in New Comedy, a genre that was attracting both audiences and readers from the educated classes in the second century. Note how much New Comedy is quoted by Plutarch.[32] Love is also, of course, much exploited by Hellenistic poets whose readership at any time has generally (and perhaps too confidently) been reckoned to be from the best-educated classes. Even historians in the second century exploit the love interest; witness the story of Stratonice in Appian's *Syriace*.[33] This is hardly surprising, given the popularity of Xenophon in the second century and the treatment in his *Cyropaedia* of the story of Araspas and Pantheia.[34]

The second argument is related, and invokes the generally low quality of the novels. This too seems to me to be a poor argument. Even where the quality is low, as it certainly is in Xenophon of Ephesus and from time to time in Achilles Tatius, that actually tells us little about their intended or actual audience. And those critics who condemn all the exponents of the genre have done so with historical hindsight, aware of the ways in which the modern world has developed the novel and contrasting the ancient genre to its predictable disadvantage.

Third, there is the absence of an ancient name for the genre. A balanced and representative view is that of Hägg: "The novel is a whole class of literature, and a prolific one at that, lacking a learned designation of its own. The main reason for this, besides their postclassical start, seems to be that early novels, like early Christian writings, were not regarded as true literature by literary theorists and critics. There is no positive evidence for the acceptance in such quarters even of the sophisticated novels of imperial times, in spite of the obvious stylistic ambitions of their authors. Novels were most probably also read in highbrow circles, but they were not acknowledged or seriously discussed."[35] Since generic classification was principally the work of Alexandrian scholarship in the Hellenistic period (as Hägg earlier noted), it is not at all surprising that a later genre went without a label. Some parallel, though I concede it is not a close one, may be found in the fact that neither the prose hymn developed by Aristides nor the satirical dialogue or narrative developed by Lucian acquired a special name.[36] It is doubtless because Hägg sees the weakness of this argument that he attempts to bolster it by adducing another, the silence of ancient authors. To this argument, the fourth, I now turn, but again I doubt if it should be given so much weight as it has been.

Consider chronology. Our earliest attestation of the genre remains the fragments of the *Ninus* romance. This is certainly not later than A.D. 101, as is shown by the accounts on the verso of the papyrus, and palaeographic arguments suggest that the text was written not later than A.D. 50 and perhaps as early as 50 B.C. The work's composition has been attributed to the early date of 100 B.C., chiefly to bring it back nearer to such works as Xenophon's *Cyropaedia*, but neither that nor other reasons offered are compelling.[37] *Ninus* and two other fragments apart,[38] papyri so far bring us no earlier than the second century A.D., and indeed are more numerous for the second half of the second and for the third century. It is partly on the slippery ground of development of the genre, partly because of his relative immunity to atticism, that some scholars have dated Chariton as early as the first century B.C.[39] But atticism surely reached different places at different times, and in Asia it may have been resisted longer than in Rome and Athens. I have never been persuaded that a date earlier than A.D. 50 is mandatory, and am attracted by arguments of Marie-Françoise Baslez and Christopher Jones that would put him as late as the reign of Hadrian.[40] Chariton's earliest papyrus published so far dates to the middle of the second century. Both language and the classicizing historical context for its love story links *Metiochus and Parthenope* with *Chaereas and Callirhoe,* and a date from the first century A.D. has been asserted as the date of the work's composition.[41] Perhaps that is right, but again papyri are from the second century.

When we begin to get nonpapyrological evidence for dates, it all takes us well into the second century. Xenophon, in some ways associable with

Chariton, mentions the local office of eirenarch first known under Trajan. Iamblichus's claim to have predicted Verus's Parthian victory puts him after 165, perhaps by a decade or two. Lucian's *Metamorphoses* probably belongs between 155 and 180, and, to note a by-product of the novel, Philostratus's *Apollonius* was published about A.D. 230. I believe Heliodorus belongs there as well, and indeed that the author of the *Aethiopica* is Heliodorus the Arab of Philostratus's *Lives of the Sophists,* but this *lis* is still *sub judice,* and a late-fourth-century date for Heliodorus could yet be proved.[42] The papyri tell a similar story. Apart from three antedating A.D. 100, their distribution when allocated to twenty-five-year spans is as follows:[43]

ca. A.D. 150	15
ca. A.D. 175	2
ca. A.D. 200	7
ca. A.D. 225	1
ca. A.D. 250	7
ca. A.D. 275	0
ca. A.D. 300	4
ca. A.D. 550/600	3

The production of the genre could therefore cover as short a span as the years A.D. 60–A.D. 230, with a concentration in the second half of the second century and first half of the third, and only *Ninus* and two other lost works certainly antedating A.D. 100.

Why this insistence on chronology? It will be useful later, but for the moment the point is this: where should we *expect* to hear about novels and novelists? Of works on literary theory they come too late for Demetrius, for Dionysius of Halicarnassus, perhaps even for Longinus (though he would be unlikely to seek examples of sublimity from Chariton or Xenophon). Chronology alone would permit the technical writers on rhetoric to notice the novels, but are novels a suitable authority for the points these writers want to make? They would indeed have provided them with examples of rhetorical schemata, but not backed up by a context in a well-known and respected classical text. Absence from their citations shows that the novels never acquired the status of classics, but there is a substantial middle ground between that and the total neglect and contempt that is alleged. Perhaps when we encounter a list of suggested reading, such as Dio 18, the absence of novels might be thought more significant, but even there the established constituents of an educational curriculum are clearly not conceived as forming the totality of "serious literature," and it is observable that the only genre of which modern representatives are admitted is oratory, the very skill the addressee seeks to acquire.

When we turn to nontechnical works, in other literary genres, the argument from silence becomes precarious. For a start, as in the rhetorical handbooks, the vast bulk of quotation and allusion is deliberately from works of the classical period, and references to contemporary writing are a rarity. If Plutarch mentions his eminent contemporary Favorinus only five times in the *Moralia* and not at all in the *Lives,* should we expect him to mention novels or novelists if he knew them? Again, Plutarch knows a contemporary poet, Sarapion of Athens, and even gives him a part in his dialogue *On the Pythian Oracles,* but he quotes none of his or any other contemporary's poetry.[44] Finally, it is clear that Plutarch's chief circle of Greek acquaintance is from Achaea, though there are some Asian friends like Menemachus of Sardis, whereas hints in our texts suggest that the novel chiefly flourished east of the Aegean. That might also explain the silence of Gellius. Lamentably, we have no Plutarch or Gellius for a city of Asia Minor. Aristides, Galen, and Artemidorus are all silent on the novel, but given the broad spectrum of cultural activities to which they do allude, the novel's absence can hardly be attributed to its falling below their intellectual sights. It must simply be chance that it escaped Galen, Artemidorus, and the *Sacred Tales* of Aelius Aristides, while the formal speeches of the last naturally draw only on classical writers.

Lucian is a different matter. It is true that he names no novelist, nor does he show explicit awareness of the genre of ideal romance, but in judging the first of these points we should recall that Lucian himself was thought to have passed unnoticed by contemporary writers until it was recently observed that he lurked in an Arabic translation of a work of Galen.[45] In judging the second, we must also assess the exploitation of themes related to those of the novel in the *Toxaris* and *Philopseudes,* the relationship of the *Verae historiae* to Antonius Diogenes' *Wonders beyond Thule,* and finally the fact that Lucian himself seems to have composed a novelistic work, the *Metamorphoses,* which survives in Photius's epitome and in the abridged version Λούκιος ἢ ὄνος, which has been transmitted among Lucian's works.[46] That Lucian knew only romances in which travel dominated and was unfamiliar with the sentimental "ideal" romance is highly improbable.[47]

When we reach Philostratus, it is no longer a matter of explaining silence but assessing whether two references are indeed to novels. The stronger candidate is *Epistle* 66:

Χαρίτωνι

Μεμνήσεσθαι τῶν σῶν λόγων οἴει τοὺς Ἕλληνας, ἐπειδὰν τελευτήσῃς· οἱ δὲ μηδὲν ὄντες, ὁπότε εἰσιν, τίνες ἂν εἶεν ὁπότε οὐκ εἰσίν:

To Chariton

You think that the Greeks will remember your words when you are dead; but those who are nobodies while they exist, what will they be when they exist not? (trans. Benner and Fobes)

There is no good reason to doubt that the addressee is the novelist. The reference to λόγοι shows that he is a literary figure, and one can see why Philostratus might have thought that depreciation of a writer in a recent and innovative genre would make good copy. On the other hand, Philostratus's dismissal of Chariton cannot be used to support the view that novels were in general regarded as trash by sophists. Such seems to be Perry's view: "The writing of that kind of romance in prose, at least in the early stages of its development, was left to authors who were nobodies (as Philostratus says of Chariton)."[48] It would be equally unwise to generalize from Philostratus's criticism of Plutarch for himself attacking sophists (*Ep.* 73 ad fin). Rather, Philostratus's letter indicates that by his time novels and their creators had a claim to belong to the world of λόγοι, and that Philostratus might expect his cultivated readers to recognize both the individual and his genre.

The second Philostratean passage is less straightforward. In his life of Dionysius of Miletus, Philostratus impugns the ascription to Dionysius of a work called "Araspas in Love with Pantheia" and asserts that it was by his enemy, the *technographos* Celer.[49] Both men were rhetors who made it to the rank of *ab epistulis Graecis,* but Philostratus manifestly has a lower opinion of Celer, giving him no *Life* of his own and (in this same passage) criticizing his capacity for declamation, μελέτη. What was the work in question? It could have been a declamation, as Anderson, for example, takes it to be. But since it is mentioned by Philostratus in the context of Dionysius's blameless life, unmarred by any ἐρωτικὴ αἰτία, something more seems to be indicated, and I share Perry's view that this was a novel.[50] It is less easy to follow Perry in his view—which he actually presents falsely as a statement by Philostratus—that Celer ascribed the book to Dionysius in order to disgrace him. Philostratus does not suggest that there is anything disgraceful about the work, although he does by implication suggest that it might be adduced as evidence by anyone wanting to draw attention to the author's erotic proclivities. He denies it to Dionysius not on moral but on stylistic grounds: it did not display Dionysius's rhythms, ἑρμηνεία or ἐνθυμήματα.

If the work was a novel, then we learn that a novel could be written in the middle of the second century by a rhetor who had come near to the top of his profession—it matters little whether it was Dionysius or Celer—and could be read carefully enough by Philostratus around A.D. 230 for him to form a stylistic judgment. That should not surprise anyone who has read Philostratus's *Life of Apollonius,* a work that in a number of ways resembles novels, particularly those of Achilles Tatius and Heliodorus. It has also been suggested that the *Metamorphoses* reported by Photius were composed by one of Philostratus's sophists, Hadrianus of Tyre, appointed to the imperial chair of rhetoric in Athens circa A.D. 176, and then were parodied in the extant *Lucius, or the Ass* by one of the Thessalian sophists,

Flavius Phylax and Flavius Phoenix, the latter also given a brief *Life* by Philostratus.[51] The proposal has not received much scholarly assent, and is certainly not my own view of these works' genesis.

In the second half of the third century, Porphyrius of Tyre knew the *Wonders beyond Thule* of Diogenes and drew on them for his life of Pythagoras,[52] but this is clearly a special case, since he would have been drawn to the work not as novelistic entertainment but as a repository of Pythagorean lore.

Thereafter there is indeed silence on the novel for over half a century, until the 360s A.D. But that period is one for which our literary texts are very much fewer than for the preceding centuries. Then Julian offers two pieces of evidence. First, writing from Antioch about January of A.D. 363 to the *archiereus* of Asia, Theodorus, whom he had appointed to oversee cults in the Greek East, Julian clearly refers to novels as a category of literature to be avoided (along with iambic poetry and Old Comedy): ὅσα δέ ἐστιν ἐν ἱστορίας εἴδει παρὰ τοῖς ἔμπροσθεν ἀπηγγελμένα πλάσματα παραιτητέον, ἐρωτικὰς ὑποθέσεις καὶ πάντα ἁπλῶς τὰ τοιαῦτα (We must eschew the fictions reported in the shape of history by earlier writers, love themes and all that sort of stuff).[53] This could, at a pinch, refer to Herodotus or Xenophon, but ἐρωτικὰς ὑποθέσεις point rather to works in which love was a central theme, not incidental decoration, and I share the view that Julian is here referring to novels. If he is, then it is of interest that he treats them as a genre produced by earlier and not contemporary writers.

That should be borne in mind when we consider the second piece of evidence in Julian, his description in *Orations* 1 and 3 of Sapor's siege of Nisibis in A.D. 350. There are, notoriously, close parallels between this and Heliodorus's description of a siege of Syene in the *Aethiopica,* 9.3ff. That the parallels show the use of one writer by the other is widely agreed, but not so which used which. The controversy cannot be pursued in detail here. I have myself been disposed to accept the view of Szepessy and Maróth that Heliodorus is prior; Szepessy in particular seems to have showed that Julian's picture of the siege does not cohere with the eyewitness account of Ephraim of Nisibis.[54] Discussion with John Morgan in the course of the Dartmouth conference persuaded me that the question remains open. But if Julian were to be shown to be using Heliodorus, he would emerge as a reader of novels himself (something his epistolary remark suggests rather than excludes), and Heliodorus would have to antedate A.D. 357.

With the final triumph of Christianity, the world changed in a number of important ways, and evidence from the fifth century and later cannot be deployed to identify the first readers of novels. But it is convenient to notice here how the novels gradually join the mainstream of the classical tradition.

Diverse witnesses attest some knowledge of the novels in the first half of the fifth century. Around 400 the physician Theodorus Priscianus recommended the reading of erotic novels as a cure for impotence: he specifies Iamblichus and Herodian, the latter name perhaps a corruption of Heliodorus.[55] Presumably another motive led the church historian Socrates Scholasticus to know of Heliodorus, whom he asserts to have become a bishop of Trikka in Thessaly.[56] It may also have been in the fifth century that Aristanenetus composed his collection of love letters, which appear to show a knowledge of Xenophon of Ephesus. Toward the end of the same century, Musaeus's epyllion *Hero and Leander* draws certainly on Achilles Tatius and perhaps on Chariton.[57]

Two of these names recur among the three novelists with entries in the Suda—Xenophon, Iamblichus, and Achilles Tatius—entries that probably stem from the fifth- or sixth-century lexicon of Hesychius of Alexandria. But it would be rash to insist that only these three were known to Hesychius. Certainly neither Heliodorus nor Chariton had been wholly forgotten in Egypt, since we have a fragment of a parchment codex of Heliodorus copied about A.D. 550, and the parchment codex of circa A.D. 600 transported by Wilcken to Hamburg, only to be destroyed by fire before much had been transcribed, contained texts of Chariton and of the *Chione* romance.[58]

A different selection was known to Photius in the second half of the ninth century: Antonius Diogenes, the *Metamorphoses* that Photius ascribes to Lucius of Patrae, and Iamblichus, Achilles Tatius, and Heliodorus, whom he groups together.[59] The *Palatine Anthology* also ascribes either to Photius, or to his friend and contemporary Leon the philosopher, an epigram on Achilles Tatius (9.203) that seems to be intended for the frontispiece of an edition.

In the second half of the eleventh century, Michael Psellus wrote a syncrisis of Achilles Tatius and Heliodorus. That is also the date of our earliest manuscript of Heliodorus.[60] Finally, in the twelfth century four novels were composed that showed knowledge of and admiration for the sophistic novels of the high empire, particularly Achilles Tatius and Heliodorus, though Longus's *Daphnis and Chloe* was also familiar to Theodorus Prodromus, author of *Rhodanthe and Dosicles,* and to Nicetes Eugenianus, author of *Drosilla and Charicles.*[61] These, like Constantine Manasses' now fragmentary *Aristandros and Callithea,* were in verse, while Eustathius Macrembolites' *Hysmine and Hysminias* was in prose. Knowledge of another text, that of Xenophon, is shown by the twelfth-century commentator Gregory of Corinth, who refers to Achilles, Xenophon, and τὰ ἄλλα ἐρωτικά.[62] The late thirteenth century saw the transcription of the novels of Chariton and Xenophon into the manuscript that is the only medieval witness to their texts and one of two chief witnesses to the texts of Longus and Achilles Tatius. Investigation of the ownership and location of these and of the more numerous manuscripts of Heliodorus would make an important contribution to our understanding of the novels' readership in this period. This is not, however, the place for that investigation.

I return again to late antiquity. Before a brief foray into the geographical spread of the novels' readers, I will attempt to summarize what has been argued concerning their intellectual level. I hope I have shown that there are insufficient grounds for denying that the novel was known in intellectual circles. If this is accepted, then the positive indications in the novels that an educated readership is expected, and in particular the relation to sophistic products of the novels of Longus, Achilles Tatius, and Heliodorus, should be taken as evidence that their writers were steeped in sophistic literature, if not practising sophists themselves, as the titles of their manuscripts claim for Achilles Tatius and Longus. It should also be taken as evidence that their readership overlapped with the educated classes who attended the lectures of sophists and philosophers and who read poetry, history, and occasionally philosophy. Chariton is just as allusive, and his novel's relative immunity to atticism and to sophistic elaboration should not be attributed to unambitious literary objectives. In *Metiochus and Parthenope* we also have a historical context that would evoke nostalgia in educated readers brought up on Herodotus. For this novel we may also have, in evidence from the visual arts, a possible corroboration of the postulate of an educated readership, as well as some evidence for an aspect I have so far neglected, the novel's geographical spread.

Two mosaics from Daphne, the suburb of Syrian Antioch, depict Metiochus and Parthenope; in one both lovers are clearly labeled, in the other only the tag identifying Metiochus survives. The house in which they were found is not among the most opulent, but it is not small, and certainly does not belong to the poor in spirit or in worldly goods. It was dated by its excavators, who called it "the house of the man of letters," to the Severan period (A.D. 193–235). That the mosaics illustrate the novel, rather than some other literary treatment of the story, might be suggested by the presence in the same house of a mosaic whose subject can be identified as Ninus contemplating a portrait, presumably of Semiramis: the identification is established by a mosaic of the same subject labeled "Ninos" from nearby Alexandreia ad Issum (Iskenderun).[63] We thus seem to have a pair of illustrations of novels used in the same way as the mosaic floors in all the other numerous houses at Daphne deployed standard mythological themes, and it is tempting to think that here, at least, in the very place where Philostratus had his conversations with Gordian, a well-to-do Antiochene was a fancier of novels; and not of the sophistic novel, but of the supposedly less pretentious *Parthenope* and even less advanced *Ninus*.

Before succumbing to this temptation, however, another piece of evidence from the Syrian region must be weighed. As Doro Levi noted in his full publication of the Antioch mosaics, Ninus and Metiochus are linked by Lucian.[64] Here, however, they are introduced as examples not of characters in a novel, but of characters in a theatrical performance. Attacking the sophist who is the pamphlet's ostensible victim, Lucian makes the sophist's tongue say of the stages that preceded his activity as a primary teacher:

πένητα καὶ ἄπορον παραλαβοῦσα καὶ βίου δεόμενον τὰ μὲν πρῶτα ἐν
τοῖς θεάτροις εὐδοκιμεῖν ἐποίησα, νῦν μὲν Νίνον, νῦν δὲ Μητίοχον,
εἶτα μετὰ μικρὸν Ἀχιλλέα τιθεῖσα.

I found you poor and destitute and without a livelihood, and first secured you a reputation in theaters, making you now Ninus, now Metiochus, and then a little later Achilles.

That the activity is more disreputable than elementary teaching excludes the possibility that the reference is to declamation.[65] Nor is the supposition that it refers to recitations from novels consonant with the clearly *dramatic* role being alleged. Most probably, then, it is indeed a reference to drama, and in particular mime, whether involving plots influenced by the novel or plots that themselves influenced the novel.[66] This cannot be certain, but at least doubt is cast on the hypothesis that the Daphne mosaics illustrate novels, though it cannot be disproved.

If it were the case that these mosaics did illustrate novels, however, they would constitute a large proportion of our knowledge of the geographical spread of the readership. Our other data are too scanty to allow anything but the most precarious inferences, and it would be unwise to use them to limit readership to a particular quarter of the Greek-speaking world, or to suggest that one type of novel found favor in one part, another in another. There is, for instance, no easily interpreted distinction in Egyptian papyri between the sophistic novels and what are often seen as "the popular type of novel."[67] We have papyri of the *Ninus*, Chariton's *Chaereas and Callirhoe*, *Parthenope and Metiochus* (if that was of the "popular" sort); of stories involving Iolaus and Sesonchosis; and of Antonius Diogenes' *Wonders beyond Thule* and Lollianus's *Phoenicica*. But we do not as yet have papyri of Xenophon of Ephesus, Lucian's *Metamorphoses,* or Iamblichus's *Babyloniaca*. This last is admittedly a borderline case: from some points of view "popular," it does have "sophistic features." Within the triad of developed novels, both Achilles Tatius and Heliodorus have appeared on papyrus, but not (so far) Longus. It might be tempting to argue that Longus was as widely read elsewhere, but not in Egypt, as members of the first category; and to explain Achilles' and Heliodorus's appearance on Egyptian papyri on the grounds that Achilles is a local author—from Alexandria—who gives his novel much local color, and that this also abounds in Heliodorus. But I doubt if the evidence from papyri is voluminous enough to justify this distinction, and would register no surprise if a papyrus of Longus were to be published.

No help can be sought from the writers from the third to the fourth centuries whom I argued above show knowledge of novels; Lucian, Philostratus, Porphyry, and Julian were not tied to one part of the empire, but traversed many of its provinces, eastern and western alike, and knew Italy too. That the Greek novel was as well known in Rome as in the Greek East is likely for the second to fourth centuries, and virtually certain for the first. Even if Persius's half-line *post prandia Callirhoen do* (1.134) does not refer to Chariton's work (I doubt that it does), Petronius's *Satyrica* shows that in the 60s A.D. he at least knew some form of the Greek novel.

Nor is the geographical setting of a novel's story a reliable guide to the location of readers, since the exotic ambience of Babylon or Egypt must have been more fascinating to an Aegean or Anatolian city-dweller than to a civil servant in Mesopotamia or the Fayum. But something can perhaps be made of the origins boasted by the writers themselves. Iamblichus and Lucian both claim to have grown up with Aramaic as their mother tongue, Iamblichus in an unspecified part of Syria, Lucian in Commagenian Samosata. Heliodorus belongs to the same general area, coming from Emesa, now Homs. But at least one of these, Lucian, had his literary career in Ionia, Achaea, and the West; and if Heliodorus of Homs is the same as the sophist Heliodorus the Arab in Philostratus, he too went west, holding the post of *advocatus fisci* and living in retirement in Rome.[68] Iamblichus may have been working on his novel in the Near East, but we cannot safely assume that he was. Achilles Tatius was an Alexandrian, according to the Suda, and he certainly offers detailed descriptions of both Alexandria and up-country Egypt. On the other hand, Byzantium, Tyre, and Ephesus are important in his plot, and although papyri show he had Egyptian readers, we would be rash to exclude others in the sophistic centers too.

It is western Asia Minor to which the claimed *patrides* of Chariton and Xenophon take us, Aphrodisias and Ephesus respectively: were the Lollianus who wrote the *Phoenicica* to be identified with Philostratus's sophist, he too had Ephesus as his *patris,* but that identification is not easy.[69] That another of the apparently early novels, *Metiochus and Parthenope,* has important scenes on Samos and the Thracian Chersonese might be taken along with the origins of Chariton and Xenophon to indicate that this stage of the genre at least flourished chiefly in western Asia Minor: this is Hägg's conclusion,[70] and I would like to offer a further possible argument.

Where was the *Ninus* romance conceived? On the analogy of Iamblichus, with his Babylonian setting, and in the light of the Antioch mosaics, a Near Eastern context might be tempting. But there is no evidence that the author is trying to glorify Ninus as a national hero.[71] There is, on the other hand, a city in western Asia Minor with a special interest in Ninus: Aphrodisias, which gave him a place in its foundation legend, and commemorated Ninus and Semiramis on reliefs. That one of our other early novels was written by a man claiming to be from Aphrodisias, Chariton, may be sheer coincidence, but I am not the only person to have been tempted by the thought that a city whose chief deity was Aphrodite may have been a suitable nursery for the early novel.[72]

Finally, I turn to the particular case of Longus's *Daphnis and Chloe,* the work whose problems were in fact responsible for my attempting this study in the first place. It might of course be argued that *Daphnis and Chloe* is so different from the other novels that a different class of reader might legitimately be postulated. Indeed, Richard Hunter in his excellent study comes near to excluding it from the genre entirely.[73] But there are enough shared features to justify its classification with the others, and I shall proceed on the hypothesis that Longus knew other examples more typical of the genre, such as the works of Chariton, Xenophon, and Achilles Tatius.[74]

That the educated classes of *provincia Asia* were indeed foremost among the intended readership of novels in general would certainly suit what little can be inferred about the readership of *Daphnis and Chloe.* That readership is expected to recognize the names of the chief cities of Lesbos—Mytilene, Methymna, perhaps Pyrrha—and to know something of its landscape, but not to know it well. A native of Lesbos would be puzzled by a number of features Longus attributes to his scene. The city of Mytilene is said to be distinguished by canals and bridges. So far excavation has revealed only one canal, separating the island on which the acropolis is built from the mainland, and over the canal only one bridge.[75] Perhaps, of course, the plural is rhetorical. The same argument certainly has to be used to deal with the plural rivers in which Daphnis bathed, since few parts of Lesbos have one perpetual stream deep enough to swim in, and none has two. But there are other ways in which Longus's topography does not fit, as I have tried to show elsewhere,[76] and it seems best to conclude that Longus does not expect readers to demand a depiction of Lesbos that is *both* realistic *and* accurate. This conclusion could accommodate readers familiar with Lesbos but not expecting accuracy or realism in a novel. On the other hand, Longus makes so many gestures toward topographic exactitude that it is easier to infer that his readers were expected to know Lesbos from geographers and other literary sources, but not by close personal acquaintance, and to enjoy recognizing what they knew. Indeed, the sort of acquaintance that Longus as narrator seems to claim—that acquired on a hunting or tourist trip—is what I would set as the maximum expected in a reader, and perhaps as much as Longus had himself.[77]

That Longus's readers should know Lesbos principally from their reading but might possibly be expected to have made a tourist visit suits a geographical catchment area of *provincia Asia,* within which indeed the island was included for administrative purposes. Lesbos was never a sophistic center like Pergamon, Smyrna, or Ephesus, but some sophists must have gone there to perform, and Dionysius of Miletus, the man to whom Philostratus denies the work on Araspas and Panthea, taught there in his youth before moving down the coast and upmarket to Ephesus.[78] We do not know whether all his pupils were from Lesbos or some went there from overseas. We can also detect some links with the religious and sophistic center, Pergamon, adumbrated by Louis Robert.[79]

If we return from the geographical to the intellectual horizons of Longus's readers we are taken firmly into the educated class. Knowledge of Alcaeus is necessary to appreciate Longus's picture of a Lesbian winter with its ice and *silvae laborantes,* knowledge of Sappho to appreciate the apple ἐν αὐτοῖς ἄκροις ἀκρότατον that Daphnis plucked and placed in Chloe's bosom. Allusions to Theocritus are naturally numerous, and there is also, I have argued, allusion to Philetas.[80]

The four-book structure might also be allusive. Clearly the scale of the work is largely a function of the miniature plot and landscape, but Longus cannot have been ignorant of the historiographic model chosen by Chariton and Xenophon, and he himself moves into a para-Thucydidean mode in narrating the πόλεμος between Methymna and Mytilene.[81] But whereas Thucydides wrote eight books and Herodotus nine, one historian of the late fifth century had a penchant for shorter works, usually in two books, sometimes in three or perhaps four, and that was Hellanicus of Lesbos.[82] Is one facet of Longus's Lesbian setting an evocation of that historian? I have no verbal echoes to point to, and given our scanty remains of Hellanicus I do not expect to find any, but if there *is* any sort of allusion here to Hellanicus, it argues an expectation of readers, some of whom have a very good knowledge of classical literature. Indeed, many of the authors to whom Longus alludes indicate a higher level of education than would follow from allusions to more accessible texts like the *Odyssey,* Herodotus, or New Comedy. The range and exploitation of Longus's allusion is admirably discussed by Richard Hunter in his monograph, and I am sure he is right to insist "that in the majority of cases . . . an echo of earlier literature invests a scene with a layer of meaning which would be difficult otherwise to fit into the artificially simple narrative; it allows the author to direct a reader's reacton without in fact having to intrude directly into the narrative."[83] This requires readers who are mature, alert, and well-educated.

The case cannot be made so forcefully for the sort of allusion we find in the nonsophistic novels, but I hope that the evidence and arguments contemplated soberly have shown that an educated readership for these too should not be excluded, and that the hypothesis of a readership either intended or actual that centered on women, juveniles, and "the poor in spirit" has little to recommend it.

NOTES

This chapter was presented as a paper at a London seminar and a colloquium in Paris in 1987, and an abbreviated version appeared as "Les lecteurs du roman grec" in *Le monde du roman grec,* ed. M.-F. Baslez, P. Hoffmann, and M. Trédé, Etudes de littérature ancienne, vol. 4 (Paris, 1992), 55–61. Only in 1989 did I see B. Wesseling, "The Audience of the Ancient Novels," in *Groningen Colloquia on the Novel* I, ed. H. Hofmann (Groningen, 1988), 67–79. I am reassured that independently we have reached similar conclusions.

1. E.g., T. Hägg, *The Novel in Antiquity* (Oxford, 1983), 94. Although I take issue with Hägg on a number of points, his chap. 3, "The Social Background and the First Readers of the Novel," 81–108, is an excellent account of the problem of readership. So too, with conclusions much closer to my own, is that of C. W. Müller, "Der griechische Roman," in *Neues Handbuch der Literaturwissenschaft,* vol. 2, *Griechische Literatur,* ed. E. Vogt (Wiesbaden, 1981), 377–412, esp. the section "Der antike Romanleser" (392–96). There are also discussions by G. Schmeling in his *Chariton* (New York, 1974), 27–33, and *Xenophon of Ephesus* (New York, 1980), 131–38. I have not found much that I can both understand and assent to in D. N. Levin, *Rivista di studi classici* 25 (1977): 18–29.

2. B. E. Perry, *The Ancient Romances* (Berkeley and Los Angeles, 1967), 5.

3. Ibid., 98. The low opinion of Chariton goes back at least as far as Rohde. Perry himself was able to discern merit in the work; cf. "Chariton and His Romance from a Literary-Historical Point of View," *American Journal of Philology* 51 (1930): 93–134. For still more sympathetic approaches to his artistry, see T. Hägg, *Narrative Technique in Ancient Greek Romances* (Stockholm, 1971), and B. P. Reardon, "Theme, Structure, and Narrative in Chariton," *Yale Classical Studies* 27 (1982): 1–27.

4. Perry, *Ancient Romances,* 164, "an obscure Greek romancer addressing himself to juvenile readers." The idea of teenage readership goes back to Gilbert Highet, but Highet added an important qualification. "They are meant for the young, or those who wish they were still young" (*The Classical Tradition* [Oxford, 1949], 165).

5. Ibid., 7.

6. Strabo 1.2.8, 19–20C; Macrobius, *In somnium Scipionis* 1.2.7ff.

7. Hägg, *Novel in Antiquity,* 96.

8. Ibid., 95–96, more cautiously than the caption to his illustration on 97, which reads, "The cover girl—a woman novelist in her hour of inspiration?"

9. B. Egger, "Zu den Frauenrollen im griechischen Roman: Die Frau als Heldin und Leserin," in *Groningen Colloquia on the Novel* I, ed. H. Hofmann (Groningen, 1988), 33–66.

10. Women: Achilles Tatius 5.11ff., Longus 3.15–19; homosexuality: Achilles Tatius 2.36–38. On attitudes to homosexuality, cf. R. MacMullen, "Roman Attitudes to Greek Love," *Historia* 31 (1982): 484–502.

11. Photius, *Bibliotheca* 111a30–b31. For my interpretation of Antonius Diogenes'

prefatory letters I am indebted to the commentary on the fragments of Greek novels by
S. A. Stephens and J. J. Winkler, *Ancient Greek Novels: The Fragments* (Princeton, 1993).

12. For the problem of literacy in the Roman Empire, see W. V. Harris, *Ancient
Literacy* (Cambridge, Mass., 1989), with a brief but trenchant discussion of the readership of novels at 227–28, and *Literacy in the Roman World*, Journal of Roman Archaeology, supp. series, no. 3, ed. J. H. Humphrey (Ann Arbor, Mich., 1991). Earlier works I
found helpful include R. Duncan-Jones, "Age-rounding, Illiteracy, and Social Differentiation in the Roman Empire," *Chiron* 7 (1977): 333–53, and W. V. Harris, "Literacy and
Epigraphy I," *Zeitschrift für Papyrologie und Epigraphik* 52 (1983): 87–111. The problem
of female literacy is discussed by S. B. Pomeroy, "Technikai kai mousikai," *American
Journal of Ancient History* 2 (1977): 51; Pomeroy, "Women in Roman Egypt," in *Reflections of Women in Antiquity,* ed. H. P. Foley (New York, 1981), 303–22, esp. 309ff; and
S. G. Cole, "Could Greek Women Read and Write?" in Foley, *Reflections,* 219–45. An
inscription from Teos of the second century B.C. attests the education of girls as well as
boys for the first three levels; *SIG*³, no. 578. Texts from Pergamum show that some
girls studied epic, elegiac and lyric poetry, reading, and *kalligraphia;* cf. H. Hepding,
"Die Arbeiten zu Pergamon, 1908–1909: II. Die Inschriften," *Mitteilungen des Kaiserlichen Deutschen Archäologischen Insituts, Athenische Abteilung* 35 (1910): 401–93, esp.
436, no. 20; L. Robert, *Etudes Anatoliennes: Recherches sur les inscriptions grecques de l'Asie
Mineure* (Paris, 1937), 58–59. We also know of a *gymnasiarchos* from Dorylaum who was
in charge of women; *Mitteilungen des Kaiserlich Deutschen Archäologischen Instituts, Athenische Abteilung* 22 (1897): 480–81. For a dossier of letters about the education in
second-century A.D. Egypt of a girl named Heraidous, *P. Giessen* 80–85, cf. C. Préaux,
"Lettres privées grecques d'Egypte relatives à l'éducation," *Revue Belge de philologie et
d'histoire* 8 (1929): 757–800, esp. 772–78.

13. See Wesseling, "Audience," 71, no. 25.

14. Molinié, in his Budé edition of Chariton, notes thirty-one citations of twenty-
eight different passages of Homer (p. 12 and footnotes): cf. A. D. Papanikolaou,
Chariton-Studien, Hypomnemata, no. 37 (Göttingen, 1973), 14–16. For allusions to
Sappho, see 1.1.13, 1.1.15; to Sophocles, 3.8.8 (cf. Papanikolaou, *Chariton-Studien,* 16);
to Menander, 1.4.2, 1.4.3, 1.7.1, 2.1.5 (cf. also Papanikolaou, *Chariton-Studien,* 23–24);
to Apollonius, 1.774–80, and Theocritus, 2.79–80; see 1.1.5. The historians are evoked
constantly (cf. Papanikolaou, *Chariton-Studien,* 16–22); the orators occasionally (ibid.,
22–23).

15. See Suda, s.v. T 139; Photius, *Bibliotheca* cod. 175, esp. 119b16–25 and 38–40; cf.
M. R. Lefkowitz and M. B. Fant, *Women's Life in Greece and Rome,* 2d ed. (London,
1992), 168, no. 219. The authenticity of the work περὶ ἀφροδισίων is doubted by L.
Holford-Strevens, *Aulus Gellius* (London, 1988), 21 n. 13, but the name Pamphile does
not seem to me in itself sufficiently suggestive to father the treatise. For other such
works ascribed to *hetairai* (Astyanassa and Elephantine) and to Philaenis from the fourth
century B.C. (with a scrap surviving on *POxy.* 39 [1972]: 2891), cf. Lefkowitz and Fant,
Women's Life, 348 n. 25. An overall description of literature produced by women in antiquity is offered by J. M. Snyder, *The Woman and the Lyre: Women Writers in Classical Greece
and Rome* (Carbondale, Ill., 1989).

16. Cf., from Sparta, Aur. Oppia and her daughter Heraclia, *IG* 5.1.598 (= *SEG*
11.814), 599. From Apollonia ad Rhyndacum in Mysia, Magnilla, daughter of Magnus
and wife of Menius, all three philosophers, *IGR* 4.125.

17. For the *Consolatio, Mor.* 608b. For the work of his wife (also Timoxena), περὶ
φιλοκοσμίας, 145a: the Lamprias catalogue ascribes a work with this title (no. 113) to
Plutarch, and U. von Wilamowitz-Moellendorf, *Kleine Schriften* 4 (Berlin, 1962), 655,

thought him to have written it himself and ascribed it to his wife—I think it plausible enough that she wrote it and that it was to be found among Plutarch's own writings.

18. For the dedication of the *Praecepta conjugalia,* see 138a, with Eurydice addressed at 145a and e; dedications to Clea are at 242e and 351c.

19. The honorific degree is published in *Fouilles de Delphes* 3.4 (1930) as no. 79 by G. Colin, whose dating and interpretation I follow. The missing ethnic name (or cognomen?) at 3–4 Αὐφρίαν [. . .] νην could be, e.g., [Βιθυ] νήν. Note an addressee of a work of Plutarch, περὶ φιλίας called Βιθυνός, Lamprias Catalogue no. 83.

20. Eunapius, *Lives* 466ff. = p. 398ff. Loeb. There is a late and presumably apocryphal tradition that claimed female pupils for Plato: Lastheneia of Mantinea, Diog. Laert. 3.46; Axiothea of Phlius, ibid., and Themist., *Or.* 23.295c. For women who seem to have been drawn to philosophy by fathers or husbands, note Aristippus's daughter and pupil, Arete of Cyrene (also claimed as teacher of her own son Aristippus by Diog. Laert. 2.86); Crates' wife, Hipparchia, ibid., 6.96–98, Magnilla, above n. 16; and the five daughters of Diodorus Cronus and the wife of Epicurus's pupil Leontes, Clement Alex., *Strom.* 4.19. For pseudepigrapha attributed to Pythagorean women, cf. Diels-Kranz, 1.448 50a, and (for the texts) H. Thesleff, *The Pythagorean Texts of the Hellenistic Period* (Åbo, 1965); an excerpt in Lefkowitz and Fant, *Women's Life,* no. 208; see also *POxy.* 52 (1984): 3656.

21. See A. Bernand and E. Bernand, *Les inscriptions grecques et latines du Colosse de Memnon* (Paris, 1960), nos. 28–31, 83, and 92–94. For Balbilla, see E. L. Bowie, "Greek Poetry in the Antonine Age," in *Antonine Literature,* ed. D. A. Russell (Oxford, 1990), 61–83.

22. For Plotina's interest in the Epicurean succession, see *IG* 2/3² 1099 = *ILS* 7784 = *SIG*³, no. 834 = F. Martin, *La documentacion griega de la cancilleria del emperador Adriano* (Pamplona, 1982), no. 12.

23. On Julia Domna, see esp. G. W. Bowersock, *Greek Sophists in the Roman Empire* (Oxford, 1969), 101–9.

24. See Cole, "Greek Women," suggesting that Hermione might have been a secretary and comparing for female scribes the κόραις εἰς καλλιγραφίαν ἠσκημέναις mentioned by Eusebius, *HE* 6.23.

25. Hägg, *Novel in Antiquity,* 93, Reardon, "Theme," 15. The idea of "recitations in private circles" is supported by Hägg by reference to the narrative technique of the nonsophistic novels (foreshadowings, regular plot summaries). Appropriate as these are to a work recited bit by bit, they also suit works that are so read by an individual, as modern literature demonstrates.

26. The term "populaire" was perhaps rather loosely used by Reardon in *Courants littéraires grecs* (Paris, 1971), 323. He tells me (*per litteras*) that he meant literature aimed at people without critical standards or a wider background of reading, and was in any case discussing the early novels.

27. Note Chariton's somewhat dismissive reference to *demodesteron plethos,* 3.2.15.

28. Cf. Harris, *Ancient Literacy,* 228 n. 274; R. A. Pack, *The Greek and Latin Literary Texts from Greco-Roman Egypt,* 2d ed. (Ann Arbor, 1965); W. H. Willis, "A Census of the Literary Papyri from Egypt," *Greek, Roman, and Byzantine Studies* 9 (1968): 205–41. The opposite conclusion might be advocated on the basis of our papyrus texts: a number of these are fragments of elegant, and therefore relatively expensive, books. *POxy.* 42.3012 (Antonius Diogenes) is from a handsomely set out book roll. *Pubblicazioni della Società Italiana per la ricerca dei Papiri greci e latini in Egitto,* Papiri Greci e Latini, no. 8, ed. G. Vitelli (Florence, 1927), no. 981 (the Calligone fragment) "conveys the impression of a most luxurious edition" (Stephens and Winkler, *Ancient Greek Novels*). The two Berlin

fragments of the *Ninus* romance (*P. Berolinensis* 6929) are from the same well-made book roll. These indications point to prosperous readers.

29. Munich Staatsbibliothek, *Papyrus Graecus* 128 (fourth century A.D.): see K. Weitzmann, *Ancient Book Illumination* (Cambridge, Mass., 1959), 32ff., arguing for a cycle of illustrations as early as the Hellenistic period.

30. Hägg, *Novel in Antiquity*, 93. The four codices are of Achilles Tatius (ca. A.D. 150), Lollianus (ca. A.D. 175), *Sesonchosis* (ca. A.D. 300), and Heliodorus (ca. A.D. 550). My figures are drawn from the tables used by Susan Stephens to illustrate her paper at ICAN II (see above, chap. 22). The most obvious conclusion is that which she drew in that paper—that the novels are on the same footing as classical texts.

31. For a useful review of inferences from the sentimentality of the novels to a particular class of reader, see Schmeling, *Xenophon*, 131–38. Schmeling's position had by then (1980) changed slightly from that formulated in *Chariton* (1974), where he suggested (cf. 30–34) that writers came from the middle classes and spoke to an audience of the middle classes. In writing on Xenophon, Schmeling wished rather to see the readership "as a sentimental group, i.e., one which suspends its intellectual judgments and appreciation for reality and adopts a view that events in life are simple, rather than as a middle-class audience" (*Xenophon*, 133). On p. 137, however, Schmeling again endorses Scobie's view of the audience as "middle-class readers who enjoy reading fiction which mirrors their own ideals and unfulfilled longings" (A. Scobie, *More Essays on the Ancient Romance and Its Heritage* [Meisenheim am Glan, 1973], 96).

32. W. C. Helmbold and E. N. O'Neill, *Plutarch's Quotations,* Monographs of the American Philological Society, no. 19 (1959): around fifty for Menander (50), six for Philemon (54). So too Lucian alludes regularly to New Comedy; cf. F. W. Householder, *Literary Quotation and Allusion in Lucian* (New York, 1941). Again, the evidence of papyri, which have so greatly augmented the twentieth century's knowledge of New Comedy, is telling; cf. the fingers for Menander in Willis, "Census," 212, 229.

33. Appian, *Syriace* 308–27, and note too Plutarch's *Antony,* with S. C. R. Swain, "Novel and Pantomime in Plutarch's *Antony*," *Hermes* 120 (1992): 76–82.

34. For Xenophon's popularity, see K. Münscher, *Xenophon in der griechisch-römischen Literature,* Philol. Supplement no. 13.2 (Leipzig, 1920); for the *Cyropaedia,* see now J. Tatum, *Xenophon's Imperial Fiction* (Princeton, 1989).

35. Hägg, *Novel in Antiquity*, 3–4.

36. For Aristides' use of prose for hymns, cf. his hymn to Sarapis, 45.1–5k, with G. W. Bowersock, in *The Cambridge History of Classical Literature,* ed. P. E. Easterling and B. M. W. Knox (Cambridge, 1985), 659–60, and D. A. Russell, *Antonine Literature* (Oxford, 1990), 199–219. Wessling, "Audience," 69, compares the omission of lyric poetry in Aristotle's *Poetics*—which would not be surprising in that curiously slanted work, but is not strictly correct, since he does mention dithyramb (1449a11).

37. Perry, *Ancient Romances,* 153, asserting also the relevance of the decline of drama on the stage after Terence, as if the fashions of Latin Rome were a guide to those of the cities of the Eastern Mediterranean, where in fact drama did not disappear from the repertory of city entertainment until late antiquity.

38. *The Rendel Harris Papyri,* ed. J. E. Powell (Cambridge, 1936), no. 18, and the Tithraustes papyrus, *The Oxyrhynchus Papyri,* vol. 6, ed. B. P. Grenfell and A. S. Hunt (London, 1908), no. 868 (= Pack, *The Greek and Latin Literary Texts* . . . , no. 2630), written in the first century B.C. but not certainly novelistic.

39. For a tabulation of the novels' chronology, see Easterling and Knox, *Cambridge History of Classical Literature* 1:684, with brief citation of evidence for the date of individual novelists in the bibliographical appendix, 879–86. For the linguistic arguments for an early date for Chariton, see Papanikolaou, *Chariton-Studien,* with a summing up on

160–63: his dating to the first century B.C. was accepted by Dihle; cf. below, n. 41. A more precise definition of the linguistic habits of Chariton has been constructed by C. Ruiz-Montero, "Aspects of the Vocabulary of Chariton of Aphrodisias," *Classical Quarterly* 41 (1991): 484–89.

40. M.-F. Bazlez, "De l'histoire au roman: La Perse de Chariton," in Baslez, Hoffmann, and Trédé, *Le monde du roman grec*, 199–204; here, 204; G. W. Bowersock and C. P. Jones in *Approaches to the Second Sophistic*, ed. G. W. Bowersock (University Park, Penn., 1974), 38.

41. For the dating of *Metiochus and Parthenope*, see A. Dihle, "Zur Datierung des Metiochos-Romans," *Würzburger Jahrbücher für die Altertumswissenschaft*, n.s. 4 (1978): 47–55, and *Der griechische und lateinische Literatur der Kaiserzeit* (Munich, 1989), 147.

42. On the date of Heliodorus, see below, n. 54.

43. Again I am indebted to Susan Stephens's table.

44. Plutarch, *Quaest. Conv.* 1.10.628a, *De Pyth. orac.* 5.396dff. For Sarapion, see J. H. Oliver, "Two Athenian Poets," *Hesperia*, supp. 8 (1949): 243f., and R. Flacelière, "Le poète stoicien Sarapion d'Athènes, ami de Plutarque," *Revue des études grecques* 64 (1951): 323–27.

45. G. Strohmaier, "Übersehenes zur Biographie Lukians," *Philologus* 120 (1976): 117–22.

46. On the *Toxaris* and *Philopseudes*, see G. Anderson, *Studies in Lucian's Comic Fiction, Mnemosyne*, supp. 43 (Leiden, 1976), 12–33.

47. See Anderson, *Studies*, 83–94, on Lucian's links with novels, observing (89) "Lucian knew the Ideal Romance but opted out of writing it."

48. Perry, *Ancient Romances*, 89. G. Anderson, *Philostratus* (London, 1986), 276, thinks Philostratus is drawing a distinction between the jejune style of Chariton and such contemporary work as that of Heliodorus; perhaps.

49. *Lives of the Sophists* 1.22 (524).

50. Anderson, *Studies*, 29; Perry, *Ancient Romances*, 169.

51. H. van Thiel, *Der Eselsroman: Zetemata 54* (Munich, 1971), 1:37ff. For Hadrianus, see Philostratus, *Lives of the Sophists* 2.10; for Phoenix, ibid. 2.22 and *Prosopographia Imperii Romani*, ed. E. Groag and A. Stein, 2d ed. (Berlin, 1933–), F 199. Arguments against van Thiel's position are put by Anderson, *Studies*, 35ff.

52. *Life of Pythagoras* 10, 32; cf. W. Burkert, *Lore and Science in Ancient Pythagoreanism* (Cambridge, Mass., 1972), 99 n. 9 (= 88 of original German edition).

53. Julian, *Letter* 63, p. 301b = *Letter* 89, p. 169 in the Budé edition edited by Bidez.

54. See T. Szepessy, "Le siège de Nisibe et la chronologie d'Héliodore," *Acta Antiqua Hungarica* 24 (1976): 247–76; M. Maróth, "Le siège de Nisibe en 350 ap. J.-C. d'après des sources syriennes," *Acta Antiqua Hungarica* 27 (1979): 239–43; C. S. Lightfoot, "Fact and Fiction—The Third Siege of Nisibis (A.D. 350)," *Historia* 37 (1988): 107–25.

55. Theodorus Priscianus, *Euporista* 2.11.34 (133 Rose), "Uti sane lectionibus animum ad delicias petrahentibus. Ut sunt . . . aut Herodiani aut Syri Iamblichi, vel ceteris suaviter amatorias fabulas describentibus." Although an unknown novelist, Herodianus, cannot be excluded, the hazards of transmission make it more likely that Heliodorus is meant (cf. the grouping of Iamblichus, Achilles Tatius, and Heliodorus by Photius, *Bibliotheca* cod. 94, 73b). Our Latin version of Theodorus was translated by him from a work he originally wrote in Greek; it would be dangerous to assert on its basis that he knew Latin translations of the two novelists he cites, but the case of *Apollonius, King of Tyre* (and, in a related genre, Dictys) shows that they may have existed.

56. *Hist. Eccl.* 5.22.

57. For the possible influence of Xenophon on Aristaenetus, see H. Gärtner, "Xeno-

phon von Ephesos," in *Real-Encyclopaedie der classischen Altertumswissenschaft,* ed. A. Pauly, G. Wissowa, and W. Kroll, 2d ser. (Stuttgart, 1967), 9:2055–89; Schmeling, *Xenophon,* 141. Schmeling also argues (141–46) for the influence of Xenophon on the Pseudo-Clementine *Recognitions* and on the apocryphal *Acts.* For Achilles Tatius in Musaeus, see K. Kost, *Musaios, Hero und Leander* (Bonn, 1971), 29ff. P. Orsini, *Musée, Héro et Léandre* (Paris, 1968), xv–xvii, also asserts the influence of Chariton 1.4–7, but I doubt if the parallels are close enough.

58. The Heliodorus parchment was published by M. Gronewald, "Ein Fragment aus dem Aithiopica des Heliodoros," *Zeitschrift für Papyrologie und Epigraphik* 34 (1979): 19–21.

59. Heliodorus, *Cod.* 73; Achilles Tatius, *Cod.* 87; Iamblichus, *Cod.* 94 (compared with Achilles Tatius and Heliodorus at 73b); *Metamorphoses, Cod.* 129; Antonius Diogenes, *Cod.* 166.

60. Cf. Michael Psellus, *De oper. daem.* 48ff., and A. R. Dyck, ed., *Essays on Euripides and George of Pisidia and on Heliodorus and Achilles Tatius* (Vienna, 1986).

61. For bibliography on the Byzantine novels, see Hägg, *Novel in Antiquity,* 240–41, and R. Beaton, *The Medieval Greek Romance* (Cambridge, 1989). For knowledge of Longus, cf. M. D. Reeve, ed., *Longus* (Leipzig, 1982), v n. 5.

62. Gregory of Corinth, in *Rhetores Graeci* 7, ed. C. Walz (Stuttgart, 1834), 1236.

63. D. Levi, *Antioch Mosaic Pavements* (Princeton, 1947), 1:117–19; 2, pl. 20, 107f. (cf. Levi, "The Novel of Ninus and Semiramis," *Proceedings of the American Philosophical Society* 87 [1944]: 420–28). For the chronology, cf. the table on p. 625 of Levi, *Antioch,* and for the mosaic from Alexandria ad Issum, 118. There is a good discussion of the problem of interpreting the mosaics by H. Maehler, "Der Metiochus-Parthenope-Roman," *Zeitschrift für Papyrologie und Epigraphik* 23 (1976): 1–20, and most recently, M.-H. Quet, "Romans grecs, mosaïques romaines," in Baslez, Hoffmann, and Trédé, *Le monde du roman grec,* 125–60, arguing that one of the Metiochus-Parthenope mosaics does indeed depict a stage performance. For the linking of novel writing with the writing of mime, cf. Epiphanius, *Adv. haer.* 1.33.8 (*Patrologia Graeca* 41.568), bracketing Philistion and Antonius Diogenes.

64. *Pseudologistes* 25.

65. As suggested, e.g., by C. W. Müller, "Der griechische Roman," 393.

66. Both Parthenope (as noted by Müller, ibid.) and Achilles were also characters in pantomime; cf. Lucian, *De saltat.* 2 and 54 (Parthenope) and 46 (Achilles). This helps establish Parthenope as a suitable subject for mime too, but the *Pseudologistes'* attack on the victim's tongue shows that it, at least, cannot refer to pantomime.

67. Hägg, *Novel in Antiquity,* 3.

68. Aramaic mother tongue: Iamblichus, scholium at the beginning of Photius, *Cod.* 94, in manuscript A; Lucian, *Bis acc.* 27. For the sophist Heliodorus, cf. Philostratus, *Lives of the Sophists* 2.32. The view that he may be identical with the novelist has also been advanced by G. W. Bowersock and C. P. Jones, in *Approaches to the Second Sophistic,* ed. G. W. Bowersock (University Park, Pa., 1974): 38.

69. For a stylistic argument against the identification, cf. M. D. Reeve, *Classical Quarterly* 21 (1971): 514–39.

70. Hägg, *Novel in Antiquity,* 98.

71. Cf. the forceful rhetoric of Perry, *Ancient Romances,* 164.

72. For reliefs of Ninus and Semiramis from Aphrodisias, see K. Erim, *Aphrodisias: City of Venus-Aphrodite* (New York, 1986), 20–21. I am grateful to Dr. Charlotte Roueché, who had independently developed the same idea, for discussion of the evidence.

73. R. L. Hunter, *A Study of "Daphnis and Chloe"* (Cambridge, 1983).

74. For the unity of the genre, see C. W. Müller, "Der griechische Roman," 387–92.

75. Longus 1.1: I owe the information about the archaeological evidence to Prof. E. H. Williams of the University of British Columbia, who has recently been excavating in Mytilene.

76. For the rivers in which Daphnis bathes, see Longus 1.23.2, 2.24.2; cf. E. L. Bowie, "Theocritus' Seventh *Idyll*, Philetas and Longus," *Classical Quarterly* 25 (1985): 89.

77. For Longus's possible origin in Lesbos, see most recently Hunter, *Study*, 2–3 (overestimating the accuracy of Longus's picture).

78. Philostratus, *Lives of the Sophists* 1.22 (526).

79. L. Robert, "Deux poètes grecs à l'époque impériale," ΣΤΗΛΗ, Festschrift Kontoleon (Athens, 1980), 1–9.

80. 3.3.33–34; cf. Hunter, *Study*, 59–83, and Bowie, "Theocritus' Seventh *Idyll*," esp. 74–86.

81. 2.19.3ff., 3.1–2: cf. Hunter, *Study*, 4 n. 18.

82. Cf. the evidence collected by F. Jacoby in *Die Fragmente der griechischen Historiker* (Berlin, 1923), vol. 1, no. 4 (Hellanikos von Lesbos).

83. Hunter, *Study*, 59.

NOTES ON CONTRIBUTORS

W. Geoffrey Arnott is Emeritus Professor of Greek Language and Literature at the University of Leeds, England. He has published widely on Greek and Roman drama, Hellenistic poetry, and ancient bird names. He is the author of *Menander, Plautus, Terence* (1975), and is editing and translating Menander for the Loeb Classical Library (volume 1 appeared in 1979).

Peter Bien is Professor of English and Comparative Literature at Dartmouth College. Currently the editor of the *Journal of Modern Greek Literature,* he has published extensively on Kazantzákis, Cavafy, and Rítsos, and has translated Modern Greek prose and poetry. At present he is preparing an edition of the selected letters of Níkos Kazantzákis.

John Bodel is Associate Professor of Classics at Rutgers. He is the author of *Roman Brick Stamps in the Kelsey Museum* (1983), *Graveyards and Groves: A Study of the Lex Lucerina* (1993), and several articles on Latin inscriptions and Roman literature.

Ewen Bowie is Praelector in Classics at Corpus Christi College, Oxford, and University Lecturer in Greek and Latin Language and Literature at the University of Oxford. He has published articles on early Greek elegiac poetry, Aristophanes, Theocritus, and the Second Sophistic, and contributed major sections on the Greek literature of the Roman Empire, including the novels, to *The Cambridge History of Classical Literature.* He is preparing a commentary on Longus's *Daphnis and Chloe.*

Margaret Anne Doody, Andrew W. Mellon Professor of Humanities and Professor of English at Vanderbilt University, is currently the director of the Comparative Literature Program at Vanderbilt. She has written numerous books and articles on eighteenth-century poetry and fiction, and two novels—one of these, *Aristotle Detective* (1978), indicating her interest in matters classical. She is now working on a book on the novel from antiquity to the present day.

Faustina C. W. Doufikar-Aerts studied Turkish and Arabic languages, cultures, and literatures at the Universities of Leiden and Utrecht. She is a specialist in comparative medieval literature and the dialectology of Moroccan Arabic. She has held a lectureship in the Oriental department of the University of Utrecht, and is now writing her dissertation on the manuscript of an Arabic biography of Alexander the Great.

Ken Dowden is Senior Lecturer in Classics at the University of Birmingham. He specializes in the novel, religion, and mythology. He has written several articles on Apuleius, translated the *Alexander Romance,* and written *Death and the Maiden:*

461

Girls' Initiation Rites in Greek Mythology (1989), *Religion and the Romans* (1992), and *The Uses of Greek Mythology* (1992).

BRIGITTE EGGER is Assistant Professor of Classics at Rutgers University. She has published on gender in the Greek novels.

DAVID KONSTAN is the John Rowe Workman Distinguished Professor of Classics and Comparative Literature at Brown University. He has published books on Catullus, Epicurean psychology, and Roman comedy, and a translation of Simplicius's commentary on book 6 of Aristotle's *Physics*. His latest book is *Sexual Symmetry: Love in the Ancient Novel and Related Genres* (1993).

SUZANNE MACALISTER is Lecturer in Greek Language and Literature in the Department of Classics at the University of Sydney. She has published on the ancient and Byzantine Greek novels, Byzantine epic, the social construction of gender, dreams in the ancient and Byzantine world, and Aristotle on dreams. She is currently at work on *Dreams and Suicides: The Greek Novel in Antiquity and the Byzantine Empire.*

REINHOLD MERKELBACH is Professor Emeritus of Classical Philology at Cologne University. He has published *Fragmenta Hesiodea* (with M. L. West, 1967); *Roman und Mysterium in der Antike* (1962); *Mithras* (1984); *Die Hirten des Dionysos* (1988); *Abrasax 1–2* (with M. Totti, 1990–91); *Abrasax 3* (1992); and *Die Bedeutung des Geldes für die Geschichte der griechisch-römischen Welt* (1992).

STEFAN MERKLE teaches at the University of Munich. He has published on Ovid and on the ancient novel, and is the author of *Die Ephemeris belli Troiani des Diktys von Kreta* (1989). He is at work on a book about the fabulist Phaedrus.

HOLLY W. MONTAGUE teaches in the Department of Classics at Amherst College. She is working on a book about Cicero's trial speeches.

JUDITH PERKINS is Professor of Classics and English at Saint Joseph College, West Hartford, Connecticut. She is writing a book about the social implications of early Christian narrative representation.

B. P. REARDON is Professor of Classics at the University of California, Irvine. He has written on late Greek literature and the Greek novel, and organized the 1976 International Conference on the Ancient Novel. He is the editor of *Collected Ancient Greek Novels* (1989) (translations) and author of *The Form of Greek Romance* (1991). He is currently editing Chariton.

DAVID ROLLO is Assistant Professor of French at Dartmouth College. His current project deals with formulations of the Other in twelfth- and thirteenth-century Latin, French, and Provençal literature, with specific studies of alterity in the contexts of history, nature, gender, race, and nation.

JAMES ROMM is Assistant Professor of Classics at Bard College. His book *The Edges of the Earth in Ancient Thought: Geography, Exploration, and Fiction* (1992) examines the relationship between science and myth in Greek and Roman accounts of distant places. He has also done substantial research on Renaissance appropriations of ancient discovery literature, and the debate over Greco-Roman discoveries of the New World.

SUZANNE SAÏD is Professor of Greek Literature at Columbia University, where she chairs the Department of Classics. She has published extensively on Homer, Greek tragedy and comedy, and the Greek novel. Her books include *La faute tragique* (1978), *Sophiste et Tyran ou le problème du Prométhée enchaîné* (1985), and *La littérature grecque d'Alexandre à Justinien* (1990).

DANIEL L. SELDEN teaches classics at the University of California, Santa Cruz. He has recently coedited and published *Innovations of Antiquity* (1993), and is completing a book on Alexandrianism.

SUSAN A. STEPHENS is Professor of Classics at Stanford. She is the author of *Yale Papyri in the Beinecke Rare Book and Manuscript Library* (1985), and has contributed to the *Oxyrhynchus Papyri* (vols. 45 and 49). Her edition of *Ancient Greek Novels: The Fragments,* produced in collaboration with the late Jack Winkler, will appear in 1993.

WALTER STEPHENS is Associate Professor of French and Italian and Comparative Literature at Dartmouth College. He is the author of *Giants in Those Days: Folklore, Ancient History, and Nationalism* (1989), and coeditor of *Discourses of Authority in Medieval and Renaissance Literature* (1989). He is completing a book on Tasso.

DIANA DE ARMAS WILSON teaches Renaissance Studies in the Department of English at the University of Denver. She has published widely on Cervantine topics and is the author of *Allegories of Love: Cervantes's "Persiles and Sigismunda"* (1991). She has coedited *Quixotic Desire: Psychoanalytic Perspectives on Cervantes* (1993). She is at work on a book about Cervantes and "the Matter of America."

JOHN J. WINKLER taught classics at Stanford University until his death in 1990. He delivered the Martin Classical Lectures in 1988, was the author of *Auctor and Actor: A Narratological Reading of Apuleius' "Golden Ass"* (1985) and *The Constraints of Desire: The Anthropology of Sex and Gender in Ancient Greece* (1989), and was a coeditor of and contributor to two volumes of essays, *Nothing to Do with Dionysos?* (1990) and *Before Sexuality* (1990).

FROMA I. ZEITLIN is Charles Ewing Professor of Greek Language and Literature and Professor of Comparative Literature at Princeton University. She is author of *Under the Sign of the Shield: Semiotics and Aeschylus' Seven against Thebes* (1982), as well as numerous articles on Greek myth and literature, with special emphasis on the genre of tragedy. She coedited *Before Sexuality: The Construction of Erotic Experience in the Ancient Greek World* (1990) as well as *Nothing to Do with Dionysos? Athenian Drama in Its Social Context* (1990), and has recently published an edition of the selected essays of Jean-Pierre Vernant, *Mortals and Immortals*. Her current research focuses on iconography and representation.